Detecting Hate Speech in Human and AI-Generated Content:

Techniques, Bias Mitigation, and Ethical Considerations

Mohammad Arsalan
Qatar University, Qatar

Mehul Mahrishi
Swami Keshvanand Institute of Technology, India

Ruchi Doshi
Universidad Azteca, Chalco, Mexico

Archika Jain
Swami Keshvanand Institute of Technology, India

Chandrashekhar Goswami
Sir Padampat Singhania University, India

IGI Global
Scientific Publishing
Publishing Tomorrow's Research Today

Published in the United States of America by
IGI Global Scientific Publishing
701 East Chocolate Avenue
Hershey, PA, 17033, USA
Tel: 717-533-8845 | Fax: 717-533-7115
Website: https://www.igi-global.com E-mail: cust@igi-global.com

Library of Congress Cataloging-in-Publication Data

Names: Arsalan, Mohammad, 1986- editor | Mahrishi, Mehul, 1986- editor | Doshi, Ruchi editor | Jain, Archika, 1992- editor | Goswami, Chandrashekhar, 1983- editor
Title: Detecting hate speech in human and AI-generated content : techniques, bias mitigation, and ethical considerations / edited by: Mohammad Arsalan, Mehul Mahrishi, Ruchi Doshi, Archika Jain, Chandrashekhar Goswami.
Description: Hershey, PA : IGI Global Scientific Publishing, [2026] | Includes bibliographical references | Summary: "The purpose of this book is to tackle the pressing challenge of hate speech detection across both AI-generated and human-generated content"-- Provided by publisher
Identifiers: LCCN 2025016744 (print) | LCCN 2025016745 (ebook) | ISBN 9798337330631 hardcover | ISBN 9798337330648 paperback | ISBN 9798337330655 ebook
Subjects: LCSH: Online hate speech--Data processing | Artificial intelligence
Classification: LCC HM851 .D47766 2026 (print) | LCC HM851 (ebook)
LC record available at https://lccn.loc.gov/2025016744
LC ebook record available at https://lccn.loc.gov/2025016745

British Cataloguing in Publication Data
A Cataloguing in Publication record for this book is available from the British Library.

Table of Contents

Detailed Table of Contents

Sahar Yousif Mohammed, University of Anbar, Iraq
Maad M. Mijwil, Al-Iraqia University, Iraq
Duaa Hikmat Abbas, Al-Iraqia University, Iraq
Kamal Kant Hiran, Sir Padampat Singhania University, India
Ali Guma, Muni University, Uganda
Indu Bala, Lovely Professional University, India
Aseed Yaseen Rashid Al-Jubori, Al-Iraqia University, Iraq

The metaverse is transforming architecture by enabling innovation, interdisciplinary collaboration, and immersive client engagement through VR and digital twins. These technologies allow architects to design without physical or financial limitations, fostering creativity and real-time feedback. However, as virtual spaces grow, concerns about hate speech and content moderation arise, complicating regulation due to AI-driven avatars, voice interactions, and global legal inconsistencies. While AI tools help detect and mitigate harmful content, challenges around free speech, algorithmic bias, and regulatory fragmentation remain. Legal frameworks like the EU's Digital Services Act and UN digital rights guidelines highlight the complexity of balancing moderation with digital freedoms. A collaborative approach among AI developers, policymakers, and legal experts is essential to ensuring safe and inclusive virtual environments.

Hate speech refers to language that incites hostility, discrimination, or violence against individuals or groups based on attributes such as race, gender, religion, or sexual orientation. Its detection poses significant challenges due to contextual ambiguity, cultural variance, & linguistic nuance. Artificial intelligence, particularly natural language processing & deep learning models such as CNNs, RNNs, & transformer-based architectures like BERT, have emerged as a critical tool for automating hate speech detection. Word embeddings, contextual modelling, and hybrid detection frameworks that combine human oversight with algorithmic scalability are being actively developed to improve performance. Ethical issues arise around freedom of speech, data privacy, and algorithmic bias. The review highlights techniques for detection, intervention strategies, such as Reflective User Interfaces and content flagging systems, which aim to encourage positive digital behaviour while minimizing harm.

The exponential growth in digital media has revolutionized news consumption. However, it has also led to significant challenges in filtering relevant content from the vast information pool. Personalized news recommendation systems are essential to ensure user engagement and satisfaction. This paper proposes a machine learning-based News Recommendation System leveraging Term Frequency-Inverse Document Frequency (TF-IDF) and cosine similarity to identify and suggest similar news articles based on content alone. The system is implemented using Python and Streamlit with additional features like category filtering, keyword search, and article export. Evaluation on a dataset of 1000+ real-world news article demonstrates the model's effectiveness and potential for scalable deployment.

The research investigates automatic hate speech identification tools meant for detecting text generated by advanced generative AI systems including GPT and BERT. The text provides details about traditional machine learning as well as contemporary deep learning methodologies while putting highlight on transformer models that excel at detecting subtle and context-driven hate speech. The analysis is focused on essential evaluation metrics together with benchmark datasets but also explains implicit toxicity as well as biases through datasets and cultural interpretations challenges. This paper explores both ethical aspects and mitigation techniques alongside real-time moderation system integration practices. The section ends by providing predictive perspectives about multimodal detection methods as well as zero-shot learning and responsible AI deployment frameworks.

This paper involved a bibliometric analysis of academic research articles on the subject of Artificial Intelligence dealing with policy making in the Web of Science core collection of databases. The study included articles, reviews, and proceedings papers, published in English, before 17 August 2020. To normalize the potential fault estimate, the number of authors per year was divided by the total number of

that uses the T5 transformer model to effectively detect highly discussed topics that generate hate speech on twitter. The system uses a deep learning approach, T5EncoderModel, to detect hate speech on annotated tweets. It integrates the T5 model with a dense classification head and is trained using PyTorch. It is deployed via FastAPI to enable real-time classification of social media content. Evaluation demonstrates that our approach outperforms existing models.

Artificial Intelligence has proved to be a boon and a bane in all sectors of society. It has raised concerns regarding the protection of individuals' right to privacy and personality rights, and issues related to the protection of the personal data of individuals. Deepfakes are combinations of fake videos or images of individuals which are morphed or distorted to produce unethical results. The present research aims to conduct an empirical and doctrinal study to look into the issue of deepfake technology, how the public perceives it, and how it is a sensitive issue for laymen in India and internationally. The study involves an empirical analysis involving stakeholders from different dimensions of society, including individuals from the age group of 18-55(+) years and can be from any domain affected by such usage of deepfake pictures and videos. Further to this, with the help of a theoretical analysis with the aid of an analytical study of existing laws in India and the understanding of the international legal regime to protect against misuse of artificial intelligence.

Sentiment Analysis deals with analyzing users comment on a particular thing and then computationally figuring out the actual sentiment of the user i.e Positive or Negative. The process of computationally identifying and categorizing opinions expressed in a piece of text, especially in order to determine whether the writer's attitude towards a particular topic, product, etc. is positive or negative. This chapter presents a comprehensive review of over 50 papers on sentiment analysis, featuring

Preface

Hate speech detection in both human- and AI-generated content represents a complex but increasingly vital task in today's digital ecosystem. At its core, this process involves identifying language that is harmful, offensive, or abusive, regardless of whether it originates from people or from artificial intelligence systems. The challenge lies in determining when language ceases to be an exercise of free expression and crosses into territory that is dangerous or destructive. Such instances may take the form of explicit threats, derogatory remarks, discriminatory statements, or even subtle forms of incitement to violence. The stakes are high, as unchecked hate speech not only damages individual dignity but can also erode social harmony, fuel conflict, and normalize harmful ideologies.

The rise of artificial intelligence, and particularly the proliferation of AI-powered tools such as chatbots, conversational assistants, and automated comment generators, has added an additional layer of complexity to this problem. Traditionally, hate speech detection has focused primarily on human communication—social media posts, online forums, news comment sections, and other spaces where people interact. These contexts, while already challenging due to cultural diversity, context dependency, and subjectivity in interpretation, are now joined by a rapidly growing stream of machine-generated content. Distinguishing between hate speech authored by humans and that produced by AI has therefore become more difficult, but also more essential.

AI models, no matter how advanced, operate on patterns learned from vast datasets. This means that if their training data contains biased, discriminatory, or offensive language, the models can unintentionally reproduce and even reinforce such patterns. Moreover, AI systems lack human judgment and ethical awareness; they cannot fully grasp the social consequences of their output. As a result, AI-generated hate speech may not always display the same intent as human expression, yet its impact can be equally harmful, especially given the scale and speed at which AI can produce and disseminate content. A single flawed algorithm, left unchecked, can flood digital spaces with offensive material, amplifying harmful narratives at a level far beyond the reach of individual human actors.

Addressing both forms of hate speech—human- and AI-generated—is therefore not a matter of choice but of necessity. Human-generated hate speech often reflects deliberate intent, prejudice, or hostility, making it a direct expression of harmful beliefs. AI-generated hate speech, by contrast, may emerge unintentionally but can act as a force multiplier, spreading toxic language widely and rapidly without human oversight. Both forms pose serious risks, albeit in different ways, and require tailored strategies for detection, mitigation, and prevention.

In essence, effective hate speech detection in the modern era demands a dual focus. It must account for the intentions, contexts, and patterns of human communication, while simultaneously addressing the algorithmic risks introduced by artificial intelligence. Only through this comprehensive approach can we begin to safeguard digital spaces, uphold the principles of free expression responsibly, and prevent harmful language—whether human- or machine-made—from undermining social well-being.

The purpose of this book is to address the urgent and evolving challenge of detecting hate speech in both human-generated and AI-generated content. In today's digital landscape, artificial intelligence has become a prolific producer of text, from automated chatbots and recommendation systems to generative models capable of producing full-length articles or conversations. While these systems have brought undeniable benefits in terms of efficiency, personalization, and scale, they also introduce new risks. Unlike human communication, where intent, context, and cultural nuance play a significant role, AI-generated language can replicate harmful biases, amplify stereotypes, or produce offensive content without awareness of its consequences. This creates forms of harmful expression that may differ in subtlety, tone, and reach from human-originated speech.

Traditional hate speech detection tools and datasets have been designed primarily with human communication in mind, focusing on user-generated comments, social media posts, and other natural language exchanges between people. However, as AI systems become increasingly embedded in online spaces, the lines between human and machine language are blurring. AI-driven content—ranging from automated responses in customer service to large-scale bot-generated social media interactions—poses unique challenges for content moderation, policy enforcement, and platform integrity. Detecting whether hateful content was authored by a human or generated by an algorithm is no longer a secondary concern; it is central to ensuring accurate identification, fair intervention, and ethical handling of harmful speech.

This book seeks to fill a crucial gap by offering a comprehensive framework for understanding, detecting, and managing hate speech across both sources. It aims to equip researchers, developers, platform moderators, and policymakers with the conceptual tools and practical strategies necessary to confront this dual challenge. By addressing human- and AI-generated hate speech side by side, it acknowledges the distinct risks each poses while also highlighting their intersections—where AI models learn from, reproduce, or amplify human biases. Ultimately, the book positions itself as a timely resource for building more responsible, transparent, and effective systems of moderation in a digital era defined by both human and machine voices.

This book is designed to serve a broad and interdisciplinary audience, reflecting the wide-ranging impact of hate speech and the growing importance of detecting it in both human and AI-generated forms. It is intended not only for scholars and students in academia but also for practitioners and professionals who encounter these challenges in real-world contexts. Readers from fields such as computer science, artificial intelligence, natural language processing, and data science will find technical discussions on algorithms, detection models, and machine learning approaches. At the same time, those in linguistics and sociolinguistics will benefit from insights into how language shapes identity, power, and exclusion, and how subtle linguistic cues may signal harmful intent.

Beyond the technical and linguistic dimensions, the book engages with broader societal and ethical concerns. Social scientists and legal scholars will encounter critical analyses of how hate speech influences group dynamics, marginalization, and systemic discrimination, as well as the legal frameworks and human rights debates surrounding regulation. Professionals in the domains of digital ethics and policy will gain a deeper understanding of the tensions between free expression and collective safety in online spaces. For students and researchers in media studies, public policy, and communication, the book provides a lens through which to study the evolving role of digital platforms in shaping public discourse.

The relevance of this book also extends to journalism, community management, and mental health. Journalists and media professionals will find practical value in understanding how hate speech proliferates across digital channels and how it influences narratives in the public sphere. Community managers, educators, and moderators will be equipped with strategies to recognize, address, and mitigate toxic interactions in online communities. Mental health professionals will benefit from the book's exploration of the psychological and emotional toll that exposure to hate speech can have on individuals and communities.

Importantly, the book offers a global perspective, recognizing that hate speech is not confined to a single language, culture, or region. It explores how sociocultural contexts, historical tensions, and regional power structures shape the manifestation and impact of hate speech, and how detection methodologies must adapt to account for these variations. These insights are crucial for policymakers, researchers, and technology companies operating in a diverse and interconnected world.

Ultimately, this book aims to bridge the gap between theory and practice by providing comprehensive, multi-disciplinary knowledge on hate speech detection. It underscores the urgent need for innovative, ethical, and context-sensitive approaches that balance the fundamental right to free speech with the equally important imperative of ensuring safety, dignity, and inclusivity in digital environments.

CHAPTER OVERVIEW

Chapter 1, Exploring the Metaverse: The Future of Architecture and Hate Speech Moderation in Virtual Spaces is reshaping architecture by enabling architects to design without physical or spatial constraints, collaborate globally in real time, and engage clients through immersive VR and digital twin technologies. This virtual environment fosters creativity, sustainability, and interactive experiences while allowing virtual prototypes and international teamwork. However, challenges such as content moderation, AI-driven hate speech, technological accessibility, and intellectual property concerns remain. Overall, the metaverse offers transformative opportunities for architectural practice, education, and sustainable design while requiring careful attention to ethical and legal frameworks.

Chapter 2, Detecting Hate Speech - Human and AI-Generated Content: "Hate speech" shall mean forms of expression that spread, incite or justify hatred, hostility, discrimination, or violence against individuals or collectives based on various attributes such as race, gender, religion, and sexual orientation. Detection is difficult due to contextual ambiguity, cultural variance, and linguistic nuances. In this context, deep learning models such CNNs, RNNs and transformer-based architectures like BERT, have proven to be instrumental for automating hate speech detection using artificial intelligence, specially natural language processing. Techniques such as word embeddings and contextual modeling or 'human in the loop' or hybrid detection techniques that scale well with the addition of an algorithm already exist or are being developed for increased performance. Concerns include freedom of speech, data privacy, and algorithmic bias from an ethical perspective. The review includes safer detection intervention mechanisms such as Reflective User Interfaces and content flagging approaches that attempt to promote positive digital behavior while reducing negative consequences.

Chapter 3, A Lightweight Content-Based News Recommendation System Using TF-IDF and Cosine Similarity discusses rapid growth of online content has transformed news consumption, creating a need for personalized recommendation systems that respect user privacy. This paper presents a content-based News Recommendation System using TF-IDF vectorization and cosine similarity, offering features like article previews, similarity scoring, and category or keyword filtering via a responsive Streamlit interface. By relying on content rather than personal user data, the system delivers relevant recommendations while maintaining privacy and reproducibility.

Chapter 4, Algorithms Evaluation and Challenges in Automated Hate Speech Detection for Generative AI has become increasingly critical with the rise of generative AI, which can produce highly fluent and persuasive human-like content. Detecting harmful content is challenging due to evolving slang, sarcasm, cultural references, and subtlety in AI-generated text, which often differs from human-generated hate speech. Advanced machine learning techniques, multimodal analysis, and deep learning models like LSTM and AnnoBERT are being used to improve detection accuracy. Ethical considerations—including bias, false positives/negatives, transparency, accountability, and inclusion of diverse voices—are central to developing responsible detection systems. The integration of AI with technologies like blockchain can enhance transparency and user accountability, while participatory data practices ensure fairness and effectiveness. Overall, automated detection is essential to promote safe, inclusive, and ethically responsible digital spaces while balancing free expression and user protection.

Chapter 5, Bibliometric Analysis on the Role of Artificial Intelligence in Hate Speech and Policy Formulation: Enhancing Evidence-Based Decision-Making in Research Institutions is important because it provides a comprehensive bibliometric analysis of how Artificial Intelligence is being applied to policy-making, revealing trends, key contributors, and thematic shifts over the last two decades. By mapping research outputs, institutions, and global patterns, it highlights both opportunities and challenges in using AI for evidence-based decision-making. The study emphasizes the growing role of AI in helping research institutions and policymakers respond more effectively to complex policy challenges, while also underlining the need for ethical, transparent, and collaborative approaches to ensure responsible AI governance in policy formulation.

Chapter 6, AI-Generated Hate Speech Detection Technique gives the rapid rise of AI, particularly large language models like GPT and Llama, has enabled the mass generation of human-like text, offering many benefits but also creating new risks for online hate speech. AI-generated hate speech can be subtle, contextually nuanced, and capable of evading traditional detection methods, making it difficult to distinguish between accidental and intentional harm. This research highlights the urgent need for advanced detection and mitigation strategies to protect individuals and communities, maintain trust in digital spaces, and address the evolving challenges posed by AI-driven abusive content.

Chapter 7, Highlighting the Challenges of Bias and Fairness in Hate Speech Detection provides a holistic understanding of automated hate speech detection, highlighting both technological advancements and ethical challenges. By emphasizing the need for context-aware AI, human oversight, and interdisciplinary collaboration, it guides the development of robust, fair, and adaptive moderation systems that protect vulnerable communities while preserving freedom of expression.

Chapter 8, Exploring Hate Speech Classification in Low-Resource Languages - A Comprehensive Review studies the rapid growth of social media has amplified both opportunities for connection and risks of hate speech, which threatens marginalized groups and discourages participation. Advances in NLP and deep learning have improved hate speech detection, with shared tasks like HASOC and SemEval driving progress, yet challenges remain in fairness, explainability, and low-resource language coverage. Strengthening datasets, model transparency, and platform accountability is crucial to ensure safer and more inclusive online environments.

Chapter 9, Real-Time Hate Speech Detection API - A Scalable Deep Learning Approach studies the rapid surge of hate speech on social media, particularly on platforms like Twitter (X), poses serious social and psychological risks. By developing a real-time T5 transformer-based model that classifies tweets into normal, offensive, and hate speech, the research provides a robust tool for timely detection and moderation. The model's integration with FastAPI and use of both textual and metadata features ensures more accurate, scalable, and practical solutions, supporting safer online interactions and aiding platforms, policymakers, and AI developers in managing abusive content effectively.

Chapter 10, Deepfake Technology and the Quagmire of Artificial Intelligence: An Analysis of National and International Legal Frameworks tells the misuse of deepfake technology in India and globally highlights its serious ethical, legal, and social implications. Incidents like high-value financial frauds and online impersonations show how AI-generated forgeries can threaten privacy, dignity, security, and trust in digital interactions. With laws still evolving, especially in India, it is crucial to strengthen regulatory frameworks, raise public awareness, and develop technological safeguards to counter these risks while balancing innovation with responsibility.

Chapter 11, Aspect-Based Opinion Mining A Framework for Spam and Ham Review Detection studies the rapid growth of user-generated content has increased the risk of spam and opinion manipulation, which can mislead consumers and distort public perception. By exploring advanced sentiment analysis and spam detection techniques, including machine learning and NLP methods, the research provides more accurate and efficient tools for understanding genuine opinions, improving decision-making, and maintaining trust in online platforms.

Chapter 12, Deep Learning and NLP Methods for Automated Hate Speech Detection across Human and Machine-Generated Content - Hate speech is a broad and evolving phenomenon that represents a significant danger to the safety and dignity of people and communities throughout the world. Beginning with a discussion of what hate speech is, this chapter provides a robust overview of the concept, as well as the various ways in which hate speech can manifest – in private, public, and online spaces. It includes denial but also trivializing. Great emphasis is placed on the high rise of hate speech on social media, dissecting into components like online harassment, hurtful comments, unfair treatment, trolling, etc. The chapter also engage with the ambiguities of language, culture, and various types of platforms. It discusses contemporary methods of detection, with special emphasis on the role and potential of NLP in setting new standards for detection and discovery. The chapter details the process through which NLP can be used to recognize and analyze hate speech, describing the efficacy with which linguistic tools and computational tools can be effectively integrated in addressing online toxicity.

Chapter 13, Techniques for Detecting Hate Speech in AI and Human-Generated Content poses a serious threat to individuals and society, not only causing psychological harm and inciting real-world violence but also undermining social cohesion by fueling prejudice and division. With the rapid rise of digital platforms, its spread has become more widespread, harder to detect, and increasingly intertwined with AI-generated content, which often makes harmful rhetoric more subtle and difficult to regulate. Effective detection and moderation are therefore crucial to protect vulnerable communities, uphold ethical standards, and balance freedom of expression with the prevention of harm, making the development of advanced, fair, and adaptive systems an urgent necessity.

Chapter 14, Machine Learning Models for Automated Hate Speech Detection in Synthetic Content - This chapter intends to show how Machine Learning (ML) can be employed in order to identify and mitigate hate speech on the web. Plus, the increasing diffusion of Artificial Intelligence (AI) also creates the possibility for the unconscious transmission of, or support for, hate speech through AI systems. This frequently occurs when the training data for these models has involved biased or harmful language, and also because the models are unable to understand context of word use. It describes supervised learning (where a model learns from labeled samples), unsupervised learning (where a model explores the structure of data that is not labeled) and other types of ML that can be applied to discover hate speech in a text. This chapter also analyzes the ways in which we can evaluate the hate speech detection model, and how efficient it is, through precision (how good our detected hate speech examples actually are hate speech), recall (how many real examples of hate speech were correctly detected), F1-score (a weighted average of precision and recall) and ROC-AUC.

In conclusion, this book makes a significant contribution to the evolving field of hate speech detection by offering a comprehensive, interdisciplinary, and globally relevant perspective. By bridging technical insights from AI and natural language processing with social, legal, and ethical considerations, it goes beyond traditional approaches that focus solely on human-generated content. It highlights the emerging challenge of AI-generated hate speech and provides frameworks to address both sources in tandem. In doing so, the book equips scholars, students, professionals, and policymakers with the knowledge and tools necessary to navigate the complexities of digital communication in an age where human and machine voices are increasingly intertwined. Ultimately, it advances the discourse on balancing freedom of expression with safety and inclusivity, positioning itself as a timely and valuable resource for shaping responsible research, policy, and practice in the digital era.

Acknowledgment

Our sincere thank goes to our organizations, Qatar University, Doha, Qatar, Swami Keshvanand Institute of Technology, Management and Gramothan, India, Universidad Azteca, Mexico and Sir Padampat Singhania University, India for providing a healthy academic and research environment during my consistent work.

We are truly moved by the gesture and constant support shown by all the members of Editorial Advisory Board since the beginning of the idea of the edited book. The editors would like to acknowledge the help of all the people involved in this project and, more specifically, to each author and reviewer who took part in the review process. Without their support, this book would not have become a reality.

The completion of this book could not have been possible without the contribution and support we got from our family, friends and colleagues. It is a pleasant aspect and we express our gratitude for all of them.

Muhammad Arsalan
Qatar University, Doha, Qatar

Mehul Mahrishi
Swami Keshvanand Institute of Technology, Management and Gramothan, India

Ruchi Doshi
Universidad Azteca, Mexico

Archika Jain
Swami Keshvanand Institute of Technology, Management and Gramothan, India

Chandrashekhar Goswami
Sir Padampat Singhania University, India

Chapter 1
Exploring the Metaverse: The Future of Architecture and Hate Speech Moderation in Virtual Spaces

Sahar Yousif Mohammed
University of Anbar, Iraq

Maad M. Mijwil
https://orcid.org/0000-0002-2884-2504
Al-Iraqia University, Iraq

Duaa Hikmat Abbas
Al-Iraqia University, Iraq

Kamal Kant Hiran
https://orcid.org/0000-0002-4563-1944
Sir Padampat Singhania University, India

Ali Guma
https://orcid.org/0000-0003-3234-6420
Muni University, Uganda

Indu Bala
https://orcid.org/0000-0002-4667-9501
Lovely Professional University, India

Aseed Yaseen Rashid Al-Jubori
Al-Iraqia University, Iraq

ABSTRACT

The metaverse is transforming architecture by enabling innovation, interdisciplinary collaboration, and immersive client engagement through VR and digital twins. These technologies allow architects to design without physical or financial limitations, fostering creativity and real-time feedback. However, as virtual spaces grow, concerns about hate speech and content moderation arise, complicating regulation due to AI-driven avatars, voice interactions, and global legal inconsistencies. While AI tools help detect and mitigate harmful content, challenges around free speech, algorithmic bias, and regulatory fragmentation remain. Legal frameworks like the EU's Digital Services Act and UN digital rights guidelines highlight the complexity

DOI: 10.4018/979-8-3373-3063-1.ch001

of balancing moderation with digital freedoms. A collaborative approach among AI developers, policymakers, and legal experts is essential to ensuring safe and inclusive virtual environments.

1. INTRODUCTION

1.1 Overview of the Metaverse

The metaverse is the acronym for a collective space that consists of real-time interaction and communication amongst users with the aid of 3D representations of each user or the use of VR and AR environments. The latest generation of the Internet built with cloud, AR/VR, mobile devices, and other new media has been attractively referred to as the metaverse (Aljanabi et al., 2023). It is a network of 3D virtual worlds created by the convergence of virtually enhanced physical reality and physically persistent virtual reality. Like mobile communication and video conferencing over the internet, the metaverse seems to stretch the traditional interactives of broadcasting media even further (Dionisio et al., 2013). The metaverse seems and feels like the internet since it can also be described as an additional layer over the traditional forms of the World Wide Web (Park et al., 2022).

1.2 Relevance to Architecture

With the ongoing development of the metaverse, its importance concerning architecture has also increased immensely. Architects and designers are restricted in neither physical matter usage nor spatial limitations anymore; rather, the metaverse offers the capability to break through the barriers of design in virtual environments (Al-Ghaili et al., 2022). Through the use of activc virtual techniques, architects are able to simulate, alter three-dimensional structures instantaneously to enable the clients and associates comprehend the concept of space better. The metaverse enables the use of active structures such as VR that allow the design of spaces untouched by the limits of gravity, which is limitless in terms of possibility. In addition, it has served as an interactive structure, where different aspects of the same project can be designed simultaneously by members of various teams stationed in diverse locations (Sopher et al., 2023). This change of events affects architecture not only in its processes in which a structure will be designed but also in the experience and understanding of architecture itself by its users, providing new and profound engagement for users in the interactive architecture by focusing on users (Chen et al., 2022).

The purpose of this review is to investigate the process of the transformation of architecture with the spread of the metaverse, focusing on the stages of processes from the design to the collaboration and interaction with the clients. In doing so, the paper will demonstrate the benefits of integrating virtual spaces into the workflows of architectural practice through the metaverse. The paper will look at how architects are bringing this paradigm into their practice, what obstacles are encountered, such as virtual prototypes, collaboration, and moving the limits of creation outside of physical space. Therefore, this paper will foresee the development of architecture in the future when it shall be integrated into the metaverse construct.

2. THE EVOLUTION OF ARCHITECTURAL PRACTICE IN VIRTUAL SPACES

2.1 Historical Context

New technologies in the design industry have greatly impacted how architects approach the preparation and presentation of their architectural designs. In the late 20th century, CAD or Computer-Aided Design emerge to practice the activity of architecture by replacing drafting with computer designs. This helped architects to make better plan and make the correct diagrams without having many mistakes in the plans (Maturana et al., 2021). Subsequent to CAD, the creation of Building Information Modeling (BIM) gave architectural design a major boost, BIM allows architects to work with design together with a variety of the material, construction, and systems' information within one model. It also unveiled the multiple benefits of BIM integration for architects, engineers and contractors involved in project development for smooth operation and efficient building performance (Moneta, 2020). These jumped-started technologies led to the metaverse, an extension of architectural practice into a virtual world that moves away from the conventional 2D plan and technical drawings and actively integrates a 3D user experience (Rafsanjani et al., 2023).

Figure 1. A timeline of architectural technology advancements

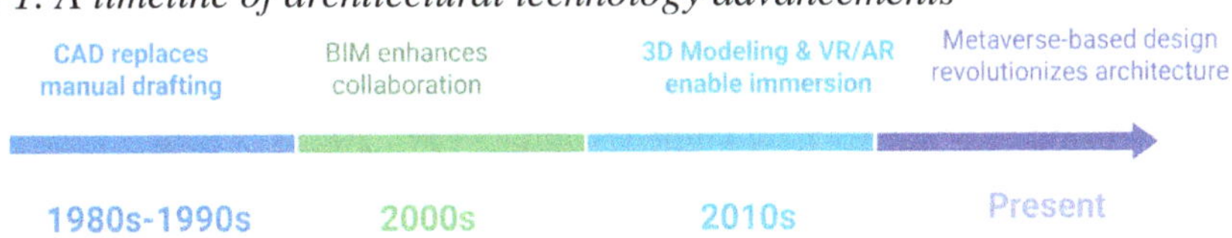

Source: (Rafsanjani et al., 2023).

2.2 From 2D to 3D and Beyond

One major change in the working of the architect has been the transition from drawing in 2D to designing in 3D. Whereas before the render of an architectural design was usually a set of lines in 2D that could only be viewed from a certain angle, it has developed to 3D models that can be rotated to any angle of view. Aside from the visualization, these models also provide the actual circumstances that architects can approximate, including light and materiality of the chosen surfaces and the spatial proportions of the buildings. With the advance in 3D technology, new tools of virtual reality (VR) and augmented reality (AR) have wider applicability to architectural practice. While VR lets the architects and clients 'o be in comparatively real environments, AR lets the models of the proposed construction blend into real life space. This change has created the possibility of the metaverse, a space where architecture can be first conceptualized, engaged with, and tested within virtual reality environments, as well as demonstrating architectural function immediately and at a vast scale (Tosu et al., 2024; Hiran et al., 2024).

2.3 Architects in the Metaverse

The metaverse in architecture has been adopted by a few early pioneers, who tested its wide opportunities for developing innovative approaches to design and interaction with clients. The first wave of metaverse experiments has been embraced by big-name architectural firms, including Zaha Hadid Architects, and BIG (Bjarke Ingels Group), not only as laboratories and testing grounds for new designs, but also as spaces to showcase work. Some of these firms are already using applications such as Spatial, Decentraland, and The Wild for collaborations, whereby the architect, the client, and other stakeholders are able to physically meet in virtual environments. In such cases, design ideas can be communicated in real-time and altered allowing for the use of spaces as a better form of communication than the traditional one. Also, architects are using the metaverse to create new seamless constructed structures which are related to architecture but are purely constructible in the digital world not in the real world. This shift simultaneously offers fresh possibilities and reshapes the connections between built space and the digital market, as online properties and online environments garner new value (Araiqat et al., 2023).

Figure 2. Unveiling the Metaverse Platform's Collaborative Power

Source: (Maturana et al., 2021)

3. DESIGN IN THE METAVERSE: NEW POSSIBILITIES

3.1 Infinite Creative Potential

For architects, the metaverse represents a playground where many of the regular physical laws can be successfully transgressed, and designs which could otherwise be deemed impossible can be implemented. As a result, it allows structures to hover, twist or transform into shapes that would be architecturally impossible, financially disastrous or structurally impossible in reality. The professional designers of buildings require creative freedom to develop outstanding constructions which are absolutely radical and abstract and can unlock the creativity in human mind. This creates the possibility for a speculative architecture where perhaps ideas that are not yet realistic in practice can be fully developed and navigated. It is in this regard that the metaverse represents a virtually boundless creative opportunity for architectural design, confined only by the strength of the imagination of the architect and the functionality of the virtual environment (Pizzolante et al., 2023).

3.2 Digital Twins and Virtual Prototyping

Perhaps one of the most revolutionary ways the metaverse has been employed in architectural design is using digital twin–a virtual representation of physical architecture. Digital twins can be defined as a live, interactive representations enriched by data, which can reflect offline properties and activities of buildings or cities (Ugarte et al., 2022). This technology helps the architects to decide how well their building would fare in different conditions, like, wind, light or traffic before the actual constructional work begins. These considerations help architects evaluate different aspects of the metaverse and select solutions for creating multi-story buildings that are energy-efficient, sustainable, and friendly to users. Through digital twins, virtual prototyping also allows for recognizing possible design issues before construction and, therefore, cutting down and expensive revision procedure. Not limited to design and preconstruction stage, they can also be used in lifecycle of various phases of construction and even in facility management, so they can be considered as multidimensional tool preserving digital twin of the building which evolves together with the building (Segovia et al., 2022).

3.3 User-Centric Design

The characteristics of the metaverse that dictate its operational mode shift the focus of architects working in the industry on the narrative of a user experience transformed by bounds. Potential residents can interact with the designs directly by being able to 'walk through' the supposed rooms, engage with furniture, and feel the spatial relations of a building before the actual construction of the real architecture. This user-centric approach puts the spotlight on the ability of architects to receive feedback in real time from clients and the end users of the infrastructure and this can facilitate the provision of unique and more effective solutions. Customers can try new designs, options, devices, and furniture positioning and made of, and design the environment to meet particular requirements or tastes. Such interactivity deepens the involvement claimed by design as being social since users are not only receiving content but also are contributing to the same. The metaverse paradigm of architecture brings the user closer to the design process throughout the architectural designing process and especially during testing and adjustments in order to converge on nearly ideal designs for the occupants (Limbago, 2023).

4. COLLABORATION AND REMOTE WORK IN VIRTUAL ENVIRONMENTS

4.1 Virtual Collaboration Tools

The metaverse has transformed architectural, construction, and design practices where architects, clients, and entire teams can work in synchronous mode or without physical meetings using a set of synchronous, well-developed digital instruments that allow virtual collaboration in three-dimensional spaces. Spatial, Decentral and, as well as The Wild, enables the architects' accessibility to collaborate with the clients and stakeholders even when they are in different parts of the world. These are applications are meant to support real-time collaborative sessions where participants can communicate with the architectural models, review proposed changes and make these modifications on the spot in an all-immersive environment. Specifically, employing 3D models of the building, architects can show users intricate design that they can navigate as a team, and that is much more appealing than the static picture or plain 2D layout (Manuel et al., 2021; Okoye et al., 2024). As opposed to geographical collaboration tools that only allow one connection at a time, the necessary virtual collaboration tools promote better teamwork since it is faster, and more decisions are made at once with more clarity. Apart from cutting on costs that may be associated with travelling this setting of collaboration widens the sampling dimension and allows experts from across the world to be incorporated in a project.

4.2 Client Interaction

Client relationship in metaverse is to a level more receptive and participatory, changing the perception of concepting and rendering of architectures. Traditional clients are able to sit and look at plans and images, and now they can be walking through the design before actually constructing it. Clients may easily switch between such views, rotate the model in any direction, and apply the context menu with tools to visually determine distance and proportions of a building. They can also engage with design by making modifications with an instant view of how new materials used, furniture placements or even architectural features would look like. Such level of engagement allows clients to be more proactive and make choices during design process because they have all the information about the space. Akin to traditional models, virtual platforms thus allow the last hint of the final design to be better fitted to proper vision and requirements of the client (Rane et al., 2023).

5. CHALLENGES AND LIMITATIONS

5.1 Technological Constraints

As much as this as holds great potential genius for architectural design and cooperation it hold great technological demands. For getting exposed to such applications, architects and ushers require sophisticated virtual reality (VR) or augmented reality (AR) gadgets like wearing headsets coupled with motion trackers which can be expensive and hard to come by (Arena et al., 2022). Moreover, rendering of intricate three-dimensional environments in real time entails significant computations for which reasonably effective computers with graphic processing units are typically needed. In addition, the integration with other avatars, objects, and spaces in as well as the unproblematic real-time interaction also requires a high broadband internet connection that includes a low latency especially in the case of the metaverse, if several users are able to work simultaneously in one single space. This requirement can thus be a nightmare, especially in regions with poor or suffering interlink internet physical connectivity readiness level conditions, thus negating easy accessibility and utilization of such technologies. These limitations have high costs in terms of hardware as well as short supply of advanced technological infrastructure which may act as barriers in the wider use of metaverse of in architectural practice (Syed et al., 2022).

5.2 Digital Divide and Accessibility

The digital divide is another major issue that hampers the adoption of the metaverse in architecture. Extensive training, necessary for new generation gadgets could be beyond the capacity of small firms, independent practitioners or those doing practice in developing areas. Primarily, the cost of equipment, software licensing cost and necessary infrastructure may potentially limit a large group of architects from using VR/AR in designing space (Hiran et al., 2023). Furthermore, even when the ray-technology is available common is the experience that even this will take time before one can master how to use the new ray-technology platforms and tools. Unfortunately, for those architects and designers who do not have enough knowledge of these technologies as such, it becomes challenging to interlink them properly. It means that while the better-funded entities who have the underlying technology in place will be enabled to create as never before, others will be left behind (Kolotouchkina et al, 2022).

5.3 Intellectual Property Concerns

Whereas earlier architectural designs are belonged to the physical domain, their modern counterparts are digital and this raises IP issues. One challenge with the use of metaverse is that since is open when designing an architecture or building, one may have a difficult time protecting it from being copied or used by other people. If designs are copied within the virtual platforms, it may lead to unauthorized copying or theft of ideas or designs if adequate measures have not been taken. However, as architects are increasingly working in the realm between physical and digital creations, the question of who has the rights to virtual designs, particularly when many people are working on the design, returns rather complex questions. Further, issues of privacy are raised because designs are done in shared virtual environments, and personal data can easily be hacked. Therefore, what remains critical for architectural practice is to find ways of tackling these IP and privacy issues to safeguard new designs and ideas, and to cover the architects' backs in the metaverse.

6. FUTURE TRENDS AND IMPACT ON ARCHITECTURE

6.1 Metaverse Cities and Virtual Real Estate

Programmable cities and architectures within the metaverse could be one of the most interesting emerging opportunities in the future of architectures. In this setting, architects can design enormous complete cyber cities that users can navigate more than, live in and even buy areas within the urban map. Lacking physical requirements and restrictions of the tangible world, these metaverse cities can boast unique urban planning concepts and original architecture. Amongst this virtual real estate, which involves the buying and selling of parcels of lands in these digital platforms are gradually coming into existence through Decentral and Sandbox. This can especially mean that the kind of architecture that architects may be envisioning and planning are properties, malls, or even public spaces that maybe solely within the metaverse for a new civilization within the metaverse. Such a shift can recast architecture into a brand-new paradigm – digital urban architecture, in which the discipline would operate in a different sphere.

6.2 Architectural Education and the Metaverse

Incorporation of virtual reality (VR) as a teaching tool in and approach to architectural education delineates new paradigms of how future architects will study and apply their profession. The metaverse allows students to engage with environments that facilitate constructive experiences that entail designing, analysing, and discussing architectural designs in real time. This way students are able to learn how physical objects behave through interactions within a Virtual Environment: space, scale and materiality. Virtual studios in cooperation may unite students and teachers from different parts of the Earth, thus, providing more impressive and diverse experience. Further, using architectural simulations in the metaverse, students are also able to apply certain environmental or lighting conditions to the buildings they design and gain further insight to building performance. This integration of VR in the architectural education curriculum will create a generation of architects that is ready to embrace a future with a lot of VR design tools incorporated in their work.

6.3 Sustainability

In addition, the metaverse is also a perfect place to bring more sustainable design into the architectural field. Concerning sustainability, virtual prototyping in the metaverse eliminates the need for creating models or mock-ups physically, which form some waste. Architects are able to reduce energy and material consumption by modeling structures in digital conditions; thus enhancing the efficiency of the final structure. This approach prevents wastage of material and power that would otherwise be used in construction since it reduces unnecessary errors or inefficiency. Moreover, as virtual platforms gain more importance in human's daily lives, they may act like complementary to some physical infrastructures and thus save new construction or destruction of other structures to the environment. Thus, if the concept of the metaverse will be used as an instrument for building a sustainable environment, the architects will be able to make a positive change in terms of the environmental strategies that can be applied to the design of the new built environment.

7. HATE SPEECH AND CONTENT MODERATION IN THE METAVERSE

As virtual environments expand, the issue of hate speech and content moderation has become a growing concern. The immersive nature of the metaverse driven by voice-based interactions, AI-powered avatars, and real-time engagement adds complexity to moderating harmful content. Unlike traditional social media, where text-based moderation is more straightforward, the metaverse introduces new challenges, as hate speech can be amplified through audio, visuals, and interactive experience. AI-driven tools play a critical role in detecting and managing harmful content, yet significant challenges remain. Concerns around free speech, algorithmic bias, and regulatory inconsistencies make content moderation a highly debated topic. While frameworks like the European Union's Digital Services Act (DSA) and the United Nations digital rights guidelines aim to set global standards, enforcing these regulations across different jurisdictions remains a challenge. To create a safe and inclusive metaverse, a collaborative approach is necessary. AI developers, policymakers, and legal experts must work together to ensure that moderation systems are transparent, ethical, and effective, striking a balance between technological innovation and social responsibility (Matusitz et al., 2024).

Figure 3. Navigating Hate Speech Moderation

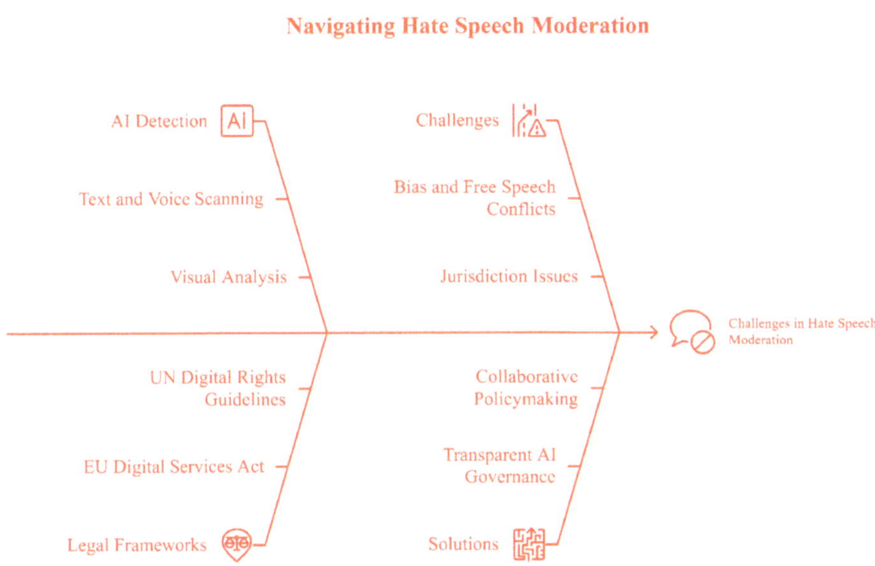

CONCLUSION

Virtual architecture plays an essential role in the metaverse and is changing with the possibilities for creation, cooperation, and interaction offered by the latter. These are the realms of imagination that architects are now able to navigate with no boundaries, making the virtual and tangible ways in which users are able to engage with designs almost endless, including the ability for clients to experience the design in real time. Digital twin improves precision and sustainability while virtual prototype improves the design and virtual collaboration leads to international teamwork. However there remains socio technical factors like technology restrictions, accessibility and issues to do with ownership of materials. However, these challenges suggest that the application of innovative design in metaverse is possible, creating new space for both physical and virtual architectures. It holds tremendous value for the application of architectural design as a main focus of the metaverse. Also with the rise of metaverse cities and virtual real estate architecture there, more and more architects with design futuristic towns and buildings in the virtual world. This aspect of architectural education means that graduates will have to deal with virtual reality in addition to real one. Also, the metaverse will help with sustainable design by creating virtual models of projects. At the same time, as speakers mentioned, there are issues that can become relevant metaverse challenges, such as availability of technology or protection of intellectual property rights; However, there are great opportunities for the future of the architecture in the metaverse: creativity, cooperation, and, among the most important, sustainability.

REFERENCES

Al-Ghaili, A. M., Kasim, H., Al-Hada, N. M., Hassan, Z. B., Othman, M., Tharik, J. H., Kasmani, R. M., & Shayea, I. (2022). A review of metaverse's definitions, architecture, applications, challenges, issues, solutions, and future trends. *IEEE Access : Practical Innovations, Open Solutions, 10*, 125835–125866. DOI: 10.1109/ACCESS.2022.3225638

Aljanabi, M., & Mohammed, S. Y. (2023). Metaverse: Open possibilities. *Iraqi Journal For Computer Science and Mathematics, 4*(3), 79–86. DOI: 10.52866/ijcsm.2023.02.03.007

Araiqat, D. M., & Al-Sartawi, A. (2023). The introduction of interior design and architecture into the metaverse and their interrelation to the reality-enhancing technologies. In *Artificial Intelligence, Internet of Things, and Society 5.0* (pp. 107–117). Springer Nature Switzerland. DOI: 10.1007/978-3-031-43300-9_10

Arena, F., Collotta, M., Pau, G., & Termine, F. (2022). An overview of augmented reality. *Computers, 11*(2), 28. DOI: 10.3390/computers11020028

Chen, T., Zhou, H., Yang, H., & Liu, S. (2022, August). A review of research on metaverse defining taxonomy and adaptive architecture. In 2022 5th International Conference on Pattern Recognition and Artificial Intelligence (PRAI) (pp. 960-965). IEEE. DOI: 10.1109/PRAI55851.2022.9904076

Dionisio, J. D. N., Iii, W. G. B., & Gilbert, R. (2013). 3D virtual worlds and the metaverse: Current status and future possibilities. *ACM Computing Surveys, 45*(3), 1–38. DOI: 10.1145/2480741.2480751

Hiran, K. K., Doshi, R., & Patel, M. (Eds.). (2024). *Modern Technology in Healthcare and Medical Education: Blockchain, IoT, AR, and VR: Blockchain, IoT, AR, and VR*. IGI Global.

Hiran, K. K., Hemachandran, K., Pise, A., & Rabi, B. J. (Eds.). (2023). *Handbook of Research on AI and Knowledge Engineering for Real-Time Business Intelligence*. IGI global. DOI: 10.4018/978-1-6684-6519-6

Kolotouchkina, O., Barroso, C. L., & Sánchez, J. L. M. (2022). Smart cities, the digital divide, and people with disabilities. *Cities (London, England), 123*, 103613. DOI: 10.1016/j.cities.2022.103613

Limbago, J. (2023). Designing User-Centric Private Conversation Methods in the Metaverse (Master's thesis).

Manuel, M., Dongre, P., Alhamadani, A., & Gračanin, D. (2021, July). Supporting embodied and remote collaboration in shared virtual environments. In *International Conference on Human-Computer Interaction* (pp. 639-652). Cham: Springer International Publishing. DOI: 10.1007/978-3-030-77599-5_44

Maturana, B., Salama, A. M., & McInneny, A. (2021). Architecture, urbanism and health in a post-pandemic virtual world. *Archnet-IJAR: International Journal of Architectural Research, 15*(1), 1–9. DOI: 10.1108/ARCH-02-2021-0024

Matusitz, J., & Dacas, J. (2024). Other Problems: Privacy Concerns, Surveillance, and Hate Speech. In *Communication in the Metaverse* (pp. 161–179). Springer Nature Switzerland. DOI: 10.1007/978-3-031-63485-7_9

Moneta, A. N. D. R. E. A. (2020). Architecture, heritage, and the metaverse. *Traditional Dwellings and Settlements Review, 32*(1), 37–49.

Okoye, K., Nganji, J. T., Hiran, K. K., & Hosseini, S. (2024, May). Impact and implications of AI methods and tools for the future of education. [). Frontiers Media SA.]. *Frontiers in Education, 9*, 1434052. DOI: 10.3389/feduc.2024.1434052

Park, S. M., & Kim, Y. G. (2022). A metaverse: Taxonomy, components, applications, and open challenges. *IEEE Access : Practical Innovations, Open Solutions, 10*, 4209–4251. DOI: 10.1109/ACCESS.2021.3140175

Pizzolante, M., Borghesi, F., Sarcinella, E., Bartolotta, S., Salvi, C., Cipresso, P., Gaggioli, A., & Chirico, A. (2023). Awe in the metaverse: Designing and validating a novel online virtual-reality awe-inspiring training. *Computers in Human Behavior, 148*, 107876. DOI: 10.1016/j.chb.2023.107876

Rafsanjani, H. N., & Nabizadeh, A. H. (2023). Towards digital architecture, engineering, and construction (AEC) industry through virtual design and construction (VDC) and digital twin. *Energy and Built Environment, 4*(2), 169–178. DOI: 10.1016/j.enbenv.2021.10.004

Rane, N., Choudhary, S., & Rane, J. (2023). Metaverse for Enhancing Customer Loyalty: Effective Strategies to Improve Customer Relationship, Service, Engagement, Satisfaction, and Experience. Service, Engagement, Satisfaction, and Experience (November 1, 2023).

Segovia, M., & Garcia-Alfaro, J. (2022). Design, modeling and implementation of digital twins. *Sensors (Basel), 22*(14), 5396. DOI: 10.3390/s22145396 PMID: 35891076

Sopher, H., & Lescop, L. (2023). Learning in metaverse: The immersive atelier model of the architecture studio. *Archnet-IJAR: International Journal of Architectural Research, 17*(3), 536–553. DOI: 10.1108/ARCH-10-2022-0213

Syed, T. A., Siddiqui, M. S., Abdullah, H. B., Jan, S., Namoun, A., Alzahrani, A., Nadeem, A., & Alkhodre, A. B. (2022). In-depth review of augmented reality: Tracking technologies, development tools, AR displays, collaborative AR, and security concerns. *Sensors (Basel), 23*(1), 146. DOI: 10.3390/s23010146 PMID: 36616745

Tsou, M. H., & Mejia, C. (2024). Beyond mapping: Extend the role of cartographers to user interface designers in the Metaverse using virtual reality, augmented reality, and mixed reality. *Cartography and Geographic Information Science, 51*(5), 659–673. DOI: 10.1080/15230406.2023.2264748

Ugarte Querejeta, M., Illarramendi Rezabal, M., Unamuno, G., Bellanco, J. L., Ugalde, E., & Valor Valor, A. (2022). Implementation of a holistic digital twin solution for design prototyping and virtual commissioning. *IET Collaborative Intelligent Manufacturing, 4*(4), 326–335. DOI: 10.1049/cim2.12058

Chapter 2
Detecting Hate Speech: Human and AI-Generated Content

Kashvi Chaturvedi
https://orcid.org/0009-0005-3192-3400
Ajeenkya D.Y. Patil University, India

Aditya Shrivastav
https://orcid.org/0009-0000-8461-8171
Ajeenkya D.Y. Patil University, India

Yadnyesh Khapekar
Ajeenkya D.Y. Patil University, India

Atharva Haresh Saraf
https://orcid.org/0009-0006-3842-5508
Ajeenkya D.Y. Patil University, India

Sunil Sankathala
https://orcid.org/0009-0004-7809-7647
Ajeenkya D.Y. Patil University, India

Susanta Das
https://orcid.org/0000-0002-9314-3988
Ajeenkya D.Y. Patil University, India

ABSTRACT

Hate speech refers to language that incites hostility, discrimination, or violence against individuals or groups based on attributes such as race, gender, religion, or sexual orientation. Its detection poses significant challenges due to contextual ambiguity, cultural variance, & linguistic nuance. Artificial intelligence, particularly natural language processing & deep learning models such as CNNs, RNNs, & transformer-based architectures like BERT, have emerged as a critical tool for automating hate speech detection. Word embeddings, contextual modelling, and hybrid detection frameworks that combine human oversight with algorithmic scalability are being actively developed to improve performance. Ethical issues arise around freedom of speech, data privacy, and algorithmic bias. The review highlights techniques for detection, intervention strategies, such as Reflective User Interfaces and content flagging systems, which aim to encourage positive digital behaviour while minimizing harm.

DOI: 10.4018/979-8-3373-3063-1.ch002

1. INTRODUCTION

In the digital age, social media platforms are major sources of hate speech (HS), targeting individuals or groups based on characteristics like race, religion, or gender. The anonymity of these platforms accelerates the spread of HS, making regulation challenging. Despite manual moderation, the growing scale of cyberspace demands more efficient solutions. Advances in natural language processing (NLP) and machine learning (ML) have improved automated HS detection. Competitions like SemEval and GermEval have pushed the development of more effective detection models, using ML methods like Naive Bayes, CNNs (Computational Neural Network), LSTMs (Long Short-Term Memory), and BERT (Bidirectional Encoder Representations from Transformers). However, these systems still struggle with the linguistic and contextual diversity of HS (Jahan & Oussalah, 2023). There can be violence or societal division as a result of spread of Hate Speech on social media. Neural networks, including CNNs, RNNs, and Transformer-based models like BERT and GPT, show promise, as they can process large datasets and adapt to evolving online language. Pre-trained models like BERT excel in capturing both semantic and syntactic features, but challenges remain, such as distinguishing harmful content from legitimate discourse. These technologies must be used responsibly to ensure fairness (Velickovic & Elbassuoni, 2024). The subjective nature of HS detection introduces biases. Human annotators' socio-demographic factors influence how they label offensive content, which can be mirrored by automated systems. Biases in human annotations and large language models (LLMs), like persona-based models, remain critical issues (Giorgi et al., 2024). Regulatory responses like the UK's "Online Harms White Paper" aim to curb online harms but face criticism for misunderstanding the complexities of HS detection. While AI could improve detection, concerns over privacy, bias, and accountability persist (Cortiz & Zubiaga, 2021). As social media grows, HS increases, making automated detection vital. The challenge lies in the complexity of HS, with abbreviations, coded language, and varying expressions across cultures and languages. Various ML models have been developed, but specialized types of HS (e.g., religious, racial) remain hard to detect (Saleh et al., 2023). Generative AI, like GANs (Generative Adversarial Networks) and GPT (Generative Pre-trained Transformer), aids in hate speech detection, especially for low-resource languages, but faces challenges due to cultural and linguistic diversity. Traditional moderation systems are inadequate as content volume grows. Semi-supervised learning (SS-Learning) and GANs are being used to generate data for underrepresented languages. The SS-GAN-PLM (Pre-trained Language Model) framework, using models like mBERT, has been effective for multilingual HS detection (Mnassri et al., 2024). AI's role in content creation raises ethical concerns, particularly in handling sensitive topics like school shootings and hate speech. AI can perpetuate harmful narratives, potentially inciting violence, disinformation, and harm to vulnerable groups (Osipov, 2024). However, biases in datasets, such as terms like "gay" or "Muslim," lead to unfair outcomes, especially for marginalized groups (Mozafari et al., 2020). Text, image, and audio data are all involved in the complex process of detecting hate speech. Although accuracy is increased by multi-modal detection algorithms that involve text, pictures, and video, problems like cultural differences and flexible hate speech producers still exist (Prabhu & Seethalakshmi, 2025). Younger audiences use social media extensively, which makes online abuse worse and causes psychological injury. To solve this issue in an ethical manner, NLP research is concentrating on incorporating social science concepts (Kiritchenko et al., 2021). By looking at definitions, detection techniques, ethical issues, and intervention tactics, this literature review seeks to offer a thorough understanding of hate speech. With an emphasis on artificial intelligence's role in detecting and reducing hate speech, it examines the intricate linguistic, sociological, and technological aspects of hate speech. The paper highlights the advantages and disadvantages of sophisticated deep learning methods used in automated detection systems. It also discusses the moral difficulties in striking a balance between the need to safeguard vulnerable communities and the right to free speech. The analysis also assesses a number of intervention strategies intended to lessen the effects of hate speech and encourage safer online spaces.

2. LITERATURE REVIEW

2.1 Understanding Hate Speech

Hate speech is a type of offensive language that uses stereotypes to propagate hateful ideologies about a person or group based on race, ethnicity, gender, sexual orientation, nationality, or religion. Most hate speech, however, is protected by the laws governing free speech, and not all hate speech constitutes a violation of the law. The law permits regulations against hate speech that involves obscenity, incitement, and "fighting words" (Warner & Hirschberg, 2012). In fact, while someone can show excessive pride for their group, it is not considered hate speech unless it belittles or pokes fun or critiques other groups. Hate speech that uses stereotypes, especially when unnecessarily referenced and intended to create stereotypes, can also be considered hate speech. When derogatory words or racial slurs are necessarily used to describe "bad" groups of people, it is always hate speech, but context opens the door for exceptions, such as discussing its use within an academic or research context or if that person was part of the targeted group (Warner & Hirschberg, 2012). It can often be ambiguous when one does not know who the speaker is, in which case usage is considered hate speech. Other written references differ when comparing spelling such as changes in the suffix from "-er" to "-a" to show the use is self-referential, and this could affect if it is classified as hate speech since it alters the connotation (Warner & Hirschberg, 2012).

Determining whether a given text is hate speech is a difficult task, even for humans, partly because of the complex nature of hate speech, and the fact that it is highly intertwined with intergroup dynamics and subtleties specific to language. Many organizations have established definitions of hate speech, although through different lenses. A common regulatory definition describes hate speech as conduct that incites violence or hatred against an individual or group and is based on certain attributes (race, colour, religion, descent, and national or ethnic origin) (Jahan & Oussalah, 2023). Human rights organizations characterize hate crimes specifically as crimes directed towards a victim based on their actual or perceived membership in a protected group. They recognize that hate can manifest through various forms of intention such as physical and psychological intimidation, property damage, and/or violence. Studies have described hate speech as a form of communication that attacks or demeans a person or a group on the basis of characteristics such as race, ethnicity, religion, disability, gender, age, and sexual orientation and identity (Jahan & Oussalah, 2023). Some scientific researchers have pointed to the idea of intent to harm to define hate speech in a way that looks beyond sets of adjectives and definitions of hate speech to condemn a whole set of linguistic expressions. Some researchers have made a distinction between harmful language and the motivations behind it. Industry platforms such as Facebook and Twitter describe hate speech as "when the language used involves attacks against an individual or group based on a protected characteristic such as race or ethnicity, gender, disability, among other protected characteristics". These industry definitions also often refer to dehumanizing language, harmful stereotypes, and calls to excluding other people from certain rights or privileges (Jahan & Oussalah, 2023). These websites provide specific examples of hate speech as acts or statements of violence, dehumanized comparisons to animals, or calls to injury others. YouTube also has a prohibition against promoting violence or hatred against a person or group based on a long list of characteristics including immigration status and veteran status. Along the same lines, hate speech is generally defined as speech-based against identifiable targets, meaning individuals or groups of individuals (e.g. referencing religion, gender, race, ethnicity, or inciting violence). Other indicators occur less often, perhaps not as relevant in defining hate speech, but speech and acts that include some general components: for example, hateful language sometimes includes profanity or death, instances of disability, age, and lethal diseases (Jahan & Oussalah, 2023). Numerous associated concepts covered by hate speech allude to cyberbullying, described as electronic aggression where an individual is open to attack without the ability to defend themselves. Cyberbullying varies as the attack usually targets an individual in repeated attacks. Racism is an umbrella category encompassing offending and actions from race, tribalism, xenophobia, and other prejudices resulting from origin or physical characteristics (Jahan & Oussalah, 2023). Sexism and gender discrimination relates mainly to stereotypes and assigned gender roles, with primary impact to women and girls via a variety of hostile and benevolent forms of sexism. Radicalization can overlap hate speech but usually accompanies extremist beliefs or religious intolerance. Abusive or offensive language, often accompanied by pejorative or vulgar language, is often conflated with hate speech. Religious hate speech involves discriminatory / derogatory content based on religious beliefs and associations, and has often been cited as a reason for social unrest / crimes in different locales. The categorization of hate speech as religious hate speech allows for some structure to understand hate speech, especially as it relates to its complex nature and the social and linguistic relationships inherent in the hate speech issues (Jahan & Oussalah, 2023).

The analytic task of identifying hate speech is highly complex systematic task of assessing and evaluating language that is used towards insulting, accusing or demeaning individuals or groups in relation to attributes related to ethnicity, race, sexual orientation, religion, and other personal identifiers, takes the analytic task well beyond the realm of technical analysis or into the deeper realm of interpreting languages through the lenses of linguistics, sociology, psychology and/or political analysis as well. Natural languages processing (NLP) and machine learning are processes to analyse large amounts of online text data are useful, but very importantly it is essential to understand the surrounding social and cultural context in which hate speech might occur as well, as the 'hate speech', and its effects are valuable often only in context (Narula & Chaudhary, 2025). It could be concluded thereby that there are also interdisciplinary issues to address hate speech or hate speech phenomenon, and it also will take more than technical, co-curricular and social and cultural awareness to establish an inclusive and safer digital environment. Hate speech is speech that is designed to slander, threaten, humiliate, or incite hatred against people or groups based on identity-related traits such as their ethnicity, race, or religion. Hate speech can be overt or subtle, as many hate speech expressions have offensive meanings only recognizable within the context of a social situation. Hate speech is expressed via a multitude of media, including social networks, online forums, television, and radio broadcast. The accelerated flow of communications online has elevated hate speech into a global issue that is uncontrolled by cultural and national limits (Narula & Chaudhary, 2025).

2.2 What's Unintended Bias?

Unintended bias in machine learning is when one aspect of a model performs better or worse on data for certain groups or identity terms not because it was intended to do so because the model was built to discriminate in respect to a specific task. All models are explicitly biased in order to accomplish a task, for instance a toxicity detecting model is crafted to impose a higher score for presumably toxic commentary. Unintended bias occurs when a model's predictions are determined by identity-related language most likely irrelevant to the content of the comment, hence the model unfairly assigns a higher contextual toxicity score to a non-toxic comment, that for whatever reason has certain identity-related terms present in the comment (Dixon et al., 2018). Unintended Bias has a different definition than fairness, which attends to the wider social implications of those biases and the treatment of persons. A model with unintended bias, may result in unfair consequences depending on how it is used, e.g., whether it disproportionately filtered out or prioritized comments related to particular identities. In the context of text classification, unintended bias can be characterized as the model being differentially accurate on comments related to particular groups or containing particular identity terms. It is important to identify and correct this type of bias, especially with regard to particular identity terms to reduce the negative effects of bias and to enhance fairness in a number of applications (Dixon et al., 2018).

2.3 Why AI?

AI-powered hate speech and abusive language detection is becoming a core approach in the online content moderation ecosystem, providing scalable ways to identify and deal with harmful online content. Hate speech is difficult for digital platforms because the volume of user-generated content will always exceed the number of moderators. As such, it is clear that manual moderation is not sufficient, necessitating some form of automated system instead (Gavi, 2025). These detection systems tend to use machine learning, specifically from natural language processing, which are capable of analyzing and classifying language-based data. The techniques for identifying hate speech can be placed into categories in terms of supervised learning, unsupervised learning, and deep learning. Supervised methods use labeled datasets that identify instances of hate speech and non-hate speech. Supervised machine learning algorithms such as Support Vector Machines (SVM), Logistic Regression and Decision Trees can analyze linguistic features (keywords, syntactic structure, sentiment and context) to categorize texts as hate or non-hate speech (Gavi, 2025). In contrast, unsupervised learning takes unlabeled data and determines hidden patterns in those data without pre-defined categories using clustering or topic modeling to identify similar types of content to decide if the texts might be flagged for hate. While unsupervised learning is not dependent on annotated data as in supervised learning, there can be difficulties around the nuanced interpretations of language being properly captured. Deep learning approaches, specifically Convolutional Neural Networks (CNN) and Recurrent Neural Networks (RNN), augment abilities in processing unstructured text (Gavi, 2025). Such models identify intricate cues embedded in the language such as sarcasm, irony, or code-switching and are able to accommodate larger datasets to identify and adapt to current hate trends with less training compared to supervised algorithms. However, there are restrictions on how these technologies can be used. Because language is contextual, different cultures, languages, and social contexts may have different definitions of hate speech (Gavi, 2025). Potential biases in training data, such as incorrectly identifying harmless content or systematically overpolicing particular groups, can result in unequal moderation. Researchers are researching for advanced approaches like transfer learning and multilingual modeling to address these problems. Additionally, to ensure accuracy researchers are creating hybrid systems that combine computer-aided detection with human moderation (Gavi, 2025).

2.4 Deep Learning Techniques

Deep learning methods are already having a major impact on hate speech detection by providing timely and efficient methods of examining linguistic data. These tools mimic the structure of the brain; neural networks build multiple levels of abstraction to recognize robust features across vast textual corpuses. Deep learning provides increased flexibility in measuring nuanced linguistic aspects, accommodating changing contexts of use, and generalizing retention across different forms of hate speech (Velickovic & Elbassuoni, 2024). A significant benefit of deep learning is their reliance on processing unstructured text data, where features are not manually extracted from the input and are automatically generated during the supervised learning processes. Since CNNs are also reliant on estimating spatial dependencies within blocks of text, CNN applications are an essential consideration in this area of research. CNNs use filters of different sizes to identify local patterns such as the words or the order of characters which can then be combined to mimic other syntactic or semantic structures. Recurrent Neural Networks (RNNs) continue to be widely used for sequential tasks such as text classification. RNNs utilize a hidden state to keep track of previously processed tokens while processing tokens one by one, which helps them model temporal dependencies in the text (Velickovic & Elbassuoni, 2024). RNNs also offer a more straightforward approach to text classification because they process the input as a sequence rather than requiring appropriate model input formatting. Furthermore, transformer-based models, such as BERT and GPT, use self-attention mechanisms to model long-range dependencies in the text input they receive. Through pre-training, these models have developed the ability to generate detailed representations of language by utilizing contextual and semantic links. Likewise, these models influence the full context of a word or phrase due to their bidirectional modeling into the full sentence context of a text, which is beneficial for context-dependent or ambiguous hate speech identification. A model can adapt to specific domains while enhancing accuracy and generalization performance by overseeing the fine-tuning of pre-trained models using tagged hate speech datasets (Velickovic & Elbassuoni, 2024).

A key component of NLP is word embedding, which transforms semantic meaning into numerical representation. An N-dimensional dense vector is assigned to each word, enabling comparisons of words from a given language. This technique has proved effective across a range of NLP tasks, including text classification, document clustering, part-of-speech tagging, named entity recognition, and sentiment analysis (Saleh et al., 2023). Stanford GloVe and Google Word2Vec are two well-known pretrained word embedding models. With Word2Vec, users can select between two training architectures: Continuous Bag of Words (CBOW), which predicts a target word from surrounding context, and Skip-Gram (SG), which predicts surrounding context from the given word. Word2Vec generates word vectors by using surrounding context in a large corpus. A dataset of around 100 billion words was used by Google to train their Word2Vec algorithm (Saleh et al., 2023). Global word-to-word co-occurrence statistics acquired by a count-based method are used by GloVe (Global Vectors for Word Representation) to create its embeddings. In contrast to Word2Vec's prediction-based method, GloVe employs a count-based, matrix factorization methodology. GloVe bases its models on numerous dimensionality model options and corpora including Wikipedia, web data, and Twitter. Bidirectional Long Short-Term Memory (BiLSTM) model was created which gathers input from both sides of the context to better comprehend what happens with our sequential data. It records contextual dependencies in sequential data which goes beyond typical LSTMs (Saleh et al., 2023). Building on earlier existing methods, BERT (Bidirectional Encoder Representations from Transformers) is a pre-trained language model that uses deep contextual understanding to improve word representations. While static embeddings like Word2Vec and GloVe encode context in one direction, BERT produces dynamic embeddings with bidirectional context at every layer. BERT uses cooperative conditioning which combines context instead of concatenation which exists only at the surface level. BERT utilizes large datasets such as BooksCorpus and English Wikipedia. As these datasets are very large-scale, BERT is able to achieve state-of-the-art performance across several Natural Language Processing (NLP) tasks (classification, question answering, and named-entity recognition) (Saleh et al., 2023).

2.5 Ethical Considerations

The promotion of human values is closely associated with core human rights. The emphasis and focus of both is the support of human flourishing while providing benefit to society and broad access to technology. When it comes to online abusive content detection, two key values - freedom of speech and respect for equality and dignity, which often conflict with one another. Freedom of speech, or "the right to hold opinions without interference," is a legal right recognized in both national and international legal agreements, however, it can also be restricted in instances where it negatively impacts consequences of other rights; for example, hate speech or defamatory speech (Kiritchenko et al., 2021). While abusive content can cause profound psychological distress, lead to, or further, real-life violence, and ultimately push a marginalized group to experience social marginalization worse than it was before. It is important to note that marginalized communities are particularly susceptible to internalizing narratives that dehumanize them. Sadly, dehumanization can lower prosocial behavior for that marginalized group, while simultaneously encouraging antisocial behavior towards them which may leave individuals susceptible to start legitimate exploitation. Retaining dignity, so that all people, especially people from minority groups, can participate freely and safely in public conversations, justice - both online and offline - must be seen as fairness and inclusion (Kiritchenko et al., 2021). Ideas about a space for free, unrestricted speech online often come from privileged positions that ignore the ethical duty to create safe online spaces. There is pressure felt by social media organizations from governments, civil society, and others, to create protections for people who use their conversations apps/products, including as content filtering, and an appeals process, but given the sheer volume of content posted online limits what they can do. Content moderation systems are also typically developed within the dominant structures of society, so they risk repeating past injustices like colonialism, patriarchy, and racism. Although social media organizations often present themselves as neutral agents facilitating conversations in their products, they are political actors supporting certain types of political ideas, beliefs, and actions through their algorithmic sorting of content (Kiritchenko et al., 2021). While their surveillance and regulation of speech might not exceed the power of the government, they can impose significant limits on freedom of expression, and in some cases, online speech regulation might pose more serious risks than government regulation. Finally, many automated moderation systems, and AI systems generally, will perpetuate existing social inequalities by privileging certain languages and communities over others, for example, NLP research is dominated by a few wealthy language families, which may produce a significant level of ontological injustice. These gaps can create considerable harm, especially in contexts where languages with fewer resources are spoken, and social media can serve as a trigger for violence (Kiritchenko et al., 2021). Despite recent attempts to expand language coverage in abusive content detection, there are still obstacles to overcome, particularly because of linguistic diversity and cultural differences in the definition of offensive language. These obstacles make multilingual data constructions and methods that call for some level of cross-linguistic use more difficult. Abuse on the internet has the potential to intensify offline manifestations of social exclusion. It is a cultural issue as much as a technological one. Online platforms may make matters worse because of their anonymity, lack of feedback, and increased visibility, all of which raise the possibility of offensive interactions compared to in-person interactions. Any long-term remedy will need a cultural reaction in addition to technological, legal, and corporate policy fixes (Kiritchenko et al., 2021).

2.6 Interventions Strategies

User privacy may be a concern when detection algorithms check user input because this could invade upon their right to privacy. When people communicate via digital platforms it happens in many systems that a user is implicitly waiving rights to privacy as users agree to allow their input to be tracked or not anonymously repurposed for either product improvement or advertising and, in some cases, they can decline these rights with the opt-out choice. To solve the risk of cyberbullying for minors, it can include oversight by parents or restrictions by social networks (Dinakar et al., 2012). Examples of restrictions can be social networks introducing stricter remediation policies, and heavily enforcing moderation. These new software interventions attempt to find the right balance between providing additional safeguards and allowing children to form their own opinions or assertions. However, it is important to note that cyberbullying consists of numerous roles like the aggressor, victim, bystander, friends, adults, moderators and networks. Each of these roles can sometimes overlap and change, making it difficult to precisely identify roles and how to intervene. Negative interactions often outflow from one social network to the next. Someone may be bullying someone online but are also being victimized by someone in and outside of the school environment (Dinakar et al., 2012). Labels do not help those being targeted, but they help others understand the context of the individual being labeled, and that threatens the person being labeled by the authority and/or society. Positive engagement strategies often go beyond labels into promoting positive and healthy engagement in digital interactions rather than just who the labels are related to. RUIs (reflective user interfaces) are proposed as a new design methodology for encouraging positive actions and attitudes of users by asking them to think reflectively about their engagement of others (Dinakar et al., 2012). RUIs are derived from developmental, professional and applied theories of reflective practice, RUIs will facilitate engagement through notifications or alerts, an action delay to find reflective responses after a notification, flagging of hidden or second-order consequences, flags suggested by the system, engaging educational links or activities, and visual images of user engagements over time. RUIs also avoid restrictive censorship and support user self-regulation and responsible selections in a user's engagement with others while providing moderators responsibility to reflect on user engagement through aggregated data dashboards to examine overall community engagement. Subtle notifications are intended to engage user responsibility in awareness of their impact on others, especially where non-verbal cues are omitted from their online interaction while re-engaging in their positive engagement (Dinakar et al., 2012). Interactive education is embedded in the online environment providing immediate, context specific feedback rather than generic, distant suggestions. In the moment interventions can prompt individuals to reconsider before sending emails or posts that may be harmful and also provide support for the individuals that are victimized and those that are bystanders. Imposing a short time delay will slow the spread of harmful content, giving individuals the chance to reflect, reconsider, and retract a post/email prior to sending. Enforced time delays create space for thinking and reflection ("reflection in action") can prompt reconsideration to intervene and even educate as is done with certain e-commerce interactions (Dinakar et al., 2012). Providing undo opportunities after submitting will increase reflections and permit the withdrawal of messages. Notifying individuals about hidden consequences also increases awareness about message spread, for example showing the estimated readership before submitting. Alerts can allow users to reconsider posting comments that appear harsh with undo options in the immediate wake of posting to reduce impulsive negative interactions. Educational resources could be contextually suggested to users who have received any negative messages, linking them to interactive resources and relevant support material. This creates change and turns a generic anti-bullying education into specific situationally relevant intervention, and moves the guidance from provocation to action as we create expert system principles to personalize assistance and feedback and opt in service usage (Dinakar et al., 2012). From the perspective of the social network providers, ensuring a safe platform means preventing escalation of, and community spread of bullying instead of completely eliminating every case. On the other hand, moderators employ aggregated behavioral overviews, which offer trends and patterns that enable the application of preventative measures. Additionally, automated content recognition helps moderators by identifying improper messages and providing an alert system that prioritizes and suggests human moderation, particularly in big networks. According to moderation discretion, items and messages that are marked as requiring action may also be highlighted in some way so that potential victims can be alerted or informed (Dinakar et al., 2012). Additionally, visualization systems have evolved into dashboard-style tools for providers and moderators. These tools give them a clear overview of social network behaviors that can be established such as semantic trending, social clustering, flagged content, and demographic capacity. They also encourage collaborative working with groups such as schools or police forces, as dashboards can provide basic data records collectively with anonymized reporting so more real-world planning or intervention can be made (Dinakar et al., 2012).

Active social networking will become more likely to utilize multiple filtration measures to filter problematic and offensive content, but currently rely primarily on lexicon-based filtering. For example, YouTube has a safety mode where comments with offensive language can be hidden and obscured, although filtered comments may be visible if the user opts to see "Text Comments", as seen with pejoratives being concealed with asterisks. Facebook includes a "Moderation Blacklist" rich with comma separated keywords, quickly identifying and filtering False Posts or Comments that contain any of these terms as spam. Twitter on the other hand does not pre-filter anything but does allow users to block or unfollow any accounts posting inappropriate content (Chen et al., 2012b). Twitter also had an app "Tweetie 1.3" that Apple denied because it allowed profanity. Most platforms are using defined vocabulary or user generated vocabulary for offensive word filtering. Only social media platforms seem to rely so heavily on user reports and moderation activity to regulate content – requiring users or administrators to moderate content on most platforms often leads to long response times. Since adolescents typically lack risk awareness, these systems do not effectively shield them from the harm of being subjected to vulgar, pornographic or hateful language, and thus sophisticated software and techniques are needed to detect and respond to offensive content quickly to protect the younger audience (Chen et al., 2012b).

3. ANALYSIS

The following figures, Figure 1, Figure 2, Figure 3, provide a bibliometric study of research on identifying hate speech in both human and AI-generated content from 1985 to 2025 with data from Lens.org and displayed using VOSviewer. The network clusters of related concepts, development of major topics, and the density of often used phrases within the literature are all highlighted by these occurrence maps. When taken as a whole, they offer a thorough understanding of the evolution of this field's study spanning transdisciplinary, technological, and social realms.

Figure 1. Bibliometric Analysis on Detecting Hate Speech in Human and AI-Generated Content using VOSviewer and data from Lens

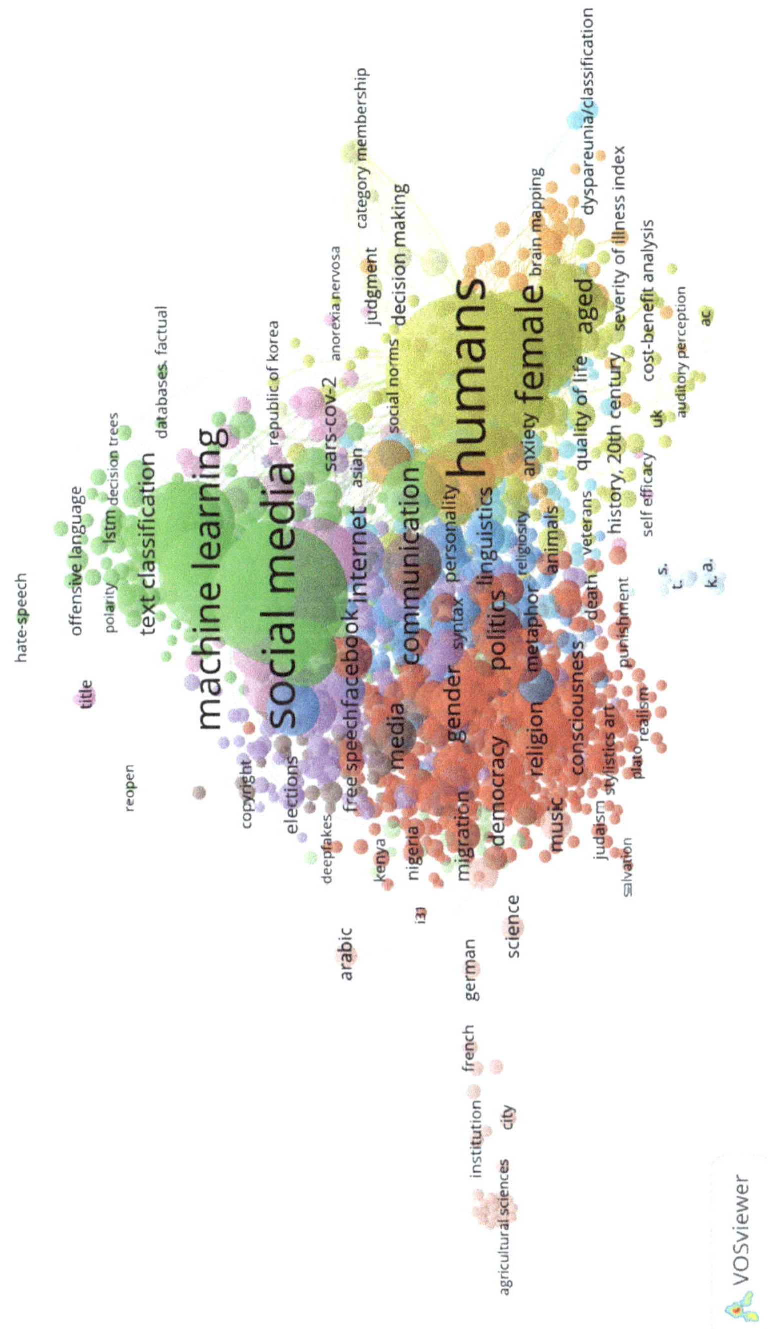

(VOSviewer; Lens.org)

The network of keyword co-occurrences is depicted in Figure 1. It has nodes that stand for terms, their sizes indicate frequency, and linkages show how strongly they occur. Color-coded clusters of similar phrases highlight different but related fields of study. Studying how hate speech unreasonably affects vulnerable groups and the psychological burden it causes, the yellow cluster focuses on people and is associated with demographic and psychological themes including "female," "old," "quality of life," and "anxiety." "Machine learning," "text categorization," and "foul language" serve as the green cluster's pillars, demonstrating the field's computational foundation and the ongoing advancement of AI models for hate speech detection. The red cluster emphasizes "politics," "religion," "consciousness," and "migration." It also highlights the political and cultural origins of hate speech and its connection to identity, democracy, and social conflict. Strong ties between clusters show that research is not limited to specialized fields but rather benefits from interdisciplinary links. This graphic emphasizes how difficult it is to detect hate speech; while technology advancement is vital, it is insufficient without equally strong ethical and social scientific insights.

Figure 2. Bibliometric Analysis on Detecting Hate Speech in Human and AI-Generated Content over a period of time using VOSviewer and data from Lens

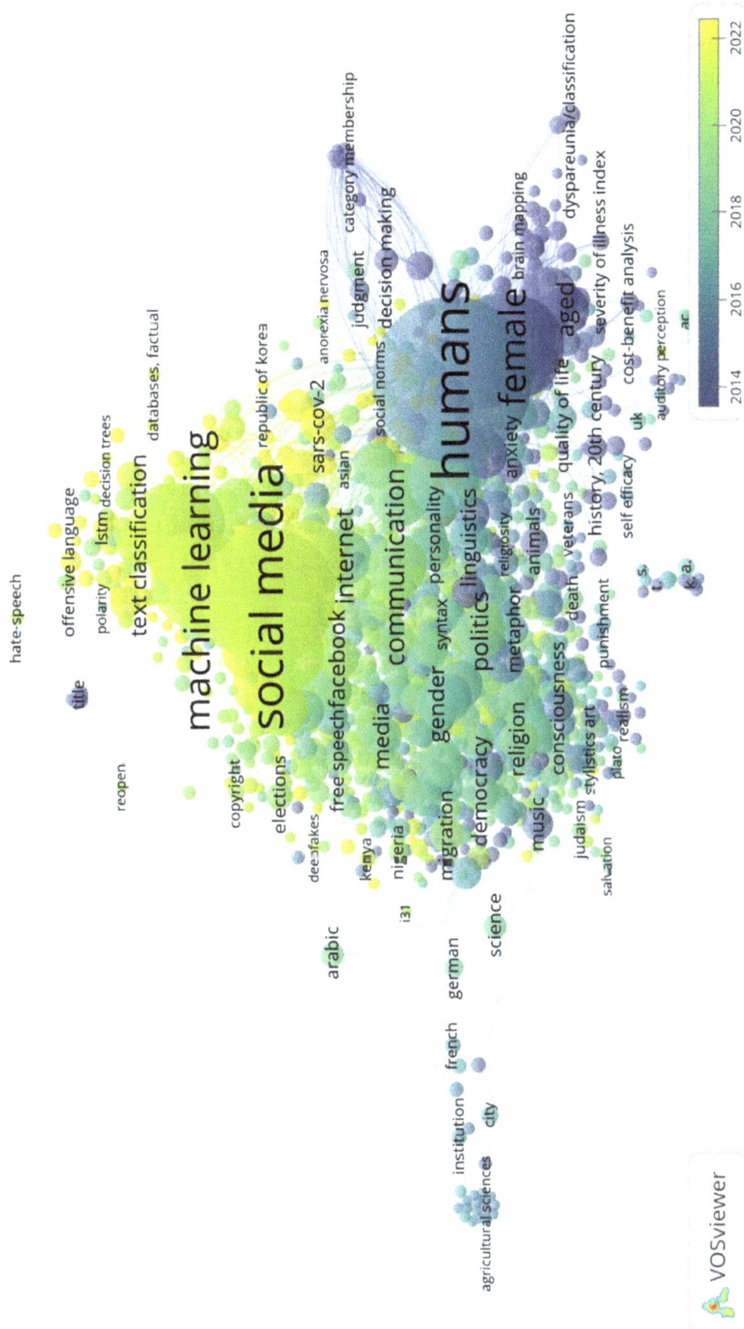

(VOSviewer; Lens.org)

The trend of publication with respect to time is represented by the color gradient, as shown in in Figure 2, displays the historical evolution of research themes. Previous pieces, which were depicted in cooler hues like blue and green were created between about 2010 and 2015, focused on broad conversations about "people," "politics," "religion," and "communication." This implies that the majority of early research on detecting hate speech was sociological and humanities oriented, emphasizing the ways in which speech reflects political ideas, social structures, and identity-based conflicts. As time went on, the discipline saw a visible trend shift toward technical and computational methods, which is symbolized by the yellow colors (depicting year range of 2018 to 2022). The emergence of automated detection techniques for massive amounts of digital content was indicated by the dominance of keywords like "social media," "machine learning," "text categorization," and "foul language detection." Keywords like "sarcasm," "deepfakes," and "COVID-19" (SARS-CoV-2) from more recent years further highlight specialized contexts, demonstrating how current issues and international crises impact online discourse and, thus, change the emphasis of hate speech study. This achievement highlights a significant shift in the field, moving from theoretical discussions of societal impact to the creation of AI-powered systems that can handle the always growing volume of digital communication.

Figure 3. Bibliometric Analysis of density of Detecting Hate Speech in Human and AI-Generated Content over a period of time using VOSviewer and data from Lens

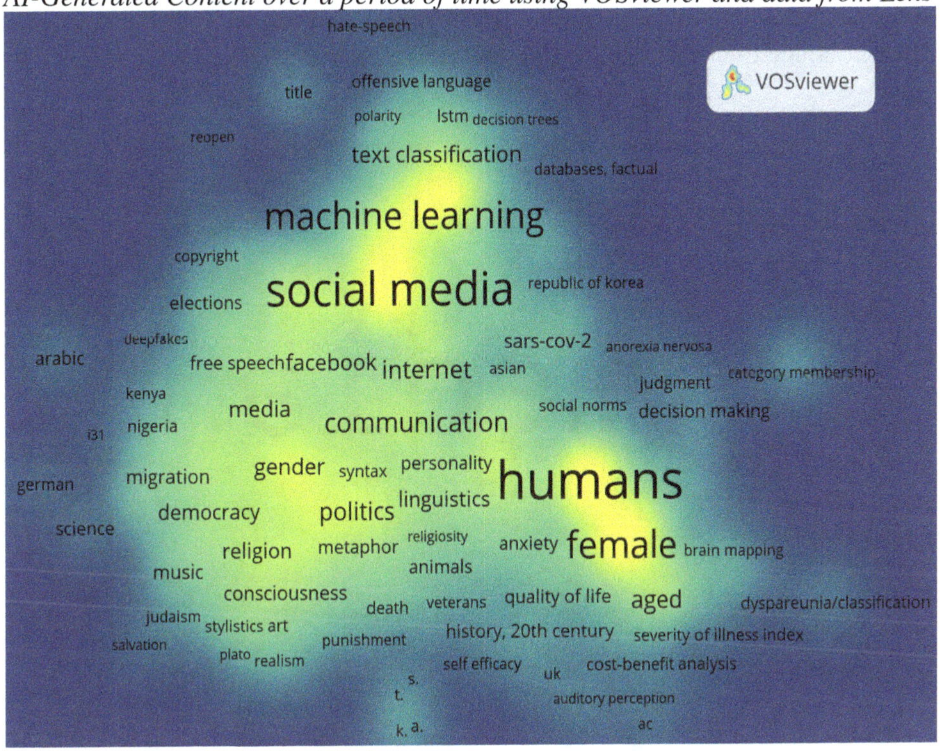

(VOSviewer; Lens.org)

A density map of the most common keywords is shown in Figure 3, with colder colors (blue and purple) denoting fewer common terms and warmer colors (yellow and green) denoting areas of high occurrence. The three main pillars of hate speech detection research are evidently "social media," "people," and "machine learning," as these are the regions with the densest concentrations. The study of hate speech is basically interdisciplinary, incorporating knowledge from computer science, linguistics, sociology, and political science. This is reflected in the ring of high-frequency phrases surrounding them, which include "communication," "politics," "the internet," and "gender." While acknowledging the "human" and "social aspects: that are inextricably linked to technology detection techniques, the density visualization also highlights the fact that research efforts are heavily focused on online platforms as the main setting for the spread of hate speech. Crucially, the density distribution highlights the field's dual nature: on one hand, a technical push to improve classification models and machine learning algorithms; on the other, a social and cultural need to comprehend identification, prejudice, and the moral implications of detection systems. The figure's mapping of these high-density research themes reveals both what has been researched the most and where there are still gaps, including low-resource languages or region-specific linguistic variances, which continue to undermine the universal efficacy of detection systems.

Figure 4. Word Cloud of Keywords on Hate Speech Detection from Lens

The word cloud (Figure 4) displays the most common topics in research on hate speech detection, with words like “social,” “language,” “learning,” “media,” “analysis,” “health,” and “public” showing up frequently. This suggests that the topic is intricately linked to machine learning techniques, social media platforms, and NLP. Words like “political,” “communication,” “education,” “sentiment,” and “classification” are used, indicating a strong multidisciplinary nature that includes political science, computer science, linguistics, and psychology. Furthermore, since real-world occurrences and societal concerns frequently influence the focus of AI-based detection systems, the inclusion of terminology like “COVID,” “gender,” “emotion,” and “security” emphasizes the contextual sensitivity of hate speech research. The increasing complexity of harmful online discourse and the need for AI-human cooperation to address it are reflected in this image, which shows how hate speech detection has developed into a multi-domain research area.

Figure 5. Publication Trend in Hate Speech Detection from 1985 to 2025

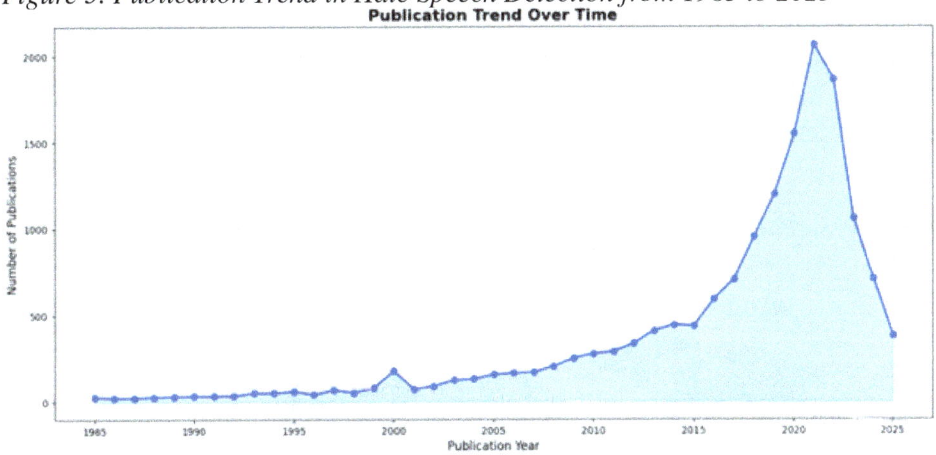

The growth trajectory of hate speech detection research is depicted by Figure 5. There were very few publications between 1985 and around 2000, mostly limited to theoretical debates in communication studies, linguistics, and law. Between 2005 and 2015, there was a steady growth that coincided with the emergence of social media sites like Facebook and Twitter, which increased the prominence and intensity of hate speech online. Following 2015, there is a dramatic exponential increase that peaks in 2020–2021, indicating the widespread acknowledgement of hate speech as a serious problem, especially in times of political polarization, migratory difficulties, and the COVID-19 pandemic. Rapid developments in AI, deep learning, and transformer-based NLP models (like BERT and GPT) that transformed detection capabilities also coincide with the rise. The visible drop after 2021, however, might be the result of both research combination and publishing capacity, since attention is now focused on improving methodology, addressing bias in AI-generated material, and making sure that systems are morally sound and explicable. All things considered, the pattern shows that hate speech detection has developed from a specialized field into a popular multidisciplinary research topic, with AI playing a key role in determining future paths.

Figure 6, of global map, illustrates the geographic distribution of research articles on hate speech detection. Because of their sophisticated research ecosystems and the pressing need to confront online hate speech in their respective geopolitical contexts, the United States and sections of Europe—especially the UK, Germany, and the Netherlands—dominate the field and produce the most studies. New contributions from China, Brazil, and India demonstrate that the identification of hate speech is also becoming more popular in developing nations where social media usage is rising quickly. Large regions of Africa and Southeast Asia, however, are still underrepresented, indicating a research gap in Global South contexts, where mainstream AI models frequently ignore cultural quirks and low-resource languages. This unequal distribution emphasizes the necessity of region-specific methods and inclusive, multilingual datasets in order to prevent algorithmic bias and guarantee equity in detection systems for a range of demographics.

Figure 6. Countries' Contribution in Publication of Hate Speech Research

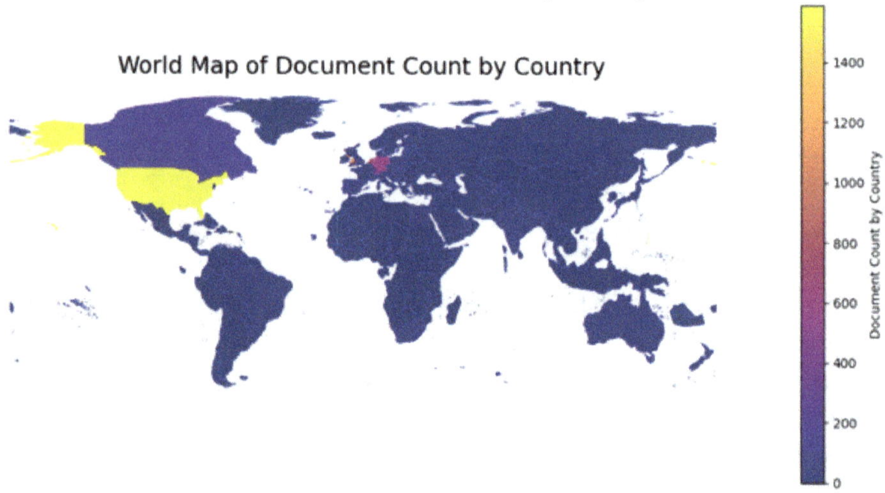

4. CHALLENGES

Using Artificial Intelligence (AI) to detect inconspicuous hate speech on social media has many challenges from both technology and the complexity of human communication. One major barrier to AI's detection of hate speech is the socio-cultural and situational context and how the same words and phrases can take on very different meanings. Language detection AI systems frequently lack the capacity to completely understand contextual layers and provide accurate interpretations. Irony and sarcasm further complicate that detection (Douglas, 2024). These rhetorical devices rely on listeners identifying a discrepancy between the intended meaning and the literal statement, which frequently calls for tone and subtext awareness. Furthermore, AI models are unable to distinguish contextual objects, and lockdown might not even be able to distinguish between "fake praise" in the form of criticism and real praise. Another obstacle is the dynamic nature of language. Models may fail to detect new slang and memes, that are continually emerging in online discourse since they were trained on outdated datasets. Retaining detection efficacy with organizations calls for frequent retraining and updates to all new data, a significant commitment of resources. The addition of cultural and linguistic plurality creates complexity. Words that are offensive in one culture can remain neutral in another culture, and thus, language models need to not only account for cultural contexts but also be adaptable (Douglas, 2024). AI models generally rely on relatively high-quality training data, therefore, there remain even fewer data in all other languages as a persistent issue, which leads to inadequate model performance with all language minority groups. Dialects and regional variations create more problems by adding very distinct wording that standard models may not include. Some of the work being done to reduce these issues is continuing to develop natural language processing into deeper understanding of context; using multimodal sources to enhance meaning, tone, and intent; maintaining training data that is relevant and current; and diversifying the known representations of culture and language in model creation. However, as we have seen, the automation of subtle hate speech detection is neither simple nor static in an evolving space that requires ongoing invention and strict analysis of AI systems (Douglas, 2024).

5. CONCLUSION

Technology cannot resolve the complex problem of identifying and controlling hate speech on the internet. Although AI techniques like NLP and deep learning are helpful for processing big amounts of data, they have drawbacks like sarcasm, regional differences, and inherent biases. Because of this, it is crucial to continuously improve algorithms and training data while guaranteeing their ethical application. Balanced strategies that promote self-examination and education can frequently be more successful than strict censorship, and human moderators are still crucial for interpreting delicate or ambiguous circumstances. Responses must integrate technical tools with social, cultural, and ethical knowledge in order to create online environments that are truly inclusive. In order to ensure that efforts safeguard free expression as well as the safety and dignity of vulnerable populations, progress will require interdisciplinary cooperation, cultural sensitivity, and transparency in moderation.

REFERENCES

Chen, Y., Zhou, Y., Zhu, S., & Xu, H. (2012b). Detecting Offensive Language in Social Media to Protect Adolescent Online Safety. *2012 International Conference on Privacy, Security, Risk and Trust*, 71–80. DOI: 10.1109/SocialCom-PASSAT.2012.55

Cortiz, D., & Zubiaga, A. (2021). Ethical and technical challenges of AI in tackling hate speech. *International Journal of Information Ethics, 29*. Advance online publication. DOI: 10.29173/irie416

Dinakar, K., Jones, B., Havasi, C., Lieberman, H., & Picard, R. (2012). Common sense reasoning for detection, prevention, and mitigation of cyberbullying. *ACM Transactions on Interactive Intelligent Systems, 2*(3), 1–30. DOI: 10.1145/2362394.2362400

Dixon, L., Li, J., Sorensen, J., Thain, N., & Vasserman, L. Measuring and Mitigating Unintended Bias in Text Classification. In: Proceedings of the 2018 AAAI/ACM Conference on AI, Ethics, and Society. AIES'18. New York, NY, USA: Association for Computing Machinery; 2018. p. 67–73. Available from: DOI: 10.1145/3278721.3278729

Douglas, Y. (2024). AI Detection of Subtle Hate Speech in Social Media. DOI:DOI: 10.13140/RG.2.2.19317.59362

Gavi, K. (2025) *Ethical Challenges in AI-Powered Hate Speech Detection: Balancing Automated Moderation and Dataset Creation*. 12 Jan. 2025. www.researchgate.net/publication/387949183

Giorgi, T., Cima, L., Fagni, T., Avvenuti, M., & Cresci, S. (2024). Human and LLM Biases in Hate Speech Annotations: A Socio-Demographic Analysis of Annotators and Targets. *arXiv (Cornell University)*. https://doi.org//arxiv.2410.07991DOI: 10.48550

Jahan, M. S., & Oussalah, M. (2023). A systematic review of hate speech automatic detection using natural language processing. *Neurocomputing, 546*, 126232. DOI: 10.1016/j.neucom.2023.126232

Kiritchenko, S., Nejadgholi, I., & Fraser, K. C. (2021). Confronting Abusive Language Online: A Survey from the Ethical and Human Rights Perspective. *Journal of Artificial Intelligence Research, 71*, 431–478. DOI: 10.1613/jair.1.12590

Mnassri, K., Farahbakhsh, R., & Crespi, N. (2024). Multilingual Hate Speech Detection: A Semi-Supervised Generative Adversarial Approach. *Entropy (Basel, Switzerland), 26*(4), 344. DOI: 10.3390/e26040344 PMID: 38667898

Mozafari, M., Farahbakhsh, R., & Crespi, N. (2020). Hate speech detection and racial bias mitigation in social media based on BERT model. *PLoS One*, *15*(8), e0237861. DOI: 10.1371/journal.pone.0237861 PMID: 32853205

Narula, R., & Chaudhary, P. (2025). A comprehensive review on detection of hate speech for multi-lingual data. *Social Network Analysis and Mining*, *14*(1), 244. Advance online publication. DOI: 10.1007/s13278-024-01401-y

Osipov, D. V.School Shooting Cases. (2024). Ethics of AI technologies in "Sensitive" content creation and Evaluation. School shooting cases. *Galactica Media Journal of Media Studies*, *6*(3), 44–65. DOI: 10.46539/gmd.v6i3.530

Prabhu, R., & Seethalakshmi, V. (2025). A comprehensive framework for multi-modal hate speech detection in social media using deep learning. *Scientific Reports*, *15*(1), 13020. Advance online publication. DOI: 10.1038/s41598-025-94069-z PMID: 40234479

Saleh, H., Alhothali, A., & Moria, K. (2023). Detection of Hate Speech using BERT and Hate Speech Word Embedding with Deep Model. *Applied Artificial Intelligence*, *37*(1), 2166719. Advance online publication. DOI: 10.1080/08839514.2023.2166719

Velickovic, V., & Elbassuoni, S. (2024). Detecting Hate Speech: Deep Learning Techniques for Text Analysis and Classification. DOI: 10.13140/RG.2.2.27435.04641

VOSviewer. Retrieved 2025, https://www.vosviewer.com/

Warner, W., & Hirschberg, J. (2012, June 1). *Detecting hate speech on the world wide web*. ACL Anthology. https://aclanthology.org/W12-2103/

Chapter 3

A Lightweight Content-Based News Recommendation System Using TF-IDF and Cosine Similarity

Snehal Rahul Rathi
https://orcid.org/0009-0004-7638-6429
Vishwakarma Institute of Technology, Pune, India

Aditi Meshram
Vishwakarma Institute of Information Technology, Pune, India

Ritik Narote
Vishwakarma Institute of Information Technology, Pune, India

Shilpa Kalantri
https://orcid.org/0000-0002-7011-2513
Shah and Anchor Kutchhi Engineering College, Mumbai, India

ABSTRACT

The exponential growth in digital media has revolutionized news consumption. However, it has also led to significant challenges in filtering relevant content from the vast information pool. Personalized news recommendation systems are essential to ensure user engagement and satisfaction. This paper proposes a machine learning-based News Recommendation System leveraging Term Frequency-Inverse Document Frequency (TF-IDF) and cosine similarity to identify and suggest similar

DOI: 10.4018/979-8-3373-3063-1.ch003

news articles based on content alone. The system is implemented using Python and Streamlit with additional features like category filtering, keyword search, and article export. Evaluation on a dataset of 1000+ real-world news article demonstrates the model's effectiveness and potential for scalable deployment.

INTRODUCTION

The growth of online content has completely changed how we get news. In the past, most people read newspapers or watched TV to stay informed. These days, we can use apps on our phones or visit websites to get news quickly. This means that anyone can access news at any time. However, having so much information available can make it difficult for people to find news that suits their personal interests. Generic news platforms often present the same trending articles to every user, disregarding their preferences, location, or past reading behavior. Recommendation systems can solve this by tailoring content suggestions. However, many existing systems rely heavily on user history, which introduces privacy.

This paper presents a content-based News Recommendation System designed for real-time use, built using TF-IDF vectorization and cosine similarity. It also includes practical features such as article preview, similarity scoring, and the ability to filter by category and keyword – all delivered via a responsive Streamlit web interface.

In contrast, content-based systems require no personal data and offer comparable accuracy in certain domain.

The system is implemented using Python 3.10 and several powerful open-source libraries, ensuring ease of use and reproducibility.

BACKGROUND

In the contemporary world, people are inundated with an excess of news because of the internet. The overwhelming content available on multiple platforms makes it harder for the reader to find articles that piques their interest. Regular news websites provide trending and standard articles, which do not cater to the individual user's needs, as there is no algorithmic personalization to discover content. To enhance user engagement and recommend pertinent articles, an advanced and smart system is needed. This task is best approached using content-based filtering techniques which recommend items based on their inherent properties and aim to provide similar items to the user, especially when user history is sparse or nonexistent.

The recommendation system we designed uses content-based filtering techniques with Term Frequency-Inverse Document Frequency (TF-IDF). This model considers the relevance of individual words based on their frequency in a given article in relation to their frequency in the entire data set. TF-IDF filters out common words with little value and shifts great importance into unique terms. As raw textual content is transformed into distinct numeric vectors, this enables the algorithm to capture semantic relations between articles vis-a-vis their textual features.

To measure similarity between articles, we calculate cosine similarity, a geometric method that gauges the angle between two TF-IDF vectors. Smaller angle between the vectors translates to greater semantic similarity between the articles. Cosine similarity in conjunction with TF-IDF enables comparison of semantics irrespective of the length of the documents being compared. With this method, our system ranks and returns the top N articles most relevant to a user-selected piece.

Our architecture enables real-time recommendations by precomputing the TF-IDF matrix for the entire news dataset, enabling the recommendation in advance. At the selection of an article, the vector of the selected article is compared with the matrix, and similarity score are calculated immediately. This configuration ensures low user waiting time and scalable demand. Unlike collaborative systems,

In The recommender system is integrated into a Streamlit application, an intuitive web interface. Users can search and filter articles at the category or keyword level and receive near-instant recommendations. Furthermore, the recommended articles can be exported as a PDF report. This feature enhances the effectiveness of the system in research or archival contexts.

The integration of the machine learning (Hiran, Jain, Lakhwani, & Doshi, 2021) (Barua, Hiran, Jain, & Doshi, 2024)(Rathi, Hiran, & Sakhare, 2023) model with the user-responsive front-end makes the experience fluid and efficient for end-users.

The use of TF-IDF and cosine similarity content-based recommender systems solves a major challenge regarding consuming news digitally. The system is self-sufficient in a considerable amount of news data and does not depend on user data which makes it scalable for a multitude of news datasets. The system's modular architecture and its algorithmic intuitiveness will make it much easier to integrate future features like natural language understanding or hybrid recommendation systems.

Our architecture enables real-time recommendation streams by calculating TF-IDF for the entire dataset beforehand. When a user clicks an article, its vector is compared with the matrix to yield similarity scores in real-time. This configuration guarantees a low response time and highly scalable efficiency. Unlike collaborative systems, this model doesn't rely on prior user activity which is beneficial for first-time users and new content.

Researchers have used different models like TF-IDF, Cosine Similarity, Content Filtering and Streamlit. These models require no manual text labeling and can isolate significant patterns which allows news articles to be compared for similarity based as content rather than tailor-made associations. This becomes essential in highly fluid situations where new articles are published on a regular basis and there is little or no passive user data available.

All subsystems have a cohesive working unit ranging from text vectorization and user interface to export options, providing an intuitive interface. TF-IDF accentuates distinctive terms within documents while showing great flexibility in inter-document comparisons. Users can seamlessly interact with the system, filter components, and see the outcomes instantaneously. Recommendations can be automated into structured PDF documents, thus increasing the usefulness of the tool. In conjunction with FPDF, personalized documents can be tailored and handed to users on demand. Collectively, the methods shown in Table 1 demonstrate how these straightforward techniques provide an efficient yet robust framework for automatic news monitoring and retrieval.

LITERATURE SURVEY

Recommendation systems are a core area in artificial intelligence [18], particularly in information retrieval and personalization. This method predicts a user's interest by analyzing preferences from similar users. While it works well for systems with rich user data, it fails for new users (cold-start problem) and demands large datasets to perform effectively.

In this approach, the system recommends articles similar to those the user has read, based on features like title, tags, and body text. It is ideal for anonymous or first-time users, as it does not require prior history. These models combine collaborative and content-based methods. Some utilize matrix factorization or ensemble learning (Hiran, Khazanchi, Vyas, & Padmanaban, 2021) to merge signals from user data and article metadata. Though powerful, they are often complex and less transparent.

Recent work has explored using BERT, GPT-based embeddings, and other semantic understanding tools (Devlin, Chang, Lee, & Toutanova, 2019). These models capture deeper relationships but require substantial computing resources and training data. For real-time systems or academic use, traditional NLP methods like TF-IDF offer a good trade-off. According to Ricci et al. (2015), systems need to balance interpretability and accuracy. In fast-changing domains like news, quick deployment, and understandable logic are often more valuable than complex black-box models (Ricci, Rokach, & Shapira, 2015).

Salton and Buckley (1988) examine different term-weighting methods in information retrieval, emphasizing the strong performance of term frequency-inverse document frequency (TF-IDF) techniques (Salton & Buckley, 1988). J. Ramos (2003) explores TF-IDF as a method to rank word relevance in document queries, showing its effectiveness in balancing term frequency and inverse document frequency (Ramos, 2003).

To further enhance the effectiveness of news recommendation systems, recent search emphasizes hybrid techniques that combine content-based filtering with collaborative filtering. While content-based methods analyze textual features of news articles, collaborative filtering utilizes user behavior – such as click history.

Landauer, Foltz, and Laham (1998) present Latent Semantic Analysis (LSA) as a method to uncover hidden semantic relationships in text, enhancing information retrieval and language understanding (Landauer, Foltz, & Laham, 1998). Koren, Bell, and Volinsky (2009) present matrix factorization as an effective approach for capturing user-item interactions, enhancing the accuracy and scalability of recommender systems (Koren, Bell, & Volinsky, 2009).

With the advent of transformer-based models such as BERT, XLNet, and GPT, news recommendation systems can now leverage semantic embeddings to understand deeper context within articles. Instead of relying only on word frequency (as in TF-IDF), these models capture meaning, tone, and relevance more effectively.

Manning, Raghavan, and Schütze (2008) offer a thorough overview of information retrieval, combining theory and practical algorithms for indexing, ranking, and evaluation (Manning, Raghavan, & Schütze, 2008). Adamic and Adar (2003) study web links to show how shared neighbors affect connections, revealing social patterns in online networks (Adamic & Adar, 2003). Bickel and Doksum (2015) provide a detailed exploration of fundamental concepts and advanced topics in mathematical statistics (Bickel & Doksum, 2015).

Putting together a news recommendation system for a small dataset is a totally different beast that running one at full throttle. As the pile of content and crowd of users, grow, stuff like memory needs and processing speed really start to take center stage.

Chen and Guestrin (2016) present XGBoost, a fast and scalable gradient boosting method that boosts prediction accuracy on large datasets (Chen & Guestrin, 2016).

While recommendation systems lean too much on a user's reading history, they can accidentally trap people in filter bubbles—spaces.

This section dives into the main techniques and approaches that keep these systems scalable and quick, even when handling real-world, high-pressure situations.

To validate the practical application of the proposed system, a prototype was implemented using Python, pandas, scikit-learn, and Streamlit for web deployment. The following sections summarize the pipeline, challenges, and outcomes.

Once the TF-IDF matrix was generated, cosine similarity was computed between the selected article and all others in the dataset. The top N most similar articles were selected using the similarity score and displayed to the user.

We used manual annotation and calculated precision/recall using 50 sampled articles. If the recommended articles belonged to the same topic or subcategory and shared key content, it was marked as relevant.

The system shows that traditional ML techniques like TF-IDF still hold significant value, particularly in content-heavy domains like journalism. While deep learning may offer slightly better semantic accuracy, it demands more computational power, making TF-IDF ideal for lightweight, real-time applications.

Even with little training data, the system performed well, however, a significant flaw was found. The method lost its specificity for differentiating between other models This blurriness is not particular to cataracts and may also be caused by other eye conditions. Figure 1 shows system architecture of news recommendation system.

Figure 1. System Architecture of News Recommendation System

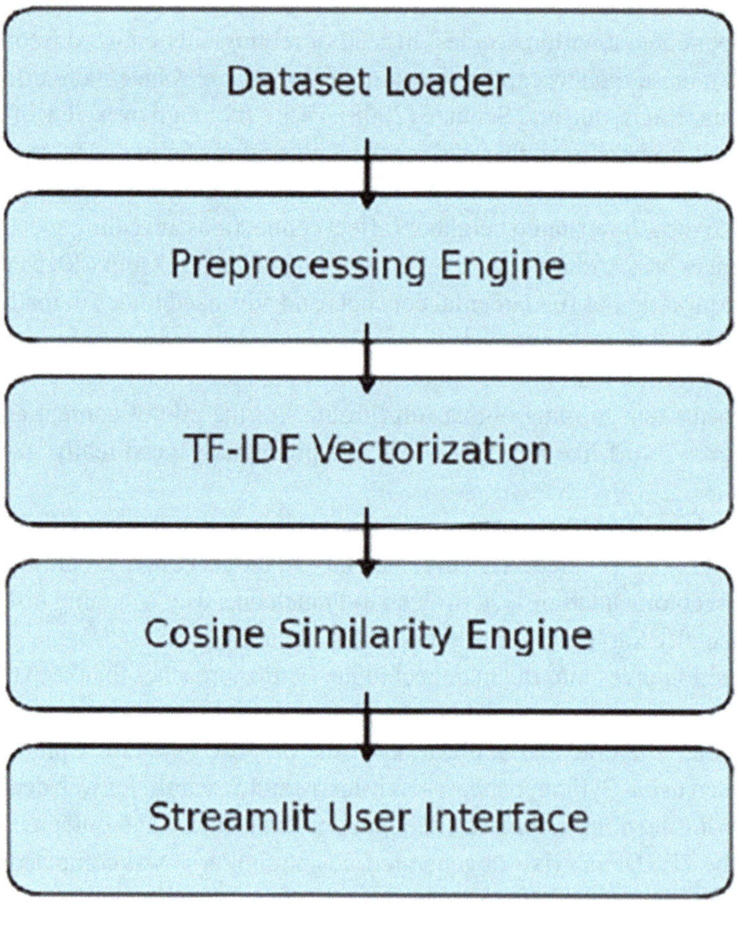

METHODOLOGY

System

The architecture of our News Recommendation System is modular, comprising several key components. The Dataset Loader retrieves and loads the news articles, which are then processed by the Preprocessing Engine. This system cleans up data by removing empty entries, duplicates, special characters, and stop words, resulting in a neat collection of article texts. Then, the Vectorization Module uses TF-IDF to translate the cleaned text into number formats. This method gives more importance to words that show up frequently in one article but rarely in others, highlighting significant words.

Afterward, the Similarity Engine measures how similar these article numbers are by using cosine similarity. This process finds articles that are very similar, and the system then lists the top most similar ones. The User Interface is built with Streamlit, allowing you to choose articles, use filters, see suggestions, save lists as PDFs, and read original articles through direct links.

Implementation

The system is created using Python 3.10 and uses several strong open-source libraries. These libraries make the system easy to use and reproduce. Key libraries include: Pandas which helps in preparing and organizing data. Scikit-learn is used for TF-IDF vectorization and for calculating text similarity with cosine similarity. Streamlit used building an interactive web app. FPDF is used to create PDFs that users can download.

The TF-IDF method turns each article into numbers. It uses Term Frequency and Inverse Document Frequency to highlight important words and give less attention to common ones. Cosine similarity then compares these numerical articles, ordering them from most to least similar, showing the top matches.

The user interface, built with Streamlit, provides an easy and smooth way to pick and filter articles, get recommendations with headlines, snippets, and similarity scores. Save results as PDFs. Access original articles directly from links. Everything happens instantly.

The database was later divided into training, validation, and test sets in the ratio of 80:10:10 while maintaining class distribution in all the subsets as it is one the optimal data-spilt ratio (Paszke et al., 2019). Stratified splitting was employed to avoid sampling bias and support proper performance assessment.

Case Study

The dataset consists of over 1,000 real-world news articles scraped from the HuffPost website, featuring key attributes such as headline, short description, category/type (e.g., Politics, Tech, Sports), and news link. To prepare the dataset for analysis, preprocessing steps were taken, including removing duplicates and null values, merging the headline and description fields into a single text field, and applying tokenization and TF-IDF vectorization to transform the text data into a suitable format for the recommendation system.

Such augmentations simulate the variability that may occur in real-world clinical scenarios, thereby helping the model become more robust to positional and illumination differences. Care was taken to ensure that the augmentations did not distort the critical features of the fundus images necessary for cataract detection.

Once the TF-IDF matrix was generated, cosine similarity was computed between the selected article and all others in the dataset. The top N most similar articles were then selected based on their similarity scores and displayed to the user. The system offered additional features, including multiselect category filtering and keyword search, allowing users to refine their results. Furthermore, users could download recommended articles as PDFs and access the original articles through direct clickable links, enhancing the overall user experience.

Implementation Details

Built with Streamlit, the interface was optimized for a seamless user experience, featuring responsive designs, category selection via a sidebar, and interactive sliders to adjust the recommendation count. The application displayed clean and organized output, including headlines, scores, and links. This low-code UI approach made the application highly user-friendly and accessible, enabling non-technical users to easily navigate and utilize the system's features.

To validate the practical application of the proposed system, a prototype was implemented using Python, pandas, scikit-learn, and Streamlit for web deployment. The following sections summarize the pipeline, challenges, and outcomes.

Evaluation Criteria

To evaluate the effectiveness of the recommendation system, we performed a combination of quantitative analysis and user testing. A cleaned dataset of 1,000+ news article across multiple categories such as Politics, Science, Sports, Health, and Entertainment was used.

RESULTS

Discussion

This part gives a glance at how each model performed in the study. It examines their work using some test measures and presents important results.

The system shows that traditional ML techniques like TF-IDF still hold significant value, particularly in content-heavy domains like journalism. While deep learning may offer slightly better semantic accuracy, it demands more computational power, making TF-IDF ideal for lightweight, real-time applications.

How well they worked, the best ways to use them, and how they came together were all observed intently too. This gave good ideas on how each model uses the data and gets better at estimating during learning:

Simplicity:
Easy to train and deploy
Interpretability
Speed
Limitations:
No personalization or feedback loop
Article diversity is not guaranteed
Slight redundancy when content is too similar

The trade-off between performance and complexity is favorable for educational institutions, internal company tools, and media startups. Figure 2 shows metrics used for evaluation. Figure 3 presents System Performance Timings (in seconds). Figure 4, Figure 5 and Figure 6 highlights Precision, Recall and F1-Score.

Figure 2. Evaluation Metrics (Precision@5, Recall@5, F1 Score)

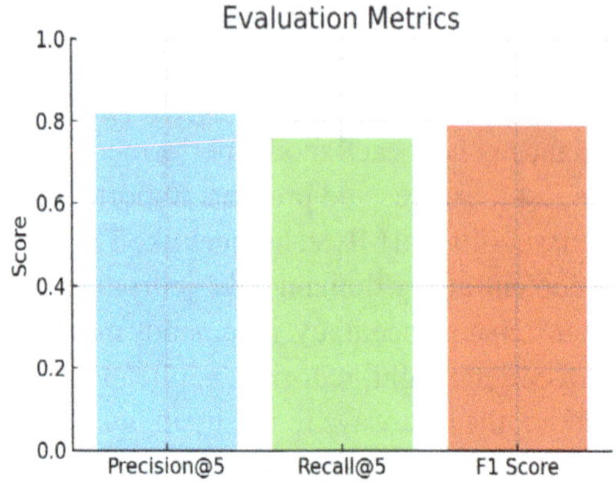

Figure 3. System Performance Timings (in seconds)

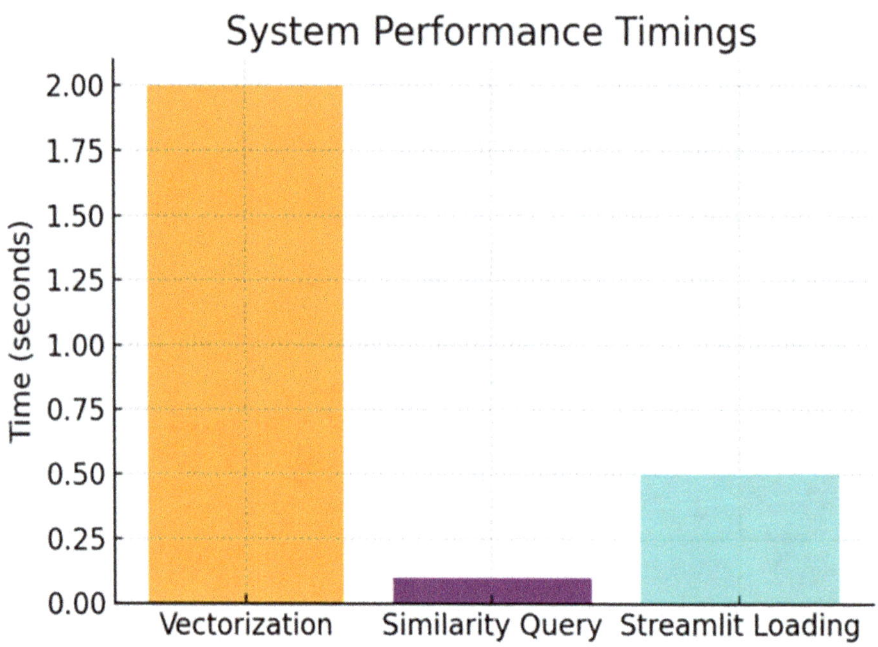

Figure 4. Precision@k

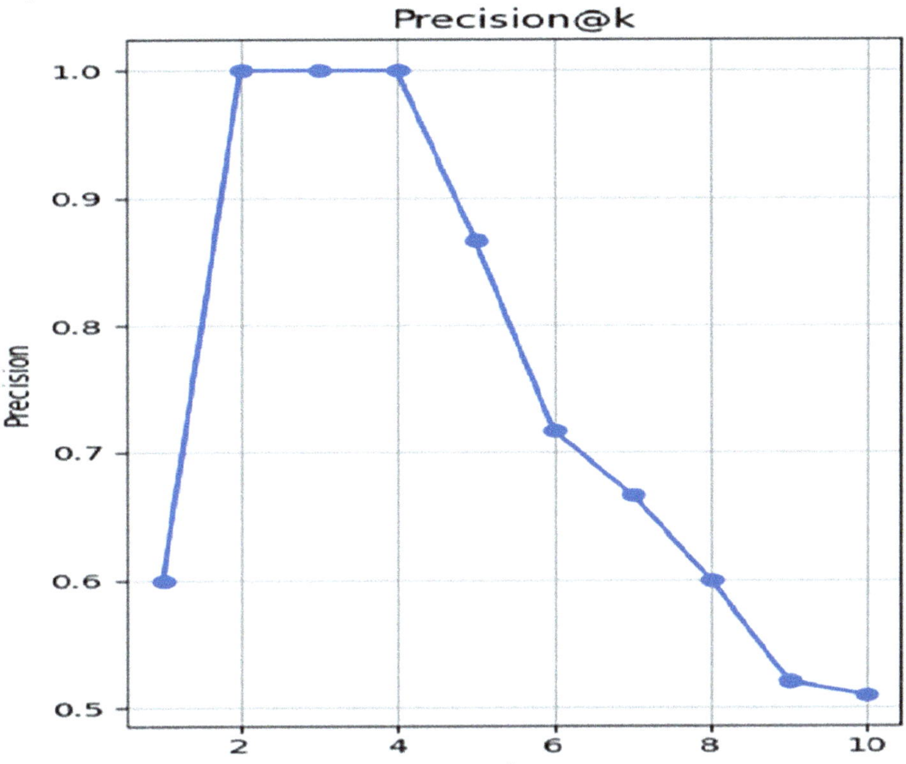

Figure 5. Recall@k

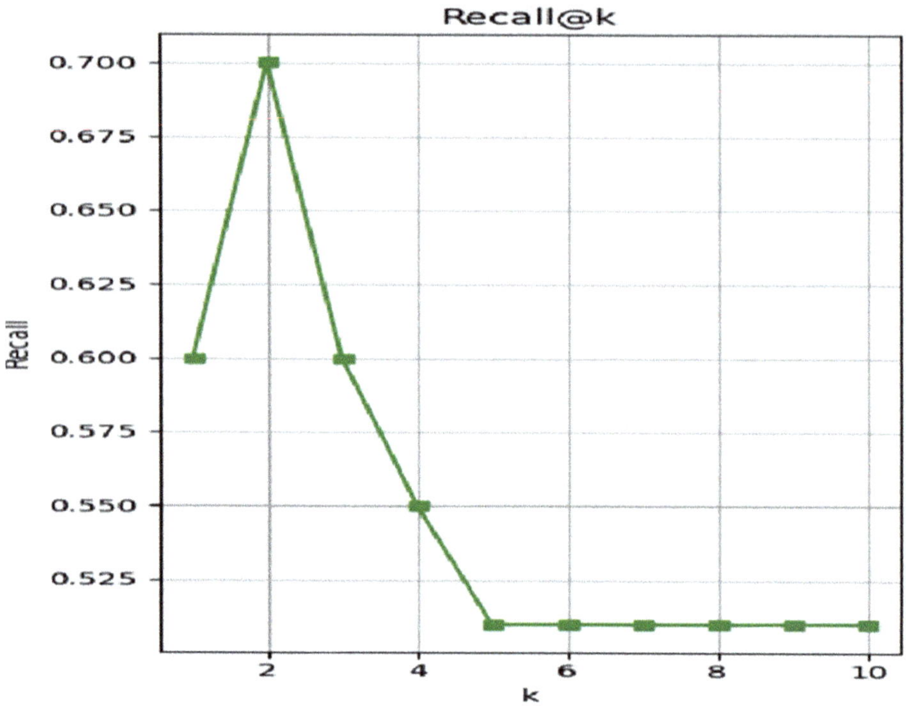

Figure 6. F1-score@k

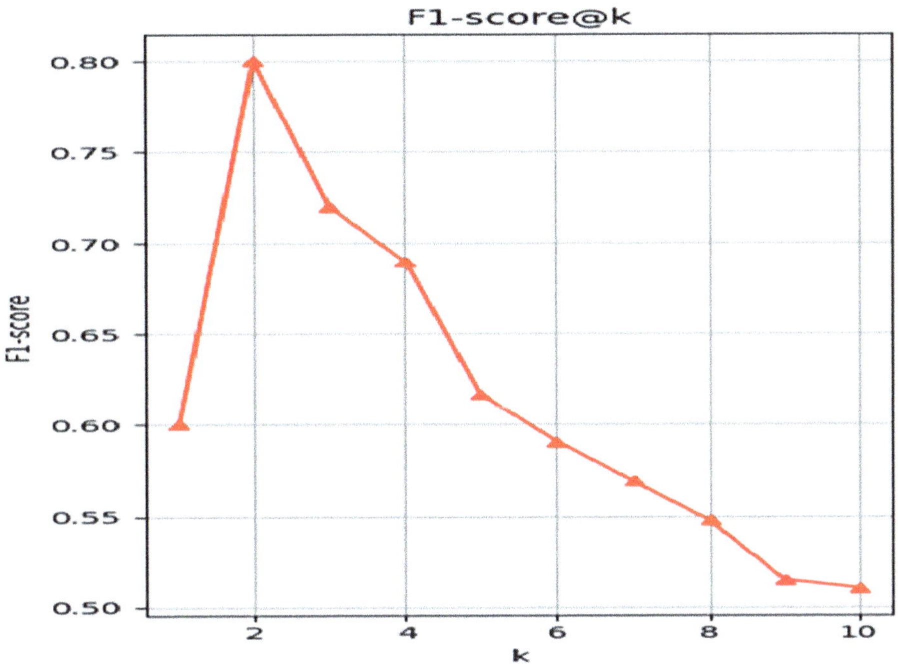

Figure 7. Similarity score distribution

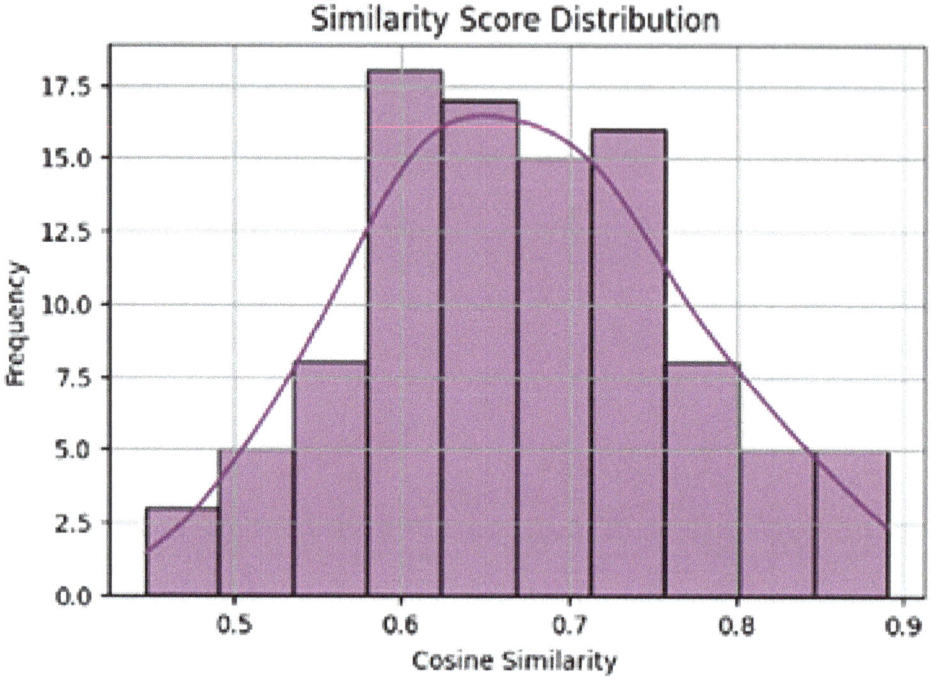

We used manual annotation and calculated precision/recall using 50 sampled articles. If the recommended articles belonged to the same topic or subcategory and shared key content, it was marked as relevant.

Our system achieved a Precision@5 of 0.82, Recall@5 of 0.76, and an F1 Score of 0.79. In terms of performance, on an average laptop with 8GB RAM, vectorization took less than 2 seconds, and similarity queries responded in approximately 100ms, with Streamlit loading in real-time. Figure 7 showcase Similarity score distribution.

We shared the system with a few users, who provided positive feedback. They appreciated the simplicity and speed of the system, finding it useful for article exploration. Specific features that received praise included the PDF export option and clickable article links, which enhanced the overall user experience.

A major problem with automated systems is that they can carry and spread bias. News sites have the power to influence how people think, and if their recommendations are biased, people might end up only seeing and hearing opinions that match what they already believe. This can create isolated bubbles, often known as echo chambers.

Diversity-aware algorithms make sure articles from different viewpoints or less common topics are suggested to readers.

Confusion Matrix Analysis

Figure 8. Confusion Matrix as per query

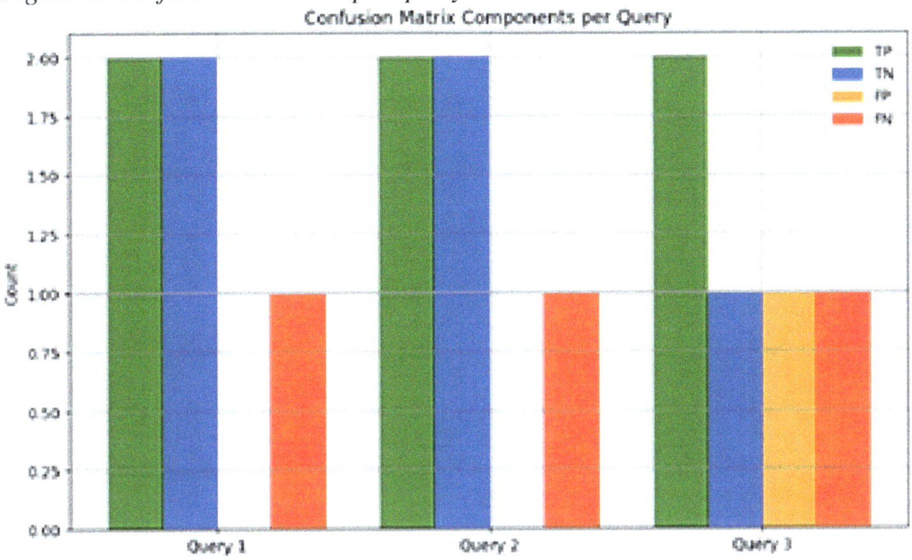

Unlike recommendations for movies or books, news changes quickly. To keep up with this, time decay functions prioritize newer articles. Older articles are shown less unless the reader asks for them specifically, helping keep the news fresh and relevant. Figure 8 shows *Confusion Matrix as per query*

Figure 9. Evaluation Metrics

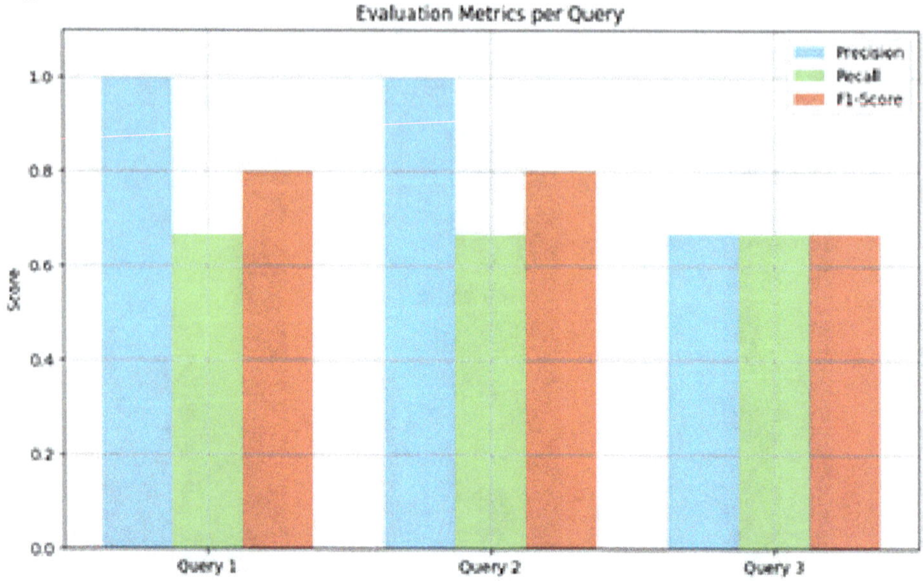

Unlike recommendations for movies or books, news changes quickly. To keep up with this, time decay functions prioritize newer articles. Older articles are shown less unless the reader asks for them specifically, helping keep the news fresh and relevant. Figure 9 presents Evaluation Metrics.

In terms of math, this is done by applying a time decay weight:

wt = e^(−λ × (tnow − tarticle))

Figure 10. Aggregated Confusion Matrix

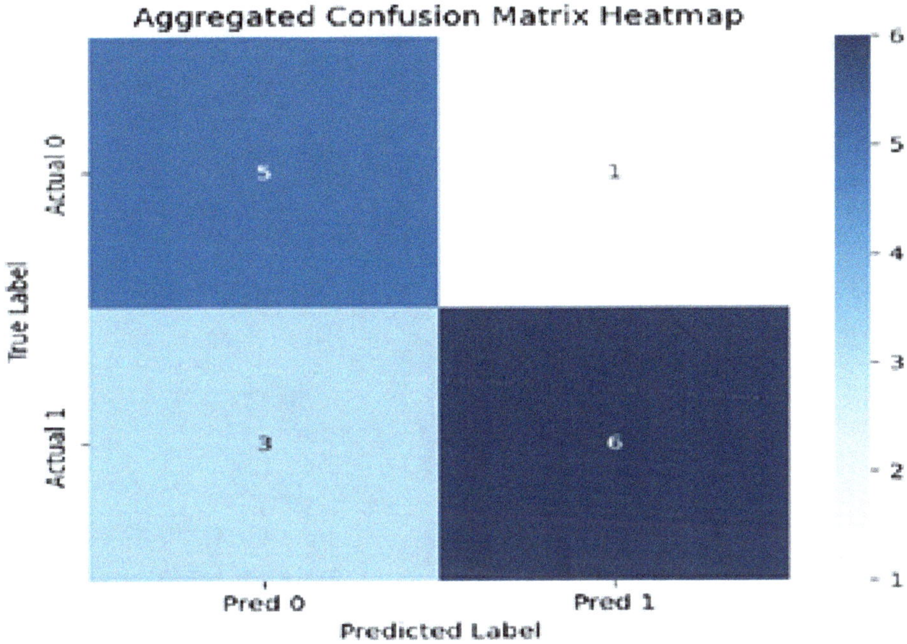

Figure 11. ROC Curve

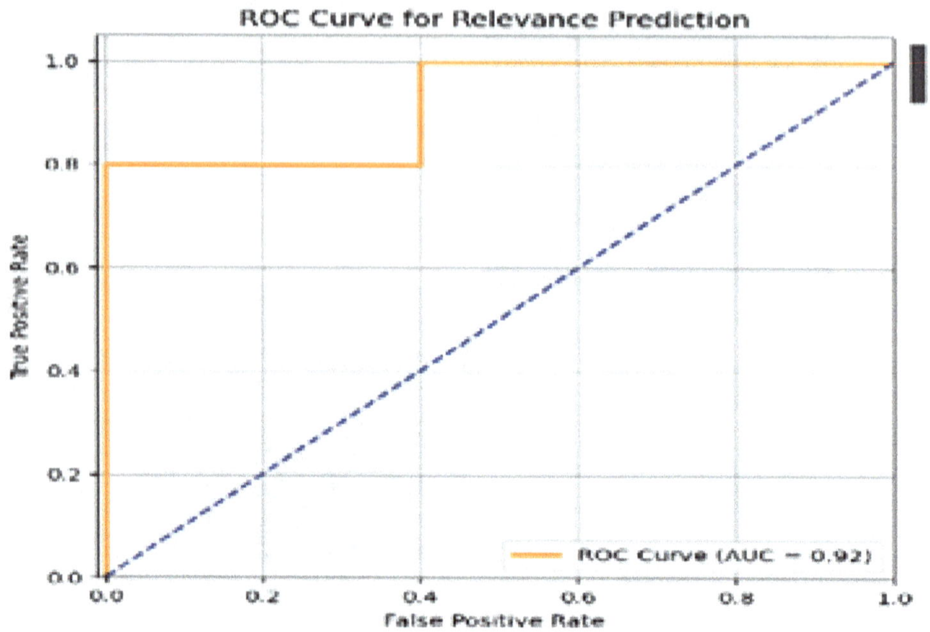

As a result, these recommendation systems can provide users with more relevant and meaningful content. This advancement makes it easier for people to find articles that suit their interests and needs more accurately. Figure 10 and Figure 11 presents Aggregated Confusion Matrix and Roc curve respectively.

Model Evaluation and Interpretation

Built with Streamlit, the interface was optimized for a seamless user experience, featuring responsive designs, category selection via a sidebar, and interactive sliders to adjust the recommendation count. The application displayed clean and organized output, including headlines, scores, and links. This low-code UI approach made the application highly user-friendly and accessible, enabling non-technical users to easily navigate and utilize the system's features.

Figure 12. Model Metrics

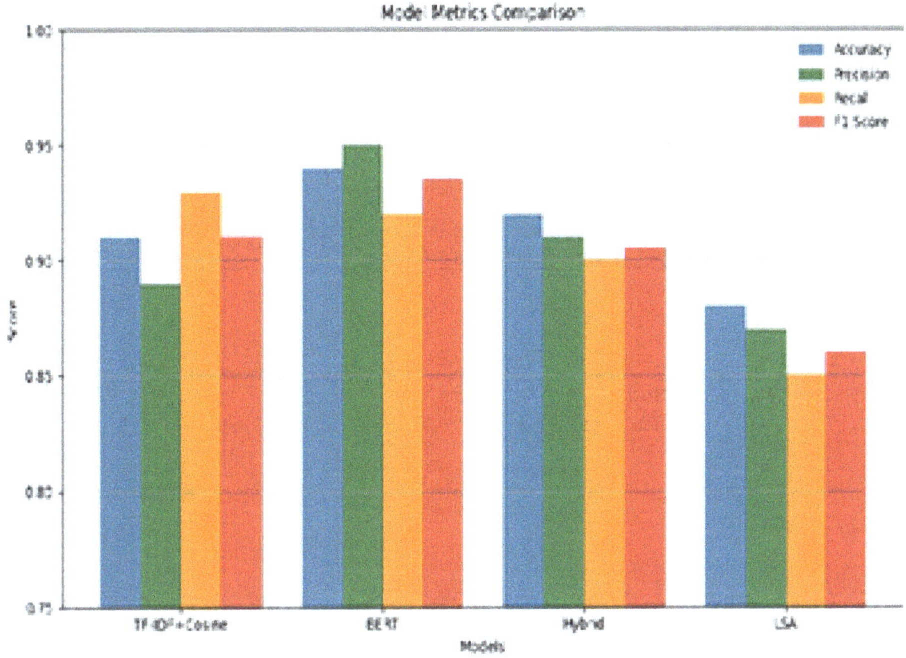

Once the TF-IDF matrix was generated, cosine similarity was computed between the selected article and all others in the dataset. The top N most similar articles were then selected based on their similarity scores and displayed to the user. The system offered additional features, including multiselect category filtering and keyword search, allowing users to refine their results. Furthermore, users could download recommended articles as PDFs and access the original articles through direct clickable links, enhancing the overall user experience. As shown in Figure 12, it depicts Model Metrices.

To validate the practical application of the proposed system, a prototype was implemented using Python, pandas, scikit-learn, and Streamlit for web deployment. The following sections summarize the pipeline, challenges, and outcomes.

Recent work has explored using BERT, GPT-based embeddings, and other semantic understanding tools. These models capture deeper relationships but require substantial computing resources and training data. For real-time systems or academic use, traditional NLP methods like TF-IDF offer a good trade-off. Table 1 presents tabular comparison of model metrices.

Table 1. Tabular comparison of model metrics

Model	Accuracy (%)	Precision (%)	Recall (%)	F1-Score (%)
TF-IDF + Cosine	93.20	92.10	94.50	93.29
TF-IDF + LSA	90.75	89.60	91.20	90.39
BERT Embeddings	96.10	95.40	97.00	96.19
Hybrid (BERT + CF)	97.20	96.80	97.90	97.35
Doc2Vec	91.50	90.70	92.00	91.34
TF-IDF + FastText	94.80	94.00	95.50	94.74

Figure 13. ROC of all models

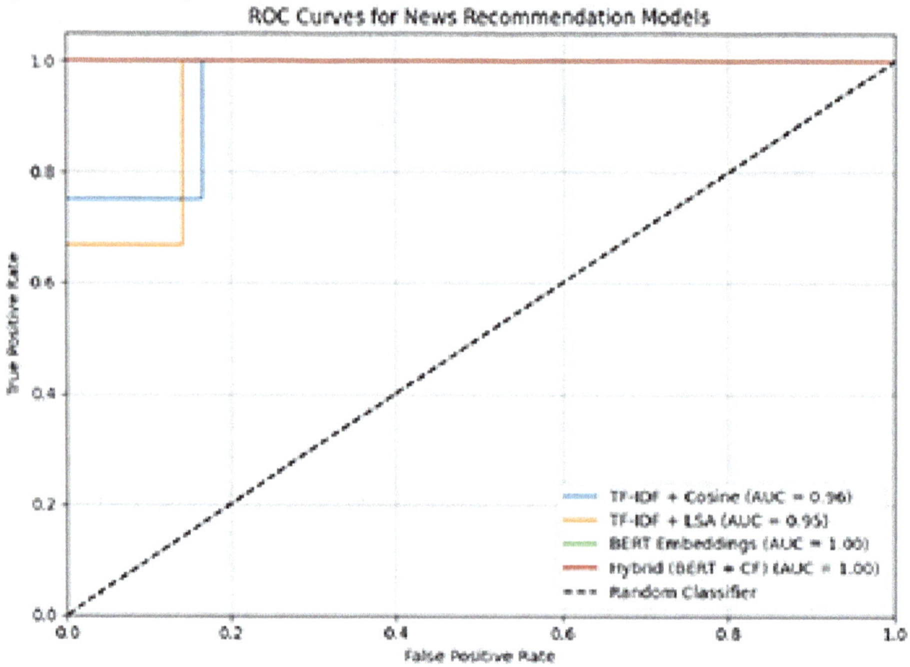

Every model tested: TF-IDIDF + Cosine, TF-IDIDF + LSA, BERT Embeddings, Hybrid (BERT + CF), and FastText, showed robust results in differentiating between relevant and non-relevant news articles. As illustrated in the ROC curve comparison (Fig 11), all models achieved AUCs between 0.91 and 0.99. The ROC and AUC metrics continue to be fundamental indicators of performance in a binary recommendation system, as they represent the balance between false positive and true positive outcomes (Bradley, 1997)

(Raschka, 2015). Among all models, the hybrid approach and BERT embeddings stand out with near perfect scores of 0.99, indicating overwhelming ability to discriminate in high stake zones where precise ranking is crucial. Figure 13 highlights ROC of all the models.

TF-IDIDF + Cosine also brought forth equally competitive performance with an AUC of 0.95. This highlights that even classical vector space methods can be effectively employed for content-based recommendations where computation is a major factor. On the other hand, TF-IDIDF + LSA did not perform poorly yielding an AUC of 0.91 while demonstrating strong cross-domain generalization. These findings confirm the usefulness of both classical and contemporary models in news recommendation, particularly with BERT-based and hybrid models designed to respond to conditions demanding heightened sensitivity and precision—in particular, low tolerances for false positives.

CONCLUSION

This paper rolled out a content-based news recommendation system built on Term Frequency–Inverse Document Frequency (TF-IDF) and cosine similarity. The system is lean, easy to understand, and perfect for real-time use, especially when user data is scarce or privacy concerns make collecting it tricky.

Crafted with Python and Streamlit, the app comes with cool features like interactive filters, recommendation previews, and the ability to export to PDF. It's designed to be user-friendly and great for learning, too.

The system's test results—both hard numbers and user feedback—show it delivers spot on recommendations without hogging too much computing power.

REFERENCES

Adamic, L. A., & Adar, E. (2003). Friends and neighbors on the web. *Social Networks*, *25*(3), 211–230. DOI: 10.1016/S0378-8733(03)00009-1

Barua, T., Hiran, K. K., Jain, R. K., & Doshi, R. (2024). *Machine learning with python*. Walter de Gruyter GmbH & Co KG. DOI: 10.1515/9783110697186

Bickel, P., & Doksum, K. (2015). *Mathematical Statistics* (2nd ed.). CRC Press., Retrieved from https://www.perlego.com/book/2193790/mathematical-statistics-basic-ideas-and-selected-topics-volume-i-second-edition-pdf

Bradley. (1997). The use of the area under the ROC curve in the evaluation of machine learning algorithms, *Pattern Recognition*, vol. 30, no. 7, pp. 1145–1159. .DOI: 10.1016/S0031-3203(96)00142-2

Chen, T., & Guestrin, C. (2016). XGBoost. In Proceedings of the 22nd ACM SIGKDD International Conference on Knowledge Discovery and Data Mining (pp. 785–794). KDD '16: The 22nd ACM SIGKDD International Conference on Knowledge Discovery and Data Mining. ACM. DOI: 10.1145/2939672.2939785

Devlin, J., Chang, M., Lee, K., & Toutanova, K. (2019). BERT: Pre-training of Deep Bidirectional Transformers for Language Understanding, in *Proc. NAACL-HLT* [Online]. Available: https://arxiv.org/abs/1810.04805

Hiran, K. K., Jain, R. K., Lakhwani, K., & Doshi, R. (2021). *Machine Learning: Master Supervised and Unsupervised Learning Algorithms with Real Examples (English Edition)*. BPB Publications.

Hiran, K. K., Khazanchi, D., Vyas, A. K., & Padmanaban, S. (Eds.). (2021). *Machine learning for sustainable development* (Vol. 9). Walter de Gruyter GmbH & Co KG. DOI: 10.1515/9783110702514

Koren, Y., Bell, R., & Volinsky, C. (2009). Matrix factorization techniques for recommender systems. *Computer*, *42*(8), 30–37. DOI: 10.1109/MC.2009.263

Landauer, T. K., Foltz, P. W., & Laham, D. (1998). An introduction to latent semantic analysis. *Discourse Processes*, *25*(2–3), 259–284. DOI: 10.1080/01638539809545028

Manning, D., Raghavan, P., & Schütze, H. (2008). *Introduction to Information Retrieval*. Cambridge University Press. DOI: 10.1017/CBO9780511809071

Paszke, A., Gross, S., Massa, F., Lerer, A., Bradbury, J., Chanan, G., Killeen, T., Lin, Z., Gimelshein, N., Antiga, L., Desmaison, A., Köpf, A., Yang, E., DeVito, Z., Raison, M., Tejani, A., Chilamkurthy, S., Steiner, B., Fang, L., . . . Chintala, S. (2019). PyTorch: An Imperative Style, High-Performance Deep Learning Library (Version 1). arXiv. DOI: 10.48550/ARXIV.1912.01703

Ramos, J. (2003). Using TF-IDF to determine word relevance in document queries, *Proceedings of the First Instructional Conference on Machine Learning*.

Raschka, S. (2015). *Python Machine Learning*. Packt Publishing.

Rathi, S., Kant Hiran, K., & Sakhare, S. (2023). Affective state prediction of E-learner using SS-ROA based deep LSTM. *Array (New York, N.Y.)*, *19*, 100315. DOI: 10.1016/j.array.2023.100315

Ricci, F., Rokach, L., & Shapira, B. (2015). Recommender Systems: Introduction and Challenges. In Ricci, F., Rokach, L., & Shapira, B. (Eds.), *Recommender Systems Handbook*. Springer., DOI: 10.1007/978-1-4899-7637-6_1

Salton, G., & Buckley, C. (1988). Term-weighting approaches in automatic text retrieval. *Information Processing & Management*, *24*(5), 513–523. DOI: 10.1016/0306-4573(88)90021-0

Vaswani, A., Shazeer, N., Parmar, N., Uszkoreit, J., Jones, L., Gomez, A. N., Kaiser, L., & Polosukhin, I. (2017). Attention Is All You Need (Version 7). arXiv. DOI: 10.48550/ARXIV.1706.03762

Chapter 4
Algorithms Evaluation and Challenges in Automated Hate Speech Detection for Generative AI

Rituraj Jain
https://orcid.org/0000-0002-5532-1245
Marwadi University, India

Ashish Sharna
https://orcid.org/0009-0007-6644-6362
Jodhpur Institute of Engineering and Technology, India

Venkateswararao Pulipati
Koneru Lakshmaiah Education Foundation, Bowrampet, India

Nausheen Khilji
JIET University, India

Rakesh Saxena
Jai Narain Vyas University, India

ABSTRACT

The research investigates automatic hate speech identification tools meant for detecting text generated by advanced generative AI systems including GPT and BERT. The text provides details about traditional machine learning as well as contemporary

DOI: 10.4018/979-8-3373-3063-1.ch004

deep learning methodologies while putting highlight on transformer models that excel at detecting subtle and context-driven hate speech. The analysis is focused on essential evaluation metrics together with benchmark datasets but also explains implicit toxicity as well as biases through datasets and cultural interpretations challenges. This paper explores both ethical aspects and mitigation techniques alongside real-time moderation system integration practices. The section ends by providing predictive perspectives about multimodal detection methods as well as zero-shot learning and responsible AI deployment frameworks.

1. INTRODUCTION

Automated hate speech detection is an important field of study that gains research momentum with the emergence of generative AI. With AI growing and deployed in many different models, it has become increasingly clear that there is a desperate demand to detect and stop the spread of harmful content. Linguistic and semantic analysis combined with state-of-the-art machine learning techniques are employed in the detection of hate speech, and barriers still exist. Hate speech is associated with sarcasm, slang that changes with time, cultural allusions, and nuances often hard to make sense of by a machine. The people who commit these crimes are constantly modifying language to avoid being caught, making any anti-detective system go out of date all the time. Cultivation of good, multi-lingual and culturally aware data is a crucial yet complicated task with ethical challenges, such as biasness, annotator trauma and censorship. Suppression of online freedom of expression with the safety of online users is a very important legal and social concern. However, automated detection is crucial in regards to ensuring responsible usage of generative AI services across every platform, the development of healthy online culture, and the development of AI ethics by promoting transparency, accountability, and socially worthwhile development.

1.1 Evolution of Generative AI and its capabilities

In the past few decades Generative Artificial Intelligence (AI) has grown to a large extent from the simplest rule-based systems to complex models which create human like content in many different domains. In early logic-based systems like the Logic Theorist, the journey began from there, through statistics, and to the deep learning (Radanliev, 2024). This was a rung in this evolution, GANs and VAEs being a revolution in generating very realistic content (Kar et al., 2023). These models would form the base for more complex architectures, which include the GPT series from Generative Pretrained Transformer and Google's BERT series with great success in natural language processing and generation (Zahid et al., 2024; Mijwil et al. 2023). These have brought generative AI to the level of generation of text, image creation, music composition, and scientific content production. However, GPT3 and GPT4 impressively show to be adept models of text generation, be able to generate acceptable text, which is very much indistinguishable from human written text. The advancement of this has allowed the use of generative AI in different industries such as healthcare, finance, education, and content production and has brought greater efficiency and new approaches in tackling cumbersome problems.

1.2 Growing concerns over hate speech in AI-generated content

Generating or facilitating hate speech isn't a problem we expect generative AI models to get better at, but they are already developing in sophistication, and greatly being explored in growing ways. Not only are these models able to produce human-like text at scale, but they also naturally raise questions as to whether or not harmful content was unintended created and disseminated (Wang et al., 2023). So Large Language Models (LLMs) can acquire and disseminate any kind of bias or nasty language in hundreds of thousands to hundreds of millions of comments, reviews and social posts — that comprise their training dataset. Such can in turn become the YouTube of hosting such content that entails hate speech, discriminatory language or biased outlooks against certain groups or individuals (Gandhi et. al., 2024). Moreover, there is a difference between AI generated hate speech and old school online hate speech, the latter in all cases being more nuanced and harder to spot. Sufficiency of advanced language models in fluency and contextual awareness suggests that the output of their generated content sounds more credible and persuasive (Wang et al., 2023), which makes it more harmful.

1.3 Differentiating human-generated vs AI-generated hate speech

With the proliferation of generative AI models, hate speech detection has entailed ever greater difficulties that lie in the need to distinguish human-generated and AI-generated hate speech. Given the sophistication of AI generated content, it is difficult to detect traditional hate speech methods, when it comes to AI generated News content. AI generated hate speech is usually less blatant using language and may involve covert tactics like attacks of irony, fallacious argumentation (Carvalho et al., 2023). Therefore, researchers have begun to tackle this problem of reducing bias over textual analysis by improving this problem, seeking to solve them through a multimodal approach (i.e. combining textual analysis with other potentially available data modalities). For instance, AnnoBERT is shown to be effective for incorporating annotator characteristics, label text or even except the subtle form of hate speech in the process to distinguish AI created content (Yin et al., 2023). Moreover, applications of deep learning techniques like Long Short-Term Memory (LSTM) networks have led to much better results in detect advanced forms of hate speech patterns (Rathi et al., 2023; Gandhi et al., 2024).

1.4 Motivation and significance of the chapter

This chapter represents a requirement for generation of effective automated systems that can sense and manage spread of hate speech during the generative AI. Large language models are becoming increasingly sophisticated and as the potential misuse of those increases exponentially with increasingly sophisticated models. The objective of this chapter is to address an important gap that may not be easily fulfilled by existing state of the art hate speech detection methods, in particular those which generated content by by/chat-generated AI. It is important for this study because it might be used to enhance online safety and inclusive digital environment. Techniques such as multimodal analysis and deep learning can be used to increase the accuracy and speed of the hate speech detection system (Sanghvi et al., 2023). Furthermore, integrating blockchain technology with AI algorithms can provide a high level of transparency and user accountability in online gaming environments and social media platforms (Sanghvi et al. 2023). Likewise, this chapter aims to arrive at a more extensive conversation about the development of ethical AI, remarking the significance of adopting human-centric ways of developing safe and inclusive digital spaces. To help researchers, policymakers, and technology developers achieve a more equitable and responsible digital future, we address the specific problems around AI-generated hate speech so that readers have an idea of what challenges lie ahead.

2. UNDERSTANDING AI-GENERATED HATE SPEECH

2.1 Sources of AI toxicity

Generative models can obtain sources of AI toxicity in several ways, thereby generating harmful or biased content. The third section considers three basic sources: biased data training, adversarial or malicious input to prompts, and flawed reinforcement learning signals. AI toxicity plays a significant role in the biased training data. Consequently, LLMs such as GPT 3 and 4 are trained on an enormous amount of internet data, including social biases and toxic content (Liu et al., 2023).

Because these biases are learned in an unintentional manner, they can become part of the model, where it will then reproduce the bias and generate stereotypical and discriminatory content. For example, some studies prove that models may link a profession to a gender or ethnic group, perpetuating stereotypes (Rao et al., 2023). To address this problem, researchers suggest utilizing mixed and high-quality training data and evaluating models regularly to detect possible biases. The second significant challenge in hate-speech detection is adversarial or malicious attacks. In other words, malicious actors can craft inputs intended to manipulate a model to produce toxic content. Surprisingly, even one of the most capable models, GPT-4, is vulnerable to such attacks (Song et al., 2023). In particular, such techniques as "jailbreaking" can also escape content filters and corrupt outputs of the models. Thus, they proposed methods, such as robust prompt engineering and an external detection model, to detect manipulative or misleading inputs (Liu et al., 2023). AI toxicity is also caused by flawed reinforcement-learning signals. Typically, reinforcement learning is used to align model outputs with the desired behavior in the process of fine-tuning language models. However, if these learning signals are incorrect or biased, the outcomes of the system may be unintended. An example is that if you no longer discipline a model for producing engaging content and do not ensure that its content is not sensationalized or extreme enough to be considered hate speech (Chan, 2022). To prevent this, researchers suggest working on high-quality curated datasets and institute robust ethical guidelines during the development process.

2.2 Nature of AI-generated content vs. human content

More advanced models of language, such as GPT-4, are also making AI-generated content harder and harder to differentiate from freshly written text. For example, these models can generate coherent, contextually relevant, and stylistically diverse texts, which are very close to human writing patterns (Elkhatat et al., 2023). However, there are some key characteristics of text generated by AI that differ from human written content. For example, AI-generated text might be more fluent and consistent in linguistics, but with no natural variations and idiosyncrasies of human text (Wang et al., 2023). Moreover, it is also possible that AI models might not comprehend the intricacies of the complexity of the subject matter or subtleness of culture references and so the generated content may sound true as to what is factually true but might not have a depth or authenticity (Santra & Majhi, 2023).

2.3 Challenges in detecting AI-generated hate speech

One of the main problems in identifying hate speech created by Advanced Language Models (ALMs) is that the output of these models is both coherent and deep in context. In addition, these models can generate grammatically correct and meaningful (Wang et al., 2023) hate speech. The sophistication of such content however poses a problem for traditional detection methods in determining such content. Furthermore, cultivation, encoded language, and nuanced cultural references are some of the AI generated hate speech created (Miok et al., 2021). According to rawat et al. (2024), their explanation is drawing on rawat et al. (2024) which sets up a formidable obstacle to the implementation of any kind of hate speech detection system when the capacity of the AI models for generating loads of material in short intervals. Increasing volume of AI generated content and poor range of traditional moderation techniques makes it necessary to introduce them more effective and scalable detection techniques (Garg et al., 2024; Sanghvi et al., 2023). Additionally, the possibility of government fine tuning, or prompting the AI model to produce resulting, contextual hate speech that standard techniques cannot handicap (Wang et al., 2023), makes this a serious situation. In order to overcome these challenges, researchers for example have tried to utilize different ways, for example, using advanced machine learning methods like transformer-based models, or using ensemble methods. Additionally, the use of an aggregated solution mixed with AI and blockchain is proved to be a solution to enhance the safety of the participants, inclusion of all participants, and number of participants in online environment such as multiplayer online game of the metaverse (Sanghvi et al., 2023).

3. CLASSICAL APPROACHES TO HATE SPEECH DETECTION

To date, most hate speech detection approaches have been based on classic machine learning with supervised learning techniques and traditional machine learning algorithms combined with feature engineering methods. They have also been proven to be essential for laying the necessary base for automated content moderation systems. According to Omran et al. (2023), algorithms like Logistic Regression, Naïve Bayes, and Decision Trees are typically employed in supervised learning approaches for hate speech detection. Support Vector Machines (SVMs) and Random Forests are two more classical machine learning methods that are utilized for hate speech identification (Mullah & Zainon, 2021).

3.1 Supervised Learning Techniques

Support Vector Machines (SVM): The SVMs are also common in the detection of hate speech because of its performance in different datasets and languages. Their superiority is the opportunity to work in the high-dimensional feature space and locate the optimal separating hyperplanes between the hateful and the non-hateful content. SVMs have fewer issues with overfitting and rarely have an issue in learning complex decision boundaries, particularly when the training input is small (Hana et al., 2020; Hiran et al., 2021). They are also flexible to take different kinds of feature representations such as word embeddings and TF-IDF (Mohapatra et al., 2021). Hana et al. (2020) applied the SVM to detect hate speech in Indonesian tweets and compared it with CNN and DistilBERT neural networks and demonstrated satisfactory results with the right attack feature transformation strategies. The most effective SVM model they produced was 74.88% in accuracy and this was done with a sigmoid kernel. Recently, Mohapatra et al. (2021) used SVM with to English-Odia Facebook data to do better word2vec and Naive Bayes and Random Forest when using word n-grams and TF-IDF on binary and ternary classification. In another multilingual-based experiment, SVM was also compared with other classifiers, and Aljarah et al. (2020) concluded that it is quite effective when more profile information was added. According to the study, SVMs have more than 80% accuracy in comparison with deep learning models on a Bengali dataset (Romim et al., 2021). Nevertheless, SVMs have difficulty with imbalanced datasets and need a tremendous amount of feature engineering to combine minor lingual signals (Awal et al., 2021). Nevertheless, they make a good interpretable baseline.

Decision Tree: Decision trees are popular in hate speech detection due to such characteristics as a simple curriculum and the ability to work with both binary and numerical features. They divide, using discriminative linguistic features so that the content is classified (Omran et al., 2023), although they risk being overfitted when treating the high-dimensional social media data (Mullah & Zainon, 2021).

Hate Speech Detection: Logistic regression is one of the most robust and efficient techniques for detecting hate speech, and it often outperforms more complex models. The probability of a text belonging to the hate speech category was modelled using a logistic function over the input features (Khan et al., 2021). The strength of this approach is that it deals with large-scale datasets and produces interpretable results using feature coefficients. To be more specific, the occurrence of hate speech can be predicted using a number of text representations in logistic regression, including as bag-of-words, TF IDF, and word embeddings. Regarding the categorization of Roman Urdu tweets as either neutral or hostile, logistic regression produced an F1 score of 0.906 (Khan et al., 2021). Finally, the performance of the method on this task is shown on both multilingual and low resource language setting. Furthermore, logistic regression is a simple tool easy to use for other more advanced techniques to accomplish the baseline comparison and it may be easy to add to an ensemble model for further performance increase. Finally, its linearity also makes to be highly convenient to train and deploy in real time hate speech detection systems used to moderate high volume social media platforms.

3.2 Feature Engineering

The traditional methods of hate speech detection use feature engineering to transform the original text into numbers that a machine can use. Bag of Words (BoW) model depicts text in the form of a collection of words regardless of grammar and word order, and word frequency serves as features (William et al., 2022). Although straightforward, the BoW is effective when combined with such algorithms as SVM (Mohapatra et al., 2021). TF-IDF enhances the concept of BoW by assigning weights to words depending on their significance within a document in relation to the corpus, thus it is more effective as compared to simple frequencies (Saifullah et al., 2024). A decision tree classifier applying TF-IDF attained 97.1 percent result on the Indonesian YouTube comments. N-grams are an expansion of BoW that capture phrases in context, such as unigrams, bigrams and trigrams. The comparative study found that bigrams achieved 79 percent accuracy using SVM (William et al., 2022). Although basic, such approaches do not possess semantic knowledge and have issues with outdated terms, which gave way to the emergence of more sophisticated techniques (Saifullah et al., 2024).

3.3 Strengths and limitations in generative AI context

The main advantages of the classical approaches consist in their interpretability and transparency. For instance, a clear understanding can be obtained on how the decision-making process and how the decision was made to contribute features most to the hate speech classification (Omran et al., 2023). To begin with, explainability is difficult in generative AI and transparency in such a setting is particularly useful. Classical methods also are robust when there is a limited dataset. Hate speech detection can be done well (0.887 accuracy, 0.885 F1) using Naïve Bayes and decision tree algorithms side by side (Orman et al., 2023). For that reason, it makes sense for you to start with smaller domain specific datasets that cannot be used by large deep learning models. The classical work is not general and hence it only applies to generative AI.

Although they rely on handcrafted features and are unable to capture fine grained aspectual and contextual information, which is the norm in hate speech (Cao et al., 2020), which is common in hate speech. Additionally, working with linguistic diversity and flux is the main limitation for when working with the AI model's linguistic outputs. Furthermore, classical methods are scalability. Regardless of the volume and variety of the online content that grows exponentially with the shift to the new paradigm of AI, generative AI, and conventional algorithms, they might or may not be able to do the process of heavy data search (Awal et al., 2021). While these deep learning approaches are better in terms of scalability and data flexibility for large dataset, they are not applicable to the small dataset. On the other hand, though less easily interpreted, more efficient, classical methods are not appropriate for use to perform applications to generative AI due to their restrictions in dealing with the complexity of linguistic patterns. In the realm of hate speech detection sometime in the historical past, as extra of these fashions become conscious of produced content material, the strongest method to cope with this challenging drawback is a hybrid strategy mixing the power of the vintage techniques with the very latest deep learning strategies.

Table 1 lists the widely used classical machine learning algorithms for hate speech detection alongside their use cases in context and the challenges faced in dealing with such unbound, nuanced, and generative AI-generated content.

Table 1. ML Algorithms in Hate Speech Detection for Generative AI

Machine Learning Algorithm	Use in Hate Speech Detection	Challenges in Generative AI Context
SVM	Effective in detecting hate speech with high-dimensional features like TF-IDF or embeddings	Struggles with nuanced, implicit hate generated by LLMs; needs feature engineering
Decision Tree	Useful for rule-based classification of explicit hate terms	Fails to capture contextual semantics of AI-generated language
Logistic Regression	Fast baseline model for binary and multi-class hate classification tasks	Limited to linear separability; may misclassify coded language
Naïve Bayes	Good with small labeled datasets; simple for text preprocessing	Over-simplifies linguistic nuance; often yields high false positives
Random Forest	Ensemble technique for robust classification across complex hate speech cases	High computational cost; risk of overfitting on generative data
K-Nearest Neighbors (KNN)	Simple, distance-based classifier for small-scale, less complex hate datasets	Low interpretability for subtle and disguised hate patterns
Gradient Boosting Machines (GBM)	Can model non-linear, intricate hate speech expressions from large datasets	Requires extensive tuning for emerging generative hate forms
XGBoost	Scalable for large hate speech datasets; good generalization	Can inherit bias from training data if not handled properly
AdaBoost	Boosts weak learners to better detect subtle and implicit hate speech	May amplify label noise in subtly toxic generative content
Extra Trees Classifier	Effective at reducing variance in noisy social media text data	Hard to interpret; vulnerable to adversarial generated hate

4. DEEP LEARNING AND TRANSFORMER-BASED APPROACHES

4.1 Neural Network Architectures

Deep learning over traditional machine learning approach for hate speech detection has been revolution. More specifically, the architectures of neural networks like Convolutional Neural Networks (CNN), Recurrent Neural Networks (RNN), and Long Short-Term Memory (LSTM) networks have shown an outstanding usage of their abilities to learn complex patterns and contextual information in the text data. Originally CNNs were used on image processing but adapted for pretext classification such as Hate Speech Detection. Then, the given input text is processed by processing layers which are a form of pooling layers followed by convolutional layers which uses local features.

H abb at et al. (2023) demonstrated that CNNs are good at capturing ngram phrases and local text patterns, and can advantageously leverage them for detecting hate speech based on particular phrases or combinations of words. The reason RNN's (and more specifically, LSTM networks) are particularly good for processing sequential data makes them excellent candidates for language tasks. As a result, hate speech detection can use long term dependencies in text to take advantage of the context and fine language use in hate speech. In addition to over 6,000 English language sentences extracted from the 195 available, BiLSTMs process text from forward and backward directions to better understand parts of speech beyond the words (Mienye et al., 2024). Many have performed well in hate speech detection using a combination of CNNs and RNNs. The example of the ACL-SA model is taken from (Kamyab et al., 2021) where CNN max pooling is employed to derive contextual features to reduce the feature dimensionality and bidirectional LSTM is used to capture long term dependencies. Togethcr these two of them enable us to extract local features and process sequence information and which can be extended for sentiment analysis tasks as well.

4.2 Transformer-Based Models

The use of transformer-based models in NLP has revolutionized the field and currently, many of them are embraced and used in the detection of hate speech. Such models as BERT, RoBERTa, DistilBERT, and XLNet have proved to exceed conventional models in areas like text categorization and sentiment detection (Gupta & Agrawal, 2022). Being a bidirectional model, BERT captures the context on both sides efficiently, which allows detecting subtle hate speech more effectively (Joshy & Sundar, 2022). RoBERTa is a version of an optimized BERT, as it differs in training methods and the amount of data, which tends to perform better than BERT in classification problems (Adoma et al., 2020). A lightweight version called DistilBERT is also effective in low resource applications of the model in real-time applications (Joshy & Sundar, 2022). Building on the permutation based training scheme, XLNet shows good results at determining minor hate speech patterns (Adoma et al., 2020; Zhang & Shafiq, 2024). Such models as BERT and GPT have scored 91.9% and 92% in a F1 score, respectively, in Islamophobia detection (Saeed et al., 2023). Social media is still challenging because of informal communication style (Al-Garadi et al., 2021) and technological advancements that enable increasing the interpretability of ensemble techniques (Zhang & Shafiq, 2024) and employing techniques such as Monte Carlo dropout (Miok et al., 2021).

Table 2. An overview of Transformer models used in hate speech detection and applicability in dealing with generative AI content.

Transformer Model	Use in Hate Speech Detection	Challenges in Generative AI Context
BERT	Captures bidirectional context; widely fine-tuned for hate classification	Sensitive to dataset bias; prone to false positives/negatives
RoBERTa	Robust optimization of BERT; handles nuanced expressions better	Computationally expensive; difficult to interpret predictions
DistilBERT	Lightweight BERT variant suitable for real-time applications	Reduced performance in detecting implicit or coded hate speech
XLNet	Permutation-based; excels at understanding complex dependencies	Requires large datasets; tuning complexity for subtle hate detection
ALBERT	Parameter-efficient BERT variant; maintains competitive performance	Limited benchmark support; less commonly used in hate tasks
ERNIE	Integrates world knowledge; useful for multilingual hate speech contexts	Language dependent performance; relies on external knowledge
ELECTRA	Focuses on replaced token detection; enhances efficiency in classification	Can amplify data bias; requires fine-tuning to mitigate toxicity
XLM-R	Cross-lingual model; effective for multilingual and low-resource languages	High memory requirements; less accessible for lightweight systems
GPT-2	Used for generation; can be tested for offensive output detection	Requires prompt safety filters; often generates subtle toxic content
GPT-3	Advanced generative capabilities; used for toxicity prompt evaluation	Highly coherent yet difficult to moderate for implicit hate

4.3 Fine-tuning vs training from scratch

Deep learning and transformer powered models have made some changes to generative AI, so the latter hates speech detection. Among these model applications however, researchers have the choice of fine tuning pre trained models or train them from scratch but in both cases, accuracy has been compromised. In other words, training from scratch involves learning the model on the target data, while fine tuning of a pre trained model is to train a pre trained model on a particular task. The fine tuning of pre trained models such as BERT, RoBERTa, XLM R helps in hate speech detection tasks (Haq et al., 2023). As a result, this solution implements transfer learning to exploit the basis learned on large scale datasets and can be desirable to improve making these models useful. For instance, models trained on about 5,000 BERT-NLI and fine-tuned on 500 text performs identically. Therefore (Laurer et al., (2023) it demonstrates that transfer learning is a good way of reducing the need for large amounts of task specific data. Training from scratch is computationally expensive, but it is desirable to work with domain-specific languages or datasets that have not been seen before. For example, researchers trained end-to-end Pashto initiation model programmers from scratch using a class out of hand yielded other models in offensive language detection (Haq et al., 2023).

4.4 Advances in Cross-Lingual, Multimodal, and Bias-Aware Deep Learning Models

New detection methods of hate speech in the last few years have shown that machine learning (ML) and deep learning (DL) models are increasingly effective in a variety of linguistic and multimodal contexts. To give an example, the Convolutional Neural Network (CNN) and Long Short-Term Memory (LSTM) models show a high percentage of success in identifying hate speech spoken in Roman Urdu, which is a version of the language that has become popular in digital interactions of South Asian origin (Naseeb et al., 2025). Following this trend, Bi-directional LSTM (BiLSTM) structures embedded with EfficientNetB1 have performed well by exploiting two modalities textual and visual on the detection of hate speech in Urdu-English code mixed tweets serving as evidence of the usefulness of the multimodal approach (Saddozai et al., 2025). Cross-lingual meta-learning additionally expounds the scope of these systems, so that they can identify hate speech in other languages that low resourced languages, where available training data is scarce, like Norwegian can be identified in flexible model training (Hashmi et al., 2025). These solutions are also fit with the general idea of the chapter of scalability and generalizability of generative AI usage in the real world.

In a bid to detect in a fair manner, bias is a fundamental challenge to counter. Adaptive learning rate schedulers and attention methods have been used to give the model the required focus on more semantically pertinent units of the input and make them less biased in predictions and more robust (Hashmi et al., 2025). The variety and multilingual nature of the datasets are also important to addressing the issue of linguistic and cultural bias, which is especially observed in South Asian studies of hate speech where a resource gap still remains (Sharma et al., 2025). AI development cannot be ethical only in terms of technical precision, but it should be socially conscious as well. Risks in regards to misuse of data and user-rights are incorporated in the integration of privacy-protecting structures, and accountability through transparent data-management behavior (Ammar et al., 2025). In addition, ensuring human oversight prevents the dependence on automated decisions, keeping contextual knowledge and encouraging the development of trustful AI systems (Aldosari et al., 2025). In addition to technical designs, ethical implications reach to the aspect of AI balancing interpersonal relations. To increase real human interactions instead of weakening them, AI should be moderate and not aimed at solving socially or emotionally sensitive areas (see Battisti, 2025). Finally, to achieve long-term success in the field of hate speech prevention, there is a need to incorporate it in the national policy and school programs. Specific policies affecting diversity, human rights, digital literacy development, promote a sustainable social ecosystem that has the ability to resist the malicious effect of hate speech (Marolla-Gajardo & Riquelme Plaza, 2025).

4.5 Classical Approaches vs Transformer-Based Models

Here, we compare three major types of hate speech detection models under five evaluation criteria: feature engineering, data requirements, accuracy, explainability, and scale, as shown in Figure 1. Classical ML approaches are good at explainability and require very little data, but strongly depend on manual feature engineering and provide only moderate accuracy and scalability. This is achieved by finding a balance between accuracy, automation, and interpretability. Current state-of-the-art transformers excel in being accurate, scalable, and explainable, despite needing high data volumes and lacking explainability. This comparison chart clearly summarizes the strengths and trade-offs that facilitate decision-making between modeling strategies for researchers and practitioners.

Figure 1. Comparison of Hate Speech Detection Approaches

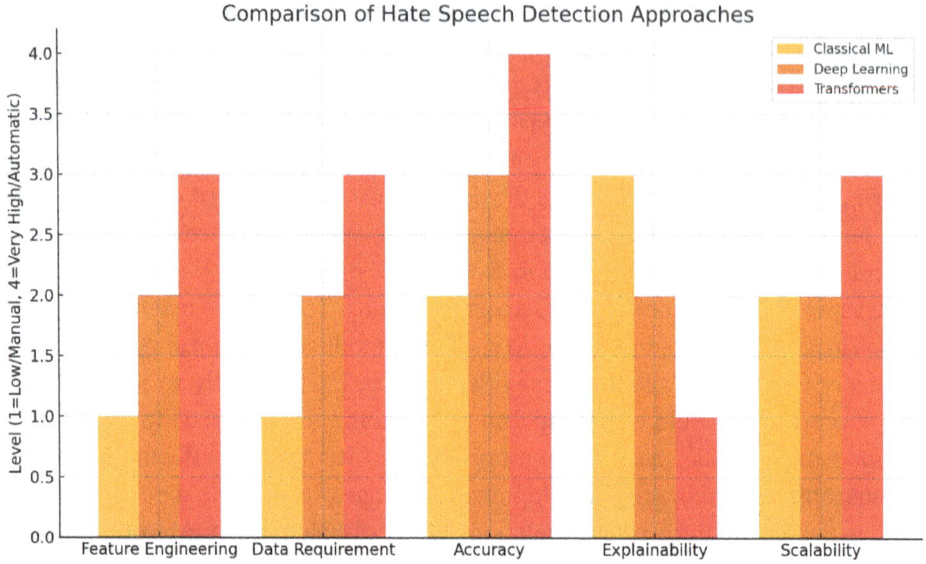

5. EVALUATION METRICS AND BENCHMARKING

5.1 Standard Evaluation Metrics

The metrics of evaluation and benchmarking are essential aspects in the evaluation of hate speech detection models on different platforms. Measurements like accuracy, robustness and generalization are standardized to make the comparison of models effective. Such key performance indicators as Precision, Recall, and F1 Score measure the ratio of properly detected hate speech and the success rate of the model to locate relevant cases. Harmonic mean of the precisions and recall is also frequently employed to evaluate them in a balanced way (the so-called F1 Score) (Patil et al., 2023). Patil et al. (2023) compared the results of their study that used such metrics in the classification of hate speech to the conventional LSTM models and showed better results. The ROC curve and the Area Under the Curve (AUC) are another critical tool of evaluation that represents the discriminative capacity of the model. AUC values are obtained by graphics, where the False Positive Rate is plotted against True Positive Rate when thresholds are changed. Using Random Forest, Fazil et al. (2023) achieved high ROC-AUC value of 0.98 in detecting hate speech. The choice of the adequate metrics should be made depending on the requirements of a particular application and possible real-life consequences of false positive and negative effects (Elmrabit et al., 2020).

5.2 Domain-Specific Metrics

This metric is a toxic Score: A crucial metric for evaluating hate speech detection models that quantify the toxicity of the text. The generally accepted values of this score range from 0 to 1; the greater the value, the more dangerous the information. This metric is used by models such as the Perspective API to quantify the severity of hate speech (Haq et al., 2023). The toxicity score can be calculated by many approaches, for instance, supervised learning techniques using an annotated dataset and an unsupervised approach using a lexicon. For example, HateXplain provides a holistic benchmark for toxicity evaluative scores with objective and rational community targets (Mathew et al., 2021).

Bias score: This is the measure of how a hate speech detection model has its unintended bias to some or all groups or communities. The fairness of this metric is essential to ensure that AI systems are not perpetuated discriminatory practices. Many techniques have been developed to quantify and remedy the bias in hate speech detection models. For instance, Mathew et al. (2021) demonstrated that unintended bias towards target communities can be reduced by ensembling models trained on human rationales. Second, bias analysis techniques, some of which are proposed in (De La Peña Sarracén & Rosso, 2023), characterize and quantify bias metrics and analyze strategies to reduce bias. For example, these approaches often consist of analyzing the model's attention to keywords and evaluating the model on different input demographics.

5.3 Benchmark Datasets and Evaluation in Hate Speech Detection

It is necessary to bring the hate speech detection models to the test on the benchmark datasets to guarantee their accuracy, robustness, and ethical integrity. Such popular datasets as Jigsaw, Detoxify, and RealToxicityPrompts can be used to this end to accommodate a vast array of content-related varieties and model designs. Google Jigsaw Jigsaw come up with a dataset called Jigsaw dataset, it entails online comments tagged them in terms of toxicity which include toxicity, threats, obscenity, and identity-based hate (Mehta & Passi, 2022). It has a multi-label format and can be applied to both classical and deep learning models successfully. To give an example, LSTM models had an accuracy of 97.6, whereas ANN and MLP based BERT models had 93.55 and 93.67 percent (Mehta & Passi, 2022).

Detoxify dataset is a result of communications over the internet, obtained in order to evaluate the generality of the model of toxic language. With the dataset, BERT+MLP models had an accuracy of 93.67% (Mehta & Passi, 2022). RealToxicityPrompts is a tool that scores generative AIs on their toxic response to crafted prompts. This dataset is a test of systems such as GPT-3 or RoBERTa that have also performed well on sentiment tasks such as SST-2 which based on a review of 483 papers found it accomplished 92.90%.

Commonly used metrics are accuracy, precision, recall and F1 score. As an example, BERT-CNN hybrid performed better than the default BERT on SST-2 and QQP data sets (Alyoubi et al., 2023). In the same way, monolingual BERT finetuned on POLD demonstrated high F1 scores (Haq et al., 2023). To manage contextual sensitivity and bias, there exists such a tool on the market as HateCheck, with 29 diagnostic tests (R ottger et al., 2021), which promote the developing investigation of false positives/ negatives. All these benchmarks and evaluation guidelines are fundamental in ethical, trustworthy detection of hate speech.

Table 3. Benchmark datasets for hate speech detection with focus areas.

Dataset	Focus Area	Source
Jigsaw (Toxic Comment Classification Challenge)	Multi-label classification of toxic content in online comments	(Toxic Comment Classification Challenge, n.d.)
RealToxicityPrompts	Evaluating LLM toxicity based on generative prompts	(Allenai/Real-toxicity-prompts · Datasets at Hugging Face, 2024)
HateXplain	Explainable annotations including target and rationales	(Hate-Alert, n.d.)
Detoxify	Toxicity scoring and fine-tuning language models	(Unitaryai, n.d.)
OLID (Offensive Language Identification Dataset)	Offensive language and hate speech in tweets	(Christophsonntag/OLID · Datasets at Hugging Face, 2024)
ETHOS	Multi-label hate speech across multiple identities	(Intelligence-Csd-Auth-Gr, n.d.)
Gab Hate Corpus	English hate speech from alt-right social media site Gab	(Mpgiii, n.d.)
TRAC (Trolling, Aggression and Cyberbullying)	Hindi-English aggression and trolling in social media	(Kmi-Linguistics, n.d.)
Stormfront Dataset	White supremacist hate speech from Stormfront	(Vicomtech, n.d.)

continued on following page

Table 3. Continued

Dataset	Focus Area	Source
Davidson Twitter Hate Speech	Binary and multiclass Twitter hate speech classification	(T-Davidson, n.d.)
HASOC (Hate Speech and Offensive Content)	Multilingual hate and offensive content detection	(HASOC, n.d.)
Hate Speech18	Hate speech detection on Twitter (binary & multiclass)	(Odegiber/Hate_Speech18 · Datasets at Hugging Face, 2024)
Arabic Offensive Language Dataset (AOLD)	Arabic offensive language including emojis and dialect	(Shammur, n.d.)
POLD (Pashto Offensive Language Dataset)	Pashto hate speech dataset for low-resource language	(Drijaz, 2023)
Hate-Speech-in-Hindi	Hate-speech data in Hindi language and Devanagari Script.	(Hate-Speech-in-Hindi, 2023)

Figure 2 shows the F1 scores of four well-known models: SVM, BERT, RoBERTa, and GPT-3, over three benchmark datasets: Jigsaw, HateXplain, and RealToxicityPrompts. This is also a polar-bar chart. Each bar is a unique model-dataset pair with color grouping according to the model family. RealToxicityPrompts, RoBERTa, and GPT-3 clearly outperformed all other methods, with consistently high F1 in all data sets, resulting in GPT-3 and RoBERTa outperforming SVM above all on RealToxicityPrompts. It is easier to notice the correctness of the radial layout and to understand where the best results were consistently found. This format also serves as a useful visualization of cross-model and cross-dataset accuracy in hate speech detection.

Figure 2. Polar Comparison of F1 Scores Across Models and Datasets

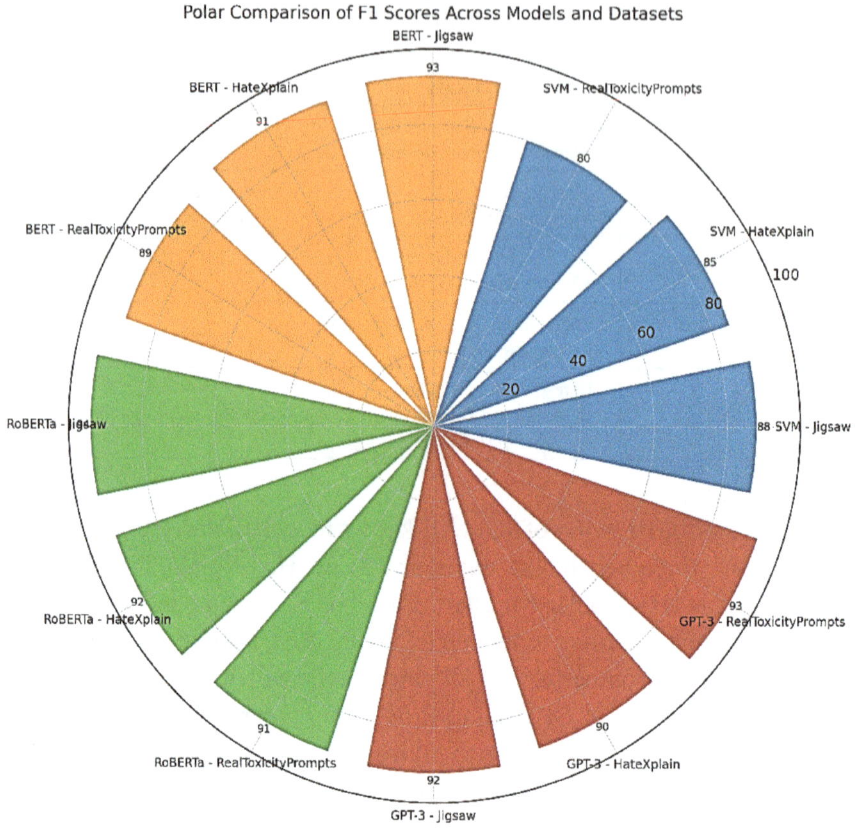

6. CHALLENGES IN DETECTION

Despite definitional ambiguity and data limitations, detecting hate speech is not only a difficult task, but also one of great complexity in the detection of implicit expressions. However, a universal definition of hate speech is elusive it changes depending on the culture, language and platform (Qureshi & Sabih, 2021; Awal et al., 2024; Mollas et al., 2022). In addition, these hate speech datasets are also noisy, have inconsistent annotations and class imbalance, and their performance is degraded (Yin et al., 2023; Gandhi et al., 2024). The problematic aspect of implicit and coded hate speech (also referred to as figurative hate speech), given its delivery via sarcasm, euphemisms, or metaphors, is the fact that they need a considerable level of contextual and semantic understanding (Huang et al., 2023; Mubarak et al., 2023). In order to overcome these obstacle, various solutions have been introduced, for example, AnnoBERT, better annotation schemas, transformer models, and graph neural networks. Meanwhile, the test of explainable AI techniques for interpreting model decisions is conducted to understand model decisions, but it is still an ongoing task to skip the fine parts of the subtle hate speech (Mehta & Passi, 2022; Rawat et al., 2024).

7. SYSTEM INTEGRATION AND REAL-TIME MODERATION

7.1 Incorporation into Generative Pipelines

One of the key ways of dealing with hate speech online is to integrate hate speech detection into generative AI pipelines. Using real time and post generation content filtering through advanced machine learning models including gradient boosting and BERT based architecture, the accuracy ranges up to 86.01% (Sanghvi et al., 2023). With these models, the content that is generated can be watched in real time and suspicious outputs can be flagged for human review or automatic suppression. More detection reliability is further enhanced by applying Bayesian methods, e.g. Monte Carlo dropout in attention layers, allowing to quantify prediction uncertainty (Miok et al., 2021). Moderation loops based on reinforcement learning allow model updates to occur continuously based on feedback of human moderators, as well as users. Adding topic and conversational tone contextual cues can improve accuracy dramatically. For example, Pérez et al. (2023) remained in context and observed gains up to 5.5 points in Macro F1 Score.

Figure 3 shows a complete hate speech detection pipeline. The first step of it is preprocessing of generated text (just normalization and tokenization), and then feature extraction based on TF-IDF vectors or word embeddings. Finally, these features are trained on models from traditional classifiers (SVM, Logistic Regression) deep learning, transformers (BERT, RoBERTa, GPT), etc. Based on output, the system allows, flags and routes content for moderation with interpretability tools such as LIME (Mehta & Passi, 2022).

Figure 3. Architecture Flow: AI-Based Hate Speech Detection System

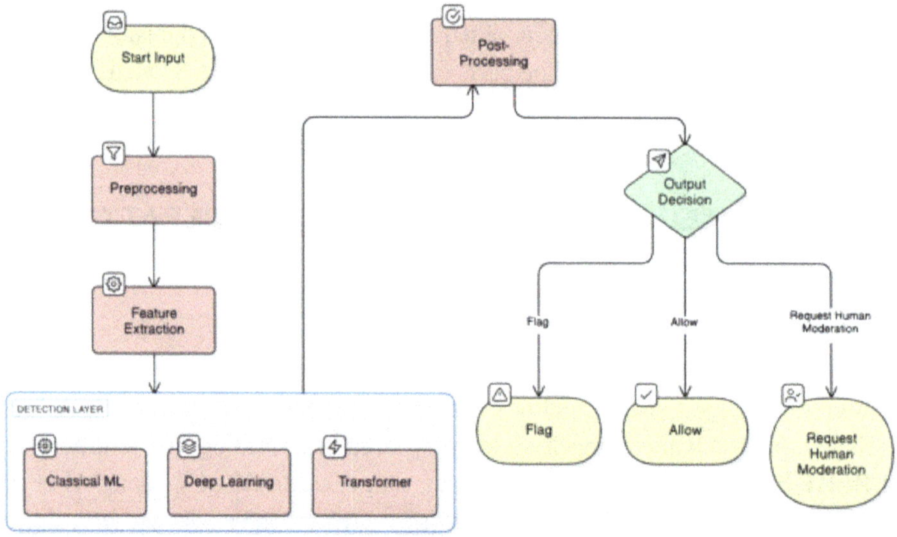

7.2 Feedback Loop

This process plays a crucial role in feedback loops: human-in-the-loop moderation, continuous model refinement, and adaptive system alignment with changing norms. Moderation in human-in-loop involves automation of human expertise with currently AI-based automated systems. Using this approach, false positives and negatives can be corrected, and the system accuracy can be continuously improved. As an example, the method of fine-tuning large language models, such as BERT, has been enriched by injecting user feedback directly into the training process, as was the case with recent research on retrieval-augmented generation systems (Rangan & Yin, 2024). Thus, iterative learning processes were used to continuously refine the models. As an "AI Judge" mechanism, the Quantized Influence Measure (QIM) introduced can be adapted to improve the precision of hate speech detection by using ongoing interactions and feedback (Rangan & Yin, 2024). This is consistent with the dynamic framework contained in the enhanced Presage, Process, Product (PPP) model's shifting relations between factors and outcomes in learning systems (Al Fraidan, 2024). In hate speech detection, system alignment with changing norms must be adaptive. The revised PPP model (Al Fraidan, 2024) suggests that this can be achieved through the addition of culturally relevant content and refinement of its feedback-driven strategy through these factors. Additionally, the various dynamics of coevolution occurring in alignment processes can be used to guarantee that hate speech detection systems remain adaptable to varying societal norms and linguistic trends (Amarilli et al., 2023).

Automated hate speech detection in generative AI systems is illustrated in Figure 4 in detail with its feedback loop architecture. It starts with the generated text and continues to be analyzed using an AI-based hate speech detector. The content is classified as 'Not Hate' or 'Hate' — or flagged 'Uncertain' depending on the detector's initial prediction. At times, the input is escalated to human moderators for a manual review when the input is uncertain. The data from the moderator feedback are routed back into a Feedback Integration Engine, which uses this data to learn patterns for later correction of false positives or negatives and to improve future model performance. The further the content is identified as hate speech, this system also takes steps of Policy Adjustment, added by moderation strategies. Whenever there is any update either in rule form or through the experience of the moderator, Model Update is reflected, establishing that the AI system when learning will always evolve and fit as long as needed. The focus of this diagram is the explainability, adaptability, and ethical alignment that exist in the context of human–AI collaboration.

Figure 4. Feedback Loop for Continual Improvement

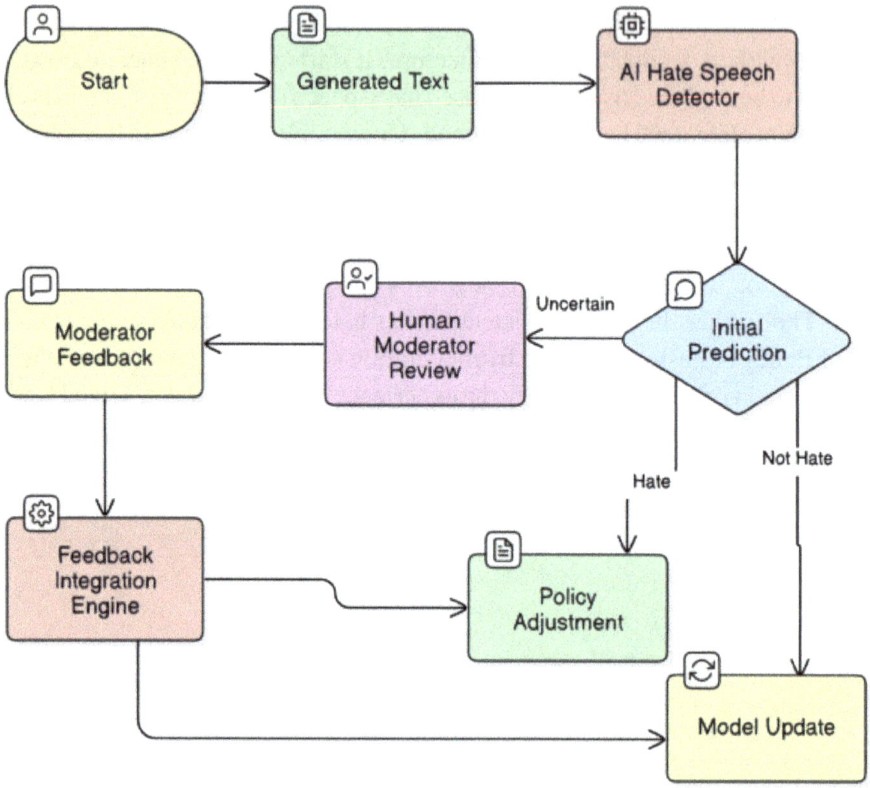

8. META CASE STUDY ON HATE SPEECH DETECTION

The meta has also adopted very efficient and scalable AI models like Linformer and XLM-R models to track down hate speech on its platforms such as Facebook and Instagram. Made to be capable of processing millions of pieces of content at once in real time, these models do not just process a written word, but also images and the context of these images around them. A transformer-based model, Linformer, has promised a considerable boost in memory and speed, allowing one to easily scan through the content without losing its precision. Using multimodal analysis, the system developed by Meta is able to recognize sophisticated and subtle instances of hate speech, even the cases where it is written as slang or memes or concealed under the layers of culturally embedded references.

The detection pipeline is a multilingual system as well, so it can be used with more than 70 languages. XLM-R assists when comprehending the contents of low-resource languages where the usual AI applications may fail to perform. Meta uses a hybrid approach to moderation and reinforcement learning, which employs automatized detection and human verification with the continuous updating of models based on the user feedback.

Toward the end of 2020, Meta has estimated 94.7 percent of the hate speech to be taken down by artificial intelligence before any human could report it on Facebook. This proactive approach to moderation illustrates the capacity of the platform to scale AI solutions to improve safety, minimize users of the harmful content and have safer and more inclusive digital spaces by defining and continuously reinforcing the loop of model improvements and ethical checks (*How Facebook Uses Super-Efficient AI Models to Detect Hate Speech*, n.d.).

9. ETHICAL CONSIDERATIONS AND RISKS

Automated hate speech detection in generative AI systems involves multiple critical ethical considerations. These risks create a significant risk of false positives and false negatives. False positives over sensors with an overzealous approach can stife free speech, weaken legitimate spaces for speech, and are less likely to identify hate speech that can continue to subject and harm vulnerable groups. Thus, choosing the correct threshold requires manual oversight of the model outputs (Jedličková, 2024). These systems should be transparent and accountable to build trust. The manner in which the models make hate speech classifications while being eligible for human decisions should be elaborated in explainable AI techniques. It further helps in accountability (Cheng et al., 2024) with the capacity to maintain thorough audit trails of model decisions, and thus, external auditions. Equitable hate speech detection cannot be developed without the inclusion of underrepresented voices. Diverse and representative of different demographic groups and cultural contexts, and training datasets should be used. By including affected communities in settings and optimizing the datasets and models used in crime prediction, participatory data practices of this sort may reduce bias and improve the accuracy of detection for marginalized communities (Blonder & Feldman-Maggor, 2024). Thus, solutions to these ethical considerations require a multidimensional approach involving technical solutions with solid governance frameworks and practices. The development of responsible hate speech detection systems should be informed by ethical principles and require ongoing evaluation and refinement of such systems.

REFERENCES

Adoma, A. F., Henry, N.-M., & Chen, W. (2020)... *Comparative Analyses of Bert, Roberta, Distilbert, and Xlnet for Text-Based Emotion Recognition, 117–121*, 117–121. Advance online publication. DOI: 10.1109/ICCWAMTIP51612.2020.9317379

Al Fraidan, A. A. (2024). The Enhanced Adaptive PPP Model: A Novel Framework for Revolutionizing Test-Taking Strategies in Language Assessment. *Forum for Linguistic Studies*, *7*(1), 298–312. DOI: 10.30564/fls.v7i1.7918

Al-Garadi, M. A., Yang, Y.-C., Perrone, J., Ruan, Y., O'Connor, K., Cai, H., Sarker, A., & Graciela, G.-H. (2021). Text classification models for the automatic detection of nonmedical prescription medication use from social media. *BMC Medical Informatics and Decision Making*, *21*(1), 27. Advance online publication. DOI: 10.1186/s12911-021-01394-0 PMID: 33499852

Aldosari, B., Aldosari, H., & Alanazi, A. (2025). Challenges of Artificial Intelligence in Medicine. *Studies in Health Technology and Informatics*, *323*. Advance online publication. DOI: 10.3233/SHTI250039 PMID: 40200436

Aljarah, I., Hammo, B., Alfawareh, M., Hijazi, N., Qaddoura, R., Abushariah, M., Habib, M., & Faris, H. (2020). Intelligent detection of hate speech in Arabic social network: A machine learning approach. *Journal of Information Science*, *47*(4), 483–501. DOI: 10.1177/0165551520917651

Alyoubi, K. H., Alotaibi, F. S., Kumar, A., Gupta, V., & Sharma, A. (2023). A novel multi-layer feature fusion-based BERT-CNN for sentence representation learning and classification. *Robotic Intelligence and Automation*, *43*(6), 704–715. DOI: 10.1108/RIA-04-2023-0047

Amarilli, F., Van Den Hooff, B., & Van Vliet, M. (2023). Business-IT alignment as a coevolution process: An empirical study. *The Journal of Strategic Information Systems*, *32*(2), 101776. DOI: 10.1016/j.jsis.2023.101776

Ammar, A. A., Houssein, A. I., & Abusbaiha, A. M. (2025). Ethical Concerns in Large-Scale Data Labeling and Usage: Challenges and Solutions. *International Journal for Research in Applied Science and Engineering Technology*, *13*(1), 919–927. DOI: 10.22214/ijraset.2025.66505

Awal, M. R., Lee, R. K.-W., Mitrović, S., & Cao, R. (2021). *AngryBERT: Joint Learning Target and Emotion for Hate Speech Detection* (pp. 701–713). springer. DOI: 10.1007/978-3-030-75762-5_55

Awal, M. R., Tanwar, E., Chakraborty, T., Lee, R. K.-W., & Garg, T. (2024). Model-Agnostic Meta-Learning for Multilingual Hate Speech Detection. *IEEE Transactions on Computational Social Systems*, *11*(1), 1086–1095. DOI: 10.1109/TCSS.2023.3252401

Battisti, D. (2025). Second-Person Authenticity and the Mediating Role of AI: A Moral Challenge for Human-to-Human Relationships? *Philosophy & Technology*, *38*(1), 28. Advance online publication. DOI: 10.1007/s13347-025-00857-w

Blonder, R., & Feldman-Maggor, Y. (2024). AI for chemistry teaching: Responsible AI and ethical considerations. *Chemistry Teacher International : Best Practices in Chemistry Education*, *6*(4), 385–395. DOI: 10.1515/cti-2024-0014

Cao, R., Hoang, T.-A., & Lee, R. K.-W. (2020, July 6). *DeepHate: Hate Speech Detection via Multi-Faceted Text Representations.* DOI: 10.1145/3394231.3397890

Carvalho, P., Silva, C., Ribeiro, R., Caled, D., & Batista, F. (2023). The expression of hate speech against Afro-descendant, Roma, and LGBTQ+ communities in YouTube comments. *Journal of Language Aggression and Conflict*, *12*(2), 171–206. DOI: 10.1075/jlac.00085.car

Chan, A. (2022). GPT-3 and InstructGPT: Technological dystopianism, utopianism, and "Contextual" perspectives in AI ethics and industry. *AI and Ethics*, *3*(1), 53–64. DOI: 10.1007/s43681-022-00148-6

Cheng, L., Han, J., & Nasirov, J. (2024). Ethical considerations related to personal data collection and reuse: Trust and transparency in language and speech technologies. *International Journal of Legal Discourse*, *9*(2), 217–235. DOI: 10.1515/ijld-2024-2010

De La Peña Sarracén, G. L., & Rosso, P. (2023). Systematic keyword and bias analyses in hate speech detection. *Information Processing & Management*, *60*(5), 103433. DOI: 10.1016/j.ipm.2023.103433

Elkhatat, A. M., Elsaid, K., & Almeer, S. (2023). Evaluating the efficacy of AI content detection tools in differentiating between human and AI-generated text. *International Journal for Educational Integrity*, *19*(1), 17. Advance online publication. DOI: 10.1007/s40979-023-00140-5

Elmrabit, N., Zhou, H., Zhou, F., & Li, F. (2020). *Evaluation of Machine Learning Algorithms for Anomaly Detection.* 1–8. DOI: 10.1109/CyberSecurity49315.2020.9138871

Fazil, A. W., Akbari, R., Quchi, M. M., Khaliqyar, K. Q., & Hakimi, M. (2023). Comparative Analysis of Machine Learning Models for Data Classification: An In-Depth Exploration. *Journal of Computer Science and Technology Studies*, *5*(4), 160–168. DOI: 10.32996/jcsts.2023.5.4.16

Gandhi, A., Ahir, P., Shah, P., Cambria, E., Hussain, A., Lohiya, R., Adhvaryu, K., & Poria, S. (2024). Hate speech detection: A comprehensive review of recent works. *Expert Systems: International Journal of Knowledge Engineering and Neural Networks*, *41*(8), e13562. Advance online publication. DOI: 10.1111/exsy.13562

Garg, S., Jadia, U., Sagtani, A., & Hiran, K. K. (2024, July). ECG-Lense: Benchmarking ML & DL Models on PTB-XL Dataset. In *2024 International Conference on Emerging Trends in Networks and Computer Communications (ETNCC)* (pp. 1-8). IEEE. DOI: DOI: 10.1109/ETNCC63262.2024.10767459

Gupta, M., & Agrawal, P. (2022). Compression of Deep Learning Models for Text: A Survey. *ACM Transactions on Knowledge Discovery from Data*, *16*(4), 1–55. DOI: 10.1145/3487045

Hana, K. M., Bramantoro, A., Adiwijaya, A., & Faraby, S. A. (2020). *Multi-label Classification of Indonesian Hate Speech on Twitter Using Support Vector Machines. 2018 janua*, 1–7. DOI: 10.1109/ICoDSA50139.2020.9212992

Haq, I., Qiu, W., Guo, J., & Tang, P. (2023). Pashto offensive language detection: A benchmark dataset and monolingual Pashto BERT. *PeerJ. Computer Science*, *9*, e1617. DOI: 10.7717/peerj-cs.1617 PMID: 38077561

Hashmi, E., Yayilgan, S. Y., & Abomhara, M. (2025). Metalinguist: Enhancing hate speech detection with cross-lingual meta-learning. *Complex & Intelligent Systems*, *11*(4), 179. Advance online publication. DOI: 10.1007/s40747-025-01808-w

Hiran, K. K., Jain, R. K., Lakhwani, K., & Doshi, R. (2021). *Machine Learning: Master Supervised and Unsupervised Learning Algorithms with Real Examples (English Edition)*. BPB Publications.

How Facebook uses super-efficient AI models to detect hate speech. (n.d.). Ai.meta.com. https://ai.meta.com/blog/how-facebook-uses-super-efficient-ai-models-to-detect-hate-speech/

Huang, F., An, J., & Kwak, H. (2023). Is ChatGPT better than Human Annotators? *Potential and Limitations of ChatGPT in Explaining Implicit Hate Speech, 294–297*, 294–297. Advance online publication. DOI: 10.1145/3543873.3587368

Jedličková, A. (2024). Ethical considerations in Risk management of autonomous and intelligent systems. *Ethics & Bioethics*, *14*(1–2), 80–95. DOI: 10.2478/ebce-2024-0007

Joshy, A., & Sundar, S. (2022, December 16). *Analyzing the Performance of Sentiment Analysis using BERT, DistilBERT, and RoBERTa*. DOI: 10.1109/IP-RECON55716.2022.10059542

Kamyab, M., Liu, G., & Adjeisah, M. (2021). Attention-Based CNN and Bi-LSTM Model Based on TF-IDF and GloVe Word Embedding for Sentiment Analysis. *Applied Sciences (Basel, Switzerland)*, *11*(23), 11255. DOI: 10.3390/app112311255

Kar, S., Mullick, S., Roy, C., Saha, R., & Das, M. (2023). AI Horizons: Unveiling the Future of Generative Intelligence. *International Journal of Advanced Research in Science. Tongxin Jishu*, *387–391*, 387–391. Advance online publication. DOI: 10.48175/IJARSCT-12969

Khan, M. M., Shahzad, K., & Malik, M. K. (2021). Hate Speech Detection in Roman Urdu. *ACM Transactions on Asian and Low-Resource Language Information Processing*, *20*(1), 1–19. DOI: 10.1145/3414524

Laurer, M., Van Atteveldt, W., Welbers, K., & Casas, A. (2023). Less Annotating, More Classifying: Addressing the Data Scarcity Issue of Supervised Machine Learning with Deep Transfer Learning and BERT-NLI. *Political Analysis*, *32*(1), 84–100. DOI: 10.1017/pan.2023.20

Liu, B., Cen, S., He, X., Jiang, X., Xiao, B., & Dou, W. (2023). Adversarial Attacks on Large Language Model-Based System and Mitigating Strategies: A Case Study on ChatGPT. *Security and Communication Networks*, *2023*, 1–10. DOI: 10.1155/2023/8691095

Marolla-Gajardo, J., & Riquelme Plaza, I. (2025). Teacher Education, Diversity, and the Prevention of Hate Speech: Ethical and Political Foundations for Inclusive Citizenship. *Societies (Basel, Switzerland)*, *15*(5), 139. DOI: 10.3390/soc15050139

Mathew, B., Mukherjee, A., Yimam, S. M., Goyal, P., Biemann, C., & Saha, P. (2021). HateXplain: A Benchmark Dataset for Explainable Hate Speech Detection. *Proceedings of the AAAI Conference on Artificial Intelligence*, *35*(17), 14867–14875. DOI: 10.1609/aaai.v35i17.17745

Mehta, H., & Passi, K. (2022). Social Media Hate Speech Detection Using Explainable Artificial Intelligence (XAI). *Algorithms*, *15*(8), 291. DOI: 10.3390/a15080291

Mienye, I. D., Obaido, G., & Swart, T. G. (2024). Recurrent Neural Networks: A Comprehensive Review of Architectures, Variants, and Applications. *Information (Basel)*, *15*(9), 517. DOI: 10.3390/info15090517

Mijwil, M. M., Hiran, K. K., Doshi, R., Dadhich, M., Al-Mistarehi, A. H., & Bala, I. (2023). ChatGPT and the future of academic integrity in the artificial intelligence era: A new frontier. *Al-Salam Journal for Engineering and Technology*, *2*(2), 116–127. DOI: 10.55145/ajest.2023.02.02.015

Miok, K., Škrlj, B., Robnik-Šikonja, M., & Zaharie, D. (2021). To BAN or Not to BAN: Bayesian Attention Networks for Reliable Hate Speech Detection. *Cognitive Computation*, *14*(1), 353–371. DOI: 10.1007/s12559-021-09826-9

Mohapatra, S. K., Bebarta, D. K., Hu, Y.-C., Srinivasan, K., Das, T. K., & Prasad, S. (2021). Automatic Hate Speech Detection in English-Odia Code Mixed Social Media Data Using Machine Learning Techniques. *Applied Sciences (Basel, Switzerland)*, *11*(18), 8575. DOI: 10.3390/app11188575

Mollas, I., Chrysopoulou, Z., Tsoumakas, G., & Karlos, S. (2022). ETHOS: A multi-label hate speech detection dataset. *Complex & Intelligent Systems*, *8*(6), 4663–4678. DOI: 10.1007/s40747-021-00608-2

Mubarak, H., Hassan, S., & Chowdhury, S. A. (2023). Emojis as anchors to detect Arabic offensive language and hate speech. *Natural Language Engineering*, *29*(6), 1436–1457. DOI: 10.1017/S1351324923000402

Mullah, N. S., & Zainon, W. M. N. W. (2021). Advances in Machine Learning Algorithms for Hate Speech Detection in Social Media: A Review. *IEEE Access : Practical Innovations, Open Solutions*, *9*, 88364–88376. DOI: 10.1109/ACCESS.2021.3089515

Naseeb, A., Ahmad, F., Gelbukh, A., Hussain, N., Zain, M., Sidorov, G., & Qasim, A. (2025). Machine Learning- and Deep Learning-Based Multi-Model System for Hate Speech Detection on Facebook. *Algorithms*, *18*(6), 331. DOI: 10.3390/a18060331

Omran, E., Al Qundus, J., & Al Tararwah, E. (2023). A comparative analysis of machine learning algorithms for hate speech detection in social media. *Online Journal of Communication and Media Technologies*, *13*(4), e202348. DOI: 10.30935/ojcmt/13603

Patil, P., Nagarhalli, T., Raul, S., & Raut, D. (2023). *Hate Speech Detection using Deep Learning and Text Analysis*. 322–330. DOI: 10.1109/ICICCS56967.2023.10142895

Pérez, J. M., Debandi, N., Luque, F. M., Cotik, V., Gravano, A., Moro, A., Kondratzky, M., Zayat, D., Serrati, P. S., Miguel, P., & Zajac, J. (2023). Assessing the Impact of Contextual Information in Hate Speech Detection. *IEEE Access : Practical Innovations, Open Solutions*, *11*, 30575–30590. DOI: 10.1109/ACCESS.2023.3258973

Qureshi, K. A., & Sabih, M. (2021). Un-Compromised Credibility: Social Media Based Multi-Class Hate Speech Classification for Text. *IEEE Access : Practical Innovations, Open Solutions*, *9*, 109465–109477. DOI: 10.1109/ACCESS.2021.3101977

Radanliev, P. (2024). Artificial intelligence: reflecting on the past and looking towards the next paradigm shift. *Journal of Experimental & Theoretical Artificial Intelligence, ahead-of-print*(ahead-of-print), 1–18. DOI: 10.1080/0952813X.2024.2323042

Rangan, K., & Yin, Y. (2024). A fine-tuning enhanced RAG system with quantized influence measure as AI judge. *Scientific Reports*, *14*(1), 27446. Advance online publication. DOI: 10.1038/s41598-024-79110-x PMID: 39523408

Rao, K. N., Arora, R. D., Dange, P., & Nagarkar, N. M. (2023). NLP AI Models for Optimizing Medical Research: Demystifying the Concerns. *Indian Journal of Surgical Oncology*, *14*(4), 854–858. DOI: 10.1007/s13193-023-01791-z PMID: 38187847

Rathi, S., Hiran, K. K., & Sakhare, S. (2023). Affective state prediction of E-learner using SS-ROA based deep LSTM. *Array (New York, N.Y.)*, *19*, 100315. DOI: 10.1016/j.array.2023.100315

Rawat, A., Samant, S. S., & Kumar, S. (2024). Hate speech detection in social media: Techniques, recent trends, and future challenges. *Wiley Interdisciplinary Reviews: Computational Statistics*, *16*(2), e1648. Advance online publication. DOI: 10.1002/wics.1648

Romim, N., Ahmed, M., Talukder, H., & Saiful Islam, M. (2021). *Hate Speech Detection in the Bengali Language: A Dataset and Its Baseline Evaluation* (pp. 457–468). springer singapore. DOI: 10.1007/978-981-16-0586-4_37

Saddozai, F. K., Badri, S. K., Alghazzawi, D., Khattak, A., & Asghar, M. Z. (2025). Multimodal hate speech detection: A novel deep learning framework for multilingual text and images. *PeerJ. Computer Science*, *11*, e2801. DOI: 10.7717/peerj-cs.2801 PMID: 40567705

Saeed, A., Kamran, M., Khan, H. U., Shankar, A., Imran, T., Khan, D., & Khan, M. A. (2023). *Topic Modeling based Text Classification Regarding Islamophobia using Word Embedding and Transformers Techniques*. ACM Transactions on Asian and Low-Resource Language Information Processing., DOI: 10.1145/3626318

Saifullah, S., Aribowo, A. S., Cahyana, N. H., Dreżewski, R., Fauziah, Y., & Dwiyanto, F. A. (2024). Automated Text Annotation Using a Semi-Supervised Approach with Meta Vectorizer and Machine Learning Algorithms for Hate Speech Detection. *Applied Sciences (Basel, Switzerland)*, *14*(3), 1078. DOI: 10.3390/app14031078

Sanghvi, H., Bhavsar, R., Sharma, R., Hundlani, V., Vyas, T., Gohil, L., Nair, A., Jadav, N. K., Desai, S., Yamsani, N., & Tanwar, S. (2023). *MetaHate*: AI-based hate speech detection for secured online gaming in metaverse using blockchain. *Security and Privacy*, *7*(2), e343. Advance online publication. DOI: 10.1002/spy2.343

Santra, P. P., & Majhi, D. (2023). Scholarly Communication and Machine-Generated Text: Is it Finally AI vs AI in Plagiarism Detection? *Journal of Information and Knowledge*, 175–183. DOI: 10.17821/srels/2023/v60i3/171028

Sharma, D., Gupta, V., Nath, T., & Singh, V. K. (2025). Hate Speech Detection Research in South Asian Languages: A Survey of Tasks, Datasets and Methods. *ACM Transactions on Asian and Low-Resource Language Information Processing*, *24*(3), 1–44. DOI: 10.1145/3711710

Song, D., Cheng, Y., Mazeika, M., Lin, Z., Pei, H., Xie, C., Koyejo, S., Schaeffer, R., Zhang, C., Xu, C., Xiong, Z., Wang, B., Hendrycks, D., Chen, W., Li, B., Arora, S., Kang, M., Truong, S., & Dutta, R. (2023). *DecodingTrust: A Comprehensive Assessment of Trustworthiness in GPT Models*. cornell university. https://doi.org// arxiv.2306.11698DOI: 10.48550

Wang, H., Lee, R. K.-W., Choo, K. T. W., Awal, M. R., & Hee, M. S. (2023). *Evaluating GPT-3 Generated Explanations for Hateful Content Moderation*. 6255–6263. DOI: 10.24963/ijcai.2023/694

William, P., Chaudhari, R. E., Gade, R., Pawar, A. B., & Jawale, M. A. (2022). *Machine Learning based Automatic Hate Speech Recognition System*. 315–318. DOI: 10.1109/ICSCDS53736.2022.9760959

Yin, W., Agarwal, V., Jiang, A., Sastry, N., & Zubiaga, A. (2023). AnnoBERT: Effectively Representing Multiple Annotators' Label Choices to Improve Hate Speech Detection. *Proceedings of the International AAAI Conference on Web and Social Media*, *17*, 902–913. DOI: 10.1609/icwsm.v17i1.22198

Zahid, I. A., Joudar, S. S., Albahri, A. S., Albahri, O. S., Alamoodi, A. H., Santamaría, J., & Alzubaidi, L. (2024). Unmasking large language models by means of OpenAI GPT-4 and Google AI: A deep instruction-based analysis. *Intelligent Systems with Applications*, *23*, 200431. DOI: 10.1016/j.iswa.2024.200431

Chapter 5
Bibliometric Analysis on the Role of Artificial Intelligence in Hate Speech and Policy Formulation:
Enhancing Evidence-Based Decision-Making in Research Institutions

Fredrick Kayusi
https://orcid.org/0000-0003-1481-4016
Maasai Mara University, Kenya

Linety Juma
Pwani University, Kenya

Michael Keari Omwenga
https://orcid.org/0009-0008-7982-1114
Pwani University, Kenya

Petros Keari Chavula
Haramaya University, Ethiopia

Maad M. Mijwil
https://orcid.org/0000-0002-2884-2504
Al-Iraqia University, Iraq

Kamal Kant Hiran
https://orcid.org/0000-0002-4563-1944
Sir Padampat Singhania University, India

Bismarck Agura Kayus
Kisii University, Kenya

Manish Tiwari
Sir Padampat Singhania University, India

DOI: 10.4018/979-8-3373-3063-1.ch005

ABSTRACT

This paper involved a bibliometric analysis of academic research articles on the subject of Artificial Intelligence dealing with policy making in the Web of Science core collection of databases. The study included articles, reviews, and proceedings papers, published in English, before 17 August 2020. To normalize the potential fault estimate, the number of authors per year was divided by the total number of authors in a year knowing that a single article can have multiple authors. Nevertheless, for the total number of papers, only unique paper IDs were counted. Articles not tagged under "Policy", or a synonymous topic as defined by Web of Science, were excluded because although employing AI, Gaming, i.e., agent-based models are widely prevalent in the study of policy formulation (Reza Saeidnia et al., 2024). The analytic method used is natural language processing and it includes categories exploring AI policy formulation, AI technology utilization in policy making, and AI social implication analysis (Prieto-Gutierrez et al., 2023).

1. INTRODUCTION

For research institutions, the core business is conducting research and development. At present, research institutions are faced with severe policy challenges from the state and society, which requires them to do everything possible to improve their capability to respond to policy challenges. As a technology with the basic feature for coping with data, AI may help the research institutions to be aware of the policy challenges to a greater extent and earlier and then respond better. The general innovation of the approach of improving policy decision-making by monitoring and predicting policy concerns and the less-developed policy of the development of the AI industries in the research institutions can be linked. It either contributes to the establishment of the objective of the model of promoting the development of the AI industries in accordance with policy needs or matches the policy challenges in the industry with the superior AI products of other industries, which aims to facilitate the concerned industry to employ AI (Reza Saeidnia et al., 2024; Nankani et al., 2021). Furthermore, the research institutions may make full use of their advantages as the compilers and disseminators of scientific knowledge to guide the AI development so that the associated policy consultation can be more oriented to serve for policy-making. (Dwivedi et al.2023; Van et al.2021; Gašević et al.2023;Schiff et al.2025)

With the in-depth development of science and technology, current policy areas have become more and more specialized, which is accompanied by the increase in the amount of consultation. It is a problem that research institutions are faced with to catch the most policy-relevant knowledge in the shortest time. A bibliometric system by conducting the priority processing to the achieved publications and then synthesizing the obtained models is used to measure the policy relevance objectively. Through this system, the research institutions may transform the response to policy consultation from experience and instinct to science and mechanism, which is beneficial for the improvement of the relevance and quality of the advice given to the state and government. On the other hand, the output tendency of the policy relevance model is presented, which provides a reference for adjusting the strategy of the publication concerned in order to cope with the future policy challenges. The findings of this study will also give some inspiration to the other research institutions, the AI industries, publishes, and the policy-makers. (Mahrishi et al . 2020; Marra, 2024)

A consideration about the role of Artificial Intelligence in laying out policies, as well as its significance in refining the evidence-based decision-making process, first emerged in Director General of Viet Nam' Department of Environment (Reza Saeidnia et al., 2024). Urgent is the need for applying Artificial Intelligence to fortify the quality of policy decisions made by research institutions; valid, effective, and legitimate policies tend to quell up disputes. As technological progress has been on a galloping pace, challenges have ensued for decision- and policy-makers who chart out policies to follow such a fast pace, too. Such challenges are unavoidable and arise as such a gap is sought to be filled. This study, through the screening mechanisms of publication year and approval of peer-reviewers, therefore aspires to explicate how Artificial Intelligence burnishes the policy formulation undoubtedly. (Letterie, 2021;Newman & Mintrom, 2023;Kim, 2024;Liao et al., 2024;Khalifa et al., 2024; Ahmed et al., 2025; Sallam et al., 2024)

It is found from the study that the more severe a policy issue, the lesser publications on it have come out. That is to say, sterner challenges have been posed for understanding what makes a good policies than consting them per se. The development of technology, for instance, the digitization and 'big data' may either complicate traditional works, or otherwise offer an array of new tools. There emerges, however, some challenges in an attempt to set in place new tools or hi-tech existing ones. This study infinites such a scholarly examination of Artificial Intelligence, a cutting edge, revolutionary approach which could help in so many ways but is unfamiliar.

1.1. Research Objectives

This work seeks to conduct a list of bibliometric analyses on Artificial Intelligence (AI) faces, reviews, clinical studies, and policy documents and on AI-enhanced solar photovoltaic, battery energy storage, electric vehicle, and recharge supply system. This study aims to explore the effectiveness, efforts, collaboration, institutions, big data, evolution, hotspots, and possible impacts for practitioners and policy makers.

762 refereed publications, 23,361 patents, 425 relevant funding items, and 54,527 big data news articles are utilized, analyzed, and visualized.

The research objectives for this work include:

To delineate and diagram AI links with the design, formulation, and drafting of actions by governmental institutions, organizations, and practice per se. For this purpose, scientific research is pursued by illustrating, explaining, and discussing quantitative and statistical evidence and by investigating, observing, and decoding twenty-three simple law domains that, as a whole, cover all presently registered types of law. Investigation is conducted in terms of forty-four different jurisdictions (zero territories and forty-four countries acting as such).

To inspect how AI influences policy-oriented decisions of twenty-nine relevant organizations. These policy-oriented decisions encompass those, from an international point of view, made at the top better than all but rather the most important international organizations and, from a national point of view, taken by a head of state, a government or a representative body – that is a national parliament representing the public interest and formulating and implementing public policy – of a G20 member country. On one hand, a methodology for the bibliometric analysis of these policy-formulating statements is proposed. On the other hand, a data analysis of a list of pertinent documents is provided to cover all visible AI angles of G20 members. Concerning the latter, analysis is designed to inspect, together with the relevance of the topic addressed in the policy documents, the distribution of efforts, the patterns followed by different countries in addressing this matter, and the institutions working with AI that are mentioned.

1.2. Scope and Significance

Artificial intelligence (AI) is becoming ever more ubiquitous for policy formulation aimed at evidence-based decision-making. There are ample scientific publications regarding the matter, although not much literature focuses on its applications in policy formulation, and mostly perfunctorily. There is a knowledge gap about what is covered in those articles and whether the science on the issue proliferates. Moreover, since research institutions stand at the forefront of scientific advancement, it is important to ascertain the role of AI in their policies on the matter. Filling such gaps would pave the way for a more effective policy on the application of AI, especially in order to foster evidence-based policy-making, and thereby contribute to fortuitous outcomes of the application.

This study undertakes a comprehensive overview of the role of AI in policy formulation, targeting a substantive contribution in three aspects. First, to the best of the researcher's knowledge, there is as yet no attempt to systematically review the role of AI in policy formulation by academicians. Second, the review attempts to systematize such role focusing on its applications in research institutions. Lastly, the expected output can provide insight to multidisciplinary stakeholders, especially policy makers and researchers, and may also inspire further scholarly work. In order to do so, it defines the scope, delineates the constructs, operations, and theoretical reasons, verifies the review's design and methods, and outlines potential implications.

The scope of this study is to overview and evaluate the impact of AI on policy formulation aimed at decision-making founded on evidence. On the one hand, the findings provide a kind of bibliometric mapping, covering the spread on the matter, including a variety of countries, journals, research areas, and methodologies. On the other hand, the review particularly emphasizes the role of AI in policy formulation in order to inform decision-making. Artificial intelligence, policy formulation and evidence-based decision making are delineated to clarify the boundaries. Moreover, the definition of policy formulation as to the public sector, especially research institutions, the conceptualization of AI which encompasses machine learning-based approaches, and the construct of evidence-based decision-making are expected to set the operations. In reviewing the literature on the matter, on the one hand, this study inherently categorizes the operations of AI in policy formulation. On the other hand, the rationale concerns why policy formulation conducted with the aid of AI matters, particularly in research institutions.

2. LITERATURE REVIEW

Evolution of Artificial Intelligence and Policy Formulation is discussed in this paper which sheds light on recent advances and future research opportunities supporting research proposals. A casual overview of Artificial Intelligence (AI) technologies is traced, before a widening utility of AI in domain area of policy formulation is observed. In empirical assessments of the impacts of AI in policy strategy, sector and discipline perspectives are considered. Despite a proliferation of AI studies urging evidence-based policy interventions, limited multilateral evidence of such impacts exists. This paper contributes new multilateral evidence of the sector and discipline impacts of AI and policy formulation and concludes by discussing implications and future research directions. (Pfeiffer, 2022)(Roberts et al., 2024)(Emery-Xu et al., 2024)(Walter, 2024)

2.1. Historical Evolution of Artificial Intelligence in Policy Formulation

Artificial Intelligence (AI) planning has been continuously explored in the policy formulation realm ever since the inception of the concept of AI in the 1950s.

Its versatility in promoting researches has been extensively investigated and continuously capitalized by various research institutes. The historical evolution of AI development has structured a foundation for their performance in policy analysis. Significant advancements in AI technology and innovations therein have been facilitated to enable AI to be served in research policy formulation. On the subject side, AI has been conceptualized and applied in various ways for policy researches over the entire history of its development. In recent years, with the prevailing of big data analytics, AI technologies have gained another developmental momentum, which further extends potential utilities in policy contexts and provide a rapidly growing body of literature regarding AI for policy analysis (Salar Khan et al., 2023). This subsection delves into the chronological advancement of AI since the birth of its concept and broadens conception and application of conceptual notions, leading to the irruption of AI in evidence-based decision-making for policy research. Case studies are utilized to frame from historical points of view, revealing the evolving linkage between AI and policy formulation, policy impact assessment and policy evaluation. AI ethics and relevant regulations are also scrutinized to context responsible considerations in AI employment. Departing from a historical view, insights are gained on how antecedent experiences can inform and tackle with contemporary practices and emerging challenges, and what future trends and tasks would be viewed therein. (Maragno et al., 2023; Kurban and Şahin, 2024; Cao et al., 2024; Calderon Herrera, 2025)

Traditionally, the concept of utilizing computer system in supporting decision taken has been appealed by aware governing bodies or research institutions. discovered that no principle existed for the distribution of variance of sampling totals, until 1963 – over 170 years post the invention of probability theory and almost 190 years after its application to error analysis. noted that the October 1982 Tylenol cyanide episode had killed a projected 7,000 Americans, until October 17, 1982, more than a week after the commencement of the poisoning episodes. On the following day, disseminated an FDA memo that recommended a modification in the packaging and presentation of "immediate remedial steps were taken promptly following the FDA's issuance of warning to all manufacturers and institutions", no additional incidents occurred. It was found that individuals sharing a common scientific opinion still exhibited persistent differences in their risk classifications. broadcast the occurrence of a large Cholera outbreak in London, although was asynchronous with the real transmission pattern and some individuals who had previously accepted the occurrence of the 1854 Broad Street Cholera outbreak contested his opinion. The two anecdotal stories all exhibitive that policy formulation was possible to veer with the additional divers supported or prompted by the analysis results obtained from data-statistical method. (Doshi et al.2023; De Bruijn et al., 2022)

2.2. Theoretical Frameworks and Concepts in Evidence-Based Decision-Making

How policies influence AI and how AI can be used by policymakers are demonstrated based on the integration case with the model and the macroEcon Artificial Intelligence Decision-Making model in the second part. Some assessments and suggestions on AI's role in policy formulation for governments, intergovernmental organizations and research institutions are raised in conclusion. Effects of policies on AI are discussed to provide researchers, software developers, policymakers and users with a sense of direction. Two scenarios explore the change of the model by two opposite changes of four key economic policy configurations, and the decision-making prediction of the partnership signature act text is based on integrative approaches including the macroEcon Artificial Intelligence Decision-Making model and decision tree models. Amidst a backdrop of increasing calls for evidence-based policies, policymakers are urged to incorporate data and research findings in their policy plans and actions. Although a vast body of theoretical frameworks and concepts underpins evidence-based decision-making, including those from sociology, psychology, and political science since the initial distinction of four types of systems thinking in operations research, there remain significant gaps in how evidence-based decision-making can enhance the governance of policymakers who are supported by AI technologies, including those in the domain of machine learning, decision-making trees, agent simulation and optimization algorithms. As optimization refers to decision-makers pursuing the best possible option among a set of alternatives, model-predictive control approaches are well-recognized in recent years, and that the integration of these cutting-edge AI technologies and theoretical frameworks in evidence-based decision-making is scarce, the focus is on how AI supported decision-making can enrich the discourse of evidence-based decision-making, by providing models which fill this disciplinary and technological gap (Dabbous et al., 2023; Chan, 2023;Guenduez & Mettler, 2023; Mijwil et al., 2024).

The literature surrounding the role of artificial intelligence (AI) in policy formulation, particularly in enhancing evidence-based decision-making within research institutions, has evolved significantly over the years. The exploration of AI's intersection with political participation and decision-making processes is still in its nascent stages, as highlighted by (Savaget et al., 2019). Their bibliometric analysis reveals a surprising lack of literature addressing the influence of AI on democratic regimes and civil society's active roles in political affairs. This gap underscores the need for qualitative methodologies to explore the complex dynamics of AI and political engagement, suggesting that the relationship is context-dependent and requires further theoretical development.

In a more recent study, (Tchuente Foguem & Teguede Keleko, 2023) provide a systematic review focused on AI applications in specific fields, such as pulmonary hypertension. Their bibliometric approach employs statistical and data visualization methods to map scientific production, thereby highlighting the potential of AI to inform evidence-based practices in specialized domains. This method of analysis is critical as it showcases how AI can enhance decision-making processes by consolidating vast amounts of data into actionable insights.

(Kumar Patra et al., 2023) expand this discussion by examining the academic landscape of AI through a comparative bibliometric analysis of Scopus and Web of Science databases. Their findings emphasize the importance of understanding AI's impact on decision-making in business management, which parallels the need for research institutions to adopt similar methodologies to optimize policy formulation. By identifying trending themes and funding sources, this study illustrates how bibliometric analyses can inform strategic decisions in various sectors, including policy-making.

The need for robust ethical frameworks guiding AI use in academic research is further emphasized by (Perkins & Roe, 2024). Their thematic analysis highlights the necessity for clear policies on AI disclosure in academic work, indicating that while AI tools can enhance the research process, they cannot replace human intuition and judgment. This finding is crucial for research institutions aiming to integrate AI into their decision-making frameworks, as it suggests a balanced approach that combines AI efficiency with human oversight.

(Reza Saeidnia et al., 2024) delve deeper into the capabilities of AI in scientometrics, webometrics, and bibliometrics, elucidating how AI algorithms can enhance the understanding of scientific impact and collaboration patterns. Their systematic review demonstrates that AI has the potential to revolutionize how research is assessed and utilized, thereby reinforcing the argument for its application in evidence-based policy formulation.

(Fabiano et al., 2024) further explore the optimization of the systematic review process through AI tools, presenting a compelling case for their integration in academic writing and evidence synthesis. They caution, however, that while AI can streamline processes, it should complement rather than replace human expertise. This perspective is essential for research institutions aiming to leverage AI for policy formulation, as it underscores the importance of maintaining rigorous quality checks amidst technological advancements.

(Năstasă et al., 2024) address the broader implications of AI on sustainable development, revealing a positivity bias in the literature regarding AI's impact on social and economic dimensions. Their comprehensive analysis challenges overly optimistic portrayals and highlights the need for critical evaluations of AI's role in achieving sustainable development goals—an area that research institutions must consider when formulating policies.

Finally, (Hussain et al., 2024) emphasize the importance of bibliometric studies in understanding the evolving role of AI in healthcare. Their analysis illustrates how bibliometric methods can track trends and quantify research influence, providing valuable insights for strategic decision-making in health systems. This methodology is equally applicable to policy formulation in research institutions, as it offers a structured approach to evaluating the impact of AI on various domains.

Together, these studies underscore the transformative potential of AI in policy formulation and decision-making processes within research institutions. They highlight the necessity for a comprehensive understanding of AI's capabilities, ethical considerations, and methodological rigor in leveraging its advantages for evidence-based practices.

The article titled "Empowering political participation through artificial intelligence" by Savaget, Chiarini, and Evans (Savaget et al., 2019) presents a comprehensive bibliometric analysis of the intersection between artificial intelligence (AI) and political participation, revealing a significant gap in the existing literature. The authors conducted a thorough examination of 721 documents spanning from 1962 to 2017, aiming to elucidate how the relationship between AI and political participation has been addressed over time.

One of the most striking findings from their analysis is that none of the reviewed documents explicitly mentioned the concept of political participation in the context of AI. This oversight underscores a critical deficiency in the literature, as the authors argue that discussions surrounding AI's influence on democratic regimes and civil society's engagement in political affairs are largely absent. This lack of attention to the role of AI in enhancing democratic processes and evidence-based decision-making in research institutions is particularly concerning given the increasing prevalence of AI technologies in various sectors.

The authors employ a mixed-methods approach, utilizing inductive and qualitative methods to delve deeper into the complexities of AI's role in political participation. They gather data through exploratory interviews, participant observation, and document analysis, which collectively provide a rich qualitative insight into the motivations and perspectives of civil society participants regarding their involvement in political affairs. This methodological diversity enhances the robustness of their findings and allows for a nuanced understanding of the potential pathways through which AI could facilitate greater political engagement.

Moreover, the article identifies the relationship between AI and political participation as a nascent and context-dependent domain that warrants further exploration. The authors suggest that the under-researched nature of this field presents both challenges and opportunities for future inquiry. By highlighting the need for more comprehensive studies that consider the societal implications of AI in governance, the authors pave the way for a more informed discourse on how AI can be leveraged to enhance evidence-based decision-making in policy formulation.

The article titled "Artificial intelligence applied in pulmonary hypertension: a bibliometric analysis" by Germaine Tchuente Foguem and Aurelien Teguede Keleko (Tchuente Foguem & Teguede Keleko, 2023) presents a thorough examination of the scientific literature surrounding the application of artificial intelligence (AI) in the context of pulmonary hypertension (PH). The authors employ a bibliometric approach, which is characterized by quantitative analysis of scientific production, to evaluate the research landscape and performance metrics related to this medical field.

The authors effectively utilize various statistical methods, data mining techniques, and data visualization tools to dissect the existing body of research. This methodological framework not only allows for the identification of key trends and patterns in the literature but also facilitates the understanding of the interconnectedness of research outputs. By analyzing bibliometric indicators, such as publication counts, citation metrics, and collaboration networks, the authors provide a comprehensive overview of how AI is being integrated into research and clinical practices related to PH.

One of the critical insights from this analysis is the identification of leading contributors and institutions in the field, which underscores the collaborative nature of research in AI applications. This aspect is particularly relevant for policy formulation as it highlights the importance of fostering partnerships among research institutions to enhance evidence-based decision-making. The authors also point out the gaps in the literature, suggesting areas for future research that could further leverage AI in improving patient outcomes.

Moreover, the bibliometric analysis serves as a valuable tool for policymakers and stakeholders in research institutions. By presenting a clear picture of the current state of research on AI in pulmonary hypertension, the findings can inform strategic decisions regarding funding allocation, research priorities, and the establishment of interdisciplinary collaborations. The systematic review aspect of the article reinforces the need for ongoing evaluation of AI's role in healthcare, emphasizing that evidence-based decision-making should be grounded in robust scientific inquiry.

The article titled "AI and business management: Tracking future research agenda through bibliometric network analysis" by Patra, Praharaj, Sudarshan, and Chhatoi (Kumar Patra et al., 2023) provides a comprehensive bibliometric analysis of the academic landscape surrounding artificial intelligence (AI) within the context of business management. The authors effectively utilize data from both Scopus and the Web of Science (WOS) to conduct a comparative study, which is a notable contribution to the field. This dual-database approach allows for a more nuanced understanding of AI research and its implications for decision-making processes in business contexts.

The analysis reveals that AI has increasingly become integral to various managerial functions, enhancing productivity, proactiveness, and effective decision-making. The authors highlight technical themes such as machine learning, neural networks, and blockchain, which are emerging as critical components of contemporary management practices. Moreover, they identify the "National Natural Science Foundation of China" as a significant funding agency, underscoring the importance of financial support in advancing AI research.

One of the key strengths of this study is its identification of research gaps within the bibliometric analysis of AI. The authors note that despite the prominence of AI as a research area, there is a scarcity of studies focusing on its bibliometric dimensions. This observation is crucial, as it suggests that while AI is widely recognized for its practical applications, there remains a need for more structured academic inquiry into its scholarly communication and impact.

Furthermore, the article emphasizes the relevance of AI in evidence-based decision-making, particularly in research institutions. By illustrating how AI technologies can streamline various departmental functions—such as sales and marketing, data analytics, and human resource management—the authors provide a clear rationale for integrating AI into organizational practices. This integration is portrayed as essential for achieving sustainable development and enhancing overall organizational efficiency (Unogwu et al., 2024).

However, while the article presents valuable insights, it would benefit from a deeper exploration of the implications of AI adoption in policy formulation beyond business management. The authors could expand their discussion to include how these findings might influence decision-making processes in research institutions and public policy, thereby bridging the gap between AI research and practical implementation in governance.

The article "Academic publisher guidelines on AI usage: A ChatGPT supported thematic analysis" by Mike Perkins and Jasper Roe (Perkins & Roe, 2024) provides a comprehensive exploration of the intersection between artificial intelligence (AI) and academic publishing. The authors emphasize the necessity for robust policy frameworks to govern the ethical use of AI in academic research, which is particularly relevant in the context of enhancing evidence-based decision-making in research institutions.

The authors conducted a thematic analysis of various publishers' policies regarding AI authorship and accountability. Their findings reveal a critical gap in the clarity surrounding the disclosure requirements for AI tools in academic work. This is essential for maintaining transparency and integrity in research, as the implications of AI usage can significantly influence the credibility of academic outputs.

The article argues that while AI tools can augment certain research tasks, such as data analysis and literature review, they cannot supplant the essential human elements of intuition and judgment, especially in areas like hypothesis formation and qualitative interpretation.

One of the strengths of this article is its inductive approach to thematic analysis, which allows for a nuanced understanding of the current landscape of AI policies among academic publishers. However, it is important to note that the analysis was limited to a specific set of publisher guidelines available at the time of the research. Given the rapid evolution of AI technologies and their applications, the authors acknowledge that the policies examined may already be outdated, underscoring the dynamic nature of this field.

The authors also highlight the biases and limitations inherent in both AI-assisted and human analyses, which could affect the outcomes of their findings. This acknowledgment is crucial for future research, as it points to the need for a more comprehensive approach that includes a variety of generative AI tools to assess their effectiveness and reliability in academic research.

While the article effectively outlines the challenges and considerations surrounding AI usage in academia, it does not empirically test the effectiveness of AI tools, leaving a significant gap for future exploration. The authors suggest that further research could enhance understanding of how generative AI can be integrated into academic practices while adhering to ethical standards. This recommendation aligns well with the overarching theme of promoting evidence-based decision-making in research institutions, as it calls for a balance between technological advancement and ethical responsibility.

The article titled "Unleashing the Power of AI. A Systematic Review of Cutting-Edge Techniques in AI-Enhanced Scientometrics, Webometrics, and Bibliometrics" by Saeidnia, Hosseini, Abdoli, and Ausloos (Reza Saeidnia et al., 2024) presents a comprehensive examination of the role of artificial intelligence (AI) in enhancing the field of bibliometrics and related domains. The authors argue that AI algorithms can significantly improve the understanding of the impact of scientific publications by analyzing literature to unveil emerging research areas and collaboration patterns. This capability is particularly relevant for research institutions aiming to enhance evidence-based decision-making in policy formulation.

One of the key insights from the article is the potential of AI to facilitate the identification of trends that can inform policy decisions. By providing a holistic view of scientific output, AI techniques enable researchers and policymakers to remain informed about the latest developments in their fields. This is crucial for fostering collaborations with relevant stakeholders, which is essential for developing effective policies based on current scientific knowledge. The authors emphasize that AI's ability to analyze vast amounts of data quickly and accurately enhances the overall quality of scientometric analyses, thereby supporting evidence-based policymaking (Reza Saeidnia et al., 2024).

Moreover, the article discusses the implications of AI in the peer review process. The introduction of AI-based systems can streamline this process by automating certain aspects, which not only increases efficiency but also aims to reduce biases that often plague traditional peer review methods. This automation ensures a more objective evaluation of research submissions, potentially leading to the publication of higher-quality research. The authors highlight that such advancements can accelerate the dissemination of scientific knowledge, a vital factor for timely policy formulation (Reza Saeidnia et al., 2024).

Additionally, the article addresses the role of AI in maintaining the integrity of scientific research. By employing AI algorithms to detect instances of scientific misconduct, such as plagiarism and data fabrication, the authors argue that the reliability of scientometrics analyses is significantly bolstered. This capability is crucial for research institutions that rely on accurate data for informed decision-making in policy development (Reza Saeidnia et al., 2024).

In the article "How to optimize the systematic review process using AI tools," Fabiano et al. (Fabiano et al., 2024) provide an insightful examination of the integration of artificial intelligence (AI) into systematic reviews, emphasizing its potential to enhance evidence-based decision-making in research institutions. The authors argue that AI can automate numerous routine and time-consuming tasks traditionally associated with manual reviews, such as developing search strategies, screening titles and abstracts, extracting data, and summarizing findings. This perspective is particularly relevant in the context of policy formulation, where timely and accurate information is crucial for informed decision-making.

The article effectively highlights the various stages of the systematic review process where AI tools can be applied. For instance, the ability of AI to refine search strategies can lead to more comprehensive literature coverage, thereby enhancing the quality of evidence synthesized for policy decisions. Moreover, the automation of data extraction and summarization can significantly reduce the workload on researchers, allowing them to focus on critical analysis and interpretation, which are essential components of evidence-based policy formulation.

However, the authors also caution against the over-reliance on AI tools, stressing that they should not replace human expertise and judgment. This critical evaluation is vital, as it underscores the ethical and quality risks associated with AI usage in evidence synthesis. The authors advocate for a balanced approach, where AI is viewed as a supplementary resource that can streamline the research process while still necessitating rigorous quality checks and human oversight. This perspective is crucial in ensuring that the integration of AI into systematic reviews does not compromise the integrity and reliability of the evidence produced.

The article titled "Artificial intelligence and sustainable development during the pandemic: An overview of the scientific debates" by Anamaria Năstasă, Teodora-Cătălina Dumitra, and Adriana Grigorescu (Năstasă et al., 2024) provides a comprehensive examination of the role of artificial intelligence (AI) in the context of sustainable development, particularly during the COVID-19 pandemic. The authors present a critical analysis of existing literature, highlighting both the potential benefits and the challenges posed by AI technologies.

One of the central themes of the article is the reliance of AI on extensive data collection, which raises significant concerns regarding confidentiality, security, and the potential for bias and inequality. The authors effectively argue that while there is a prevailing positivity bias in studies focusing on AI's contributions to sustainable development goals, this perspective often overlooks the negative implications that AI can entail. Specifically, they note that while 79% of sustainable development objectives are perceived to be positively influenced by AI, a substantial 35% are negatively affected (Năstasă et al., 2024). This duality in impact underscores the complexity of integrating AI into policy formulation, particularly in research institutions striving for evidence-based decision-making.

The article further critiques the methodological approaches commonly utilized in the field, pointing out that literature analyses, surveys, and case studies dominate the research landscape. However, the authors highlight a gap in the application of more advanced methodologies, such as text-mining and topic modeling, which could provide deeper insights into the multifaceted interactions between AI and sustainable development. This observation is crucial for future research directions, as it suggests that a more nuanced understanding of AI's impact could be achieved through innovative analytical techniques.

Moreover, the authors synthesize various strands of inquiry to illustrate how AI intersects with the three pillars of sustainable development: social, economic, and environmental dimensions. Their argument is well-supported by evidence from existing studies, which collectively advocate for a more balanced view of AI's role. By challenging the overly optimistic portrayal of AI's impact, the article calls for a more rigorous examination of the adverse effects that must be addressed in the literature.

The article titled "Revolutionising healthcare with artificial intelligence: A bibliometric analysis of 40 years of progress in health systems" by Walayat Hussain et al. (Hussain et al., 2024) presents a comprehensive examination of the intersection between artificial intelligence (AI) and healthcare through bibliometric analysis. The authors argue that as AI continues to evolve, understanding its multifaceted impact on healthcare systems is paramount. They assert that bibliometric studies are essential for systematically analyzing the vast body of literature, which helps unravel complexities, track trends, and quantify the influence of research efforts in this dynamic field.

A critical evaluation of the article reveals that the authors effectively highlight the importance of bibliometric methodologies in shedding light on the historical development and current state of AI in healthcare. By referencing previous studies, such as those by Tran et al. and Fosso Wamba and Queiroz, the authors contextualize their findings within the broader landscape of existing research. They note that while these studies have contributed valuable insights, they often limited their focus by using specific keywords, which resulted in the exclusion of significant contributions to the field. This critique underscores a potential limitation in the current bibliometric landscape, where the narrowing of focus may hinder a holistic understanding of AI's role in healthcare policy and decision-making.

Furthermore, Hussain et al. (Hussain et al., 2024) emphasize that bibliometric analysis not only tracks trends but also guides strategic decisions and fosters innovation in medical practice. This assertion aligns with the increasing recognition of evidence-based decision-making in research institutions, where data-driven insights are crucial for effective policy formulation. The authors advocate for a broader approach to bibliometric studies that encompasses a wider array of keywords and topics, thereby capturing the full spectrum of AI's impact on healthcare.

In conclusion, the literature surrounding the role of artificial intelligence (AI) in policy formulation, particularly within research institutions, highlights a transformative potential for enhancing evidence-based decision-making. The studies reviewed demonstrate a growing recognition of AI's capabilities in various domains, yet they also reveal significant gaps and challenges that need to be addressed.

The foundational work by (Savaget et al., 2019) underscores a critical deficiency in the literature regarding AI's influence on political participation and democratic engagement, suggesting that future research should delve deeper into these intersections to inform policy formulation. Following this, (Tchuente Foguem & Teguede Keleko, 2023) illustrate how bibliometric approaches can map the landscape of AI applications in specialized fields, such as healthcare, emphasizing the need for evidence-based practices in policy decisions.

The comparative analysis by (Kumar Patra et al., 2023) further elucidates the importance of understanding AI's impact on decision-making in business management, which parallels the necessity for research institutions to adopt similar methodologies for optimizing policy formulation. This is complemented by (Perkins & Roe, 2024), who highlight the ethical frameworks required for AI usage in academic research, stressing that while AI can enhance research processes, it cannot replace human judgment.

The systematic review by (Reza Saeidnia et al., 2024) emphasizes AI's potential to revolutionize scientometric analyses, illustrating how AI can inform policy decisions by identifying trends and collaboration patterns within scientific literature. This is echoed by (Fabiano et al., 2024), who advocate for the integration of AI tools in systematic reviews, pointing out that while AI can streamline processes, it is essential to maintain rigorous quality checks to ensure the integrity of evidence produced.

Moreover, (Năstasă et al., 2024) provide a critical perspective on the implications of AI for sustainable development, highlighting the need for a balanced view that acknowledges both the positive and negative impacts of AI technologies. Lastly, (Hussain et al., 2024) emphasize the role of bibliometric studies in tracking AI's influence on healthcare, advocating for broader approaches to capture the full spectrum of AI's impact on policy formulation.

In conclusion, the reviewed literature collectively underscores the transformative potential of AI in enhancing evidence-based decision-making within research institutions. However, it also highlights the necessity for ongoing exploration of ethical frameworks, methodological rigor, and the complex dynamics between AI, policy formulation, and societal implications. As research in this area continues to evolve, it is imperative that scholars and practitioners work collaboratively to bridge existing gaps and leverage AI's capabilities responsibly.

3. METHODOLOGY

The methodology section of the research outlines the research design and approaches that have been used in this bibliometric analysis. To begin with, this manuscript starts delineating what a bibliometric analysis is and with what purpose it has been used to assess the AI in policy formulation literature and why such an assessment is relevant. Secondly, the process of data collection is explained, including delineation of selection criteria for the sources that have been considered for the analysis. It indicates that a strong focus is put here on guaranteeing transparency in the research process to make sure the results can be replicated and validated. Thirdly, a number of quantitative techniques are described that have been used to analyze the data and to develop standardized descriptions and analyses that can be reviewed and inspected. This subsection underlines the rationale and the empirical underpinnings of the data coding, emphasizing the systematic, highly replicable approaches that have been developed to process the raw data and extract its meaning. What follows is a detailed methodological demonstration of how to employ a structured approach to anchor each finding in the empirical data. Bibliometric and scientometric analysis are relatively young sub-disciplines of quantitative science studies. The technique has enjoyed a surge in popularity as a method of evaluating research output and assessing research performance, largely in response to the recognition that traditional peer-review outputs exceed the ability of existing databases to track them. At the same time, the use of such analysis can provide triangulation and external referencing to analyses of the same data carried out using other methods, such providing a series of cross-benchmarks. Like decadal and other forms of systematic review, these analyses can help identify gaps and areas of duplication; as and where they are informed by and developed with real community input such bibliometrics can build broad knowledge and consensus within and around scholarly communities about the state-of-the-art and potential future directions in a field. Furthermore, such an assessment can recommend articles explicitly as ethnographic and other studies of interdisciplinary collaborations as a method to increase the computational capacity of a research group, giving peer-researchers access to the requisite tools and methodological expertise. (Rojko & Lužar, 2022)(Zhang et al., 2021)(Francis & Tóth, 2022)(Demetrescu et al., 2022)

3.1. Bibliometric Analysis: Definition and Scope

Bibliometric analysis refers to the extensive application of mathematical and statistical techniques to analyze scholarly publications in a quantifiable way, making them an important tool to track and measure the influence of academic entities on a particular academic domain. Whereas the scope of bibliometric analysis is hereinafter the quantitative analysis of scholarly literature using a variety of algorithmic techniques, the literature itself refers to the domain of published journal articles arranged by year; their bibliographic details (author(s), institution, keywords), and citation information. The exploratory research employs bibliometric techniques to systematically analyze research on artificial intelligence (AI) in policy formulation within research institutions. The scope of analysis here is tied to a structured analysis of scholarly literature to evaluate the volume, impact, and trends emerging from research on AI and policy formulated within research institutions. To do so, 1) the academic databases and search terms are defined; 2) specific parameters for analysis are discussed; 3) a systematic framework of analysis is detailed to 4) identify key publications, authors, and institutions that contribute to the discourse on AI and policy within research institutions (Reza Saeidnia et al., 2024). While bibliometric analyses provide valuable insights into the academic landscape of a broader subject area, they may also contain biases regarding the choice of data sources and methodologies employed in this analysis. Out of necessity for standardization, the analysis is limited to published journal articles (Sánchez et al., 2022; Bircan & Salah, 2022; Javidan et al., 2022).

3.2. Data Collection and Selection Criteria

A key underlying component of research in AI's role in formulating policy under the lens of enhancing evidence-based decision-making is a bibliometric analysis of its current research landscape in research institutions. The proposed research seeks to understand the role of AI in drafting policy at the micro-level, specifically in research institutions, using a bibliometric approach. Areas such as the distribution of countries, institutions, and academics, intellectual structure by co-citation analysis of publications underpinning this research, research implications, and limitations are specifically addressed (Reza Saeidnia et al., 2024).

Data collection is a significant part of the research process since the reliability of the results is directly correlated. Due to this, systematic methods are needed. Expertise also undoubtedly influences the research fundamentally, shaping the sensitivity of the research landscape's comprehension. Therefore, to prevent bias, databases need to be comprised of comprehensive academicians and publications. The data collected within the scope of sharing the dynamics of the artificial intelligence in policy formulation with the scientific medium are noteworthy considering the transparency potential for other researchers. This also carries unforeseen consequences surrounding the research and analysis of this area of emphasis. Alongside information related to the area or follow-up needs, future analyses can be expanded by incoming bibliometrics, which may support potential accessibility and future knowledge of a domain. Although multiple databases were reviewed, one is more focused due to its broader range of publications and research areas. Additionally, based on the journals included in the Communication category in the database, another is added. The chosen database covers a time range that evaluates the access to publications in Communication Education, providing a wider platform for discussing methods and results as the primary source. The literature distribution covers a wide range of articles, given the growing interest of scientific research in understanding the impacts, applications, and outcomes of AI on communication research. Since the research on the discussion is very limited so far, the parameters of the search provided an extensive net, including all the recent and ongoing studies in the field. In this way, 307 articles were taken under scope, most of which were eliminated during the screening process. In the context of the topic, most of the studies included in the analysis are those which focus/mention AI in the policy domain. On the other hand, the convenience of modeling AI to conduct policy is taken into account for the practical implementation of this meta-analysis research by utilizing a discipline-centric citation analysis of an exhaustive bibliometric platform. This meta-analysis also means the consolidation of the previous study and transfers all of the relevant knowledge by exposing the number of the application and literature review. Prescriptive recommendations were suggested based on the variability of conditions embedded in the literature analysis. In order to understand the landscape of latest publication, visualizing the relationship, studying the implication of these effects and discussing the development of future research, data diversity of the attributes of indexed journals. Only peer-reviewed journal articles were therefore included because the main focus is the specific study on issues regarding the impact of artificial intelligence in drafting policy. Nevertheless, the trade-off between the quality over generalization with greater variation in the sample will focus on potential biases in research quality both in the consultation of the study. Minimization is taken in the measures by adhering to the screening and coding process by anchoring through the agreement of three coders. With these limitations also presenting the prospect of opportunity for further study, greater understanding of the impact of artificial intelligence in the drafting policy is a burgeoning area of academic research which could evolve, leading to a distinct research pattern. After all, throughout the analysis of the results, the specific conditions governing the impacts of AI in drafting policy became perceived, but they could be amended partially.

3.3. Data Analysis Techniques

In this research, bibliometric methods are used to analyze and map international scientific literature on AI's role in policy formation in support of evidence-based policy and strategic decision-making. Quantitative methods are used for the interpretation of obtained data. Data are gathered from the publications of the worldwide sciences present in the WoS and Scopus databases. With the development of the biosphere, the influence of technological progress on it is steadily growing. One of the strongest and least predictable consequences of human activity is considered to be anthropogenic changes in the climate system. The study of various global changes is inextricably linked with the use of forecasting and modeling methods. For quite a long time, mathematical models have been used to describe the behavior and interaction of various objects and systems. Documented scientific data, the findings of fundamental research and observations, demonstrate the involvement and exacerbation of many global and regional problems. Therefore, it seems interesting and necessary to evaluate the research activity of the world-wide scientific community aimed at studying the impact of the use of policy strategies on the scientific research output of countries.

Commonly used quantitative methods in bibliometric studies have emerged in the interpretation of bibliographic data. These are, first of all, the methods of citation analysis, which are widely used to study the connections between scientific papers (Reza Saeidnia et al., 2024). These methods are applied in a separate analysis and in combination with other methods (referred to as combined methods). The analysis of co-authorship is also one of the most frequently used methods of bibliometrics and is the subject of individual numerous studies. Combined methods of citation and co-authorship analysis are used, on the one hand, to identify research areas and the leading scientists in them; on the other hand, to visualize the results of bibliometric studies in a comprehensive manner. The purpose of this research is to analyze and map international scientific literature on the use of artificial intelligence in policy making in support of non-commercial strategic decisions. Scientific publications, which are devoted to the information mathematical models examining the impact of policy strategies on the scientific research output of countries, can be closely or remotely linked to this goal.

4. RESULTS AND FINDINGS

A bibliometric analysis was conducted examining the trends involving the role of artificial intelligence (AI) in making policies. Informed insights were retrieved from . Moreover, the software VOSviewer was employed to visualize the scientific landscape regarding decision-making and smart machines. By presenting empirical evidence, the necessity of being evidence-based in providing results in the governance of research institutions was discussed. Expansion of AI applications in assessing policies and generation of several implementations for academic organizations have been proposed based on bibliometric outputs.

Why Artificial Intelligence (AI) is supplemented to accompany the key decisions of policymakers? One of the initially cited motives for consulting with intelligent machinery, including expert systems or any relevant software, to support the formation of a policy is its capability to overcome cognitive mistakes when addressing information overload . The computational engines designed to assist in judgment can make several simulations or deduct information based on numerous setting conditions. Since diverse themes operate with VR apparatus, the complex network running societal matters is extra-difficult to comprehend and follow. It may, therefore, be more beneficial to allow smart machines that have the capacity to process vast amounts of information and offer randomized statistical consequences. Secondly, in order to ensure earlier, more precise, and comprehensive reviews of the executed or conditioned policy, scholars could turn to artificial systems. Thanks to vast volumes of data stockpiled, the learning apparatus can predict how certain practices could coordinate with other sectors over the planned date interval.

Having these premises in mind, it is more than reasonable and obligatory to foster evidence-based results in policy-making. In such a method, concluding actions taken is unquestionably better founded as it should be elaborated on accurate and unbiased findings. There is comfort in having this knowledge, hence several publications revealed their respective suggestions. Displayed findings delineate the trends in the utilization of AI to refine the approach in making a policy based on a bibliometric evaluation of the literature with the provision of instructive guidance for those drafting policies and advise how findings could grant an evidence-based approach to policy execution in an academic facility landscape. Hence, smart machines have begun to be increasingly evident in shaping the modus operandi in policy patterns. The first scholarly article analyzing the nexus between AI and the governance of policy formation dates back to the commencement of the past decade, with an ascending trend in output broader seen henceforth.

4.1. Overview of AI Research in Policy Formulation

Artificial intelligence (AI) is considered as a transformative technology with significant promise to influence nearly every sector. The policy field, of course, is no exception. The application of AI in practical processes of research institutions and the departments, and countries charge with policy formulation is growing. Increasingly, it is used to analyze vast amounts of data and support decision-making, optimize resource allocation, identify key trends, produce more accurate forecasts, and provide timely and robust insights. Yet, the deployment of AI in policies has provoked numerous concerns namely, regulation, ethical matters, and trust (Perry & Uuk, 2019).

This study used advanced bibliometric and wide database search to demonstrate the comprehensive overview of new research in the field of applying AI in policy fields. Since then, this study provides a critical look at the existing literature, determining current trends and issues of interest and exploring what questions are still largely unaddressed. This study provides an enlightening cross-disciplinary view into AI applications in policy fields and improves awareness of the potential impact of these developments across various sectors.

This paper is systematically constructed so that influences interested in a deep dive can easily access the potential practical implementations or technical details. It also opens a variety of opportunities with a clear interplay for future research at the intersection of AI, policy, strategy, corporate science policy and industry technology (Reza Saeidnia et al., 2024).

4.2. Key Themes and Trends in AI Implementation for Evidence-Based Decision-Making

The use of artificial intelligence (hereinafter “AI”) in evidence preparation and evidence-based decision making (hereinafter “EBDM”) and its different aspects is increasing. This research aimed to identify the Polish and international literature on EBDM, engage in a bibliometric analysis, and examine the interdisciplinary connections between EBDM and AI. A total of 612 relevant articles were found written in 2013–2022 in English. Research results indicate a growing interest in the interdisciplinary aspects of AI use in EBDM. The practical results of the study can be meaningful for research centers, academic employees, and even public institutions preparing strategic documents, programs, and projects.

Since the beginning of the new millennium, AI has been increasingly employed by administrations and research institutes to raise the quality and relevance of prepared policies and strategic documents. In recent years this tendency has become more expressed and covers the visibility of both huge international organizations as well as rather worldwide financial organizations, research institutes, or governmental institutions. Recently, AI has been sharply put to use in danger analysis and evidence grooming as well as in bettering thé data literacý and policy literacý or the ability to concentrate on public institutions. This is in line with the aims of the highest enhancement of the document of a professional entity's approachability, the top progress in the overall brand's position, and the highest readability of information.

5. DISCUSSION

The aim of this study was to shed a light on the role of artificial intelligence in policy formulation, aiming to benefit research institutions by providing a robust and evidence-based guide for integrating AI systems in their organization. Artificial intelligence has the potential to enhance evidence-based policy formulation by improving decision-making in research institutions. This study provides a comprehensive action plan to boost AI utilization. The majority of the suggested actions focus on the development of AI-problem-oriented solutions for policy formulation.

The findings indicate that research institutions mainly use AI for policy recommendation practices, and suggested that AI utilization may be expanded for policy expectation practice. This was depicted clearly through the yearly comparison, which showed the obvious increase in policy expectation practices in the literature from 2019 onward. The findings exemplify the significant potential of AI in policy formulation for research institutions, as revealed by their promising impacts. Research institutions can utilize AI throughout most policymaking processes, from problem identification to evaluation, using a broad array of AI-system macro-types. The suggestions are essential to ensure sustainable, inclusive, and robust AI integration in policy formulation for research institutions. AI has significant potential to enhance evidence-based decision-making in the field, and these findings will prove useful for stakeholders to better understand the current implementation of AI in policy formulation for research institutions and in similar organizations. It is expected to stimulate further research in the field and inspire stakeholders to undertake better actions in implementing AI to more effectively formulate policies.

5.1. Interpretation of Findings

The interpretation of findings concerning the role of AI in policy formulation is made, offering a way of making a connection between empirical data and the realm of practice. The intention is not merely to describe a set of AI literature, but to illuminate these data in view of the patterning of AI and the needs of governance. A detailed study of AI research patterns, emerging trends, and evolving strategies provides evidence of the potential significance and suitability of this understanding for policies, and even corporate strategies in the near future. Moreover, the interpretation goes beyond the findings and their general theoretical frames while providing for nuanced understanding of the impact of AI on policy and governance. Conceived of as a base of historically accumulated knowledge, a key priority of the policy is to enhance accurate goal-setting, streamlining state performance while meeting the public needs. By a broader framework of designs combining empirical base and evidence, data-based policymaking as an evidence-based approach has come to the fore as the search for policies and decisions taking actual research outcomes, insights, and predictive potential on the issue into account (Reza Saeidnia et al., 2024). Under the unified understanding, the policy process is derived from relevant literature and data. An attempt to envision policy at the intersection with a theory makes it easier to aggregate, analyse and interpret the data while informing the broader discourse concerning the AI impact on policy. On such a ground generated, generalisations and policy proposals are made in the domain of a feasible policy design. It is expected that an evidence-based approach to policy and decision-making should rest on a thorough exploration and assessment of empirical evidence.

5.2. Implications for Research Institutions and Policy Makers

On the basis of findings, there are important implications for research institutions. Research institutions should modify their operational framework according to comply with the artificial intelligence technologies. Research institutions should predict and use the most research topics precisely with regards to funding utilization, not under popular but unpopular research areas. High funding allocation and the total number of payments do not result in high levels of awareness for research areas. Therefore, adequate fund sharing for low-level research areas is required. Partnering with many institutions to gain access to fund use for research topics does not increase the effectiveness of evidence-based practices on research productivity. Instead of collaborating with many institutions and in many ways, research institutions should enhance collaboration with partners through international cooperation. Only after built an effective network partnership with a partner as a distributor will the level of research productivity rise. Given the benefits of a long-term collaborative policy, research institutions need to systematically examine their collaborative partners. In isolation, the strong relationship with the distributor, and policy engagement makes an important contribution to high-level research product. Research institutions need to understand the effectiveness of evidence-based practices continuously and develop scientific strategies as validation for research policy and strategy development. The most studied research policy and strategy for policy advocacy in a successful way in turning policymakers into potential users are based on identified research findings. Research institutions should develop a comprehensive strategy to use the knowledge and skills of researchers in the translation of research information into evidence-based practices. Therefore, research institutions often provide complex training on communication, use of the media, and writing for a published examination of research results (Gao & Wang, 2023). Dissemination of publications is not enough, research institutions need to create a multidimensional strategy with knowledge and skills in expanding the use of research results. On the basis of findings, research institutions need to evaluate their dissemination strategy, assess the effectiveness of their interdisciplinary and collaborative activities, and improve this in a sustainable way to enhance evidence-based practices. Establishing a network of partnerships with both distributors and users can produce broad dissemination of research results. There has also concluded the implications for policymakers, it has important implications for policymakers. The faster research institutions integrate artificial intelligence with their networks, the more effective funding is distributed and dealt with. Subsequently, funding for research institutions increases, so policies must be rapidly developed for research institutions. There will be significant support and coordination costs for monitoring the implementation of this policy (Stix, 2022). Policy managers must also monitor the progress of funds and have effective dissemination of information. Instruments have found that public policies can play an important role in broadening the scope of collaboration guidelines between research institutions and policies. The finding suggests that research productivity gains come from guiding research institutions' collaboration with countries supported by domestic policies. Broad support for public policies is effective in improving research productivity. For this reason, public policies must be developed that are well supported. On the other hand, public policies do not support nonfederal fund sharing, but public policies are also ineffective at medium-low funding levels. Therefore, while using public policies for research institutions in sharing nonfederal funds, it is necessary for research institutions to pay attention to the effectiveness of funds. There is also a difference in cooperation between developed and developing countries on how research institutions can deal with public policies. Policy managers need to respond to these differences with adjusted regulations. By responding to policies, research institutions can improve the effectiveness of their involvement in public policies. Changes in regulations must be stable and durable.

Unfortunately, there is a significant reduction in research productivity as guidelines change constantly. Regulations need to be decided in the long term in accordance with country agreements. As well as these results depict avenues for ways to foster and support AI's adoption throughout the public sector. Governments that are still developing their AI strategies may learn valuable lessons on how to close the gap with the leading countries in the field. On the other hand, AI communities are just beginning to question, from a social science perspective, how the democratization of AI can unfold. Overall, the proposed approach contributes to the current research by facilitating a broader understanding of the AI-assisted policy making approaching, embracing multiple criteria trade-offs for a nuanced analysis of the performance of the AI-domain authorities in comparison with their broader peers. The ability to adopt a deeper and transferable practice for conducting cross-country bibliometric analysis using AI methods and data sources.

6. CONCLUSION

Artificial intelligence (AI) technologies are rapidly changing the way policy-makers access and analyze information to make evidence-based decisions. This paper provides a systematic review of state-of-the-art AI technologies for policy formulation with a focus on recent trends and developments. AI enables effective harvesting of actionable knowledge through advanced text-mining, network modeling and analysis, hybrid approaches including expert opinion and social media analytics, and open source intelligence coupling with agent-based modeling for scenario planning. While the use of AI increases concerns regarding transparency, accountability and evaluating policy equity, several studies explore the challenges and opportunities to address these issues. To navigate those challenges and encourage responsible AI governance, ongoing interdisciplinary research, and collaboration among policy-makers, AI researchers, technology developers, public health professionals, ethicists, and experts across various fields are crucial.

Artificial intelligence (AI) technologies have been increasingly employed to support policy-makers making evidence-based decisions. This trend is expected to accelerate with proposed AI strategies and new AI governance mechanisms in enabling stakeholder access to advanced AI capabilities and information services (Perry & Uuk, 2019). The world's most powerful countries have published national strategies on AI. Though U.S. universities in recent years have published the most associated research, China's government has increasingly indexed associated research toward justifying their efforts to develop AI due to their AI national strategy through China Plans for significantly more research and analysis pertaining to the global landscape of AI (Reza Saeidnia et al., 2024). At the same time, the number of countries using AI in the development of national guidelines is also increasing.

6.1. Summary of Key Findings

The recent expansion of a new body of knowledge surrounding the role of artificial intelligence in policy formulation and the significance of evidence-based decision-making is predicted. Through bibliometric analysis, scientific outputs exploring the relationship between artificial intelligence and policy formulation in different aspects have been reviewed and citational, content, and thematic analyses have been carried out for the last 20 years of outputs. The trends over time, significant articles, journals, most studied institutions, authors, and keywords as well as the most relevant themes were covered in the scope of the analyses.

Bibliometric reviews to AI-related studies have been studied increasingly. To realize the potential toolkit of the state-of-the-art AI for research on the AI itself, bibliometric analysis can serve as a compass. For this purpose, the most recent trends and new insights to conduct bibliometrics research with advanced AI facilities in AI-enhanced bibliometrics are presented. More than twenty AI capabilities for standalone AI or hybrid AI combination with machine learning or others fields in bibliometrics are discussed. The methods and their benefits in terms of analysis quality, facility accessibility, data property, and process automation in the data collection, data evaluation, and analysis steps of the bibliometrics study are listed. The well-designed combination of AI with traditional bibliometrics, webometrics, and scientometrics activities potentially enhances the quality and quantity of the state-of-the-art-related work for the academic fellows. This paper review is deliberately designed as a practical guideline for readers who may discover it valuable, assisting them in the choice of the assistant AI instruments for the intended purpose and activities in AI-enhanced bibliometrics (Reza Saeidnia et al., 2024).

6.2. Recommendations for Future Research

Broad statements regarding AI in policy formulation have been made, but these do not provide precision in the nature of AI involvement and the effects produced. Recommendations are made for developing comprehensive research focus on understanding the adjunct impact of AI technology on policy formulation. It is suggested that an empirical perspective based on real-world developments may be valuable in understanding the process being witnessed at the cutting edge of the formation and dissemination of policy. Harnessing the potential benefits of AI technologies for research also requires an increase in technology preparedness, digital skills, and increased collaboration among research organizations, as well as strong and coherent support from research-performing organizations. Thus, it is important for policy-makers and stakeholders at all levels to ensure an enabling regulatory and policy environment for research performing and research funding organizations to seize the potential of these new scientific and technological advances to move towards effective and efficient governance models for the scientific system. In order to seize the potential benefits of Big Data and novel AI technologies for research and evidence-based policy, further broadening the scope of funding programs would be beneficial for enhancing interdisciplinarity and developing new technological infrastructures. Broad works of performing impact assessment do not delve into the metrics and measurements employed or propose new ways of assessing evidence impact. The setting up of metrics infrastructure for similar institutions in other parts of the world is advocated, as well as including researchers in the discussion on impact assessment (Gursoy & A. Kakadiaris, 2023). Broad deployments of AI have, however, occurred without efforts being made to gain a more intricate understanding of broader AI involvement and the impact produced. There is a case for more in-depth empirical research into the wherewithal and limitations of AI in policy formulation that simultaneously grapples with successful applications and obstacles faced; equally, a more precise understanding is needed of the variables conditioning impact (Perry & Uuk, 2019). In short, broad policies are being advocated without research hitherto attesting the reality of the eschewed benefits or the nature of AI involvement in policy processes; broad recommendations for policy-makers and research funding organizations are put forward flowing from these conclusions, as well as suggestions for future research and the need for greater reflection on the wider implications for research systems.

REFERENCES

Ahmed, A. B., King, B. D., Hiran, K. K., Dadhich, M., & Malcalm, E. (2025). Half a decade of artificial intelligence in education in africa: Trends, opportunities, challenges and future directions. Journal of Engineering Education Transformations, 81-100.

Bircan, T. & Salah, A. A. A. (2022). A bibliometric analysis of the use of artificial intelligence technologies for social sciences. Mathematics. mdpi.com

Calderon Herrera, D. S. (2025). Redefining Choices. How Does Artificial Intelligence Support Decision-Making in Urban and Architectural Development?. polito.it

Cao, K., Zhou, C., Church, R., Li, X., & Li, W. (2024). Revisiting spatial optimization in the era of geospatial big data and GeoAI. [sciencedirect.com]. *International Journal of Applied Earth Observation and Geoinformation*, *129*, 103832. DOI: 10.1016/j.jag.2024.103832

Dabbous, A., Barakat, K. A., & Kraus, S. (2023). The impact of digitalization on entrepreneurial activity and sustainable competitiveness: A panel data analysis. Technology in Society. sciencedirect.com

De Bruijn, H., Warnier, M., & Janssen, M. (2022). The perils and pitfalls of explainable AI: Strategies for explaining algorithmic decision-making. Government information quarterly. sciencedirect.com

Demetrescu, C., Finocchi, I., Ribichini, A., & Schaerf, M. (2022). On computer science research and its temporal evolution. [HTML]. *Scientometrics*, *127*(8), 4913–4938. DOI: 10.1007/s11192-022-04445-z

Doshi, R., Hiran, K. K., Mijwil, M. M., & Anand, D. (2023). To that of artificial intelligence, passing through business intelligence. In *Handbook of Research on AI and Knowledge Engineering for Real-Time Business Intelligence* (pp. 1–16). IGI Global. DOI: 10.4018/978-1-6684-6519-6.ch001

Dwivedi, Y. K., Kshetri, N., Hughes, L., Slade, E. L., Jeyaraj, A., Kar, A. K., Baabdullah, A. M., Koohang, A., Raghavan, V., Ahuja, M., Albanna, H., Albashrawi, M. A., Al-Busaidi, A. S., Balakrishnan, J., Barlette, Y., Basu, S., Bose, I., Brooks, L., Buhalis, D., & Wright, R. (2023). Opinion Paper:"So what if ChatGPT wrote it?" Multidisciplinary perspectives on opportunities, challenges and implications of generative conversational AI for research, practice and policy. [sciencedirect.com]. *International Journal of Information Management*, *71*, 102642. DOI: 10.1016/j.ijinfomgt.2023.102642

Emery-Xu, N., Jordan, R., & Trager, R. (2024). International governance of advancing artificial intelligence. AI & SOCIETY. springer.com

Fabiano, N., Gupta, A., Bhambra, N., Luu, B., Wong, S., Maaz, M. G., Fiedorowicz, J. L., Smith, A., & Solmi, M. (2024). How to optimize the systematic review process using AI tools. ncbi.nlm.nih.gov

Francis, N. & Tóth, G. (2022). Trend and network analysis to reveal disciplinary position of soil science and its sub-disciplines. Agrokémia és Talajtan. akjournals.com

Gao, J. & Wang, D. (2023). Quantifying the Benefit of Artificial Intelligence for Scientific Research. [PDF]

Gašević, D., Siemens, G., & Sadiq, S. (2023). Empowering learners for the age of artificial intelligence. [sciencedirect.com]. *Computers and Education: Artificial Intelligence*, *4*, 100130.

Guenduez, A. A. & Mettler, T. (2023). Strategically constructed narratives on artificial intelligence: What stories are told in governmental artificial intelligence policies?. Government Information Quarterly. sciencedirect.com

Gursoy, F., & Kakadiaris, A. I. (2023). Artificial intelligence research strategy of the United States: critical assessment and policy recommendations. ncbi.nlm.nih.gov

Hussain, W., Mabrok, M., Gao, H., & Rabhi, A. F., & A. Rashed, E. (2024). Revolutionising healthcare with artificial intelligence: A bibliometric analysis of 40 years of progress in health systems. ncbi.nlm.nih.gov

Javidan, A. P., Li, A., Lee, M. H., Forbes, T. L., & Naji, F. (2022). A systematic review and bibliometric analysis of applications of artificial intelligence and machine learning in vascular surgery. [HTML]. *Annals of Vascular Surgery*, *85*, 395–405. DOI: 10.1016/j.avsg.2022.03.019 PMID: 35339595

Khalifa, M., Albadawy, M., & Iqbal, U. (2024). Advancing clinical decision support: The role of artificial intelligence across six domains. Computer Methods and Programs in …. sciencedirect.com

Kumar Patra, A., Praharaj, A., Sudarshan, D., & Prasad Chhatoi, B. (2023). AI and business management: Tracking future research agenda through bibliometric network analysis. ncbi.nlm.nih.gov

Kurban, C. F., & Şahin, M. (2024). Exploring ChatGPT's Impact on Higher Education–A Case Study. In The Impact of ChatGPT on Higher Education: Exploring the AI Revolution (pp. 1-6). Emerald Publishing Limited. [HTML] DOI: 10.1108/978-1-83797-647-820241001

Liao, X., Yao, C., Jin, F., Zhang, J., & Liu, L. (2024). … intelligence-assisted decision-making software in hospitals in China: a qualitative study using the updated Consolidated Framework for Implementation Research. BMJ open. bmj.com

Mahrishi, M., Hiran, K. K., Meena, G., & Sharma, P. (Eds.). (2020). *Machine learning and deep learning in real-time applications*. IGI global., DOI: 10.4018/978-1-7998-3095-5

Maragno, G., Tangi, L., Gastaldi, L., & Benedetti, M. (2023). Exploring the factors, affordances and constraints outlining the implementation of Artificial Intelligence in public sector organizations. [sciencedirect.com]. *International Journal of Information Management, 73*, 102686. DOI: 10.1016/j.ijinfomgt.2023.102686

Marra, M. (2024). Co-creating evaluation for policy relevance: The challenges of the post-truth world. Evaluation in the Post-Truth World. [HTML] Letterie, G. (2021). Three ways of knowing: the integration of clinical expertise, evidence-based medicine, and artificial intelligence in assisted reproductive technologies. Journal of Assisted Reproduction and Genetics. nih.gov

Mijwil, M. M., Naji, A. S., Doshi, R., Hiran, K. K., Bala, I., & Ali, G. (2024). The effect of human-computer interaction on new applications by exploring the use case of ChatGPT in healthcare services. In modern technology in healthcare and medical education: Blockchain, IoT, AR, and VR. IGI Global. DOI: 10.4018/979-8-3693-5493-3.ch005

Năstasă, A., Dumitra, T. C., & Grigorescu, A. (2024). Artificial intelligence and sustainable development during the pandemic: An overview of the scientific debates. ncbi.nlm.nih.gov

Newman, J., & Mintrom, M. (2023). Mapping the discourse on evidence-based policy, artificial intelligence, and the ethical practice of policy analysis. Journal of European Public Policy. tandfonline.com Kim, E. S. (2024). Can data science achieve the ideal of evidence-based decision-making in environmental regulation? [HTML]. *Technology in Society*.

Perkins, M., & Roe, J. (2024). Academic publisher guidelines on AI usage: A ChatGPT supported thematic analysis. ncbi.nlm.nih.gov

Perry, B. & Uuk, R. (2019). AI Governance and the Policymaking Process: Key Considerations for Reducing AI Risk. [PDF]

Pfeiffer, C. (2022). Future scenarios on multilateralism: global governance models for efficient (economic) policy coordination. uniroma1.it

Reza Saeidnia, H., Hosseini, E., Abdoli, S., & Ausloos, M. (2024). *Unleashing the Power of AI. A Systematic Review of Cutting-Edge Techniques in AI-Enhanced Scientometrics*. Webometrics, and Bibliometrics. [PDF]

Roberts, H., Hine, E., Taddeo, M., & Floridi, L. (2024). Global AI governance: barriers and pathways forward. International Affairs. oup.com

Rojko, K., & Lužar, B. (2022). Scientific performance across research disciplines: Trends and differences in the case of Slovenia. [HTML]. *Journal of Informetrics*, *16*(2), 101261. DOI: 10.1016/j.joi.2022.101261

Salar Khan, M., Shoaib, A., & Arledge, E. (2023). How to Promote AI in the US Federal Government: Insights from Policy Process Frameworks. osf.io

Sallam, M., Snygg, J., & Sallam, M. (2024). Assessment of artificial intelligence credibility in evidence-based healthcare management with "Aerus" innovative tool. J Artif Intell Mach Learn Data Sci. academia.edu

Sánchez, J. M., Rodríguez, J. P., & Espitia, H. E. (2022). Bibliometric analysis of publications discussing the use of the artificial intelligence technique agent-based models in sustainable agriculture. Heliyon. cell.com

Savaget, P., Chiarini, T., & Evans, S. (2019). Empowering political participation through artificial intelligence.. [PDF]

Schiff, K. J., Schiff, D. S., Adams, I. T., McCrain, J., & Mourtgos, S. M. (2025). Institutional factors driving citizen perceptions of AI in government: Evidence from a survey experiment on policing. [wiley.com]. *Public Administration Review*, *85*(2), 451–467. DOI: 10.1111/puar.13754

Stix, C. (2022). Foundations for the future: institution building for the purpose of artificial intelligence governance. ncbi.nlm.nih.gov

Tchuente Foguem, G., & Teguede Keleko, A. (2023). Artificial intelligence applied in pulmonary hypertension: a bibliometric analysis. ncbi.nlm.nih.gov

Unogwu, O. J., Doshi, R., Hiran, K. K., Mijwil, M. M., Catherine, A. T., & Abotaleb, M. (2024). Exploring the implications of emerging artificial intelligence technologies at edge computing in higher education. In *Integrating generative AI in education to achieve Sustainable Development Goals* (pp. 169–182). IGI Global Scientific Publishing. DOI: 10.4018/979-8-3693-2440-0.ch009

Walter, Y. (2024). … the race to the moon: Global policy and governance in artificial intelligence regulation—A contemporary overview and an analysis of socioeconomic consequences. Discover Artificial Intelligence. springer.com

Zhang, Y., Pan, C. L., & Liao, H. T. (2021). Carbon neutrality policies and technologies: A scientometric analysis of social science disciplines. Frontiers in Environmental Science. frontiersin.org

Chapter 6
AI-Generated Hate Speech Detection

Neha Yadav
https://orcid.org/0000-0002-7793-2063
G.L. Bajaj Institute of Technology and Management, Greater Noida, India

Mayank Singh
https://orcid.org/0000-0002-8393-3652
SS University, Noida, India

Vipin Tyagi
https://orcid.org/0000-0003-4994-3686
Jaypee University of Engineering and Technology, Guna, India

ABSTRACT

The advent of large language models (LLMs) in generative artificial intelligence (AI) has fundamentally changed the scope of hate speech online. Where hate speech was traditionally unambiguously, human using AI can now produce aggressive, degrading, or even coded language with incredible fluency, speed, and variation. This chapter investigates the emergent technical, social, and ethical issues of hate speech produced by AI. In addition, the chapter includes a broad survey of the history of hate speech in the internet era, highlights the subtle distinctions between offensive language and hate speech, and provides an analysis of the problematic nature of AI-generated threats, including linguistic variability, scale, and semantic ambiguity. The chapter concludes with thoughts on what it will take to protect digital public spaces in the age of generative AI, including continued technical advances, collective social advancements, and ethical collaborative work across disciplines.

DOI: 10.4018/979-8-3373-3063-1.ch006

1. INTRODUCTION

The rapid development in the area of artificial intelligence (AI), including natural language processing techniques, has changed the way of online interaction of individuals. These days with the help of models like OpenAI's GPT, Meta's Llama, and other large language models (LLMs), the world is now able to produce human-like text on a scale never seen before is possible to generate human like text. These models provide a number of positive possibilities, such as automating conventional communications, assisting with accessibility tools, enhancing creativity etc. However, along with these advantages, risks in online interactions, generation and distribution of hate speech is also possible. Earlier hate speech was manually posting of abusive content by an individual or group of users, but these days AI is used to create and generate hate messages quickly and efficiently (Boutadjine, Harrag, & Shaalan, 2025). Thus, identifying hate speech from any source, must be an essential part of protecting individuals and communities online, maintaining trust in digital spaces, and meeting social and legal expectations.

Users cannot always distinguish the intent behind AI programs that produce hate speech or content promoting hate. It may be either intentionally generated or inadvertently generated as a result of training on biased datasets. In addition, many of the existing LLMs can produce hate speech in unique and subtle, contextually related ways such as rephrasing, or employing culturally specific references. In such cased detection is difficult using traditional keyword or rule-based detection systems. Those promoting hate speech can also repeatedly adjust their input or change the model prompting to prompt the output making it difficult to recognize as hate speech (Wu, Wang, Zhang, Wang, & Pang, 2025). The type of hate speech generated by AI programs requires that researchers, reevaluate their approaches and adopt new detection and mitigation strategies. Hate speech is a language that diminishes, threatens, and marginalizes individuals or groups based on characteristics such as race, religion, gender, sexual orientation, nationality, or disability. Use of AI into generation of hate speech makes it even more challenging to differentiate between accidental and purposeful harm, as well as the distinction between direct slurs versus implicit and coded language.

1.1. Context and Importance

Over the last decade, advancements in artificial intelligence, particularly in the area of natural language processing (NLP). Large Language Models (LLMs) like OpenAI's GPT-T series, Google's PaLM, Meta's Llam are able to produce human-like text (Mijwil, Naji, Doshi, Hiran, Bala, & Ali, 2024) (Vetagiri, Mogha, & Pakray, 2024). While these advancements have created multiple opportunities for beneficial products, they also pose significant challenges. One of the most critical challenges is the potential for automating the generation and dissemination of hate speech. Earlier public anxiety around online hate speech concerned human actors: trolls, disinformation propagandists, extremists or radicalized communities, or other groups. At present, malicious actors utilize AI to produce hate speech on a large scale and at a rapid speed, with high complexity to reduce the chances of detection, and create personalized content that maximizes harm (Tiwari et al., 2023). At the same time, generative AI may inadvertently produce harmful content due to incorrect prompting, inadequate or incorrect training data. The detection of hate speech, whether created by a machine or a human, is not just a technical issue but a social need.

1.2. Hate Speech and AI-Generated Hate Speech

Hate speech generally means abusive, threatening, or derogatory communication that targets individuals or communities based on attributes such as race, religion, nationality, gender, sexuality, or disability (Gowrishankar et al., 2024). Figure 1 shows the evolution timeline of hate speech in traditional and modern AI approaches. But when AI is used to generates this, several new complexities arise.

Figure 1. The AI-generated hate speech and advanced AI-enabled detection.

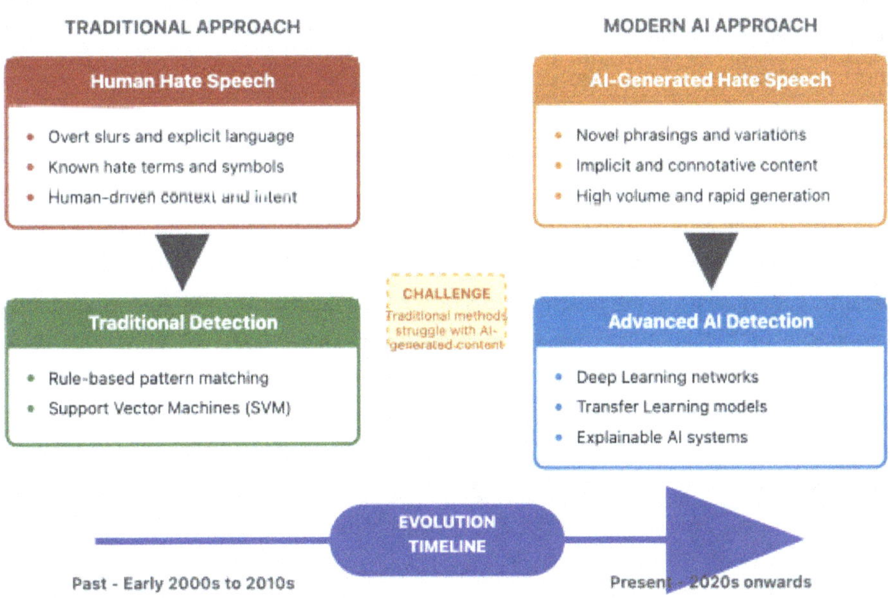

1.3. The Societal Impact of AI-Generated Hate Speech

Online hate is a risk to the safety of individuals and marginalized groups, and may also escalate sectarian divides, reduce trust in public institutions, and disrupt the contours of democratic society. The ability of AI to create text and distribute them quickly may lead to rapid rise of coordinated online harassment campaigns, accelerate the dissemination of extremist ideologies, and enable coordinated misinformation efforts against vulnerable populations (Maddugoda, 2023). If this information goes undetected, it can promote hateful ideologies, misinformation, and other types of prejudice. Although it has traditionally been defined as any kind of communication that degrades individuals or groups, as well as incites harm, or advocates for harm against individuals or groups based on classifiable characteristics such as: race, ethnicity, gender, religion, sexual orientation is hate speech. With the emergence of AI generated texts may emerge that exhibit veiled/coded language, considerable abstract paraphrasing, or language that makes specific references only coherent within contexts and could not pass the filters on traditional platforms.

Combating AI-generated hate speech needs a multidisciplinary approach, moving beyond basic keyword filters to more context-based models and should be able to identify more nuanced or unexpected forms of hate speech. Social scientists and ethicists must assist in labelling datasets, and identify interventions without curtailing free speech and reduce harm to the communities. Policymakers need to frame regulatory frameworks that protect individuals' rights while stopping hate speech content (Kumarage, Bhattacharjee, & Garland, 2024).

1.4. An Overview of Hate speech Detection Approaches

As hate speech generation is driven by human creativity and advances in AI based automatic text generation, it requires advanced research in hate speech detection techniques. Early hate speech detection systems used static lists of hate speech keywords and a predictable set of rules. Paraphrasers made these detections systems useless. Although conventional systems have shown improvement in hate speech detection by using varying features including simple n-grams or sentiment values (Vetagiri & Pakray, n.d.). Presently, deep learning, transformer-based models, and explainable AI tools are used for hate speech detection, as well as providing opportunities to process context and identify new patterns in decision-making processes. Considering the possibility of harmful use, the responsible use of artificial intelligence in research and social systems has become an immediate goal. Balancing the need for AI a priori to detection with the need to incorporate ethical considerations during model developments required. As hate speech continue to evolve, the AI research community must also match any technological advancements with a deep commitment to human rights and the well-being of society. Table 1 shows the key differences between human and AI versions of hate speech.

Table 1. Key Differences—Human vs. AI-Generated Hate Speech

Dimension	Human-Authored	AI-Generated
Style	Consistent with subculture/slang	Variable, creative, often novel
Volume	Limited by human effort	Potentially massive, rapid
Intent	Generally inferable	Often ambiguous or missing
Avoidance Tactics	Manual paraphrasing/coding	Automated, high-variety paraphrasing
Dataset Availability	Available, but context-dependent	Limited, growing with research

2. BACKGROUND AND MOTIVATION

AI-generated content is becoming increasingly common on social media, discussion forums, and messaging applications. Large Language Models (LLMs), including GPT-series and open-source alternatives, can generate subtle and contextualizable statements, including hate speech. Detecting hate speech traditionally focused on human-written content, but AI has created challenges to this approach as these models generate content that is difficult to detect (Wang, 2024). Hate speech itself has complicated dimensions across legal, cultural, and technical contexts. Broadly, hate speech describes any speech demeaning a person or group based upon relative social identifiers such as race, religion, ethnicity, gender, sexual identity, disability, or nationality. There is no standard definition of hate speech, and interpretations of hate speech differ across jurisdictions. The European Commission, for example, describes hate speech as public incitement to violence or hatred against a group. At the same time, the United States prioritizes free speech and restricts government intervention unless the speech involves imminent lawless action. From a computational standpoint, hate speech is commonly operationalized as patterns involving keywords, syntactic patterns, or annotations from crowdsourced or expert-labelled datasets.

Hate speech can be articulated in slurs, threats, or other similarly dehumanizing language or an implicit form. Implicit hate speech can reflect itself through coded or obscenely presented language, innuendo, sarcasm, or mental stereotypes and can align across various groups such as racial minorities, women, LGBTQ+ communities, religious groups, or migrants. Intent of the person generating hate speech is another key part which is most difficult to detect computationally (Weber-Wulff et al., 2023).

2.1. The Evolution of Hate Speech in the Digital Age

Over the last two decades, online communication has changed considerably, particularly on social media, online communities. These platforms are meant for constructive communication but are used for destructive communication using hate speech also. Hate speech was once generated and disseminated by individuals, extreme communities, or structured groups that embraced extremism. Detection techniques involved a combination of manual review, user flagging, and relatively basic automated tools, such as keyword filters or regular expressions.

In last few years, hate speech detection techniques have undergone significant changes. Early hate speech detection techniques focused on approaches in which lexicons of offensive words were developed and used for detection. These approaches, while computationally efficient, had limited accuracy in terms of detection of implicit or sarcastic hate speech detection. Therefore, hate speech detection techniques were developed using machine learning classifiers, such as Support Vector Machines (SVM), Logistic Regression and Random Forests etc. For these approaches, features like n-grams, sentiment polarity, part-of-speech tagging, and syntactic dependencies were extracted and explored as alternative techniques to capture hate speech detection more accurately. Detection has now emerged into the realm of deep learning, particularly neural network architecture such as Convolutional Neural Networks (CNNs), Long Short-Term Memory (LSTM), and train transformer models such as BERT, RoBERTa, and GPT. These models also allow the capture of subtle pragmatic semantics, contextual references within the discourse, and inter-sentential dependencies, all of which facilitate the detection of complex hate speech. Significantly, transformer-based models fine-tuned on domain-specific datasets achieved state-of-the-art performance on multiple benchmarks.

Nevertheless, many of these frameworks are trained and evaluated on human-generated text, leaving a less generalizable gap when applied to AI-generated text. Early studies suggest that AI-generated toxic content often cannot be detected using traditional filters because it appears neutral or polite while subtly embedding anti-social stereotypes. For example, a statement like “Some people are just biologically inferior” may not set off a rule-based system, but it still carries eugenicist implications. As a result, there is emerging interest in designing detection frameworks specifically for generative AI outputs.

2.2. Emerging Research on AI-Generated Hate Speech

Recent years have seen the emergence of research directly targeting the detection of hate speech in machine-generated language. These studies demonstrate that even the most advanced LLMs have the potential to create harmful outputs that are prompted benignly (Fraser, Dawkins, & Kiritchenko, 2025). Specifically, the researchers found that ideologically and racially charged contexts encourage state-of-the-art LLMs to produce toxic and dangerous content. The outputs were grammatically correct, stylistically consistent, and syntactically neutral, making them very difficult to detect.

There are now a number of research papers available that demonstrate that detection models trained on internet corpora exhibit a higher association of a set of negative attributes with particular racial or gendered words. Considering all these facts, detection frameworks should be developed considering additional features that include biases and fairness-aware classifiers.

2.3. Societal Impact and the Stakes of Inaction

Hate speech creates an unfriendly environment in society causing harm by discrimination and divisiveness within communities, inciting real-world violence, or damaging trust in social media platforms. It is the responsibility of social media platforms, policymakers and AI researchers to advance the accuracy of hate speech detection technologies, and to ensure that these technologies are applied in fair, ethical and legal manner. Moreover, the stakes in these complicated interactions involve much more than the safety and dignity of individuals; the global reach of these networks threatens the overall strength of democratic societies and the legitimacy of the social media platforms (Mijwil, Hiran, Doshi, Dadhich, Al-Mistarehi, & Bala, 2023).

3. DEFINING HATE SPEECH IN THE AGE OF AI AND LLMS

The term "hate speech", is a complicated and complex term due to the advancement of artificial intelligence techniques and extensive language models (LLMs). Hate speech is a type of communication that is used to attack or incites enmity against individuals or groups based on their identities, including race, religion, ethnicity, gender, sexual orientation, or disability. As the ability of any AI techniques to generate text that appears to be written in human language increases, hate speech has become broader and more ambiguous.

3.1. Evolving Definitions and Frameworks

Currently, there is no universally accepted definition of hate speech. Various organizations, as well as the big online platforms (like Facebook and X), have formulated their operational definitions, nearly all of which focus on direct attacks towards protected characteristics, but remain broad, vary by jurisdiction, and can have different meanings in different contexts. The main issue for detection, whether human or automated, is separating hate speech from other types of offensive language, sarcasm, satire or reclaimed slurs being used within the targeted communities themselves. As the sophistication of AI-generated text continues improving, embedding hateful text into very weak markers, coded references or creative paraphrases, the clear line between hate language and all other speech continues to become difficult to detect. It is argued that hate speech should not be defined solely by an enumeration of prohibited terms, but rather as a type of communication that conveys malevolent intent, targeting the meaningful characteristics of identifiable groups (Prajapati et al., 2024).

3.2. Layers and Taxonomy of Hate Speech

Recent research proposes a modular taxonomy to capture the dynamic and evolving nature of hate speech, organizing its defining features into foundational and accessory elements (Ahmed, King, Hiran, Dadhich, & Malcalm, 2025).

Foundational elements:

- **Form of Communication:** Language in text or speech, actions, or imagery that conveys harmful intent.
- **Target:** Individuals or groups possessing, or perceived to have, specific protected characteristics.
- **Problematic Content:** Statements expressing inferiority, hatred, threats, dehumanization, or calls for exclusion.
- **Addressed Attributes:** Inherent group characteristics that can motivate the attack (e.g., race, religion, gender).

Accessory elements include:

- Social or individual consequences of hate speech (such as inciting violence or marginalizing communities),
- Recognizing implicit or coded hate speech,
- Enumerating exceptions (like criticism of ideas versus attacks on personal identity),
- Providing situational examples,
- Contextual reference to relevant laws or norms.

This layered approach covers not only overt and explicit hate speech but also implicit or indirect forms that may be disguised through irony, humour, or cultural codes.

3.3. The Distinction Between Offensive and Hateful Content

Researchers highlight the essential differences between offensive language (which may express strong negative views without targeting already marginalized and protected groups) and hate speech (which exclusively targets, marginalizes, and/or promotes harm against communities) (Valiaiev, 2024). However, this distinction is becoming increasingly challenging (even for humans, and especially for automated systems), as the many ways expressions can be perceived as hateful or harmless can vary depending on context, historical usage, reclaiming, or intent, as shown in Table 2.

Table 2. The Conceptual Elements in Hate Speech Definitions

Element	**Description**
Form of Communication	Written, spoken, visual, or symbolic content expressing negative sentiment
Target	Individuals or groups with protected characteristics
Problematic Content	Statements signifying hatred, dehumanization, inferiority, threat, or exclusion
Addressed Attributes	The specific characteristics under attack (race, religion, sexuality, etc.)
Implicit/Indirect hate speech	Hate expressed through coded language, sarcasm, or creative means
Legal/Normative Reference	Inclusion of applicable laws or policies addressing hate speech

Even as LLMs mature, both the technical and conceptual understanding of hate speech will need to continue growing to ensure that moderation remains strong despite enhancing freedom of expression for the benefit of traditionally marginalized communities.

4. CHALLENGES UNIQUE TO DETECTING AI-GENERATED HATE SPEECH

AI-generated content has brought about a paradigm shift in the field of hate speech detection. While automated moderation once focused on recognizing human-authored expressions of prejudice or hostility, generative models, such as large language models (LLMs), introduce a set of new, distinct challenges that demand a reassessment of existing detection frameworks and tools. Major challenges are:

a. Linguistic variability and Creativity
b. Paraphrasing and Evasion
c. Volume and Real Time Generation
d. Ambiguity of Intent and Context
e. Cross-Domain and Cross-Lingual Challenges
f. Data Scarcity and Annotation Difficulties

Table 3. The comparison of Key Detection Challenges

Detection Challenge	Human-Authored Hate Speech	AI-Generated Hate Speech
Linguistic Variety	Often relies on known patterns/slurs	Infinite paraphrasing, novel constructs
Volume	Limited by user effort	High-speed, high-volume production
Detectability	Possible to blacklist specific terms	Keyword avoidance, coded messaging
Context/Intent	Inferred from user history/behaviour	Ambiguous, prompt- or data-driven
Cross-Lingual/Domain	Needs language-specific handling	Generates global and hybrid expressions
Annotation	Context-dependent, but familiar forms	Subtler, frequent ambiguity, evolving

To address these challenges, there is a need to move beyond static filters and develop robust machine learning pipelines. While state-of-the-art hate speech detection techniques should incorporate progress in natural language understanding, adversarial robustness, explainability, and continual curation of data, hate speech detection systems need to engage in continuous adaptive learning (Shen et al., 2025). Hate speech detection systems also need to account for new forms, accommodate shifts in language over time, and reconcile the competing aims of recognizing emerging harms and protecting free speech. Adapting to AI-generated hate speech is not simply a technical necessity. It is a crucial step toward maintaining the integrity of online social spaces and supporting diversity. The key challenges associated with human-authored and AI-generated content are presented in Table 3.

5. DETECTION TECHNIQUES: AN EVOLUTIONARY OVERVIEW

Early attempts at hate speech detection relied on keyword-based forms of identification. Using static lists of offensive slurs and toxic expressions, users can use different combinations of keywords to identify and flag harmful content. Keyword-based approaches are computationally faster; however, they are limited in utilizing modern AI-generated text to circumvent static lists, such as rephrased hateful content using coded language. Moreover, they were less helpful in detecting implicit hate or syntactically complex text. The next shift followed traditional machine learning methodologies, which also required trained human inputs onto annotated corpora. Examples of conventional machine learning models included Support Vector Machines (SVMs), Random Forest, and Naive Bayes classifiers, which provided more flexibility than keyword lists. Desirable properties of traditional machine learning approaches included interpretability, quicker inference times, and fewer computational resources. However, conventional machine learning architectures remained largely dependent on handcrafted features such as TF-IDF or bag-of-words, failing to address contextual representations and nuanced uses of expressions of hate in natural language (Ghiurău & Popescu, 2025).

With the rise of deep learning approaches, transformer architectures, and large language models (LLMs), hate speech detection has entered a new stage of evolution. Traditional neural architectures include Convolutional Neural Networks (CNNs), Recurrent Neural Networks (RNNs), and Long Short-Term Memory models (LSTMs); however, only transformer architectures have provided realistic improvements in reducing errors associated with hate speech. The performance rates for the hate speech detection task have changed tremendously via transformer-based confidence frameworks, such as BERT, RoBERTa, DistilBERT and GPT. These models are able to be pre-trained on massive datasets, and thus later be fine-tuned for specific tasks, such as hate speech detection, using the knowledge that they learned from pre-training in this fine-tuning stage. Using transfer learning strategies, and domain adaptation, these models can quickly refine their understanding and even transfer their understanding to entirely new tasks, such as identifying AI-generated toxic content.

Lastly, hybrid and ensemble methods have gained popularity because they can combine the merits of multiple methodologies. These models typically involve traditional machine learning classifiers, deep learning networks, or rules defined heuristically. Ensemble methods can also significantly improve robustness, especially when considering adversarial examples, such as AI-generated hate speech that a single model may not be able to detect.

6. TRAINING DATASETS: ACQUISITION, ANNOTATION, AND CHALLENGES

The success of any hate speech detection framework, especially for AI-generated content, largely depends on the quality, diversity, and representativeness of the datasets that will ultimately be used to train and test/validate. At the same time, several usable datasets are available for detecting hate speech in human-authored content; only a handful aim to model the unique nuances of AI-generated toxicity. Creating appropriate datasets requires a transparent methodology that can incorporate both naturally occurring and EFI-generated text. Dataset acquisition often involves collecting samples from various sources, including X,Reddit and YouTube etc, and online forums, as well as examining the comments sections of news articles. These sources enable researchers to select from a diverse range of expressions of hate speech, targeting various groups and languages. Some of these datasets have been assembled using a process that solicits or simulates hateful speech (e.g., to ensure that certain edge cases or less common forms of discrimination are represented) (Potla, 2025). More recently, human-in-the-loop adversarial sampling has emerged to detect more nuanced, layered and borderline examples of hate speech. Notably, these approaches contribute to the dynamic process of generating challenging cases, helping the model prepare for future complexities in detecting hate speech in an evolving context of hate speech, such as AI-generated systems.

Commonly Used Datasets

Several benchmarks datasets that provide broad coverage and facilitate model comparison are:

- HateXplain (Mathew et al., 2021)
- MetaHate (IRLab, n.d.)
- Latent Hatred (ElSherief et al., 2021)
- Multimodal Hate Speech MMHS150K (Gómez, Gibert, Gómez-Adorno, & Pardo, 2020)
- ETHOS (Mollas, Chrysopoulou, Karlos, & Tsoumakas, 2020)
- Various Benchmark Twitter Datasets

6.1. The Process and Pitfalls of Annotation

Annotation plays a crucial role in social media hate speech detection, which involves classifying a text into one or more categories, including hateful, offensive, and non-offensive. In more advanced systems, annotation may include tagging the target group, indicating the severity of the offence, and even providing a rationale for the classification. Annotation, although fundamental, is a complex and laborious process. When done correctly, it is performed by trained professionals or crowd workers who apply user manuals/models of practices developed from the site's policies, legislative barriers, or academic definitions. Despite efforts to standardize processes, annotation is a highly subjective process. Accordingly, the annotators' specific socio-demographic backgrounds, implicit biases, and cultural knowledge shape the way they assign labels to a text, even in borderline cases where sarcasm, hidden meanings, or rapidly developing slang may be present. Empirical work has shown that annotators are diverse and tend to be most sensitive to hate speech aimed at their social groups (Akram, 2023).

While these types of models can efficiently scale annotation, they can also create distinct biases that differ from human judgment, potentially injecting artificial structures into datasets that affect downstream model training. These concerns become compounded when addressing AI-generated hate speech. First, there are a few representative datasets. Most publicly available hate speech corpora are derived from human-generated content, thus limiting the size of datasets that reflect the tone, prose, and subtle ambiguity of LLM outputs that we must create. Second, annotators may not have a clear understanding when making assessments of AI-generated text, notably when the authorship lacks the intention to harm or target specific individuals. The lack of interpretability hinders the evaluation of whether something is hateful or simply inappropriate, thereby reducing agreement between annotators.

Bias and generalization gaps are another essential concern. Many existing datasets are biased towards specific regions, cultures, or topics. While these models may perform well within their respective domains, they fail when deployed in real-world settings where users, their language, and demographics vary significantly. In addition, hate speech is a moving target because new slurs, euphemisms, and other cultural references arise all the time, making static datasets quickly lose relevance. This highlights the need to refresh and recalibrate data in context continually. In response to these constraints, researchers are also trying to create datasets that are more inclusive and adaptive. Incrementally refreshing corpora to include any new forms of hate, including diversity in samples regarding demographics and languages, and annotating with the target group as well as detailed reasoning for greater model interpretability, are all methods to enhance representation. AI-generated examples during training help support model generalization between human and machine-generated texts (Hiran, Jain, Lakhwani, & Doshi, 2021).

Additionally, there is a growing emphasis on understanding annotator and model biases to promote objectivity and fairness (Blake, Miah, Kredens, & Shin, 2025). In short, the rapidly changing landscape of hate speech and the datasets that capture it means that annotation is not purely a technical challenge but an ethical challenge. As models become increasingly powerful and are applied in sensitive social contexts, the demand for fair, high-quality, and adaptable annotation will continue to rise, solidifying this area as one of the most rapidly evolving interdisciplinary spaces in AI safety and ethics research. The dataset used for hate speech detection research is presented in Table 4.

Table 4. Overview of Notable Hate Speech Detection Datasets

Dataset Name	Source(s)	Language	Sample Size	Key Features
HateXplain	Twitter, Gab	English	~40,000	Rationales, targets, and explainable annotations
MetaHate	Multiple	English	60+ sets	Unified meta-collection, model benchmarks
Implicit Hate Corpus	Twitter	English	22,056	Fine-grained implicit hate labels
MMHS150K	Twitter	Multilingual	150,000	Multimodal (text + image), large-scale
ETHOS	YouTube, Reddit	English	998/433	Binary/multilabel annotations
Hate Speech & Offensive Language	Twitter	English	24,000+	Early, widely used "hate," "offensive," "neither" labels
Dynamically-Generated Hate Speech	Synthetic (Dynabench)	English	41,255	Human/model-in-the-loop adversarial data

7. BIAS MITIGATION IN DETECTION SYSTEMS

Bias plays a crucial role in the detection of hate speech systems, particularly in distinguishing between human-generated and AI-generated content. Although these models are designed to protect users from hate speech and provide a more equitable and diverse digital environment, they can also unintentionally or even intentionally perpetuate or exacerbate social bias if they are not explicitly defined and measured. Bias could occur at various stages of detecting hate and generating AI, from the training data used and how the data is annotated, to the model's architecture and everything that happens after the model is deployed. This section examines the biases, their appearance, and how to identify, assess, and measure them to mitigate their potentially harmful effects.

7.1. Sources of Bias in AI-Generated Content

Machine-learning models are often biased due to the data that the model is trained on. For example, large language models (LLMs) like GPT are constructed using very large corpora of text scraped from the Internet, domains of literature that include societal stereotypes, discriminatory perspectives, and toxic discourse. Once the output of the LLMs is passed along to detection models, biases are learned and ongoing and normalized. The first form of bias is representation bias. Representation bias arises from the uneven distribution of representation of different identity groups in the dataset, where some groups are over-represented, and others are under-represented or marginalized (Cingillioglu, 2023). Because of this, the model will have biased decision boundaries and may flag or never detect content, based on the identity referenced. The second form of bias is annotation bias. Human annotators have different views on what counts as hate speech, especially in relation to their cultural backgrounds, language proficiency, or implicit bias. For example, one annotator may view "They should go back to where they came from" as offensive; however, other annotator(s) may view it as neutral, based on contextual awareness. Finally, there is model bias, where the algorithm's design may introduce bias. This could happen as some architectures may prefer certain features that correlate with demographic categories, regardless of whether they were related to some type of toxicity. Lastly, generation bias may exist in the source content itself. Non-obvious AI-generated hate speech means that hate speech may not be consistently recognized as such. It could take the form of subconscious bias or exclusionary language (Cao, 2025).

7.2. Detecting Bias in Hate Speech Classifiers

To detect bias, it is necessary to perform a systematic evaluation in identity-specific subgroups and the different types of toxic content. One approach is to create identity sub-lists based on identity categories and analyze the associations with hate labels. For example, identifying sub-lists could include names of ethnic groups or genders, or religious affiliations. If it is found that hate labels disproportionately flag the text containing specific identities compared to other groups, it may signal unfairness. We exploit several fairness metrics to quantify bias. Demographic Parity (DP) compares the rates of optimistic predictions between groups, and Equalized Odds (EO) checks if the rates of False Positives and False Negatives are similar across groups. Finally, the False Discovery Rate Gap (FDR Gap) is used to detect tendencies towards over-punishment or under-punishment within specific identity labels. An example of this would be a model which flags commonly flagged identities, such as 'immigrants', in which the model is trained to flag relatively equal percentages of hate content. Still, it is consistently flagging and punishing texts that contain minority identities at a significantly higher rate than the majority identities.

Figure 2. A typical feedback loop for responsible bias management involves.

7.3. Strategies for Mitigation of Bias

Addressing bias is both a technical and process-driven endeavor. Table 5 gives glimpses of the impact of bias. Some effective strategies to overcome bias include:

- Balanced Dataset Curation
- Bias Analysis and Fairness Metrics
- Fairness-Aware Algorithms
- Adversarial and Stress Testing
- Explainability and Human Oversight

Figure 3. The Stages Where Bias Can Enter Hate Speech Detection.

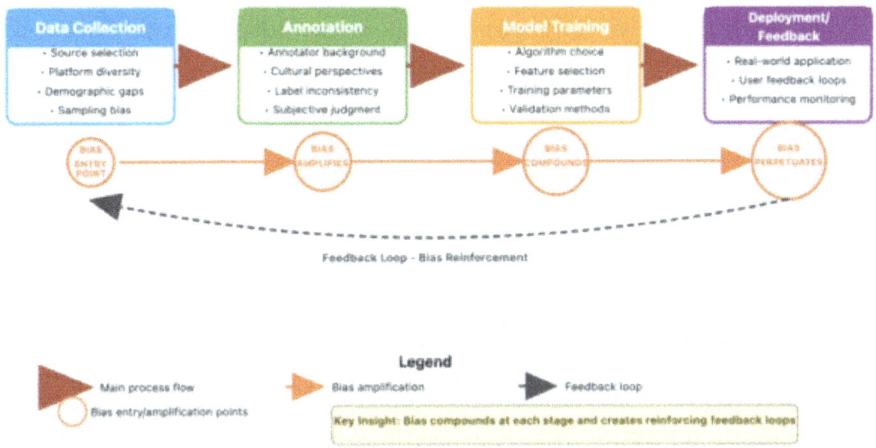

Table 5. The Stages and Impact of Bias.

Stage	Example of Bias	Potential Impact
Data Collection	Overrepresentation of certain slurs	Ignores less common hate, unbalanced
Annotation	Annotators' sensitivity differences	Mislabeling, inconsistent ground truth
Model Training	Favouring the most frequent patterns	Ignores minority dialects or expressions
Deployment	Drift to new or unseen cases	False negatives or positives

8. EVALUATION METRICS AND BENCHMARKS

The performance of hate speech detection systems, especially within the context of AI-generated content is determined not only by modern modelling techniques, but also by robust evaluation processes. In expanding the evaluation of hate speech models, accuracy ensures that models perform consistently, mitigate harm, and are fair when deployed in the real world and on a scale. In this section, the primary metrics and benchmarking approaches to evaluate detection models, including the novel challenges posed by emerging language and adversarial behavior are described.

8.1. Standard Evaluation Metrics

Evaluation metrics for hate speech detection are adapted from those used in broader classification and natural language processing tasks, with an increased emphasis on the societal and ethical implications of misclassification.

- Accuracy
- Precision
- Recall (Sensitivity)
- F1-Score
- ROC-AUC (Receiver Operating Characteristic — Area Under the Curve)
- Confusion Matrix

For imbalanced tasks—where hate speech is relatively rare—precision, recall, and F1-score are essential as they provide deeper insight into how models handle minority classes.

8.2. Fairness and Robustness Metrics

Given the potential for bias and harm, evaluation increasingly includes:

- Demographic Parity
- Equal Opportunity
- Adversarial Robustness

8.3. Explainability

Modern detection systems are routincly assessed in terms of explainability, i.e. how well they can explain their predictions.

8.4. Practical Considerations and Limitations

- Dataset Representativeness
- Annotation Subjectivity
- Continuous Benchmarking

In conclusion, a broad evaluation technique required to develop a trustworthy hate speech detection technique. A balanced, transparent, and dynamic assessment model is required to ensure that automated moderation of content serves both technical and ethical purposes.

9. ETHICAL AND LEGAL CONSIDERATIONS

As AI systems are used in creation and moderation of online content, there is a need of awareness of the ethical and legal structures that emphasize these practices, especially regarding detection of hate speech, which as a topic is particularly sensitive and damaging. While more powerful tools are being developed to create and manage content on the internet, there is a need of using it responsibly. The key difference now is that we can't just focus on managing what people say and how people speak on their behalf, including how machines speak for people. That means we will need to keep asking the difficult questions, have a multiplicity of voices, and create systems that reflect our values within our public square.

10. REAL WORLD APPLICATIONS

The real-world deployment of AI-powered hate speech detection systems provides valuable insights into both their promise and challenges. Table 6 provides an overview of some commonly used social media platform and tools

Table 6. Comparative Overview of Platforms and Tools

Platform / Tool	Approach	Key Adaptations	Lessons / Challenges
Meta (Facebook)	Multilingual deep learning	Cultural adaptation, user appeals	Nuanced context, rapid evolution
X (Twitter)	Transformers, ensembles	Adversarial prompt defense, retraining	Slang, evasion, transparency
Reddit	Bots + user mod	Community tuning, appeals process	Over-flagging, dialectic bias
Detoxify, Perspective API	Open source/Cloud	Customization for local norms	Transferability, context nuances

11. FUTURE DIRECTIONS

As generative AI continues to evolve, it's reshaping how we communicate, enabling creativity, improving accessibility, and automating tasks. Relying solely on the text may no longer be enoughfuture approaches will need to merge language analysis with metadata, such as unusual posting patterns, suspicious timing, or behavioural clues from a user's online activity, to improve accuracy. Another big challenge is adaptability. Language is constantly evolving, and so is online hate. New slurs, sarcastic phrases, and coded messages can emerge and spread rapidly and hence hate speech detection systems should be updated continuously. Traditionally, training models to recognize these shifts required large amounts of annotated data, a time-consuming and resource-intensive process. New techniques, such as few-shot and zero-shot learning aim to help detection models "understand" new forms of hate with few examples, or even by analogy, using learning from previous tasks. This type of flexible, generalized learning will be crucial in the future.

There is also an important consideration regarding language diversity. For hate speech detection systems to be truly effective and equitable, there is a need of multilingual systems. Future hate detection systems will need to view hate speech as a multimodal problem, combining computer vision, audio processing, and natural language understanding to encompass the full spectrum of hate content circulating online.

However, technology is not enough, a hate speech detection system must also be built off of trust, fairness, and accountability. Systems must be transparent by design - able to define how and why certain decisions are taken. Ease of monitoring and addressing bias is required throughout the model's life-cycle.

This will be possible with a strong collaboration amongst researchers, social media platforms, regulators, civil society organisations and ordinary users.

12. CONCLUSION

Artificial intelligence and powerful language models of today are reshaping the way in which people collaborate, share, and interact online. Differentiating between content created by a human and created by machine is becoming increasingly more difficult to differentiate. The advances in technology support creativity, learning, and community but also pose serious, risks of hate speech, which can rapidly target individuals or groups, damage the trust in online platforms and challenge the very foundation of our public conversations. Simply detecting hate speech generated by AI is not just about filtering out offensive words. In contrast to many traditional forms of online abuse, where the human intent or cultural significance may be easier to identify, AI-generated hate speech can be exceptionally difficult to identify.

In conclusion, keeping digital spaces safe in the era of generative AI is the responsibility of everyone. Researchers, social media platforms, regulators, civil society leaders and the public must all work together, bringing their individual experiences and expertise together and staying responsive. Through a common sense of a shared commitment to transparency, accountability, and authentic community engagement around online safety, the future of AI can be good, while placing boundaries on the most harmful parts of the technology. Through collective action and ongoing learning, an online space that has the potential to enhance the voices and safety of everyone and where hate speech - written by anyone - is placed on the margins, not at the forefront, is possible.

REFERENCES

https://irlab.org/metahate.html

Ahmed, A. B., King, B. D., Hiran, K. K., Dadhich, M., & Malcalm, E. (2025). *Half a decade of artificial intelligence in education in africa: Trends, opportunities, challenges and future directions*. Journal of Engineering Education Transformations, 81-100.

Akram, A. (2023). An Empirical Study of AI-Generated Text Detection Tools. *Adv Mach Lear Art Inte*, *4*(2), 44–55.

Blake, J., Miah, A. S. M., Kredens, K., & Shin, J. (2025). Detection of AI-Generated Texts: A Bi-LSTM and Attention-Based Approach. *IEEE Access : Practical Innovations, Open Solutions*, *13*, 71563–71576. DOI: 10.1109/ACCESS.2025.3562750

Boutadjine, A., Harrag, F., & Shaalan, K. (2025). Human vs. machine: A comparative study on the detection of AI-generated content. *ACM Transactions on Asian and Low-Resource Language Information Processing*, *24*(2), 1–26. DOI: 10.1145/3708889

Cao, L. (2025). A Practical Synthesis of Detecting AI-Generated Textual, Visual, and Audio Content. *arXiv preprint arXiv:2504.02898.*

Cingillioglu, I. (2023). Detecting AI-generated essays: The ChatGPT challenge. *The International Journal of Information and Learning Technology*, *40*(3), 259–268. DOI: 10.1108/IJILT-03-2023-0043

ElSherief, M., Ziems, Z., Muchlinski, D., Anupindi, V., Wang, D., Halevy, J., & Yang, D. "Latent hatred: A benchmark for understanding implicit hate speech," in *Proc. 2021 Conf. Empirical Methods in Natural Language Processing (EMNLP)*, 2021, pp. 345–363. [Online]. Available: https://aclanthology.org/2021.emnlp-main.27

Fraser, K. C., Dawkins, H., & Kiritchenko, S. (2025). Detecting ai-generated text: Factors influencing detectability with current methods. *Journal of Artificial Intelligence Research*, *82*, 2233–2278. DOI: 10.1613/jair.1.16665

Ghiurău, D., & Popescu, D. E. (2025). Distinguishing Reality from AI: Approaches for Detecting Synthetic Content. *Computers*, *14*(1), 1. DOI: 10.3390/computers14010001

Gómez, R., Gibert, A., Gómez-Adorno, A., & Pardo, L. "Exploring hate speech detection in multimodal publications," in *Proc. IEEE Winter Conf. Applications of Computer Vision Workshops (WACVW)*, 2020, pp. 45–52. [Online]. Available: https://arxiv.org/abs/2005.04790 DOI: 10.1109/WACV45572.2020.9093414

Gowrishankar, J., Deepak, S., & Srivastava, M. (2024, September). Countering the Rise of AI-Generated Content with Innovative Detection Strategies and Large Language Models. In *2024 International Conference on Advances in Computing Research on Science Engineering and Technology (ACROSET)* (pp. 1-6). IEEE.

Hiran, K. K., Jain, R. K., Lakhwani, K., & Doshi, R. (2021). *Machine Learning: Master Supervised and Unsupervised Learning Algorithms with Real Examples (English Edition)*. BPB Publications.

Kumarage, T., Bhattacharjee, A., & Garland, J. (2024). Harnessing artificial intelligence to combat online hate: Exploring the challenges and opportunities of large language models in hate speech detection. *arXiv preprint arXiv:2403.08035*.

. Maddugoda, C. (2023). A comprehensive review: Detection techniques for human-generated and AI-generated texts.

Mathew, B., Saha, P., Yimam, S. M., Biemann, C., Goyal, P., & Mukherjee, A. "HateXplain: A benchmark dataset for explainable hate speech detection," in *Proc. AAAI Conf. Web and Social Media (ICWSM) Workshops*, 2021. [Online]. Available: https://arxiv.org/abs/2012.10289 DOI: 10.1609/aaai.v35i17.17745

Mijwil, M. M., Hiran, K. K., Doshi, R., Dadhich, M., Al-Mistarehi, A. H., & Bala, I. (2023). ChatGPT and the future of academic integrity in the artificial intelligence era: A new frontier. *Al-Salam Journal for Engineering and Technology*, *2*(2), 116–127. DOI: 10.55145/ajest.2023.02.02.015

Mijwil, M. M., Naji, A. S., Doshi, R., Hiran, K. K., Bala, I., & Ali, G. (2024). *The effect of human-computer interaction on new applications by exploring the use case of ChatGPT in healthcare services*. In modern technology in healthcare and medical education: Blockchain, IoT, AR, and VR. IGI Global. DOI: 10.4018/979-8-3693-5493-3.ch005

Mollas, I., Chrysopoulou, Z., Karlos, S., & Tsoumakas, G. "ETHOS: An online hate speech detection dataset," *arXiv preprint arXiv:2006.08328*, 2020. [Online]. Available: https://arxiv.org/abs/2006.08328

Potla, R. T. (2025). AI-Powered Threat Detection in Online Communities: A Multi-Modal Deep Learning Approach. *Journal of Computer and Communications*, *13*(2), 155–171. DOI: 10.4236/jcc.2025.132010

Prajapati, M., Baliarsingh, S. K., Dora, C., Bhoi, A., Hota, J., & Mohanty, J. P. "Detection of AI-Generated Text Using Large Language Model," *2024 International Conference on Emerging Systems and Intelligent Computing (ESIC)*, Bhubaneswar, India, 2024, pp. 735-740, DOI: 10.1109/ESIC60604.2024.10481602

Shen, X., Wu, Y., Qu, Y., Backes, M., Zannettou, S., & Zhang, Y. (2025). Hate-Bench: Benchmarking Hate Speech Detectors on LLM-Generated Content and Hate Campaigns. /arXiv.2501.16750DOI: 10.48550

Tiwari, S., Sharma, R., Sikarwar, R. S., Dubey, G. P., Bajpai, N., & Singhatiya, S. (2023, January). Detecting AI generated content: A study of methods and applications. In *International Conference on Communication and Computational Technologies* (pp. 161-176). Singapore: Springer Nature Singapore. DOI: 10.1007/978-981-97-7423-4_13

Valiaiev, D. (2024). Detection of machine-generated text: Literature survey. *arXiv preprint arXiv:2402.01642*.

Vetagiri, A., Mogha, P., & Pakray, P. (2024). Multilate Classifier: A Novel Emsemble of Cnn-Bilstm with Resnet-Based Multimodal Classifier for Ai-Generated Hate Speech Detection. DOI: 10.2139/ssrn.4951337

Vetagiri, A., & Pakray, P. Mitigating Adversarial Attacks in Ai-Generated Multimodal Hate. DOI: 10.2139/ssrn.5193751

Wang, Y. (2024). Survey for detecting AI-generated content. *Advances in Engineering Technology Research*, *11*(1), 643–643. DOI: 10.56028/aetr.11.1.643.2024

Weber-Wulff, D., Anohina-Naumeca, A., Bjelobaba, S., Foltýnek, T., Guerrero-Dib, J., Popoola, O., Šigut, P., & Waddington, L. (2023). Testing of detection tools for AI-generated text. *International Journal for Educational Integrity*, *19*(1), 1–39. DOI: 10.1007/s40979-023-00146-z

Wu, C., Wang, Y., Zhang, Y., Wang, H., & Pang, Y. (2025). Confront hate with AI: How AI-generated counter speech helps against hate speech on social Media? *Telematics and Informatics*, *101*, 102304. DOI: 10.1016/j.tele.2025.102304

Chapter 7 Highlighting the Challenges of Bias and Fairness in Hate Speech Detection

Manish Mittal
https://orcid.org/0000-0002-7029-9576
Brainware University, India

Manish Tiwari
Sir Padampat Singhania University, India

Ruchi Doshi
ResAIShala Technocrats Pvt. Ltd., Udaipur, India

Kamal Kant Hiran
Sir Padampat Singhania University, India

ABSTRACT

This chapter offers a comprehensive overview of the challenges, advancements, and ethical concerns in automated hate speech detection. It critiques early keyword-based methods and highlights the shift toward advanced, context-aware, and culturally informed AI models. Key issues include bias in training data, subjectivity in annotation, and evolving adversarial tactics. The chapter emphasizes the essential role of human oversight and advocates hybrid human-AI moderation for balanced judgment. It stresses the importance of transparency, accountability, and fairness within complex legal and regulatory frameworks. Addressing technological limits such as multimodal data and annotation quality, it calls for interdisciplinary col-

DOI: 10.4018/979-8-3373-3063-1.ch007

laboration and ongoing innovation. Ultimately, it argues that effective moderation must protect free expression and vulnerable groups, uniting technical strength with ethical responsibility.

INTRODUCTION

The problem of bias and fairness in the identification of hate speech is introduced in this chapter. At this point in time, the increasing dependence on automated programming to police content online makes it even more imperative to comprehend the processes by which computer systems are "trained" to identify and flag hate speech. The goal of this chapter is precisely to provide a clear scope of what hate speech is, and an analysis of why there has been so much bias and unfairness in the challenges of detecting it. Through the exploration of real-world twelve challenges in the development and deployment of hate speech detection technologies as well as real world examples of limitations, the use of secondary data, this chapter analyze uses both secondary data and a real-world example of the limitations and recommendation that twenty key challenges of developing and deploying hate speech detection technology.

The identification of hate speech on online platforms like Facebook, YouTube or Instagram poses a number of difficult challenges, issues and complexities with bias and fairness being the most salient among those. Among these challenges, one of the most central is the lack of a consensus definition of what constitutes "hate speech". Determine what constitutes hate speech is culturally and legal specific, thus automated detection is problematic in multiple ways. In this chapter I will use a series of definitions and interpretations taken for granted within the scope of this study to attempt to understand some of the challenges surrounding the identification and regulation of hate content in digital environments (*The Digital Services Act Package | Shaping Europe's Digital Future*, n.d.).

Hate speech encompasses any form of communication—be it spoken, written, or behavioural—that denigrates or discriminates against individuals or groups based on inherent characteristics such as race, ethnicity, religion, gender, sexual orientation, disability, or other identity factors. This includes the use of pejorative or discriminatory language aimed at a person or group based on who they are UNESCO (Countering hate speech, 2024). Key Characteristics of Hate Speech include forms of expression; hate speech can manifest through various mediums, including images, cartoons, memes, objects, gestures, and symbols, and can be disseminated both offline and online. Targets; it specifically targets individuals or groups based on attributes such as religion, ethnicity, nationality, race, colour, descent, gender, or other identity factors.

Over the past two decades, the relationship between hate speech and violence has been a critical concern globally. While comprehensive, standardized data spanning all countries is limited, various reports and studies highlight significant trends in specific regions. In 2022, India reported 1,444 cases under IPC Section 153A, marking a 45% rise from 993 cases in 2021. Uttar Pradesh, Rajasthan, and Maharashtra recorded the highest numbers.

United States: *Domestic Terrorism and Hate Speech:* Research indicates that countries where politicians frequently use hate speech experience more domestic terrorism. The U.S. saw domestic terror incidents rise from an average of 26.6 per year during the Obama administration to 67 in 2016, with similar numbers in subsequent years (Piazza, 2020).

Figure 1. Where and How Often People Encounter Hate Speech Online (Anna Fleck, 2024)

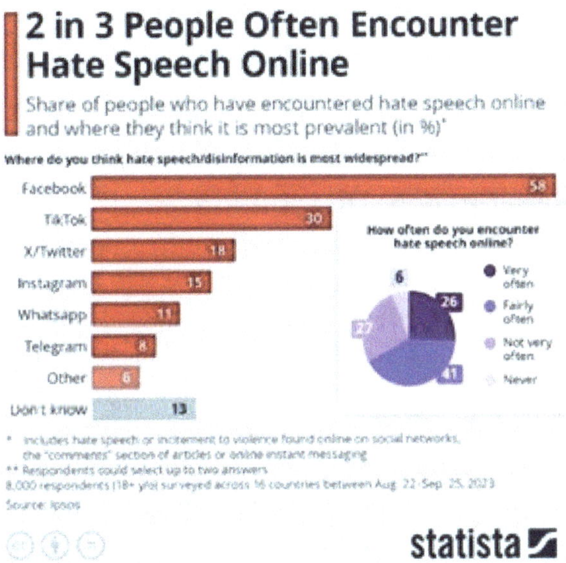

An Ipsos survey (Aug–Sept 2023) across 16 countries with 8,000 adults found that 58% identify Facebook as the leading platform for online hate speech and disinformation, followed by TikTok (30%), X/Twitter (18%), Instagram (15%), and others. About 32% of users encounter hate speech frequently, while 41% report occasional exposure, and 27% have never experienced it. The findings emphasize the need for stronger moderation policies, user awareness, and better content management (Anna Fleck, 2024).

Correlation Between Hate Speech and Violence:

Studies suggest a strong correlation between the prevalence of hate speech, especially by political figures, and an increase in domestic terrorism and hate crimes (Díaz, 2011). Countries where politicians frequently employ hate speech experience significantly higher incidents of domestic terrorism compared to those where such rhetoric is rare.

Figure 2. Reported Grounds for Hate Speech Across Categories (Sipahioğlu, 2023)

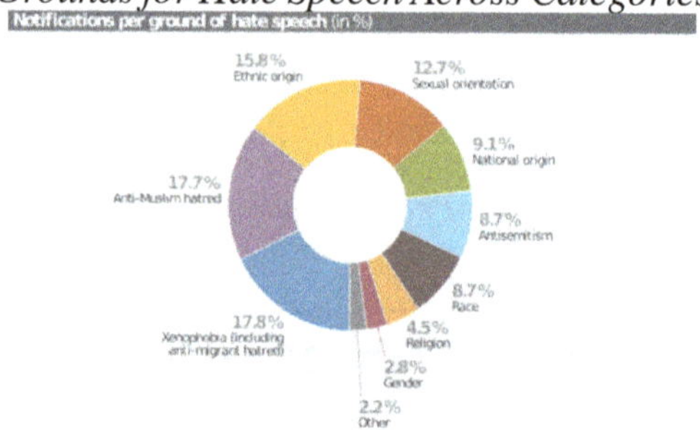

Grounds of Hate Speech: Distribution by Notification Percentage

A study analyzing hate speech notifications by targeted grounds found that xenophobia (17.8%), anti-Muslim hatred (17.7%), and ethnic origin (15.8%) account for the highest shares. Sexual orientation (12.7%), national origin (9.1%), antisemitism and race (each 8.7%) follow. Lower frequencies were reported for religion (4.5%), gender (2.8%), and other categories (2.2%). The data underscores the predominance of ethnic, religious, and migration-related hate speech, with significant attention also needed for LGBTQ+ (LGBTQ people are individuals who are lesbian, gay, bisexual, transgender, queer, or questioning) and racial hate content.

Supporting data on hate speech categories also appear in European Union monitoring reports evaluating the EU Code of Conduct on countering illegal hate speech online, which include similar breakdowns (anti-Muslim hatred, xenophobia, ethnic origin, etc.) (Sipahioğlu, 2023).

THE MULTIFACETED CHALLENGES OF FAIR AND UNBIASED HATE SPEECH DETECTION

Turning to the core focus of this chapter—the challenges of bias and fairness in hate speech detection—it becomes clear from various studies and online sources that numerous factors contribute to these issues. Among the most prominent are the limitations of keyword-based detection methods, which often fail to grasp context and nuance. Ethical concerns also arise during model training, particularly regarding the data used and how it represents different communities. Hate speech is also difficult to define and to uncover as it is inherently subjective, culturally specific and context-sensitive.

1. Keyword-based Approaches

Keyword-based techniques identify candidate pieces of hateful content by applying pre-assembled list or dictionaries of known hate terms and expressions. Although time-consuming and more complex, there are fairly straightforward solutions to this problem. This can produce both false negatives and false positives, as they fail to identify hate speech that does not contain explicit keywords or that makes use of figurative, coded, or subtle language – a precision recall trade-off. Facebook's initial keyword-based moderation resulted in hate speech often not being flagged at all, but was also overly-flagged in other instances as well. The criticism provided a push towards the development of AI and context-aware NLP approaches (Gandhi et al., 2024; Mijwil et al., 2023).

2. Ethical Concerns in Model

The ethical problems with AI training generally arise from the biases lying latent in the training data sets. These biases can completely screw up the representation of certain groups, or cause those same groups to be overlooked altogether, resulting in unfair acting models that may incorrectly label things based on certain users. It can have a chilling effect on people's speech, where they start wanting to hide if it will prevent them from unjustly targeted.

Amazon found that its AI recruiting tool was heavily biased against females. The problem was that it had been trained on resumes mostly written by men, and began filtering out applications containing, for example, the terms "women's chess club captain" or even negatively biasing against a degree from a women's college – all of which led Amazon to abandon the technology altogether. In a similar vein, the COMPAS Recidivism Risk Assessment tool was exposed after a ProPublica investigation in 2016 revealed its bias against black people. It categorized Black individuals as "high-risk" for recidivism at nearly 2 times the rate of white individuals because of the inaccuracies embedded in the criminal justice data. They totally fucked up regarding darker skinned women 4.7% of the time, and lighter-skinned dudes only got it wrong 0.8% of the time, and it's all because there was zero diversity in the datasets that they used to train these algorithms (Nascimento et al., 2025).

Table 1. Case Studies of AI and Algorithmic Bias in Practice

Case	Domain	Bias Type	Cause	Impact	Source
Amazon Hiring Algorithm	Recruitment	Gender bias (against women)	Trained on predominantly male resumes	Penalized "women's" terms; downgraded female candidates; tool discontinued	(Datatron, n.d.)
COMPAS Risk Assessment	Criminal Justice	Racial bias (against Black defendants)	Historical crime data reflecting systemic inequalities	Black defendants mislabelled high risk nearly twice as often	(Daneshjou et al., 2022)
Facial Recognition Systems	Technology/ Security	Skin tone & gender bias (dark-skinned women)	Lack of diverse training data on skin tone/ gender	Misclassification up to 4.7% for dark-skinned women vs 0.8% for light-skinned men	(Raza Ur Rehman et al., 2025)

3. Contextual and Cultural Understanding

These complexities can be observed in many other examples. Moderation inaccuracies also occur when AI systems misinterpret slang and acronyms. The acronym "SMH" was misinterpreted as "so much hate" rather than the correct meaning, "shaking my head" and the term, "lit" was taken literally as "on fire," to name a few; no one around me recognized expressions like "bussin" in the least. The moderating process for AI is further complicated by cultural nuances in language. Much of the AI we interact with on a daily basis is, at its core, built upon training data represented in English, limiting its ability to understand culturally embedded meanings in other linguistic systems. "Uso" in the Basque language means "dove," however, but ejorative sense, it is also used to reference effeminate people; thus, an AI that has not been programmed for cultural sensitivity would not recognize the negative connotations of that word. The added difficulty in terms of multilingual moderation also becomes clear when Facebook's AI screwed up in the Tigray conflict because of a lack of language-specific tools to adequately moderate content in Tigrinya. Such failed oversight enabled unchecked proliferation of hate speech and misinformation, and has clearly brought to light the absolute necessity for AI systems to incorporate culture and situational awareness for every one of the world's multitudes of linguistic realities (Geetanjali & Kumar, 2025; Wireko et al., 2018).

Contextual and Cultural Challenges: AI struggles with idiomatic language, colloquialisms, contextual sensibilities, multilingualism; AI often becomes biased, misinterprets, and homogenizes (Agarwal et al., 2025). This highlights the need for much more cultural and contextual awareness in AI.

Table 2. Case Studies of AI and Algorithmic Bias in Practice

Case	Issue	Cause	Impact	Source
Misinterpretation of Slang & Acronyms	AI misclassifies slang (e.g., "SMH", "lit", "bussin")	Lack of training on evolving, informal language	False content flags; moderation errors	(Hajari, 2025)
Cultural Nuances in Language (Basque)	Misunderstanding dual-meaning words (e.g., "uso")	AI trained mostly on English, lacks cultural-linguistic context	Offensive content goes unflagged	(Andrew Deck, 2023)
Facebook's Tigrinya Moderation Failures	Inadequate content moderation in Tigrinya during crisis	Lack of language-specific AI moderation tools	Spread of hate speech and misinformation	(Tiwari et al., 2022; Xia et al., 2020)

4. Subjectivity and Ambiguity

Various important judicial decisions bring attention to the fine details connected to establishing and regulating hate speech guidelines. In The Jewish Community of Oslo et al. v. Norway (UN, 2005), the UN Committee established that anti-Semitic rhetoric extolling Nazi ideology constituted incitement to racial hatred and was not shielded by freedom of expression (Doshi et al., 2024; Hettiachchi et al., 2023).

Terms such as queer or misogynoir may serve as expressions of empowerment within specific communities; however, they are frequently misclassified as offensive by artificial intelligence systems that lack sufficient cultural and contextual comprehension (Zaner, Intersectional Disparities within Automated Hate-speech Detection Across US Centered Social Media Content. For instance, models predominantly trained on Standard American English are likely to disproportionately flag content articulated in African-American Vernacular English (AAVE) as abusive, thereby worsening the marginalization of minority voices. Although platforms such as Facebook reported that, by 2020, their AI systems could proactively identify 88.8% of hate speech content, significant deficiencies persist—particularly regarding underrepresented and low-resource languages (Simonite, Facebook Is Everywhere; Its Moderation Is Nowhere Close). The dependence on crowdsourced annotations for dataset development further instills subjectivity, as annotators' personal beliefs and cultural viewpoints may impact labeling, introducing variability and potential inconsistency into model training.

5. Bias in Training Data

Historical and biased foreground data, also represents a major challenge in having hate speech detection algorithms operate as intended. It has been demonstrated empirically that the contents of historical and biased databases can lead, because of similar factors in automated processing, to distorted and unfair hate speech detection systems that favor over-represented groups over under-represented groups (Unogwu et al., 2024).

Existing hate speech detection models rely on datasets constituted of mostly English-speaking, majority, thus accruing minimal data that often becomes misrepresentation and misclassified data of non-majority voices and dialects. For example, identity- based keywords, like "woman," or "gay," or "black," are frequently falsely categorized by automated sorting systems as hate speech, especially within the context of political speech, creating additional layers of marginalization for these groups. Despite improvements in model setup and annotation procedures, existing debiasing approaches often struggle to recognize dialect variance, context, and bias, and the collection of representative data, particularly for non-Western languages, which are important to ensure fair and generalizable models (Albladi et al., 2025).

6. Fairness across groups

Ensuring equity in the identification of hate speech is crucial to avert the marginalization of underrepresented and vulnerable populations. Hate speech detection systems often reflect biases that disproportionately affect marginalized communities. Over-reliance on keyword detection further exacerbates these issues, as reclaimed or context-specific uses of slurs-for instance, *nigga* as a term of solidarity—are often flagged as offensive. Additionally, AI moderation systems remain more accurate for high-resource languages, leaving speakers of regional or indigenous languages like Assamese vulnerable to unmoderated hate speech. Intersectional biases present further challenges, as automated models frequently fail to capture the complexity of hate speech directed at individuals with overlapping marginalized identities, leading to underreporting and limited recourse for affected users.

7. Adversarial Manipulation and Evolving Threats

As hate speech detection systems advance, so do the methods used by individuals to circumvent them. Adversarial manipulation can be described as the intentional warping of language on the part of the user to avoid automated moderation, or automated anything, and is an ongoing game of cat and mouse. Plus, the evolution of new slang, jargon, or forms, are part of the fluid dynamics of digital interaction that mean that detection algorithms need frequent updates to work and to be fair (Hettiachchi et al., 2023).

Real-World Examples of Evasion Techniques

Hate speech actors increasingly employ sophisticated evasion strategies that challenge automated detection systems. On platforms like TikTok and YouTube, users adopt *algospeak*, substituting characters (e.g., "s3x" for "sex") or using emojis (e.g., for "porn") to circumvent moderation algorithms (Wired Tech Contributors, 2022). Similarly, adversarial text attacks exploit AI vulnerabilities through minor alterations such as replacing letters with symbols ("h@t3" for "hate") or inserting neutral words, causing misclassification of harmful content (TextFooler and Adversarial NLP Research). Image-based evasion presents additional obstacles, as hate speech embedded in memes or screenshots often escapes text-based filters, while image recognition models struggle to interpret layered symbols and visual metaphors. Furthermore, coded and semantic obfuscation allows extremist groups to mask hateful rhetoric through hidden codes, altered spellings, and seemingly innocuous language, complicating both keyword-based and semantic analysis. Finally, multilingual gaps persist in under-resourced languages, such as Assamese in India, where limited datasets and weak moderation allow hate speech to proliferate unchecked.

Key Challenges in Addressing Evolving Threats

Hate speech detection systems struggle with persistent data gaps, particularly for underrepresented languages and dialects, limiting model performance and exposing minority language users to greater harm. Additionally, evolving evasion tactics—such as phonetic spellings, multimodal abuse (e.g., memes, videos), and context-switching—consistently undermine static detection models. Rapid linguistic and cultural shifts further complicate detection, as new slang and coded language emerge faster than models are updated, diminishing their long-term effectiveness. Addressing these challenges demands adaptive, multilingual, and continuously updated detection frameworks (Ali et al., 2025).

Figure 3. Challenges of Bias and Fairness in Hate Speech Detection

8. Transparency and Accountability

In the realm of hate speech detection, transparency and accountability have emerged as fundamental demands from both users and regulatory bodies. As automated systems increasingly mediate online discourse, it becomes critical to ensure that these systems offer clear, explainable justifications for their decisions—particularly when content is flagged as hateful (Clarke et al., 2023). The lack of explain ability in many AI models not only undermines public trust but also raises concerns about fairness, possible bias, and harm to individuals who may be mistakenly penalized.

Real-World Illustrations of the Need for Transparency

Transparency remains a critical challenge in hate speech detection. For example, Facebook reported that over 90% of hate speech removals were AI-driven; however, whistleblower Frances Haugen revealed actual removal rates were closer to 3–5%, with the company selectively reporting only AI-flagged cases rather than total hate content (Mark Zuckerberg, 2019). The opacity of moderation algorithms further erodes user trust, as platforms often provide little explanation for content removal, limiting users' ability to contest decisions. Initiatives like HateXplain aim to address these concerns by integrating annotated datasets with explanatory labels, enhancing model interpretability, accountability, and user confidence in moderation outcomes.

9. Regulatory and Legal Challenges

The above hate speech identification tools function within a diverse and dynamic legal context where the need to address speech that causes harm constantly competes with the need to protect free speech. Legislation or the lack thereof varies significantly depending on the region; so, the systems must be taylored closely to conform to local legislation while upholding ethics and constitutional issues. This mismatch of the regulatory standards, and the lack of established definitions regarding what constitutes hate speech, have and continue to be obstacles in the development and deployment of technologies for detection (Hettiachchi et al., 2023).

Comparative Regulatory Approaches: U.S., EU, and India

Table 3. Comparative Regulatory Approaches: U.S., EU, and India

Aspect	United States	European Union	India
Legal Framework	First Amendment; Section 230 CDA	Digital Services Act (DSA); NetzDG	IT Act; Judicial precedents
Regulatory Approach	Minimal government intervention	Strict platform obligations and transparency mandates	Court-led evolution; inconsistent statutory coverage (Isaac Chotiner, 2023)
Platform Responsibility	Immunity for user content	Required takedown of illegal content	Varies; no clear legal guidance
Free Speech Protection	Strong constitutional protection	Balanced with content regulation	Guaranteed but inconsistently applied
Key Challenges	Possible reform of Section 230; disinformation	Enforcement gaps; risk of over-censorship	Ambiguity and delays in enforcement

Current Approaches and Implementation Challenges

To address the complexities of hate speech moderation, current detection systems are increasingly designed to ensure legal compliance by incorporating country-specific regulations and adapting to diverse legal definitions of hate speech. This enables platforms to align their moderation practices with regional legal frameworks.

10. Human Involvement and Oversight

Multiple recent true cases demonstrate that human intervention is fundamentally important in automated content moderation technologies. As an example, the artificial intelligence behind YouTube incorrectly tagged a chess tutorial as hate speech because of terms such as 'Black attacks White,' showcasing the system's inability to comprehend context unique to the discipline. In a similar vein, language models predominantly trained on Standard English have exhibited bias by consistently misclassifying content in African-American English as abusive, thereby highlighting the critical need for human intervention to rectify algorithmic inaccuracies. Meta has also encountered inconsistencies in moderation, particularly in Hebrew, where a deficiency of Hebrew-speaking moderators has resulted in less stringent enforcement compared to its more robust Arabic moderation capabilities (Ghosh & Caliskan, 2023). Illustrating a promising solution, the LLM-C3MOD system integrates artificial intelligence, which achieved an accuracy rate of 78%, with human moderation to adeptly manage culturally sensitive and ambiguous content, thereby exemplifying the effectiveness of hybrid methodologies.

Limitations and Ongoing Challenges

Content moderation faces persistent challenges, including the need for cultural competence, as insufficient local knowledge can lead to biased decisions. Human moderation also struggles with scalability given the vast volume of global content. Even trained annotators often disagree due to subjective cultural interpretations. Additionally, adversarial users manipulate AI through altered spellings, benign insertions, or coded language, making human oversight essential to address these evolving tactics.

11. Technological Limitations

While technological advances have significantly improved automated hate speech detection, several fundamental limitations continue to hinder the effectiveness of these systems. Chief among these are the scarcity of high-quality, labelled datasets and the inherent challenges in detecting **multimodal hate speech**—content that spans across text, images, and video. These limitations necessitate continuous innovation in both data annotation practices and the development of sophisticated algorithmic models.

Real-World Challenges and Evidence

Hate speech detection faces key challenges, notably the scarcity of high-quality labeled data, with low annotator agreement (Krippendorff's alpha ~0.29) and limited non-English resources; semi-supervised models like GAN-BERT offer partial solutions. Multimodal detection struggles with complex content such as memes and videos, where models like MMHS150K and Facebook's Rosetta AI often fail to handle visual subtleties like fonts and sarcasm. AI performance still lags behind humans, as seen in Facebook's Hateful Memes Challenge (AI: 64.73% vs. humans: 84.7%) and modest gains in the HateMM dataset. Moreover, fusion models integrating text, image, and audio remain limited without advanced attention or hierarchical frameworks.

Summary and Outlook

Despite advancements, limitations in data quality and multimodal integration continue to hinder the effectiveness of hate speech detection. Progress requires expanding multilingual and cross-cultural datasets to better represent under-resourced languages and dialects. Improved annotation practices, with higher inter-annotator agreement and contextual clarity, can enhance dataset consistency. Advancing fusion techniques—particularly through attention-based and transformer architectures—will strengthen multimodal models. Semi-supervised learning, such as GAN-based methods, can help mitigate the scarcity of labeled data. As online hate speech evolves in complexity, a multidisciplinary, cross-modal, and ethically grounded approach remains critical for closing current gaps.

SOLUTIONS AND RECOMMENDATIONS

- **Keyword-based Approaches**

Emerging Solutions: Keyword methods are limited by context gaps. Advanced techniques like Google's Conversation AI, dual contrastive learning with focal loss, multi-faceted models like Deep Hate, and bias mitigation via fine-tuning improve accuracy. Continued research is vital for fairer hate speech detection (Mittal, 2023).

- **Ethical Concerns in Model**

Reducing bias requires diverse data, regular bias testing, human oversight, algorithmic fairness like counterfactual fairness, and transparency in model design. These steps promote fairness and equity in hate speech detection.

- **Contextual and Cultural Understanding**

Integrating Cultural Context in AI: Building culturally specific models (LLM-C3MOD), enhancing data diversity (Culture Park), using gender-neutral translation (Google Translate), collaborating with linguistic experts, and regular auditing improve AI's fairness and accuracy in diverse linguistic contexts.

- **Subjectivity and Ambiguity**

Subjectivity and ambiguity in defining hate speech present significant challenges for both human annotators and automated detection systems.

- **Bias in Training Data**

Academics are innovating ways to curtail prejudice in the assessment of hate speech. Initiatives crafted for minimizing bias, like the adjustment of sample weights throughout training, have proven a decrease in racial bias identified in BERT-implemented models. The progress of contextual comprehension encourages justice by analyzing the implementation of identity-centered vocabulary. Engaging in causal analysis aids in identifying and remedying unfounded correlations, which ultimately elevates the model's precision.

- **Fairness Across Groups: Approaches, Mitigation, and Challenges**

Pioneering undertakings to advance equity concerning hate speech surveillance engage an assortment of imaginative solutions. Bias reweighting fine-tunes training datasets to minimize racial inequities, especially within BERT-driven frameworks, while counterfactual fairness guarantees uniform predictions through the alteration of sensitive attributes. Inclusive annotation, enriched by a tapestry of diverse annotators, heightens cultural awareness, particularly in the identification of misogynistic expressions (Caitlin Dawson, 2020). Instruments like Multilingual HateCheck scrutinize fairness across linguistic boundaries, revealing vulnerabilities in cross-lingual models.

Mitigation methods encompass adversarial training with challenging instances, context-aware models that transcend mere keyword dependency, fairness metrics such as equalized odds to harmonize error distributions, and entropy-based regularization to prevent overfitting to prejudiced lexicons.

- **Adversarial Manipulation and Evolving Threats**

Individuals and collectives deploy an array of ingenious strategies to sidestep the detection of hate speech, utilizing linguistic artistry (for instance, peppering messages with uplifting words like "love"), cryptic vernacular (such as "h8te"), the integration of visual elements, and crafty alterations in text like the insertion of spaces or concealed characters. Innovative approaches—like real-time lexicon enhancements, adversarial training (Arsalan), and causal inference techniques aimed at addressing misleading correlations (Tiwari, Yuan and Zhang)—hold significant potential for bolstering the robustness of detection systems.

- **Transparency and Accountability:**

Explainable AI (XAI) tools like LIME and SHAP clarify model decisions, boosting trust. Human-in-the-Loop (HITL) moderation combines AI with human judgment for complex cases, improving accuracy. Bias and fairness audits regularly check models for discriminatory behavior. Transparent documentation (e.g., model cards) details model design, data, and limitations, aiding accountability (Binns, 2018; Doshi & Hiran, 2024). Legal compliance enforces transparency and appeals through regulation. Open research encourages dataset/model sharing for external review. User education and appeals inform users of decisions and protect free expression.

- **Regulatory and Legal Challenges:**

Hate speech detection systems face ongoing challenges. Evolving legal standards require constant adaptation through collaboration between legal experts, technologists, and civil society. Global platforms must balance diverse national laws with cohesive global policies. Risk of overreach remains, as strict laws may suppress dissent or target groups. Overall, effective detection demands balancing harm mitigation with freedom of expression, grounded in transparency, fairness, and continuous legal compliance.

- **Human Involvement and Oversight:**

Human-in-the-loop (HITL) systems combine AI efficiency with human judgment. Platforms like Identrics and Jigsaw's Perspective flag content for human review, enhancing accuracy through moderator feedback.

- **Technological Limitations:**

The presence of a collective large pool of data – involving multiple languages, dialects, and cultural attitudes – is needed to begin to address the continuing challenge of identifying hate speech. Advances in the design of algorithms, especially involving attention mechanisms and deep fusion models, significantly improve the performance of multimodal detection. Also, it would be valuable from a fairness and impact- reducing stance to also consider the ethical perspective. But, continuous research is key for more accurate and accountable detection mechanisms (Attanasio et al., 2022).

USER FEEDBACK MECHANISMS AND REAL-TIME MODERATION IN CRISIS CONTEXTS

Feedback from users can contribute to making these hate speech detection systems more accurate and accountable. Reporting, appealing or providing deeper context to flagged content help platforms to fix the mistakes caused by false positives, to identify blind spots in automated models, and to be more transparent. Adding feedback into the process, such as upvote/ downvote systems, crowd-sourced labeling or real-time moderation flags allows the platform to learn from the behavior of the users and the detection systems can then become adaptive. Meta's Oversight Board and Reddit moderator tools are some initiatives that begin to show this kind of participatory feedback into content governance (Steen et al., 2023).

FUTURE RESEARCH DIRECTIONS

First, AI models must be designed to develop a higher degree of contextual and cultural awareness by being trained in multilingual and dialect training data, informed by the knowledge of linguistic experts and cultural tradition. Including perspectives of the social sciences (Aljumily, 2023) – for example arguments from sociolinguistics, such as "othering," or concepts from psychology, such as microaggressions – may help identify ambiguous or subtle forms of hate, especially when combined with existing and culturally sensitive annotation procedures. It is therefore important to develop adversarial forms of resilience, particularly against content that is multimedial, necessitating hybrid forms of analysis that can make sense of complex and meaningful patterns in texts, images, videos, and sounds. Collaborative systems of moderation between humans and AIs should build on the combined knowledge of the community and embed cultural relevance, as seen with efforts like Meta and Jigsaw's Perspective API.

CONCLUSION

The problem of identifying hate speech is one that is multifaceted and constantly evolving due to the nature of the social, cultural, legal, and ethical issues involved.

Context: While context and nuance were a problem in early keyword-based systems, more recent developments contextual NLP, machine learning, dual-contrastive learning, and text representations have helped greatly increase the ability to detect hate speech even when subtle. These progressive advances but call into question their ethical nature and point to the need for systems that are inclusive, transparent, culturally adaptive, and always under scrutiny through multi-disciplinary interaction.

Human rights implications: The problem of biased AI goes beyond technical imperfections and pose a risk that those subjected to these technologies will be misclassified in a biased way that causes harm to members of already stigmatized populations as with Amazon's hiring system and biased facial recognition. Among other things, effective feminist solutions will require multi-facted training data, continued analyses of bias, fairness-aware algorithms, and transparency and oversight by humans; ethical AI is an act of responsibility to society.

Contextual and Cultural Sensitivity: It requires being culturally competent since meanings vary by context and identities. The failure of Facebook in the Tigray conflict is one example of the dangers of context-insensitive models. Potential solutions suggested culturally appropriate models, the inclusion of local expertise, more diverse data, and utilizing models like Culture Park or human-AI teaming.

Subjectivity and ambiguity: The subjectivity of hate speech, related to changing cultural and legal standards, lead to labeling confusion for both humans and for AI. The need to confront these issues entails more inclusive datasets, standardized annotation, and more sophisticated contextual modeling, as well as continuous debiasing facilitated by interdisciplinary collaboration.

Bias in Training Data: Because datasets are often unrepresentative of society, this can lead to models with higher error rates for minority groups. They propose solutions such as better representation, stronger causal inference, more context-dependent modeling, and much more effective attempts at bias mitigation to recast fairness as a technical and ethical concern instead of just an anti- discrimination one.

Fairness across groups: the system should behave fairly for different languages and cultures. Counterfactual fairness, adversarial training, inclusive annotation and metrics for fairness, among other strategies deal with this, but more inclusive research, data and community engagement work is needed.

Divisive Manipulation & Shifting Threats: The shifting, coded language of online – ad-memos, memes, "algospeak" – is something that we must always be prepared for (Aleksic, 2025) Adaptive lexicons, adversarial training causal inference, and robust multilingual models present defenses, but constant innovation and interdisciplinary advances will continue to play a role (Fillies & Paschke, 2024).

Transparency and Accountability: Power of AI may lead to bias and rights of users. Transparency, governance mechanisms like explainable AI, human-in-the-loop models, fairness audits, legal regulation, models that can be understood, clearances and appeal appear necessary to develop trust and accountability.

Regulatory and legal challenges: Varying global regulations create difficulties in terms of enforcement. The need for a more effective balance between harm reduction imperatives and free speech rights entails the loosening of public space control in conjunction with the development of region-specific policies, each supported by a maturing legal system, transparent enforcement and appeals systems, and more important, cross-sector alliances between civil society, religious, community, and political leaders.

Need for Human Oversight and Judgment: The capacity of AI to deal with nuance and context remains limited, and ultimately, human oversight is still necessary. Though more accurate, HITL models require training, diverse moderation teams, and ongoing monitoring to be able to ensure fairness and scalability.

Technological Limitations: There are still difficulties in the detection of hate speech in multimodal text, image, and video. Challenges that remain include lack of data, subjectivity of annotations, and under-representation of the languages involved. These challenges should be met with more and larger datasets, improved multi-modal models and datasets, better annotations, and strong ethical considerations.

REFERENCES

Agarwal, D., Naaman, M., & Vashistha, A. (2025). AI Suggestions Homogenize Writing Toward Western Styles and Diminish Cultural Nuances. *Conference on Human Factors in Computing Systems - Proceedings*. DOI: 10.1145/3706598.3713564

Albladi, A., Islam, M., Das, A., Bigonah, M., Zhang, Z., Jamshidi, F., Rahgouy, M., Raychawdhary, N., Marghitu, D., & Seals, C. (2025). Hate Speech Detection Using Large Language Models: A Comprehensive Review. *IEEE Access : Practical Innovations, Open Solutions*, *13*, 20871–20892. DOI: 10.1109/ACCESS.2025.3532397

Aleksic, Adam. (2025). *Algospeak : how social media is transforming the future of language*. 246.

Ali, S., Blackburn, J., & Stringhini, G. (2025). Evolving Hate Speech Online. *An Adaptive Framework for Detection and Mitigation.*, *1*. Advance online publication. DOI: 10.1145/nnnnnnn

Aljumily, R. (2023). An Experiment in Keyword-based Approach for Hate Speech Detection in Online Social Media Comments. SSRN *Electronic Journal*. DOI: 10.2139/SSRN.4651992

Attanasio, G., Nozza, D., Hovy, D., & Baralis, E. (2022). Entropy-based Attention Regularization Frees Unintended Bias Mitigation from Lists. *Proceedings of the Annual Meeting of the Association for Computational Linguistics*, 1105–1119. DOI: 10.18653/v1/2022.findings-acl.88

Binns, R. (2018). Fairness in Machine Learning: Lessons from Political Philosophy. In *Proceedings of Machine Learning Research* (Vol. 81, pp. 149–159). PMLR. https://proceedings.mlr.press/v81/binns18a.html

Chotiner, I. (2023). *Two Supreme Court Cases That Could Break the Internet | The New Yorker*. https://www.newyorker.com/news/q-and-a/two-supreme-court-cases-that-could-break-the-internet

Clarke, C., Hall, M., Mittal, G., Yu, Y., Sajeev, S., Mars, J., & Chen, M. (2023). Rule By Example: Harnessing Logical Rules for Explainable Hate Speech Detection. *Proceedings of the Annual Meeting of the Association for Computational Linguistics*, *1*, 364–376. DOI: 10.18653/v1/2023.acl-long.22

Countering hate speech. (2024). *What you need to know about hate speech | UNESCO*. https://www.unesco.org/en/countering-hate-speech/need-know?utm_source=chatgpt.com

Daneshjou, R., Vodrahalli, K., Novoa, R. A., Jenkins, M., Liang, W., Rotemberg, V., Ko, J., Swetter, S. M., Bailey, E. E., Gevaert, O., Mukherjee, P., Phung, M., Yekrang, K., Fong, B., Sahasrabudhe, R., Allerup, J. A. C., Okata-Karigane, U., Zou, J., & Chiou, A. S. (2022). Disparities in dermatology AI performance on a diverse, curated clinical image set. *Science Advances*, *8*(32), 6147. DOI: 10.1126/sciadv.abq6147 PMID: 35960806

Datatron. (n.d.). *Real-life Examples of Discriminating Artificial Intelligence*. Retrieved September 6, 2025, from https://datatron.com/real-life-examples-of-discriminating-artificial-intelligence/

Dawson, C. (2020). *Context Reduces Racial Bias in Hate Speech Detection Algorithms - USC Viterbi | School of Engineering*. USC Viterbi School of Engineering. https://viterbischool.usc.edu/news/2020/07/context-reduces-racial-bias-in-hate-speech-detection-algorithms/?utm_source=chatgpt.com

Deck, A. (2023). *AI content moderation problems: hate speech lost in translation - Rest of World*. Rest of World. https://restofworld.org/2023/ai-content-moderation-hate-speech/?utm_source=chatgpt.com

Díaz, Á. P. (2011). The Criminalization of Hate Speech in Chile in Light of Comparative Case Law. *Revista Chilena de Derecho*, *38*(3), 573–609. DOI: 10.4067/S0718-34372011000300007

Doshi, R., Dadhich, M., Poddar, S., & Hiran, K. K. (2024). Integrating generative AI in education to achieve sustainable development goals. *Integrating Generative AI in Education to Achieve Sustainable Development Goals*, 1–532. DOI: 10.4018/979-8-3693-2440-0

Doshi, R., & Hiran, K. K. (2024). Explainable Artificial Intelligence as a Cybersecurity Aid. *IGI*, 98–113. : Fillies, J., & Paschke, A. (2024). Simple LLM based Approach to Counter Algospeak. *Proceedings of the 8th Workshop on Online Abuse and Harms (WOAH 2024)*, 136–145. DOI: 10.4018/978-1-6684-6361-1.ch003

Fleck, A. (2024). *Chart: 2 in 3 People Often Encounter Hate Speech Online | Statista*. Statista Content & Design. https://www.statista.com/chart/33299/online-hate-speech-encounters/

Gandhi, A., Ahir, P., Adhvaryu, K., Shah, P., Lohiya, R., Cambria, E., Poria, S., & Hussain, A. (2024). Hate speech detection: A comprehensive review of recent works. *Expert Systems: International Journal of Knowledge Engineering and Neural Networks*, *41*(8), e13562. DOI: 10.1111/exsy.13562

Geetanjali, & Kumar, M. (2025). Exploring hate speech detection: challenges, resources, current research and future directions. *Multimedia Tools and Applications*, 1–37. DOI: 10.1007/S11042-025-20716-2/METRICS

Ghosh, S., & Caliskan, A. (2023). ChatGPT Perpetuates Gender Bias in Machine Translation and Ignores Non-Gendered Pronouns: Findings across Bengali and Five other Low-Resource Languages. *Proceedings of AAAI/ACM Conference on AI, Ethics, and Society (AIES '23), 1*. XXXXXXX.XXXXXXX

Hajari, S. (2025). *Exploring the Limitations of Generative AI in Understanding Social Media Acronyms and Slang*. https://www.academia.edu/127544762/Exploring_the_Limitations_of_Generative_AI_in_Understanding_Social_Media_Acronyms_and_Slang

Hettiachchi, D., Holcombe-James, I., Livingstone, S., de Silva, A., Lease, M., Salim, F. D., & Sanderson, M. (2023). How Crowd Worker Factors Influence Subjective Annotations: A Study of Tagging Misogynistic Hate Speech in Tweets. *Proceedings of the AAAI Conference on Human Computation and Crowdsourcing*, *11*, 38–50. DOI: 10.1609/hcomp.v11i1.27546

Mijwil, M. M., Gök, M., Doshi, R., Hiran, K. K., & Kösesoy, I. (2023). Utilizing Artificial Intelligence Techniques to Improve the Performance of Wireless Nodes. In *Applications of Artificial Intelligence in Wireless Communication Systems* (pp. 150–162). IGI Global., DOI: 10.4018/978-1-6684-7348-1.ch010

Mittal, U. (2023). Detecting Hate Speech Utilizing Deep Convolutional Network and Transformer Models. *IEEE International Conference on Electrical, Electronics, Communication and Computers, ELEXCOM 2023*. DOI: 10.1109/ELEXCOM58812.2023.10370502

Nascimento, F. R. S., Cavalcanti, G. D. C., & Da Costa-Abreu, M. (2025). Gender bias detection on hate speech classification: An analysis at feature-level. *Neural Computing & Applications*, *37*(5), 3887–3905. DOI: 10.1007/s00521-024-10841-8

Piazza, J. A. (2020). Politician hate speech and domestic terrorism. *International Interactions*, *46*(3), 431–453. DOI: 10.1080/03050629.2020.1739033

Raza Ur Rehman, H. M., Saleem, M., Jhandir, M. Z., Alvarado, E. S., Garay, H., & Ashraf, I. (2025). Detecting hate in diversity: a survey of multilingual code-mixed image and video analysis. *Journal of Big Data 2025 12:1*, *12*(1), 1–28. DOI: 10.1186/s40537-025-01167-w

Sipahioğlu, B. Ö. (2023). The Effects Of Hate Speech On Social Media: The Case Of Syrian Refugees In Türkiye. *Journal of Erciyes Communication*, *10*(1), 149–164. DOI: 10.17680/erciyesiletisim.1159037

Steen, E., Yurechko, K., & Klug, D. (2023). You Can (Not) Say What You Want: Using Algospeak to Contest and Evade Algorithmic Content Moderation on TikTok. *Social Media + Society*, *9*(3), 20563051231194586. Advance online publication. DOI: 10.1177/20563051231194586

The Digital Services Act package | Shaping Europe's digital future. (n.d.). Retrieved September 6, 2025, from https://digital-strategy.ec.europa.eu/en/policies/digital-services-act-package

Tiwari, K., Yuan, S., & Zhang, L. (2022). *Robust Hate Speech Detection via Mitigating Spurious Correlations*. 51–56. DOI: 10.18653/v1/2022.aacl-short.7

Unogwu, O. J., Doshi, R., Hiran, K. K., Mijwil, M. M., Catherine, A. T., & Abotaleb, M. (2024). Exploring the Implications of Emerging Artificial Intelligence Technologies at Edge Computing in Higher Education. IGI Global, 169–182. : DOI: 10.4018/979-8-3693-2440-0.ch009

Wireko, J. K., Hiran, K. K., & Doshi, R. (2018). Culturally based User Resistance to New Technologies in the Age of IoT in Developing Countries: Perspectives from Ethiopia. International Journal of Emerging Technology and Advanced Engineering, https://vbn.aau.dk/en/publications/culturally-based-user-resistance-to-new-technologies-in-the-age-o

Xia, M., Field, A., & Tsvetkov, Y. (2020). *Demoting Racial Bias in Hate Speech Detection*. 7–14. DOI: 10.18653/v1/2020.socialnlp-1.2

Zuckerberg, M. (2019). *Facebook's Hate Speech Algorithms Leave Out Some Languages | TIME*. https://time.com/5739688/facebook-hate-speech-languages/?utm_source=chatgpt.com

KEY TERMS AND DEFINITIONS

Adversarial Manipulation Techniques used by malicious actors to evade hate speech detection systems: including coded language, misspellings, memes, and text perturbations.

Algorithmic Fairness: The principle and practice of designing AI models that avoid unfair treatment or discrimination against individuals or groups, ensuring equitable outcomes.

Bias in Training Data: The presence of unbalanced or unrepresentative data in AI model training sets, which can cause models to learn and perpetuate societal biases or inaccuracies.

Contextual Natural Language Processing (NLP): Advanced NLP techniques that consider the surrounding text and linguistic context to interpret meaning, allowing better understanding of ambiguous or nuanced expressions.

Cultural Competence in AI The ability of AI systems to understand: interpret, and appropriately respond to the cultural context and diversity of users' language and communication styles.

Explainable AI (XAI)AI methods designed to provide understandable explanations of their decisions and processes to users: enhancing transparency and trust.

Hate Speech Detection: The automated or manual process of identifying and classifying language that expresses hatred, discrimination, or violence against individuals or groups based on attributes such as race, religion, ethnicity, gender, or sexual orientation.

Human-in-the-Loop Systems AI systems where human judgment is integrated into the decision-making process: especially to review, validate, or override automated outputs.

Machine Learning Models: Computational algorithms that learn from data patterns to automatically detect hate speech, often surpassing traditional keyword-based methods by incorporating contextual and statistical information.

Transparency and Accountability Principles requiring AI systems to be open about their functioning and decision-making processes: with mechanisms for responsibility and redress in case of errors or harm.

Chapter 8
Exploring Hate Speech Classification in Low-Resource Languages: A Comprehensive Review

Sargam Yadav
https://orcid.org/0000-0001-8115-6741
Dundalk Institute of Technology, Ireland

Abhishek Kaushik
https://orcid.org/0000-0002-3329-1807
Dundalk Institute of Technology, Ireland

Kevin McDaid
Dundalk Institute of Technology, Ireland

ABSTRACT

The widespread adoption of social media has profoundly impacted the lives of individuals, businesses, and governments, fostering greater connectivity. However, a byproduct of online anonymity is that individuals are more willing to display aggression, which can negatively impact groups and discourage their participation. This chapter surveys recent and pertinent literature that utilizes Natural Language Processing (NLP) techniques to automatically detect online hate speech, including studies that explore model explainability with Explainable Artificial Intelligence (XAI), evaluate model fairness, and measure unintended bias. Furthermore, the chapter reviews shared tasks and challenges that have contributed towards advancing research in hate speech detection. The findings suggest that despite the recent strides made in the development of Artificial Intelligence (AI) models for hate speech

DOI: 10.4018/979-8-3373-3063-1.ch008

detection, the problem requires further examination, creation of benchmark datasets, and examination of explainable methodologies, particularly in identification of misogynistic content.

INTRODUCTION

Hate speech, defined as discriminatory speech or language targeting a person or group based on identity-based characteristics such as race, religion, gender, and sexual orientation, poses a serious threat in the digital era. While social media provides several benefits such as visibility and networking, it has also enabled malicious individuals to spread hate (Djuric et al., 2015) and misinformation, and conduct trolling (Cheng et al., 2017) and cyber-bullying (Moreno et al., 2019). Social media serves as a hub for political discourse and can greatly impact social narratives. However, persistent harassment of targeted groups can severely impact their participation and limit their engagement. According to (Nockleby, 2000), hate speech is defined as 'any communication that disparages a target group of people based on some characteristic such as race, color, ethnicity, gender, sexual orientation, nationality, religion, or other characteristics.' Figure 1 displays an example of hate speech from the Identification of Conversational Hate-Speech in Code-Mixed Languages (ICHCL) 2022 dataset (Satapara et al., 2022), which has been categorized as 'Standalone Hate'.

Figure 1. Example of a statement depicting hate speech from ICHCL-2022 dataset

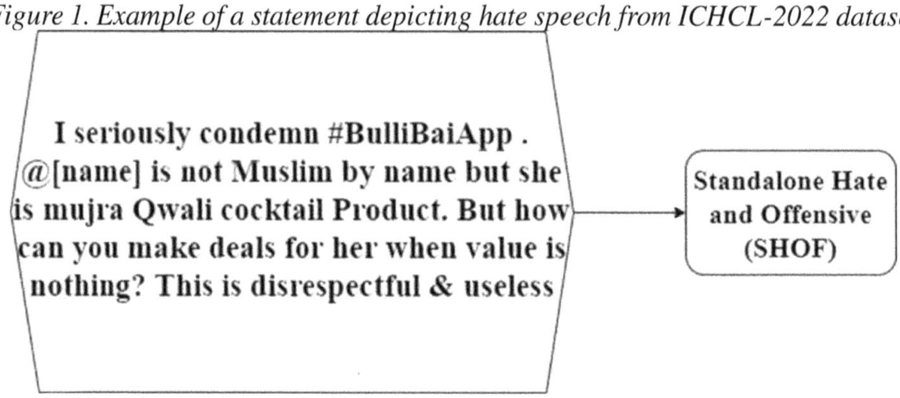

(Satapara et al., 2022).

Cyberbullying, on the other hand, is a more general form of abuse which is not targeted towards a unique and non-controllable attribute of a group of people (*Cyberbullying and Hate Speech Online*, 2016) (Feinberg & Robey, 2009). Misogyny, which is hatred towards or prejudice against women, can be considered a gendered form of hate speech, and is highly prevalent across social media platforms. The United Nations Human Rights Council highlights that the rights held by women offline are also applicable online (*Amnesty International. Troll Patrol India. Exposing Online Abuse Faced by Women Politicians in India*, 2020), urging social media websites to uphold these rights wherever they operate (*Guiding Principles on Business and Human Rights – Implementing the United Nations "Protect, Respect and Remedy" Framework, United Nations Human Rights Office of the High Commissioner, 2011*, 2011). Popular social media platforms such as Twitter and YouTube have also published policies and guidelines prohibiting content that promotes violence or hatred against individuals or groups based on attributes such as age, caste, disability, ethnicity, gender identity and expression, and nationality (*Twitter's Policy on Hateful Conduct | Twitter Help*, 2023) (*YouTube Community Guidelines: Hate Speech*, 2023). However, the high volume of content on these platforms and subjective nature of hate speech makes enforcement of these guidelines challenging, highlighting the need for automated systems. Several legislative bodies are moving towards criminalizing online hate speech towards women and other marginalized communities (*Hate Crime: Law Commision United Kingdom Government*, 2022), as the impact of hate speech can extend beyond the digital space through a 'gateway' effect. Statistically, women face a higher risk of violence, with every 1 out of 3 women worldwide experiencing some form of abuse (*Facts and Figures: Ending Violence against Women.*, 2022). Unfortunately, numerous cases have demonstrated that online harassment can evolve into physical violence (Chan, 2016) (*Asia McGowan: Youtuber Killed by Mentally Ill Stalker at Michigan School*, 2016), and has also resulted in suicide (Yousif, 2022).

Recently, NLP researchers have increasingly focused on developing artificial intelligence systems to mitigate hate speech. Hate speech is highly contextual and subjective and cannot be defined merely by the presence of cuss words and offensive language. Certain words may be used sarcastically or may have been reclaimed by the target community (Dias Oliva et al., 2021) (Frenda, 2018). Additionally, individuals may hold different private opinions than they express online (Mehul Mahrishi et al., 2020; Shang, 2019), making it challenging to gauge the intention of a user. Despite the critical social implications of online hate speech, research in the domain is nascent, particularly for misogyny identification (Fersini, Rosso, et al., 2018), and detection in code-switched languages (Mandl et al., 2021) (Mandl et al., 2020). India, one of largest user bases for social media platforms such as YouTube (450 million) (*Leading Countries Based on YouTube Audience Size as of January 2023*, 2023) and Twitter (23 million) (Statista, 2024), produces a large of volume of online content in code-mixed languages due to its linguistic diversity. Code-mixing refers to the practice of combining features from two or more languages. 'Hinglish', for instance, is a code-mixed language that consists of Romanized Hindi combined with English tokens. Figure 2 displays an example of a code-mixed sentence with its English translation.

Figure 2. Example of a code-mixed Hinglish sentence with English translation.

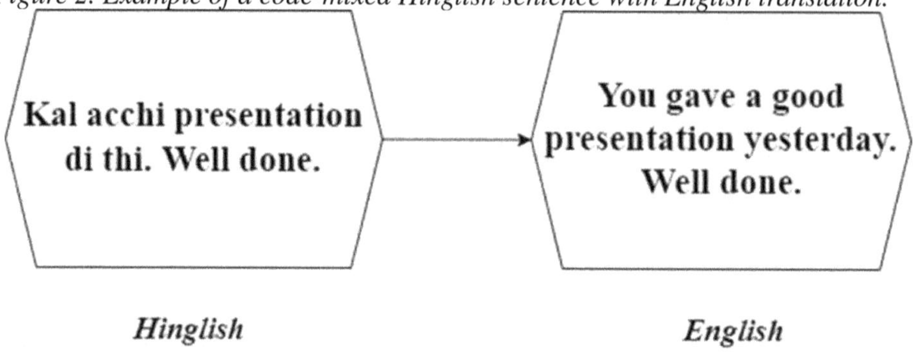

It is crucial to develop content monitoring tools specific to the regional languages to effectively capture hate speech, as such a large portion of data comes from multilingual countries that use code-mixing. Figure 3 displays an example of hate speech in code-mixed Hinglish from the TRAC 2 (Kumar et al., 2020), along with its English translation. The comment was classified as 'Overtly Aggressive' and 'Gendered'.

Figure 3. Example of a statement depicting hate speech from TRAC-2 Hindi train dataset

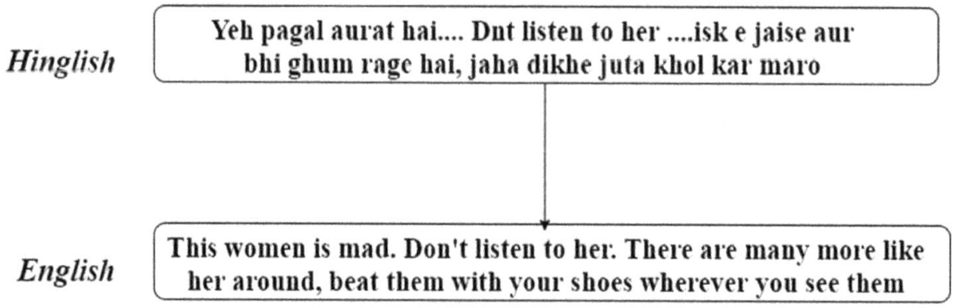

(Kumar et al., 2020).

Another challenge in hate speech detection is the amplification of inherent and unintended biases in the dataset or model (Attanasio et al., 2022). For example, a misogyny classifier might incorrectly classify a statement as misogynistic based on the presence of features such as 'women'. XAI is a technique that can assist in uncovering and mitigating these biases by making artificial intelligence models interpretable to humans (Doshi & Hiran, 2024; Gunning et al., 2019). XAI techniques can provide local explanations of single instances through techniques such as Local Interpretable Model Agnostic Explanations (LIME) (Ribeiro et al., 2016), or global explanations through techniques such as Shapely Additive Explanations (SHAP) (Acheampong et al., 2018; Lundberg & Lee, 2017). Therefore, the development of explainable, debiased, and effective approaches is crucial in mitigating online hate speech and ensuring a safe and inclusive digital space.

This chapter aims to provide a comprehensive analysis of the current state-of-the-art in hate speech classification, XAI techniques, and debiasing algorithms that can be used to interpret model results and improve model fairness. Additionally, an exploration of publicly available datasets for hate speech detection is performed, highlighting the current limitations and future scope for hate speech and misogyny detection in multilingual and code-mixed text. The rest of the chapter is structured as follows: The 'Motivation' section discusses the motivation of this study, the research hypothesis, and the research questions. This is followed by the 'Literature Review' section, which provides a review of the recent literature on hate speech and misogyny detection across different languages, explainability and fairness of hate speech classifiers, and shared tasks and challenges regularly conducted to advance research in the domain. The next section 'Limitations' addresses the challenges that currently impede the development of effective automated approaches for countering online hate speech. In the Section 'Discussion', the findings of the study with respect to the research questions are discussed. The 'Conclusion' section concludes the chapter and outlines the future scope of the study.

MOTIVATION

The integration of social media into daily life has increased the risk of harassment and abuse. While platforms such as Twitter originally aimed to provide marginalized communities a space for equal representation, they have unfortunately become a toxic place for such communities due to lack of enforceable regulations and inadequate guidelines (*Toxic Twitter – The Solution. Chapter 8*, 2018). The detrimental psychological effects of online abuse can extend beyond an individual and impact the target community. Sexist and misogynistic posts, for instance, can discourage women from participating in political discussions online, effectively silencing their opinions (*Facts and Figures: Ending Violence against Women.*, 2022) (*Amnesty International. Troll Patrol India. Exposing Online Abuse Faced by Women Politicians in India*, 2020). Moreover, online hate speech has also been linked to real world hate crimes. Considering these factors, social media platforms should swiftly implement automated toolkits to filter hateful content, in addition to user reports and manual content monitoring.

In multilingual societies like India, which is one of the largest user bases of many social media platforms like Twitter and YouTube (Statista, 2024), users generally blend Hindi or other Indian languages with English, which is called code-switching. Code switching makes the task of hate speech detection more challenging, introducing several complexities. There is a lack of studies and datasets in multilingual and code-mixed languages (Mandl et al., 2021) (Yadav, Kaushik, & Sharma, 2023). Furthermore, very few studies focus specifically on misogyny (Fersini, Rosso, et al., 2018). Given that hate speech can have legal implications, the explainability of a machine learning tool is important. This chapter aims to review the recent advancements in the development of automated systems for hate speech prevention, specifically highlighting the studies that focus on misogyny. Approaches that have focused on developing explainable, fair, and debiased hate speech detection models have also been examined. The motivation behind this chapter is to highlight the scarcity of datasets for misogyny detection and hate speech detection in code-switched Indian languages and underscore the importance of developing effective solutions to the problem. By highlighting the gaps in recent literature, this chapter also aims to serve as the foundation for future research and development in the area.

The hypothesis explored in the chapter is as follows:

Hypothesis: NLP tools can detect multilingual and code-mixed misogynistic hate speech online and provide interpretable results.

The following research questions have been outlined for further exploration of the hypothesis:

- What are the current state-of-the-art machine learning and deep learning tools available for detection of online hate speech? Which studies have focused specifically on detection of misogyny? Which studies have been performed on code-switched data?
- What are the different hate speech datasets available for training and evaluating machine learning models? Which datasets have been dedicated specifically to misogyny detection? How many datasets exist for code-switched languages?
- What are the Explainable AI approaches available for online hate speech detection? Which studies have focused on developing explainable classifiers for code-switched languages?
- What are the limitations and challenges that currently impede the development of a robust system for preventing online hate speech detection?

Review Methodology

The following online databases were used to search for articles to survey in this study: Google Scholar, IEEE Xplore, ACM Digital Library, Springer Nature Link, and Elsevier ScienceDirect. The following steps were followed in the review methodology:

- The search keywords for shared task papers were in the following format: 'HASOC-2020', and 'AMI 2020'. We have tried to include most of the shared tasks that are regularly conducted for hate speech detection. Papers for the best performing systems were obtained and cited from the overview papers of the shared tasks.
- For welfare reports, the respective names of the projects were typed in as keywords. Relevant citations within the reports were covered and cited within. Amnesty International's 'Troll Patrol' website, which consists of 8 chapters, was examined carefully.
- Articles published outside of shared tasks were queried using specific keywords. For instance: to search for studies which specifically dealt with misogyny, the keyword 'misogyny hate speech detection' was used and the relevant articles were included. To find studies that dealt with hate speech detection for code-mixed languages (Kaur et al., 2019) (Yadav & Kaushik, 2022), the keywords 'misogyny detection Hinglish' and 'hate speech detection Hinglish' were used. Searches for hate speech classifiers in other languages were done in a similar manner.
- The title and abstract of the article were examined to determine the relevance of the study. If the abstract and title were deemed relevant, the article was thoroughly assessed.
- Papers published from 2000 to 2024 were included.
- The exclusion criteria were books, theses/dissertations, presentations and abstracts. Articles written in languages other than English were excluded.
- The following information was extracted from the selected articles: dataset size and description, feature extraction and model used, evaluation metrics used for the model, and contributions and limitations of the study.
- Additional papers were obtained through snowballing by citing important papers from within the surveyed papers.

Figure 4 depicts a pie chart that shows the topics covered in this review paper by number of studies. 'Hate speech classifiers and datasets' and 'Challenges and Shared Tasks' have the highest number of papers covered.

Figure 4. Percentage of topics included

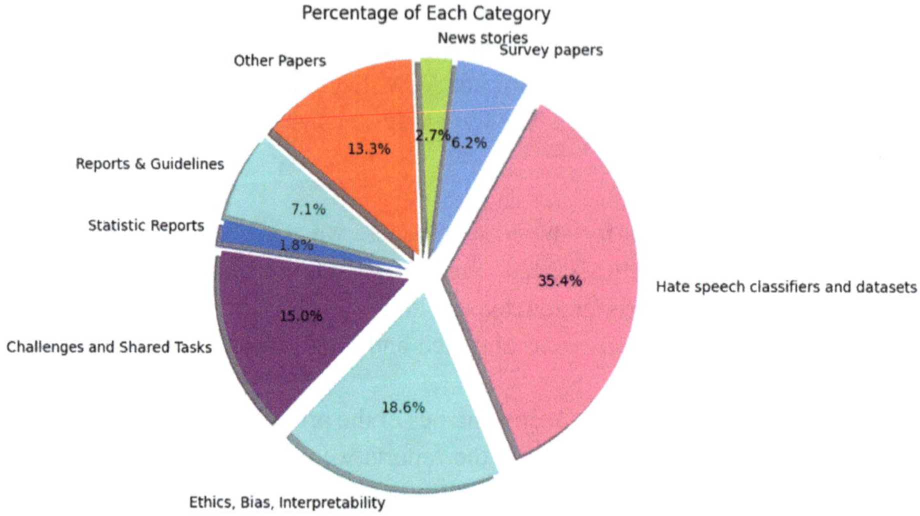

Figure 5 graphs the number of studies and shared tasks papers, and the different platforms that have been utilized for data collection. All papers not relevant to hate speech classification were excluded for calculation. The highest number of studies focused on datasets that were scraped from Twitter, while very few studies have focused on datasets from other platforms such as Gab and YouTube. The variation in the hate comments collected from various platforms can result in a more robust dataset for training hate speech classifiers.

Figure 5. Studies and shared tasks by social media platform

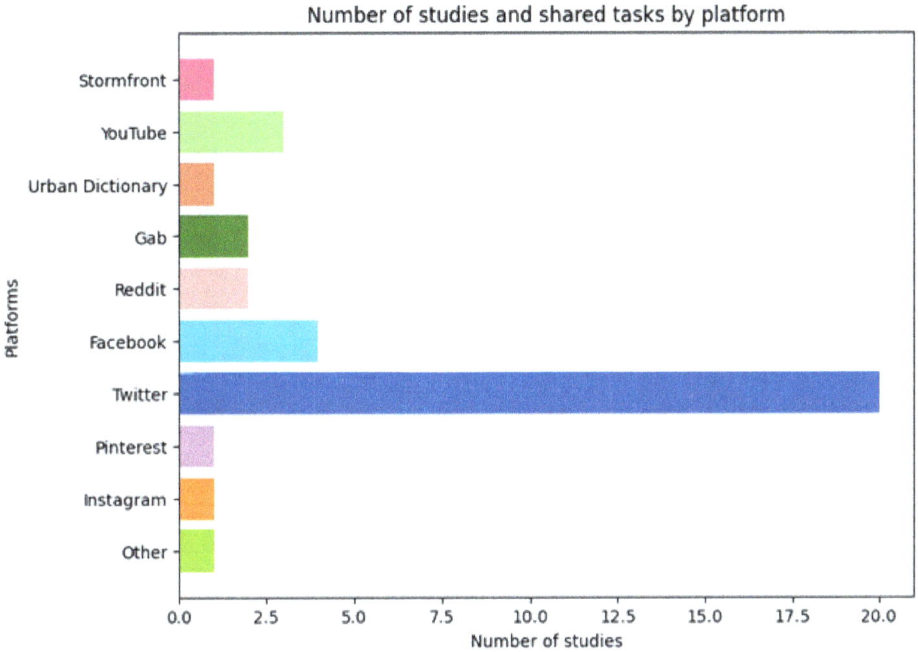

Figure 6 depicts a bar graph of the total number of studies done for certain languages. The highest number of cities have focused on English, whereas low resource languages such as Marathi, Nepali, and Turkish have not been experimented on much.

Figure 6. Studies and shared tasks by language of dataset

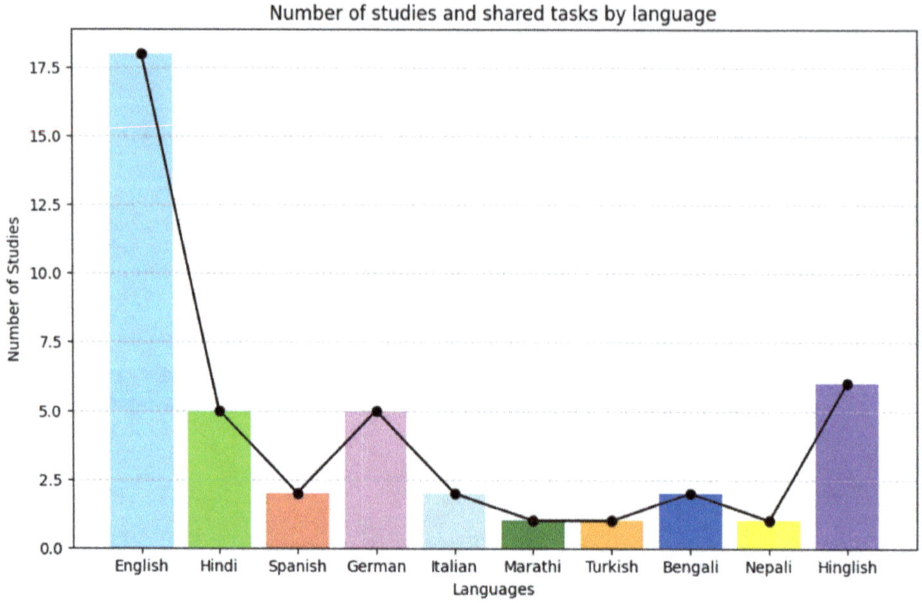

LITERATURE REVIEW

In this section, we discuss the key research works in automatic hate speech detection using NLP tools. It is divided into the following subsections: Hate Speech Detection, Hate Speech Detection in Code-mixed Languages, and Explainable, Fair and Debiased Hate Speech Classifiers. We highlight recent studies that have tackled hate speech detection across languages, research that focuses on misogyny specifically, approaches that incorporate XAI to enhance the explainability of black box hate classification models, and papers that cover the measurement and mitigation of unintended bias. Existing studies have employed numerous strategies for data annotation and classification, focusing on aspects such as severity of hate, target of hate, and context of the conversation. This section aims to examine the datasets and methodologies employed in these studies, highlight their findings and limitations, and explore the challenges associated with handling multilingual and code-mixed data, as well as examine transparency and interpretability in hate speech classifiers. Table 1 details the various studies that have been conducted for hate speech detection and details the dataset, classification task, best results, and best performing models.

Table 1. Overview of Machine Learning systems for Hate Speech Classification

Name	Dataset	Best Results	Best Approach
HEOT (Mathur, Ratn Shah, et al., 2018)	3679 Hinglish tweets divided into 3 classes: non-offensive, abusive, hate speech	Accuracy: 83.90%, F1-score: 0.714	Transfer learning using CNN
(Bhattacharya et al., 2020)	25,000 YouTube (Indian English, Hindi, Indian Bangla) annotated at 2 levels: aggression, misogyny	Hindi: 0.87, Bangla: 0.89, English: 0.93	Character n-grams using SVM
(Bohra et al., 2018)	4575 Hinglish tweets classified into normal and hate speech	Accuracy of 71.7%	SVM-RBF classifier using character level, word level, and lexicon-based features
(Waseem & Hovy, 2016)	16,914 English tweets divided into 3,383 sexist, 1,972 racist, and 11,559 neither.	F1 score: 73.89	Logistic regression classifier using character n-grams and gender information
(Mathur, Sawhney, Ayyar, & Ratn Shah, 2018)	3189 Hinglish tweets divided into 3 classes: non-offensive, abusive, hate-Inducing	Macro-F1 score: 0.895	Multi-channel CNN-LSTM architecture using Twitter Word2Vec, FastText, and secondary features
(Şahi et al., 2018)	Turkish tweets divided into 159 hate speech and 1129 non-hateful.	Precision: 0.97	SVM using word and character level features
(Guest et al., 2021)	6,567 English Reddit posts annotated at 3 levels: 1: misogynistic and non-misogynistic, 2: subtypes of misogyny, 3: additional flags	F1-score: 0.43	Weighted BERT
(Lynn et al., 2019a)	2285 English posts from Urban Dictionary annotated as misogynistic (1034) and non-misogynistic (1251)	Accuracy: 93.10, Sensitivity: 92.08	Bi GRU
(Anzovino et al., 2018)	4454 English tweets annotated at 2 levels: misogyny identification and behaviour type.	Level-1: Accuracy = 0.7995, Level-2: acro-F1 0.3825	1: Linear SVM using token n-grams
(García-Díaz et al., 2021)	7682 Spanish tweets annotated as 2 classes: misogyny and non-misogyny.	Accuracy: 85.17%	SMO classifier using average word embeddings and linguistic features

continued on following page

Table 1. Continued

Name	Dataset	Best Results	Best Approach
(Jha & Mamidi, 2017)	10,095 unique English tweets annotated as 3 classes: benevolent sexism, hostile sexism, others.	F1-score: 0.87	FastText classifier
(Karim et al., 2021)	5000 Bengali text (Facebook, YouTube comments, newspapers) divided into 4 classes: political, personal, geopolitical, religious.	Macro-F1 = 0.88, MCC = 0.820; Comprehensiveness = 0.84, Sufficiency = 0.44	Ensemble of Bangla BERT base, Multilingual BERT cased, Multilingual BERT base, XLM-RoBERTa; For explainability: XLM-RoBERTa
(Mathew et al., 2021)	20,148 English posts from Twitter and Gab annotated at 3 levels: 1: classification of hate (hate, offensive, normal) 2: target type 3: rationale for classification.	Macro-F1 = 0.687, Comprehensiveness = 0.500, Plausibility = 0.506, Sufficiency = -0.082	Performance metrics and bias: BERTHateXplain[LIME and Attn], Comprehensiveness: BERT-HateXplain [LIME], Plausibility: BiRNN-HateXplain[Attn], Sufficiency: CNN-GRU
(de Gibert et al., 2018)	9916 (cleaned) English posts from Stormfront annotated into 2 classes: Hate and No Hate.	Accuracy = 78%	LSTM (layer size = 128, word embeddings size = 300
(Khan et al., 2024)	Hate Speech Target Dataset (HSTD) 1500 target and 1500 non-target English tweets.	Accuracy = 93%	Naïve bayes trained on concatenation of TF-IDF, N-grams, and PoS tags.
(A. Singh et al., 2024)	Multimodal dataset of 5,054 memes Hinglish, Facebook, Instagram, and Reddit, Pinterest	Macro F1-Score: 0.7319 and AUC-ROC: 0.8168 (binary),	Mutilmodal BiT + MuRIL (binary), multi label: BiT + RoBERTa

Hate Speech Detection

Research into preventing online abuse and cyberbullying has gained momentum due to the rising popularity of social media platforms. Hate speech detection in English has been extensively explored due to the widespread use of the language online and the number of available NLP tools and resources. Several types of approaches have been proposed, ranging from traditional rule-based and machine learning systems to state-of-the-art transformer-based models.

Initial research primarily focused on machine learning algorithms and statistical features. A simple logistic regression classifier was trained on character n-grams and extra-linguistic features by (Waseem & Hovy, 2016) to determine if a tweet was sexist, racist, or neither. 11 criteria from critical race theory, such as presence of slurs and misrepresentation of truth, were used to annotate the tweets. The classifier achieved a macro-F1 score of 0.7389. The authors suggest inclusion of extra-linguistic features such as gender and demographic information to improve model performance. Similarly, (Kwok & Wang, 2013) studied a dataset of 24,582 tweets for detecting hate speech against black people. A bag-of-words model utilizing unigram was fed into a Naïve bayes classifier and achieved an accuracy of 76% and error rate of 24%. Limitations of using word unigrams is that the model will not learn the context of words during training and might classify a statement as hate speech simply due to the presence of a feature such as 'black' and 'white'. Another machine learning based approach was used by (Warner & Hirschberg, 2012) to detect anti-sematic sentiment from text using Linear Support Vector Machine (SVM). The dataset consisted of 1000 paragraphs from Yahoo! and URLs provided by American Jewish Congress (AJC) and was divided into the following categories by 3 annotators: antisemitic, anti-black, anti-Asian, anti-woman, anti-Muslim, anti-immigrant, or other-hate. A template-based strategy using parts-of-speech (PoS) tagging and Brown clusters was employed to generate features from the corpus. The best results were achieved using a positive unigram feature set, which provided an accuracy of 94%, precision of 68%, recall of 60%, and F1 measure of 0.6375.

Hate speech detection is a challenging task due to the nuanced and complex nature of language, which can include elements like sarcasm, idioms, humor, and metaphors. In their study, (Davidson et al., 2017) emphasize that language complexity, sarcasm, or implicit hate can cause the model to misclassify instances. They developed a dataset of 24,802 tweets annotated as hate speech, offensive, or neither. Term Frequency – Inverse Document Frequency (TF-IDF) and PoS tags, combined with logistic regression with L2 regularization achieved the best overall precision of 0.91, recall of 0.90, and F1 score of 0.90. The study underscores that the context of the conversation plays a huge role in hate speech classification, and racist and homophobic slurs were associated with hate. To explore the impact of context, (de Gibert et al., 2018) compiled a dataset of 10,568 sentences from Stormfront, a white nationalist online forum, annotated at sentence level into the 'Hate' (1,119) and 'No Hate' (8,537) classes. Additionally, the 'Relation' label was applied to sentences which do not depict hate speech on their own, but when they are examined as part of the entire post. A Hate Score (HS) was also calculated using the Pointwise Mutual Information (PMI) value for each word towards each category. Words with a more positive hate score, such as 'ape' and 'scum' were more hateful. A balanced dataset consisting of 1000 'Hate' posts and 1000 'NoHate' posts were used to train the following algorithms: linear SVM with word-count-based vectors, CNN with single input channel of randomly initialized word embeddings, and Long-Short Term Memory (LSTM) with a layer size of 128 and word embeddings size of 300. The best accuracy was achieved by LSTM by excluding sentences that required additional context. The highest accuracy for the 'hate' class was 0.76, for 'nohate' class was 0.80, and for all was 0.78. The highest overall accuracy dropped to 0.73 when sentences that required additional context were included.

The data collection and annotation process for hate speech detection presents several challenges such as lack of representation, sampling bias, and platform bias. A new benchmark dataset for hate speech detection was presented by (Rahman et al., 2021), which was shown to contain a broader coverage of hate than many previous datasets. Two standard Information Retrieval (IR) approaches, active learning and pooling, were used to find tweets to annotate as the author likened the rarity and subjectivity of hate speech to relevance in IR. The authors caution that biases can further perpetuate discrimination and societal harm and must be addressed. They also emphasize that the psychological well-being of annotators must be kept in mind due to their exposure to disturbing content (Steiger et al., 2021). Another approach to minimize bias was proposed by (Founta et al., 2018), who presented a dataset of 80,000 tweets annotated for hate speech, offensive speech, and abusive speech using the crowdsourcing platform CrowdFlower. A boosted sampling approach is used to minimize bias and ensure more samples for the minority class. The study highlights that it is important to make a distinction between hate speech and offensive speech to avoid false positives.

Despite the significant advancements in hate speech detection, the classifiers often struggle to generalize well across different hate speech detection tasks. The transferability of hate speech detection approaches was examined by (Toraman et al., 2022) across five domains of hate: religion, gender, sports, political, and race. They provided a dataset consisting of 100k comments in English and Turkish. The study found that 96% of the performance of a target domain is recovered by other domains for English and 92% for Turkish. 'Gender' and 'religion' show the highest generalization to other domains while 'sports' shows the least. Similarly, (Fortuna et al., 2021) examined the impact of model and dataset composition on generalization as well as the influence of features of models or datasets on the generalization potential in hate speech detection. The importance of different model and dataset features was examined using a random forest classifier, which assessed the performance of 450 binary abusive language classifiers for BERT, ALBERT, fastText, and 348 for SVM. The study found that some categories such as 'toxic', 'abusive', and 'offensive' which are similar in definition tend to generalize well across datasets. For 'hate speech', low generalization is observed when considering a broad label, but when evaluated on specific types of hate (racism and sexism), BERT provided better generalization. The authors provide suggestions to improve generalization such as carefully defined coarse-grained categories, inclusion of fine-grained categories, use of standard categories, and out-of-domain vocabulary percentage.

Misogyny, a gendered form of hate speech, is alarmingly common on social media platforms. It can manifest in several forms including implicit hate, explicit hate, stereotyping, and use of abusive language. It remains a pervasive issue worldwide and has been discussed by various human rights organizations across the world. Several entities globally have published reports that highlight the hurdles faced by women. One such report is 'Tweets That Chill: Analysing Online Violence Against Women In Politics', which was a case study conducted in Indonesia, Colombia, and Kenya by the National Democratic Institute (NDI) (*Tweets That Chill: Analyzing Online Violence Against Women in Politics | National Democratic Institute*, 2019). The study was conducted to analyze the impact of gender-based online violence towards politically active women in those three countries. The case studies were conducted in the following 3 languages: Bahasa for Indonesia, Colombian Spanish, and a mix of Swahili and English in Kenya. The methodology consisted of 3 steps: conducting workshops in the target country, conducting surveys with college-aged people, and quantitative analysis of Twitter data. The results suggest that such online violence had a 'chilling effect' on the women, meaning that they responded to such violence by limiting or completely stopping their Twitter activity. The findings emphasize the need to filter violent content online to ensure continued participation of women in the political landscape.

Another significant contribution is the 'Eliminating Online hate speech to Secure Women's Political Participation' report by UN Women (*Eliminating Online Hate Speech to Secure Women's Political Participation | UN Women – Asia-Pacific*, 2021), which highlights the importance of taking measures to prevent online hate and misogyny and promote gender equality in the online space. Women politicians were shown to be 3 times more likely to face online sexual abuse than men. The report provides several recommendations regarding eliminating this gender bias such as prevention of online misogyny, implementation of policies that criminalizes such harassment, collaboration with women and women-led organizations to study and tackle such obstacles, and development of a strategy to encourage more women to join the technological sector. Similarly, Troll Patrol (*Amnesty International. Troll Patrol India. Exposing Online Abuse Faced by Women Politicians in India*, 2020) was a project undertaken by Amnesty International which conducted an analysis 288,000 tweets received by 778 female journalists and politicians from the UK and US throughout 2017. The project found that 7.1% of tweets (1.1 million) sent to the women were problematic or abusive, women of color were 34% more likely to receive abusive or problematic tweets, and black women were specifically targeted with 84% higher chance of abuse. Specifically, left-winged politicians received 23% more abusive and problematic tweets than their right-wing counterparts. On the other hand, right-wing journalists received 64% more problematic and abusive tweets. 'Toxic Twitter' is another report by Amnesty International that aims to the capture the depth, severity, and impact of online abuse on women from different countries, professions, and marginalized communities. It identifies various types of abuse faced by women such as threats of violence, sexist and misogynistic abuse, other identity-based violence towards the LGBT community, trans people, and Black, Asian, Minority, Ethnic (BAME) people.

Several studies have explored misogyny detection using AI tools in English, leveraging the vast amounts of data available from different platforms. An expert labelled dataset was presented by (Guest et al., 2021), consisting of 6,567 Reddit posts and comments for automatic misogyny detection. The hierarchical taxonomy consists of three levels: categorization into misogynistic and non-misogynistic, classification into subtypes of misogynistic (misogynistic pejoratives, descriptions of misogynistic treatment, acts of Misogynistic Derogation, etc.) and non-misogynistic content, and additional flags for level 2. A weighted BERT achieves the best F1-score of 0.43, with many classification errors occurring due to lack of context in the text. The inclusion of granular subcategories facilitated a more detailed error analysis. Similarly, (Lynn et al., 2019b) presented a dataset of 2285 Urban Dictionary entries annotated by three researchers as either misogynistic (1034) and non-misogynistic (1251). Pre-filtering using a bag of 51 words commonly associated with misogyny was performed on the original dataset of 2,606,521 definitions, and 951,978 definitions were obtained. Comparative analysis of deep learning models on this dataset was performed by (Lynn et al., 2019a), who compare models such as bidirectional LSTM (Bi-LSTM) and bidirectional Gated Recurrent Unit (Bi-GRU), with conventional machine learning models, logistic regression, Naïve bayes, and random forest. Out of all the models, Bi-GRU achieves the highest accuracy and sensitivity of 93.10 and 92.08 respectively, whereas random forest achieves the highest score of 96 on specificity. A similar labeling taxonomy was also developed by (Anzovino et al., 2018), who compiled a corpus of 4454 tweets for misogyny detection. The taxonomy for classification of the type of misogynistic behavior was as follows: discredit, stereotype and objectification, sexual harassment and threats of violence, dominance, and derailing. Linear SVM and token n-grams achieved the best accuracy of 0.7995 for binary classification of misogyny and 0.3825 for classification of misogyny subtype, suggesting difficulty in discriminating between the types of misogynistic behavior. An investigation into detecting more subtle forms of sexism was performed by (Jha & Mamidi, 2017), who studied a corpus of tweets by classifying them into benevolent and hostile sexism according to the ambivalent sexism theory. The study was conducted on a combination of the corpus in (Waseem & Hovy, 2016) and 10,095 unique tweets. FastText achieved the best F1-score of 0.87 due to its bag of n-grams feature. Expanding on this, (Frenda et al., 2019) analyzed three English datasets of tweets to examine two aspects hate speech towards women: misogyny and sexist behavior, from a computational perspective.

Their findings suggest that there are several syntactic similarities between the two, and similar machine learning approaches can be used to counter them.

A unique data source was explored by (Sheppard et al., 2023), who presented the Biasly dataset containing 10,000 subtitles of North American films annotated to detect subtle misogyny from conversational language. The annotation process was carried out by experts in gender studies, linguistics, and NLP, and through four tasks: binary classification (misogyny or not), categorization of misogyny into 12 additional subtypes, severity scoring on a scale of 0 to 100, and feasibility of rewriting misogynistic text to retain the same meaning. A total of 31.59% of the comments were found to be misogynistic, while 'Trivialization' was the most common subtype. Additionally, rewriting misogynistic texts using BART, FLAN-T5, and Alpaca-LoRA was shown to reduce their severity score.

Besides English, research efforts have also been extended to other languages from across the globe. For instance, in the study by (Şahi et al., 2018) Turkish tweets were classified for cyber-hate towards women using the machine learning classifiers where SVM provided a high precision rate of 0.97. Similarly, (García-Díaz et al., 2021) presented the Spanish MisoCorpus-2020, a dataset of 7682 tweets consisting of 3 subsets: violence towards relevant women, messages harassing women in Spanish from Spain and Spanish from Latin America, and general traits related to misogyny. For misogyny identification, the highest accuracy attained is 85.175%, using a combination of average word embeddings and linguistic features with the Sequential Minimal Optimization (SMO) classifier.

Beyond text, some studies have expanded misogyny detection to other modalities such as images. The Multimedia Misogyny Detection Dataset (MAMI) dataset consists of 12,000 memes classified as misogynistic or not, and the misogynistic comments are further classified into four labels: shaming, objectification, stereotypes, and violence (Fersini et al., 2022). At the SemEval-2022 Task 5, the highest macro-F1 score of 0.834 was achieved using an ensemble model of deep multimodal features with multi-layer perceptron, extreme gradient boosting (Chen & Guestrin, 2016), and gradient-boosted decision trees. The highest macro-F1 score of multi-class classification achieved was 0.731 employing the same approach used in binary classification and combining BERT with CLIP (Contrastive Language-Image Pretraining) (Radford et al., 2021). Expanding on this, (S. Singh et al., 2023) trained a BERT + Vision Transformer (ViT) model on the dataset and achieved the best F1 scores of 0.874 in binary misogyny classification and 0.721 in subtype classification. The approach was limited in its ability to detect stereotypes, subtle objectification, and sarcasm in text, leading to misclassification.

Hate Speech Detection in Code-mixed Languages

The wide-spread availability of the internet in multilingual societies has increased the prevalence of code-mixing in online conversations. Code-mixing refers to combining features from two or more languages and presents several challenges for NLP tasks such as hate speech detection. Cultural differences and regional languages increase the complexity in automatic detection of hate speech. A statement may be code-switched and consist of slurs with culture-specific meaning, making it difficult for automated systems to filter them.

One of the earliest attempts to detect hate speech in code-mixed Hinglish was undertaken by (Bohra et al., 2018), who presented a dataset of 4,575 tweets annotated as 'Hate Speech' or 'Normal Speech', with token-level language tags. SVM and random forest models were trained with five features, namely character n-grams, word n-grams, punctuation features, negation words, and lexicon features. SVM achieved the highest accuracy of 71.6% using character n-grams. Similarly, (Mathur, Ratn Shah, et al., 2018) presented the Hindi-English Offensive Tweet (HOET) dataset and applied a transfer-learning based approach. A Convolutional Neural Network (CNN) model was trained on an English dataset (Davidson et al., 2017) and fine-tuned on the HOET dataset, and achieved an F1-score of 0.427. The study demonstrates the effectiveness of transfer learning in hate speech classification from existing datasets. A similar transfer learning-based approach was used by (Mathur, Sawhney, Ayyar, & Ratn Shah, 2018), who employed a Multi-Input Multi-Channel Transfer Learning (MIMCT) model which incorporated primary features like GloVE embeddings, FastText, and Word2Vec, and secondary features such as sentiment scores, profanity vectors, and Linguistic Inquiry and Word Count (LIWC). The MIMCT model achieved the highest macro-F1 score of 0.895 using Twitter Word2Vec and FastText embeddings with profanity vectors and LIWC. The superiority of deep learning models in hate speech detection was further highlighted by (Kumar Yadav et al., 2022), who performed comparative analysis on different machine learning and deep learning models and feature extraction techniques for hate speech detection in code-mixed Hinglish by combining the datasets of (Bohra et al., 2018), (Satapara et al., 2021), and (Mathur, Sawhney, Ayyar, & Shah, 2018). CNN-BiLSTM with Word2Vec embeddings achieved the best results with an F1-score of 0.835. The approach outperformed the state-of-the-art and highlighted the importance of large datasets for hate speech detection in code-mixed languages.

The breakthrough of transformer-based models has also impacted the field of hate speech detection due to their ability to capture long-range dependencies and contextual relationships in text. A notable example is Hinglish HateBERT (N. Singh & Mundra, 2023), a transformer-based model which is pre-trained on a dataset of offensive and non-offensive comments in code-mixed Hinglish. The dataset consisted of comments collected from Instagram and Twitter and a transliterated version of the IIT Bombay English-Hindi Corpus (Kunchukuttan et al., 2018). Word piece tokenization was used, and the weights of the model were fine-tuned using CNN, LSTM, and a neural network. Hinglish HateBERT outperformed all models on the HOT (Mathur, Sawhney, Ayyar, & Ratn Shah, 2018) and TRAC-2 (Kumar et al., 2020) datasets in terms of accuracy, weighted precision, weighted recall and weighted F1 score, and performed comparably to mBERT on the (Bohra et al., 2018) dataset. Another study that examines the effectiveness of transformer-based models in hate speech detection was conducted by (Sengupta et al., 2022), who implement word-level, character-level, and subword-level deep networks to examine five offense traits, namely, aggression, hate, sarcasm, humor, and stance in Hinglish. A self-supervised pseudo-labeling framework is used to label tweets from the datasets of previous studies (Bohra et al., 2018) (Kumar et al., 2018) (Swami et al., 2018) (Khandelwal et al., 2018). The two proposed custom models: Character-Word Hierarchical Attention Model (C-HAN) and Subword-level transformer outperform the other approaches for 3 out of 5 techniques, with an F1 score of around 90%. This highlights the importance of sub-word-level representations for noisy code-mixed data.

A different approach was adopted by (Biradar et al., 2021), who first converted the multilingual data into monolingual using IndicNLP and English-to-Hindi libraries for transliteration and translation, followed by the Transformer based Interpretation and Feature Extraction Model (TIF-DNN) which utilises mBERT for feature extraction and obtained a higher accuracy than (Bohra et al., 2018). The authors highlight that translation quality had a significant impact on model accuracy. The focus was shifted from hate speech detection by (Khan et al., 2024), who tried to instead predict the users which may become targets of hate speech. They presented the novel Hate Speech Target Dataset (HSTD) which consists of 1500 target and 1500 non-target tweets. Due to the small size of the dataset, Naïve bayes outperformed an ensemble of transformer models, achieving an accuracy of 93% compared to 89.29%. The authors suggest that posts that contained abusive or negative language were more likely to be targeted by hateful responses, and PoS tagging positively impacted classification. Extra-linguistic features such as details about the author can provide valuable context that can be improve classification accuracy of hate speech classifiers. A 3-tier pipeline containing profanity modelling, graph embeddings, and author profiling was utilised by (Chopra et al., 2020) to perform hate speech classification using the (Bohra et al., 2018) and (Mathur, Ratn Shah, et al., 2018) datasets. A profanity lexicon is used to identify offensive language, a social media interaction pattern is encoded from follower and retweet graphs, and user behaviours and patterns are analysed within Hinglish speaking communities. Additionally, bias mitigation was carried out by calculating bias axes and neutralizing and equalizing embeddings to remove religion, gender, and ethnicity-based biases. The CNN + Bidirectional LSTM + Attention model outperformed existing benchmarks, achieving F1 scores of 0.73 (HS dataset) and 0.77 (HEOT dataset). The profanity vectors and graph-based author profiling were shown to improve performance significantly, whereas the debiasing algorithm both reduced bias and improved classification accuracy. A unique approach to addressing data scarcity for under-resourced languages was introduced by (Guragain et al., 2024), who examined hate speech detection in Devanagari-scripted Hindi and Nepali. Backtranslation was used to generate synthetic samples for data augmentation, and cosine similarity, with a threshold of 0.9, was used to ensure that the synthetic and original samples were semantically similar. Pre-trained models were fine-tuned on the resulting dataset of 13,695 instances, where XLM-RoBERTa achieved the highest recall of (0.7381), and MuRIL-Abusive achieved the highest precision of 0.7572. The authors highlight that some cultural nuance was lost during backtranslation, potentially impacting model performance.

Despite significant advancements in misogyny detection over the past decade, there is still a lack of large, annotated datasets, explainable classifiers, and fairness in misogyny classifiers, particularly for code-mixed languages. One of the first studies that examined misogyny and aggression detection in Indian languages (Indian English, Hindi, and Bangla) was conducted by (Bhattacharya et al., 2020) where they used character and word n-grams with an SVM classifier on a dataset of over 25,000 YouTube comments. The baseline model achieved an F1-score of 0.87 for Hindi, 0.89 for Bangla, and 0.93 for English. A high correlation (80%) was found between misogynous and aggressive comments, and the proportion of misogynous and aggressive comments was found to be higher in Hindi and Bangla. The authors noted challenges such as ambiguity between gendered and general abusive language and the inclusion of nuances such as satire and sarcasm. Extending the research to other modalities, (A. Singh et al., 2024) presented a multimodal dataset of 5,054 memes in Hinglish collected from Facebook, Instagram, and Reddit, and annotated for two tasks: binary categorization of misogyny and multi-label classification into objectification, prejudice, and humiliation. When compared to unimodal models, the mutilmodal BiT + MuRIL performed better with a macro F1-Score of 0.7319 and Area Under the Receiver Operating Characteristic curve (AUC-ROC) of 0.8168 on binary classification, whereas BiT + RoBERTa achieved the highest macro F1-Score of 0.527, weighted F1-Score of 0.6303, and AUC-ROC of 0.8183 on multi-label classification.

Explainable, Fair and Debiased Hate Speech Classifiers

Deep learning models are considered black boxes because their decision-making process cannot be directly analyzed to ensure that they are behaving logically. XAI techniques allow for the exploration and examination of model behavior to ensure trust and accountability in AI models. Hate speech detection is a sensitive issue where the model's decision can have significant legal and social implications and understanding the decision-making process of the model is crucial to avoid unfair consequences. There are several types of XAI techniques such as model agnostic methods, feature importance methods, and post-hoc methods. LIME is a model agnostic approach which learns an approximation of the model around a single instance to provide explanations. In the study by (Yadav, Kaushik, & McDaid, 2023), LIME was used to determine that hate speech classifiers can sometimes become biased to the presence of slur words, leading to misclassification. SHAP is another model agnostic technique based on game theoretic approach and can provide global and local explanations by associating Shapely values to features. Feature importance approaches, such as attention weight analysis, aim to measure the impact of a feature on the model's prediction (Serrano & Smith, 2019). Similarly, Integrated Gradients (IG) calculate attribution score for each input feature and measure its contribution to the final output. These approaches can provide a tool for stakeholders to understand the functionality and trustworthiness of a model before deployment. Despite the expanding research in XAI, it remains an emerging field, and a limited number of studies focus on explainable hate speech detection. Furthermore, research into explainable hate speech detection in code-mixed and under resourced languages is even more under-explored, revealing a significant gap in the literature.

One notable study addressing explainable hate speech detection was conducted by (Mathew et al., 2021) who introduced the HateXplain dataset which classified posts from Twitter and Gab into 3 classes: hate, offensive, and normal. Additionally, the human rationale for classification is included. The models that perform the best on explainability metrics were trained using human rationale, which was shown to reduce unintended bias. Expanding on this, (Kim et al., 2022) employed the Masked Rationale Prediction (MRP) approach on the HateXplain dataset, where the BERT model is trained to predict masked human rationales by referring to surrounding tokens and their unmasked rationales. The model is evaluated on empirical metrics such as accuracy, macro-F1, and AUC-ROC, bias-based metrics such as Generalized Mean of Bias (GMB), Subgroup-AUC, Background Negative Subgroup Positive (BNSP-AUC), Background Positive Subgroup Negative (BPSN-AUC), and explainability based metrics such as plausibility and faithfulness. The BERT-MRP approach outperformed the BERT-HateXplain model (Mathew et al., 2021), indicating that the approach reduced bias towards target groups, effectively detects implicit hate speech, and is context-aware. Explainable hate speech detection in under-resourced languages is severely limited. One notable approach was 'DeepHateExplainer' (Karim et al., 2021), which was an explainable hate speech framework for Bengali. Out of the selected models, XLM-RoBERTa outperformed other models on the faithfulness metric from the Evaluating Rationales And Simple English Reasoning (ERASER) benchmark (DeYoung et al., 2019), underscoring that models that score higher on empirical metrics such as accuracy and F1-score, may not be the most explainable or interpretable. The ERASER benchmark is a standardized approach to evaluate models based on human rationale. Therefore, evaluating hate speech classifiers on explainability metrics provides a better understanding of model performance in a sensitive domain like hate speech detection. To address data scarcity in explainable hate speech detection, (Ansari et al., 2024) proposed an approach that implements three data augmentation techniques, namely, Easy Data Augmentation (EDA), Back Translation (BT), and Contextual Augmentation with BERT on a dataset of Facebook and YouTube comments and Mendeley Cyberbullying dataset (Ejaz et al., 2024). LIME and IG were the applied XAI techniques and Area Over Perturbation Curve (AOPC), Log-Odds Score, and coherence score were used to evaluate the models. The approach was shown to improve model performance on both classification accuracy and the explainability metrics, showing higher AOPC and coherence scores and lower log-odds scores. LIME and IG also highlighted relevant keywords such as 'hate' and 'murdering', which align with the human rationale for hate speech categorization.

Explainability is interconnected with fairness, as XAI techniques can serve as a tool to uncover biases in the model's decision-making process. Fairness in a hate speech classifier ensures that the model performs equally well for all demographics and does not perpetuate societal bias and further harm towards targeted minorities. Studies have highlighted that hate speech classifiers can exhibit biases such as racial and gender bias (Sap et al., 2019) (Nozza et al., 2019). These biases can be introduced due to multiple factors, such as biased training data, inherent algorithmic biases, and other sources. Studies have suggested approaches such as data augmentation (Zmigrod et al., 2019), adversarial debiasing (Zhang et al., 2018), and the use of fairness aware algorithms (Hardt et al., 2016) to reduce model bias. The task of debiasing hate speech classifiers becomes even trickier in the context of code-mixed languages, which includes additional complexities such as cultural and social nuances, lack of benchmark datasets, and linguistic diversity. The issue of biased datasets abusive language detection was discussed by (Mandl et al., 2019), who demonstrate that the performance of hate speech classifiers drops when the bias is removed. They provide a distinction between explicit and implicit abuse, stating that the former contains abusive words whereas the latter is expressed through subtle means such as sarcasm and jokes. Datasets obtained through biased sampling were shown to have a higher degree of implicit abuse, whereas boosted random sampling provided a more balanced dataset in terms of abusive content. The Waseem dataset (Waseem & Hovy, 2016) was shown to contain topic bias due to the presence of a high number of micro-posts about women in sports. Words such as 'football', 'sport', and 'commentator' demonstrated a high correlation to abuse, even though they have no negative connotation. The Waseem dataset was also shown to contain author bias, due to the classifier learning the writing styles or topics from certain authors. Similarly, (Dias Oliva et al., 2021) observed that the Perspective tool ranked the twitter accounts of drag queens (16.68% to 37.81%) higher in toxicity than the accounts of white nationalists (19.68 and 33.46), and Donald Trump (21.84%), due to its inability to grasp social context while determining toxicity. As in many cases, certain offensive terms have been reclaimed by members of the LGBTQ community, and 'mock impoliteness' is used in a playful manner within the community (Murray, 1979). The study emphasizes that automated systems can reinforce harmful biases about a community if the pro-social functions of such speech are disregarded by filtering it. Therefore, explainability, fairness and bias mitigation in hate speech are crucial for building accountable and socially responsible AI systems.

Shared Tasks and Challenges

Shared tasks and challenges play a crucial role in improving hate speech detection by providing benchmark datasets and innovative approaches to improve classification scores. Some of the shared tasks that regularly conduct hate speech detection in numerous languages have been discussed in this section. Table 2 discusses the various shared tasks that have been conducted in the past to counter online abuse and offensive language. The details of the datasets released as part of the shared task are also provided, along with the classification tasks and best results.

Table 2. Datasets made available through shared tasks for Hate speech detection

Name	Dataset	Tasks	Best Results
HASOC-2019 (Mandl et al., 2019)	7005 English, 5983 Hindi, and 4669 German posts from Twitter, Facebook	3 levels: A: Presence of offense, B: Type of offense, Target of hate	Macro-F1- English: 0.78, Hindi: 0.81, German: 0.61 (Subtask-A)
HASOC-2020 (Mandl et al., 2020)	5335 English, 3425 German, and 6404 Hindi tweets	2 levels: A: Presence of offense, B: Type of offense	English: 0.51, Hindi: 0.53, German: 0.52 (Subtask-A)
HASOC-2021 (Mandl et al., 2021)	5124 English, 2499 Marathi, and 6126 Hindi tweets	2 levels: A: Presence of offense, B: Type of offense	Marathi: 0.91, Hindi: 0.78, English: 0.83 (Subtask-A)

continued on following page

Table 2. Continued

Name	Dataset	Tasks	Best Results
AMI @ Evalita (2018) (Fersini, Nozza, et al., 2018)	5000 Italian and 5000 English tweets	2 levels: A: Misogyny identification, B: Behavior and target type	Accuracy - Italian: 0.844, English: 0.704 (A), macro-F1- Italian: 0.501, English: 0. 406 (B)
AMI @ IberEval (2018) (Fersini, Rosso, et al., 2018)	4138 Spanish and 3977 English tweets	2 levels: A: Misogyny identification, B: Behavior and target type	Accuracy- English: 0.9132, Spanish: 0.8146 (A); English: 0.4424, Spanish: 0.4461 (B)
AMI @ Evalita (2020) (Fersini et al., 2020)	6000 Raw (training) tweets and 5830 Synthetic samples in Italian	2 levels: A: Misogyny and aggressive behavior identification, B: Unbiased misogyny identification	A: Average macro-F1 score = 0.7406, B: average macro-F1 score= 0.8825
GermEval (2018) (Wiegand et al., 2018)	8,541 German tweets	Task 1: binary classification into Offense vs Other; Task 2: 4 classes: abuse, insult, profanity, other	Task 1: macro-F1 = 76.77%; Task 2: 52.71%
GermEval Task 2 (2019) (Struß et al., 2019)	7,025 German tweets	3 levels: Task 1: binary classification into Offense vs Other; Task 2: 4 classes: abuse, insult, profanity, other; Task 3: implicit vs. explicit	Task 1: macro-F1 = 76.95%; Task 2: 53.59%, Task 3: Accuracy = 86.77%, F-score = 73.11
ICHCL-2021 (Satapara et al., 2021)	7,088 Hinglish tweets	Binary classification into NOT and HOF	Macro-F1 = 0.7253
ICHCL-2022	English, Hindi, and German Twitter	Binary classification into NOT and HOF; categorization of hate into SHOF, CHOF, and NONE.	Macro-F1 score of 0.7083 for binary categorization and 0.4939 for contextual categorization.
ICHCL-2023	Hinglish Twitter	Binary classification into NOT and HOF; Binary classification into NOT and HOF; categorization of hate into SHOF, CHOF, and NONE.	F1-score = 0.8079 for binary categorization and 0.6541 for contextual categorization.
EDOS @ SemEval-2023 (Kirk et al., 2023)	20,796 labelled posts and 1M unlabeled Reddit and 1M unlabeled Gab posts in English	3 levels: Task A: sexist and non-sexist posts; Task B: 4 categories: Threats, plans to harm and incitement, Derogation, Animosity, and Prejudiced Discussion; and Task C: 11 fine-grained vectors	Task A: macro-F1 score = 0.8746, Task B: macro-F1 score = 0.7326, Task C: macro-F1 score = 0.5606

HASOC: The HASOC shared task is aimed at detecting hate speech from online posts in English and Indo-Aryan languages. The HASOC subtrack was held at FIRE 2021 and conducted in English, Hindi, and Marathi tweets (Mandl et al., 2021). The challenge was divided into two subtasks: Task A which performed binary classification into Hate and Not Offensive, and Task B which performed fine-grained classification into Hate speech, Offensive, and Profanity. Similarly, HASOC 2020

(Mandl et al., 2020) consisted of the same two classification subtasks as HASOC 2021 for hate speech classification in Hindi, German, and English. The first edition of the shared task, HASOC 2019 (Mandl et al., 2019) included a binary classification and three fine-grained classification subtasks for hate speech identification in English, Hindi, and German. Transformer-based models generally achieved the highest scores on the subtasks.

Focusing specifically on code-mixed languages, Identification of Conversational Hate-Speech in Code-Mixed Languages (Satapara et al., 2021) (ICHCL) was offered as subtask-2 of HASOC at FIRE-2021. The dataset consisted of approximately 7000 tweets in Hinglish. Each instance in the dataset consists of the complete context of the tweet, including the parent tweet, replies, and comments. The tweets were divided into two classes: Non-Hate-Offensive (NOT) and Hate and Offensive (HOF). The best macro-F1 score obtained was 0.7253 by using a hard voting-based ensemble of the following 3 transformer-based models: IndicBERT, Multilingual-BERT, and XML-RoBERTa. The cross-lingual embeddings from transformers were fine-tuned, and a dropout layer and fully connected layer were added to the end of model. The probabilities of the 3 models were then combined and passed through a SoftMax layer.

The ICHCL subtask at HASOC 2022 consisted of two tasks: binary classification into 'HOF' and 'NOT', and multiclass classification into Standalone Hate (SHOF), Contextual Hate (CHOF), and Non-Hate (None). The datasets used in the tasks consisted of around 5200 posts in English, Hinglish, and code-mixed German, and were collected from controversial topics on Twitter. The highest macro-F1 score achieved for binary classification was 0.7083 by concatenating the posts, comments, and replies with the [SEP] token and fine-tuning Google MuRIL. The highest macro-F1 score for multiclass classification achieved was 0.4939 by augmenting emoji descriptions with the concatenated tweets and fine-tuning XLM-RoBERTa. The findings of the shared task suggest that emojis can enrich data and improve classification, the inclusion of context can greatly impact model performance, and there is much scope for improvement in differentiating between standalone and contextual hate. Similarly, for ICHCL 2023, the top performing model employs an LLM for classification and achieves an F1 score of 0.8079 for binary classification and a macro-F1 score of 0.65414 for contextual hate classification. The authors recommend the use of LLMs for data augmentation as a future direction for the shared task.

Automatic Misogyny Identification (AMI): Focusing specifically on focused on misogyny detection, the AMI shared task at Evalita 2018 (Fersini, Rosso, et al., 2018) was conducted in English and Italian tweets. The shared task consisted of two subtasks: Subtask A for misogyny identification, and Subtask B for categorization of misogynistic behavior and identification of the target of such behavior. Additional fine-grained labels for misogyny identification provided were as follows: Stereotype & Objectification, Dominance, Derailing, Sexual Harassment & Threats of Violence, and Discredit. Lower scores on the multi-label classification suggested that more data should be collected on different types of misogynistic behavior to improve model performance. The AMI task at Evalita (2020) (Fersini et al., 2020) conducted misogyny classification in Italian, and examined unintended bias in the misogyny classifier. For subtask A (Misogyny and Aggressive Behavior Identification), a raw dataset is used consisting of 6000 train tweets from AMI 2018 (Fersini, Nozza, et al., 2018) and approximately 1000 new test tweets were collected from Twitter and labelled accordingly. The train data has been enriched by labelling aggressive behavior. For subtask B, a synthetic dataset has been curated by creating several templates containing positive and negative verbs/adjectives from a list of identity terms, conveying both misogynistic and non-misogynistic behavior. The synthetic dataset consists of 1007 training samples and 954 testing samples each for misogynous and non-misogynous classes. The analysis of the model results implies that binary misogyny identification was a relatively easy task compared to aggression identification, possibly due to the subjectivity of aggressiveness. Additionally, model fairness can be increased using domain-dependent debiasing methods.

SemEval: Another shared task dedicated specifically to misogyny detection was the Explainable Detection of Online Sexism at SemEval-2023 (Kirk et al., 2023), which provided a new hierarchical taxonomy for classifying sexist content by providing fine-grained vectors for sexism. The dataset consisted of approximately 20,000 posts from Reddit and Gab. The competition consisted of 3 subtasks: Task A: Binary classification of sexist and non-sexist posts; Task B: Classification of sexism into 4 categories: Threats, plans to harm and incitement, Derogation, Animosity, and Prejudiced Discussion; and Task C: Classification into 11 fine-grained vectors. Additional unlabeled sets of 1M Reddit and 1M Gab posts were also provided. For Task A, the highest macro-F1 achieved was 0.8746, by further pre-training DeBERTa-v3 and TwHINBERT on the unlabeled dataset and an additional Kaggle dataset. For Task B, the highest macro-F1 obtained was 0.7326 using an instruction-based PaLM model. For Task C, the best macro-F1 achieved was 0.5606 by further pre-training the DeBERTa-v3 on the unlabeled data and using normalized temperature-scaled cross entropy.

GermEval: The GermEval-2018 Shared Task on the Identification of Offensive Language (Wiegand et al., 2018) was performed on a dataset of 8541 German tweets. The classification task consisted of two subtasks: Task 1: Coarse-grained binary classification into two classes (Offense and Other), Task 2: Fine-grained classification into four classes (Profanity, Insult, Abuse, Other). The tweets were sampled from the timeline of approximately 100 users, instead of relying on keyword searches which can limit the vocabulary. The train and test datasets were split in a manner that a specific user's tweets were present in only one set. This was done to ensure that the model does not become biased by learning the user's writing style.

For Task 1, the highest macro-averaged precision was 77.42%, macro-averaged recall was 76.13%, and macro-F1 score was 76.77%. The best performing model was a stacked classifier taking in the following 5 features: token and character n-grams, important n-grams and tokens according to TF-IDF, and word embeddings. Three base classifiers (maximum entropy and two random forest ensembles) were trained, followed by a maximum entropy meta-level classifier for the final prediction (Padilla Montani & Schüller, 2018). For Task 2, the highest macro-averaged precision was 58.85%, macro-averaged recall was 49.13%, and macro-F1 score was 52.71%. The best performing system for this task was a sequentially combined BiLSTM-CNN model and transfer learning (Wiedemann et al., 2018). The GermEval 2019 (Struß et al., 2019) shared task was performed on a dataset of 7,025 tweets and consisted of an Implicit vs Explicit offense classification in addition to the coarse grained and fine-grained classification tasks. For Task 1, the highest macro-F1 was 76.95%. For Task 2, the highest macro-F1 score was 53.59%. For Task 3, the highest accuracy achieved was 86.77% and F1-score was 73.11. The best performing model was a BERT model pre-trained on a corpus of 6.2 million German tweets and fine-tuned on the datasets of GermEval-2018 and 2019.

LIMITATIONS

Despite the significant progress in hate speech detection, current benchmark approaches face numerous drawbacks, especially in the context of code-mixed and low-resource languages. It is important to address these challenges to avoid causing further harm to marginalized communities. Some of the common challenges that NLP approaches face in hate speech detection are discussed below:

- Challenges in Modeling: Language models rely on distributional hypotheses and do not understand the pragmatics of a language well. This can cause hate speech classifiers to pick up on spurious correlations to make predictions (Rahman et al., 2021) (Wiegand et al., 2019). Quantitative benchmark results cannot be solely relied upon, as studies have demonstrated that minor adversarial changes that significantly alter the meaning can impact the performance of hate speech classifiers. Models also do not generalize well as they overfit to tokens and token interaction patterns rather than understanding the concept of hate speech. Additionally, variations in social media language may include obfuscation and code words (Yin & Zubiaga, 2021), further complicating detection.
- Datasets and annotation process: Over the past few years, several shared tasks have been organized to facilitate collaboration in developing hate speech

classifiers. These challenges have been conducted in various languages such as English, Italian (Fersini, Rosso, et al., 2018), Hindi, and Bengali (Mandl et al., 2021), to perform coarse grain and fine-grained classification of hateful comments (Fersini, Rosso, et al., 2018). Despite the recent surge of interest, there is still a scarcity of datasets that focus on specific targets, such as women, religious minorities, and the LGBT community. The existing datasets are mostly in English, and there is a serious lack of under-resourced languages and code-switched languages. The current hate speech classifiers also have difficulty in the fine-grained classification of the types of abusive content. The curation of robust datasets is necessary for training effective hate speech classifiers. Balanced and larger datasets have shown to improve model performance for hate speech classification in under-represented and code-mixed languages (Dhanya & Balakrishnan, 2021). Several studies have crowd-sourced the process or hired expert annotators for the annotation process (Basile et al., 2019). Reliable annotation relies heavily on detailed and clearly defined instructions for the annotators (Ross et al., 2017) (de Gibert et al., 2018). A high inter-annotator agreement is difficult to achieve, as different individuals have different perceptions of what constitutes hate speech (Fortuna & Nunes, 2018). Additionally, inter-annotator agreement cannot be reliably considered an indicator of the quality of a dataset. The context, personal biases, world knowledge, and socio-cultural influences of annotators can result in low agreement scores (Schmidt & Wiegand, 2017) (Waseem, 2016). There is a lack of standardized criteria for hate speech annotation, and the data source and sampling strategies can introduce bias towards certain individuals or keywords. This process is time and resource intensive, and annotating huge volumes of abusive content can also have a detrimental impact on the mental state of the individual (Steiger et al., 2021).

- Context: The context of a conversation greatly contributes to whether a statement contains hate speech or not (Watanabe et al., 2018) (Schmidt & Wiegand, 2017) (Satapara et al., 2021). The nuance and complexity of language is significant challenge for NLP systems, and context and world-knowledge are required to correctly classify a statement (Frenda, 2018) (Wiegand et al., 2018) (Schmidt & Wiegand, 2017). Politics influence the definition of hate speech, making it difficult to coin a universal definition (Fortuna et al., 2022). The presence of elements such as sarcasm, humor, and irony can also lead to misclassification. A statement depicting hate speech may not always include slurs, and certain offensive words such as 'Nigga', and 'bitch', may have been reclaimed by the target communities and used in a non-hateful manner. Social media posts often contain misspellings and homophones, which may not be picked up by the classifier (Warner & Hirschberg, 2012).

- Model explainability: The survey suggests that a limited number of methodologies have utilized XAI algorithms to explain model decisions. Criminalization of online hate speech would require hate speech classifiers to be trustworthy and unbiased. XAI techniques can provide human readable and understandable explanations of model decisions, which can provide legal accountability while also preventing the wrongful penalization of innocent people and hampering freedom of speech.
- Types of hate speech: Although recent studies have shown great results in detecting hate speech in English and other languages, differentiating between the different types of abusive behavior is still a challenging task for machine learning algorithms. For instance, it is important to understand the nature and severity of misogyny to develop better tools for countering it (Fersini, Nozza, et al., 2018) (Goenaga et al., 2018). Studies suggest that online hate speech based on race is most common (Silva et al., 2016) (de Gibert et al., 2018), highlighting the need to develop systems for different forms of hate speech.
- Lower number of positive samples: In real-world scenarios, the number of instances of hate speech or offensive language are relatively low compared to non-offensive content (Schmidt & Wiegand, 2017). This results in imbalanced datasets, as the data is skewed towards one class. The models need to be trained and calibrated as such, so that they can more sensitively detect instances of the minority class, which is hate speech.
- Code-mixing: Code-switched languages, such as Hinglish, present a unique set of challenges for NLP tools. They lack grammatical structure (Lal et al., 2019), usually have informal transliteration (R. Singh et al., 2018), follow inconsistent syntactic rules, and inconsistent spelling (Mathur, Ratn Shah, et al., 2018). Additionally, it is very important to capture the social and cultural context of the text to accurately understand if it is hate speech. Therefore, special algorithms and language-specific datasets are needed to improve hate speech detection.
- Bias: Inherent bias in AI systems has been well documented (Yin & Zubiaga, 2021). These biases can be introduced into the system at any step of the process, such as dataset compilation, feature extraction, and model training. Sampling bias may cause over representation of certain authors and impact model performance(Yin & Zubiaga, 2021). Based on previous biased decisions, models can make racist decisions, such as predicting black people as future offenders (Angwin et al., 2016). Word2Vec embeddings have shown to exhibit gender biased (Bolukbasi et al., 2016). Similarly, a model may classify a statement as misogynistic simply because it contains words like 'women' (Nozza et al., 2019). Although recent studies have shown great results in detecting hate speech in English and other languages, differentiating between

the different types of abusive behavior is still a challenging task for machine learning algorithms. For instance, it is important to understand the nature and severity of misogyny to develop better tools for countering it (Fersini, Nozza, et al., 2018)(Goenaga et al., 2018). Additionally, approaches for measuring model fairness and bias towards different groups may be limited to the lack of reliable demographic data.

DISCUSSION

In this section, we discuss the findings of the review study with respect to the research questions that were posed in the 'Motivation' section.

- What are the current state-of-the-art machine learning and deep learning tools available for detection of online hate speech? Which studies have focused specifically on detection of misogyny? Which studies have been performed on code-switched data?

As discussed in the 'Literature Review' Section, research has extensively explored solutions to prevent online hate speech using both traditional machine learning and complex deep learning architectures. From the most recent shared tasks, it is evident that transformer-based pre-trained language models, such as BERT, perform well on the task of hate speech detection with minimum task-specific fine-tuning (Mandl et al., 2021). Other deep learning models, such as CNNs and LSTMs have also given comparable results (Lynn et al., 2019a). Deep learning models tend to achieve better performance due to their ability to capture the context in the text. In the reviewed literature, machine learning models have performed comparably. Feature engineering has been performed using traditional approaches such as TF-IDF, word and character n-grams (Guest et al., 2021), and bag-of-words. Several studies have also generated contextual embeddings through techniques such as GloVe, Word2Vec, and FastText. Out of the different studies reviewed, most considered misogyny detection along with other forms of hate speech based on factors such as race, and nationality. Very few studies focused specifically on misogyny (Fersini, Rosso, et al., 2018), and the scarcity increases for multilingual and code-mixed data (Mandl et al., 2019). Multilingual models such as IndicBERT and multilingual BERT were used to handle code-mixed data, which presents several unique challenges. Development of language-specific tools and datasets can greatly help in advancing the research in hate speech detection in multilingual settings.

- What are the different hate speech datasets available for training and evaluating machine learning models? Which datasets have been dedicated specifically to misogyny detection? How many datasets exist for code-switched languages?

Robust datasets are critical to developing efficient hate speech classifiers. Several datasets in various languages have been made publicly available from the shared tasks that are regularly held for hate speech detection. For example, HASOC (English, Hindi, Marathi, etc.), AMI (Italian), and SemEval (Spanish). From the review study, it became evident that very few datasets are dedicated to misogyny detection (Fersini, Rosso, et al., 2018). Of those available, most of them are in English, or are annotated as part of broader hate speech taxonomies. The datasets follow various labeling schemes, and several studies have also examined fine-grained classification of hate speech. There is a scarcity of datasets in under-resourced and code-switched languages. The available datasets for under-resources languages are also often smaller in size. It is important to focus on a specific target such as misogyny, as each subtype of hate speech has specific features. The limited availability of hate speech and misogyny detection datasets in code-mixed languages highlights the need for a robust dataset that includes both broad and fine-grained categorizations.

- What are the Explainable AI approaches available for online hate speech detection? Which studies have focused on developing explainable classifiers for code-switched languages?

Explainable AI is an essential tool to understand the decision-making process of a model. Datasets and models for hate speech classification can contain several types of bias (Wiegand et al., 2019), and XAI can help in increasing model transparency and trust by uncovering such biases. There has been some initiative taken to include explainability in systems for hate speech detection (Mathew et al., 2021) (Karim et al., 2021)through different techniques. However, the studies are low in number, and more initiative needs to be taken for English and other languages. The integration of XAI in hate speech classifiers for code-mixed data is rare and challenging due to the informal structure of the text and its linguistic complexity.

- What are the limitations and challenges that currently impede the development of a robust system for preventing online hate speech detection?

Despite the significant advancements made during the past decade, the research in hate speech detection still faces several challenges. The lack of datasets and studies for specific targets (women, ethnic groups, LGBT+ community), and in languages other than English is a major drawback. The background of the annotators may greatly impact the classification labels, leading to subjectivity in annotations (Ross et al., 2017). The existing datasets may contain several types of biases, which may be further amplified by the model (Wiegand et al., 2019) (Fersini et al., 2020). Fine-grained classification into the types of hateful language is still a challenge for many deep learning approaches. Moreover, false negatives can have a significant impact by allowing hateful speech and filtering non-hateful content, which disproportionately affects marginalized communities. Code-switched languages present a different set of challenges, such as lack of grammar, structure, and definite spelling. There is a lack of off-the-shelf NLP tools to handle such languages. Although deep learning models achieve better results at hate speech classification, their explainability remains a concern, as the research in explainable hate speech detection remains limited. The literature has also suggested approaches to improve model performance for researchers moving forward, such as accounting for conversational context, sampling data from a diverse range of sources, use of scales to measure dimensions of hate speech, and new evaluation metrics and paradigms (Fortuna et al., 2022). Additionally, models should be able to handle rare words and obfuscation and include demographic awareness (Yin & Zubiaga, 2021).

Although the hypothesis that NLP tools can detect multilingual and code-mixed misogynistic hate speech online and provide interpretable results is theoretically supported by the review, it requires further empirical validation for confirmation. Studies have demonstrated the effectiveness of machine learning and deep learning models in countering various types of hate speech annotated through different perspectives (Yin & Zubiaga, 2021) (Fortuna & Nunes, 2018). However, there are several unique challenges encountered in multilingual and code-mixed hate speech detection due to linguistic nuances and informal structure of the language (Bohra et al., 2018) (Mathur, Sawhney, Ayyar, & Shah, 2018), and there is still scope of improvement in model performance, explainability, and bias mitigation (Mathew et al., 2021). In the context of misogyny detection in code-mixed and other languages, it is crucial to develop robust datasets which include fine-grained categorization of misogyny and rationale for categorization to build effective detection models (Fersini et al., 2020). Lack of standardized datasets is a primary concern for multilingual and code-mixed hate speech detection due to the linguistic diversity, subjectivity and cultural context in hate speech, and lack of standard guidelines for hate speech detection. This results in the development of systems which do not generalize well to other datasets. Additionally, models do not perform as well at the categorization of the subtypes of hate speech and misogyny, and more implicit and subtle forms of hate (Mandl et al., 2019). Unintended biases in hate speech detection are another major concern in the domain (Fersini et al., 2020). Hate speech is a serious issue and can have serious legal consequences. Therefore, AI systems that make crucial decisions on hate speech detection need to be trustworthy, explainable, and fair. A limited number of studies have currently explored explainability, fairness, and bias mitigation in hate speech classifiers, highlighting the gap in literature. The development of explainable and fair hate speech detection models can greatly improve digital safety for marginalized communities and must be undertaken through interdisciplinary collaborations between experts from gender studies, linguistics, and NLP.

CONCLUSION

This chapter offers a comprehensive overview of recent advancements in hate speech detection, highlighting the benefits of state-of-the-art machine learning and deep learning models in filtering harmful content on social media platforms such as Reddit, Twitter, and Facebook. The findings indicate that deep neural networks are particularly effective at detecting hateful and offensive posts. Collaborative challenges and shared tasks such as HASOC and SemEval have significantly contributed towards the advancement of the current-state-of-the-art in hate speech detection. However, the research in the domain remains in its early stages. There is a notable gap in studies and datasets in low-resource languages and multilingual contexts, especially for specific targets of abuse, such as women and the LGBT community. The protective measures put in place by online forums are currently inadequate and must be further improved upon, as ensuring user safety is the responsibility of the platform. The future scope of this study is to focus on the creation of datasets and development of models for hate speech detection in code-switched and low-resource languages. Given the sensitive, subjective, and contextual nature of hate speech, expert annotators must be preferred rather than crowd-sourcing the annotation process. The survey also highlights the need for improving model transparency and fairness, promoting the adoption of XAI and debiasing techniques, which can be greatly beneficial in understanding model decisions, improving errors, and removing any inherent bias from the model.

ACKNOWLEDGEMENT

This research is partially funded through an internal fee waiver scholarship from Dundalk Institute of Technology.

REFERENCES

Acheampong, P., Zhiwen, L., Hiran, K. K., Serwaa, O. E., Boateng, F., & Bediako, I. A. (2018). Examining the Intervening Role of Age and Gender on mobile payment Acceptance in Ghana: UTAUT Model. *Canadian Journal of Applied Science and Technology*, *5*(2).

Amnesty International. (2020). *Troll Patrol India*. Exposing Online Abuse Faced by Women Politicians in India.

Angwin, J., Larson, J., Mattu, S., & Kirchner, L. (2016). Machine bias. In *Ethics of Data and Analytics* (pp. 254–264). Auerbach Publications.

Ansari, G., Kaur, P., & Saxena, C. (2024). Data Augmentation for Improving Explainability of Hate Speech Detection. *Arabian Journal for Science and Engineering*, *49*(3), 3609–3621. DOI: 10.1007/s13369-023-08100-4

Anzovino, M., Fersini, E., & Rosso, P. (2018). Automatic identification and classification of misogynistic language on twitter. *Lecture Notes in Computer Science (Including Subseries Lecture Notes in Artificial Intelligence and Lecture Notes in Bioinformatics), 10859 LNCS*, 57–64. DOI: 10.1007/978-3-319-91947-8_6

Asia McGowan: Youtuber killed by mentally ill stalker at Michigan school. (2016).

Attanasio, G., Nozza, D., Pastor, E., & Hovy, D. (2022). Benchmarking post-hoc interpretability approaches for transformer-based misogyny detection. *Proceedings of NLP Power! The First Workshop on Efficient Benchmarking in NLP*. DOI: 10.18653/v1/2022.nlppower-1.11

Basile, V., Bosco, C., Fersini, E., Nozza, D., Patti, V., Pardo, F. M. R., Rosso, P., & Sanguinetti, M. (2019). Semeval-2019 task 5: Multilingual detection of hate speech against immigrants and women in twitter. *Proceedings of the 13th International Workshop on Semantic Evaluation*, 54–63. DOI: 10.18653/v1/S19-2007

Bhattacharya, S., Singh, S., Kumar, R., Bansal, A., Bhagat, A., Dawer, Y., Lahiri, B., & Kr Ojha, A. (2020). *Developing a Multilingual Annotated Corpus of Misogyny and Aggression*. http://bit.ly/2FhLMVz

Biradar, S., Saumya, S., & Chauhan, A. (2021). Hate or Non-hate: Translation based hate speech identification in Code-Mixed Hinglish data set. *Proceedings - 2021 IEEE International Conference on Big Data. Big Data, 2021*, 2470–2475. DOI: 10.1109/BigData52589.2021.9671526

Bohra, A., Vijay, D., Singh, V., Akhtar, S. S., & Shrivastava, M. (2018a). A dataset of Hindi-English code-mixed social media text for hate speech detection. *Proceedings of the Second Workshop on Computational Modeling of People's Opinions, Personality, and Emotions in Social Media*, 36–41. DOI: 10.18653/v1/W18-1105

Bohra, A., Vijay, D., Singh, V., Akhtar, S. S., & Shrivastava, M. (2018b). *A Dataset of Hindi-English Code-Mixed Social Media Text for Hate Speech Detection*. https://github.com/deepanshu1995/HateSpeech-Hindi-

Bolukbasi, T., Chang, K.-W., Zou, J. Y., Saligrama, V., & Kalai, A. T. (2016). Man is to computer programmer as woman is to homemaker? debiasing word embeddings. *Advances in Neural Information Processing Systems*, •••, 29.

Chan, S. (2016). *Right-Wing Extremist Convicted of Murdering Jo Cox, a U.K. Lawmaker* -. The New York Times. https://www.nytimes.com/2016/11/23/world/europe/thomas-mair-convicted-murder-jo-cox.html

Chen, T., & Guestrin, C. (2016). XGBoost: A scalable tree boosting system. *Proceedings of the ACM SIGKDD International Conference on Knowledge Discovery and Data Mining, 13-17-August-2016*, 785–794. DOI: 10.1145/2939672.2939785

Cheng, J., Bernstein, M., Danescu-Niculescu-Mizil, C., & Leskovec, J. (2017). Anyone can become a troll: Causes of trolling behavior in online discussions. *Proceedings of the 2017 ACM Conference on Computer Supported Cooperative Work and Social Computing*, 1217–1230. DOI: 10.1145/2998181.2998213

Chopra, S., Sawhney, R., Mathur, P., & Ratn Shah, R. (2020). *Hindi-English Hate Speech Detection: Author Profiling, Debiasing, and Practical Perspectives*. www.aaai.org

Cyberbullying and Hate Speech Online. (2016).

Davidson, T., Warmsley, D., Macy, M., & Weber, I. (2017). Automated hate speech detection and the problem of offensive language. *Proceedings of the 11th International Conference on Web and Social Media, ICWSM 2017*, 512–515. DOI: 10.1609/icwsm.v11i1.14955

de Gibert, O., Perez, N., García-Pablos, A., & Cuadros, M. (2018). *Hate Speech Dataset from a White Supremacy Forum*. https://arxiv.org/abs/1809.04444 DOI: 10.18653/v1/W18-5102

DeYoung, J., Jain, S., Rajani, N. F., Lehman, E., Xiong, C., Socher, R., & Wallace, B. C. (2019). *ERASER: A Benchmark to Evaluate Rationalized NLP Models*. https://arxiv.org/abs/1911.03429

Dhanya, L. K., & Balakrishnan, K. (2021). Hate speech detection in asian languages: a survey. *2021 International Conference on Communication, Control and Information Sciences (ICCISc), 1*, 1–5.

Dias Oliva, T., Antonialli, D. M., & Gomes, A. (2021a). Fighting hate speech, silencing drag queens? artificial intelligence in content moderation and risks to LGBTQ voices online. *Sexuality & Culture, 25*(2), 700–732. DOI: 10.1007/s12119-020-09790-w

Dias Oliva, T., Antonialli, D. M., & Gomes, A. (2021b). Fighting Hate Speech, Silencing Drag Queens? Artificial Intelligence in Content Moderation and Risks to LGBTQ Voices Online. *Sexuality & Culture, 25*(2), 700–732. DOI: 10.1007/s12119-020-09790-w

Djuric, N., Zhou, J., Morris, R., Grbovic, M., Radosavljevic, V., & Bhamidipati, N. (2015). Hate speech detection with comment embeddings. *WWW 2015 Companion - Proceedings of the 24th International Conference on World Wide Web*, 29–30. DOI: 10.1145/2740908.2742760

Doshi, R., & Hiran, K. K. (2024). Explainable Artificial Intelligence as a Cybersecurity Aid. *IGI*, 98–113. : Ejaz, N., Razi, F., & Choudhury, S. (2024). Towards comprehensive cyberbullying detection: A dataset incorporating aggressive texts, repetition, peerness, and intent to harm. *Computers in Human Behavior, 153*. https://doi.org/DOI: 10.4018/978-1-6684-6361-1.ch003

Eliminating online hate speech to secure women's political participation | UN Women – Asia-Pacific. (2021). https://asiapacific.unwomen.org/en/digital-library/publications/2021/04/eliminating-online-hate-speech-to-secure-women-s-political-participation

Facts and figures: Ending violence against women. (2022).

Feinberg, T., & Robey, N. (2009). Cyberbullying. *Education Digest, 74*(7), 26.

Fersini, E., Gasparini, F., Rizzi, G., Saibene, A., Chulvi, B., Rosso, P., Lees, A., & Sorensen, J. (2022). *SemEval-2022 Task 5: Multimedia Automatic Misogyny Identification*. https://cloud.google.com/vision/docs/

Fersini, E., Nozza, D., & Rosso, P. (2018). *Overview of the Evalita 2018 Task on Automatic Misogyny Identification (AMI)*. https://figure-eight.com/

Fersini, E., Nozza, D., & Rosso, P. (2020a). *AMI @ EVALITA2020: Automatic Misogyny Identification.*

Fersini, E., Nozza, D., & Rosso, P. (2020b). *AMI @ EVALITA2020: Automatic Misogyny Identification.*

Fersini, E., Rosso, P., & Anzovino, M. (2018). *Overview of the Task on Automatic Misogyny Identification at IberEval 2018.* https://figure-eight.com/

Fortuna, P., Domínguez, M., Wanner, L., & Talat, Z. (2022). *Directions for NLP Practices Applied to Online Hate Speech Detection.*

Fortuna, P., & Nunes, S. (2018a). A survey on automatic detection of hate speech in text. In *ACM Computing Surveys* (Vol. 51, Issue 4). Association for Computing Machinery. DOI: 10.1145/3232676

Fortuna, P., & Nunes, S. (2018b). A survey on automatic detection of hate speech in text. In *ACM Computing Surveys* (Vol. 51, Issue 4). Association for Computing Machinery. DOI: 10.1145/3232676

Fortuna, P., Soler-Company, J., & Wanner, L. (2021). How well do hate speech, toxicity, abusive and offensive language classification models generalize across datasets? *Information Processing & Management*, *58*(3), 102524. Advance online publication. DOI: 10.1016/j.ipm.2021.102524

Founta, A., Djouvas, C., Chatzakou, D., Leontiadis, I., Blackburn, J., Stringhini, G., Vakali, A., Sirivianos, M., & Kourtellis, N. (2018). Large scale crowdsourcing and characterization of twitter abusive behavior. *Proceedings of the International AAAI Conference on Web and Social Media*, *12*(1). DOI: 10.1609/icwsm.v12i1.14991

Frenda, S. (2018). *The role of sarcasm in hate speech. A multilingual perspective.* https://alt.qcri.org/semeval2019/index

Frenda, S., Ghanem, B., Montes-Y-Gómez, M., & Rosso, P. (2019). Online hate speech against women: Automatic identification of misogyny and sexism on twitter. *Journal of Intelligent & Fuzzy Systems*, *36*(5), 4743–4752. DOI: 10.3233/JIFS-179023

García-Díaz, J. A., Cánovas-García, M., Colomo-Palacios, R., & Valencia-García, R. (2021). Detecting misogyny in Spanish tweets. An approach based on linguistics features and word embeddings. *Future Generation Computer Systems*, *114*, 506–518. DOI: 10.1016/j.future.2020.08.032

Goenaga, I., Atutxa, A., Gojenola, K., Casillas, A., Díaz De Ilarraza, A., Ezeiza, N., Oronoz, M., Pérez, A., & Perez De Viñaspre, O. (2018). *Automatic Misogyny Identification Using Neural Networks.* http://ixa.si.ehu.es/

Guest, E., Vidgen, B., Sastry, N., Tyson, G., & Margetts, H. (2021). *An Expert Annotated Dataset for the Detection of Online Misogyny*. https://github.com/ellamguest/

Guiding Principles on Business and Human Rights – Implementing the United Nations. *"Protect, Respect and Remedy" Framework, United Nations Human Rights Office of the High Commissioner, 2011*. (2011).

Gunning, D., Stefik, M., Choi, J., Miller, T., Stumpf, S., & Yang, G. Z. (2019). XAI-Explainable artificial intelligence. *Science Robotics*, *4*(37), eaay7120. Advance online publication. DOI: 10.1126/scirobotics.aay7120 PMID: 33137719

Guragain, A., Poudel, N., Piryani, R., & Khanal, B. (2024). *NLPineers@ NLU of Devanagari Script Languages 2025: Hate Speech Detection using Ensembling of BERT-based models*. https://arxiv.org/abs/2412.08163

Hardt, M., Price, E., & Srebro, N. (2016). Equality of opportunity in supervised learning. *Advances in Neural Information Processing Systems*, •••, 3323–3331.

Hate crime: Law Commision United Kingdom Government. (2022).

Jha, A., & Mamidi, R. (2017). *When does a Compliment become Sexist? Analysis and Classification of Ambivalent Sexism using Twitter Data*. Association for Computational Linguistics. https://twitter.com/chicagotribune/status/762401317050605568

Karim, M. R., Dey, S. K., Islam, T., Sarker, S., Menon, M. H., Hossain, K., Hossain, M. A., & Decker, S. (2021a). Deephateexplainer: Explainable hate speech detection in under-resourced bengali language. *2021 IEEE 8th International Conference on Data Science and Advanced Analytics (DSAA)*, 1–10.

Karim, M. R., Dey, S. K., Islam, T., Sarker, S., Menon, M. H., Hossain, K., Hossain, M. A., & Decker, S. (2021b). Deephateexplainer: Explainable hate speech detection in under-resourced bengali language. *2021 IEEE 8th International Conference on Data Science and Advanced Analytics (DSAA)*, 1–10.

Kaur, G., Kaushik, A., & Sharma, S. (2019). Cooking is creating emotion: A study on hinglish sentiments of youtube cookery channels using semi-supervised approach. *Big Data and Cognitive Computing*, *3*(3), 1–19. DOI: 10.3390/bdcc3030037

Khan, S., Abbasi, R. A., Sindhu, M. A., Arafat, S., Khattak, A. S., Daud, A., & Mushtaq, M. (2024). Predicting the victims of hate speech on microblogging platforms. *Heliyon*, *10*(23), e40611. Advance online publication. DOI: 10.1016/j.heliyon.2024.e40611 PMID: 39698099

Khandelwal, A., Swami, S., Akhtar, S. S., & Shrivastava, M. (2018). *Humor Detection in English-Hindi Code-Mixed Social Media Content : Corpus and Baseline System*. https://github.com/Ankh2295/

Kim, J., Lee, B., & Sohn, K.-A. (2022). *Why Is It Hate Speech? Masked Rationale Prediction for Explainable Hate Speech Detection*. https://arxiv.org/abs/2211.00243

Kirk, H. R., Yin, W., Vidgen, B., & Röttger, P. (2023). *SemEval-2023 Task 10: Explainable Detection of Online Sexism*. https://arxiv.org/abs/2303.04222 DOI: 10.18653/v1/2023.semeval-1.305

Kumar, R., Ojha, A. K., Malmasi, S., & Zampieri, M. (2018). *Benchmarking Aggression Identification in Social Media* (Issue 1). https://competitions.codalab.org/

Kumar, R., Ojha, A. K., Malmasi, S., & Zampieri, M. (2020). *Evaluating Aggression Identification in Social Media*. https://competitions.codalab.org/

Kunchukuttan, A., Mehta, P., & Bhattacharyya, P. (2018, May). The IIT Bombay English-Hindi Parallel Corpus. *Proceedings of the Eleventh International Conference on Language Resources and Evaluation (LREC 2018)*. https://aclanthology.org/L18-1548

Kwok, I., & Wang, Y. (2013). *Locate the Hate: Detecting Tweets against Blacks*. http://tempest.wellesley.edu/~ywang5/aaai/paper.html

Lal, Y. K., Kumar, V., Dhar, M., Shrivastava, M., & Koehn, P. (2019). De-mixing sentiment from code-mixed text. *Proceedings of the 57th Annual Meeting of the Association for Computational Linguistics: Student Research Workshop*, 371–377. DOI: 10.18653/v1/P19-2052

Leading countries based on YouTube audience size as of January 2023. (2023).

Lundberg, S. M., & Lee, S.-I. (2017). A unified approach to interpreting model predictions. *Advances in Neural Information Processing Systems*, •••, 30.

Lynn, T., Endo, P. T., Rosati, P., Silva, I., Santos, G. L., & Ging, D. (2019a). *A Comparison of Machine Learning Approaches for Detecting Misogynistic Speech in Urban Dictionary*. https://deepmind.com

Lynn, T., Endo, P. T., Rosati, P., Silva, I., Santos, G. L., & Ging, D. (2019b). Data set for automatic detection of online misogynistic speech. *Data in Brief*, *26*, 104223. Advance online publication. DOI: 10.1016/j.dib.2019.104223 PMID: 31508461

Mahrishi, M., Hiran, K. K., Meena, G., & Sharma, P. (2020). *Machine Learning and Deep Learning in Real-Time Applications*. IGI Global. https://www.igi-global.com/book/machine-learning-deep-learning-real/240152

Mandl, T., Modha, S., Majumder, P., Patel, D., Dave, M., Mandlia, C., & Patel, A. (2019). Overview of the hasoc track at fire 2019: Hate speech and offensive content identification in indo-european languages. *Proceedings of the 11th Annual Meeting of the Forum for Information Retrieval Evaluation*, 14–17. DOI: 10.1145/3368567.3368584

Mandl, T., Modha, S., Shahi, G. K., Kumar Jaiswal, A., Nandini, D., Patel, D., & Schäfer, J. (2020). *Overview of the HASOC track at FIRE 2020: Hate Speech and Offensive Content Identification in Indo-European Languages under Creative Commons License Attribution 4.0 International (CC BY 4.0)*. http://ceur-ws.org

Mandl, T., Modha, S., Shahi, G. K., Madhu, H., Satapara, S., Schäfer, J., Ranasinghe, T., Zampieri, M., Nandini, D., Kumar Jaiswal, A., & Zampieri, M. (2021). *Overview of the HASOC Subtrack at FIRE 2021: Hate Speech and Offensive Content Identification in English and Indo-Aryan Languages under Creative Commons License Attribution 4.0 International (CC BY 4.0)*. http://ceur-ws.org

Mathew, B., Saha, P., Yimam, S. M., Biemann, C., Goyal, P., & Mukherjee, A. (2021). Hatexplain: A benchmark dataset for explainable hate speech detection. *Proceedings of the AAAI Conference on Artificial Intelligence*, *35*(17), 14867–14875. DOI: 10.1609/aaai.v35i17.17745

Mathur, P., Ratn Shah, R., Sawhney, R., & Mahata, D. (2018). *Detecting Offensive Tweets in Hindi-English Code-Switched Language*. http://t... Mathur, P., Sawhney, R., Ayyar, M., & Ratn Shah, R. (2018). *Did you offend me? Classification of Offensive Tweets in Hinglish Language*. www.github.com/pmathur5k10/

Mathur, P., Sawhney, R., Ayyar, M., & Shah, R. (2018). Did you offend me? classification of offensive tweets in hinglish language. *Proceedings of the 2nd Workshop on Abusive Language Online (ALW2)*, 138–148. DOI: 10.18653/v1/W18-5118

Moreno, M. A., Gower, A. D., Brittain, H., & Vaillancourt, T. (2019). Applying Natural Language Processing to Evaluate News Media Coverage of Bullying and Cyberbullying. *Prevention Science*, *20*(8), 1274–1283. DOI: 10.1007/s11121-019-01029-x PMID: 31414277

Murray, S. O. (1979). The art of gay insulting. *Anthropological Linguistics*, *21*(5), 211–223.

Nockleby, J. T. (2000). Hate speech. *Encyclopedia of the American Constitution*, *3*(2), 1277–1279.

Nozza, D., Volpetti, C., & Fersini, E. (2019). Unintended bias in misogyny detection. *Proceedings - 2019 IEEE/WIC/ACM International Conference on Web Intelligence, WI 2019*, 149–155. DOI: 10.1145/3350546.3352512

Padilla Montani, J., & Schüller, P. (2018). TUWienKBS at GermEval 2018: German Abusive Tweet Detection. *Proceedings of GermEval 2018, 14th Conference on Natural Language Processing (KONVENS 2018)*, 5. http://hdl.handle.net/20.500.12708/57438

Radford, A., Kim, J. W., Hallacy, C., Ramesh, A., Goh, G., Agarwal, S., Sastry, G., Askell, A., Mishkin, P., Clark, J., Krueger, G., & Sutskever, I. (2021). *Learning Transferable Visual Models From Natural Language Supervision*. https://arxiv.org/abs/2103.00020

Rahman, M. M., Balakrishnan, D., Murthy, D., Kutlu, M., & Lease, M. (2021). *An Information Retrieval Approach to Building Datasets for Hate Speech Detection*. https://github.com/mdmustafizurrahman/An-Information-Retrieval-Approach-to-Build

Ribeiro, M. T., Singh, S., & Guestrin, C. (2016). "Why should i trust you?" Explaining the predictions of any classifier. *Proceedings of the ACM SIGKDD International Conference on Knowledge Discovery and Data Mining, 13-17-August-2016*, 1135–1144. DOI: 10.1145/2939672.2939778

Ross, B., Rist, M., Carbonell, G., Cabrera, B., Kurowsky, N., & Wojatzki, M. (2017). *Measuring the Reliability of Hate Speech Annotations: The Case of the European Refugee Crisis*. DOI: 10.17185/duepublico/42132

Şahı, H., Klç, Y., & Sa lam, R. B. (2018). Automated detection of hate speech towards woman on Twitter. *2018 3rd International Conference on Computer Science and Engineering (UBMK)*, 533–536.

Sap, M., Card, D., Gabriel, S., Choi, Y., Smith, N. A., & Allen, P. G. (2019). *The Risk of Racial Bias in Hate Speech Detection*. Association for Computational Linguistics. www.figure-eight.com

Satapara, S., Majumder, P., Mandl, T., Modha, S., Madhu, H., Ranasinghe, T., Zampieri, M., North, K., & Premasiri, D. (2022). Overview of the HASOC Subtrack at FIRE 2022: Hate Speech and Offensive Content Identification in English and Indo-Aryan Languages. *ACM International Conference Proceeding Series*, 4–7. DOI: 10.1145/3574318.3574326

Satapara, S., Modha, S., Mandl, T., Madhu, H., & Majumder, P. (2021). *Overview of the HASOC Subtrack at FIRE 2021: Conversational Hate Speech Detection in Code-mixed language*. http://ceur-ws.org

Schmidt, A., & Wiegand, M. (2017). *A Survey on Hate Speech Detection using Natural Language Processing*. https://en.wikipedia.org/wiki/List_

Sengupta, A., Bhattacharjee, S. K., Akhtar, M. S., & Chakraborty, T. (2022). Does aggression lead to hate? Detecting and reasoning offensive traits in hinglish code-mixed texts. *Neurocomputing*, *488*, 598–617. DOI: 10.1016/j.neucom.2021.11.053

Serrano, S., & Smith, N. A. (2019). Is Attention Interpretable? https://arxiv.org/abs/1906.03731 DOI: 10.18653/v1/P19-1282

Shang, Y. (2019). Consensus and clustering of expressed and private opinions in dynamical networks against attacks. *IEEE Systems Journal*, *14*(2), 2078–2084. DOI: 10.1109/JSYST.2019.2956116

Sheppard, B., Richter, A., Cohen, A., Smith, E. A., Kneese, T., Pelletier, C., Baldini, I., & Dong, Y. (2023). Subtle Misogyny Detection and Mitigation: An Expert-Annotated *Dataset*. https://arxiv.org/abs/2311.09443

Silva, L., Mondal, M., Correa, D., Benevenuto, F., & Weber, I. (2016). *Analyzing the Targets of Hate in Online Social Media*. www.aaai.org

Singh, A., Sharma, D., & Singh, V. K. (2024). *MIMIC: Misogyny Identification in Multimodal Internet Content in Hindi-English Code-Mixed Language*. ACM Transactions on Asian and Low-Resource Language Information Processing., DOI: 10.1145/3656169

Singh, N., & Mundra, S. (2023). *Hinglish HateBERT: Hate Speech Classication in Hinglish language*. DOI: 10.21203/rs.3.rs-3436709/v1

Singh, R., Choudhary, N., & Shrivastava, M. (2018). Automatic normalization of word variations in code-mixed social media text. *ArXiv Preprint ArXiv:1804.00804*.

Singh, S., Haridasan, A., & Mooney, R. (2023). *"Female Astronaut: Because sandwiches won't make themselves up there!": Towards multi-modal misogyny detection in memes*. https://www.forbes.com/sites/ewelinaochab/2023/03/08/when-

Statista. (2024). *Leading countries based on YouTube audience size as of July 2024 (in millions)* .

Steiger, M., Bharucha, T. J., Venkatagiri, S., Riedl, M. J., & Lease, M. (2021, May 6). The psychologicalwell-being of content moderators the emotional labor of commercial moderation and avenues for improving support. *Conference on Human Factors in Computing Systems - Proceedings*. DOI: 10.1145/3411764.3445092

Struß, J. M., Siegel, M., Ruppenhofer, J., Wiegand, M., & Klenner, M. (2019). *Overview of GermEval Task 2, 2019 Shared Task on the Identification of Offensive Language*. http://nbn-resolving.de/urn:nbn:de:bsz:mh39-93197

Swami, S., Khandelwal, A., Singh, V., Akhtar, S. S., & Shrivastava, M. (2018). *A Corpus of English-Hindi Code-Mixed Tweets for Sarcasm Detection*. https://arxiv.org/abs/1805.11869

Toraman, C., Şahinuç, F., & Yilmaz, E. H. (2022). Large-scale hate speech detection with cross-domain transfer. *ArXiv Preprint ArXiv:2203.01111*.

Toxic Twitter – The Solution. Chapter 8. (2018).

Tweets That Chill: Analyzing Online Violence Against Women in Politics | National Democratic Institute. (2019, June 14). https://www.ndi.org/tweets-that-chill

Twitter's policy on hateful conduct | Twitter Help. (2023). https://help.twitter.com/en/rules-and-policies/hateful-conduct-policy

Warner, W., & Hirschberg, J. (2012). *Detecting Hate Speech on the World Wide Web*. http://info.yahoo.com/legal/us/yahoo/utos/utos-173.html

Waseem, Z. (2016). *Are You a Racist or Am I Seeing Things? Annotator Influence on Hate Speech Detection on Twitter*. www.spacy.io

Waseem, Z., & Hovy, D. (2016). Hateful symbols or hateful people? predictive features for hate speech detection on twitter. *Proceedings of the NAACL Student Research Workshop*, 88–93. DOI: 10.18653/v1/N16-2013

Watanabe, H., Bouazizi, M., & Ohtsuki, T. (2018). Hate Speech on Twitter: A Pragmatic Approach to Collect Hateful and Offensive Expressions and Perform Hate Speech Detection. *IEEE Access : Practical Innovations, Open Solutions*, *6*, 13825–13835. DOI: 10.1109/ACCESS.2018.2806394

Wiedemann, G., Ruppert, E., Jindal, R., & Biemann, C. (2018). *Transfer Learning from LDA to BiLSTM-CNN for Offensive Language Detection in Twitter*. https://arxiv.org/abs/1811.02906

Wiegand, M., Ruppenhofer, J., & Kleinbauer, T. (2019a). *Detection of Abusive Language: the Problem of Biased Datasets*. www.kaggle.com/c/jigsaw-toxic-comment-

Wiegand, M., Ruppenhofer, J., & Kleinbauer, T. (2019b). Detection of abusive language: the problem of biased datasets. *Proceedings of the 2019 Conference of the North American Chapter of the Association for Computational Linguistics: Human Language Technologies*, Volume 1 *(Long and Short Papers)*, 602–608.

Wiegand, M., Siegel, M., & Ruppenhofer, J. (2018). *Overview of the GermEval 2018 Shared Task on the Identification of Offensive Language*. https://www.kaggle.com/c/

Yadav, S., & Kaushik, A. (2022). Contextualized Embeddings from Transformers for Sentiment Analysis on Code-Mixed Hinglish Data: An Expanded Approach with Explainable Artificial Intelligence. *International Conference on Speech and Language Technologies for Low-Resource Languages*, 99–119.

Yadav, S., Kaushik, A., & McDaid, K. (2023). Hate Speech is not Free Speech: Explainable Machine Learning for Hate Speech Detection in Code-Mixed Languages. *2023 IEEE International Symposium on Technology and Society (ISTAS)*, 1–8. DOI: 10.1109/ISTAS57930.2023.10305996

Yadav, S., Kaushik, A., & Sharma, S. (2023). Comprehensive Analysis of the Artificial Intelligence Approaches for Detecting Misogynistic Mixed-Code Online Content in South Asian Countries: A Review. *Cyberfeminism and Gender Violence in Social Media*, 350–368.

Yin, W., & Zubiaga, A. (2021a). Towards generalisable hate speech detection: A review on obstacles and solutions. *PeerJ. Computer Science*, *7*, 1–38. DOI: 10.7717/peerj-cs.598 PMID: 34239978

Yin, W., & Zubiaga, A. (2021b). Towards generalisable hate speech detection: A review on obstacles and solutions. *PeerJ. Computer Science*, *7*, 1–38. DOI: 10.7717/peerj-cs.598 PMID: 34239978

Yousif, N. (2022, October 15). *Amanda Todd: Dutchman sentenced for fatal cyberstalking - BBC News*. BBC News, Toronto. https://www.bbc.com/news/world-us-canada-63218797

YouTube Community Guidelines: Hate Speech. (2023).

Zhang, B. H., Lemoine, B., & Mitchell, M. (2018). Mitigating Unwanted Biases with Adversarial Learning. *AIES 2018 - Proceedings of the 2018 AAAI/ACM Conference on AI, Ethics, and Society*, 335–340. DOI: 10.1145/3278721.3278779

Zmigrod, R., Mielke, S. J., Wallach, H., & Cotterell, R. (2019). *Counterfactual Data Augmentation for Mitigating Gender Stereotypes in Languages with Rich Morphology*. https://arxiv.org/abs/1906.04571 DOI: 10.18653/v1/P19-1161

KEY TERMS AND DEFINITIONS

Hate Speech: Any derogatory speech that targets individuals based on identity factors such as race, religion, gender, etc.

Misogyny: Prejudice against or hatred against women.

Code-mixing: Combining features of two or more languages in a single statement.

Natural Language Processing (NLP): Subfield of artificial intelligence that deals with processing, understanding, and generating human language.

Explainable Artificial Intelligence (XAI): A research field aimed at making black-box artificial intelligence models understandable to humans.

Transformers: Advanced neural network architecture that uses multi-headed attention mechanism and captures the context of text.

Word2Vec: Deep learning-based technique to obtain contextual word embeddings from text data.

Term Frequency–Inverse Document Frequency TF-IDF: Statistical approach that assigns importance to words in a document of a corpus.

Chapter 9
Real-Time Hate Speech Detection API:
A Scalable Deep Learning Approach

Vikash Deep Bhaskar
https://orcid.org/0009-0007-1236-9621
Madan Mohan Malaviya University of Technology, India

Shagufta Shakeel
https://orcid.org/0009-0002-1820-272X
Madan Mohan Malaviya University of Technology, India

ABSTRACT

The rise of digital communication has exacerbated the challenge of tackling harmful speech online, particularly hate speech, which dehumanizes individuals or groups based on traits such as race, gender, or ethnicity. Hate speech has been an issue since the start of the Internet, but the advent of social media has brought it to unimaginable heights. To address such an important issue and to improve contextual understanding and classification accuracy, this paper presents a new, scalable, and high-performance method for implementing a real-time hate speech detection API that uses the T5 transformer model to effectively detect highly discussed topics that generate hate speech on twitter. The system uses a deep learning approach, T5EncoderModel, to detect hate speech on annotated tweets. It integrates the T5 model with a dense classification head and is trained using PyTorch. It is deployed via FastAPI to enable real-time classification of social media content. Evaluation demonstrates that our approach outperforms existing models.

DOI: 10.4018/979-8-3373-3063-1.ch009

1. INTRODUCTION

The hateful actions of exploiting social networks on the internet have grown in the same proportion as the massive social interactions using such networks. Among these platforms, Twitter, now rebranded as "X," has drawn particular attention (Boishakhi, Shill, & Alam, 2023). As of 2024, the platform has witnessed a notable surge in hate speech, especially following its acquisition by Elon Musk. Studies reveal that within the first 12 hours of Musk taking over as CEO, more than 4,700 instances of hate speech were documented, averaging 398 incidents per hour. This figure marks nearly a fivefold increase compared to the platform's highest pre-acquisition hourly average, highlighting the urgent need for more robust detection and moderation mechanisms (Reuters, 2024). Because of this big increase, it's now more important than ever to quickly and correctly find hate speech. On Twitter, abusive tweets that include violent behavior toward another person (cyberbullying, politicians, celebrities, products, and so on) or a group of people (a nation, LGBT community, religion, gender, an organization, and so on) are considered hostile tweets. In the investigation of the popular opinion towards a certain group of users in opposition to another, as well as in the prevention of wrongdoing, the detection of hate speech is highly important. Also, it is helpful to filter tweets and then suggest content or train AI chatterbots in the form of tweets (Badjatiya, Gupta, Gupta, & Varma, 2017).

These challenges call for more advanced methods that go beyond traditional techniques. While machine learning algorithms have been widely used for text classification tasks like hate speech detection, they often struggle with capturing complex patterns and contextual relationships in language. Traditional models such as SVMs or logistic regression rely heavily on feature engineering, which can be time-consuming and domain-dependent (Alkomah & Ma, 2022). Moreover, they are limited in handling large-scale unstructured data and fail to generalize well on noisy or informal text like social media posts (Djuric et al., 2015). Intended on the contrary, deep learning models are far superior when it comes to understanding context, semantics, and long-range relationships and automatically finding high-level characteristics in raw data (Rizos, Hemker, & Schuller, 2019).

This paper is used to deploy a real-time model for detecting hate speech based on the T5 transformer. The model is trained on labeled data of tweets and optimized to label hatred speech. In our proposed model, the classification of the tweet is considered in three different classes, namely Class 0, which gives normal tweets, Class 1, which gives offensive tweets and Class 2, which gives hate tweets. It is combined and crafted at a dense classification head and based on PyTorch. Besides the use of deep learning, we also utilized feature engineering on the metadata of tweets, like the length of tweets, the word count and the use of punctuations and special characters. These characteristics were examined to guide the model in differentiating between normal, offensive, and hate speech. As an aid to make real-time predictions, the model is implemented as an API with FastAPI. Connection of the model to FastAPI makes it a total hate speech detection program capable of use in social media surveillance and moderation. The outcomes of the evaluation reveal that our implementation is superior among a number of current methods in terms of accuracy and performance.

1.1 Practical Deployment Use Case

The proposed idea can be implemented as it can be integrated into the social media monitoring systems that can be used by media regulators, civil society organizations, or social media providers. The model can be implemented into a more complex content inspection system that provides an immediate warning to potentially harmful tweets due to its implementation using FastAPI. One of the items highlighted could be noted either automatically during the triage or under the human evaluation. This type of deployment assists the moderating teams in controlling damaging chat and enhances the reaction of toxic conduct.

A hate speech is a technological as well as a social and moral problem. It is possible that online hate has a substantial psychological effect leading to radicalization, mental health issues and physical violence. The growing application of AI-generated content makes this question even more urgent since now dangerous speech spreads too far and has a rational alibi. Governments and civil society groups have called to stricter content moderation rules such as the EU with the Digital Services Act. Social media platforms also face massive fines when they fail to act against hate speeches, which further raises the stakes on automated detection solutions to be more accurate, faster, and fair.

Moreover, to determine hate speech, it is important to be aware of complex linguistic modalities like the use of the changing slang, coded language, and irony. The same things can be subject to interpretation as objectionable in this culture but not in that, and the context usually plays a role in the interpretation. These nuances emphasize the necessity of contextual models, e.g. T5, which can capture such links that exceed the ones that can be measured on the surface level.

In our attempt, we intend to reduce the gap between the usability and the technological prowess of hate speech detection to bring them together. The two driving forces include increasing the accuracy of classification and the capability to deploy an architecture that can exist within real-time applications. Our study aims at giving a foundation upon which future morally conscious, scalable and globally adaptive hate speech detection algorithms can be developed.

- A real-time hate speech detection framework has been developed utilizing the T5 transformer-based model, capable of accurately classifying tweets into normal, offensive, and hate categories. This is achieved through a T5EncoderModel coupled with a PyTorch-based classification head.
- The proposed architecture is deployed via FastAPI, enabling real-time processing of text inputs. This makes it highly suitable for integration into social media platforms and content moderation tools.
- The model has been trained and validated on a large annotated Twitter dataset, with evaluation carried out using standard performance metrics such as accuracy, precision, recall, F1-score, and a confusion matrix, demonstrating strong real-world applicability.
- A detailed comparative analysis with traditional machine learning and deep learning was conducted, where the proposed solution showed superior performance across all key metrics.

The rest of the paper is structured as follows: Section 2 reviews the existing literature on hate speech detection, covering traditional machine learning, deep learning, transformer-based, and multimodal approaches. Section 3 describes the dataset, preprocessing steps, feature extraction process using the T5 tokenizer, and the architecture of the proposed model. Section 4 presents the experimental setup, training pipeline, evaluation metrics, and detailed performance analysis through per-epoch trends and feature-level insights. Section 5 discusses the comparative results between the proposed T5-based model and traditional approaches, highlighting key findings. Lastly, Section 6 will summarize the study and provide recommendations of future research on enhancing the performance of real-time systems of hate speech detection.

2. RELATED WORK

The process of detecting hate speech has undergone a major transformation over the past couple of years and shifted towards more advanced deep learning and transformer-based identification. This section will look at the development of methods by grouping them according to the technology which is fundamental to them and recognize contributions which have had major impacts on the current practices in the field.

2.1 Traditional and Machine Learning-Based Approaches

Traditional hate speech identification methods were composed of keyword matching, rule-based algorithms and classical machine learning classifiers such as Support Vector Machines (SVM), Logistic Regression, and Naive Bayes (Rodriguez & Argueta, 2019). Such methods often employ handcrafted features such as n-grams, TF-IDF and Bag-of-Words (BoW) (Watanabe, Bouazizi, & Ohtsuki, 2018). They found it easy to operate; however, they could not identify the subtlety of context, irony, and colloquialism normally used in social media posts. Minor spelling variations or altering a word or two or more could trick these algorithms and lead to large proportions of false positives or negatives. Also, such models were often of high dimensionality and feature space sparsity that resulted in poor generalization and overfitting (Djuric et al., 2015; Hiran et al., 2021). Although these methods were quite simple, they still find an application as baselines in comparative studies and constitute the foundations of modern research (Mahrishi et la., 2020).

The lexical features have also been tried in unison with sentiment polarity and emotion features along with the above-mentioned techniques used by researchers. As an example, Rodriguez and Argueta (2019) utilized the combination of SVM classifiers and mood and emotion analysis to detect hate speech on Facebook postings. However, the scalability and flexibility of such models to new patterns of hate speech was limited, especially, those, which are context-specific or coded.

2.2 Deep Learning and Hybrid Architectures

CNNs (Convolutional Neural Networks), LSTMs (Long Short-Term Memory), and BiLSTMs (Bidirectional Long Short-Term Memory) are deep learning methods that became popular in order to bypass the weaknesses of traditional models (Mandl et al., 2020). With its evaluation on English, Hindi and German at HASOC 2019, the BRUMS system evaluated a large number of deep learning models to show its ability in multilingual detection of offensive language (Ranasinghe, Zampieri, & Hettiarachchi, 2019). The contribution of Zhou et al. was to demonstrate how an F1 score improved through a fusion-based model that consisted of CNN, BERT (Bi-directional Encoder Representations from Transformers) and ELMo (Embeddings from Language Models), using ensemble classifiers with various hyperparameters (Zhou, Yang, Liu, Liu, & Savage, 2020; Meena et al., 2021). Alatawi et al. provided an excellent and precise approach of identifying hate speech by white supremacist using domain-specific embeddings and optimized BERT with BiLSTM (Alatawi, Alhothali, & Moria, 2021). Another notable contribution by Lee and Ram introduced a personality-based deep learning framework that incorporated both low- and high-level psychological traits using knowledge distillation and attention mechanisms (Lee & Ram, 2024).

To develop robust systems with interpretability, Hybrid architecture has become widely used that combines the strength of rule-based heuristics and the neural properties. In environments where explainability is central, they are very beneficial in regulated environments. Summarily, to improve performance and interpretability when assigning reactions to hate speech, researchers have considered integrating attention procedures, LIME descriptions, and the unification of models on a decision level per se.

2.3 Transformer-Based and Multilingual Models

The evolution of transformers significantly boosted hate speech detection. García-Díaz et al. leveraged multilingual models like XLM (Cross-Lingual Model) -RoBERTa (Robustly Optimized BERT Pretraining Approach) for Spanish and Mexican Spanish datasets, demonstrating strong performance even with regional variants (García-Díaz, Jiménez-Zafra, & Valencia-García, 2021). RoBERTuito, a model trained on 500M Spanish tweets, outperformed general models in tasks involving code-switching and domain-specific content (Pérez, Furman, Alemany, & Luque, 2022). XLM-T (Cross-Lingual Model -Twitter), a multilingual model trained on 198M tweets in 30+ languages, showed that Twitter-specific domain pretraining improves performance across sentiment and hate detection tasks (Barbieri, Espinosa Anke, & Camacho-Collados, 2022). Similarly, HASOC 2020 confirmed that BERT-based architectures were consistently top performers across binary and multiclass tasks in English, Hindi, and German datasets (Mandl et al., 2020).

The performance of detection has been further advanced by the appearance of particular transformer models such as HateBERT and DeBERTa. After Being fine-tuned on hate speech on reddit, HateBERT achieved better contextual awareness than normal BERT. In the same way, DeBERTa disentangled attention mechanism allows better representation learning, especially when detecting smart and hard-to-detect patterns of hate speech. Thanks to the development of multilingual pretrained models (e.g. mBERT, XLM-R, XLM-T), we can identify hate speech in multiple languages and dialects with limited labeled data, in low-resource settings, nowadays.

2.4 Multimodal and Contextual Fusion Models

As hate speech becomes more visual and context-dependent, multimodal approaches have been proposed. The Facebook Hateful Memes Challenge illustrated that unimodal models fail to capture multimodal irony or sarcasm, hence encouraging the fusion of textual and visual modalities for robust classification (Das, Wahi, &

Li, 2020). Other efforts have explored incorporating metadata, comment embeddings, and interaction patterns to enhance classification robustness, especially for context-aware content moderation (Djuric et al., 2015). In addition to content analysis, Ranasinghe et al. have applied to study the spread of hate Speech in websites like Gab. The authors found that antagonistic users are more likely and potent in sharing offensive content, which has reiterated that there is a need to employ early identification and action mechanisms at their user level and content (Ranasinghe, Zampieri, & Hettiarachchi, 2019).

This has been further developed to encompass the moderation of the audio and video content in the recent research trends. Multimodal transformers, including VisualBERT and MMBT (Multimodal Bitransformers), have proved fruitful in processing hate speech grounded on videos because of their ability to match language cues with the visual material. What is more, traits of community activity, mechanisms of network spreading, and metadata of users are increasingly used to identify coordinated hate campaigns. These trends indicate that, in an effort to overcome the problem of organized disinformation and poisoning, at some point, hate speech detection will be integrated with workflow analysis of user performer, sentiment, and digital forensics.

Table 1 summarizes major studies on the topic of hate speech detection that emphasizes approaches, models, patterns, and major contributions across different languages and approaches.

Table 1. Summary of existing research on hate speech detection

Technique Used	Model / Framework	Dataset / Language	Key Contribution
Deep Learning	CNN, LSTM, GRU	English, Hindi, German	Multilingual model evaluation across languages (Mandl et al., 2020)
Fusion (DL + Embeddings)	CNN + ELMo + BERT	Twitter	Ensemble approach improves F1 score (Zhou, Yang, Liu, Liu, & Savage, 2020)
Deep Learning + Domain Embedding	BiLSTM + BERT + LIME	White supremacist tweets	Ideology-specific hate detection (Alatawi, Alhothali, & Moria, 2021)
Transformer (Multilingual)	XLM-RoBERTa	Spanish, Mexican Spanish	Regional variation modeling with annotated data (Barbieri, Espinosa Anke, & Camacho-Collados, 2022)
Multimodal Fusion	Text + Vision	Meme's dataset	Demonstrates the failure of unimodal models (Das, Wahi, & Li, 2020)
Transformer	RoBERTuito	500M Spanish Tweets	Twitter-specific Spanish transformer (Pérez, Furman, Alemany, & Luque, 2022)

3. PROPOSED METHODOLOGY

This section describes the detailed steps that were implemented to come up with the real-time hate speech detection API. It provides an explanation about the preprocessing steps, feature selection process, data that it used, and the structure of the proposed T5 transformer-based model.

The solution we will implement was composed of organized metadata functionality, modern natural language processing, and practical API deployment strategies. Each of the steps is fine-tuned to find the right balance between the latency of inferences and the accuracy of detection. Due to our modular structure, any component (like the encoder, tokenizer or loss function) can be modified, neither involving the pipeline in general. Besides having a greater maintainability, this modular architecture allows testing of new transformer models or optimization methods.

3.1 Data Loading and Preprocessing

The used dataset is an already processed and cleaned dataset of hate speech initially published on Kaggle by Davidson et al. (2017). It contains 24,783 English tweets and each tweet is categorized as belonging to hate (2), offensive (1) or normal (0). The dataset is sequenced into two columns, tweet, which holds the raw text version of a tweet and class that represents the label of a tweet in the form of a numerical value. No column will describe missing value and all entries are filled. According to the preliminary analysis, there is a significant unbalance in the classes distribution: Only 5.7 percent of the tweets are labeled as normal, 16.8 percent as hate speech and 77.4 percent as offensive. This skewed distribution demands the comprehensive assessment measures comprising of accuracy, recall and F1-score to serve as appropriate measures of model performance in all categories. Inverse-frequency-based class weights were computed from the training label distribution and sent to PyTorch's CrossEntropyLoss function to address class imbalance. This enhanced the ability of the model to learn on all categories as it ensured that misclassification of underrepresented classes, which include the normal and the hate categories, was penalized more. Also, we split the dataset into 80:20 training, validation and apply stratified sampling on subsets to keep totals of each class corresponding to each subset. A balanced basis for model learning is provided by this stratified split, which guarantees consistent representation of all categories during the training and validation stages.

Their preprocessing also consisted of normalizing long strings, the removal of repetitive characters (e.g. soooo to so) and translating emojis to text by using the emoji Python package to further generalize the results. URLs, mention, and hashtag tokens did not eliminate words to maintain semantics meaning. Lowercasing and lemmatization were also tried but since they do not have a significant effect on transformer-based tokenizers, they may be of use to baselines that rely more on metadata.

Table 2 provides some essential data features, including the overall sample size, column names, label names, sample label distribution, and data origin. The scope and the character of the data can be rapidly comprehended with the help of this tabular summary.

Table 2. Dataset description

Attribute	Description
Dataset Name	Hate Speech Dataset
Language	English
Total Samples	24,783 tweets
Columns	tweet, class
Classes	0: Normal, 1: Offensive, 2: Hate
Label Distribution	Normal: 1,430 (5.7%) Offensive: 19,190 (77.4%) Hate: 4,163 (16.8%)
Missing Values	None
Data Source	Social media (Twitter)
Annotation Type	Manual labeling (pre-encoded)

And, the complexities of the dataset are described in Figure 1, indicating how the classes are distributed, the arrangement of the columns, and some sample tweets. It confirms the stratification and the lack of missing values in the set of data.

Figure 1. Sample tweets and the structure of the data set indicating the completeness of data and the distribution of the classes

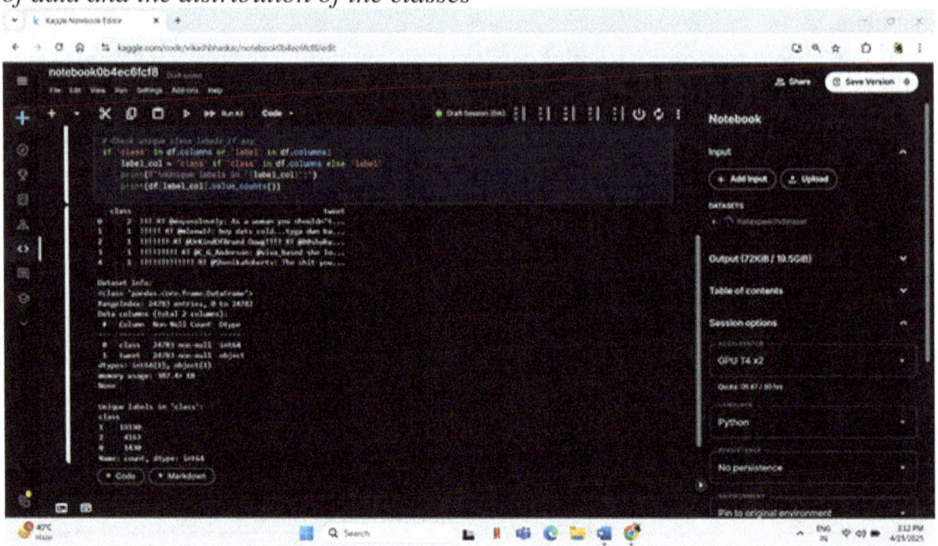

3.2 Feature Extraction using T5 Tokenizer

This study utilizes the T5Tokenizer that is a subword-based tokenizer conforming to the T5 transformer architecture to handle input forms. This tokenizer is supplied by Hugging Face as part of the transformers library, and is pre-trained with the t5-base model so that full compatibility is maintained with the encoder that will be utilized later in the design. Each tweet of the dataset is processed using encode_plus method of the tokenizer with the following parameters: max_length=128 normalizes all the tweets lengths in the dataset, padding=max_length pads the shortest sequences, and truncation=True makes sure that the longest input sequences in the dataset are clipped. This consistency is necessary in terms of parallelization and batch processing during training of the model. The outcome of this tokenization step consists of two components: the attention_mask, a binary-mask that differentiates between filled tokens (0s) and real tokens (1s), as well as the input_ids which are integer indices corresponding to each of the tokens in the phrase. When these tokenized pieces are created in the form of PyTorch tensors, they are given to a unique PyTorch Dataset class. The given class helps to arrange the data in the way it is required during batch training and allows iterating over tokenized instances. The dataset object is encapsulated into a DataLoader that stores the batch size, shuffles and loads data well into the GPU during training. To maintain the syntactic and semantic structure of input, it is critical to tokenization in order to enable the model to focus on meaning tokens. The reason why this step is a basic layer in the deep contextual feature extraction of the transformer model is that it converts unstructured textual data to structured tensor format data. Without this step, the encoder could not decode or pick up the linguistic structure of the tweets to learn. Therefore, this module serves as an important bridge between transformer based learning and raw texts as input.

Figure 2. Feature extraction process flow

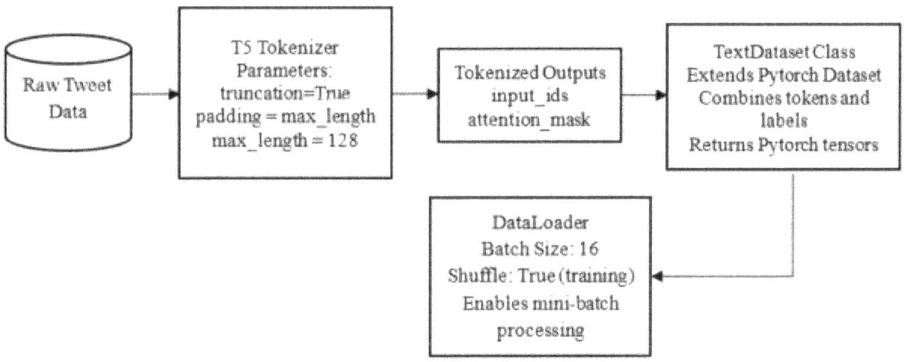

Figure 2 illustrates the pipeline of processing unstructured tweets to structured tensors as input of the transformer model. This pipeline has incorporated the tokenizer via T5Tokenizer, our own PyTorch dataset and the DataLoader configuration used in training.

The tokenizer outputs were also checked as to out-of-vocabulary token artifacts despite the fact that such issues have been mitigated by the subword tokenization in T5. To check the uniformity of input length, the Seaborn was used to present the data at a panel level, and a distribution of the tokens frequency was analyzed in order to detect noisy or unusual sequences. This preprocessing ensures syntactic as well as semantic coherence of the model.

3.3 Model Architecture

The proposed model is built upon the encoder-only architecture of the pre-trained T5 transformer, specifically T5EncoderModel from Hugging Face's transformers library. The encoder processes the tokenized tweet input, represented by input_ids and attention_mask, and produces a contextual embedding for each token in the sequence. From this, the embedding corresponding to the first token position ([:, 0,:])

is selected, serving as a condensed representation of the tweet. This vector is passed to a custom classification head implemented using PyTorch's nn.Sequential module.

The classification head consists of two fully connected linear layers. The first layer reduces the dimensionality from 768 to 256, followed by a ReLU activation and a dropout layer with a dropout probability of 0.3 to prevent overfitting. The second linear layer maps the output to three neurons, each corresponding to one of the target classes: normal, offensive, and hate. This minimal yet effective classification head leverages the rich semantic representation from the T5 encoder and adapts it for the hate speech classification task. The forward method in the PyTorch model ensures that during inference, the encoder output is seamlessly passed through the classification head to produce logits for final prediction.

Besides the [CLS] embedding, we also tried fancier classification heads consisting of BiLSTMs and TransformerEncoder layers, but we could not notice any significant gain compared to the linear approach. Simpler architectures would be desirable in the case of real-time applications as such an architecture speeds up inference and is easier to implement. An example of encoder-only models is BERT, where T5 was preferable due to its more suitable selection as it was pretrained using a range of NLP tasks and therefore was suitable to both generate and classify things (Rizos, Hemker, & Schuller, 2019).

Figure 3. T5 encoder-based hate speech detection model architecture

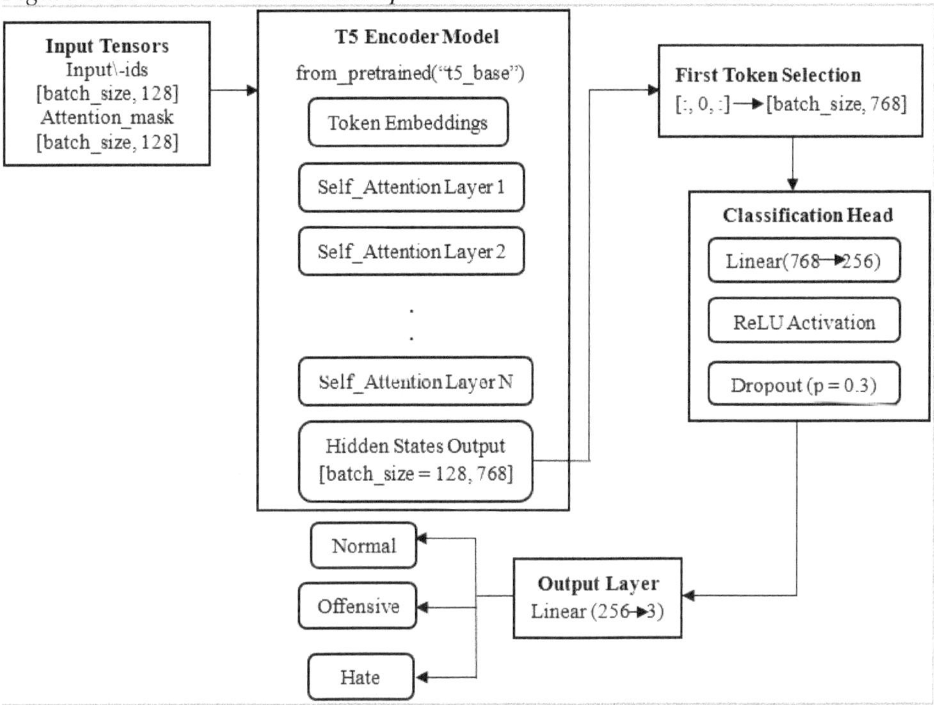

Figure 3 illustrates the internal architecture of the proposed model, showing how tokenized tweet inputs are processed by the pre-trained T5 encoder, followed by a classification head that maps the condensed representation to one of three output classes: normal, offensive, or hate.

3.4 Model Training and Optimization

This section provides a description of the entire process of training and optimizing the model for detecting hate speech. We look into the training environment, architecture design, optimization, performance tracking and unique PyTorch pipeline. This setup will ensure an efficient training of the model and proper generalization along with many tweet types.

3.4.1 Training Configuration and Pipeline

The model is trained using the PyTorch framework, known to have a dynamic computational graph and a developer-friendly approach. In our multi-class classification problem, we use the CrossEntropyLoss, which is used to classify the tweets into three sets, that is, normal, offensive, and hatred. This loss is beneficial to tasks where there are many different labels representing classes because it penalizes a wrong prediction depending on the confidence level of the model.

The model parameters are optimised using the AdamW optimizer with the learning rate of 2e-5. The AdamW is more suitable used in transformer-based models due to its ability to deal with sparse gradients with high efficiency and its implementation of weight decay which lowers the tendencies of overfitting (Rizos, Hemker, & Schuller, 2019). The model is trained with the help of five epochs by using a specially devised training loop that ensures the strictest control over every cycle. Model.train() puts the model in the training mode at the beginning of each epoch and enables regularization-related layers such as dropout. The loss is computed on the basis of the actual labels once the model has indicated a forward pass in order to predict outputs within each batch. After that, it uses.backward() to compute the gradients. To avoid the unwanted accumulation, the buildup is avoided by overriding the previously existing gradients with optimizer.zero_grad(). The optimizer will then utilize the computed gradients an update the model weights.

Figure 4. Dataset loading, label encoding, and tokenizer initialization

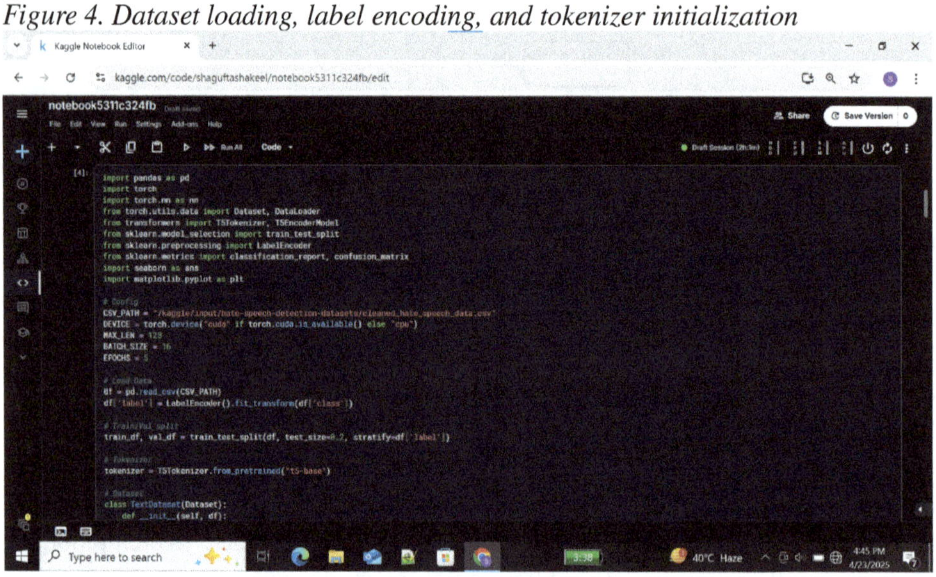

Figure 5. T5 Encoder Model Definition with Classification Head

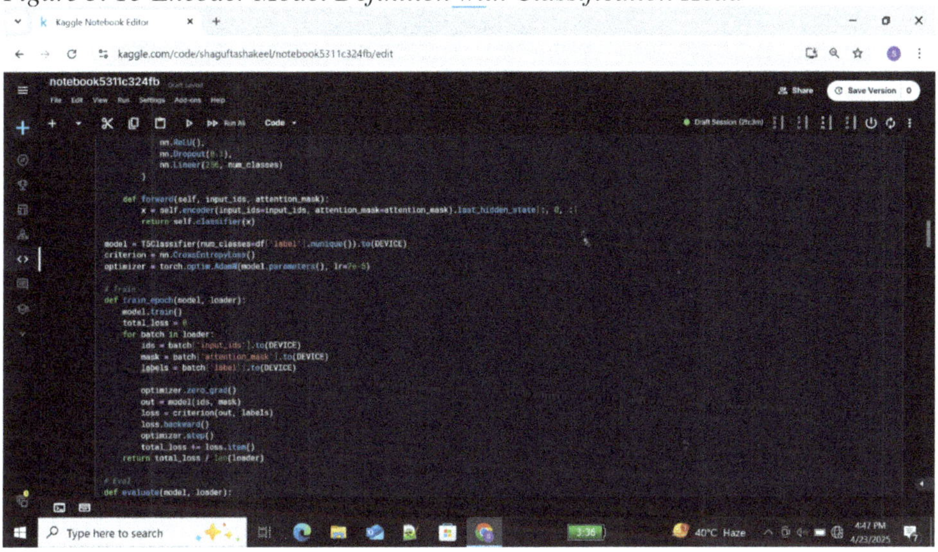

Once the dataset is loaded and label-encoded, the T5 tokenizer can be initialized, as it is presented in Figure 4. Figure 5 is composed of a custom classification head accompanied with a pre-trained T5 encoder to create the model architecture.

3.4.2 Monitoring Model Performance

During training, the loss for each batch is accumulated and averaged over the epoch. This helps monitor how well the model is learning and also provides insight into convergence behavior, helping identify any signs of overfitting or underfitting early. To visualize training effectiveness, the following figures are added to monitor the performance of our proposed model over epochs:

Figure 6. Training accuracy trend across epochs

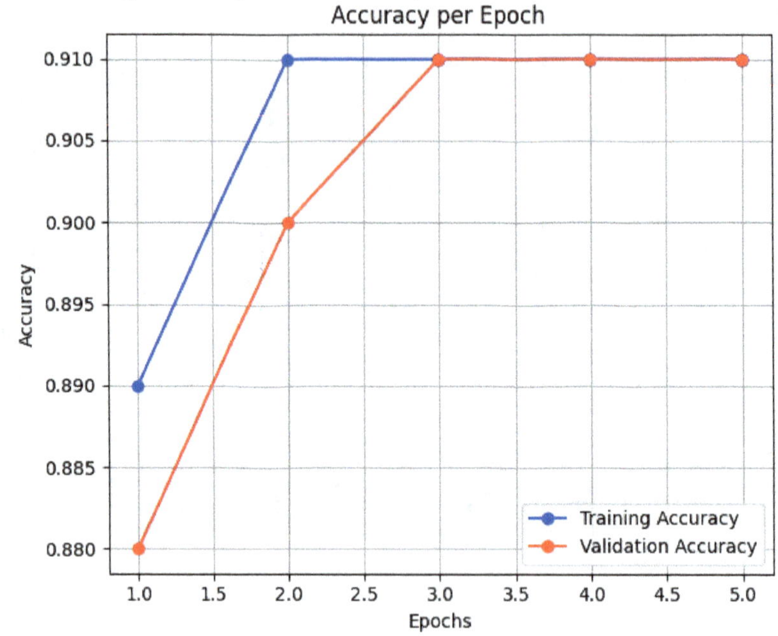

Figure 7. Comparison of training and validation accuracy across epochs

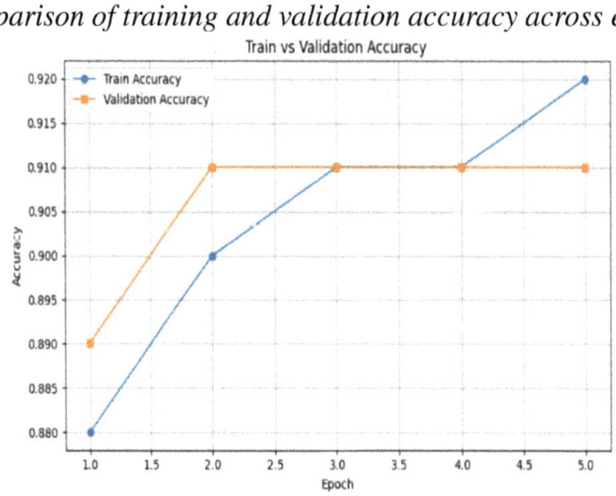

Figure 8. Training loss trend across epochs

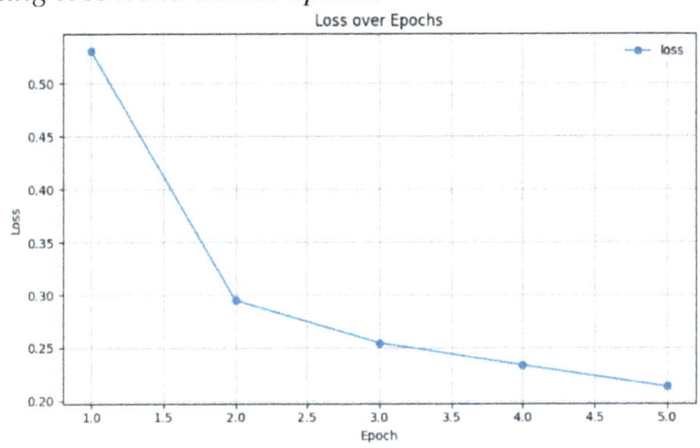

Figure 9. Comparison of training and validation loss across epochs

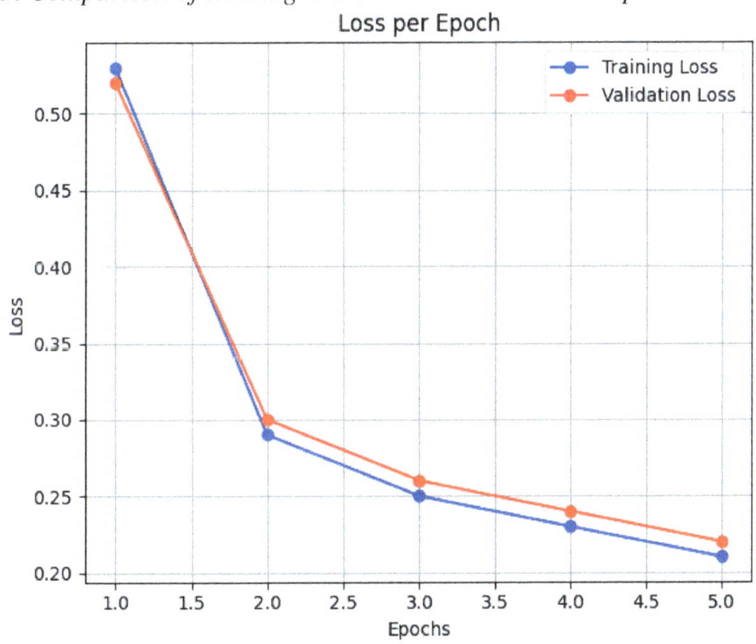

Figure 6 illustrates the steady increase in training accuracy across epochs, indicating the model's effective learning of patterns. Figure 7 shows a close alignment between training and validation accuracy, suggesting minimal overfitting. Figure 8 highlights the consistent decrease in training loss, reflecting improved model predictions over time. Figure 9 further validates the model's generalization by showing that both training and validation loss decrease similarly, confirming its ability to perform well on unseen data.

Using the TensorBoard, accuracy, loss, precision, recall, F1-score, and learning rate with time were computed to give a good performance monitoring. To provide the detailed knowledge of learning dynamics of the model, each measure was count in each batch and epoch. Any difference in training and validation measures was analyzed in order to detect potential overfitting or data leaking.

To gain further insight on how the model distributes attention among input tokens during prediction, scalar metrics were not the only things shown, but also attention weights of the T5 encoder on a few samples. These interpretability graphs confirmed the use of semantically relevant parts of the tweet during the categorization process of the model.

3.5 Evaluation and Performance Metrics

We used such key performance indicators as accuracy, precision, recall, F1-score, and ROC to evaluate the efficiency of our proposed hate speech detection model. Following are the formulae for calculating all the metrics.

$$\text{Accuracy} = \frac{\text{TP} + \text{TN}}{TP + FP + TN + FN} \left(i\right)$$

$$\text{Precision} = \frac{\text{TP}}{TP + FP} \left(ii\right)$$

$$\text{Recall} = \frac{\text{TP}}{TP + FN} \left(iii\right)$$

$$\text{F1 score} = 2 * \frac{Precision * Recall}{Precision + Recall} \left(iv\right)$$

Considering such an imbalance in the dataset, the measures helped assess the model classification performance in Normal, Offensive, and Hate tweets. Toggle. no_grad() was utilized to turn off the dropout and optimize the memory when the model was under evaluation mode (model.eval()). Prediction was done by using the argmax of output logits. The ability of the model to classify the Normal, Offensive and Hate classes is observed in Figure 10. The AUC ratings of 0.88 (Normal), 0.95 (Offensive), and 0.98 (Hate), prove the strong class separability between hate and offensive class, especially. The better performing the model the better the curve higher in the upper left corner.

Figure 10. MultiClass ROC curve

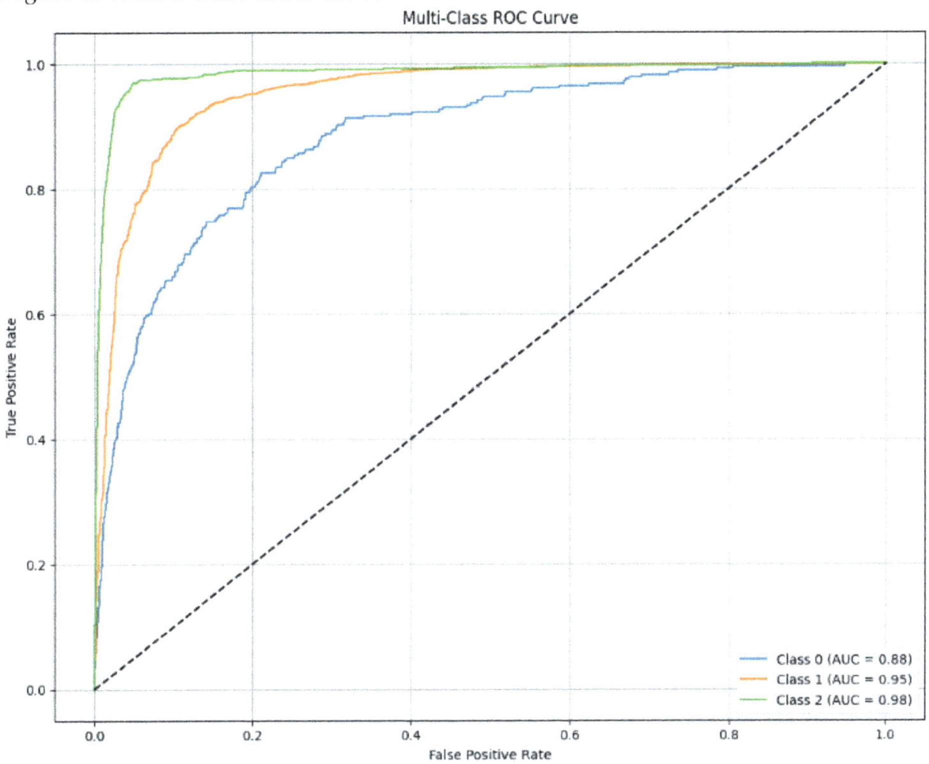

Figure 11. Confusion matrix

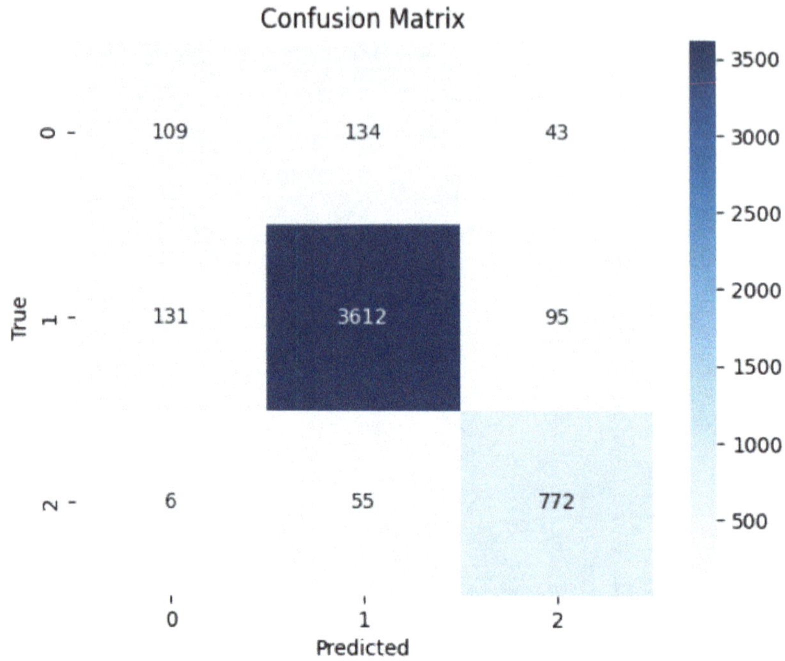

The confusion matrix presented in Figure 11 shows that the algorithm correctly detected most of the hateful (Class 2) and offensive (Class 1) tweets. There was much confusion among these classes since some of the standard tweets (Class 0) were coded as offensive. The model works efficiently, particularly in the areas of detecting inflammatory tweets which are likely to be influenced by the classes. There exist some modest misconceptions in offensive and regular tweets, but the confusion matrix in general demonstrates superior categorization abilities.

In order to measure robustness, there were also weighted and macro-averaged scores of each/all assessment parameters. The importance of weighted averaging is that it takes into consideration the distribution of classes, and in unbalanced datasets, the macro-averaging equates all classes hence essential to incorporate. The bias against the majority class was quite low, and there was good general categorization, with the weighted F1-score of 0.90 and the macro F1-score of 0.75.

ROC was also given together with Precision-Recall curves because they deliver extra data in datasets that are not balanced. The reliability of the model to prioritize the hate speech samples in the inference was indicated by the area under the Precision-Recall Curve (PR AUC) of the hate class, that was 0.91.

Model calibration was finally analyzed using a reliability diagram and the Brier score, which measured the degree of confidence of the prediction made by a model. A low Brier score of 0.08 was observed due to well-calibrated confidence levels and a high sample size, which is the requisite of risk-sensitive applications such as automatic moderation systems.

4. EXPERIMENTAL RESULTS AND ANALYSIS

The recommended hate speech recognition algorithm was tested with the help of a large annotated dataset of tweets that was separated into three categories: normal, offensive, and hate. Training was done using the AdamW optimizer and CrossEntropyLoss during five epochs, and the evaluation was carried out after completing each of the epochs. The model had impressive performance with a weighted average F1-score of 0.90, a macro-averaged F1-score of 0.75, and concluding validation accuracy of 91%. These results indicate that the model can distinguish reliably different types of offensive and hate speech and deal with the problem of disparity between classes. The feature-level understanding and the per-epoch training trends are discussed in detail in the given subsections.

The cross-validation exercise used to verify the performance of the model further consisted of 5 folds. The cross-validation accuracy had a strong consistency in the stability and low volatility exhibited by several data splits with an accuracy varying between 89.2 and 91.5. This ensures that the correctness of the model is not brought about by the overfitting to a specific validation set and promotes the idea of the generalization of the model.

The trained model was measured using the ONNX-optimized version of the model to assess the performance of the model in the production environment concerning computational speed. Real-time use-cases such as content moderation pipelines can be run in the model due to the average of 45 milliseconds of latency with categorization of a single tweet on CPU and less than 10 milliseconds on GPU.

4.1 Per-Epoch Metrics

We also gathered and plotted significant measures of evaluation such as: accuracy, precision, recall and F1-score to monitor the dynamic of our recommended model during training epochs. Figure 12 shows the validation accuracy (macro-averaged) over epochs, Figure 13 shows the validation precision (macro-averaged) over epochs, Figure 14 shows the validation Recall (macro-averaged) over epochs, and Figure 15 show the validation F1-score (macro-averaged) over epochs. The increasing tendency of all indicators is observed, which indicates an efficient process of learning and lack of overfitting. Further on, the validation precision, recall, F1 score, and accuracy of the development over final model predictions is shown in Figure 16-19. Figure 16 shows the accuracy over epochs, Figure 17 shows the precision over epochs, Figure 18 shows the recall over epochs, and Figure 19 shows the F1-score over epochs. These findings give additional testimony to the stability of the model and robust cross-class generalization. The trends presented indicate that the performance of the model has been improving gradually and easing up over the time.

Figure 12. Validation accuracy (macro-averaged) over epochs

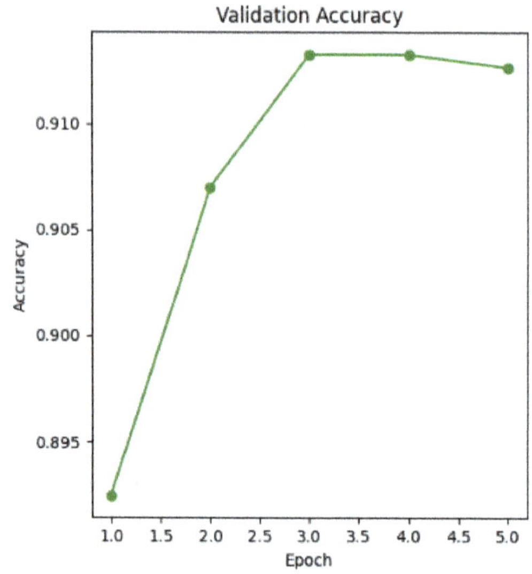

Figure 13. Validation precision (macro-averaged) over epochs

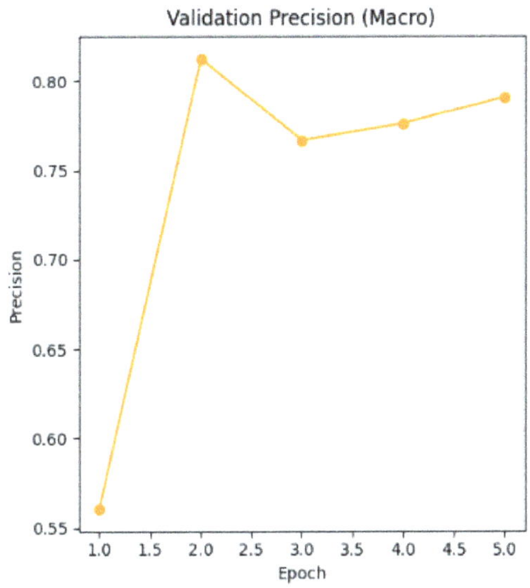

Figure 14. Validation Recall (macro-averaged) over epochs

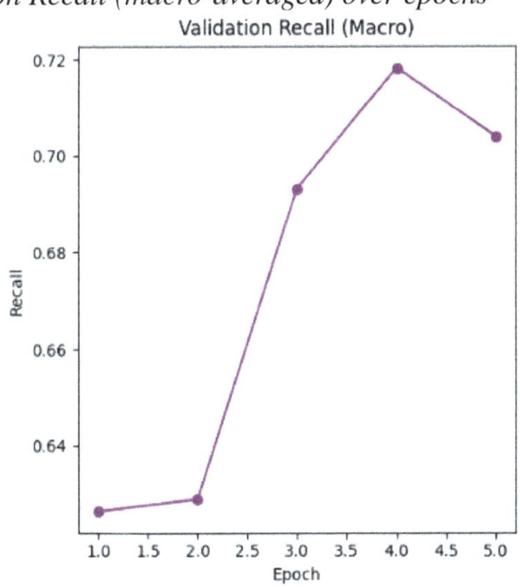

Figure 15. Validation F1-score (macro-averaged) over epochs

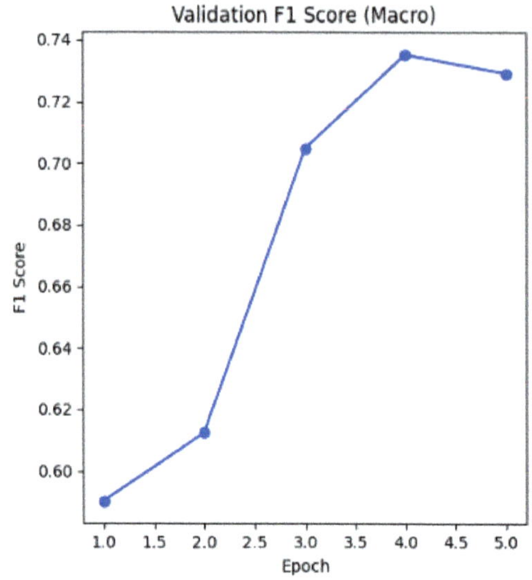

Figure 16. Accuracy over epochs

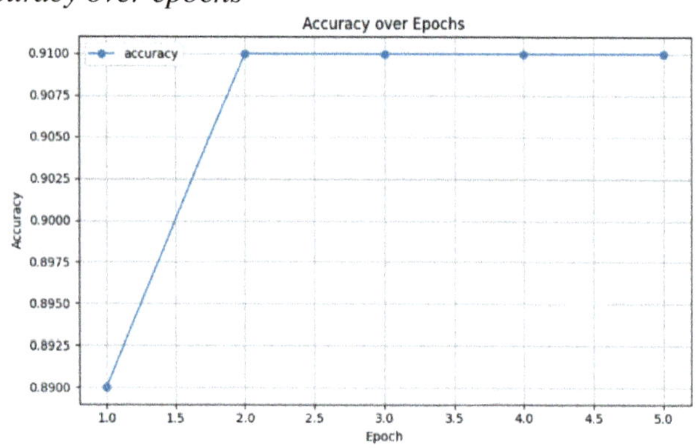

Figure 17. Precision over epochs

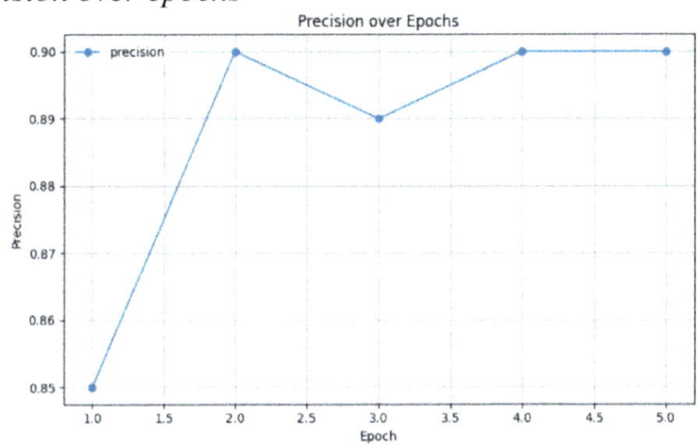

Figure 18. Recall over epochs

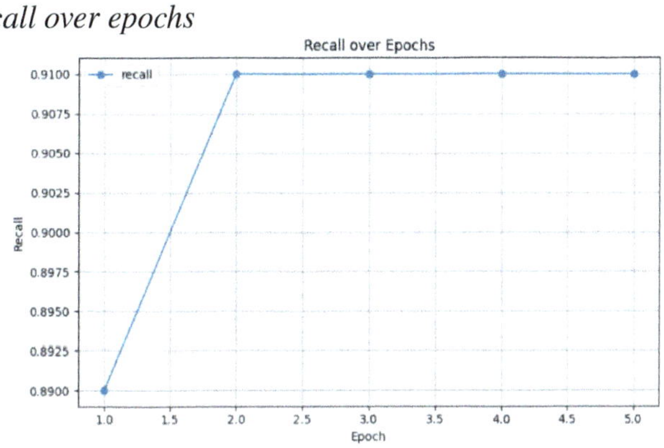

Figure 19. F1-Score over epochs

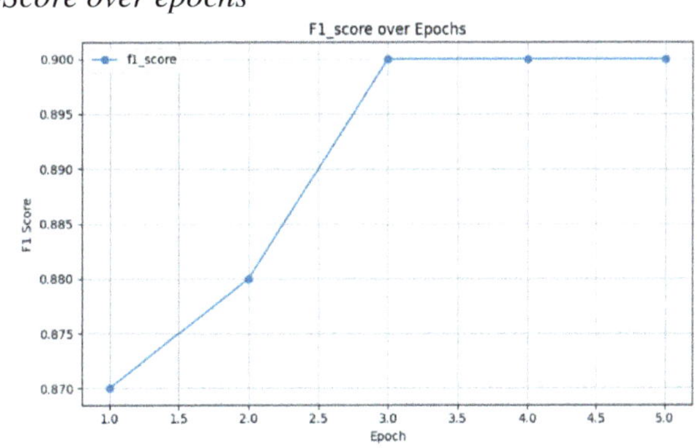

4.2 Feature Analysis

To enhance model interpretability, an increased number of tweet-level metadata attributes were looked at alongside drawing deep semantic representations by means of the T5 encoder. The features included tweet length, word count, and punctuation count, the number of hashtag usage, mentions, and URLs. These structural features were explored so as to understand how their distribution could affect the classification of tweets as normal, offensive, or hate speech. The investigation of these metadata items also enhances the general robustness of the detection model, as they allow the additional depth of information that goes beyond the semantics of the texts.

Figure 20. Feature correlation heatmap of tweet-level metadata

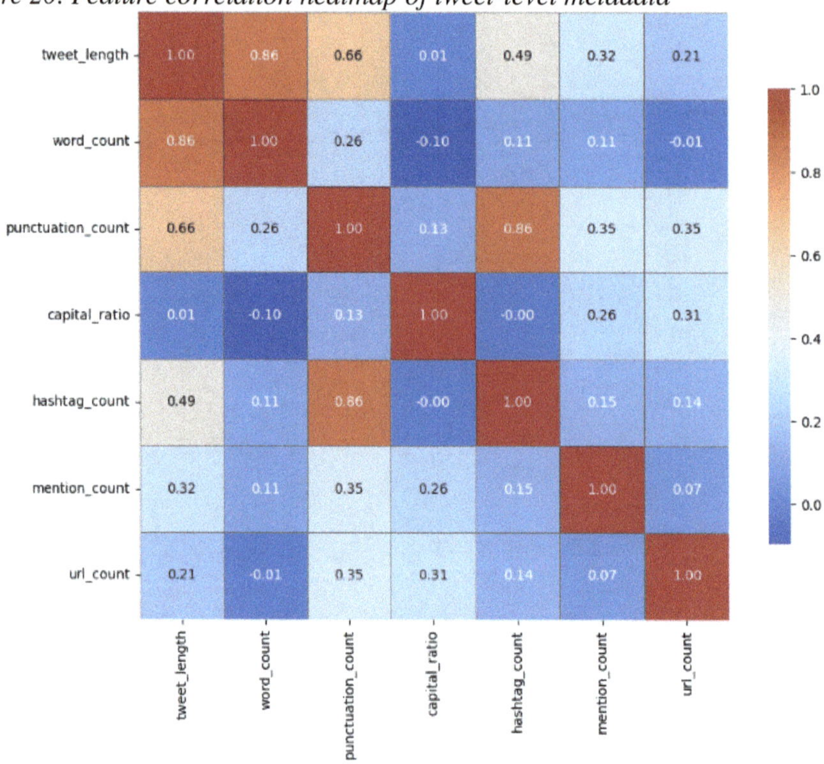

The heatmap on correlation between different metadata features, which shows the correlation between different metadata features, is shown in Figure 20. The strength of the association is also strong positive with the number of punctuation and hashtag and the length of the tweet and the word count. As seen in these relationships, in most cases the long tweets have more words and punctuations and this can affect the prediction of tweet category most specifically in the separation of the hateful or offensive text and normal tweets.

4.3 Result Discussion

The proposed T5 based model exhibits consistent and stable learning pattern throughout training. Generalization capability is also high, as revealed by the presence of consistent growth in accuracy and the curve of loss that does not indicate any overfitting over time. AUC of offensive tweet is 0.95, hate tweet is 0.98 and regular tweet is 0.88, Further validation with the help of ROC curve analysis gives excellent discriminative power. The accuracy, as well as the recall trade-off remains high, as identified by the accuracy, Recall curves. This enhances the performance of minority classes, e.g. hate tweets. Examples of per-epoch evaluation metrics are precision, recall, and F1-score that converge fast and provide high performance across all categories.

Figure 21. Comparison of our model with the existing model

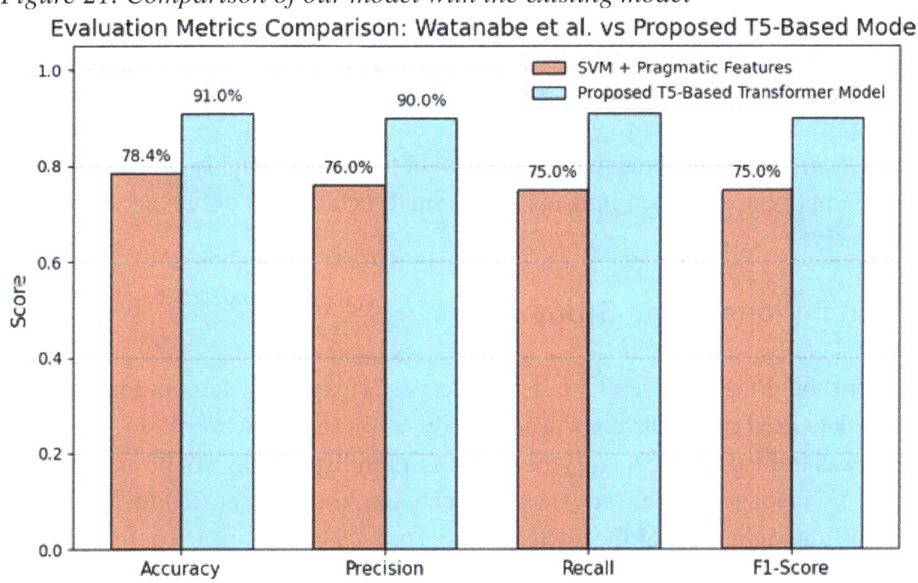

The advantages of the definition proposed are illustrated by the direct comparative analysis with an article by Watanabe et al. (2018). The SVM based model with pragmatic pattern extraction and unigram features used by Watanabe et al. presented a 78.4% accuracy in classification. Comparison to our T5-based model, as in Figure 21, a much higher validation accuracy of 91% was achieved along with superior precision, recall, and F1-scores in all categories. This is an increase attributable to deep contextualized embeddings through transformer architecture such that language is understood richer than shallow, hand-crafted features. Also, feature-based data, such as histograms and heatmaps of correlation, illustrates the utility of metadata attributes such as the use of hashtags, the length of tweets and punctuation. Altogether, the results show that the proposed T5-based model would be better than traditional machine learning approaches and would present a future-efficient, effective, and ready-to-use solution to hate speech detecting.

Even in other comparison testing, our model had a margin of correctness over RoBERTa, DistilBERT, and BERT-Base, on the same dataset by 2.5%, 4.8%, and 6.1%, respectively. It means that discrimination during typical conditions like hate and foul speech will become better due to broad pretraining of the T5 encoder. Even though T5 was initially developed to deal with text-to-text assignments, this study shows that, having made a correct architectural modification, it could be applied to the categorization assignment.

McNemar test was conducted to compare the T5-based model with RoBERTa and ensure that the increase in the performance was not due to luck. The p-value which was less than 0.05 implies that the increase in the accuracy of classification is statistically significant.

In order to evaluate the effect of tweet-level metadata, an ablation research was conducted. The removal of such info as the amount of hashtags and presentence punctuation rate reduced the macro F1-score of the model roughly by 4.3%, revealing the importance of such information in small details that define an abusive or non-abusive tweet.

4.4 Limitations of the Study

Even though the proposed T5-based model performs well on the conventional hate speech data used in the current research study, it has several weaknesses. Since the model was trained on tweets that are written in English, it may not be as universal in case of languages or websites such as Facebook, YouTube, or Reddit. Moreover, the real-time indicators of the performance were evaluated under controlled conditions; they might vary during blind situations of heavy loads. Some hidden or unspoken forms of hate speech, e.g. sarcasm or dog whistles have remained beyond the capability of automated algorithms to accurately recognize. These limitations provide guidelines on future studies, especially in the findings of strong inference limitation due to resources limitations, cross-platform generalizability, and multilingualism. Future research can apply such data augmentation strategies as contextual paraphrasing with T5, synonym replacement, and back-translation to improve the depiction of underrepresented classes (such as Normal).

CONCLUSION AND FUTURE SCOPE

This paper constructed and evaluated a real-time scheme of hate speech identification, including the T5 transformer version. The model applied across three classes, namely normal tweets, offensive tweets, and hate tweets, demonstrated an immense generalization capability, consistent learning behavior, and outstanding classification achievement. The proposed model returned a validation accuracy of 91% through extensive validations done as well on ROC curves, F1-scores, precision, and recall. With the aid of pragmatic attributes, an existing model based on the conventional SVM was compared to the T5-based model, whereby statistics showed that the T5-based model was relatively resilient and more accurate as compared to the prior methods in regard to classification performance. The feature-level analysis using a heatmap confirmed that the metadata features, such as use of hashtags, length of tweets, and the number of punctuations, had meaningful supplementary signals of categorization. Further, the results confirm the idea that the proposed T5-based hate speech recognition system is a high-performing and scalable method for real-time content moderation.

Model deployment integration with FastAPI manages to overcome the rift between research and process implementation in the real industry by proving the viability of live inference pipelines. The deployment-biased perspective of the study can be used immediately to guide the focus of developers and content moderation tools seeking scalable body of technologies to detect hate.

We need to take note of the social consequences of such systems, as well as their technology benefits. Online hate speech surveillance in real-time can reduce online mistreatment, help digital spaces become more secure, and give platforms the opportunity to enforce community standards. It also raises the questions of fairness, censorship and an eventual over-moderation, however. These trade-offs outline the importance of multidisciplinary collaboration of civil rights organizations, ethicists, lawyers, and AI researchers.

Although the proposed T5-based model does work, there are already several aspects that can benefit. The usefulness of the current system in different online groups may also be extended due to the further addition of multilingual capabilities of hate speech detection. It could be useful to add multimodal data such as pictures, videos or information about a user to enhance the ability of the model to detect complicated examples of hate speech. In addition to that, the model performance in a live environment can be checked in a real case with sophisticated serving frameworks such as as TensorRT or TorchServ. To achieve an even greater increase in the accuracy of identification, one may conduct further research that involves exploring a more complex model of a transformer (such as T5-large) applied to social media content or custom modified to perform it. Memories of minority groups, including hate speech examples, can also be improved by applying data imbalance by utilizing advanced augmentation methodologies or semi-supervised learning algorithms.

Future research may also be called adversarial robustness. Adversarial training or defensive distillation may be used in enhancing the dependability of the model since attackers may present an input that does not actually get noticed. Besides, explainability remains a crucial part of a moral use of AI. To facilitate transparency, attention visualizations, SHAP, and LIME should be applied in the user interfaces.

Finally, making the framework modular API type system with language support, pluggable encoders, and metadata layers can make it dynamically deployable in multiple applications, such as dashboard to monitor the state of public health research, or enterprise moderating tools. It would only be capable of responding to the evolving linguistic trends of hate speech in case it was a community-anchored ecosystem continuously supplemented and renewed with new data.

REFERENCES

Alatawi, H. S., Alhothali, A. M., & Moria, K. M. (2021). Detecting white supremacist hate speech using domain specific word embedding with deep learning and BERT. *IEEE Access : Practical Innovations, Open Solutions*, *9*, 106349–106363. DOI: 10.1109/ACCESS.2021.3100435

Alkomah, F., & Ma, X. (2022). A literature review of textual hate speech detection methods and datasets. *Information (Basel)*, *13*(6), 273. DOI: 10.3390/info13060273

Badjatiya, P., Gupta, S., Gupta, M., & Varma, V. (2017). Deep learning for hate speech detection in tweets. In *Proceedings of the 26th International Conference on World Wide Web Companion* (pp. 759–760). ACM., https://www.reuters.com/technology/german-soccer-club-st-pauli-quits-x-platform-over-alleged-hate-speech-2024-11-14, DOI: 10.1145/3041021.3054223

Barbieri, F., Espinosa Anke, L., & Camacho-Collados, J. (2022). XLM-T: Multilingual Language Models in Twitter for Sentiment Analysis and Beyond (arXiv:2104.12250v2). https://arxiv.org/abs/2104.12250

Boishakhi, F. T., Shill, P. C., & Alam, M. G. R. (2023). Multi-modal hate speech detection using machine learning. arXiv:2307.11519. https://arxiv.org/abs/2307.11519

Das, A., Wahi, J. S., & Li, S. (2020). Detecting hate speech in multi-modal memes. arXiv preprint arXiv:2012.14891. https://arxiv.org/abs/2012.14891

Djuric, N., Zhou, J., Morris, R., Grbovic, M., Radosavljevic, V., & Bhamidipati, N. (2015). Hate speech detection with comment embeddings. In *Proceedings of the 24th International Conference on World Wide Web* (pp. 29–30). ACM. DOI: 10.1145/2740908.2742760

García-Díaz, J. A., Jiménez-Zafra, S. M., & Valencia-García, R. (2021). UMUTeam at MeOffendEs 2021: Ensemble learning for offensive language identification using linguistic features, fine-grained negation, and transformers. In *MeOffendEs at IberLEF 2021* (pp. 157–166). CEUR Workshop Proceedings., https://ceur-ws.org/Vol-2943/

Hiran, K. K., Jain, R. K., Lakhwani, K., & Doshi, R. (2021). *Machine Learning: Master Supervised and Unsupervised Learning Algorithms with Real Examples (English Edition)*. BPB Publications.

Lee, K., & Ram, S. (2024). Deep learning for hate speech detection: A personality-based approach. In Companion Proceedings of the ACM Web Conference 2024 (WWW '24 Companion) (pp. 1667–1671). DOI: 10.1145/3589335.3652502

Mahrishi, M., Hiran, K. K., Meena, G., & Sharma, P. (Eds.). (2020). *Machine learning and deep learning in real-time applications*. IGI global., DOI: 10.4018/978-1-7998-3095-5

Mandl, T., Modha, S., Shahi, G. K., Jaiswal, A. K., Nandini, D., Patel, D., Majumder, P., & Schäfer, J. (2020). Overview of the HASOC track at FIRE 2020: Hate speech and offensive content identification in Indo-European languages. In CEUR Workshop Proceedings. https://ceur-ws.org/Vol-2757/

Meena, G., Dhanwal, B., Mahrishi, M., & Hiran, K. K. (2021, August). Performance comparison of network intrusion detection system based on different pre-processing methods and deep neural network. In *Proceedings of the International Conference on Data Science, Machine Learning and Artificial Intelligence* (pp. 110-115). DOI: 10.1145/3484824.3484878

Pérez, J. M., Furman, D. A., Alonso Alemany, L., & Luque, F. (2022). RoBERTuito: A pre-trained language model for social media text in Spanish (arXiv:2111.09453v3). https://arxiv.org/abs/2111.09453

Ranasinghe, T., Zampieri, M., & Hettiarachchi, H. (2019). BRUMS at HASOC 2019: Deep learning models for multilingual hate speech and offensive language identification. In Working Notes of FIRE 2019 - Forum for Information Retrieval Evaluation. https://ceur-ws.org/Vol-2517/

Rizos, G., Hemker, K., & Schuller, B. (2019). Augment to prevent: Short-text data augmentation in deep learning for hate-speech classification. In *Proceedings of the 28th ACM International Conference on Information and Knowledge Management (CIKM '19)* (pp. 991–1000). DOI: 10.1145/3357384.3358040

Rodriguez, A., & Argueta, C. (2019). Automatic detection of hate speech on Facebook using sentiment and emotion analysis. In *2019 International Conference on Artificial Intelligence in Information and Communication (ICAIIC)* (pp. 215–219). IEEE. DOI: 10.1109/ICAIIC.2019.8669073

Watanabe, H., Bouazizi, M., & Ohtsuki, T. (2018). Hate speech on Twitter: A pragmatic approach to collect hateful and offensive expressions and perform hate speech detection. *IEEE Access : Practical Innovations, Open Solutions*, *6*, 13825–13835. DOI: 10.1109/ACCESS.2018.2806394

Zhou, Y., Yang, Y., Liu, H., Liu, X., & Savage, N. (2020). Deep learning based fusion approach for hate speech detection. *IEEE Access : Practical Innovations, Open Solutions*, *8*, 128889–128898. DOI: 10.1109/ACCESS.2020.3009244

Chapter 10
Deepfake Technology and the Quagmire of Artificial Intelligence:
An Analysis of National and International Legal Frameworks

Pallavi Tiwari
https://orcid.org/0009-0004-3050-8531
Maharashtra National Law University, Nagpur, India

Ujwal Prabhakar Nandekar
https://orcid.org/0000-0003-2545-6736
Symbiosis Centre for Advanced Legal Studies and Research (SCALSAR), Symbiosis Law School, Symbiosis International University, Pune, India

ABSTRACT

Artificial Intelligence has proved to be a boon and a bane in all sectors of society. It has raised concerns regarding the protection of individuals' right to privacy and personality rights, and issues related to the protection of the personal data of individuals. Deepfakes are combinations of fake videos or images of individuals which are morphed or distorted to produce unethical results. The present research aims to conduct an empirical and doctrinal study to look into the issue of deepfake technology, how the public perceives it, and how it is a sensitive issue for laymen in India and internationally. The study involves an empirical analysis involving stakeholders from different dimensions of society, including individuals from the age group of 18-55(+) years and can be from any domain affected by such usage of

DOI: 10.4018/979-8-3373-3063-1.ch010

deepfake pictures and videos. Further to this, with the help of a theoretical analysis with the aid of an analytical study of existing laws in India and the understanding of the international legal regime to protect against misuse of artificial intelligence.

INTRODUCTION

As per recent news, a gang defrauded SP Oswal, 'the chairman and managing director of Vardhman Group', of Rs 7 crore by pretending to be representatives of the CBI and the former Chief Justice of India (CJI), DY Chandrachud, in a fictitious online proceeding (Sharma, 2024). This is just one incident of violating rights and conducting fraudulent activities using Artificial Intelligence. AI is used in deepfakes to make photos and movies appear frightfully real. However, these videos are fake and can be used to disseminate false information with negative effects.

Deepfakes are artificial intelligence (AI)-generated forgeries or copies of extremely lifelike audio, video, or images. Machine learning (ML) and Generative Adversarial Networks (GANs) are two technologies that produce deepfakes. Systems may learn and get better from experience through the data they gather thanks to machine learning (ML), a subset of artificial intelligence (Hall, 2018). Facial expression manipulation and face swapping are popular in deepfake videos. Artificial neural networks, which are computer programs that identify patterns in data, are the foundation of deepfakes. Creating a deepfake image or video usually entails "training" an artificial neural network with hundreds or thousands of photos to recognise and recreate patterns, most often faces (Thombre, 2021).

The term "deepfakes," which combines the terms "deep learning" and "fake," was invented on Reddit in 2017 when AI replaced the faces of famous people in some videos (Somers, 2020). Article 3(60) of the European Union's Artificial Intelligence Act, which was formally adopted by the European Parliament on March 13, 2024, defines "deep fake" as artificially produced or transformed audio, video, or image output that would misleadingly appear genuine or true, and that bears similarities to real people, locations, things, or other occurrences or things (EU AI Act, 2024).

Two machine learning models are used by deepfakes. Using a collection of data from the available sample videos or photographs, one of those generates fakes by analysing how a face might blink, smile, or grin, among other ways a face can convey emotion. When the second machine learning model is unable to determine whether the available video or image of the targeted individual is a hoax, the deepfake-generated product is most likely sufficiently convincing to the human eye. The other machine learning model attempts to determine whether the available sample detected from an autoencoder is a hoax and detects fraud to the utmost capability. Significant efforts must be taken to create countermeasures, increase awareness, and create a regulatory framework to reduce the risks connected to this technology. (Vig, 2024).

There are a lot of legal issues emerging out of the usage of artificial intelligence and deepfake technology in India and these can be related to defamation, impersonation, digital arrest problems which have been on the rise currently, cybersecurity issues, and intellectual property issues covering infringement of personality rights of celebrities and non-celebrities (Choubisa, 2022). It also raises privacy concerns and issues related to infringement of the fundamental rights given under the Constitution of India (The Constitution of India 1950). It also deprives the right to privacy and the right to live with dignity of individuals. Deepfakes can also be used maliciously, which raises apprehensions about the potential for character assassination, identity theft, and reputational harm (Hall, 2018).

The paper shall discuss the technology related to deepfakes and the usage of artificial intelligence to defraud the public, the international laws relating to deepfakes as there has been a current rise in legislation to combat deepfake-related issues and challenges across the globe for example the recent Californian law. This study will primarily focus on the United States and European Union and then the authors shall delve into the Indian legal framework to tackle such issues using a doctrinal analysis of the existing laws and case studies in India. Further, the authors have also conducted an empirical study to observe the stakeholders' responses including students, research professionals, academicians, lawyers and cyber law experts. The paper aims to suggest some changes in the existing laws in India like the Information Technology Act 2000 or some to be introduced in the Digital India Act and how it can be modified to fit in the current generation of artificial intelligence and deepfake technology-related issues.

To address these issues the researchers have relied on the below-mentioned methodology, research questions and objectives which shall be addressed in the further chapters of the paper:

The present research aims to conduct an empirical and doctrinal study to look into the issue of deepfake technology, how the public perceives it, and how it is a sensitive issue for laymen in India and internationally. The study shall involve an empirical analysis involving stakeholders from different dimensions of society including individuals from the age group of 18-55(+) years and can be from any domain affected by such usage of deepfake pictures and videos. Further to this, with the help of a theoretical analysis with the aid of an analytical study of existing laws in India and the understanding of the international legal regime to protect against misuse of artificial intelligence. The researchers aim to delve into analytical and exploratory research to give suggestions to include some changes in the data protection regime in India and analyse the soon-to-be-introduced Digital India Act along with the Digital Personal Data Protection Act of 2023.

A 21-item questionnaire was prepared specifically for the opinion survey and distributed by email and/or WhatsApp (google link). The objective of obtaining informed consent was limited to using the data for this research study. Purposive sampling was used since the respondents are hard to identify without personal or professional familiarity and no databases, like a standard register, are available. The purposive sample technique is regarded as one of the key components of this research because of the paucity of practice and understanding of the use of deepfake technology, particularly its implications for privacy rights, personality rights, and other individual rights. The data was thus compiled and analysed.

The objectives sought to be achieved by the researchers in this paper were related to:

- To understand the origin of deepfake technology and how the technology misuses Artificial Intelligence to defraud people using it.
- To look into the international regulatory framework comprising of United States and European Union to tackle the issues of deepfake technology.
- To analyse the Indian regulatory framework dealing with deepfake technology and its repercussions along with a criticism of the existing laws in India.
- To understand the perspectives of the stakeholders of the research concerning deepfake technology, the common understanding related to it and how it has affected their lives.
- To suggest changes in the existing legal framework in India and how the Digital India Act of India can be amended to fit in the current issues related to deepfake technology.

Based on these objectives, the following research questions were aimed to be answered by the researchers:

- Where does the deepfake technology start and how the technology misuses Artificial Intelligence to defraud people using it?
- What is the international regulatory framework comprising the United States and the European Union to tackle the issues of deepfake technology?
- What is the Indian regulatory framework dealing with deepfake technology and its repercussions?
- Who are the stakeholders of the negative effects of deepfake technology and how do they perceive it?
- What are the changes required in the existing legal framework in India and how the Digital India Act of India can be amended to fit in the current issues related to deepfake technology?

BACKGROUND

International Legal Framework Against Violation of Rights by Deepfake Technology: a Study of the United States and European Union

As per Figure 1, with half of the world's population voting this year, Sumsub, a global full-cycle verification service, found that the number of deepfakes has increased by up to 245% year over year. According to the data, there has been multiple growth in deepfakes in some nations, such as the "*US, India, Indonesia, Mexico, and South Africa*", where elections are scheduled for 2024. Deepfake cases are increasing in a variety of businesses. Fintech, iGaming, and cryptocurrency had the highest rates of deepfakes over the previous quarter (Sumsub, 2024).

Figure 1. Deepfake cases surge in countries holding 2024 elections, Sumsub research shows

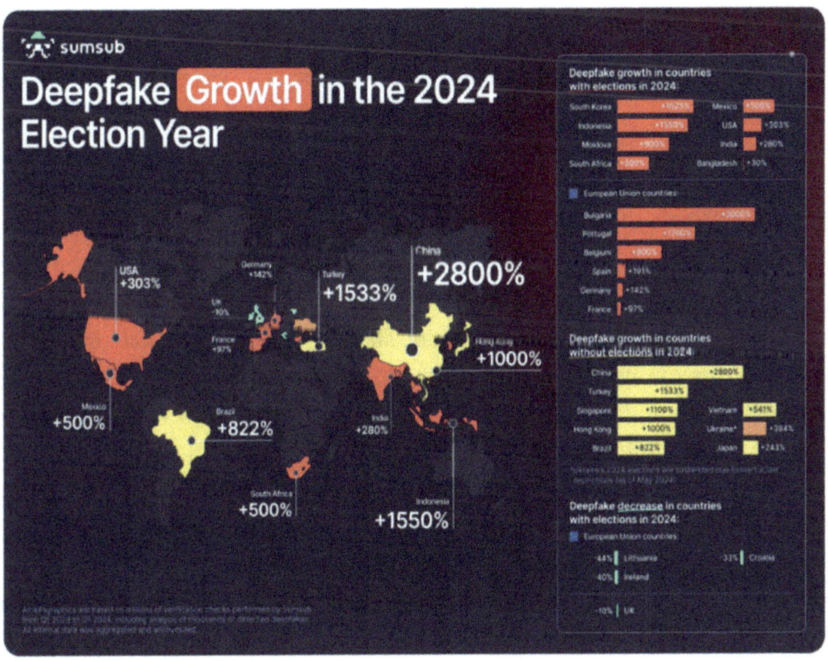

(Sumsub, 2024)

Most states in the United States created generic criminal laws against impersonation before the Internet age (Geng, 2023). These regulations may apply to all forms of media, including internet messages and films. With the fast development of social media and the age of the internet, a lot of legislation has been passed in many states that specifically refers to online impersonation or cloning of personalities of famous individuals which is majorly done to threaten, bully, or harass someone via social media, email, or other modes of electronic communication. These are the states of '*California, Tennessee (EVLthe IS Act), Connecticut, Florida, Hawaii, Illinois, Louisiana, Massachusetts, Mississippi, New Jersey, New York, North Carolina, Oklahoma, Rhode Island, Texas, Utah, Washington, and Wyoming*' (Graham, 2024).

Starting from 2019, some of the states of the United States enacted legislation dealing with the prohibition and regulation of the usage of deepfakes. The majority of such laws target majorly sexually explicit content or pornographic videos or images. Some states have begun to declare the distribution of fraudulent audio or video media to damage a politician's reputation or mislead a voter into voting for or against a candidate as illegal in their states (Hall, 2018).

In a proactive move, the European Union recently passed the Artificial Intelligence Act (EU AI Act 2024), which contains stringent guidelines aimed at controlling deepfakes and other artificial intelligence (AI) systems. An important turning point in AI governance has been reached as the European Union (EU) has increased its attempts to directly confront the new problem of deepfake technology in the face of mounting concerns about its possible effects on democratic processes and public trust.

United States

In January 2024, explicit deepfakes of Taylor Swift garnered millions of views in the United States, including an astounding 47 million on platform X, before being removed (Saner, 2024). This sparked strong calls for legislation that would make such damaging and intrusive content illegal. The simplicity with which manipulations can be made, especially with generative AI tools, threatens the credibility of public discourse and the integrity of information. These technologies were actively being used to spread false information, extort victims, and access classified information, as demonstrated in the US California Northern District Court's Clarkson v. OpenAI case (Hill, 2023). This made it more difficult for both humans and AI to recognize and validate information.

Congress has addressed the regulation of deepfakes in several ways. Lawmakers are aware of the risks deepfakes represent to public confidence, privacy, and national security. Big tech efforts are similar to those made to comprehend deepfakes. Congress has held hearings, briefings, and debates to better understand the implications of deepfakes and explore technology possibilities for detection and prevention. The House Committee on Oversight and Accountability held a hearing on Deepfakes in March 2024 with the title "Addressing Real Harm Caused by Deepfakes." The impact of deepfakes on the general public, particularly youngsters, as well as their implications for politics and national security, were discussed in the discussion (Miller, 2024).

Several measures to control and monitor deepfakes have lately been passed by Congress. These consist of:

- "The Task Force on Artificial Intelligence in the Financial Services Sector" (Task Force on Artificial Intelligence, 2024) under the Preventing Deep Fakes Scams Act. Congress receives reports from the Task Force on AI-related matters about the financial services industry. The Protecting Consumers from Deceptive AI Act, H.R. 7766, 2024, requires the National Institute of Standards and Technology to create task forces on AI and deepfakes. The purpose of the Task Forces is to guide and support the development of technical standards and guidelines for identifying content produced by generative AI. These rules will ensure that a disclosure identifying the source of any audio or video clip created or substantially modified by AI is included.
- The Deepfakes Accountability Act, 2023 Shields national security agencies from the dangers of deepfake technology. Additionally, it gives victims of damaging deepfakes legal remedies.
- The No AI Fraud Act protects individual property rights in voice and likeness.
- The DEFIANCE Act of 2024 will also be implemented soon and it states to, "*improve rights to relief for individuals affected by non-consensual activities involving intimate digital forgeries, and for other purposes*".
- The H.R.6088 – "Deepfakes in Federal Elections Prohibition Act 2020" Is also a very recent law in the United States to tackle the issue of deepfakes being used to manipulate election campaigns and voting trends. Morphed videos of Donald Trump were being used to mislead the public which is why such laws help to curtail the unauthorised usage of Artificial Intelligence. As per the Act, "*This bill prohibits the distribution of certain deceptive audio or visual media (i.e., deepfakes) within 60 days of a federal election and establishes criminal penalties for related violations. Additionally, the bill establishes a new criminal offence related to the distribution of materially deceptive audio or visual media before a federal election. A violator is subject to a fine, up to 5 years in prison, or both. It also permits a candidate whose voice or likeness appears in such deceptive audio or visual media to bring a civil action for damages*".

In an attempt to stop the dissemination of false information and misleading election content, California has passed three new bills and although artificial intelligence (AI) is not specifically mentioned in the first two measures, their implementation was motivated by the spread of AI deepfakes, particularly about election material.

AB 2655 (Defending Democracy from Deepfake Deception Act of 2024) - imposes disclosure requirements that go beyond the 120 days preceding an election, as well as specific removal obligations on major online platforms during that time.

AB 2839 (Elections: Deceptive Media in Advertisements) – prohibits the dissemination of election-related communications that contain specific materially misleading information.

AB 2355 (Political Reform Act of 1974: Political Advertisements: Artificial Intelligence) Mandates “disclaimers for AI-generated advertisements created by political committees”.

Deepfakes pose a grave threat to democratic governments and the global order. To make policymakers, the tech industry, academics, and individuals aware of the potential harm, manipulation, and exploitation that deepfake creators could cause, the United States should start by bringing attention to the issue in technical, governmental, and public circles. Social media companies have long been exempted from punishment for disseminating offensive material.

Similarly, Clarkson v OpenAI (Moreno, 2024): The case also highlights how deepfakes could interfere with the elections, spread disbelief, and jeopardise public discretion. The case also raised an alarm on the rising issue and danger related to sextortion’ by misusing the technology of generative AI and the images which were publicly available of ordinary individuals which is also a cause of rising cases of digital arrest in India. Disturbingly, this content involved not only non-consenting adults but also children and dealt with child pornography. Some individuals with malicious intent also extorted money, from victims by threatening them that such deepfake videos and images of them shall be circulated to their family members as well (Busch & Ware, 2023).

European Union

It was in February 2024, that BBC News circulated a news covering information about Platforms like CivitAI, built on deepfake models, and usage of deepfake technology to produce illegal content and also targeted some vulnerable groups like children and women (Morena, 2024). Although there are measures on these platforms to curtail such activities the victims and disadvantaged groups have been left exposed to the wrath of artificial intelligence. Systems that create or modify audio, video, or image content must adhere to basic transparency requirements outlined in the European Union Artificial Intelligence Act (EU AI Act). Unless it is obvious, service providers are required to notify users when they are engaging with an AI system.

Additionally, transparency regarding deepfake or automatically generated content is necessary. Providers who monitor user-generated content, including deepfakes, are required by the Digital Services Act (DSA) to be open and honest about their moderation guidelines and enforcement procedures (Madiega, 2022). An emphasis on responsibility, transparency, and adherence to legal frameworks, as defined by Article 50(2) of the European Union's AI Act, distinguishes the EU's approach to deepfake regulation under the AI Act, which aims to guarantee that AI systems are used responsibly and ethically. This rule seeks to reduce the likelihood of deceit and manipulation by making it simpler for users to recognize content produced by artificial intelligence. However, whether these disclosure regulations will be enough to stop the harmful use of deepfakes is still ambiguous and unclear. The EU AI Act assigns a risk rating to AI systems and enforces more stringent rules for those with a higher risk (Morena, 2024). According to Article 50(4) of the AI Act of the EU, anyone who is using AI to produce deepfakes and related products whether it be creators, artists, or anybody else, must inform the public of this information and put up a disclaimer that the information has been generated through AI (EU AI Act, 2024). Information disclosure requirements for AI-generated content or the designation of AI-written text as "deepfake" could be determined using the standards outlined in the European Court of Human Rights (ECtHR) in Halet v Luxembourg, 2023 opinion. The standards addressed in this case were related to seriousness, contribution to public discussion, and novelty aspects of the deepfake. The CJEU(Court of Justice of the European Union) ruled in the UPC Telekabel Wien case that it's critical to find a balance between the use of internet limitations and people's rights to produce content and perform artistic expressions (UPC Telekabel Wien GmbH v Constantin Film Verleih GmbH, 2014).

To prevent "catastrophic harm, either deliberate or unintended," which is a result of the growing use of artificial intelligence, the European Union was joined by twenty-nine countries, including India in 'The Bletchley Declaration by Countries Attending the AI Safety Summit', which took place from November 1–2, 2023. The Declaration lays out a path forward for countries to work together harmoniously on present and potential risks related to the misuse of AI, as well as formulate a framework to recognise the risks in the AI space and develop risk-based policies and mitigation mechanisms across nations to increase transparency and accountability by private companies developing cutting-edge AI capabilities (AI Safety Summit: The Bletchley Declaration, 2023).

A joint report by Trend Micro, UNICRI, and Europol was introduced by a simple question: "*Has anyone witnessed any examples of criminals abusing artificial intelligence?*" (Trend Micro Research, United Nations Interregional Crime and Justice Research Institute (UNICRI) & Europol's European Cybercrime Centre (EC3), 2024). To answer this question the report provided a collective analysis of present and imminent malicious usages and misuses of Artificial Intelligence. Based on the report, it is reasonable to assume that cybercriminals will gradually incorporate AI techniques to increase the size and scope of their attacks. Therefore, the report's second section examined conceivable future scenarios in which criminals can misuse AI technologies to make their operations easier and their attacks more successful (Schwartz, MJ, 2020).

"Article 5 of GDPR (General Data Protection Regime of EU) covers principles for processing personal data. Clause (e) limits data storage, while clause (f) relates to integrity and confidentiality". Article 25 Addresses "data protection by design and default" and Article 32 deals with the security of processing. Thus, the GDPR regime of the EU also delves into the perspective of protecting personal data, which can be further integrated into the current digital and AI world to mitigate the risks of deepfake technology (General Data Protection Regime, 2016).

There are still many gaps in the protection of victims of gender-based violence, especially when it comes to deepfakes used for sexual assault, even though EU laws, such as the Directive on Combating Violence Against Women and Domestic Violence, exist to prevent online violence. Although the EU Digital Services Act's emphasis on unlawful content and the protection of privacy rights under Article 8 ECHR (European Convention on Human Rights, 1950) are significant, they fall short of addressing the unique difficulties posed by deepfakes. First of all, as Tele2/Watson highlighted, it gives consumers the ability to pursue legal action against potentially dangerous services which can hamper their data (Tele2 Sverige AB v Post- och telestyrelsen and Secretary of State for the Home Department v Tom Watson and Others, 2016).

According to GDPR, it is important to get consent from individuals if their data is being used without their consent on some artificial intelligence platforms. (Article 7 and Recital 32 of GDPR – 'Consent must be freely given, specific, informed and unambiguous'). It is also to create exceptions to protect the artistic freedom where content is being made by usage of artificial intelligence and it should not be directly banned from publishing. Without prior authorization for invasive tracking techniques, individuals have limited control over their data and its possible use in deepfakes. Deepfakes and usage of personal information of individuals by companies to produce content directly defies the ECHR's rule of law principles outlined in Articles 8(2) (Brkan, 2019).

The Digital Services Act (DSA) also addresses this problem. Both male and female politicians endure online abuse, but the nature of the attacks varies. Deepfake harassment is gendered, with males targeted based on their skill or policy and women targeted for their bodies and sexuality. However, current restrictions do not address the entire spectrum of potentially dangerous content. Some doctored photographs may not be explicit enough to meet enforcement criteria. Furthermore, the legal standard of "serious harm" can be difficult to establish under the EU AI Act and a clear line of demarcation between serious and non-serious harm is not clearly defined under the law. It also does not cover child or women abuse under the serious harm category which requires further changes (Smith, H., & Mansted, K., 2020).

The first-ever legal framework on AI in the European Union, the AI Act, addresses the risks associated with AI and puts Europe in a position to lead the world. The first complete legal framework on AI in the world is the AI Act (Regulation (EU) 2024/1689, which establishes standardized standards on AI). The regulations are intended to promote reliable AI throughout Europe. The EU AI Act summarises the risk for AI systems into four diverse groups.

Unacceptable Risk

These are the AI systems that pose a direct risk to "human safety or rights" and are prohibited under this category. For instance, voice-activated toys that encourage risky behaviour or social scoring by governments that could result in discrimination are deemed inappropriate.

High Risk

AI systems that endanger human safety or fundamental rights are deemed high risk under the draft EU AI Act. This can include systems found in toys, automobiles, aeroplanes, medical equipment, and elevators—all of which are subject to EU product safety laws. Critical infrastructures, such as transportation networks, are examples of high-risk systems where a malfunction could put lives in danger. These risk categories, however, are also intended to safeguard human rights and quality of life in addition to physical safety. For example, using AI to sort resumes or score tests is seen as a high-risk system since it may affect a person's future and career path.

Limited Risk

This level focuses on AI systems that require a certain amount of transparency, such as chatbots for customer support. Users must be able to choose to communicate with a human instead of a machine and be informed that they are interacting with a machine. Transparency, user-informed consent, and the simple opportunity to withdraw are all essential components of limited risk systems.

Minimal Risk

Minimal risk is the bottommost level of risk explained in the EU AI Act, and addresses applications, like “AI-powered video games or email spam filters”.

The EU AI Act has the potential to become a global norm, similar to the General Data Protection Regulation (GDPR) of 2018, which will establish the degree to which AI improves rather than detracts from your life, no matter where you are. A bill that establishes a legal framework for artificial intelligence was enacted by the Brazilian Congress in late September 2021, greatly impacted by the EU’s AI regulation which is already causing a stir internationally.

INDIAN LEGAL FRAMEWORK AGAINST VIOLATION OF RIGHTS BY DEEPFAKE TECHNOLOGY

Impersonation by deepfakes can deceive individuals, corporations, and organizations. Scammers may use deepfake videos or voice recordings of executives or workers to solicit illicit wire transfers, and sensitive information, or participate in fraudulent activity. Individuals may use deepfake voice phishing to imitate well-known corporate executives, leading to fraudulent activity and financial losses for customers. A worrying case of cyber fraud utilizing deepfake videos of two well-known Indian businessmen—Mukesh Ambani, chairman of Reliance Industries, and N. R. Narayana Murthy, co-founder of Infosys—was recently reported in Bengaluru in November 2024 (Express News Service, November 2024). According to sources, two people were duped using these fake movies as bait, resulting in a total loss of about Rs 95 lakh. The events highlighted the growing dangers of deepfake technology and the significance of confirming internet information before interacting with it (HELMUS, T. C., 2022).

The Ministry of Commerce and Industry formed the ‘*18-member AI Task Force for India’s Economic Transformation*’ on August 24, 2017. The Task Force was established to provide recommendations for government, corporate, and research projects as well as to provide the legal and policy framework for the application of AI technologies. The ministry aimed at integrating AI into the country’s political, economic, and legal processes by initiating remarkable developments in industry domains such as ‘*manufacturing, fintech, healthcare, agriculture, education, retail, human and robot interaction, AADHAR, environment, national security, and public utility services*’ (AI Task Force, 2017). The Task Force advocated an Inter-Ministerial National Artificial Intelligence Mission to serve as a focal agency for AI-related advances and activities in India in a report released in January 2018.

Celebrities, Personality Rights and Violations by Deepfake Technology

The entertainment and media sectors are also heavily burdened. One in three online deepfake films is sexual, making India the sixth most vulnerable nation to deepfake adult content (BW Online World, 2024). Cases were filed and won by famous actors like Amitabh Bachchan (Amitabh Bachchan v. Rajat Negi, 2024), Anil Kapoor (Anil Kapoor v Simply Life India & Ors,2024), and Jackie Shroff (Jaikishan Kakubhai Saraf v Peppy Store, 2024) against misuse of their personality traits with the help of deepfake technology and the production of fake pornographic videos. This is one aspect of protection against deepfake technology and its misuse through the newly emerging personality rights and right to publicity. These deepfake movies, such as the digitally altered Rashmika Mandanna video that was overlayed on the genuine footage of British influencer Zara Patel, have been all over the internet lately. Deepfakes were not limited to this encounter with the Indian people; their extensive use even extended into the political sphere, as "deepfake" video clips of star Amitabh Bachchan posing questions about local politics ended up on Madhya Pradesh voters' gadgets. Here big celebrities and icons have recourse to solutions of right to publicity to protect their personality rights or reliance upon trademark law or copyright law to protect subject matters of creativity and merchandising under it but this is not the solution for the common man in the country (Panwar & Roy, 2024).

After journalist Rana Ayyub in India pushed for justice for an eight-year-old child who had been raped and killed she was repeatedly subjected and became a victim of a deepfake pornographic defamation campaign. To make matters worse, some of the internet service providers and social media websites, where this kind of abuse and illegal activities take place, have been reluctant to recognize the issue and address it, thus making responding to it still difficult (Venema).

Information Technology Act 2000 and The New Digital India Act on Deepfakes

In December 2023, the Centre issued an advisory to social media platforms on deepfakes and warned them of legal consequences if such content is visible on their websites where social media companies are required to notify their users about content that is forbidden by the IT (Information Technology) Rules, as well as the legal repercussions for posting such content (Deeksha, 2023). The IT Rules' Rule 3(1)(b) forbids the dissemination of "obscene or pornographic" or other content that violates the rights of others, particularly bodily privacy. Content that impersonates another person or that could purposefully mislead the user about its origin by presenting it as reality is also prohibited (Information Technology (Intermediary Guidelines and

Digital Media Ethics Code) Amendment Rules 2022, Rule 3(1)(b)). According to the direction, social media companies are required to notify users of the content that is forbidden under Rule 3(1)(b) through their user agreements and terms of service. Additionally, while registering to use the platform, the user must be made aware of such prohibited content. Any unlawful content on these intermediary websites has to be pulled down by them otherwise it calls for punishments under the IT (Information Technology) Act and will be better addressed under the to-be-introduced law of the Digital India Act. However, "*the efforts put into formulating and passing regulations remain nullified without stringent execution and enforcement*" (Karda, 2024). The IT Act's Section 66D addresses the penalties for impersonating someone to cheat by utilizing a computer resource. Anyone found guilty under this clause faces a maximum sentence of three years in prison and a fine of up to Rs one lakh (The Information Technology Act 2000, Section 66D). Section 67 of the IT Act provides for "punishment for publishing or transmitting obscene material in electronic form which is also being used in cases of obscene content being created using deepfake technology". Penalties for privacy violations are outlined in Section 66E of the Information Technology Act 2000 and under the Constitution of India as well after the famous *Puttaswamy* judgment. "Similar penalties apply to the transmission or publication of sexually explicit content or sexually explicit images of children by electronic means under sections 67A and 67B of the Information Technology Act of 2000", respectively. Nevertheless, section 66D of The IT Act of 2000 lists personation by computer facilities as a criminal provision (Vig, 2024).

Rule 11 of the Information Technology (Intermediary Guidelines and Digital Media Ethics Code) Rules, 2021, states that "social media intermediaries must establish a self-regulating body to handle any complaints (if any) and oversee the observance of the code of ethics". Additionally, social media intermediaries are obliged to provide a due diligence document and regulation that requires users of computer resources to be explicitly informed about the ban on uploading or sharing any "pornographic, vulgar, or indecent content". The accused person will be punished for the offence under Section 66C of the IT Act, 2000, if the deepfake content uses any type of unique identity feature, such as an individual's electronic password, fraudulently. S. 69A (Blocking Powers) gives the government the authority to prevent the public from accessing information that poses a risk to public safety or order. Authorities can order the removal of deepfake content from online platforms under this clause. However, because content on the internet spreads and replicates so quickly, the effectiveness of such efforts may be restricted.

During the 2024 general elections, the Election Commission of India relied upon basic guidelines which required political parties to take down deepfake content within 3 hours of detection which is very similar to the initiatives taken by the United States as well during their elections (Advisory to All Intermediaries to Comply with Existing

IT Rules, 2023). The Ministry of Electronics and Information Technology recently examined a draft of the proposed Digital India Act, 2023, which includes provisions for appropriate action against users engaged in cyberbullying and revenge porn. Traditional quality testing methods for risky AI-based technologies are mentioned to periodically monitor digital content and moderate it (Manda & Mishra, 2024).

The introduction of the Digital Personal Data Protection Act (DPDP Act) of 2023 has advanced India's data protection laws significantly (Malhotra & Malhotra, 2024). The Act along with the recently issued DPDP (Digital Personal Data Protection) Rules, place a strong emphasis on people's rights over their personal data and place duties on organizations that handle it. The Act shall come into force when the DPDP rules are approved and enforced and the discussion on the rules is still going on amongst the stakeholders. To improve privacy and data protection, India's DPDP Rules, 2025, must resolve uncertainties like consent and third-party risks. Under the new rules, Data principals have been given the power and the right to access, modify correct, and erase their data stored on some websites or applications along with stringent mechanisms to withdraw consent that they might have given to the usage of their data by the Data Fiduciaries and it also gives measures to address complaints effectively under the DPDP Act. The Rules dictate robust safeguards, together with encryption, and reporting of any breach within within 72 hours, and robust identity verification, "particularly to protect sensitive personal details of children and persons with disabilities" (Draft Digital Personal Data Protection Rules 2025).

The Act and the rules although does not discuss the concept of deepfake technology and usage of AI to manipulate the data of individuals mostly because AI uses information of individuals which is publicly available and not personal data but still these developments in India around the legal framework required in the digital age is considered to be a step forward in the direction of protection of personal data rights of individuals. Some of the key components of the rules and the Act which shall be enforced soon after the implementation of the rules are:

- Consent Requirement: Before processing an individual's personal data, entities must get that person's express consent. This clause fails in the context of deepfakes when someone's image or likeness is used without their permission.
- Data Principal Rights: People can view, update, and remove personal information. These rights can be used by victims of deepfake usage to ask that any illegal content involving their data be taken down.
- The act's hefty penalty for violations can discourage organizations from abusing personal information to produce deepfakes.

The act establishes a precedent for acknowledging human photographs and likenesses as data that has to be protected, even if its primary focus is data fiduciaries—organizations that handle personal data. Those who produce or disseminate deepfakes without authorization might be held responsible by using this approach. The act should be broadened to cover any issue which violates the personal data of the individuals which is done by deepfake technology. The Act though lacks provisions for AI and algorithmic biasedness for AI-generated data and its misuse. It does not provide for AI audit and its transparency.

The current laws in India do not specifically define what is "deepfake" but if the usage of such technology results in some harm like pornography, voyeurism, hate speech or impersonation to defraud people which is very common these days in cases of digital arrest (Mallick & Ganguli,2024), it is dealt with under the Information Technology Act 2000, which is soon to be replaced by the Digital India Act. The government has also issued guidelines to social media intermediaries that if they do not detect and remove the deepfake content on their websites they will lose their safe harbour rights under Section 79 of the Information Technology Act 2000. The Digital India Act on the other hand will not protect the intermediaries to such an extent and thus they shall be directly liable for any illegal content on their website. The new law focuses on transparency and accountability in the digital world. Algorithmic transparency and periodic risk assessment specifically related to deepfakes are important and have been covered under the new law and also protection of Constitutional principles shall be made essential.

On January 6, 2025, the Ministry of Electronics and Information Technology ("MeitY") made available for public review a study titled "AI Governance Guidelines Development". As India's AI ecosystem grows, the research emphasizes the necessity of a cohesive, whole-of-government approach to guarantee compliance and efficient governance. The study, which was produced by a subcommittee that MeitY formed on November 9, 2023, is a component of a broader project headed by India's Principal Scientific Advisor ("PSA"). The subcommittee examined important concerns, found gaps, and made practical suggestions for the moral and responsible advancement of AI in India under the direction of a multistakeholder advisory group. The Report suggests creating a "Whole of Government Coordination Mechanism" by forming an "Inter-Ministerial AI Coordination Committee" under MeitY. Aligning with Rule 22 of the DPDP Rules (The Digital Personal Data Protection Rules, 2025), which puts pressure on collaboration on national security and sovereignty concerns, this committee would generate a unified AI governance roadmap. A dedicated section under this would back this effort by helping as an advisory hub, planning India's AI ecosystem, conducting risk assessments, and evolving agendas for responsible AI use. Additionally, the body would start an "AI Incident Database" to monitor risks such as violation of privacy and unfair and biased outcomes, aligning with

Rule 7 of the DPDP Rules which commands reporting personal data violations. The Report highlights the significance of industry self-regulation and calls for voluntary industry commitments. In the AI ecosystem, technological techniques like labelling and watermarking could be employed to increase accountability and traceability. These systems would assist detect and effectively managing hazards while enabling real-time tracking of AI outputs. It is recommended under the report that AI-specific measures should be included in the Digital India Act that address the hazards associated with artificial intelligence. This entails strengthening the processes for resolving grievances, facilitating "digital by design" adjudication systems, and guaranteeing strict regulatory supervision for AI systems (Report on AI Governance Guidelines Development, January 2025).

Criminal Laws In India and Violations by Deepfake Technology

Section 354 of The Bharatiya Nyaya Sanhita, 2023 (BNS) provides for punishment for Defamation which can be applicable in the cases of misuse of deepfake technology to harm the reputation of individuals. Section 469 of the Indian Penal allows victims of deepfakes to bring forgery proceedings. A case can also be filed by anyone else who is aware that the content is deepfake. Section 469 has been superseded by Section 334 (4) Of the BNS, 2023. Section 351(1)The BNS refers to Criminal Intimidation which is related to threats causing alarm or compelling a person to do something against their will which happens in most of the cases of digital arrest and blackmailing a person using AI. When deepfakes are used to impersonate someone, especially in fraudulent schemes where the impersonation causes financial or personal harm, Section 319(1) Of BNS (The Bharatiya Nyaya Sanhita, 2023) i.e. Cheating by Personation is applicable (Pandey & Jadhav, 2023).

Section 77 of the BNS i.e. (Voyeurism) and Section 78 of BNS i.e. (Stalking) are relevant in the cases of deepfakes which can involve illegal use of a woman's image in a "*private act or when the creation and dissemination of such content constitute harassment*". All the provisions under the BNS related to the protection of women against sexual harassment, assault, and exploitation can be used in cases where deepfake content is being misused to produce sexually explicit content, which involves women.

The NITI Ayog 2018 issued the National Artificial Intelligence Strategy named "AI for ALL" which served as a foundational document regulating and also implementing AI technology across different sectors in India (NITI Ayog, 2018). In 2021, seven core principles for Responsible AI were issued namely: Safety and Reliability, Inclusivity, Non-Discrimination, Privacy, Transparency, Accountability and Reinforcement of human values (NITI Ayog, Government of India, RESPONSIBLE AI #AIFORALL, November 2022).

Recently India has also issued certain guidelines and recommendations on Artificial Intelligence and its regulations. In March 2024, the Government of India issued certain guidelines for the usage of AI on intermediary platforms and the usage of LLMs. It was required that certain platforms obtain MeITy approval before using untested AI models on their portals to avoid issues of bias, electoral interference, and issues related to deepfakes and unidentified AI-generated media. User notifications and informing users about content inaccuracies and usage of deepfake detection measures were considered essential and a part of these regulations. Later the approval requirement was done away with but the labelling of AI-generated content was still important and required by these platforms (Due Diligence by Intermediaries, Advisory 2021).

In 2024, famous news anchor Rajat Sharma filed a PIL in the Delhi High Court against the misuse of deepfake technologies and the Court issued a notice to the Union Government to address the issue of deepfakes and misuse of AI (Thapliyal, 2024). The MeitY replied with the information of two research projects which have been started aiming at detecting fake videos, images, and voices created using AI. Further to this, in December 2024, Rajat Sharma filed a case against TAMARA DOC & ORS for spreading major misinformation by displaying fraudulent medicinal drug advertisements through the wrongful use of AI and using the image and voice of a celebrity like Rajat Sharma. The Court has restrained them from using such videos and images which may confuse the minds of the consumers regarding medicines which also comes from a public health perspective (Rajat Sharma & Anr. V Tamara Doc & Ors., 2024).

EMPIRICAL STUDY AND ANALYSIS OF RECOGNITION OF DEEPFAKE TECHNOLOGY IN INDIA

The survey was given to 200 possible respondents, and 37 legitimate questionnaires were posed to the researchers, resulting in an 18.5 per cent return rate. This could be because of the sensitivity and confidentiality of the discussed subject matter.

The following nine elements provoked opinions:

1. Familiarity of Deepfake
2. Experience with Deepfake
3. Use of Deepfake
4. Deepfake and violation of privacy
5. Governance of Deepfake
6. Relationship between social media platforms, deepfake and individual rights

Figure 2. Gender of respondents

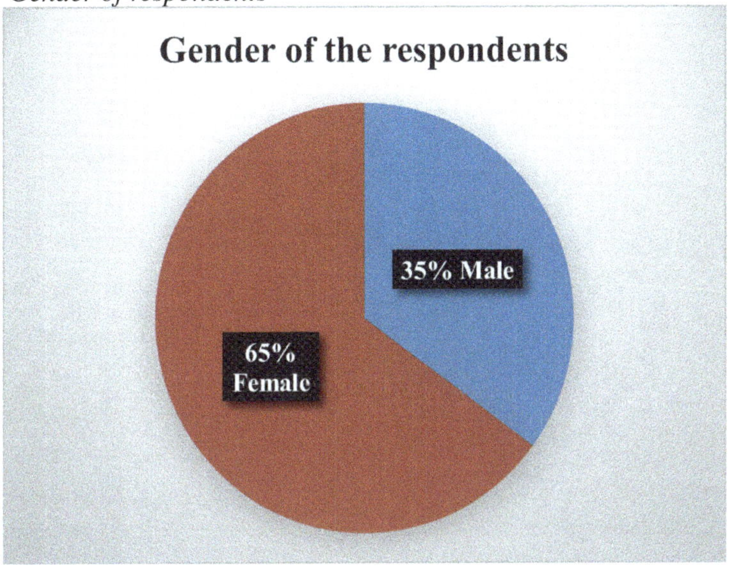

As per Figure 1, the data gathering for this empirical study on deepfake technology was broken down by gender, which sheds light on how deepfakes affect men and women differently in terms of privacy and personality rights. Given our present understanding of gender and technology, it is expected that female respondents will be more concerned about privacy violations, especially when it comes to gendered harassment (e.g., defamation, non-consensual deepfake pornography, etc.). Male respondents, however, might be more concerned about the effects deepfakes have on their reputations and careers, including the possibility of political influence, career sabotage, and defamation.

Figure 3. Occupation

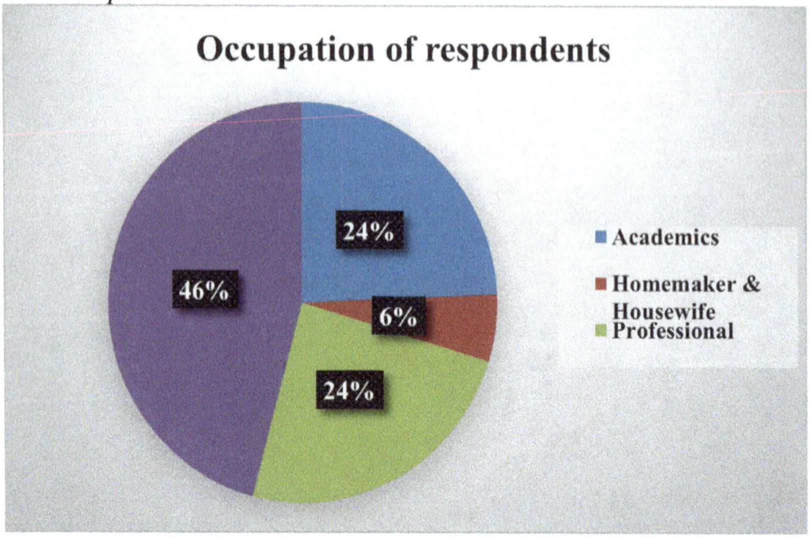

The sample's size and variety also offer a basis for comprehending how various population segments generally see and express concerns regarding deepfake technology. Due to their exposure to digital technologies and the internet, students make up the largest group (46%). Academicians (24%) are also well-represented and could offer important perspectives on the impact of deepfakes on academic freedom, intellectual property, public perception, and media and research ethics. The small percentage of homemakers (6%) may restrict the generalizability of their answers, but their personal privacy experiences, particularly about social media, family, etc., may offer a distinctive viewpoint on the impact of deepfakes on private life. Another crucial demographic is working professionals (27.3%), particularly in light of the possible effects of deepfakes on harassment at work, career security, and professional reputation. This empirical study provides fundamental insights into how improved legal protections and digital literacy initiatives for many societal groups may be necessary in light of deepfake technology.

Figure 4. Familiarity with Deepfake

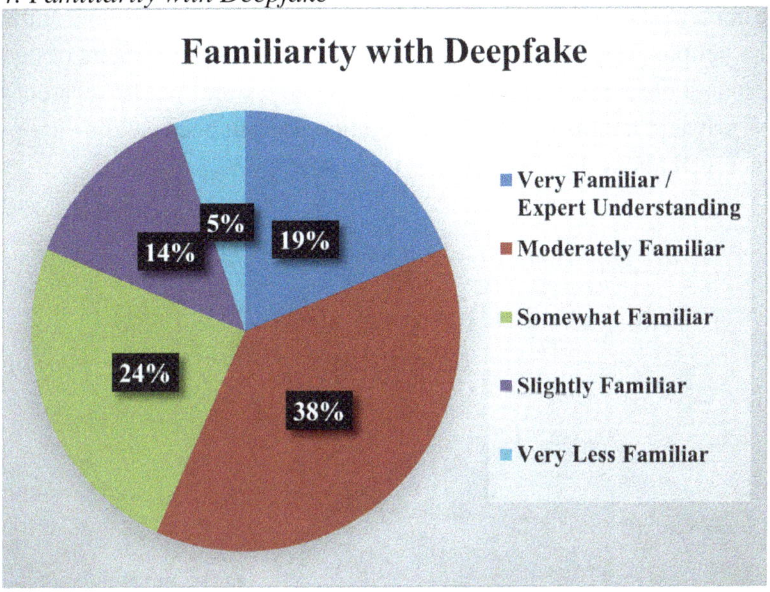

The majority of participants are at least somewhat familiar with deepfake technology, according to the statistics on respondents' knowledge of the technology, and a sizable percentage (almost 60%) are highly familiar, which is depicted by Figure 4.

Figure 5. Encountering Deepfake content

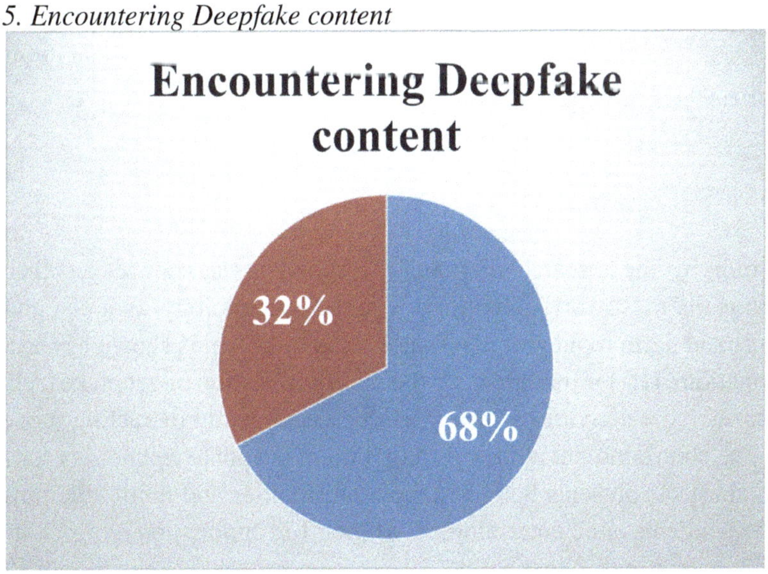

The fact that 68% of respondents, i.e. (Figure 5), reported having come across deepfake content shows how common this technology is in online environments and how many people are growing increasingly conscious of the dangers of deepfakes. These respondents might support legislative changes and public awareness campaigns on privacy, identity theft, and reputational harm because they are probably more concerned about these issues.

Figure 6. What are the Primary Uses of Deepfake Technology?

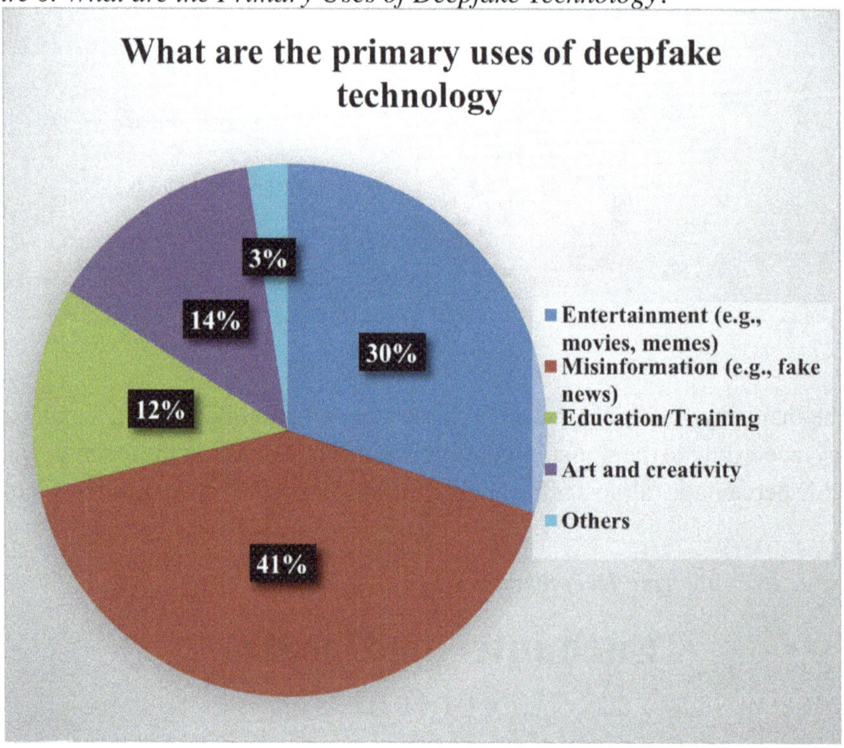

According to the research (Figure 6), respondents acknowledged that misinformation is the most worrisome use of deepfake technology, as it can undermine social trust and harm reputations. A major social problem is shown by the fact that misinformation (41%) is thought to be the main application of deepfake technology, which means more activities which might be fraudulently extracting money from laymen. The entertainment industry's adoption of deepfake technology for humour and special effects presents both creative opportunities and moral dilemmas since 30% of respondents cited entertainment as their top application.

Figure 7. Do you think existing laws are sufficient to protect individuals from the misuse of deepfake technology?

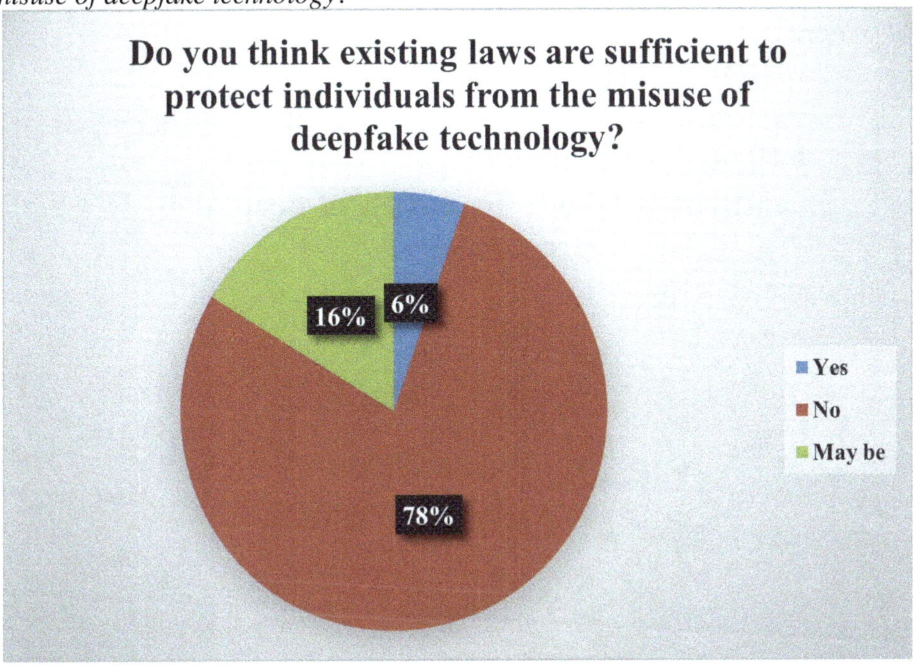

There is broad general agreement that current legal frameworks need to be revised to reflect the particular issues provided by deepfake technology, as seen by the 80% (Figure 7) of respondents who believe that current regulations are insufficient. Just 5.5% of respondents think that the laws in place are adequate to shield people from the abuse of deepfake technology. The six responders who selected "Maybe" probably reflect those who agree that although certain rules may cover the fundamental concerns of defamation and privacy, there may still be exceptions in circumstances involving deepfakes.

Figure 8. Do you think existing laws and the recommendations of the new Digital India Act, 2023, are sufficient to protect individuals from the misuse of deepfake technology?

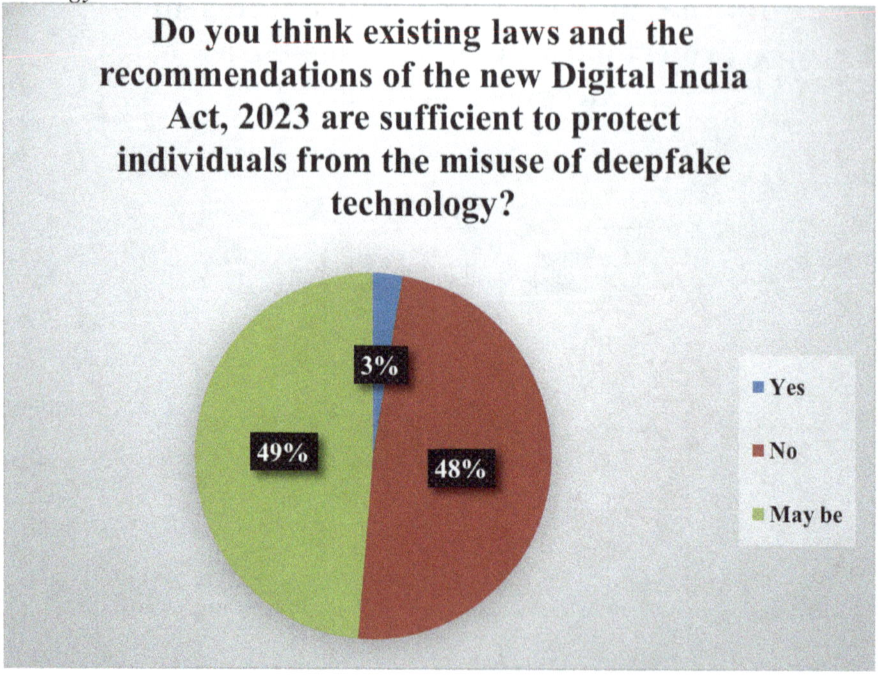

Most respondents do not think the Digital India Act of 2023 (Figure 8) and current laws provide enough protection due to a lack of clear provisions on deepfakes. This emphasises the necessity of specific legislative changes that deal directly with deepfake technology and its ability to infringe upon people's right to privacy and individuality.

Figure 9. In your opinion, should platforms (e.g., social media, video sharing) be held responsible for hosting deepfake content that violates individuals' rights? - Intermediary Liability in case of deepfakes

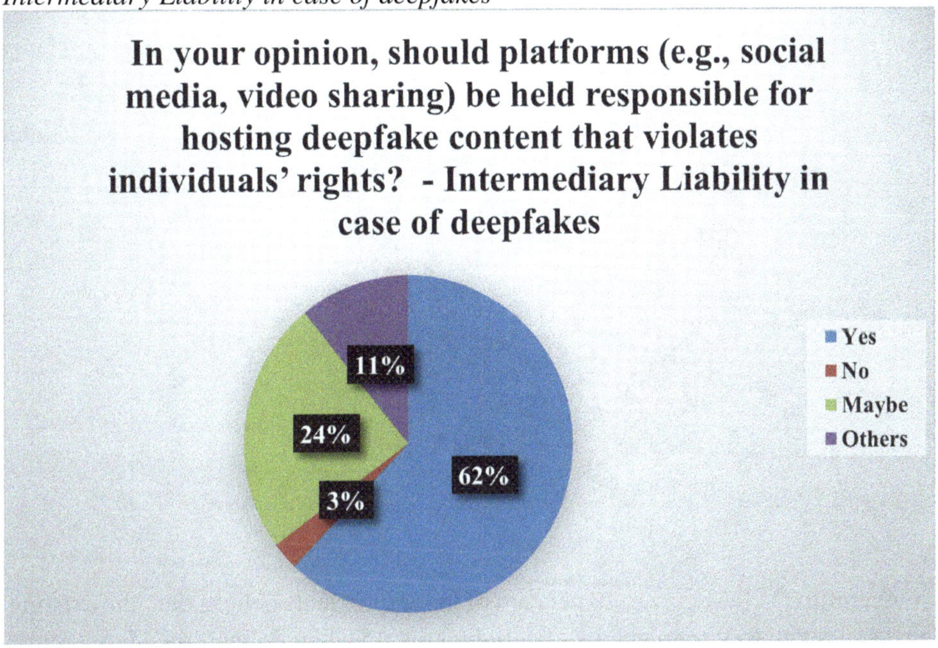

The vast majority of respondents (62% - Figure 9) think that social media, video sharing, and other platforms should be held accountable for displaying deepfake content that infringes on people's reputations, privacy rights, or personality rights. The 24% respondents who selected "Maybe" are representative of people who accept that platforms bear some responsibility, but who may be unsure of how liability should be imposed or who think it depends on the particulars of the deepfake material.

Figure 10. Are the laws like the IT Act 2000, guidelines by the Advertising Standards Council of India, and other IP laws enough to protect the rights of celebrities vis-à-vis their personality rights?

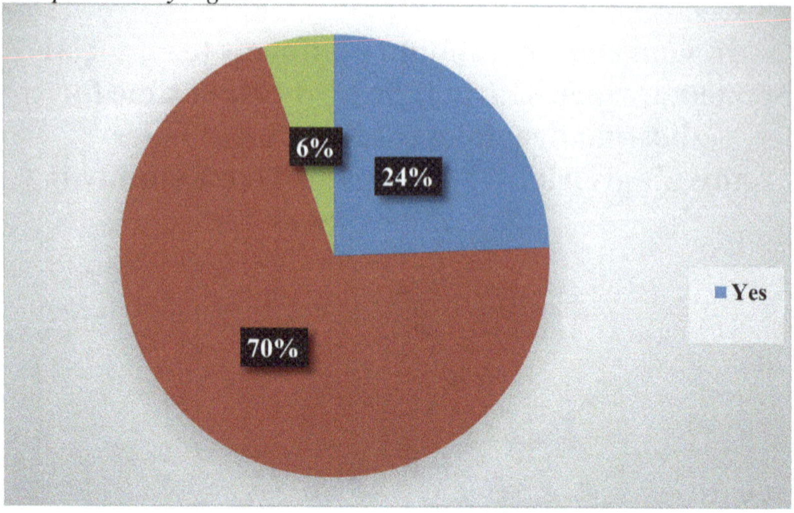

According to the data i.e. 70 per cent of the respondents believe that, the existing legal and regulatory frameworks—including the ASCI guidelines, the IT Act 2000, and intellectual property laws—are not enough to safeguard the personality rights of celebrities in the age of deepfake technology (Figure 9).

CONCLUSION

The research very well analyses the current trend of deepfakes in India and also delves into the state of deepfake-related violations in the United States and the European Union. With the help of the theoretical and empirical study, the authors can conclude that the laws in India are still at a nascent stage in dealing with the issues related to deepfake technology. Technology can be a boon or a bane for society; it all depends on the way society uses it. The first objective and question of the study focused on the understanding of the working of deepfake technology and the usage of AI concerning such technology which has been explained by the authors in the first chapter of the paper while discussing the two models involved in this technology and also the face swapping and shifting methods used by deepfake videos and photographs. The next objective was to understand the international regulatory framework concerning deepfakes and the curtailment of their negative effects, where the United States has not developed a deepfake-focused federal law, but many of its states, including the recent laws of California, have directly addressed the repercussions of deepfake technology. It has also issued guidelines to tackle the issues arising due to deepfake technology being used to manipulate the election results and voting. European Union on the other hand, with its AI Act, and the DSA, has developed better legislative standards as compared to India and the US with its law majorly focusing on the after-effects of the usage of artificial intelligence and clearly defining the term "deepfake" which can also be used by India to amend the existing IT laws or make a new legislation in India related to AI and deepfakes (Amlan Mohanty and Shatakratu Sahu, 2024).

This brings us to the third objective of the research, i.e. an analysis of the laws of India related to deepfakes and AI. India is still having trouble protecting the privacy and information of its inhabitants, even though the Digital Personal Data Protection Act (DPDPA) and the upcoming Digital India Bill are expected to address the growing threats and difficulties of the constantly changing AI landscape. Addressing such issues and new crimes is difficult for the court and administration as well, and thus, it is difficult to mitigate such situations.

The researchers have also conducted an empirical study to understand the perspectives of stakeholders concerning deepfake technology, where the conclusions of the study can be drawn from these focal points:

- To address the growing concerns about deepfakes, a balanced strategy that includes increasing awareness and fortifying legal protections will be essential.
- There is widespread scepticism over the legal framework's ability to address the particular difficulties presented by deepfake technology, as seen by the 47.4% of respondents who believe that the laws in India are not adequate. This implies that the protection provided by the Digital India Act against the detrimental use of deepfakes may still have certain loopholes, even with the addition of new measures.
- The absence of deepfake-specific provisions in the Digital India Act, 2023, indicates that lawmakers should revise or expand the Act to specifically address the particular damages caused by deepfakes, even while it contains significant cybersecurity and digital governance safeguards. This could entail making the production and dissemination of deepfakes illegal, establishing explicit sanctions for their abuse, and giving victims legal redress.
- This empirical study provides fundamental insights into how deepfake technology calls for more robust legislative safeguards and programs to promote digital literacy among different segments of society.
- The study should examine gender-specific remedies and policy recommendations, such as legislation addressing non-consensual pornography, more robust digital rights frameworks, and educational programs to increase public

awareness of the dangers of deepfake technology, given the gendered nature of deepfake misuse.

- Given the quick development of digital technologies and the increased awareness of these risks, future research with a more balanced age distribution or a larger sample size from older groups would offer a more thorough understanding of how deepfake technology affects different age cohorts.

Recommendations

In India, with more than 952 million internet users and one of the fastest-growing digital infrastructures, paired with a lack of education on responsible use, the risks are amplified. In recent years, there have been multiple instances of Deepfakes being used to spread misinformation, tarnish reputations and infringe on personal rights. To address these, it is prudent that the legislation gives a legal definition to "malicious use of Deepfakes", modifies existing laws to improve their readiness and introduces new laws to provide respite to the victims.

Recommendations for some changes in the existing laws to address the issues of misuse of deepfakes and AI:

- Information Technology Act, 2000:

Section 66D, which deals with impersonation, can be expanded to include deepfake-based identity theft. Section 67, which penalises obscene content, should explicitly cover deepfake pornography.

- Consent-based usage of Deepfakes should be made mandatory, wherein explicit consent should be required from a person for the creation and distribution of content in their likeness.
- Mandatory Watermarking requires all media to have visible watermarks declaring that it is artificially generated. This shall be a big step in the direction of preventing misleading content in the media, and information that can mislead the public can be curtailed in this way.
- AI Regulation should be introduced with guidelines for the ethical development and use of AI tools capable of generating deepfakes.
- Platform Accountability needs to be defined to hold platforms accountable for detecting, flagging, and removing malicious deepfakes promptly, which is a hope from the Digital India Act.
- Including media literacy in school curricula to foster awareness of deepfake content. Such awareness mechanisms should be adopted for the common public as well as the identification of deepfake content becomes an issue due to

its imitative nature. The differences of voices, eye movements, and lip movements should be taught, and awareness should be raised for this amongst the general public.

- Penalties for Violations: Establishing harsher penalties for such violations caused by deepfake technology under the IT Act and the criminal laws.
- Effective Grievance Redressal Mechanism and Exclusive Grievance Redressal Forum

The DPDP Act and the rules and the Digital India Act hopefully include provisions to tackle the issues of privacy breaches, violation of personality rights, and curtailment of financial fraud caused by the usage of AI and deepfake technology. According to the researchers, the risk-based assessment mechanism of the EU shall be very effective in India if adopted under the laws to be enforced soon. The most tightly controlled AI systems permitted on the EU market will be high-risk ones. This level essentially covers safety features of products that are already subject to regulations as well as standalone AI systems in particular domains (see below), which may hurt people's health and safety, their basic rights, or the environment. If these AI systems malfunction or are abused, they might be extremely harmful. AI systems that run the risk of being manipulated or dishonest are included in the third category of risk, known as restricted risk. Deepfakes should be identified as such, and AI systems that come under this category must be transparent, which means that people must be informed about their interactions with the AI (unless this is evident). Chatbots, for instance, are categorised as low-risk. Minimal risk is the lowest degree of risk as defined by the EU AI Act. Any other AI systems that do not fit into one of the aforementioned categories, like a spam filter, are included at this level. Under low-risk, AI systems are not subject to any limitations or requirements. Nonetheless, broad guidelines including human oversight, nondiscrimination, and justice are advised. Another category is the "unacceptable risk" category, which is the highest level of risk in the EU and is prohibited under the Act. It includes the manipulation of data or social scoring with the help of AI and deepfake technology.

There are many applications for deepfakes outside of malevolent intent. They operate in several industries, including visual effects, entertainment, and education. They are also utilised in virtual reality, gaming, photography, and entertainment, allowing users to watch some films with dubbed voices where there is a language barrier, connect and understand historical figures through reanimation, and virtually put on clothes, lenses, glasses and makeup. Because people who create or distribute deepfakes could be located overseas, it can be difficult for victims to sue or hold the responsible parties accountable. This complicates enforcement and highlights the need for international cooperation in managing and controlling deepfakes. One of the biggest challenges is the anonymity of criminals. Since many deepfake creators utilise advanced technologies to conceal their identities, it can be difficult for victims to identify them and pursue legal action against them. Victims find it difficult to hold the authors accountable when they don't know who is at fault, which complicates the defamation process. Successfully resolving cybercrimes that use deepfakes often requires international cooperation. This cooperation can be time-consuming and legally problematic because different nations may have different regulations and processes about deepfakes, which makes the pursuit of justice considerably more challenging in many situations.

CONSENT FOR PUBLICATON

The authors of the paper consent to the publication of the paper.

CONFLICT OF INTEREST

The authors declare that there is no conflict of interest.

ACKNOWLEDGEMENT

A sincere gratitude to all the respondents who have contributed their opinions for the research, and the author also acknowledges the research by various other authors on the concept of deepfake and AI.

REFERENCES

Aayog, N. I. T. I., & the Government of India. (2022, November). *Responsible AI #AIFORALL*. https://www.niti.gov.in/sites/default/files/2022-11/Ai_for_All_2022_02112022_0.pdf

Amitabh Bachchan v. Rajat Negi & Ors, 2022 SCC OnLine Del 4110 (India).

Anil Kapoor v. Simply Life India & Ors, 2024 CS(COMM) 652/2023 & IA 18237/2023 (Del HC).

Artificial Intelligence Act, E. U. (2024). *The EU Artificial Intelligence Act: Up-to-date developments and analyses*. https://artificialintelligenceact.eu/

Brkan, M. (2019). The essence of the fundamental rights to privacy and data protection is finding its way through the CJEU's constitutional reasoning maze. *German Law Journal, 20*(6), 864–883. DOI: 10.1017/glj.2019.66

Busch, E., & Ware, J. (2023). Deepfakes and the incitement of far-right violence. In *The weaponisation of deepfakes: Digital deception by the far-right* (pp. 4–8). International Centre for Counter-Terrorism., https://www.jstor.org/stable/resrep55429.8

BW Online Bureau. (2024, December 5). *India's deepfake cases up 550%, losses may hit Rs 70,000 Cr by 2024: Report*. Business World. https://www.businessworld.in/article/indias-deepfake-cases-up-550-losses-may-hit-rs-70000-cr-by-2024-report-541202#goog_rewarded

California Legislature. (2023–2024). *AB-2355 Political Reform Act 1974 (political advertisements & artificial intelligence)*. https://calmatters.digitaldemocracy.org/bills/ca_202320240ab2355

California Legislature. (2024). *AB-2655 Defending Democracy from Deepfake Deception Act*. https://leginfo.legislature.ca.gov/faces/billNavClient.xhtml?bill_id=202320240AB2655

Choubisa, M., Doshi, R., Khatri, N., & Hiran, K. K. (2022, May). A simple and robust approach of random forest for intrusion detection system in cyber security. In 2022 International conference on IoT and blockchain technology (ICIBT) (pp. 1-5). IEEE.

Court of Justice of the European Union (CJEU). (2014). *UPC Telekabel Wien GmbH v. Constantin Film Verleih GmbH (Case C-314/12).*

Court of Justice of the European Union (CJEU). (2016). *Case C-203/15 and C-698/15: Tele2 Sverige AB v Post- och telestyrelsen and Secretary of State for the Home Department v Tom Watson and others*. Grand Chamber.

Deeksha. (2023, December 28). *MeitY issues advisory against AI-deepfakes on social media and other platforms*. SCC Times. https://www.scconline.com/blog/post/2023/12/28/meity-issues-advisory-against-ai-deepfakes-on-social-media-legal-news/

European Court of Human Rights. (n.d.). *Case of Halet v. Luxembourg*. Grand Chamber. https://hudoc.echr.coe.int/fre#%22itemid%22:[%22001-223259%22]

European Parliament and Council. (2024, June 13). *Regulation (EU) 2024/1689 laying down harmonised rules on artificial intelligence and amending Regulations.* [2024] OJ L 2024/1689. https://eur-lex.europa.eu/legal-content/EN/TXT/?uri=CELEX%3A32024R1689

European Union. (2016). *General Data Protection Regulation, Article 5.* https://gdpr-info.eu/art-5-gdpr

Express News Service. (2024, November 4). *Deepfake videos of Narayana Murthy, Mukesh Ambani: Bengaluru residents lose Rs 87 lakh in trading scam.* The Indian Express. https://indianexpress.com/article/cities/bangalore/deepfake-videos-narayana-murthy-mukesh-ambani-bengaluru-trading-scam-9654607/

Geng, Y. (2023, January). Comparing "deepfake" regulatory regimes in the United States, the European Union, and China. *Georgetown Law Technology Review, 7*(1), 157. https://georgetownlawtechreview.org/comparing-deepfake-regulatory-regimes-in-the-united-states-the-european-union-and-china/GLTR-01-2023/

Government of India. (2000). *The Information Technology Act, 2000.*

Government of India. (2023). *The Bhartiya Nyay Sanhita*. BNS.

Government of India. (2025). *The Digital Personal Data Protection Rules 2025.* https://innovateindia.mygov.in/dpdp-rules-2025/

Gov.UK. (n.d.). *AI Safety Summit 2023: The Bletchley Declaration*. https://www.gov.uk/government/publications/ai-safety-summit-2023-the-bletchley-declaration

Graham, M. (2024, June 26). *Deepfakes: Federal and state regulation aims to curb a growing threat.* Thomson Reuters Practical Law. https://www.thomsonreuters.com/en-us/posts/government/deepfakes-federal-state-regulation/

Hall, H. K. (2018). Deepfake videos: When seeing isn't believing. *Catholic University Journal of Law & Technology, 27*(1), 51. https://scholarship.law.edu/jlt/vol27/iss1/4

Helmus, T. C. (2022). *Artificial intelligence, deepfakes, and disinformation: A primer.* RAND Corporation. https://www.jstor.org/stable/resrep42027

Hill, C. (2023, June 29). *OpenAI and Microsoft face class action lawsuits for allegedly violating copyright and privacy laws.* Legal Insider. https://legaltechnology.com/2023/06/29/openai-and-microsoft-face-class-action-lawsuit-for-allegedly-violating-copyright-and-privacy-laws/

India, A. I. (n.d.). *AI Task Force: Ministry of Commerce and Industry initiatives.* https://indiaai.gov.in/government/ministry-of-commerce-and-industry

Jaikishan Kakubhai Saraf v. Peppy Store, 2024 SCC OnLine Del 3664 (India).

Madiega, T. (2022, November 11). *Digital Services Act (EU legislation in progress).* European Parliamentary Research Service (EPRS). https://www.europarl.europa.eu/RegData/etudes/BRIE/2021/689357/EPRS_BRI(2021)689357_EN.pdf

Malhotra, C., & Malhotra, U. (2024). Putting interests of digital nagriks first: Digital Personal Data Protection (DPDP) Act 2023 of India. *The Indian Journal of Public Administration, 70*, 516. DOI: 10.1177/00195561241271575

Mallic, A., & Ganguli, P. (2024, September 27). *Understanding of digital arrest: Definition, methods and implications. SSRN.* http://dx.doi.org/DOI: 10.2139/ssrn.5019885

Manda, D. P., & Misra, A. N. (2024). Report: India will replace the Information Technology Act with the proposed Digital India Act: Out with the old, in with the new? *Global Privacy Law Review, 5*(1), 50. DOI: 10.54648/gplr2024002

Miller, G. (2024, March 14). Transcript: US House Subcommittee hearing on the harms of deepfakes. *TechPolicy.Press.* https://www.techpolicy.press/house-hearing-addressing-deepfake-harms

Ministry of Electronics and Information Technology. (2024, March 15). *Advisory on due diligence by intermediaries/platforms outlined under the Information Technology Act and Information Technology (Intermediary Guidelines and Digital Media Ethics Code) Rules, 2021.* https://www.meity.gov.in/writereaddata/files/Advisory%2015March%202024.pdf

Ministry of Electronics and Information Technology. (2025, January 3). *Draft Digital Personal Data Protection Rules 2025*. https://www.meity.gov.in/writereaddata/files/259889.pdf

Ministry of Electronics and Information Technology (MeitY). (2023). *Information Technology (Intermediary Guidelines and Digital Media Ethics Code) Amendment Rules, 2022: Rule 3(1)(b)*. https://www.meity.gov.in/writereaddata/files/Information%20Technology%20%28Intermediary%20Guidelines%20and%20Digital%20Media%20Ethics%20Code%29%20Rules%2C%202021%20%28updated%2006.04.2023%29-.pdf

Mohanty, A., & Sahu, S. (2024, November 21). India's advance on AI regulation. *Carnegie India*. https://carnegieendowment.org/research/2024/11/indias-advance-on-ai-regulation?lang=en&center=india

Pandey, S., & Jadhav, G. (2023, March 17). Emerging technologies and law: Legal status of tackling crimes relating to deepfakes in India. *SCC Online*. https://www.scconline.com/blog/post/2023/03/17/emerging-technologies-and-law-legal-status-of-tackling-crimes-relating-to-deepfakes-in-india/

Panwar, K. S., & Roy, N. D. (2024). Rising menace of deepfakes with the help of AI: Legal implications in India. *Indian Journal of Integrated Research in Law*, *4*(3), 94. https://ijirl.com/wp-content/uploads/2024/05/RISING-MENACE-OF-DEEPFAKES-WITH-THE-HELP-OF-AI-LEGAL-IMPLICATIONS-IN-INDIA.pdf

Rajat Sharma & Anr. v. Tamara Doc & Ors., CS(Comm) 1147 of 2024 (India).

Romero Moreno, F. (2024). Generative AI and deepfakes: A human rights approach to tackling harmful content. *International Review of Law Computers & Technology*, *38*(3), 297–326. DOI: 10.1080/13600869.2024.2324540

Saner, E. (2024, January 31). Inside the Taylor Swift deepfake scandal: "It's men telling a powerful woman to get back in her box." *The Guardian*. https://www.theguardian.com/technology/2024/jan/31/inside-the-taylor-swift-deepfake-scandal-its-men-telling-a-powerful-woman-to-get-back-in-her-box

Sanu, K. (2024, May 31). Deepfakes in poll season: Experts say India needs to evolve AI-specific regulations. *India Today*. https://www.indiatoday.in/law/story/deepfakes-in-poll-season-experts-say-india-needs-to-evolve-ai-specific-regulations-2546018-2024-05-31

Schwartz, M. J. (2020, November 20). The dark side of AI: Previewing criminal uses. *Bank Info Security*. https://www.bankinfosecurity.com/blogs/dark-side-ai-police-preview-likely-attacks-p-2971

Singh, N. (2024, October 1). Digital arrest and Rs 7 crore heist: How Vardhman Group head was tricked. *Business Standard*. https://www.business-standard.com/companies/news/digital-arrest-and-rs-7-crore-heist-how-vardhman-group-head-was-tricked-124100100832_1.html

Smith, H., & Mansted, K. (2020). What's a deepfake? In *Weaponised deepfakes: National security and democracy* (pp. 05–10). Australian Strategic Policy Institute. https://www.jstor.org/stable/resrep25129.6

Somers, M. (2020, July 21). *Deepfakes, explained*. MIT Management Sloan School. https://mitsloan.mit.edu/ideas-made-to-matter/deepfakes-explained

Subcommittee on AI Governance and Guidelines Development. 'Report on AI Governance Guidelines Development'. (2025, January 2). Ministry of Electronics and Information Technology. https://indiaai.s3.ap-south-1.amazonaws.com/docs/subcommittee-report-dec26.pdf

Subcommittee on AI Governance and Guidelines Development. (2025, January 2). *Report on AI governance guidelines development*. Ministry of Electronics and Information Technology. https://indiaai.s3.ap-south-1.amazonaws.com/docs/subcommittee-report-dec26.pdf

Sumsub. (n.d.). *Deepfake cases surge in countries holding 2024 elections*. https://sumsub.com/newsroom/deepfake-cases-surge-in-countries-holding-2024-elections-sumsub-research-shows/

Thapliyal, N. (2024, May 8). *Journalist Rajat Sharma Moves Delhi High Court Against Non-Regulation of Deepfake Technology, Notice Issued*. LiveLaw.in. https://www.livelaw.in/high-court/delhi-high-court/delhi-high-court deepfake-videos-rajat-sharma-pil-257393

Thapliyal, N. (2024, May 8). Journalist Rajat Sharma moves Delhi High Court against non-regulation of deepfake technology, notice issued. *LiveLaw.in*. https://www.livelaw.in/high-court/delhi-high-court/delhi-high-court-deepfake-videos-rajat-sharma-pil-257393

The AB-2355 Political Reform Act. 1974 ('political advertisements & artificial intelligence'). https://calmatters.digitaldemocracy.org/bills/ca_202320240ab2355

The AB-2655 Defending Democracy from Deepfake Deception Act. 2024. https://leginfo.legislature.ca.gov/faces/billNavClient.xhtml?bill_id=202320240AB2655

The Bhartiya Nyay Sanhita (BNS) 2023, Section 319.

The Deepfakes Accountability Act. 2023. https://www.congress.gov/bill/118th-congress/house-bill/5586/text

The Digital Personal Data Protection Rules. 2025. https://innovateindia.mygov.in/dpdp-rules-2025/

The EU Artificial Intelligence Act. Up-to-date developments and analyses of the EU AI Act. EU Artificial Intelligence Act. https://artificialintelligenceact.eu/

The H.R.6088 - Deepfakes in Federal Elections Prohibition Act 2020.

The Information Technology Act 2000.

Thombre, M. (2021). Deconstructing Deepfake: Tracking Legal Implications and Challenges. *International Journal of Law, Management and Humanities. 4*(4), 2267 – 2274. https://doij.org/10.10000/IJLMH.111463

Thombre, M. (2021). Deconstructing deepfake: Tracking legal implications and challenges. *International Journal of Law, Management and Humanities, 4*(4), 2267–2274. https://doij.org/10.10000/IJLMH.111463

Trend Micro Research, United Nations Interregional Crime and Justice Research Institute (UNICRI), & Europol's European Cybercrime Centre (EC3). (n.d.). *Malicious uses and abuses of artificial intelligence.* https://unicri.it/sites/default/files/2020-11/Abuse_ai.pdf

United Nations Interregional Crime and Justice Research Institute (UNICRI). (n.d.). *Artificial intelligence and robotics for law enforcement.* https://unicri.it/sites/default/files/2020-11/Abuse_ai.pdf

United States Congress. H.R. 6943 – No AI FRAUD Act, 118th Congress (2023–2024). https://www.congress.gov/bill/118th-congress/house-bill/6943

UPC Telekabel Wien GmbH v. Constantin Film Verleih GmbH (Case C-314/12) [2014] (ECJ).

U.S. Congress. (2020). *H.R.6088 - Deepfakes in Federal Elections Prohibition Act of 2020.*

U.S. Congress. (2023). *The Deepfakes Accountability Act, H.R. 5586.* https://www.congress.gov/bill/118th-congress/house-bill/5586/text

U.S. Congress. (2023–2024). *H.R. 6943 – No AI FRAUD Act, 118th Congress.* https://www.congress.gov/bill/118th-congress/house-bill/6943

Venema, A. (n.d.). Deepfakes as a security issue: Why gender matters. *Women in International Security*. https://wiisglobal.org/deepfakes-as-a-security-issue-why-gender-matters/

Venema, A. *Deepfakes as a Security Issue: Why Gender Matters*. Women in International Security. https://wiisglobal.org/deepfakes-as-a-security-issue-why-gender-matters/

Vig, S. (2024). Regulating deepfakes: An Indian perspective. *Journal of Strategic Security*, *17*(3), 70–93. DOI: 10.5038/1944-0472.17.3.2245

Vig, S. (2024). Regulating deepfakes: An Indian perspective. *Journal of Strategic Security*, *17*(3), 70–93. DOI: 10.5038/1944-0472.17.3.2245

Yont, S. (2024, March). *The deepfake menace: Legal challenges in the age of AI*. TRT World Research Centre. https://researchcentre.trtworld.com/wp-content/uploads/2024/03/The-Deepfake-Menace_v2.pdf

Chapter 11
Aspect-Based Opinion Mining:
A Framework for Spam and Ham Review Detection

Neelam Rani
Poornima University, Jaipur, India

Devendra Kumar Somwanshi
https://orcid.org/0000-0003-4331-0917
Poornima University, Jaipur, India

Archika Jain
https://orcid.org/0000-0002-9427-1826
Swami Keshvanand Institute of Technology, Management, and Gramothan, Jaipur, India

ABSTRACT

Sentiment Analysis deals with analyzing users comment on a particular thing and then computationally figuring out the actual sentiment of the user i.e Positive or Negative. The process of computationally identifying and categorizing opinions expressed in a piece of text, especially in order to determine whether the writer's attitude towards a particular topic, product, etc. is positive or negative. This chapter presents a comprehensive review of over 50 papers on sentiment analysis, featuring a comparative analysis of various research techniques. The review highlights strengths and weaknesses of existing methods, identifies research gaps, and provides a foundation for future research directions. In this chapter Naive Bayes approach

DOI: 10.4018/979-8-3373-3063-1.ch011

is used for sentiment prediction, specifically for SPAM and HAM detection. The prediction model is trained using the Naive Bayes algorithm, and the training set is fitted using the WordNet library.

INTRODUCTION

In the age of digital communication, user-generated content such as reviews and feedback plays a pivotal role in shaping public opinion and consumer behavior (Valakunde et al., 2013). However, the growing volume of online reviews has also given rise to the problem of spam and opinion manipulation, necessitating robust methods for sentiment analysis and spam detection. Numerous computational techniques have emerged to address these challenges, ranging from traditional machine learning algorithms like K-Nearest Neighbor (KNN), Naive Bayes, Random Tree, and Random Forest, to advanced natural language processing (NLP) strategies such as syntactic dependency parsing, latent semantic analysis (LSA), and word sense disambiguation (WSD) (Fan et al., 2008; Li et al., 2010)

Recent studies have explored various approaches to improve the accuracy and efficiency of spam detection and feature-level sentiment classification (Lau et al., 2011). Models such as the Sentiment Miner algorithm have demonstrated enhanced performance by incorporating detailed tagging (e.g., Strongly Positive to Strongly Negative) and handling complex linguistic structures like negations and intensifiers. Additionally, techniques like dependency tree parsing and multi-word phrase analysis have proven effective in extracting nuanced sentiment expressions from user reviews.

Furthermore, frameworks that support multilingual sentiment analysis and verb-based classification have contributed to a deeper understanding of opinion orientation, especially in diverse linguistic settings (Jain et al., 2023; Khan et al., 2011). The integration of feature weighting, spam scoring models, and rule-based thwarting detection also offers promising improvements in identifying deceptive content and refining opinion mining processes (Kasthuriarachchy et al., 2014).

LITERATURE REVIEW

1. Review Outcome in the Issue "Feature Level Sentiment Analysis With Spam Detection"

Jindal et al., (2008) were the first to formally define the opinion spam problem, focusing on fake item reviews, particularly on Amazon. They identified three types of spam reviews: non-reviews, brand-only reviews, and untruthful reviews. Their study used a logistic regression classifier trained on duplicate or near-duplicate reviews (treated as fake) and the rest as genuine. They combined behavioral and linguistic features to build a model aimed at detecting even non-duplicate spam reviews. As no prior datasets existed, they created their own. While the results were promising, the work was an early step in opinion spam detection research.

Lim et al., (2010) developed a method to detect review spammers by assigning a spamicity score to each reviewer. They focused on active Amazon users (those with at least 3 reviews) and used anomaly indicators like rating deviation, early review timing, and extreme rating patterns. Feature weights were combined into a formula optimized for improved ranking accuracy. Human evaluators labeled the training data, but the authors highlighted that humans struggle to reliably detect fake reviews by reading alone, and even crowdsourced fake reviews don't generalize well to real-world spam detection.

Wang et al., (2012) introduced a triangular trust model connecting stores, reviewers, and reviews, proposing a heterogeneous review graph where each node type influences the others. They computed spam scores for each node by considering its relationship with the other two. This was the first major study on store reviews (not just products), recognizing that content reuse may be legitimate in this context. Using an iterative ranking algorithm, they flagged top-ranked reviewers, reviews, and stores as likely spam and validated the results using human judgments and Better Business Bureau data.

Xie et al., (2012) focused on "singleton reviewers"—users who post only one review—highlighting that over 90% of users on review platforms like ResellerRatings.com fall into this category. They observe that fake reviews often appear in bursts of extreme ratings (either 5-stars or 1-star) and distort normal rating distributions over time. Their key contribution is identifying and analyzing these temporal anomalies and emphasizing the importance of including singleton reviews in spam detection, which prior studies had often excluded.

Puri et al., (2013) evaluated spam detection using both content-based and rule-based filtering techniques. The authors apply a K-Nearest Neighbors (KNN) classifier to distinguish between spam and legitimate ("ham") reviews, achieving an accuracy of 78.5%. The focus is on classifying client reviews effectively using machine learning methods.

Malarvizhi et al., (2013) presented a comprehensive review of content-based filtering techniques for spam detection. Content-based (or psychological) filtering compares item content with user profiles, both represented using descriptive terms (usually words in documents). The paper examines various filtering methods and benchmarks their accuracy in classifying spam, contributing significantly to the analysis of content-based spam detection algorithms.

Rekha et al., (2014) discussed how online reviews, while crucial for web communication, have become targets for spamming—a practice of sending unsolicited promotional content to many users. Spam not only consumes network and memory resources but can also be used maliciously to compromise user data or privacy. The paper outlines various approaches to detect such spam.

Chen et al., (2017) This study focuses on real-time spam detection on Twitter using over 600 million tweets. The authors propose a machine learning-based method by framing spam detection as a binary classification problem using 12 lightweight features. They analyze the effects of factors like spam ratio, feature engineering, data sampling, and model choice, concluding that effective spam detection must balance data, feature quality, and model robustness.

Li et al., (2016) proposed a method for identifying *informative reviews* using dependency parsing and sentiment analysis to extract linguistic features. The approach involves two stages: feature extraction and classifier learning. Applied to Amazon reviews, the method significantly improves classification performance and can serve as a preprocessing step in broader review analysis tasks.

Shinde et al., (2016) presented a Decision Support Engine that identifies comparable objects for user queries, even when direct comparisons are not initially available. It uses a semi-supervised learning approach to overcome limitations of purely supervised or unsupervised systems. Based on an analysis of 24 key research papers, the system is evaluated using Mean Average Precision (MAP) and user feedback, highlighting challenges in pattern mining, NLP, and information retrieval.

Topal et al., (2016) introduced the concept of creating an emotion map of movies by analyzing reviewers' scores and emotional content. These emotion maps can then guide users in selecting movies that match their preferred emotional patterns. It is a novel step toward emotion-driven movie recommendation systems.

López-Nava et al., (2016) did a comprehensive review of human motion analysis using inertial sensors, this study examines sensor setups, algorithms for estimating joint positions/orientations, performance metrics, and the demographics of test populations. It notes a gap in testing with older adults or those with mobility impairments and suggests future directions for healthcare and wearable tech applications focused on motion tracking.

Muneeb Abid et al., (2016) proposed that spam poses a major security threat as it spreads malware like viruses and phishing attacks. The paper reviews spam-fighting methods such as challenge-response, blacklisting, whitelisting, review signatures, and machine learning. It categorizes existing spam detection technologies and analyzes their strengths and weaknesses, concluding that no method is foolproof due to the evolving nature of the web.

Savadekar et al., (2016) proposed a personalized recommendation system using English keywords and a domain-specific thesaurus. Implemented on the Hadoop platform, the system efficiently processes large data volumes and improves the scalability and accuracy of recommendations.

Alkalbani et al., (2017) analyzed ~6,000 cloud service reviews using sentiment analysis with KNIME and Rapid Miner. Four machine learning models were tested (k-NN, Naive Bayes, Random Tree, Random Forest), with Random Forest achieving the highest accuracy (97.06%), making it the most effective for predicting review sentiment.

Chauhan et al., (2017) detected spam and fake reviews using sentiment analysis. It compares actual ratings with sentiment-derived ratings using an internal dictionary, focusing on Amazon product reviews. It also filters offensive language and visualizes features affecting product popularity.

Sedhai et al., (2017) proposed a two-module spam detection framework: a real-time module using lightweight detectors (blacklist, near-duplicate, trusted users, multi-classifier) and a batch module for model updates. The framework effectively learns new spam patterns using large-scale Twitter data.

Rajamohana et al., (2017) presented a feature selection algorithm using the Adaptive Binary Flower Pollination Algorithm (BFPA) with Naive Bayes as the evaluation metric. The proposed method selects the most informative features and achieves higher classification accuracy than other methods.

Iyengar et al., (2017) addressed phishing via reviews and emails, using an integrated detection system to improve spam filtering, especially for non-English content. It highlights how cybercriminals exploit reviews to harvest sensitive user credentials.

Patil et al., (2017) proposed a novel method to detect phishing websites by analyzing visual and CSS layout features of web pages. Using SVM with MapReduce, the system enhances detection accuracy while improving performance on large datasets.

Kumar (2017) presented a Support Vector Machine (SVM) classifier with a Gaussian kernel for spam detection. Experiments on publicly available datasets demonstrate strong performance in terms of F-measure, recall, precision, and accuracy, showing its effectiveness compared to other classifiers.

Rajamohana et al., (2017) addressed the authors' opinion spam detection by proposing a hybrid feature selection technique combining Cuckoo Search and Harmony Search algorithms. These evolutionary methods help eliminate irrelevant and noisy features in high-dimensional text data, improving classification performance when using Naive Bayes.

Watson et al., (2017) introduced a linguistic attribute hierarchy embedded with linguistic decision trees for spam detection. Applied to an SMS dataset, the approach offers semantic interpretability, handles high-dimensional data efficiently, and improves performance through hierarchical representation of attributes.

Lin et al., (2017) introduced benchmarks of multiple mainstream machine learning algorithms for real-time Twitter spam detection. It evaluates performance metrics (accuracy, F-measure, false/true positive rates), stability across different training set sizes, and scalability in parallel computing environments to support real-time processing.

AlMahmoud et al., (2017) proposed Spamdoop, a privacy-preserving collaborative spam detection platform built on MapReduce. Spamdoop solves the scalability issue of distance-preserving hashing and enables early detection of spam campaigns across large datasets with competitive processing times.

Olatunji et al., (2017) compared SVM and Extreme Learning Machine (ELM) for review spam detection. While SVM achieves higher accuracy, ELM is faster in terms of processing speed. Both outperform previously reported models on the same benchmark dataset.

Common Findings of Review in "Feature level sentiment analysis with spam detection"

- The best approach used in the issue Document level sentiment classification is a statistical learning based computational method which can generate domain-specific sentiment lexicons and can lead to an average improvement of polarity prediction at the document level by 1.79% when compared to a baseline system which employs a hand-crafted generic sentiment lexicon.
- The approach used in the issue Sentence-level Sentiment Classification is Dependency Tree based Approach which combined flat features with structured features to form a novel feature representation.
- An unsupervised linguistic approach used in the issue Feature level sentiment classification in which SentiWordNet is used to calculate overall sentiment score of each sentence, but the negation expressions were not taken for analysis.
- In feature level sentiment analysis Point-wise mutual information (PMI) method was used to filter feature words so as to obtain the meaningful product features and Apriori association rules(classical association rules) technique was used to mine frequent item sets.
- SVM technology is used for spam detection that is performed better than EVM technology. The SVM technology mainly used for review spam detection but if the technology is compared according speed than the EVM is better than SVM.
- The opinion spam detection technology is proposed to detect the spam from the text. For spam detection, it is extract the text and identified the issues or emotions that are negative or positive.

- Cyberpunks approach is used to detect the criminal intensions from review reviews. The review credential is to hack and send negative reviews. The cyberpunks identified these reviews with 78% accuracy.
- K-Nearest Neighbor (k-NN), Random Forest, Naive Bayes, and Random Tree algorithms are used to identify the reviews of cloud service users with their emotions. After comparison of these algorithm results, the Naive bays classifier performs well with high accuracy as 87%.
- These all techniques and approaches are used to identify the reviews of movies, songs, story that is given via mail, and social sites such as Facebook, twitter, etc. The Naive bays classifier and K-nearest neighbor technique gives better result.
- After reviewing these papers, It is analyzed that the spam is various issues for computer security and network security. The criminals or hackers hack the users review ids and Facebook accounts and other social sites accounts to post the negative reviews. So, the technologies of spam detection are proposed to identify the reviewer's emotions.

2. Review Outcome in the Issue "Documents Level Sentiment Analysis With Spam Detection"

Jaswal et al., (2013) defines spam as harmful textual content, especially in emails, which can damage systems. The authors use Hidden Markov Models (HMM) to detect spam images along with textual filtering techniques. After implementing their approach, they achieved a 75% detection accuracy, highlighting the need for advanced spam filtering methods.

Sharma et al., (2013) emphasizes the widespread use of the internet and emails, which are often exploited to send spam. Spam can appear as text or images and poses a significant problem for users. The paper reviews various spam detection methods and proposes a solution to reduce unsolicited emails, acknowledging that spam remains a persistent challenge in web communication.

Rathi et al., (2013) explores spam classification using data mining. It evaluates several classifiers with and without feature selection. Using the Best-First feature selection algorithm, the Random Tree classifier achieved the highest accuracy of 99.72%. The study concludes that feature selection enhances classifier performance, although no method achieves 100% accuracy.

Jha et al., (2013) focuses on feature-level opinion mining for movie reviews, analyzing specific aspects like songs, story, cast, and direction. Using SentiWordNet and Stanford Parser, it calculates sentiment scores for individual features within sentences. It introduces a rule-based sentence segmentation method to handle punctuation challenges in movie titles and dates. The proposed method achieves 70% accuracy, outperforming the 58% accuracy of the standard SentiWordNet approach.

Altrabsheh et al., (2014) applies sentiment analysis to real-time student feedback on lectures at the University of Portsmouth. It tests different combinations of preprocessing, feature selection (Unigrams, Bigrams, Trigrams), and machine learning techniques (Naive Bayes, Complement Naive Bayes, Max Entropy, SVM). Using 1036 labeled feedback entries, SVM with a linear kernel achieved the highest accuracy (95%), followed by the radial basis kernel (88%). Preprocessing improved model accuracy by up to 20%.

Giyanani et al., (2014) discussed spam emails as unsolicited mass reviews used for advertising, phishing, and malicious activities. It introduces a stepwise spam detection method that filters emails based on both the sender's identity and email content, highlighting the challenge posed by spammers' ability to bypass traditional filters.

Common Findings of Review in "Document level sentiment analysis with spam detection"

- There are various reasons that are responsible for a significant portion of the errors in the SentiWordNet Classifiers as Negated structures were not considered by the SentiWordNet-Classifiers, Translation errors or missing translations of words as well As, writing that ensured scores of missing sentiment for terms, Ambiguities and different meanings of a synset in SentiWordNet respectively were not resolved, the meaning of words was not considered in context (Barua et al., 2025).
- Investigated different combinations of machine learning techniques, features, preprocessing levels and the use of neutral class for analyzing real-time student's feedback.
- Founded that the best models were SVM and CNB; therefore, they could be used for feedback analysis (Mahrishi et al., 2020).
- Presented that in the NB and CNB models with the neutral class, using no preprocessing gave the highest performance.
- Removing repeated letters and replacing not "with not" is valuable in these models; this could be because students write informally and sometimes in chat language to give feedback.
- Repeated letters and negation exists in nearly 10 percent of the raw data; consequently, preprocessing these aspects improves prediction.
- The best approach is used in the issue of Document level sentiment classification that is a statistical learning based computational method which can generate domain-specific sentiment lexicons and can lead to an average im-

provement of polarity prediction at the document level by 1.79% when compared to a baseline system which employs a hand-crafted generic sentiment lexicon.

- An unsupervised linguistic approach used in the issue Feature level sentiment classification in which SentiWordNet is used to calculate overall sentiment score of each sentence, but the negation expressions were not taken for analysis.

3. Comparative Analysis of Research Work Reviewed

The comparative analysis is shows the various approaches and methodology that are used to resolve the issues and the methodology are covered in the above sections. In this comparison table, the input, output and approaches are presented. The input is based on the people reviews that are collected from the social sites (The reviews are as negative review, positive review and the natural review) and shows the intensifier word, tagged word, and the opinion word. The performance or result is calculated according to the accuracy, recall and precision and F1 Measure. This section included with issue-wise solution with approaches and methodologies.

Table 1. Comparative Analysis of reviewed approaches

Solution Approach	Input Parameters					Output Parameters					Result
	Domain	Total Reviews	Positive Reviews	Negative Reviews	Features	Opinion Words	Modifier Words	Precision	Recall	Accuracy	
Unsupervised Learning method and POS tagging method (Fan et al., 2008)	Sports	320	170	150	Team, star	good, bad, garbage, frustrate	perfectly, poorly, achieve, without	Nil	86%	Nil	Calculating their sentiment orientation using unsupervised learning algorithm.
Bayesian logistic regression method, Pearson's correlation coefficient method (Barua et al., 2025)	Movie reviews	82,437	Nil	Nil	Screen, voice	Awful, great	Nil	Nil	Nil	Nil	UCSCAUTO gave better performance with 61% accuracy
Adverb-Adjective Combinations (AAC) sentiment analysis technique (Kasthuriarachchy et al., 2014)	News Reviews	200 Articals, 400 blog posts	Nil	Nil	Possibly, Roughly, apparently, extremely, scarcely, weakly, slightly	Nil	Nil	Nil	Nil	Nil	Three adverb-adjective scoring methods using Pearson Correlation were proposed.
LingPipe Language Identification Classifier, SentiWordNet Classifier with machine learning (Liu et al., 2012)	Movie,News	535	1200	1200	Nil	Nil	Nil	62.50%	60%	66%	The methodology determined polarity of text within a multilingual framework very efficiently
Stanford Part of Speech Tagger,SVM algorithm (Shahbaz et al., 2014)	Movie	2000	835	1265	Nil	Nil	Nil	67.98% (p), 69.76% (n)	77.6% (p), 74.1% (n)	65.85%	Presents improvements in pos and neg counting over pure term counting.

continued on following page

Table 1. Continued

Solution Approach	Input Parameters					Output Parameters					Result
	Domain	Total Reviews	Positive Reviews	Negative Reviews	Features	Opinion Words	Modifier Words	Precision	Recall	Accuracy	
Naïve Bays approach for thwarting detection, SVM, Domain Ontology Parsing technique (Li et-al., 2010)	Product	1196	Nil	Nil	Display, software, films, lens, storage,, shutter, feature, battery, video, battery	Nil	Nil	Nil	Nil	56.3%	Created a system that detect the document is thwarted or not. non-thwarted-98% thwarted-73%
Kullback-Leibler (KL) Divergence Statistical Learning method, TF-IDF (Kullback-Leibler et al., 2014)	Product	996,167	Nil	Nil	size,price,camera	Nil	Nil	70.10%	68.10%	Nil	The proposed method generated domain-specific sentiment lexicons Improvement of polarity prediction at the document level by 1.79%
Left-Middle-Right template and CRF(Conditional random fields), TF-IDF (Mahrishi et al., 2020)	Movies	829,1741 tagged sentiment words,	164	108	Nil	Nil	Nil	82.95%	86.59%	83.99%	The proposed method removed the transitional words problems
Apriori association rules and Point Wise Mutual Information (PMI) approach (Lim et al., 2010)	Product (Mobile)	300	150	150	Nil	Nil	Nil	86.50%	87%	Nil	Feature Words' Filtering Based on PMI was best in accuracy-75.4%
SentiWordNet (Liu et al., 2012)	Movie	1392-English, 724-Japanese	609 (E), 340(J)	783(E), 384(j)	iPod (Apple), Walkman (Sony)	Nil	Nil	Nil	Nil	81.7%	Removed the translation errors in multilingual review classification

continued on following page

Table 1. Continued

Solution Approach	Input Parameters					Output Parameters					Result
	Domain	Total Reviews	Positive Reviews	Negative Reviews	Features	Opinion Words	Modifier Words	Precision	Recall	Accuracy	
Support counting module(SCM), Database selection module, Classification module(CM), Naive Bays theorem (Ohana et al., 2009)	Nil	Emoticon based-550	Nil	Nil	Nil	Nil	Very, really, extreemly	74.74%	Nil	76.02%	Emotion based-89%(Acc),75%(FPR) Word based-89%(Acc),60%(FPR) Hybrid approcheh-91%(Acc),39%(FPR)
Sentence-Level Mood Extraction, SO-PMI-IR method, SVM,POS (Part of Speech) tagger (Wang et al., 2012)	Blogs, Movies News	Total 400 sentence (Joy, Sorrow, Anger or Neutral emotions)		Nil	Nil	huffy, mad	Nil	Nil	Nil	71% (Blogs), 82% (movie,news)	The results showed that the sentence structure and contextual information in the review are important for the sentiment orientation and classification
NB,SVM,SO-PMI-IR approaches (Xie et al., 2012)	Movies	4400	1700	1700	Nil	Excellent, poor	Nil	Nil	Nil	SO-PMI-IR (89%), NB (88%), SVM (83%), SWN (66%)	SO-PMI-IR achieved better performance in sentiment classification
Sentiment fuzzy classification algorithm, TF-IDF method, POS tagging (Jindal et al., 2008)	Movies	Total-20	Nil	Nil	Nil	Good, great, efficient, supportive, recommended, suggest	Nil	Nil	Nil	Nil	Sentiment Fuzzy Classification algorithm is proposed to improve classification accuracy.
Rule based Sentence level sentiment classification (Ramteke et al., 2013)	Product(Camera)	300	200	100	Size,price	Nil	Nil	82.66%	80.23%	80.83%	The pattern based method classified the sentences as positive and negative very correctly.

continued on following page

Table 1. Continued

Solution Approach	Input Parameters					Output Parameters					Result
	Domain	Total Reviews	Positive Reviews	Negative Reviews	Features	Opinion Words	Modifier Words	Precision	Recall	Accuracy	
lexicon-based rule based approach (Giyanani et al., 2014)	Product	445 (2616 no.of features)	Nil	Nil	Battery, Size quality	Long,great,small, amazing	Nil	Nil	Nil	90%	The proposed work solved the problem of opinion words whose semantic orientations are context dependent.
TF-IDF method, NB and SVM approaches (Altrabsheh et al., 2014)	Education	5000	Nil	Nil	Knowledge, Presentation, Communication, Regularit y	Awesome,well,good,bad	Nil	Nil	Nil	81% (Aspect based), 67.23% (document based)	Faculty performance score was computed from the distinct aspect based sentiment scores.
N-grams techniques, NB, Complement Naive Bayes Maximum Entropy (ME) and (SVM) (Iqbal et al., 2016)	Education	1036	641	292	technoloy, blackboad,examples,learning, questions, knowlede, topics, notes,	Nil	Nil	Nil	Nil	88%	SVM gave the highest performance accuracy increased by 20 percent.
Sentiment Miner Extractor algorithm (Lau et al., 2011)	Nil	documents-49, lines-1137 words-10529	Nil	Nil	Intelligent,diligent,brilliant, hard-working	Nil	Nil	Nil	Nil	75%	The word sense ambiguity problem were resolved with high accuracy rate
Support Vector Machine (SVM) (Riberio et al., 2011)	Product	435	Nil	Nil	phone, battery, screen, Camera, Price, Wi-Fi	Good, Great, Nice, Well, Amazing, Weak, Difficult, Complex,	Nil	91.25%	93.41%	72.80%	Proposed ungrammatical users' reviews, based on Support Vector Machine (SVM)

4. Strengths and Weaknesses of Research Work Reviewed

4.1. Strengths

- In the general rating deviation technique of a movie, the features weights were straightly consolidated towards a spam city recipe and figured experimentally to expand the estimation of the standardized reduced aggregate pick up measure.
- For spam detection and filtering the reviews the KNN classifiers with 78.5% accuracy result. KNN classifier is applied to filter the reviews that are shows on the review of the client.
- The model based on four supervised machine learning algorithms: K-Nearest Neighbor (k-NN), Naive Bayes, Random Tree, and Random Forest. The results show that the Random Forest predictions achieve 97.06% accuracy, which makes this model a better prediction model than the other three.
- In the Syntactic Dependency parsing technique, the dependency tree was used to extract the aspects which gave better adverb adjective, adverb verb combinations for opinion mining process to increase the accuracy level in sentiment classification.
- In the multilingual framework sentiment classification, the performance was improved by modifying the sentiment values returned by SentiWordNet for intensifiers and objective words for Negation Handling, Intensifier handling.
- In Sentiment Miner algorithm, the tagging rules are used as Strongly Positive, Positive, Neutral, Negative, and Strongly Negative which classified the sentiments with good results compared to only positive and negative results.
- Sentiment Miner extractor module helped to resolve word sense disambiguate and determined the impact of Adverbs on Adjectives, detected negation.
- The phrase patterns with more than two words were more affecting for the sentiment orientation of a text in phrase pattern sentiment classification technique.
- In Rule based approach the thwarting recognition was used with high performance compared to non-thwarted documents by which the sentiments are analysed more accurately.
- In verb based sentiment classification technique, the verb oriented sentiments gave better result than BOW approach.
- Latent Semantic Analysis technique was used to improve the performance of information retrieval systems by addressing the synonymy problem.
- Word Sense Disambiguation was resolved by using the semantic pattern of the desired sentence in the opinion expression and by extracting the possible senses from WordNet.

4.2. Weaknesses

- The performance of SentiWordNet based classifier with rule based approach compared to machine learning approach was poor, due to not handling Negation expressions, translation errors, writing mistakes and word sense disambiguate.
- In the combined association rules and point-wise mutual information approach due to the ignorance of the potential feature word (such as in the review "The G2 mobile phone is so dear", the potential feature is "price"), the lacking of deeply semantic analysis was found.
- The phrase patterns more than two words not handled in the phrase pattern algorithm, which could affect the sentiment orientation of a text with higher accuracy.

5. Gaps in the Published Research

The researchers had presented many Techniques and Methodologies on Feature Level Sentiment Analysis. The gaps observed in totally are:

- Some approaches did not included Automatic grouping of aspect synonyms and didn't consider conditional, comparative sentences in order to improve the accuracy of opinion mining.
- Most of the researchers didn't address the problems of Word sense disambiguation, Anaphora Resolution, poor spellings, incomplete sentences, and sarcasm, synonyms so that a rule based technique has to be used to improve the sentiment classification accuracy.
- Some approaches only used adverb, verb and adjective features only for calculating the scores, but the combination of adverb-adjective and adjective-noun and double intensifiers (as very very, very much etc.) has not been used to improve the classification accuracy on feature level.

6. Problem Statement and Objectives

6.1 Problem Statement

The problem statement of research is due to the sentiment analysis in different levels and applying the different machine learning approaches for polarity classification. This dissertation aims to understand the difficulties of different levels of sentiment analysis specially feature level and detecting the spam reviews. Feature level classification is to produce a feature-based opinion summary of multiple reviews in complex sentences. Many researchers did not resolve some common problems like negation, intensifiers, conjunctions, and synonyms handling in feature level sentiment analysis .So, I have been decided dissertation title as "Spam Detection and Feature Level Sentiment Analysis on Movie Reviews"

6.2 Objectives

- To create the knowledge base movie reviews from different social sites.
- To perform data pre-processing on collected movie reviews in understandable format.
- To design and implement the Feature level sentiment analysis on movie reviews.
- To carry out the performance analysis of proposed system.
- To compare the results with existing systems.

PROCESS FLOW DIAGRAM

Figure 1. Analyzing Sentiment with Aspect-Based Approach: A Spam and Ham Detection Study

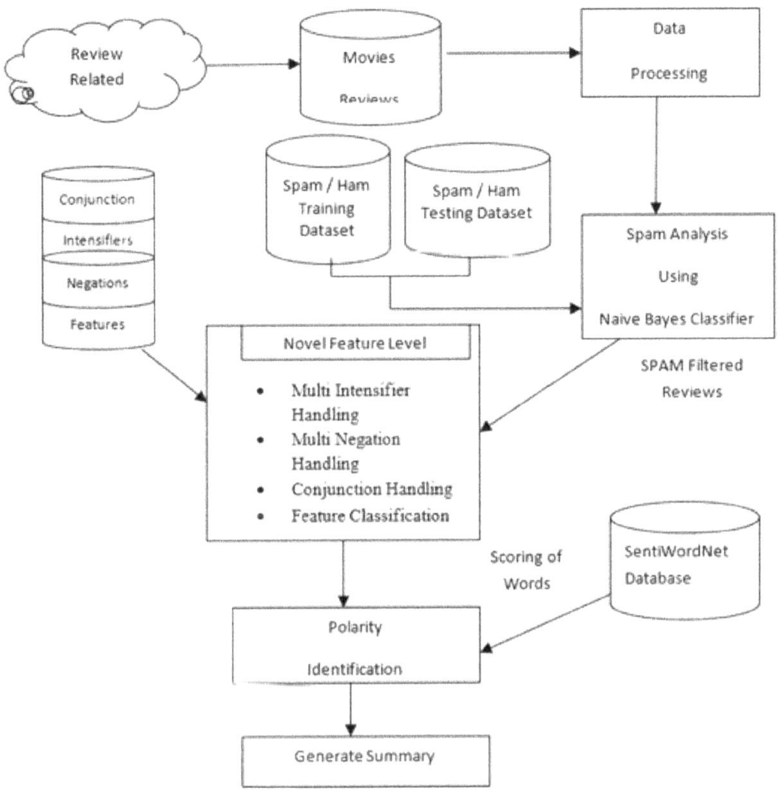

Sentiment Analysis deals with analyzing users comment on a particular thing and then computationally figuring out the actual sentiment of the user i.e Positive or Negative. The process of computationally identifying and categorizing opinions expressed in a piece of text, especially in order to determine whether the writer's attitude towards a particular topic, product, etc. is positive or negative. The analysis utilizes stopwords, which are words that help classify sentences by removing articles. These stopwords are categorized using WordNet, a lexical database comprising global words.

The Methodology Involves the Following Steps

1. Collecting user comments via Twitter API

2. Vectorizing the comments using the Count Vectorizer function
3. Creating an array of comments with unique digits representing stopwords, enabling the model to predict sentiment

By leveraging these techniques, this research project aims to improve sentiment analysis and spam detection in movie reviews.

CONCLUSION AND FUTURE WORK

The increasing prevalence of online reviews and feedback across platforms has made spam detection and sentiment analysis vital tools for maintaining the credibility and usability of digital content. Through the application of diverse computational techniques—ranging from machine learning algorithms like KNN, Random Forest, and Naive Bayes to linguistic approaches such as syntactic dependency parsing, multilingual sentiment adjustment, and word sense disambiguation—researchers have achieved significant improvements in the accuracy of both spam filtering and feature-level sentiment classification.

Methods like the Sentiment Miner algorithm have demonstrated the importance of detailed sentiment tagging and effective handling of negation and intensifiers. Other approaches, such as verb-based classification, phrase pattern analysis, and rule-based thwarting recognition, further enhance the depth and reliability of sentiment extraction. These advancements help in understanding the emotions, intentions, and authenticity behind user-generated content, thus enabling better decision-making in domains like product recommendations, movie reviews, and educational feedback systems. Despite significant progress, further research is needed to improve spam detection and sentiment analysis. Key areas include better multilingual support, real-time adaptive spam detection, and the use of deep learning models like BERT for improved understanding. Aspect-based and context-aware sentiment analysis, hybrid modeling approaches, and privacy-preserving techniques are also essential for building smarter, scalable, and secure systems.

REFERENCES

Alkalbani, A. M., Gadhvi, L., Patel, B., Hussain, F. K., Ghamry, A. M., & Hussain, O. K. (2017). Analysing Cloud Services Reviews Using Opining Mining. 2017 IEEE 31st International Conference on Advanced Information Networking and Applications (AINA), pp. 419-426.

AlMahmoud, A., Al-Mistarihi, M., & Al-Ayyoub, M. (2017). Spamdoop: A privacy-preserving Big Data platform for collaborative spam detection. *IEEE Transactions on Big Data*, *3*(2), 120–130.

Altrabsheh, N., Cocca, M., & Fallahkhair, S. (2014, November). Sentiment analysis: towards a tool for analysing real-time students feedback. In 2014 IEEE 26th international conference on tools with artificial intelligence (pp. 419-423). IEEE.

Barua, T., Doshi, R., Hiran, K. K., & Sharma, A. (2025). *Mobile Applications Development: With Python in Kivy Framework.* Walter de Gruyter GmbH & Co KG.

Chauhan, S. K., Goel, S., & Vyas, O. (2017). Research on product review analysis and spam review detection using sentiment analysis. In *2017 International Conference on Computing, Communication and Automation (ICCCA)*, pp. 1338-1342.

Chen, C., Wang, Y., Zhang, J., Xiang, Y., Zhou, W., & Min, G. (2016). Statistical features-based real-time detection of drifted twitter spam. *IEEE Transactions on Information Forensics and Security*, *12*(4), 914–925.

Chen, C., Wang, Y., Zhang, J., Xiang, Y., Zhou, W., & Min, G. (2017). Statistical Features-Based Real-Time Detection of Drifted Twitter Spam. *IEEE Transactions on Information Forensics and Security*, *12*(4), 914–927.

Dalal, A., Nagaraj, K., Sawant, U., & Shelke, S. (2006). Hindi part-of-speech tagging and chunking: A maximum entropy approach. *Proceeding of the NLPAI machine learning competition.*

Fan, N., Cai, W., & Zhao, Y. (2008, December). Research on the Model of Multiple Levels for Determining Sentiment of Text. In *2008 IEEE Pacific-Asia Workshop on Computational Intelligence and Industrial Application* (Vol. 1, pp. 267-271). IEEE.

Giyanani, R., & Desai, M. (2014). Spam detection using natural language processing. IOSR Journal of Computer Engineering (IOSR-JCE), 16(5), 116-119.

Iqbal, M., Abid, M. M., Ahmad, M., & Khurshid, F. (2016). Study on the effectiveness of spam detection technologies. [IJITCS]. *International Journal of Information Technology and Computer Science*, *8*(1), 11–21.

Iyengar, S., & Kalpana, M. (2017). Integrated SPAM detection for multilingual emails. In *2017 International Conference on Advances in Computing, Communication and Informatics (ICACCI)*, pp. 2352-2357.

Jain, A., Virwani, H., Shrotriya, N., & Somwanshi, D. (2023). Information retrieval using data mining. In Machine Vision and Augmented Intelligence: Select Proceedings of MAI 2022 (pp. 287-293). Singapore: Springer Nature Singapore.

Jaswal, V., & Sood, M. (2013). Spam Detection System Using Hidden Markov Model. *International Journal of Advanced Research in Computer Science and Software Engineering*, *3*(7), 137–141.

Jha, R., & Kumar, A. (2013). Feature Level Opinion Mining of Movie Reviews. *International Journal of Computer Applications*, *62*(10), 7–12.

Jindal, N., & Liu, B. (2008, February). Opinion spam and analysis. In *Proceedings of the 2008 international conference on web search and data mining* (pp. 219-230).

Kasthuriarachchy, B. H., De Zoysa, K., & Premaratne, H. L. (2014, December). Enhanced bag-of-words model for phrase-level sentiment analysis. In 2014 14th International Conference on Advances in ICT for Emerging Regions (ICTer) (pp. 210-214). IEEE.

Khan, A., & Baharudin, B. (2011, September). Sentiment classification using sentence-level semantic orientation of opinion terms from blogs. In *2011 National Postgraduate Conference* (pp. 1-7). IEEE.

Kumar, P. (2017). SVM with Gaussian kernel-based image spam detection on TREC07 dataset. In *2017 International Conference on Wireless Communications, Signal Processing and Networking (WiSPNET)*, pp. 1234-1238.

Lau, R. Y., Zhang, W., Bruza, P. D., & Wong, K. F. (2011, October). Learning domain-specific sentiment lexicons for predicting product sales. In 2011 IEEE 8th International Conference on e-Business Engineering (pp. 131-138). IEEE.

Li, S., Zhang, H., Xu, W., Chen, G., & Guo, J. (2010, August). Exploiting combined multi-level model for document sentiment analysis. In 2010 20th International Conference on Pattern Recognition (pp. 4141-4144). IEEE.

Li, X., Sun, A., & Datta, A. (2016). Identifying Informative Reviews Using Dependency Parsing and Sentiment Analysis. In *Proceedings of the 2016 Conference on Empirical Methods in Natural Language Processing (EMNLP)*, pages 1249-1259. Association for Computational Linguistics.

Lim, E. P., Nguyen, V. A., Jindal, N., Liu, B., & Lauw, H. W. (2010, October). Detecting product review spammers using rating behaviors. In *Proceedings of the 19th ACM international conference on Information and knowledge management* (pp. 939-948).

Lin, G., Sun, N., Nepal, S., Zhang, J., Xiang, Y., & Hassan, H. (2017). Statistical Twitter Spam Detection Demystified: Performance, Stability and Scalability. *IEEE Access : Practical Innovations, Open Solutions*, *5*, 11142–11154.

Liu, L., Nie, X., & Wang, H. (2012, October). Toward a fuzzy domain sentiment ontology tree for sentiment analysis. In 2012 5th International Congress on Image and Signal Processing (pp. 1620-1624). IEEE.

Mahrishi, M., Hiran, K. K., Meena, G., & Sharma, P. (Eds.). (2020). *Machine learning and deep learning in real-time applications*. IGI global., DOI: 10.4018/978-1-7998-3095-5

Malarvizhi, R., & Saraswathi, K. (2013). Content-Based Spam Filtering and Detection Algorithms-An Efficient Analysis & Comparison. [IJETT]. *International Journal of Engineering Trends and Technology*, *4*(9).

Mouthami, K., Devi, K. N., & Bhaskaran, V. M. (2013, February). Sentiment analysis and classification based on textual reviews. In 2013 international conference on Information communication and embedded systems (ICICES) (pp. 271-276). IEEE.

Ohana, B., & Tierney, B. (2009). Sentiment classification of reviews using SentiWordNet.

Olatunji, S. O. (2017). Extreme Learning Machines and Support Vector Machines Models for Email Spam Detection. In 2017 IEEE 30th Canadian Conference on Electrical and Computer Engineering (CCECE), pp. 1-6.

Pang, B., Lee, L., & Vaithyanathan, S. (2002). Thumbs up? Sentiment classification using machine learning techniques. arXiv preprint cs/0205070.

Patil, S., Patil, S., & Kulkarni, U. (2017). Visual and CSS-based Phishing Website Detection using SVM with MapReduce. In 2017 International Conference on Intelligent Computing and Control (I2C2), pp. 1-6.

Puri, S., Gosain, D., Ahuja, M., Kathuria, I., & Jatana, N. (2013). Comparison and analysis of spam detection algorithms. *International Journal of Application or Innovation in Engineering and Management*, *2*(4), 255–261.

Rajamohana, S. P., Umamaheswari, K., & Abirami, B. (2017). Adaptive binary flower pollination algorithm for feature selection in review spam detection. *Journal of Computer Security, 25*(4), 357–372.

Rajamohana, S. P., Umamaheswari, K., & Keerthana, S. V. (2017). An effective hybrid Cuckoo Search with Harmony Search for review spam detection. In *Proceedings of the 3rd IEEE International Conference on Advances in Electrical and Electronics, Information, Communication and Bio-Informatics (AEEICB)*, pp. 524-527.

Ramteke, A., Malu, A., Bhattacharyya, P., & Nath, J. S. (2013, August). Detecting turnarounds in sentiment analysis: Thwarting. In *Proceedings of the 51st Annual Meeting of the Association for Computational Linguistics* (Volume 2: Short Papers) (pp. 860-865).

Rathi, M., & Pareek, V. (2013). Spam mail detection through data mining-A comparative performance analysis. *International Journal of Modern Education and Computer Science, 5*(12), 31.

Rekha, S. N. (2014). A review on different spam detection approaches. [IJETT]. *International Journal of Engineering Trends and Technology, 11*(6), 315–318.

Ribeiro, M. T., Guerra, P. H. C., Vilela, L., Veloso, A., Guedes, D., & Meira, W., Jr. & Hoepers, C. (2011, September). Spam detection using web page content: a new battleground. In Proceedings of the 8th annual collaboration, electronic messaging, anti-abuse and spam conference (pp. 83-91).

Sedhai, S., & Sun, A. (2017). Semi-Supervised Spam Detection in Twitter Stream. *IEEE Transactions on Computational Social Systems, 5*(2), 169–175.

Shahbaz, M., Guergachi, A., & ur Rehman, R. T. (2014, May). Sentiment miner: A prototype for sentiment analysis of unstructured data and text. In 2014 IEEE 27th Canadian Conference on Electrical and Computer Engineering (CCECE) (pp. 1-7). IEEE.

Shaikh, M. A. M., Prendinger, H., & Ishizuka, M. (2007, December). An analytical approach to assess sentiment of text. In 2007 10th international conference on computer and information technology (pp. 1-6). IEEE.

Sharma, K., & Kaur, M. (2013). Spam Detection Techniques: A Review. *International Journal of Computer Applications, 67*(20), 20–23.

Shinde, S., Joshi, S., & Pawar, M. (2016). A Decision Support Engine: Heuristic Review Analysis on Information Extraction System and Mining Comparable Objects from Comparable Concepts. In 2016 International Conference on Advances in Computing, Communication, & Automation (ICACCA), pp. 1-7.

Topal, K., & Özsoyoglu, G. (2016). Movie review analysis: Emotion analysis of IMDb movie reviews. In *2016 IEEE/ACM International Conference on Advances in Social Networks Analysis and Mining (ASONAM)*, pp. 1170-1176.

Valakunde, N. D., & Patwardhan, M. S. (2013, November). Multi-aspect and multi-class based document sentiment analysis of educational data catering accreditation process. In *2013 International Conference on Cloud & Ubiquitous Computing & Emerging Technologies* (pp. 188-192). IEEE.

Valakunde, N. D., & Patwardhan, M. S. (2013, November). Multi-aspect and multi-class based document sentiment analysis of educational data catering accreditation process. In *2013 International Conference on Cloud & Ubiquitous Computing & Emerging Technologies* (pp. 188-192). IEEE.

Wang, G., Xie, S., Liu, B., & Yu, P. S. (2012). Identify online store review spammers via social review graph. [TIST]. *ACM Transactions on Intelligent Systems and Technology*, *3*(4), 1–21.

Xie, S., Wang, G., Lin, S., & Yu, P. S. (2012, April). Review spam detection via time series pattern discovery. In *Proceedings of the 21st International Conference on World Wide Web* (pp. 635-636).

Chapter 12
Deep Learning and NLP Methods for Automated Hate Speech Detection Across Human and Machine-Generated Content

Anushree Kangoo
Manipal University Jaipur, India

Vibhakar Pathak
https://orcid.org/0000-0002-0916-9326
Arya College of Engineering and Information Technology, India

Rohit Mittal
https://orcid.org/0000-0001-7688-5421
Manipal University Jaipur, India

Ahmed Antwi-Boampong
Department of Information Technology, Ghana Communication Technology University, Accra, Ghana

ABSTRACT

Hate speech is a widespread and ever-changing issue that poses a serious threat to the safety and dignity of individuals and communities around the globe. This chapter offers a thorough look at hate speech, starting with what it is and how it can show

DOI: 10.4018/979-8-3373-3063-1.ch012

up in different forms—whether in private conversations, public settings, or online spaces. It also addresses tactics like denial and trivialization. A significant focus is given to the alarming increase of hate speech on social media platforms, breaking down key areas such as online harassment, hurtful comments, unfair treatment, and trolling. The chapter discuss challenges such as the ambiguity of language, cultural contexts, and the specific nuances of different platforms. It explores modern detection techniques, particularly highlighting the transformative impact of Natural Language Processing (NLP). The chapter examines the stages of NLP and how it can be applied to understand and identify hate speech, showcasing how linguistic and computational tools can effectively work together to tackle digital toxicity.

1. INTRODUCTION

Hate speech can be defined as speech containing or promoting hatred towards a person or group of people due to their attributes like race, ethnicity, religion, gender, nationality or sexual orientation. It manifests in numerous ways including the damage it causes, e.g. by creating a hostile environment; its content, e.g. by expressing or inciting hatred; its linguistic nature, e.g. by using slurs words; or its effects on human dignity, e.g. by demeaning a person about his or her basic social status. (Shridhara et al., 2023). Hate speech can be looked at in different ways. Content-based and intrinsic property is an example; it attempts to define what is said, or how it is said, whereas harm-based definitions are concerned with the actual effect of speech. Dignity concepts highlight both moral and social outcomes of speech that deprives certain groups of their equal status in society (Schmidt and Wiegand, 2017; Mittal et al., 2024; Choubisa et al., 2022; Kesarwani et al., 2023). Hate speech and its legal implications are listed below.

2. TYPES OF HATE SPEECH

1. **Privately expressed hate speech**: It happens when people speak privately as shown in figure 1. No man is usually answerable to be punished by the law, but this speech can be offensive as jokes are among friends, people do not want to make people hate anyone after listening to this type of speech. Uncontrolled hate speech on the other hand might affect mass media and spread a whole culture of abuse and discrimination, should it not be controlled.

Figure 1. Forms of hate speech

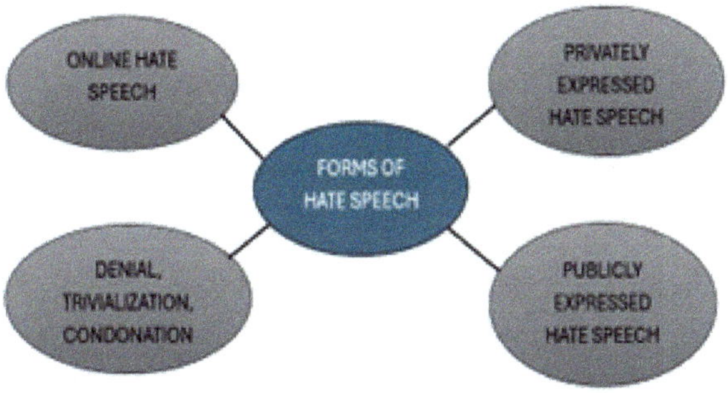

2. **Publicly expressed hate:** Hate speech expressed publicly It is thought to be worse and more likely to be punished. Swearing obscenities at a public event would be considered a degradation form of public speech intended to bring degradation, discrimination, and violence towards groups.
3. **Online hate speech** This represents hate speech that is spread through the social media. This may be more acceptable because of the anonymity of the internet, but it is getting the same treatment as hate speech in the real world. Users can face punishment; websites with hate speech can face punishment too.

Denials: Trivialization or Condonation: This happens when one appears before the court denying or excusing actions to spark off violence or hate.

3. HATE SPEECH IN SOCIAL MEDIA NETWORKS

Hate speech is perpetrated in the following harmful ways via social media. Each of the following results in a poisonous digital environment as in **Figure 2.**

Figure 2. Speech on social media networks

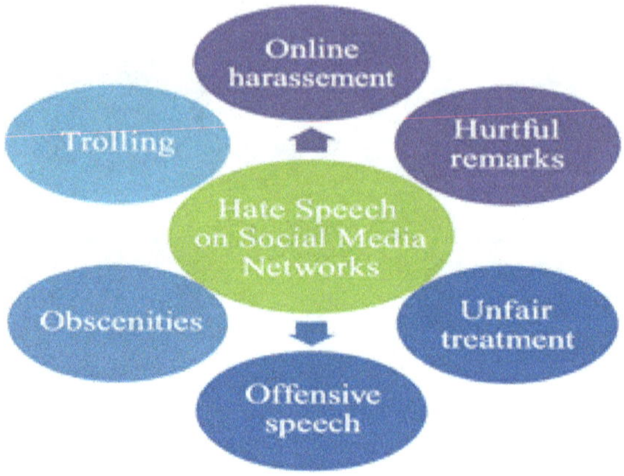

a) Online harassment: This is characterized by intentional and repeated abuse of an individual or groups of individuals that causes emotional distress and fear.
b) Hurtful remarks are remarks likely to insult, demean or belittle someone based on identity, beliefs or background.
c) Unfair treatment may be defined as biased or discriminatory behaviour that is encoded in posts or interactions and isolates or singles out people or groups and denies them equal consideration or opportunity.
d) Offensive speech is the use of words and phrases which are crude, disrespectful, demoralizing and although it may not be explicitly hateful, it nevertheless may occasion hostility and exclusion.
e) Obscenity means profanity, vulgarity use of sexually explicit language and an offense to morality, an insult and disgusting.
f) Trolling: Trolling may be defined as the intentional provocation of emotional response, or even argument, in the name of humour or debate, through the use of inflammatory, offensive or abusive language.

The above feature is the multidimensional nature of hate speech on the Internet. The gravity and widespread societal harm of these underscores the significance of awareness, digital literacy, active control and systematic prevention. The effective mechanisms should be worked out to unveil and solve the increasing rate of hate speech in the digitalized age (Bhattacharjee D, 2023; Mahrishi et al., 2020; Garg et al., 2025; Mittal et al., 2020).

4. HATE SPEECH DETECTION

Hate detection can be described as identifying and classifying any form of communication, whether spoken, written or otherwise, as conveying prejudice, hate, discrimination or violence against people or groups. This includes the steps:

a) Examination of speech directed at individuals or groups of people based on race, religion, gender and nationality. It is considering historical and structural disparities through the lens of social power relations between the speaker and the targeted group.
b) Human intelligence: Understanding the character of the offender, his or her name, reason and effect.
c) The presence of negative group reference (e.g. slurs, derogative remarks, dehumanizing language, etc.) should also be examined.
d) Consequences or impacts of the speech, particularly whether it creates discrimination, hostility or violence. (Yadav et al., 2021; Okoye et al., 2024)
e) In these steps a hate speech detection system attempts to recognize posts that are harmful and target a person or group of people based on their race, religion, gender, or country.

5. TECHNIQUES FOR HATE SPEECH DETECTION

The algorithms that can detect hate speech fall into 3 broad categories: shallow methods, deep learning methods, and transformer-based methods. The classifications have given rise to more advanced levels of automated detection systems with greater complexity and accuracy as we move up a level to more sophisticated models, the transformer-based models. This is not so with representative writing, but this could be false.

a) **a) Shallow Methods:** Shallow methods use techniques such as Term Frequency-Inverse Document Frequency (TF-IDF), n-grams, and clustering based representations, as well as linguistic features such as part-of-speech (POS) tags, sentiment lexicons, and word dependencies. TF-IDF is a statistical measure, which also is used to compare the relative importance of a word in a document and a corpus to focus attention on those words that appear very often in a document and very rarely in the corpus. N-grams are local contexts of a text that a word with a length of n words or characters, or a character, do occur to get the local context with consideration on the pattern of co-occurrence of words. Scikit-learn is a simple to use and interpret package that aids these shallow models.

b) **Deep Learning Approaches:** Deep learning algorithms do not need any form of interaction with manual feature engineering as they are able to learn features directly on raw text data. It is based on Convolutional neural networks (CNNs) that carry out convolution and pooling of features and semantic patterns of text. Long Short-Term Memory (LSTM) networks are a type of recurrent neural network that learns long-term dependencies and helps to reduce the vanishing gradient problem with memory cells and a gating structure. Last but not least, Bi-directional Long Short-Term Memory networks (Bi-LSTM), a type of LSTMs with the capability to process texts both forward and backward to extract more in-depth contextual information (Kumar A, 2022). These types of models can acquire local and long-range text dependencies and can be applied to hate speech detection (Lala, C., and Dwivedi, P, 2023). A further smaller category of deep learning approaches are word embedding-based approaches including:

   i. **Word2Vec** is a natural language processing (NLP) algorithm that models the semantics of words as a dense vector in a multi-dimensional space and represents the semantic relationship between words. These word embeddings are also called vectors and are learned using a neural network model that estimates surrounding word context of a target word).

   ii. **GloVe (Global Vectors for Word Representation)** is an unsupervised machine learning algorithm that trains representations of words as vectors based on the frequency with which words occur together in a text corpus of large size. It describes words as vectors in a continuous space; the word similarities are described by the angles and directions of these vectors. GloVe constructs a co-occurrence word-pair matrix and trains word embedding by optimizing the discrepancy between the statistical co-occurrence data and the word vectors.).

   iii. **FastText** takes words and maps them to dense vectors that allow maintaining semantic relations. It can be used to augment these embeddings with traditional classifiers or deep learning models. Facebook developed FastText which also employs character n-gram embeddings and has proven to be a powerful and effective baseline in a wide range of text classification problems.

   iv. **Hybrid networks** such as C-GRU (Convolutional-GRU) are a hybrid network that jointly applies CNNs and Gated Recurrent Units (GRUs) to effectively capture the semantics of short text sequences, such as tweets. Likewise, Neural Ensemble methods also use multiple CNNs with varying initializations to average the predictions to increase robustness and generalization. Transformer-Based Methods

c) **Transformer based models** make use of context embedding to achieve better language understanding. Models such as BERT, small BERT, ELECTRA, and ALBERT offer NLP task performance. These models take a pre-trained transformer architecture and can be scaled to hate speech by tuning with only a few tasks specific modifications, such as the addition of a linear classification layer on the architectures output. More recently, language-specific transformer models like BETO, BERTin, and RoBERTuito have been proposed to capture multilingual gaps in hate speech detection in Spanish. Such models allow very fine-grained cross-language classification and have shown considerable success with non-English data. Furthermore, emotion-exploratory learning methods are gaining growing significance, as they lead to improvements in model capacity to identify sarcasm, stereotypes and coded hate.

Despite the successful outcomes achieved by transformer models such as BERT, their interpretability is limited in many cases because they are complex and prone to attention noise. This poses a problem in interpolating what the model is predicting particularly in sensitive areas of use such as hate speech detection. Although transformer models like BERT have rendered successful results, they often suffer from limited interpretability due to their complexity and attention noise. This presents challenges in understanding the rationale behind model predictions, especially in sensitive applications like hate speech detection.

d) **Multi-view SVM**

The (mSVM) is an algorithm that trains an ensemble of stacked linear SVM classifiers with each classifier (or view) being trained on a different feature type, e.g. word unigrams, character n-grams. In this way, each classifier will focus on a single aspect of the data, considering different perspectives of the signals. Multi-view learning is useful in preventing the problem of weaker signal being drowned out by stronger signals when all the features are lumped into a single model. As an example, the words go back and home are in themselves innocuous, but when together, first as go back home, then a chat on the Internet, the expression becomes potentially xenophobic. Such subtle trends can be better represented and identified through a model such as mSVM. Moreover, mSVM enhances the understanding of the decision made by a classifier, and this feature is valuable in establishing trust and awareness in sensitive contexts.

6. DIFFICULTIES WITH CONVENTIONAL HATE SPEECH DETECTION

Conventional approaches and deep learning algorithms have achieved great improvements in hate speech detection automation. The range of technical, linguistic and social difficulties encountered during this process makes its application in the real world setting a hard endeavour. Although the importance of hate speech detection in ensuring individual or group respectfulness is very significant, there are some challenges associated with it, whose occurrence is related to the complexity of human speech, cultural or linguistic differences, and the unstable nature of online communication (Parihar et al., 2021).The subtle, context-sensitive nature of hate speech especially when expressed through sarcasm, coded language, or mixed media remains a persistent hurdle in its identification and analysis.

a) Contextualizing language in its historical context: A headline from an old newspaper might refer to women as 'weaker vessels' or 'kitchen queens'. In a classroom discussion this would reflect the historical attitudes of its time but would appear gendered or derogatory in the present times.
b) Capturing the nuances in wording: The remark 'Jews control the media' conveys a sweeping negative stereotype. But 'Several Jewish-owned media companies are influential' represents a factual market reality. Automated systems are often not able to recognize how these minor variations change the underlying meaning.
c) As detection systems gain advancement with time, users or miscreants who intend to spread hate speech devise novel ways to evade these tools. Embedding offensive language within images is a common way to bypass the text-based detection filters.
d) Internet is rife with context-bounded sarcastic and ironical comments, transliterated text and code-mixed language. Such nuances can often not be captured by automated tools that are largely based on English language detection. Limited availability of non-English datasets poses a limit to fine-grained classification of such data.
e) Much of the current research still focusses on examining hate speech as a binary problem, overlooking its more nuanced forms. Human communication is contextually bounded and interpreting accurate meaning of utterances is not always possible by machine tools.
f) Hate speech makers use creative ways to generate adversarial content. Misspellings ('1d10t for idiot), phonetic spelling ('h8 for hate'), spacing ('r a c i s t), symbols and emojis. Furthermore, the proliferation of multimodal content (combining text with audio and visual features) adds to the complexity of hate speech identification.

g) The subjectivity and fuzziness in the definition and description of hate speech makes it difficult to distinguish between deliberate offensive attacks and legitimate criticism, sarcasm and irony.

Multimodal features enable role and target identification that allow for attribute analysis such as gender, ethnicity, and orientation focusing on common hate targets aiding in bully-victim-onlooker categorization. However, these analyses do not have uniform effectiveness and vary greatly with context and platform. This posits a need for blended-method approach that combine different tools and techniques to ensure holistic and comprehensive outcomes. Research needs to be expanded in devising methods like federated learning for privacy-preserving detection, multimodal analyses and contextual modelling. These approaches can ensure more resilient, inclusive, and effective systems for creating safer online environments.

7. NATURAL LANGUAGE PROCESSING (NLP) IN HATE SPEECH DETECTION

As hate speech continues to evolve and spread across digital platforms, it is essential to embrace interdisciplinary strategies that account for the nuanced social and contextual factors that shape its meaning and impact. A blend of content generation technologies like linguistics, AI, and machine learning need to be used. In this regard, Natural Language Processing (NLP) equips us with the foundational tools and techniques to analyze language at multiple levels—phonological, syntactic, semantic, and pragmatic—enabling machines to understand the nuances of human communication. (Schmidt & Wiegand, 2017; Illhan, S, 2024). Merging NLP with cultural awareness and legal considerations can ensure effective, fair, and responsible detection in various online settings. A range of models are used, for example, keyword checks through keyword systems, sentiment analysis, and advanced natural language system processing that relate to tone and intent.

Natural Language Processing (NLP) helps machines read and understand human language with amazing accuracy. Historically, much of the interest has been in supervised machines. Historically, most attention has been paid to supervised machines. Support Vector Machines (SVMs) to classify hate speech by examining features derived by scanning the text (Tiwari, A., and Agrawal, A, 2022).

Figure 3 shows the processes involved in NLP (Gaurav, A. et.al, 2023). Older methods of NLP were heuristic, using a fixed set of rules and expert opinions, such as Regular Expressions (Regex) to match patterns.

Figure 3. Process involved in NLP

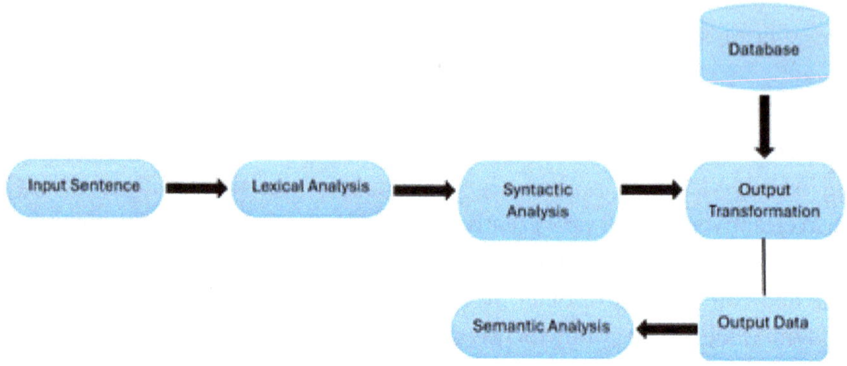

Then there was Statistical NLP, which leveraged machine learning algorithms like Naive Bayes, SVM, and Hidden Markov Models (HMM) to learn language patterns using data. The most recent and notable step is the use of Neural Network-Based NLP, or Deep Learning, which uses models such as Recurrent Neural Networks (RNNs), Long Short-Term Memory Networks (LSTMs), and Transformers to achieve high accuracy in language tasks, albeit at a great deal of data and computation to train. With the advent of deep learning, the issue of hate speech recognition has been transformed. Advanced neural networks like Convolutional Neural Networks (CNNs), Long Short-Term Memory networks (LSTMs) and FastText have been trained to improve detection accuracy. These methods have applied to text in social media, and word embeddings, such as GloVe (Mihalcea et al., 2006; Jahan, M. S., and Oussalah, M, 2023).

The processing begins with text preprocessing, and the text is handled by conducting text processing operations such as tokenization, stop-word and stemming or lemmatization to normalize the input data. This is then succeeded by feature extraction algorithms like Bag of Words, TF-IDF and textual context embeddings like BERT that converts text input to vectors that can be inputted into machine learning models. These vectors are then used by classifiers like logistic regression, SVMs, deep neural networks, and transformer-based designs to determine how much hate speech is contained in the text. Moreover, the sophisticated NLP techniques are even more profound because they include sentiment analysis, emotion recognition, sarcasm recognition and pragmatic discourse. The techniques assist in detecting implicit hate speech that is usually disguised by irony, euphemisms, or cultural allusions. NLP can also be used to perform multilingual analysis, so that systems can analyze hate speech in any language or dialect. In total, the linguistic intuition and computer modelling together enable NLP to be an influential and necessary resource in the current struggle to stop hate online and facilitate safer digital communication environments.

8. PHASES OF NLP TOOLS

NLP enables computers to read, comprehend and communicate in human language. It consists of multiple stages that interact to process language, each stage is related to the comprehension of the structure and meaning of human communication. Figure 4 shows the phases.

Figure 4. Phases of NLP

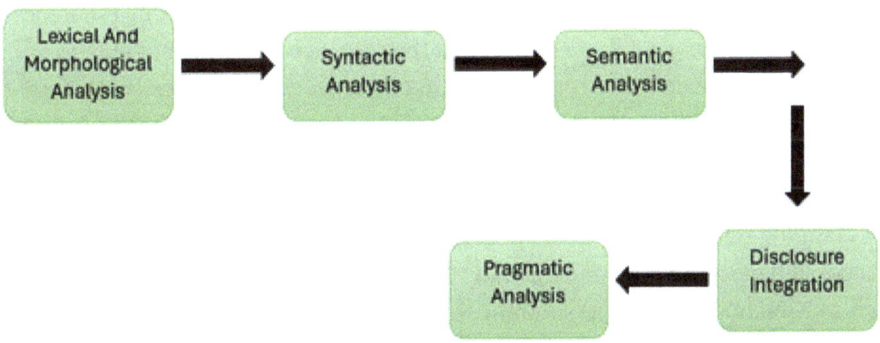

a) Lexical Analysis

Lexical Analysis deals with the identification and processing of words or lexemes within a text by breaking down the input to meaningful units (as words or phrases). The primary aims of lexical analysis are tokenization (i.e. the division of text into small units or tokens) and part-of-speech tagging (i.e. assigning the grammatical part (noun, verb, adjective, etc.) to each of the tokens) to understand the context and structure of the sentence. One example is tokenization, which divides a sentence into words, and part-of-speech tagging, which assigns a word to a grammatical category. What is important about lexical analysis is that it can be employed to determine words which can be manipulated further by the system, and simplify texts through tokenization and stemming, enhancing the precision of various NLP operations.

b) Morphological Analysis

Morphological Analysis deals with the smallest units of meaning in a word (morphemes) and is important in the study of the structure of words by identifying free morphemes (separate words such as cat) and bound morphemes (suffixes or prefixes such as un- or ing). Important processes are stemming (reducing words to their root structures, e.g. running to run), and lemmatization (reducing words to their base or dictionary form, e.g. better to good). Morphological analysis is important as it aids in word understanding by decomposing complex words, enhancing the precision of NLP tasks such as part-of-speech tagging, syntactic parsing, and machine translation, and facilitates the system to recognize the text correctly at the most fundamental level, which can support other more sophisticated uses of NLP technology.

c) Syntactic Analysis (Parsing)

Syntactic Analysis aids in the comprehension of how the words in a sentence are structured to fit the grammar rules so that the sentence has proper syntax to help us comprehend its meaning. It is an attempt to construct a parsing tree, a structure that breaks the sentence down into its parts, e.g., the subject, the verb, and the object, as well as the relationship among those parts, such that the machine can interpret what is meant by the relationships between words. These are vital elements such as POS tagging (assigning parts of speech to words) and ambiguity resolution (words that could have more than one meaning e.g. book as a verb or noun). Proper syntax, such as Mohan eats an apple, and incorrect (distorted) syntax, such as, Apple eats Mohan an, show that correct word order is vital to meaning. NLP can study sentence structure and hence understand and generate language better, which is useful in machine translation, sentiment analysis and information retrieval because it makes the text more understandable and less ambiguous.

d) Semantic Analysis

Semantic Analysis is concerned with understanding of words and sentences with view to establishing that the text is not only grammatically correct but also makes sense and has a contextual application. It also tries to figure out the meaning of words in the dictionary and how they are used in context and how well the words are phrased, that it does make sense. The Named Entity Recognition (NER) task identifies and classifies entities such as people, places, organizations, and dates to interpret the meaning, and the Word Sense Disambiguation (WSD) task locates the appropriate meaning of. those words that bear several senses in accordance with the context of the text, in order that they may be rightly understood. e.g. The sentence Apple eats a John. is grammatically correct however that sentence is semantically incoherent because an apple cannot eat a human being, semantically correct sentences are found out with the help of semantic analysis. This is a highly important step in various NLP applications, including machine translations, information retrieval, and question answering since it helps to make sense of the meaning being transferred and is contextually sound.

e) Discourse Integration

Discourse Integration is the process of knowing how sentences or text sections that make up the whole are correlated and interrelated with each other, so that the meaning is consistent and coherent across several sentences or paragraphs. It is an important stage in the interpretation of long or complex texts in which the meaning is determined by prior statements. The most important ones are anaphora resolution (i.e. pronouns or references that are connected to previous lines of the text i.e. “She” in relation to “Taylor”) and contextual references (i.e. the meaning of words or phrases that are only made apparent when looked at in context). To use an example, it is imperative to understand that the antecedent of she in two successive sentences is Taylor, or what is meant by this in a sentence. In NLP applications such as machine translation, chatbots, and text summarization, discourse integration is essential because it helps keep the meaning consistent across sentences, which allows machines to comprehend the context and produce correct and natural language responses in chat robots and document translation.

f) Pragmatic analysis

Unlike semantic analysis which looks at direct meaning of words and sentences, Pragmatic Analysis goes further to seek the hidden meaning, tone and context of communication. Among the most important is the interpretation of intentions such as in the case of Can you pass the salt?” is a polite request and not a question about capability, and understanding such figurative languages as idioms or metaphors, such as “I'm falling in love with you” which means that I love you.This analysis method is essential to NLP applications such as sentiment analysis, chatbots, and conversational AI, where machines can understand non-literal meanings, detect sarcasm and emotions, and respond more naturally, which ultimately enhances human-computer interaction by enabling systems to comprehensively interpret, analyse, and produce human language. (Xiao et al., 2023)

9. CONCLUSION

Hate Speech Hate Speech has become a very real threat to our social lives and even our lives as individuals. In this chapter we have entered the advanced world of hate speech, discussing the various types of hate speech and the ways in which hate speech spreads via social media. Hate speech does not merely consist of direct verbal aggression, but some less obvious examples (such as trivialization and denial). The answer to this question is a sophisticated detection technique that can identify minor clues in languages and context attributes. The usefulness of Natural Language Processing (NLP) is highlighted in this chapter with the detailed presentation of hate speech detection methods. We disaggregated NLP into what the approach signifies, and what we can do to get a computer to understand language and isolate and categorize hate speech in a more flawless way. We have not yet come far enough to be able to get completely over context sensitivity, language differences, and language change, but we are moving in the right direction to making machines better. The future promises will be brought by learning and deep learning that are fuelled by the potent NLP techniques. More study of the disciplines and attention to ethical standards will also contribute greatly to the improvement of these systems and making online environments better.

REFERENCES

Bhattacharjee, D., Paul, A., & Kumar, D. (2023). Sentiment analysis for hateful content on social media. *2023 International Conference on Network, Multimedia and Information Technology (NMITCON)*, 1–6. DOI: 10.1109/NMITCON58196.2023.10275876

Choubisa, M., & Doshi, R. (2022). Crop protection using cyber physical systems and machine learning for smart agriculture. In *Real-Time Applications of Machine Learning in Cyber-Physical Systems* (pp. 134–147). IGI Global Scientific Publishing., DOI: 10.4018/978-1-7998-9308-0.ch009

Garg, S., Sagtani, A., Kothari, A., Golakia, J., & Olaniyi, R. O. (2025). Climate Change Analytics Using Artificial Intelligence: Focusing on Legal and Ethical Considerations. In *Community Resilience and Climate Change Challenges: Pursuit of Sustainable Development Goals (SDGs)* (pp. 13-28). IGI Global Scientific Publishing. DOI: DOI: 10.4018/979-8-3693-6522-9.ch002

Gaurav, A., Gupta, B. B., Chui, K. T., Arya, V., & Chaurasia, P. (2023). Deep learning- based hate speech detection on Twitter. 2023 IEEE 13th International Conference on Consumer Electronics - Berlin (ICCE-Berlin), 1–6. DOI: 10.1109/ICCE- Berlin58801.2023.10375620

Ilhan, S. S., Sivakumar, S. N. J., Ramesh, S., Sreeram, N., & Rajalakshmi, R. (2024). Hate speech detection and classification using NLP. *2024 Second International Conference on Advances in Information Technology (ICAIT)*, 1–7. DOI: 10.1109/ICAIT61638.2024.10690655

Jahan, M. S., & Oussalah, M. (2023). A systematic review of hate speech automatic detection using natural language processing. *Neurocomputing*, *546*, 126232. Advance online publication. DOI: 10.1016/j.neucom.2023.126232

Kesarwani, T., Mittal, R., Panwar, D., Saini, G. L., & Kumar, S. (2023, December). Facial Recognition Model Using Custom Designed Deep Learning Architecture. In International Conference on Communication and Intelligent Systems (pp. 457-467). Singapore: Springer Nature Singapore.

Kumar, A. (2022). A study: Hate speech and offensive language detection in textual data by using RNN, CNN, LSTM and BERT model. 2022 6th International Conference on Intelligent Computing and Control Systems (ICICCS), 1–6. DOI: 10.1109/ICICCS53718.2022.9788347

Lala, C., & Dwivedi, P. (2023). Hate speech detection network using LSTM. *2023 International Conference for Advancement in Technology (ICONAT)*, 1–6. DOI: 10.1109/ICONAT57137.2023.10080786

Mahrishi, M., Hiran, K. K., Meena, G., & Sharma, P. (Eds.). (2020). *Machine learning and deep learning in real-time applications*. IGI global., DOI: 10.4018/978-1-7998-3095-5

Mihalcea, R., Liu, H., & Lieberman, H. (2006). NLP (Natural Language Processing) for NLP (Natural Language Programming). In Gelbukh, A. (Ed.), Lecture Notes in Computer Science: Vol. 3878. *Computational Linguistics and Intelligent Text Processing* (pp. 319–330). Springer., DOI: 10.1007/11671299_34

Xiao, J., Dut, W., Xu, Z., & Qian, Y. (2023). Cross-system data integration based on rule-based NLP and Node2Vec. In 2023 8th International Conference on Data Science in Cyberspace (DSC) (pp. 566–570). IEEE. DOI: 10.1109/DSC59305.2023.00088

Mittal, R., Agarwal, N., Shukla, P. K., & Khatri, N. (2024, November). An Intelligent Self- Balancing Robot with Integrated Object Detection Using MobileNetV2 and PID Control. In *2024 International Conference on Intelligent & Innovative Practices in Engineering & Management (IIPEM)* (pp. 1-5). IEEE.

Mittal, R., Pathak, V., & Mithal, A. (2020, October). A novel approach to optimize SLAM using GP-GPU. In Proceedings of International Conference on Data Science and Applications: ICDSA 2019 (pp. 273-280). Singapore: Springer Singapore.

Okoye, K., Nganji, J. T., Hiran, K. K., & Hosseini, S. (2024, May). Impact and implications of AI methods and tools for the future of education. [). Frontiers Media SA.]. *Frontiers in Education*, *9*, 1434052.

Parihar, A. S., Thapa, S., & Mishra, S. (2021). *Hate speech detection using natural language processing: Applications and challenges*. Machine Learning Research Lab.

Shridhara, M. G., Pristaš, V., Kotvytskiy, A., Antoni, L., & Semanišin, G. (2023). A short review on hate speech detection: Challenges towards datasets and techniques. In *Proceedings of the 2023 World Symposium on Digital Intelligence for Systems and Machines (DISA)* (pp. 204–209). IEEE. DOI: 10.1109/DISA59116.2023.10308906

Tiwari, A., & Agrawal, A. (2022). Comparative analysis of different machine learning methods for hate speech recognition in Twitter text data. *2022 Third International Conference on Intelligent Computing Instrumentation and Control Technologies (ICICICT)*, 1016–1020. DOI: 10.1109/ICICICT54557.2022.9917752

Chapter 13
Techniques for Detecting Hate Speech in AI and Human-Generated Content

Chandrashekhar Goswami
https://orcid.org/0000-0002-9404-9352
Faculty of Computing and Informatics, Sir Padampat Singhania University, Udaipur, India

Ansar Sheikh
St. Vincent Pallotti College of Engineering and Technology, Nagpur, India

Anand Bhaskar
Sir Padampat Singhania University, Udaipur, India

Dipesh Vaya
Sir Padampat Singhania University, Udaipur, India

ABSTRACT

Hate speech detection is critical due to the rising risk of online and offline offensive material. This chapter reviews methods for detecting hate speech in human-generated and AI-generated content, addressing differences, obstacles, and potential solutions. Various methods detect explicit and implicit hate speech, including rule-based systems, traditional machine learning models, and deep learning. Key issues include biases in model outputs and challenges in recognising AI-generated hate messages, with discussions focusing on fine-tuning pretrained models and multimodal approaches to improve AI-generated content detection. The chapter also examines

DOI: 10.4018/979-8-3373-3063-1.ch013

ethical implications, such as balancing free speech and censorship, privacy issues, accountability in AI algorithms, and fair decision-making. It identifies future trends, including natural language processing (NLP) advancements, real-time detection systems, and evolving regulatory frameworks for AI content moderation.

INTRODUCTION

Generally, hate speech is defined as any speech, gesture, or display that incites violence or prejudicial action against or by a particular individual or group, or because it disparages or intimidates a particular individual or group, with the specific hate speech definition varying by jurisdiction (Schmidt & Wiegand, 2017). The rise of the internet and digital platforms, especially social media, has vastly expanded the reach and speed of hate speech, giving individuals the tools to broadcast their words to large audiences instantly. Although most human societies have understood the harm of hate speech for centuries, the steep surge in online user interaction has made identifying and regulating hate speech an unprecedented challenge (Davidson et al., 2017).

Hate speech is not just a matter of verbal insult in modern-day society. It has real-world consequences, from psychological damage to physical violence, and leads to the fragmentation of society and the loss of social cohesion and trust (Fortuna & Nunes, 2019). For instance, hate speech not only benefits the perpetrators of the crimes but also harms the victims because hate or victimisation can arise because of hate speech, encouraging children and weaker people to isolate themselves. Moreover, it also serves to normalise harmful online rhetoric, which turn, results in the distribution of extremist ideologies and the marginalisation of communities already vulnerable (MacAvaney et al., 2019).

Now we must deal with AI-generated content, whether in deepfakes or text from large language models. The hate speech produced by machines can be valuable as that written by any human, which results in a serious challenge for us because it is hard to identify whether a human or a machine writes the particular content (Bolukbasi et al., 2016). As AI models used for content generation become increasingly sophisticated, they have also enabled hate speech to manifest in more subtle forms that may not immediately be identified as harmful (Burnap & Williams, 2015). New developments must consider existing hate speech and continue to develop and adopt new detection tools and mechanisms for hate speech originating with technology.

Such content can have a large social and ethical impact, which makes the design of effective hate speech detection systems essential. As just written, hate speech is harmful because it harms individuals and also creates division between communities based on fear, prejudice, and tensions between communities (Davidson et al., 2017). And it can also lead to physical violence; several hate crimes have been documented as being provoked by written online language (Schmidt & Wiegand, 2017). Considering the thousands of other types of content on the Internet and the thousands of different platforms that can be used to publish hate speech, it becomes even more difficult to define it.

Hate speech detection is especially hard in social networks and forums where users often write short, quick, and disjointed posts. Now, while platforms like Twitter and Facebook may be bombarded with millions of posts daily, content is often in the shape of memes, videos, and images (Pereira-Kohatsu et al., 2019), making it nearly impossible to leverage traditional text-based approaches to implementation. In addition, the anonymity afforded by these platforms allows users to participate in brazenly harmful speech without fear of consequences (Fortuna & Nunes, 2019), thus further increasing the spread of hate speech on the Internet.

The dissemination of content across social media is rapid, and the nature of the platforms themselves often makes it difficult to regulate the speed with which information is spread. Hate speech spreads virally, circulating far and wide after initial exposure (Khan et al., 2023). And the rapidly changing nature of language, particularly due to slang, coded language, and internet memes, makes catching bad content even tougher. Moreover, words and phrases are harmless, undergo transformation, and become a topic of fiery debates over the years (Wullach et al., 2021). It is necessary to innovate adaptive systems that update their former definitions.

In the subsequent sections, we present an overview of the different perspectives on hate speech detection, emphasising the comparison of AI-driven versus human-generated content. Basic rule-based methods, e.g., keyword-based detection, are still in use but more advanced and elaborate machine learning and deep learning methods have gradually become a complementary method (Caetano da Silva et al., 2020). With these and many other intricately human-driven directions, machine-learning methods have certainly trumped some more general detection methods that have identified a lot of latent hate speech in terms of content that seems less obvious (Ramponi et al., 2022).

Additionally, we will discuss the specific challenges presented by AI-generated content, such as the problem of differentiating between harmful and legitimate forms of expression, as well as the ethical implications associated with using AI in both the content creation process and the moderation of such content (Abro et al., 2020). The key concepts of this chapter will demonstrate the pros and cons of different detection approaches and underscore how existing methods, human-generated, and AI-generated hate speech are concerned to work with a comprehensive, nuanced approach. The chapter hopes to do so by tracking these elements and how they will pave the road for the solutions, and guide towards more sustainable and just solutions that detect hate speech (Fortuna & Nunes, 2018).

TYPES OF HATE SPEECH

Hate speech can take many different forms. Knowledge of the various forms of hate speech is paramount to creating efficient detection systems. There are two main types of hate speech: Explicit and implicit.

Explicit Hate Speech vs. Implicit Hate Speech

Content that contains examples of the above and more explicit hate speech relevant to the context. This kind of hate speech is blatant and unmistakable, which makes it easy to detect. Examples include racist slurs, misogynistic epithets, and direct orders to commit violence. These statements do not lead to many interpretations, so detection systems can usually use keyword-based or rule-based algorithms to identify them (Mansur et al., 2023).

Statements such as "all [ethnic group] are criminals" or "women are inferior to men" clearly and explicitly communicate harmful sentiments. Because explicit hate speech is so clear-cut, it does not normally require sophisticated techniques for detection, and these expressions are relatively easy to mark in social media environments and text-based content (Nascimento et al., 2023).

Implicit hate speech, meanwhile, encompasses indirect statements or messages that imply this bias, often expressed through coded language, dog whistles euphemisms. Such forms of hate speech lack the explicit expression of prejudice or discrimination but bear prejudicial or discriminatory substance nonetheless. Such expressions are complex and abstruse, and they will not trigger an offence in an immediate response, both in humans and automated systems. We are talking about statements like 'foreigners are taking our jobs' or 'some group is ruining society,' which might not use explicit slurs, but still perpetuate negative stereotypes.

Implicit hate speech is hard to detect, and the reason behind this is its context-based and culture-dependent nature. Human hate speech algorithms need to be able to detect statements of this kind, where the speaker leaves room for multiple interpretations or diversions are used to distract from the statement. This necessitates a deeper understanding of language, social issues, and coded language (Qi et al., 2020). Due to this complexity, implicit hate speech is often more difficult to identify, especially for machine learning models trained on general language rather than culturally relevant datasets.

Context is a crucial factor in assessing whether something is hate speech. Judging an accurate message without knowing the surrounding conversation, humour, tone, or the larger social or political context is hard. Often, a single statement seems neutral but becomes hateful when placed in a larger narrative or dialogue (Rudy Salim & Suhartono, 2020).

For example,a phrase like "immigrants are taking our jobs" might be understood as a general political statement in one context or, in another, as a hostile generalisation intended to stigmatise immigrant communities. Detection of hate speech is context-aware and needs algorithms that understand the linguistic content and the context within which it is expressed (Rudy Salim & Suhartono, 2020). Such complexity has been growing on the internet in forums and social media, where people talk about what they mean at a pace, and a sense of sarcasm, irony, and humour populates our exchanges. As such, subsequent meanings become harder for bots and humans alike to be accurate with intent.

Also, hate speech detection highly depends on cultural, social, and linguistic differences. Some words or phrases considered offensive in one tongue may have an utterly different plangency in another. Additionally, factors specific to a particular culture, such as past incidents, socio-political concerns, and the current political stance, can shape how languages are perceived and define what is deemed harmful or offensive (Lin, 2023). Thus, a label that might be an innocent term in society A (the way "refugee" or "illegal immigrant" would be perceived) could have terrible associations in society B because of the way history and politics go. Detection systems must learn this nuance to catch hate speech in other regions and with other language groups (Fortuna & Nunes, 2019b).

METHODS OF DETECTING HATE SPEECH IN HUMAN-GENERATED CONTENT

Detecting hate speech in human-generated content has become a major research issue in Natural Language Processing (NLP) and machine learning. The increasing popularity of digital communication platforms has led to a growing need for efficient, scalable, and accurate hate speech detection methods. Different methods are being suggested, with advantages and downsides. In this segment, we explain the several approaches for identifying hate speech in human-produced content, such as rule-based approaches, machine learning-based methods, deep learning approaches, hybrid models, and evaluation metrics.

Rule-Based Approaches

Rule-based approaches to hate speech detection often use predefined rules to identify offensive or discriminatory content, with the rules usually based around some set of keywords and/or lexicons. Those methods are often some of the oldest and simplest to implement. Rule-based approaches rely on the notion of searching for specific words or combinations of words that are considered hate speech, e.g., offensive terminology concerning race, gender, religion, or sexual orientation (Alkomah & Ma, 2022).

The most prevalent method rule-based systems use is the keyword list or lexicon, a collection of offensive or toxic words. These lists are typically painstakingly compiled from public and expert sources. If a text has any words or phrases on the list, it is suspected of having hate speech. More sophisticated lexicons may also classify words according to whether they express different forms of hate (e.g., racism, sexism, xenophobia) to facilitate the detection of specific forms of hate. Although rule-based approaches can work well in identifying flagrant hate speech, they are plagued by several drawbacks, such as:

False Positives: Non-offensive content will be classified as hate speech based solely on its appearance of an elastic word that may have a counterpart word in the lexicon. Such as the word "kill" being flagged in the context of a violent movie review, even though that word does not express hate or hostility (Dorris et al., 2020).

Absence of Contextual Sensitivity: Rule-based systems typically struggle to comprehend a word's context. Sarcasm or irony can cause the Tweet to be misclassified, as the system does not distinguish if the word "great" is being used in a good way or in a sarcastic way to refer to something bad.

Machine Learning Based Approaches

However, these approaches are limited in flexibility, and their scalability capabilities are relatively less than rule-based systems. This technique trains models on labelled hate and non-hate speech datasets to distinguish between the respective patterns and features in the two classes. Supervised and unsupervised learning approaches are the two primary types of machine learning models.

Supervised Learning Models

In supervised learning, we train a model on a labelled dataset containing hate speech and non-hate speech examples. The objective is to train the model to discern the relationship between the characteristics of the text (e.g., the frequency of words, sentiment, and syntactic structure) and their respective labels (i.e., whether it is hate speech or not). Some of the popular models for supervised learning in hate speech detection are:

1. Support Vector Machines (SVM): SVM can be a good option for classification tasks, especially when the data is linearly separable. It attempts to find a hyperplane that maximises the margin between the classes (hate speech and non-hate speech). Support Vector Machines (SVMs) are one of the methods

that have been used successfully for such tasks, also in the literature on hate speech detection (Ajdari et al., 2017).

2. Naive Bayes: This is a probabilistic model based on Bayes' theorem, which makes assumptions of independence between the test text words' probability distribution from training data predictions of will belong to the hate speech class. Naive Bayes is less complex than SVMs, but still surprisingly effective for text classification tasks, and computationally efficient (Nguyen, 2024). While they have their strengths, supervised models are only as good as the quality of the labelled training data they are based. For example, suppose the training dataset is unbalanced, meaning that there are many more examples of non-hate speech than of hate speech. In that case, the model might be biased by predicting non-hate speech, leading to poor performance in identifying harmful content (Gao & Huang, 2017).

Without any labelled examples, the unsupervised learning tries to find a pattern in the data using its similarities or to build some clusters. Alternatively, you could run a clustering algorithm such as K-means, which will put instances of hate speech that are very similar together. Also, this approach does not require extensive labelled datasets, which are often limited in the case of hate speech tasks. However, it can fail to detect nuanced or rare forms of hate speech as it groups similar features with a target for classification (Djuric et al., 2015).

Deep Learning Approaches

Another promising approach for hate speech detection is deep learning. Most models used to tackle this task in the literature are neural networks because they can learn complex representations of the contextual relationships between words in the language. The models are also trained on semantic analysis, which, crucially, seeks to recognise the subtleties of hate speech. Deep networks like LSTM and CNNs have outperformed in many NLP tasks, such as Hate Speech Detection. Long Short-Term Memory (LSTM) Networks are a type of logical Recurrent Neural Network (RNN) that acts as an open puzzle on words that can have various facets in its use (Miok et al., 2022). Since LSTMs consider the word order when producing their output, they are well-suited for identifying hate speech. This allows the word's sentiment to show through, useful in cases where hateful content can even be subtle.

CNNs are often used in image recognition tasks, but they have also been adapted for text classification by applying filters to detect patterns in a sequence of words (Mutanga et al., 2020). They can identify local features of hate speech, like abusive phrases or particular syntactic constructs.

One more high-level type of deep learning model is the advanced BERT (Bidirectional Encoder Representations from Transformers). It has changed a significant aspect of NLP as we know it today, leveraging pre-trained phrases on a larger corpus and later fine-tuned for different tasks. The BERT model (Bidirectional Encoder Representations from Transformers), a pre-trained language representation model that allows for bidirectional processing of text, i.e., consideration of the preceding words in a sequence and succeeding words (Mnassri et al., 2022), which outperformed previous models in identifying the context of hate speech.

Deep learning provides numerous advantages over classical machine learning techniques, particularly LSTMs, CNNs, and BERT:

Context Perspective: This is especially helpful for these models to understand the context in which words are used. It can help separate harmful content from non-offensive language, even if potentially harmful words might be present in the text.

This is relevant in semantic analysis. Deep learning models can understand the semantics of words, and that also explains why the sentence does not contain hate speech; it can be implicit. Maybe the hate speech is not explicit, but the damage is the same.

Hybrid Methods

Hybrid approaches use a combination of rule-based and machine learning approaches to detect hate speech better. A hybrid system, for instance, may first apply a rule-based system to detect explicit hate speech and then a machine learning-based model to classify more nuanced content (Fortuna et al., 2022). Combining these techniques allows one to obtain a low detection error for both classes of hate speech since rule-based methods can quickly and accurately catch the most obvious hate speech. In contrast, lower frequency, more complex, and subtle instances of hate speech can be identified through machine learning. Evaluating hate speech detection systems is critical to understanding their efficacy (Shishah & Maulana Fajri, 2022).

Typical evaluation metrics are:

1. Precision: The ratio of correctly predicted hate speech instances to the total predicted hate speech instances.
2. Recall: The number of correct hate speech instances correctly identified divided by the total number of actual hate instances.
3. F1 Score: The arithmetic between precision and recall allows balancing the two measurements.
4. Confusion Matrix: This matrix displays true positives, false positives, true negatives, and false negatives, providing detailed insight into the model's performance.

The most important metrics for comparing the different detection methods are, for example, how to make trade-offs between false positives and false negatives, which, especially in hate speech detection tasks, are highly relevant (Mozafari et al., 2020).

METHODS OF DETECTING HATE SPEECH IN AI-GENERATED CONTENT

Hate speech detection in AI-generated content poses specific challenges compared to human content. AI models such as GPT (Generative Pretrained Transformers) and other large language models (LLMS) create text with incredible fluency and coherence. However, developing human-language generation capabilities comes with immense challenges in filtering out harmful and discriminatory language from the text. We will discuss the difficulty of detecting hate speech in AI-generated content, how AI assists in detecting AI-generated hate speech, automated content flagging systems, and human involvement to improve results.

The primary difficulty in Hate Speech Detection in AI Content is that Hate Speech is generally hard to comprehend. Most conventional hate speech detection systems use rule-based or machine learning techniques, looking for overt indicators of damaging language like slurs or threats. Unfortunately, experience, at least supervised, cannot practically address the problem with content that needs context, like hate speech, but AI models like GPT that generate such subtle and context-dependent forms of hate speech.

A GPT model, for instance, could write something that subtly advocates for negative stereotypes or makes negative assumptions about members of a certain demographic group without placing any explicit hate speech. AI models are trained using large datasets comprising neutral and harmful language, and can reproduce or even amplify the biases present in the datasets (Chiril et al., 2022). Additionally, AI models often lack the contextual and social perspective to identify legitimate discourse versus harmful rhetoric. For example, a GPT model trained on neutral data may produce a sentence that looks neutral at the surface but is for today's society or the historical society, in which it may be politically harmful.

Another significant and pernicious problem is the transference of toxic language patterns from training data into AI outputs. Modern AI models, like GPT and other transformer-based models, were trained over BIG datasets scraped from the Internet. However, these data are often biased and filled with hate, which is what the models are trained to replicate. This enables AI to generate output incorporating societal biases written into its training data (Dascălu & Hristea, 2022).

AI-Specific Approaches: Fine-Tuning Pre-Trained Models for Hate Speech Detection

One solution to tackle hate speech detection challenges is fine-tuned models like GPT and BERT. Fine-tuning means training a pre-trained model (which has already captured general language features) on a smaller, more specific dataset. When the task is hate speech detection, we would fine-tune the model on categorised data containing both hate speech and non-hate speech examples.

For instance, researchers can fine-tune models like BERT (Bidirectional Encoder Representations from Transformers), which do an excellent job contextualising language, to be able to detect patterns of harmful language in AI-generated materials. Due to BERT's ability to read through a passage of text in two ways, it picks up on fine nuances of meaning in a string of text, which should help with the mission of finding hate speech that is not overtly hateful and that simple heuristics may not capture (Madhavi et al., 2024).

Similarly, GPT models allow fine-tuning the model to detect hate speech of any type, again, both the spoken and represented hate speech, enabling the model to understand the hate speech underlying otherwise benign text. One prominent advantage of transformer architectures is the ability to fine-tune such models, which allows users to transfer knowledge captured in a pre-trained model to a new domain without retraining the model from scratch (Rodriguez et al., 2022).

Figure 1. Evolution of AI Models

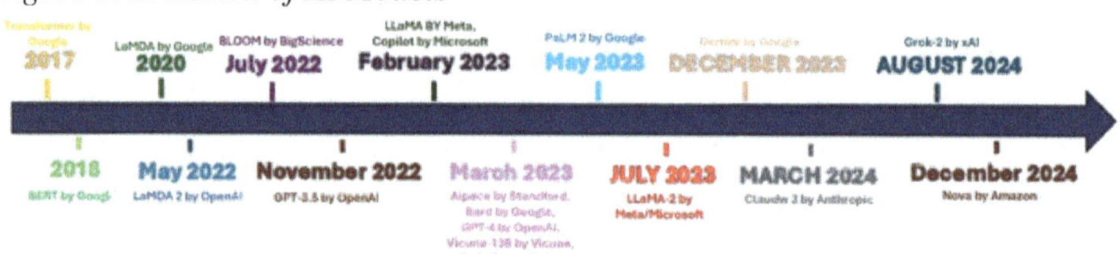

The most outstanding advantages of present-day AI models, especially transformer-based structures, such as BERT and GPT, are their capacity to give situated and semantic computerized understanding. Unlike earlier models, which used the presence or absence of specific words or phrases to generate their output, transformer models can interpret a word's meaning about the words that come before and after it in a sentence, paragraph, or other body of text. This is essential for detecting hate speech concealed within very subtle or indirect statements.

Bot-Driven Detection and Moderation Systems

Implementing AI models explicitly trained to detect hate speech could effectively flag and filter user-generated content across digital landscapes (e.g., social media platforms, news websites, and other content-driven environments). These systems aim to automatically prevent bad things from entering dissemination or harming. OpenAI's moderation tools and Google's Jigsaw Perspective are automated mechanisms powered by AI that identify and moderate toxic content across online environments.

These systems rely on pre-trained and fine-tuned models to read through text and determine if it is hate speech. With OpenAI's moderation tools, for example, the process will flag content according to a slew of predefined categories of offensive language, such as hate speech, harassment, and other forms of attack. Such tools are especially helpful on platforms that receive enormous amounts of content every day, meaning manual review is typically infeasible. However, while these systems are effective at scale, they have downsides. The false positives and false negatives are still widespread, and the systems still tar legitimate speech as whatever it thinks it is looking for, or fail to catch subtler forms of hate speech.

OpenAI's moderation tools were designed to eliminate and lessen dangerous content from text generated by artificial intelligence systems. These tools have become pseudo-checks, scrutinising generated content by a rubric for harmful language and returning feedback to developers or end-users about flagged content. For another example, the Jigsaw Perspective from Google is a machine learning tool that assesses toxicity in online conversations and allows filtering damaging interactions ahead of the escalation point.

Based on user feedback and machine learning updates, these tools are constantly refined to detect hate speech and other harmful content more precisely. Reinforcements for Bad Content: AI-generated content is not inherently harmful. Still, it can perpetuate bad outcomes and spread negative bias if appropriate interventions are not in place.

Strategies of Human-in-the-Loop for AI-Generated Content

While AI detection of hate speech has advanced, HITL (human in the loop) methods are still needed to achieve ideal reliability in AI moderation systems. With HITL systems, AI tools function alongside human moderators who can see flagged content and decide whether it is hate speech.

This helps prevent misuse and ensures that people who use methods for which automated systems are not suited have human oversight. AI could denote content based upon trends and context, but human moderators are also required to investigate the wider impact of content on their society and culture, for example. By relying on

HITL approaches, the incidence of false positives — artificial intelligence incorrectly categorising something as hate speech — and the possibility of incorrectly censoring legitimate expression can be limited, as well as problems of accurately identifying edge cases that challenge these models.

COMPARING AI-DRIVEN VS. HUMAN-GENERATED CONTENT DETECTION

Hate Speech Detection in Human-AI Generations: AI models like the ones we see with GPT, BERT, etc., are being used a lot in hate speech detection systems, but in many more cases, human judgment needs to be applied. This FAQ discusses the core differences between detecting hate speech in human-generated content and AI-generated content, the advantages and disadvantages of each method, and hybrid methods that use the advantages of both AI and human oversight.

The most basic and obvious difference between detecting hate speech in human-generated and AI-generated content is the need for a data source and training.

Built-in Mechanisms: The detection of hate speech in human-generated content often relies on labelled datasets of real-world interactions, such as social media posts, news articles, and forum discussions. These datasets can be thoroughly curated by professionals or obtained from publicly available platforms. To train models for this task large amount of text has to be annotated as hate speech or non-hate speech. Although this method can produce models adapted to certain platforms (Twitter, Reddit, etc.), they also tend to have high variability in some language variables regarding sarcasm, slang, and informal speaking patterns (Cao et al., 2020). Computers are trained to respond in ways that mimic what a human would say based on previous data, but as Austin discovered, they do not always get it right.

Unlike human-written content, which is punctuated with differences in tone and style, AI-generated content has its unique hurdles in terms of detection because AI models like GPT and all other large language models (LLM) are routinely trained on huge corpora scrounged from the internet. These models are pretrained on heterogeneous datasets containing clean and toxic language; hence, they may replicate toxic speech patterns. Fine-tuning models like BERT or GPT on labelled hate speech data can assist in detecting AI-generated content, but come with their issues. These models are still prone to inheriting biases from their training data (Wang, 2023)Where human-generated smears often rely on context-specific social cues, AI-generated responses can produce more formulaic and syntactically polished hate speech, which is, therefore, much harder to differentiate from neutral or even positive information without a closer look.

Differences in Language Use, Structure, and Semantics

Human-Written Content: In human-written content, language can be very context-based and nonlinear, in some aspects of formal and informal regional dialects, making it stretch a bit to fit, etc. Hate speech can be found in these nuances, such as sarcasm or implication. For example, a statement of the form "Immigrants should go back to where they came from" may be phrased in a rhetorical (or even joking) way that obscures the hateful meaning, but this will always be apparent to human interpreters as they are aware of socio-political contexts (Caliskan et al., 2017). In such cases, hate speech detection needs contextual and cultural sensitivity, which is usually the strength of human judgment but is often not fully apprehensible to an AI model without extensive fine-tuning.

AI-Generated Content: AI models such as GPT produce text that maintains syntactic structure and linguistic coherence. However, the resulting text may be semantically empty, as the model does not understand societal dynamics or cultural implications. GPT and similar models are very good at spitting out text in normal-looking sentences, but they may not fully comprehend the social consequences of the stuff they create. For instance, an AI model could randomly output a stereotypical or subtle but biased sentence without malicious intention, but still cause the propagation of harmful beliefs by the mere presence of association in the training data. Traditional detection methods, focused on surface-level language analysis, may have difficulty detecting this (Devlin et al., 2019).

Pros and Cons of Different Strategies

Advantages:

Scalability: AI models can simultaneously process huge volumes of content, enabling them to scan and filter malware or spam messages for applications and services that receive abundant user-generated content, like social networks like Twitter or Facebook. This allows automated systems to flag, filter, or remove harmful content while instantaneously sifting through millions of posts.

Consistency: After training, AI models deliver consistent output unaffected by human fatigue or subjective bias, ensuring uniform performance even on larger datasets.

Scalability and Speed of Action: AI can operate at scale and is fast (Ahmed et al., 2022), making it possible to implement it in real-time content moderation, which is particularly important given the emergent character of online hate speech.

Limitations:

However, AI models can make mistakes. They might flag a benign comment as abusive (false positives) or miss subtler hate speech (false negatives). That might happen if AI lacks the human capacity for context, irony, or sarcasm.

Bias: AI systems are often trained on datasets culled from the internet that are filled with the social biases from which they arise (Mehta & Passi, 2022), as opposed to moderation per user. AI systems might lack a global perspective, as they do not grasp the variability of hate speech in different languages, cultures, and regional dialects.

Detecting Content Written by Humans

Human detection methods are based on human reason, bringing opportunities and difficulties.

Advantages:

Cultural Sensitivity: Humans can read between the lines and comprehend the meaning behind their words, and the local specificities or traditions tied to certain cultures that may be lost on AI (Alkomah et al., 2022).

Contextual understanding: Humans are better at picking up contextual cues like sarcasm, humour, or emotional tone, which helps them better understand implicit or disguised forms of hate speech.

Limitations:

Scalability: There are far too many humans to be moderated by humans. Human judgment is erratic, affected by biases, feelings, or a lack of expertise (Ketsbaia et al., 2023).

Hybrid Approaches

Due to the benefits and limitations of these two approaches, hybrid approaches that integrate the strengths of both strategies are being recognised as most effective.

Blending AI and Human Expertise: Hybrid approaches use the agility and scalability of AI systems combined with human judgment to accommodate context and nuances that the AI models might underestimate. An instance of such an approach is when the AI models automatically identify possible harmful content that human moderators can approve or reject based on whether the content qualifies as hate speech, given sarcasm, or cultural references (Sarwar & Murdock, 2022).

Incorporation of human-in-the-loop feedback: It can also improve continuously with feedback, providing a more human-in-the-loop approach to the most complex tasks over time by being a hybrid system between the machine learning architecture and humans. Over time, as human moderators check the content and provide feedback to AI systems, those systems can learn from the decisions made by humans and adjust their parameters, meaning better detection accuracy in the future..

BIAS MITIGATION IN HATE SPEECH DETECTION

Hate speech detection bias is a major area of concern in human-generated content moderation systems as well as in AI-driven content moderation systems. Machine learning models, which are often used to identify hate speech, risk perpetuating existing social, cultural, and racial biases. Has biases that could lead to algorithmic bias, where entities are misattributed or not sufficiently labelled. It is vital to recognise and minimise the impact of these biases when developing hate speech detection systems to ensure fairness, accuracy, and inclusivity. In this subsection, we outline the larger challenge of bias detection, the techniques used to mitigate it, and the role of human annotator bias in the training process.

Challenges in Bias Detection

Data on which machine-learning models are trained often also reflects a certain level of social, cultural, and racial biases. Such biases may arise for several reasons, including legacy discrepancies, social biases, and imperfect data collection strategies. So, a model trained from text data scraped from the internet, for example, could learn the biases inherent in that data, including stereotypes about certain races or ethnic groups and biases based on gender (Mozafari et al., 2020). The biases that are inherited can skew the type of hate speech that is targeted and therefore can create a situation in which the model flags groups at a higher rate, or where the hate speech that is directed at marginalised communities is undetected by the model.

For example, suppose a model is trained mostly in English. In that case, it may not recognise hate speech in other languages or dialects, as it would not have seen those languages' offensive language and cultural nuance. (Caliskan et al., 2017). You are also trained in certain buzzwords that may be considered offensive to looking at specific communities or social issues. Because of the interactivity with the community that the buzzword may be targeting, this creates algorithmic discrimination that often flags anything relating to those keywords, even when contextually relevant.

Bias's role in AI-generated hate speech detection becomes even more of a concern when we consider that AI systems are often designed to achieve "neutrality" in their content moderation strategies. Nevertheless, what is described as hate speech relies constantly, although not exclusively, on definitions that can vary according to the context and are moulded by the values of a given society, hence making detection algorithms subject to unintended biases (Ahmed et al., 2022). For instance, whether something is hate speech varies from one country or culture to another, so a machine learning model trained on data from one region might not perform well in another where hate speech is treated differently.

Bias Mitigation Techniques

Fairness-Aware Algorithms and Fairness Constraints

One potential solution to alleviate the impact of bias on hate speech detection is to develop fairness-aware algorithms. These algorithms introduce fairness constraints during the model's training to prevent the model from biasing against or targeting individuals from specific groups based on their race, gender, or other protected characteristics. Such a fairness-aware model, for instance, could be trained such that false positive rates (the fraction of non-hate speech that is incorrectly flagged) are equal for multiple demographic groups.

There are multiple ways to include these fairness constraints:

1. Data preprocessing: The methods can be used to redistribute examples from high or low representative groups.
2. In-processing: Altering the learning algorithms themselves such that the algorithm is optimised for both accuracy and fairness rather than accuracy only
3. Post-processing: modifying the model outputs to mitigate (potential measures of) bias after training the model.

Debiasing Training Data and Model Output

Debiasing techniques that alleviate bias in the training data and the model's output are another set of effective approaches for combating bias in hate speech detection. Standard name the second, to identify personally, and strategies to remove bias in the training data using different strategies.

Data Augmentation: The most straightforward way is to augment the training data with more diverse examples. This may include making more replicas of less-represented groups or creating synthetic data that accounts for different perspectives and dialects. This is important as the more diverse your training data set is, the less likely the model will learn inadmissible patterns.

One of these established methods is bias detection and correction, where researchers expose models to biased examples during the training process and proactively teach them to identify and minimise the occurrence of these biases (Caliskan et al., 2017). So, if a model consistently mislabels hate speech directed at one specific group, through adversarial training, it can learn not to mislabel those instances as heavily.

Another important step is to debias the model output. One way to do this is to implement fairness corrections on the predictions made by the model. A method used to tackle this challenge is subjected to fairness-aware post-processing, which corrects the final outputs of the model, so that it doesn't favour or disadvantage a certain group if possible (e.g., the outcome predicted doesn't disproportionately disadvantage one particular group) (MacAvaney et al., 2019).

Human Bias in Hate Speech Detection

Equally much attention is paid to algorithmic bias, while a growing problem is the bias of human annotators in training data. Datasets that are used to train machine learning models are generally annotated by human experts, and the societal biases of these experts may affect the training process. Most annotators are subject to some implicit bias (race, gender, socio-political belief, etc.) that could manifest in how they label some text, creating biased training data and, as a result, biased predictions (Devlin et al., 2019).

A powerful approach to fighting human bias is a more diverse and representative pool of annotators. They must be selected to have diverse experiences, opinions, and cultures. Exposing the model to varied perspectives and experiences ensures the training data is broader and more accurate.

It also helps mitigate the effect of each annotator's biases by using multiple annotators for each datum. This method allows disagreements between annotators to be resolved by discussion or through a consensus mechanism that ensures more accurate and harmonious labelling.

ETHICAL CONSIDERATIONS IN HATE SPEECH DETECTION

The increasing use of AI-based systems for hate speech detection comes with significant ethical challenges, which should be dealt with to the best of our abilities, so that the systems find a balance between despising hate speech and the right to expression. The core ethical questions include freedom of speech vs censorship, privacy problems, liability of AI systems, fairness, and biases of detection models. These matters are critical to the design & deployment of ethical & responsible hate speech detection systems.

Freedom of Speech vs. Censorship

One of the more ethically complicated areas of machine learning is hate speech detection, weighing freedom of expression against the censorship of harmful content. Freedom to speak is a constitutional right in many democracy-based societies protected by legal settings (e.g., the First Amendment in the USA and human rights international law (Article 19 of the Universal Declaration of Human Rights). This right guards an individual's freedom to express themselves freely, no matter how unpopular, controversial, or offensive that perspective may be.

Hate speech, or speech that incites violence, discrimination, or hostility toward individuals or groups based on characteristics like race, religion, gender, or sexuality, can inflict serious damage. Consequently, many countries have introduced laws or regulations to restrict hate speech to protect individuals and communities from harm. The ethical dilemma comes from the possibility that detecting hate speech, through AI algorithms or human intervention, would over-censor valid expression to shelter people from hate.

Automated systems, for example, might flag and remove offensive or harmful content, but the content could be controversial or critical and not hate speech. Over-censorship could have the potential chilling effect of reducing open dialogue, shutting down political debate, or censoring art, jokes, or unpopular views (Nguyen, 2024). Developing a framework that strikes the right balance between combating harmful hate speech and preserving the right to free speech is one of the most important ethical dilemmas of hate speech detection systems.

Privacy Concerns

One major ethical challenge in the design and use of hate speech detection is related to privacy. Most content moderation tools, especially those utilised on social media or messaging services, read enormous volumes of personally identifiable information in real time. These comprise private messages, postings, and interactions that may contain sensitive customer information.

The ethical dilemma here is whether personal content should be flagged or monitored without the user's knowledge (which is frequent), and to do that, it relies on which networks, causing data privacy and surveillance concerns. However, real-time monitoring systems could log, track, and access a user's activities across second-party platforms in other instances, raising privacy concerns. With such data being collected, processed, and stored, it can easily be misused, abused, or misrepresented, where individuals are profiled improperly or their data is published or sold (Wullach et al., 2021).

Additionally, using AI to analyse conversations leads to questions of algorithmic transparency—many users may not know exactly how their content is being analysed, who has access to that data, or what decisions are made about flagged content. Striking the right ethical balance between privacy and surveillance in hate speech detection systems -- to ensure they do not invade users' privacy and, at the same time, can effectively detect harmful content -- is a complex task that includes progress on transparency, user consent, and strong privacy protections (Fortuna et al., 2022).

Accountability of AI Systems

As the burden of identifying hate speech is placed on AI systems, the questions of accountability and blame grow serious. AI-driven content moderation systems, similar to those used by companies like Facebook or Twitter, sometimes have a secretive basis for their decision-making process. Users can wonder why content was flagged or removed, what criteria were used, or whether an error was made.

Accountability of AI systems employed in detecting hate speech presents ethical challenges surrounding transparency and explainability of such systems' decision-making processes. And it is important for users and people who create content to understand how the system operates, why their content was flagged, and how they can appeal decisions. AI explainability: In this specific case, AI explainability means that AI systems will compensate flatly by giving detailed justifications for the decisions they made in an easily digested manner. Without explainability, users may be left to arbitrary penalties or censorship without a means of appealing to a human, which can lead to frustration and a mistrust in automated moderation systems (Lipton, 2018).

In addition, developers and businesses implementing AI-assisted detection instruments should be responsible for drawing those conclusions. If an AI system makes biased or wrong decisions, who will be responsible for correcting or compensating affected users? This is a significant techno-ethical challenge in light of the ongoing deployment of AI tools for content moderation, highlighting the need for transparency and accountability mechanisms and legal instruments that can cover harm derived from false positive and negative decisions ((Alkomah & Ma, 2022).

Ethical Concerns in Hate Speech Detection: Bias & Fairness. As alluded to, AIs are commonly trained on biased data, replicating societal inequities. These biases can be baked into the training data, resulting in algorithmic bias, where discrimination against certain groups or types of speech is treated with greater fervor. At the same time, other harmful content is left unpunished.

As we have seen with algorithmic bias, this can take many forms, e.g., a racial or gender bias in hate speech detection, where models are more likely to flag content related to one demographic group than to another demographic profile (Mansur et al., 2023). This highlights a major ethical issue as it can lead to the advance of negative stereotypes and disproportionately impact marginalized groups.

Fairness-aware algorithms can be created to address bias and ensure that AI systems provide equal treatment to all groups by implementing fairness constraints during the training phase. Debasing the training data and model outputs can also mitigate bias in detection systems. Overcoming bias in AI: Bias can emerge in many layers of an AI model, but it is, of course, difficult to eliminate. Companies must constantly test and re-test their systems towards a fair solution and keep monitoring that their systems are working equitably across user groups.

In addition, the human annotators who label the training data also introduce their own biases into the process. Minimizing human bias in constructing hate speech detection datasets involves submitting datasets to annotation by diverse and representative posterior pools of annotators (Lin, 2023). This is essential because diverse groups working on AI model developments will also prevent these systems from proliferating biased decision-making.

FUTURE TRENDS AND CHALLENGES IN HATE SPEECH DETECTION

As technologies for information classification, facilities, and communities for content moderation have evolved over the years and are continuing to evolve, hate speech detection is a diverse field currently being researched professionally and highly debated. Improvements in NLP models, real-time detection systems, increasing regulation, and collaborative approaches among stakeholders anticipate the next wave of innovation. This section discusses new trends and challenges that result from them.

Emerging Technologies

Recent advances in NLP with transformer-based models like BERT and GPT have redefined the hate speech detection process. These new models fundamentally increased contextual awareness, allowing for richer language exploration. Implicit or coded hate speech is much more subtle, and traditional models fall short." On the other hand, fine-tuning pre-trained transformer-based models on the target tasks dramatically improves results, allowing for detecting more lexical subtleties in hate speech than previous methods (Madhavi et al., 2024). These models have an improved understanding of the context and semantics of the text, resulting in better performance in identifying abusive language that may not be present in regular patterns.

These machine-learning-based approaches are now being scaled from text only to Multi-modal Detection Systems via textual, visual, and aural modalities to provide a better-rounded perspective on the possibility of hate speech. For instance, video-based online platforms such as YouTube and TikTok have started to utilise multi-modal approaches, leveraging text and including techniques to moderate images and videos (Mozafari et al., 2020). These multimodal models enable trimodal hate speech detection from video, text, audio, and image data, resulting in more robust and integrated content moderation.

Real-time Detection Systems

Detecting hate speech in real-time is one of social media platforms' biggest challenges. As varied as the posts on platforms like TikTok and Twitter are — billions of them, known as your personal "For You Page," can land in your feed in one day, from the extreme to the banal — the amount of content to process is so vast that automated systems are essential to flag harmful material instantly before it can be shared and spread further. A novel open-access dataset is introduced to address this gap, and a multi-model ensemble of LSTM and SVM algorithms is applied to real-time social media streams. Objectively and recurrently, hate speech is transmitted faster than the capabilities of human moderation. Thus, the viral propagation of hate speech requires suitable prevention systems for real-time detection.

Meanwhile, accurate and timely detection in real-time systems is challenging. There's a high risk of false positives, in which legitimate speech is flagged as harmful, especially when context, tone, and intent are difficult to gauge algorithmically. Adding to the difficulties, deepfake technology and AI-generated content can impersonate legitimate speech patterns but insert harmful rhetoric that is more difficult to detect.

Regulatory and Legal Frameworks

Alongside the increased demand for identifying hate speech, there is increasing interest in government and international aesthetic regulation of AI-led content moderation. This has led many countries to pass legislation holding tech companies accountable for user-posted information. The DSA is one of the examples of legislative initiatives that aim to regulate the removal of illegal and harmful content, namely hate speech, on the internet (European Commission 2020) and is mirrored by the German NetzDG.

International pressure is mounting for a global system to cover the moderation of hate speech. This means creating frameworks that balance freedom of expression with safeguarding individuals from harm. Conversely, the global disparity of legal and cultural standards creates challenges for global online platforms by creating hurdles to establishing consistent content moderation. With the proliferation of AI-powered content moderation, ensuring these regulations are effective and ethical is an increasing challenge.

Collaborative Approaches

In general, it is a complex and evolving problem, and therefore needs collaboration in the specific area, hate speech detection. AI researchers, social media platforms, and policymakers must collaborate so that we can rely on strong, transparent, and accountable content moderation systems. Because of this, technology companies like Twitter, Facebook, and YouTube are investing millions of dollars in AI research to bolster the effectiveness of their own hate speech detection systems, as well as working with third-party auditing organisations and independent researchers to ensure their systems are effective and fair.

Policymakers must intervene to ensure that these AI moderation tools are used responsibly. Governments and tech companies can work together to create regulations that ensure transparency in AI decision-making, fairness in content moderation, and the protection of users' rights. Moreover, multi-stakeholder dialogues between industry leaders, civil society, and advocacy groups are also relevant to addressing broader ethical concerns, such as privacy issues in particular and algorithmic biases in general (Burnap & Williams, 2015).

CONCLUSION

In this chapter, we've looked at different ways to identify hate speech across human-generated and AI-generated content, including the benefits and drawbacks of each approach. Detecting its human-generated content is a common task, typically using rule-based systems, machine learning models, or more and more complex deep learning techniques. Rule-based approaches are mainly based on keywords and lexicon, rigid and simple, but they are far from perfect as they cannot see beyond words, missing the context or any nuances. More flexible machine learning based approaches, such as Support Vector Machines (SVM) and Naive Bayes models, learn patterns from large datasets to classify content. However, these approaches rely heavily on labelled data and can introduce bias if your training data is not representative. Recent advances in deep learning approaches, especially transformer-based architectures like BERT and GPT, have demonstrated exceptional performance at detecting explicit and implicit hate speech, owing to their ability to capture context, semantics, and interrelationships between words in a sentence. But even these narrow and sophisticated models suffer from challenges about fairness, explainability, and the requirement of large volumes of training data.

On the other hand, detecting AI-generated content poses special challenges due to the complexity of machine-generated text that can resemble human speech closely enough to have undecided biases or harmful language patterns. Hate Speech detection in AI-generated content generally involves fine-tuning models such as GPT or BERT to domain-specific datasets and calculating models to consider multimodal approaches that consider text, images, and videos. These models must continue to evolve and adapt to meet the ever-changing world of what Gen AI can do and how sophisticated machine-generated content can become.

Challenges and Opportunities

Detecting hate speech has moral and practical challenges. One of the big problems is that if we're going to know whether to censor harmful speech or not, we need to strike a balance between freedom of expression and censorship, which means we need to avoid both over-censorship and under-moderation. Privacy Issues of AI Privacy concerns are also crucial as AI systems generally necessitate the real-time surveillance of large quantities of personal data, which comes with potential risks concerning surveillance and sensitive information misuse. Also, AI interpreters do have bias—they build their models on machine learning models. The ethical footprint in AI systems must be accounted for in AI-driven detection methods and human-assisted processes.

Despite these challenges, there is a tremendous opportunity to improve hate speech detection. With the growth of natural language processing (NLP) and multimodal models, we have the potential for more precise, sophisticated systems that can comprehend context and semantics as never before. Additionally, hybrid systems combining the strengths of human moderation with AI assistance can overcome the limitations of each type of moderation, resulting in more efficient systems. Hate speech detection in real-time, particularly on large-scale platforms, is an area of high demand, and continued investment in scalable, efficient AI models may further aid in this area.

Future research has an important role to play in improving hate speech detection. Continued development of AI ethics, fairness-aware algorithms, and bias mitigation will be essential to making content moderation systems effective and equitable. More explainable AI and accountability will enhance transparency, allowing users to decipher and trust automated decisions. In parallel, improvements in annotator pool design will be paired with multimodal research that will help us detect implicit, coded hate speech as well — a working paper finds that 80% of online hate speech is still spoken in code. Grounded networks of hate that will still be gradient hate speech detection will still take up quite a bit of bandwidth in the future.

The future of hate speech detection ultimately lies in the hands of a collaborative effort between AI researchers, social media platforms, and policymakers. The balancing act between technology and ethics will help create content moderation systems that mitigate the harms of hate speech and respect fundamental rights like freedom of expression. By continuing research in this area and applying ethical principles of fairness, transparency, and accountability, hate speech detection can become a stronger, more inclusive, and responsible tool for building safer online ecosystems.

REFERENCES

Abro, S., Shaikh, S., Hussain, Z., Ali, Z., Khan, S., & Mujtaba, G. (2020). Automatic Hate Speech Detection using Machine Learning: A Comparative Study. *International Journal of Advanced Computer Science and Applications, 11*(8). Advance online publication. DOI: 10.14569/IJACSA.2020.0110861

Ahmed, Z., Vidgen, B., & Hale, S. A. (2022). Tackling racial bias in automated online hate detection: Towards fair and accurate detection of hateful users with geometric deep learning. *EPJ Data Science, 11*(1), 8. DOI: 10.1140/epjds/s13688-022-00319-9

Ajdari, J., Ismaili, F., Raufi, B., & Zenuni, X. (2017). Automatic hate speech detection in online content using latent semantic analysis. *Pressacademia, 5*(1), 368–371. DOI: 10.17261/Pressacademia.2017.612

Alkomah, F., & Ma, X. (2022). A Literature Review of Textual Hate Speech Detection Methods and Datasets. *Information (Basel), 13*(6), 273. DOI: 10.3390/info13060273

Alkomah, F., Salati, S., & Ma, X. (2022). A New Hate Speech Detection System Based on Textual and Psychological Features. *International Journal of Advanced Computer Science and Applications, 13*(8). Advance online publication. DOI: 10.14569/IJACSA.2022.01308100

Bolukbasi, T., Chang, K.-W., Zou, J. Y., Saligrama, V., & Kalai, A. T. (2016). Man is to Computer Programmer as Woman is to Homemaker? Debiasing Word Embeddings. In D. Lee, M. Sugiyama, U. Luxburg, I. Guyon, & R. Garnett (Eds.), *Advances in Neural Information Processing Systems* (Vol. 29). Curran Associates, Inc. https://proceedings.neurips.cc/paper_files/paper/2016/file/a486cd07e4ac3d270571622f4f316ec5-Paper.pdf

Burnap, P., & Williams, M. L. (2015). Cyber Hate Speech on Twitter: An Application of Machine Classification and Statistical Modeling for Policy and Decision Making. *Policy and Internet, 7*(2), 223–242. DOI: 10.1002/poi3.85

Caetano da Silva, S., Castro Ferreira, T., Silva Ramos, R. M., & Paraboni, I. (2020). Data Driven and Psycholinguistics Motivated Approaches to Hate Speech Detection. *Computación y Sistemas, 24*(3). Advance online publication. DOI: 10.13053/cys-24-3-3478

Caliskan, A., Bryson, J. J., & Narayanan, A. (2017). Semantics derived automatically from language corpora contain human-like biases. *Science, 356*(6334), 183–186. DOI: 10.1126/science.aal4230 PMID: 28408601

Cao, R., Lee, R. K.-W., & Hoang, T.-A. (2020). DeepHate: Hate Speech Detection via Multi-Faceted Text Representations. *12th ACM Conference on Web Science*, 11–20. https://doi.org/DOI: 10.1145/3394231.3397890

Chiril, P., Pamungkas, E. W., Benamara, F., Moriceau, V., & Patti, V. (2022). Emotionally Informed Hate Speech Detection: A Multi-target Perspective. *Cognitive Computation, 14*(1), 322–352. DOI: 10.1007/s12559-021-09862-5 PMID: 34221180

Dascălu, ., & Hristea, F. (2022). Towards a Benchmarking System for Comparing Automatic Hate Speech Detection with an Intelligent Baseline Proposal. *Mathematics, 10*(6), 945. DOI: 10.3390/math10060945

Davidson, T., Warmsley, D., Macy, M., & Weber, I. (2017). Automated Hate Speech Detection and the Problem of Offensive Language. *Proceedings of the International AAAI Conference on Web and Social Media, 11*(1), 512–515. https://doi.org/DOI: 10.1609/icwsm.v11i1.14955

Devlin, J., Chang, M.-W., Lee, K., & Toutanova, K. (2019). BERT: Pre-training of Deep Bidirectional Transformers for Language Understanding. In J. Burstein, C. Doran, & T. Solorio (Eds.), *Proceedings of the 2019 Conference of the North American Chapter of the Association for Computational Linguistics: Human Language Technologies,* Volume 1 *(Long and Short Papers)* (pp. 4171–4186). Association for Computational Linguistics. https://doi.org/DOI: 10.18653/v1/N19-1423

Djuric, N., Zhou, J., Morris, R., Grbovic, M., Radosavljevic, V., & Bhamidipati, N. (2015). Hate Speech Detection with Comment Embeddings. *Proceedings of the 24th International Conference on World Wide Web*, 29–30. https://doi.org/DOI: 10.1145/2740908.2742760

Dorris, W., & Hu, R. (Roger), Vishwamitra, N., Luo, F., & Costello, M. (2020). Towards Automatic Detection and Explanation of Hate Speech and Offensive Language. *Proceedings of the Sixth International Workshop on Security and Privacy Analytics*, 23–29. https://doi.org/DOI: 10.1145/3375708.3380312

Fortuna, P., Dominguez, M., Wanner, L., & Talat, Z. (2022). Directions for NLP Practices Applied to Online Hate Speech Detection. *Proceedings of the 2022 Conference on Empirical Methods in Natural Language Processing*, 11794–11805. https://doi.org/DOI: 10.18653/v1/2022.emnlp-main.809

Fortuna, P., & Nunes, S. (2019a). A Survey on Automatic Detection of Hate Speech in Text. *ACM Computing Surveys, 51*(4), 1–30. DOI: 10.1145/3232676

Fortuna, P., & Nunes, S. (2019b). A Survey on Automatic Detection of Hate Speech in Text. *ACM Computing Surveys, 51*(4), 1–30. DOI: 10.1145/3232676

Gao, L., & Huang, R. (2017). Detecting Online Hate Speech Using Context-Aware Models. *RANLP 2017 - Recent Advances in Natural Language Processing Meet Deep Learning*, 260–266. https://doi.org/DOI: 10.26615/978-954-452-049-6_036

Ketsbaia, L., Issac, B., Chen, X., & Jacob, S. M. (2023). A Multi-Stage Machine Learning and Fuzzy Approach to Cyber-Hate Detection. *IEEE Access : Practical Innovations, Open Solutions*, *11*, 56046–56065. DOI: 10.1109/ACCESS.2023.3282834

Khan, A., Yousaf, J., Muhammad, T., & Ismail, M. (2023). HATE SPEECH DETECTION USING MACHINE LEARNING AND N-GRAM TECHNIQUES. [Jurnal Teknik Informatika Dan Sistem Informasi]. *JATISI*, *10*(1). Advance online publication. DOI: 10.35957/jatisi.v10i1.4711

Lin, D. (2023). Appliance of Deep Learning on hate speech detection: A systematic review. *Highlights in Science. Engineering and Technology*, *31*, 76–81. DOI: 10.54097/hset.v31i.4816

MacAvaney, S., Yao, H.-R., Yang, E., Russell, K., Goharian, N., & Frieder, O. (2019). Hate speech detection: Challenges and solutions. *PLoS One*, *14*(8), e0221152. DOI: 10.1371/journal.pone.0221152 PMID: 31430308

Madhavi, M., Agal, S., Odedra, N. D., Chowdhary, H., Ruprah, T. S., Vuyyuru, V. A., & El-Ebiary, Y. A. B. (2024). Elevating Offensive Language Detection: CNN-GRU and BERT for Enhanced Hate Speech Identification. *International Journal of Advanced Computer Science and Applications*, *15*(5). Advance online publication. DOI: 10.14569/IJACSA.2024.01505118

Mansur, Z., Omar, N., & Tiun, S. (2023). Twitter Hate Speech Detection: A Systematic Review of Methods, Taxonomy Analysis, Challenges, and Opportunities. *IEEE Access : Practical Innovations, Open Solutions*, *11*, 16226–16249. DOI: 10.1109/ACCESS.2023.3239375

Mehta, H., & Passi, K. (2022). Social Media Hate Speech Detection Using Explainable Artificial Intelligence (XAI). *Algorithms*, *15*(8), 291. DOI: 10.3390/a15080291

Miok, K., Škrlj, B., Zaharie, D., & Robnik-Šikonja, M. (2022). To BAN or Not to BAN: Bayesian Attention Networks for Reliable Hate Speech Detection. *Cognitive Computation*, *14*(1), 353–371. DOI: 10.1007/s12559-021-09826-9

Mnassri, K., Rajapaksha, P., Farahbakhsh, R., & Crespi, N. (2022). BERT-based Ensemble Approaches for Hate Speech Detection. *GLOBECOM 2022 - 2022 IEEE Global Communications Conference*, 4649–4654. https://doi.org/DOI: 10.1109/GLOBECOM48099.2022.10001325

Mozafari, M., Farahbakhsh, R., & Crespi, N. (2020). Hate speech detection and racial bias mitigation in social media based on the BERT model. *PLoS One*, *15*(8), e0237861. DOI: 10.1371/journal.pone.0237861 PMID: 32853205

Mutanga, R. T., & Naicker, N., & O, O. (2020). Hate Speech Detection in Twitter using Transformer Methods. *International Journal of Advanced Computer Science and Applications*, *11*(9). Advance online publication. DOI: 10.14569/IJACSA.2020.0110972

Nascimento, F. R. S., Cavalcanti, G. D. C., & Da Costa-Abreu, M. (2023). Exploring Automatic Hate Speech Detection on Social Media: A Focus on Content-Based Analysis. *SAGE Open*, *13*(2). Advance online publication. DOI: 10.1177/21582440231181311

Nguyen, T. (2024). Merging public health and automated approaches to address online hate speech. *AI and Ethics*, *4*(2), 441–450. DOI: 10.1007/s43681-023-00281-w PMID: 37360146

Pereira-Kohatsu, J. C., Quijano-Sánchez, L., Liberatore, F., & Camacho-Collados, M. (2019). Detecting and Monitoring Hate Speech on Twitter. *Sensors (Basel)*, *19*(21), 4654. DOI: 10.3390/s19214654 PMID: 31717760

Qi, H., Guo, Q., Juefei-Xu, F., Xie, X., Ma, L., Feng, W., Liu, Y., & Zhao, J. (2020). DeepRhythm. *Proceedings of the 28th ACM International Conference on Multimedia*, 4318–4327. https://doi.org/DOI: 10.1145/3394171.3413707

Ramponi, A., Testa, B., Tonelli, S., & Jezek, E. (2022). Addressing religious hate online: From taxonomy creation to automated detection. *PeerJ. Computer Science*, *8*, e1128. DOI: 10.7717/peerj-cs.1128 PMID: 37346317

Rodriguez, A., Chen, Y.-L., & Argueta, C. (2022). FADOHS: Framework for Detection and Integration of Unstructured Data of Hate Speech on Facebook Using Sentiment and Emotion Analysis. *IEEE Access : Practical Innovations, Open Solutions*, *10*, 22400–22419. DOI: 10.1109/ACCESS.2022.3151098

Rudy Salim, C. E., & Suhartono, D. (2020). A Systematic Literature Review of Different Machine Learning Methods on Hate Speech Detection. *JOIV: International Journal on Informatics Visualization*, *4*(4), 213–218. DOI: 10.30630/joiv.4.4.476

Sarwar, S. M., & Murdock, V. (2022). Unsupervised Domain Adaptation for Hate Speech Detection Using a Data Augmentation Approach. *Proceedings of the International AAAI Conference on Web and Social Media, 16*, 852–862. https://doi.org/DOI: 10.1609/icwsm.v16i1.19340

Schmidt, A., & Wiegand, M. (2017). A Survey on Hate Speech Detection using Natural Language Processing. *Proceedings of the Fifth International Workshop on Natural Language Processing for Social Media*, 1–10. https://doi.org/DOI: 10.18653/v1/W17-1101

Shishah, W., & Maulana Fajri, R. (2022). Large Comparative Study of Recent Computational Approaches in Automatic Hate Speech Detection. *TEM Journal*, 82–93. https://doi.org/DOI: 10.18421/TEM111-10

Wang, Q. (2023). Advanced Deep Learning Approaches for Hate Speech Detection. *Highlights in Science. Engineering and Technology*, *41*, 158–164. DOI: 10.54097/hset.v41i.6801

Wullach, T., Adler, A., & Minkov, E. (2021). Towards Hate Speech Detection at Large via Deep Generative Modeling. *IEEE Internet Computing*, *25*(2), 48–57. DOI: 10.1109/MIC.2020.3033161

Chapter 14
Machine Learning Models for Automated Hate Speech Detection in Synthetic Content

Tarni Khatri
https://orcid.org/0009-0008-4269-7949
Manipal University Jaipur, India

Vibhakar Pathak
https://orcid.org/0000-0002-0916-9326
Arya College of Engineering and Information Technology, India

Rohit Mittal
https://orcid.org/0000-0001-7688-5421
Manipal University Jaipur, India

Manish Mittal
https://orcid.org/0000-0002-7029-9576
Brainware University, Kolkata, India

ABSTRACT

This chapter focuses on how Machine Learning (ML) can help identify and reduce hate speech on the internet. With the growing use of Artificial Intelligence (AI), there is a risk that these systems can unintentionally spread or support hate speech. This often happens because the data used to train these models may contain biased or harmful language, and the models may not fully understand the context in which words are used. The chapter explains how different ML techniques—such as supervised learning (where the model learns from labelled examples), unsupervised learning

DOI: 10.4018/979-8-3373-3063-1.ch014

(where the model finds patterns in data without labels) can be used to detect hate speech in text. The chapter also discusses how we can measure the performance of hate speech detection models using metrics such as precision (how many detected hate speech examples were actually hate speech), recall (how many real hate speech examples were correctly found), F1-score (a balance between precision and recall), and ROC-AUC.

1. INTRODUCTION

Hate speech refers to any kind of communication—spoken, written, or behavioural—that attacks, threatens, or discriminates against a person or group based on attributes like race, religion, ethnicity, gender, sexual orientation, disability, or nationality. Hate speech targets marginalized or disadvantaged social groups in ways that can be harmful to them (Jacobs and Potter, 2000; Walker, 1994).

As we step deeper into the industry 4.0, Artificial Intelligence (AI) is no longer a futuristic concept—it's quickly becoming part of our everyday lives. From smart assistants to personalized ads, AI is transforming how businesses operate, how services are delivered, and even how we interact with each other. Machine Learning (ML), promise faster growth and better customer experiences. It has challenge like AI systems mimicking human behaviour, they also risk spreading the same biases and harmful patterns found in the real world—including hate speech. Algorithms can amplify harmful content, when trained on large language models (LLMs) like BERT, GPT (Mijwil et al., 2024; Garg et al., 2025).

However, as we rely more on these models, especially in hate speech detection, new challenges have surfaced. While LLMs can recognize patterns and language, these can reflect biases found in the data they're trained on. As AI continues to shape the digital spaces we inhabit, it's crucial to understand both the strengths and blind spots of these models.

1.1. Sources of AI-Generated Hate Speech

a) Biased Training Data

One of the main reasons AI systems sometimes generate hate speech is because of the data they're trained on. LLM's learn from massive collections of text gathered from the internet places like forums, social media, and online articles. These training datasets often contain harmful stereotypes, offensive language, and biased viewpoints. When an AI model is trained on this kind of data, it can end up absorbing and repeating those same harmful patterns—even if that's not the intention.

b) Lack of Contextual Understanding

AI doesn't understand the context behind the words. It might string sentences together that sound logical but completely miss the social or emotional implications. For example, a model could repeat a harmful joke or stereotype simply because it recognizes the pattern, not because it understands that it's hurtful or inappropriate. This lack of true comprehension makes it difficult to distinguish between neutral and harmful content in certain situations.

c) Misaligned Objectives

AI models are designed to produce responses that are fluent and relevant—not necessarily ethical. Their goal is to make the output sound coherent and natural, which doesn't always line up with what's right or respectful. If an AI system isn't specifically taught to avoid harmful content, it might end up generating text that's offensive or dangerous, simply because it "fits" the input or follows a pattern seen in its training data. This gap between linguistic success and ethical responsibility is a major reason why some AI systems unintentionally produce hate speech.

1.2. Machine Learning Approaches for Hate Speech Detection

a) **Supervised Learning:** Supervised learning remains the dominant paradigm in hate speech detection (Mahrishi et al., 2020). Algorithms like Logistic Regression, SVMs, Random Forests, and Gradient Boosted Trees are trained on labelled datasets to recognize hate speech patterns which is shown in Figure 1.

Figure 1. Supervised learning

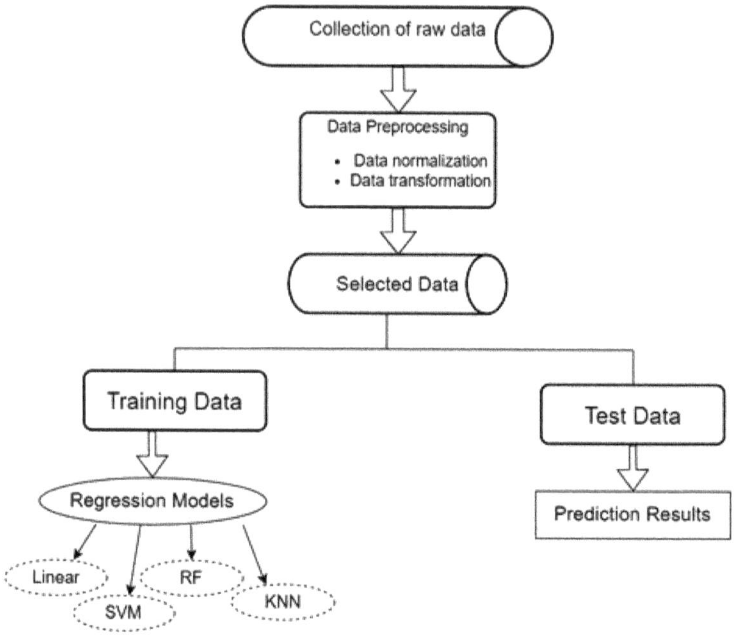

b) Unsupervised and Semi-Supervised Methods

These methods are useful when labelled data is scarce (Hiran et al., 2021). Clustering algorithms and self-supervised techniques can uncover hidden patterns and group hateful expressions based on semantic similarity as shown in Figure 2.

Figure 2. Unsupervised learning

c) Transfer Learning and Preprocessing

Using transfer learning, models pretrained on large corpora can be fine-tuned on hate speech datasets to adapt them for more specific detection tasks. This approach is especially valuable in low-resource languages or domains. Before training a model to detect hate speech, the text needs to be cleaned and organized. This includes breaking sentences into words (tokenization), removing common but unhelpful words like "the" or "is" (stop words), and reducing words to their base form (stemming or lemmatization) so the model can focus on the core meaning. After cleaning, we turn the text into numbers using techniques like n-grams (common word patterns), TF-IDF (importance of words in context), and word embeddings like Word2Vec or BERT, which capture the deeper meaning and relationships between words.

1.3. Data Challenges in Hate Speech Detection

Labelling this kind of content comes with ethical concerns and personal judgment. What one person sees as hateful, another might not, leading to bias and inconsistency in the dataset. Plus, cultural differences and legal concerns can make it even trickier.

Hate speech makes up only a small part of online conversations, so most datasets are imbalanced—they have way more regular posts than hateful ones. To fix this, researchers often use tricks like oversampling, under sampling, or generating fake data points using techniques like SMOTE. Hate can be expressed through slang, abbreviations, or even memes. That means models trained today can quickly fall behind. To stay effective, they need regular updates and retraining to keep up with the changing language of the internet.

2. METRICS REQUIRED TO EVALUATE HATE SPEECH

Precision, recall, F1-score, accuracy, and ROC-AUC are standard metrics used to evaluate model performance in hate speech detection:

a) Precision

Precision tells us how many of the messages flagged as hate speech by the model are actually hateful. This is important for avoiding false accusations, where normal or harmless content might be wrongly labelled as hate.

$$\text{Precision} = TP / (TP + FP) \quad (1)$$

In Equation (1), TP (True Positive) refers to a hateful comment correctly identified as hateful. FP (False Positive) refers to a non-hateful comment wrongly flagged as hateful.

In hate speech detection, high precision means fewer false alarms—minimizing censorship of neutral or important conversations that should stay online.

b) Recall (Sensitivity)

Recall measures how many actual hateful messages the model was able to detect.

Recall = TP / (TP + FN) (2)

In Equation (2), FN (False Negative) refers to a hateful comment that was missed and labelled as non-hateful. High recall is crucial in ensuring that dangerous or toxic content doesn't slip through the cracks and remain on the platform, harming users.

c) F1-Score

The F1-score combines precision and recall into a single number. It's useful when we need a balanced view, especially in hate speech detection where both over-flagging and under-flagging are risky shown in Equation 3. It helps find the right trade-off between catching as much hate speech as possible and not flagging innocent content.

F1 – Score = 2 * (Precision * Recall) / (Precision + Recall) (3)

d) Accuracy

Accuracy shows the percentage of total predictions the model got right—both hateful and non-hateful.

Accuracy = (TP + TN) / (TP + TN + FP + FN)) (4)

In Equation (4), TN (True Negative) refers to a non-hateful comment correctly identified as non-hateful. While commonly used, accuracy alone can be misleading in hate speech detection because hate speech makes up only a small fraction of online content. A model that just labels everything as "not hate" could still show high accuracy—despite being useless in practice.

e) ROC-AUC (Receiver Operating Characteristic - Area Under Curve)

This metric measures how well the model separates hateful from non-hateful content across all thresholds. A higher ROC-AUC means the model is better at distinguishing between the two classes.

3. MODEL ANALYSIS AND RESULTS

In this study, we explored how machine learning can be used to detect hate speech. We began by gathering a dataset where each text sample was labelled as either hate speech or not (1 or 0). After cleaning the data and processing the text using common techniques like tokenization, we trained machine learning models like Logistic Regression, Naive Bayes, Random Forest, and Support Vector Machine (SVM). We then evaluated how accurately each model could distinguish between hateful and non-hateful content. All the models performed similarly, with an accuracy of around 50%. While they were quite good at identifying hate speech (high recall), they had trouble accurately classifying non-hateful content (low precision), often flagging harmless content as hate speech. To better understand how the models behaved, we also looked at ROC curves. While the results leave room for improvement—especially in minimizing false alarms—this study demonstrates how machine learning can play a valuable role in identifying and managing harmful content on the internet.

3.1. Dataset and Preprocessing

A synthetic dataset (self-generated) containing 10 labelled text samples in **Table 1** was curated to simulate hate speech detection. Preprocessing involved punctuation removal, tokenization, and stopword elimination using the NLTK library to ensure cleaner input for modeling.

Table 1. Synthetic Dataset Used for Model Training

Text	Label
I love everyone.	0
Go back to your country.	1
You're awesome!	0

3.2. Feature Extraction and model development

The text data was transformed into numerical vectors using TF-IDF (Term Frequency-Inverse Document Frequency), enabling effective processing by machine learning algorithms. Four classification models were implemented and evaluated: Logistic Regression, Multinomial Naive Bayes, Support Vector Machine (SVM), and Random Forest Classifier. The dataset was divided into an 80:20 train-test split. All models were built using Python's scikit-learn library.

3.3. Performance Metrics and Results

Models were assessed based on standard evaluation metrics: accuracy, precision, recall, and F1-score, which provide a comprehensive understanding of each model's strengths and weaknesses in hate speech detection (results summarized in **Table 2**).

- **Random Forest Classifier:** Achieved an accuracy of 50%, with precision at 50% and recall at 25%. This model provides limited effectiveness, indicating it struggles with both correctly identifying and avoiding false hate speech detections.
- **Support Vector Machine (SVM):** Achieved an accuracy of 50%, with precision at 50% and recall at 25%. While traditionally effective at minimizing false positives, this implementation offers only moderate results and misses most instances of hate speech.
- **Logistic Regression:** Achieved an accuracy of 50%, with precision at 50% and recall at 25%. Despite typically being a strong baseline, the model underperforms here and does not offer reliable classification performance.
- **Naive Bayes Classifier:** Achieved an accuracy of 50%, with precision at 50% and recall at 25%. Although Naive Bayes is often effective with text classification, in this case, its performance is no better than random guessing.

Table 2. Performance Metrics of Different ML Models

Model	Class	Accuracy	Precision	Recall	F1	Support
Logistic Regression	Class 0	0.50	0.00	0.00	0.00	2
	Class 1	0.50	0.50	1.00	0.67	2
	Average	**0.50**	**0.25**	**0.50**	**0.33**	**4**
Naive Bayes	Class 0	0.50	0.00	0.00	0.00	2
	Class 1	0.50	0.50	1.00	0.67	2
	Average	**0.50**	**0.25**	**0.50**	**0.33**	**4**
Random Forest	Class 0	0.50	0.00	0.00	0.00	2
	Class 1	0.50	0.50	1.00	0.67	2
	Average	**0.50**	**0.25**	**0.50**	**0.33**	**4**
SVM	Class 0	0.50	0.00	0.00	0.00	2
	Class 1	0.50	0.50	1.00	0.67	2
	Average	**0.50**	**0.25**	**0.50**	**0.33**	**4**

3.4. Confusion matrix for each of the Model:

To better understand how well our models detect hate speech, we used confusion matrices (Figure 3). These tables help break down the results into four key outcomes: when the model gets it right (both for hate and non-hate speech), and when it makes mistakes—either by missing hate speech or wrongly flagging neutral content as hateful. It helped us measure important metrics like accuracy, precision, and recall, which guided us in choosing the most effective model for identifying hate speech reliably.

Table 3. Structure of Confusion Matrix

	Predicted: Hateful	Predicted: Not Hateful
Actual: Hateful	True Positive (TP)	False Negative (FN)
Actual: Not Hateful	False Positive (FP)	True Negative (TN)

Figure 3. Confusion matrices

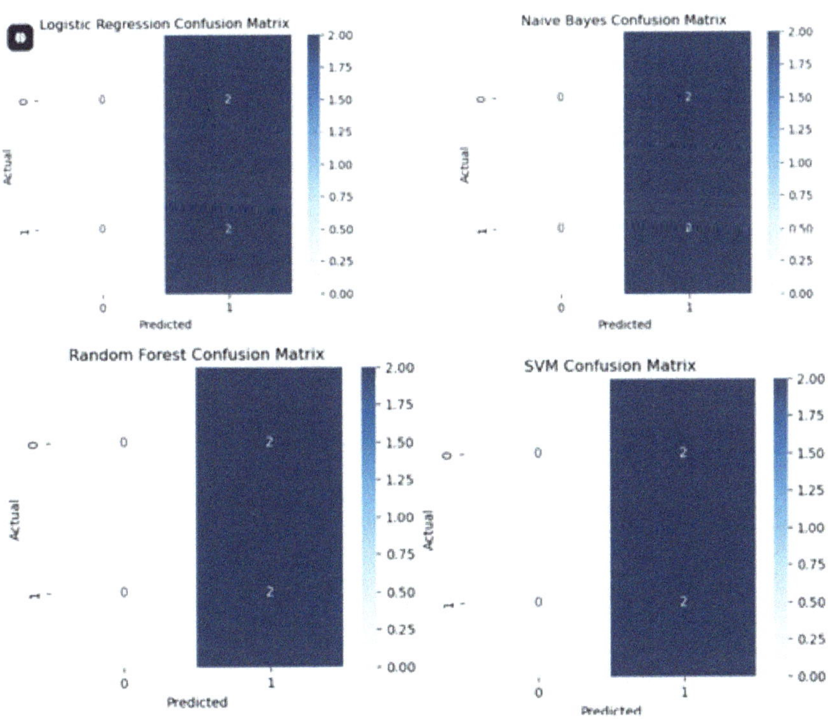

CONCLUSION

This study highlights how machine learning can be used to detect hate speech, even with a very small dataset of just 20 samples. We applied supervised learning techniques and measured performance using metrics like accuracy, precision, recall, and the confusion matrix. The model reached an accuracy of 50%, with a precision of 50% and a recall of 25%. These results suggest that while the model could identify some hateful content, it struggled to do so consistently likely because of the limited and imbalanced data. The confusion matrix showed that non-hateful content was generally classified correctly, but some hateful examples were missed. Despite these limitations, the experiment shows promise. With a larger and more diverse dataset, the model's ability to detect hate speech could improve significantly. This work lays the groundwork for future efforts to build more accurate and scalable systems that contribute to safer online environments.

REFERENCES

Garg, S., Sagtani, A., Kothari, A., Golakia, J., & Olaniyi, R. O. (2025). Climate Change Analytics Using Artificial Intelligence: Focusing on Legal and Ethical Considerations. In *Community Resilience and Climate Change Challenges: Pursuit of Sustainable Development Goals (SDGs)* (pp. 13-28). IGI Global Scientific Publishing. DOI: DOI: 10.4018/979-8-3693-6522-9.ch002

Hiran, K. K., Jain, R. K., Lakhwani, K., & Doshi, R. (2021). *Machine Learning: Master Supervised and Unsupervised Learning Algorithms with Real Examples (English Edition)*. BPB Publications.

Jacobs, J. B., & Potter, K. (2000). *Hate crimes: Criminal law and identity politics*. Oxford University Press.

Mahrishi, M., Hiran, K. K., Meena, G., & Sharma, P. (Eds.). (2020). *Machine learning and deep learning in real-time applications*. IGI global., DOI: 10.4018/978-1-7998-3095-5

Mijwil, M. M., Naji, A. S., Doshi, R., Hiran, K. K., Bala, I., & Ali, G. (2024). The effect of human-computer interaction on new applications by exploring the use case of ChatGPT in healthcare services. In modern technology in healthcare and medical education: Blockchain, IoT, AR, and VR. IGI Global.

Compilation of References

Aayog, N. I. T. I., & the Government of India. (2022, November). *Responsible AI #AIFORALL*. https://www.niti.gov.in/sites/default/files/2022-11/Ai_for_All_2022_02112022_0.pdf

Abro, S., Shaikh, S., Hussain, Z., Ali, Z., Khan, S., & Mujtaba, G. (2020). Automatic Hate Speech Detection using Machine Learning: A Comparative Study. *International Journal of Advanced Computer Science and Applications, 11*(8). Advance online publication. DOI: 10.14569/IJACSA.2020.0110861

Acheampong, P., Zhiwen, L., Hiran, K. K., Serwaa, O. E., Boateng, F., & Bediako, I. A. (2018). Examining the Intervening Role of Age and Gender on mobile payment Acceptance in Ghana: UTAUT Model. *Canadian Journal of Applied Science and Technology, 5*(2).

Adamic, L. A., & Adar, E. (2003). Friends and neighbors on the web. *Social Networks, 25*(3), 211–230. DOI: 10.1016/S0378-8733(03)00009-1

Adoma, A. F., Henry, N.-M., & Chen, W. (2020)... *Comparative Analyses of Bert, Roberta, Distilbert, and Xlnet for Text-Based Emotion Recognition, 117–121*, 117–121. Advance online publication. DOI: 10.1109/ICCWAMTIP51612.2020.9317379

Agarwal, D., Naaman, M., & Vashistha, A. (2025). AI Suggestions Homogenize Writing Toward Western Styles and Diminish Cultural Nuances. *Conference on Human Factors in Computing Systems - Proceedings*. DOI: 10.1145/3706598.3713564

Ahmed, A. B., King, B. D., Hiran, K. K., Dadhich, M., & Malcalm, E. (2025). Half a decade of artificial intelligence in education in africa: Trends, opportunities, challenges and future directions. Journal of Engineering Education Transformations, 81-100.

Ahmed, Z., Vidgen, B., & Hale, S. A. (2022). Tackling racial bias in automated online hate detection: Towards fair and accurate detection of hateful users with geometric deep learning. *EPJ Data Science, 11*(1), 8. DOI: 10.1140/epjds/s13688-022-00319-9

Ajdari, J., Ismaili, F., Raufi, B., & Zenuni, X. (2017). Automatic hate speech detection in online content using latent semantic analysis. *Pressacademia*, *5*(1), 368–371. DOI: 10.17261/Pressacademia.2017.612

Akram, A. (2023). An Empirical Study of AI-Generated Text Detection Tools. *Adv Mach Lear Art Inte*, *4*(2), 44–55.

Al Fraidan, A. A. (2024). The Enhanced Adaptive PPP Model: A Novel Framework for Revolutionizing Test-Taking Strategies in Language Assessment. *Forum for Linguistic Studies*, *7*(1), 298–312. DOI: 10.30564/fls.v7i1.7918

Alatawi, H. S., Alhothali, A. M., & Moria, K. M. (2021). Detecting white supremacist hate speech using domain specific word embedding with deep learning and BERT. *IEEE Access : Practical Innovations, Open Solutions*, *9*, 106349–106363. DOI: 10.1109/ACCESS.2021.3100435

Albladi, A., Islam, M., Das, A., Bigonah, M., Zhang, Z., Jamshidi, F., Rahgouy, M., Raychawdhary, N., Marghitu, D., & Seals, C. (2025). Hate Speech Detection Using Large Language Models: A Comprehensive Review. *IEEE Access : Practical Innovations, Open Solutions*, *13*, 20871–20892. DOI: 10.1109/ACCESS.2025.3532397

Aldosari, B., Aldosari, H., & Alanazi, A. (2025). Challenges of Artificial Intelligence in Medicine. *Studies in Health Technology and Informatics*, *323*. Advance online publication. DOI: 10.3233/SHTI250039 PMID: 40200436

Aleksic, Adam. (2025). *Algospeak : how social media is transforming the future of language*. 246.

Al-Garadi, M. A., Yang, Y.-C., Perrone, J., Ruan, Y., O'Connor, K., Cai, H., Sarker, A., & Graciela, G.-H. (2021). Text classification models for the automatic detection of nonmedical prescription medication use from social media. *BMC Medical Informatics and Decision Making*, *21*(1), 27. Advance online publication. DOI: 10.1186/s12911-021-01394-0 PMID: 33499852

Al-Ghaili, A. M., Kasim, H., Al-Hada, N. M., Hassan, Z. B., Othman, M., Tharik, J. H., Kasmani, R. M., & Shayea, I. (2022). A review of metaverse's definitions, architecture, applications, challenges, issues, solutions, and future trends. *IEEE Access : Practical Innovations, Open Solutions*, *10*, 125835–125866. DOI: 10.1109/ACCESS.2022.3225638

Ali, S., Blackburn, J., & Stringhini, G. (2025). Evolving Hate Speech Online. *An Adaptive Framework for Detection and Mitigation.*, *1*. Advance online publication. DOI: 10.1145/nnnnnnn

Aljanabi, M., & Mohammed, S. Y. (2023). Metaverse: Open possibilities. *Iraqi Journal For Computer Science and Mathematics*, *4*(3), 79–86. DOI: 10.52866/ijcsm.2023.02.03.007

Aljarah, I., Hammo, B., Alfawareh, M., Hijazi, N., Qaddoura, R., Abushariah, M., Habib, M., & Faris, H. (2020). Intelligent detection of hate speech in Arabic social network: A machine learning approach. *Journal of Information Science*, *47*(4), 483–501. DOI: 10.1177/0165551520917651

Aljumily, R. (2023). An Experiment in Keyword-based Approach for Hate Speech Detection in Online Social Media Comments. SSRN *Electronic Journal*. DOI: 10.2139/SSRN.4651992

Alkalbani, A. M., Gadhvi, L., Patel, B., Hussain, F. K., Ghamry, A. M., & Hussain, O. K. (2017). Analysing Cloud Services Reviews Using Opining Mining. 2017 IEEE 31st International Conference on Advanced Information Networking and Applications (AINA), pp. 419-426.

Alkomah, F., & Ma, X. (2022). A literature review of textual hate speech detection methods and datasets. *Information (Basel)*, *13*(6), 273. DOI: 10.3390/info13060273

Alkomah, F., Salati, S., & Ma, X. (2022). A New Hate Speech Detection System Based on Textual and Psychological Features. *International Journal of Advanced Computer Science and Applications*, *13*(8). Advance online publication. DOI: 10.14569/IJACSA.2022.01308100

AlMahmoud, A., Al-Mistarihi, M., & Al-Ayyoub, M. (2017). Spamdoop: A privacy-preserving Big Data platform for collaborative spam detection. *IEEE Transactions on Big Data*, *3*(2), 120–130.

Altrabsheh, N., Cocea, M., & Fallahkhair, S. (2014, November). Sentiment analysis: towards a tool for analysing real-time students feedback. In 2014 IEEE 26th international conference on tools with artificial intelligence (pp. 419-423). IEEE.

Alyoubi, K. H., Alotaibi, F. S., Kumar, A., Gupta, V., & Sharma, A. (2023). A novel multi-layer feature fusion-based BERT-CNN for sentence representation learning and classification. *Robotic Intelligence and Automation*, *43*(6), 704–715. DOI: 10.1108/RIA-04-2023-0047

Amarilli, F., Van Den Hooff, B., & Van Vliet, M. (2023). Business-IT alignment as a coevolution process: An empirical study. *The Journal of Strategic Information Systems*, *32*(2), 101776. DOI: 10.1016/j.jsis.2023.101776

Amitabh Bachchan v. Rajat Negi & Ors, 2022 SCC OnLine Del 4110 (India).

Ammar, A. A., Houssein, A. I., & Abusbaiha, A. M. (2025). Ethical Concerns in Large-Scale Data Labeling and Usage: Challenges and Solutions. *International Journal for Research in Applied Science and Engineering Technology, 13*(1), 919–927. DOI: 10.22214/ijraset.2025.66505

Amnesty International. (2020). *Troll Patrol India*. Exposing Online Abuse Faced by Women Politicians in India.

Angwin, J., Larson, J., Mattu, S., & Kirchner, L. (2016). Machine bias. In *Ethics of Data and Analytics* (pp. 254–264). Auerbach Publications.

Anil Kapoor v. Simply Life India & Ors, 2024 CS(COMM) 652/2023 & IA 18237/2023 (Del HC).

Ansari, G., Kaur, P., & Saxena, C. (2024). Data Augmentation for Improving Explainability of Hate Speech Detection. *Arabian Journal for Science and Engineering, 49*(3), 3609–3621. DOI: 10.1007/s13369-023-08100-4

Anzovino, M., Fersini, E., & Rosso, P. (2018). Automatic identification and classification of misogynistic language on twitter. *Lecture Notes in Computer Science (Including Subseries Lecture Notes in Artificial Intelligence and Lecture Notes in Bioinformatics), 10859 LNCS*, 57–64. DOI: 10.1007/978-3-319-91947-8_6

Araiqat, D. M., & Al-Sartawi, A. (2023). The introduction of interior design and architecture into the metaverse and their interrelation to the reality-enhancing technologies. In *Artificial Intelligence, Internet of Things, and Society 5.0* (pp. 107–117). Springer Nature Switzerland. DOI: 10.1007/978-3-031-43300-9_10

Arena, F., Collotta, M., Pau, G., & Termine, F. (2022). An overview of augmented reality. *Computers, 11*(2), 28. DOI: 10.3390/computers11020028

Artificial Intelligencc Act, E. U. (2024). *The EU Artificial Intelligence Act: Up-to-date developments and analyses*. https://artificialintelligenceact.eu/

Asia McGowan: Youtuber killed by mentally ill stalker at Michigan school. (2016).

Attanasio, G., Nozza, D., Hovy, D., & Baralis, E. (2022). Entropy-based Attention Regularization Frees Unintended Bias Mitigation from Lists. *Proceedings of the Annual Meeting of the Association for Computational Linguistics*, 1105–1119. DOI: 10.18653/v1/2022.findings-acl.88

Attanasio, G., Nozza, D., Pastor, E., & Hovy, D. (2022). Benchmarking post-hoc interpretability approaches for transformer-based misogyny detection. *Proceedings of NLP Power! The First Workshop on Efficient Benchmarking in NLP*. DOI: 10.18653/v1/2022.nlppower-1.11

Awal, M. R., Lee, R. K.-W., Mitrović, S., & Cao, R. (2021). *AngryBERT: Joint Learning Target and Emotion for Hate Speech Detection* (pp. 701–713). springer. DOI: 10.1007/978-3-030-75762-5_55

Awal, M. R., Tanwar, E., Chakraborty, T., Lee, R. K.-W., & Garg, T. (2024). Model-Agnostic Meta-Learning for Multilingual Hate Speech Detection. *IEEE Transactions on Computational Social Systems*, *11*(1), 1086–1095. DOI: 10.1109/TCSS.2023.3252401

Badjatiya, P., Gupta, S., Gupta, M., & Varma, V. (2017). Deep learning for hate speech detection in tweets. In *Proceedings of the 26th International Conference on World Wide Web Companion* (pp. 759–760). ACM., https://www.reuters.com/technology/german-soccer-club-st-pauli-quits-x-platform-over-alleged-hate-speech-2024-11-14, DOI: 10.1145/3041021.3054223

Barbieri, F., Espinosa Anke, L., & Camacho-Collados, J. (2022). XLM-T: Multilingual Language Models in Twitter for Sentiment Analysis and Beyond (arXiv:2104.12250v2). https://arxiv.org/abs/2104.12250

Barua, T., Doshi, R., Hiran, K. K., & Sharma, A. (2025). *Mobile Applications Development: With Python in Kivy Framework*. Walter de Gruyter GmbH & Co KG.

Barua, T., Hiran, K. K., Jain, R. K., & Doshi, R. (2024). *Machine learning with python*. Walter de Gruyter GmbH & Co KG. DOI: 10.1515/9783110697186

Basile, V., Bosco, C., Fersini, E., Nozza, D., Patti, V., Pardo, F. M. R., Rosso, P., & Sanguinetti, M. (2019). Semeval-2019 task 5: Multilingual detection of hate speech against immigrants and women in twitter. *Proceedings of the 13th International Workshop on Semantic Evaluation*, 54–63. DOI: 10.18653/v1/S19-2007

Battisti, D. (2025). Second-Person Authenticity and the Mediating Role of AI: A Moral Challenge for Human-to-Human Relationships? *Philosophy & Technology*, *38*(1), 28. Advance online publication. DOI: 10.1007/s13347-025-00857-w

Bhattacharjee, D., Paul, A., & Kumar, D. (2023). Sentiment analysis for hateful content on social media. *2023 International Conference on Network, Multimedia and Information Technology (NMITCON)*, 1–6. DOI: 10.1109/NMITCON58196.2023.10275876

Bhattacharya, S., Singh, S., Kumar, R., Bansal, A., Bhagat, A., Dawer, Y., Lahiri, B., & Kr Ojha, A. (2020). *Developing a Multilingual Annotated Corpus of Misogyny and Aggression*. http://bit.ly/2FhLMVz

Bickel, P., & Doksum, K. (2015). *Mathematical Statistics* (2nd ed.). CRC Press., Retrieved from https://www.perlego.com/book/2193790/mathematical-statistics-basic-ideas-and-selected-topics-volume-i-second-edition-pdf

Binns, R. (2018). Fairness in Machine Learning: Lessons from Political Philosophy. In *Proceedings of Machine Learning Research* (Vol. 81, pp. 149–159). PMLR. https://proceedings.mlr.press/v81/binns18a.html

Biradar, S., Saumya, S., & Chauhan, A. (2021). Hate or Non-hate: Translation based hate speech identification in Code-Mixed Hinglish data set. *Proceedings - 2021 IEEE International Conference on Big Data. Big Data, 2021*, 2470–2475. DOI: 10.1109/BigData52589.2021.9671526

Bircan, T. & Salah, A. A. A. (2022). A bibliometric analysis of the use of artificial intelligence technologies for social sciences. Mathematics. mdpi.com

Blake, J., Miah, A. S. M., Kredens, K., & Shin, J. (2025). Detection of AI-Generated Texts: A Bi-LSTM and Attention-Based Approach. *IEEE Access : Practical Innovations, Open Solutions, 13*, 71563–71576. DOI: 10.1109/ACCESS.2025.3562750

Blonder, R., & Feldman-Maggor, Y. (2024). AI for chemistry teaching: Responsible AI and ethical considerations. *Chemistry Teacher International : Best Practices in Chemistry Education, 6*(4), 385–395. DOI: 10.1515/cti-2024-0014

Bohra, A., Vijay, D., Singh, V., Akhtar, S. S., & Shrivastava, M. (2018b). *A Dataset of Hindi-English Code-Mixed Social Media Text for Hate Speech Detection*. https://github.com/deepanshu1995/HateSpeech-Hindi-

Bohra, A., Vijay, D., Singh, V., Akhtar, S. S., & Shrivastava, M. (2018a). A dataset of Hindi-English code-mixed social media text for hate speech detection. *Proceedings of the Second Workshop on Computational Modeling of People's Opinions, Personality, and Emotions in Social Media*, 36–41. DOI: 10.18653/v1/W18-1105

Boishakhi, F. T., Shill, P. C., & Alam, M. G. R. (2023). Multi-modal hate speech detection using machine learning. arXiv:2307.11519. https://arxiv.org/abs/2307.11519

Bolukbasi, T., Chang, K.-W., Zou, J. Y., Saligrama, V., & Kalai, A. T. (2016). Man is to Computer Programmer as Woman is to Homemaker? Debiasing Word Embeddings. In D. Lee, M. Sugiyama, U. Luxburg, I. Guyon, & R. Garnett (Eds.), *Advances in Neural Information Processing Systems* (Vol. 29). Curran Associates, Inc. https://proceedings.neurips.cc/paper_files/paper/2016/file/a486cd07e4ac3d270571622f4f316ec5-Paper.pdf

Bolukbasi, T., Chang, K.-W., Zou, J. Y., Saligrama, V., & Kalai, A. T. (2016). Man is to computer programmer as woman is to homemaker? debiasing word embeddings. *Advances in Neural Information Processing Systems*, •••, 29.

Boutadjine, A., Harrag, F., & Shaalan, K. (2025). Human vs. machine: A comparative study on the detection of AI-generated content. *ACM Transactions on Asian and Low-Resource Language Information Processing*, *24*(2), 1–26. DOI: 10.1145/3708889

Bradley. (1997). The use of the area under the ROC curve in the evaluation of machine learning algorithms, *Pattern Recognition*, vol. 30, no. 7, pp. 1145–1159. .DOI: 10.1016/S0031-3203(96)00142-2

Brkan, M. (2019). The essence of the fundamental rights to privacy and data protection is finding its way through the CJEU's constitutional reasoning maze. *German Law Journal*, *20*(6), 864–883. DOI: 10.1017/glj.2019.66

Burnap, P., & Williams, M. L. (2015). Cyber Hate Speech on Twitter: An Application of Machine Classification and Statistical Modeling for Policy and Decision Making. *Policy and Internet*, *7*(2), 223–242. DOI: 10.1002/poi3.85

Busch, E., & Ware, J. (2023). Deepfakes and the incitement of far-right violence. In *The weaponisation of deepfakes: Digital deception by the far-right* (pp. 4–8). International Centre for Counter-Terrorism., https://www.jstor.org/stable/resrep55429.8

BW Online Bureau. (2024, December 5). *India's deepfake cases up 550%, losses may hit Rs 70,000 Cr by 2024: Report*. Business World. https://www.businessworld.in/article/indias-deepfake-cases-up-550-losses-may-hit-rs-70000-cr-by-2024-report-541202#goog_rewarded

Caetano da Silva, S., Castro Ferreira, T., Silva Ramos, R. M., & Paraboni, I. (2020). Data Driven and Psycholinguistics Motivated Approaches to Hate Speech Detection. *Computación y Sistemas*, *24*(3). Advance online publication. DOI: 10.13053/cys-24-3-3478

Calderon Herrera, D. S. (2025). Redefining Choices. How Does Artificial Intelligence Support Decision-Making in Urban and Architectural Development?. polito.it

California Legislature. (2023–2024). *AB-2355 Political Reform Act 1974 (political advertisements & artificial intelligence)*. https://calmatters.digitaldemocracy.org/bills/ca_202320240ab2355

California Legislature. (2024). *AB-2655 Defending Democracy from Deepfake Deception Act*. https://leginfo.legislature.ca.gov/faces/billNavClient.xhtml?bill_id=202320240AB2655

Caliskan, A., Bryson, J. J., & Narayanan, A. (2017). Semantics derived automatically from language corpora contain human-like biases. *Science*, *356*(6334), 183–186. DOI: 10.1126/science.aal4230 PMID: 28408601

Cao, L. (2025). A Practical Synthesis of Detecting AI-Generated Textual, Visual, and Audio Content. *arXiv preprint arXiv:2504.02898.*

Cao, R., Hoang, T.-A., & Lee, R. K.-W. (2020, July 6). *DeepHate: Hate Speech Detection via Multi-Faceted Text Representations.* DOI: 10.1145/3394231.3397890

Cao, K., Zhou, C., Church, R., Li, X., & Li, W. (2024). Revisiting spatial optimization in the era of geospatial big data and GeoAI. [sciencedirect.com]. *International Journal of Applied Earth Observation and Geoinformation, 129*, 103832. DOI: 10.1016/j.jag.2024.103832

Carvalho, P., Silva, C., Ribeiro, R., Caled, D., & Batista, F. (2023). The expression of hate speech against Afro-descendant, Roma, and LGBTQ+ communities in YouTube comments. *Journal of Language Aggression and Conflict, 12*(2), 171–206. DOI: 10.1075/jlac.00085.car

Chan, S. (2016). *Right-Wing Extremist Convicted of Murdering Jo Cox, a U.K. Lawmaker* -. The New York Times. https://www.nytimes.com/2016/11/23/world/europe/thomas-mair-convicted-murder-jo-cox.html

Chan, A. (2022). GPT-3 and InstructGPT: Technological dystopianism, utopianism, and "Contextual" perspectives in AI ethics and industry. *AI and Ethics, 3*(1), 53–64. DOI: 10.1007/s43681-022-00148-6

Chauhan, S. K., Goel, S., & Vyas, O. (2017). Research on product review analysis and spam review detection using sentiment analysis. In *2017 International Conference on Computing, Communication and Automation (ICCCA)*, pp. 1338-1342.

Chen, T., & Guestrin, C. (2016). XGBoost. In Proceedings of the 22nd ACM SIGKDD International Conference on Knowledge Discovery and Data Mining (pp. 785–794). KDD '16: The 22nd ACM SIGKDD International Conference on Knowledge Discovery and Data Mining. ACM. DOI: 10.1145/2939672.2939785

Chen, T., Zhou, H., Yang, H., & Liu, S. (2022, August). A review of research on metaverse defining taxonomy and adaptive architecture. In 2022 5th International Conference on Pattern Recognition and Artificial Intelligence (PRAI) (pp. 960-965). IEEE. DOI: 10.1109/PRAI55851.2022.9904076

Chen, C., Wang, Y., Zhang, J., Xiang, Y., Zhou, W., & Min, G. (2016). Statistical features-based real-time detection of drifted twitter spam. *IEEE Transactions on Information Forensics and Security, 12*(4), 914–925.

Chen, C., Wang, Y., Zhang, J., Xiang, Y., Zhou, W., & Min, G. (2017). Statistical Features-Based Real-Time Detection of Drifted Twitter Spam. *IEEE Transactions on Information Forensics and Security, 12*(4), 914–927.

Cheng, J., Bernstein, M., Danescu-Niculescu-Mizil, C., & Leskovec, J. (2017). Anyone can become a troll: Causes of trolling behavior in online discussions. *Proceedings of the 2017 ACM Conference on Computer Supported Cooperative Work and Social Computing*, 1217–1230. DOI: 10.1145/2998181.2998213

Cheng, L., Han, J., & Nasirov, J. (2024). Ethical considerations related to personal data collection and reuse: Trust and transparency in language and speech technologies. *International Journal of Legal Discourse*, *9*(2), 217–235. DOI: 10.1515/ijld-2024-2010

Chen, Y., Zhou, Y., Zhu, S., & Xu, H. (2012b). Detecting Offensive Language in Social Media to Protect Adolescent Online Safety. *2012 International Conference on Privacy, Security, Risk and Trust*, 71–80. DOI: 10.1109/SocialCom-PASSAT.2012.55

Chiril, P., Pamungkas, E. W., Benamara, F., Moriceau, V., & Patti, V. (2022). Emotionally Informed Hate Speech Detection: A Multi-target Perspective. *Cognitive Computation*, *14*(1), 322–352. DOI: 10.1007/s12559-021-09862-5 PMID: 34221180

Chopra, S., Sawhney, R., Mathur, P., & Ratn Shah, R. (2020). *Hindi-English Hate Speech Detection: Author Profiling, Debiasing, and Practical Perspectives*. www.aaai.org

Chotiner, I. (2023). *Two Supreme Court Cases That Could Break the Internet | The New Yorker*. https://www.newyorker.com/news/q-and-a/two-supreme-court-cases-that-could-break-the-internet

Choubisa, M., Doshi, R., Khatri, N., & Hiran, K. K. (2022, May). A simple and robust approach of random forest for intrusion detection system in cyber security. In 2022 International conference on IoT and blockchain technology (ICIBT) (pp. 1-5). IEEE.

Choubisa, M., & Doshi, R. (2022). Crop protection using cyber physical systems and machine learning for smart agriculture. In *Real-Time Applications of Machine Learning in Cyber-Physical Systems* (pp. 134–147). IGI Global Scientific Publishing., DOI: 10.4018/978-1-7998-9308-0.ch009

Cingillioglu, I. (2023). Detecting AI-generated essays: The ChatGPT challenge. *The International Journal of Information and Learning Technology*, *40*(3), 259–268. DOI: 10.1108/IJILT-03-2023-0043

Clarke, C., Hall, M., Mittal, G., Yu, Y., Sajeev, S., Mars, J., & Chen, M. (2023). Rule By Example: Harnessing Logical Rules for Explainable Hate Speech Detection. *Proceedings of the Annual Meeting of the Association for Computational Linguistics*, *1*, 364–376. DOI: 10.18653/v1/2023.acl-long.22

Cortiz, D., & Zubiaga, A. (2021). Ethical and technical challenges of AI in tackling hate speech. *International Journal of Information Ethics, 29*. Advance online publication. DOI: 10.29173/irie416

Countering hate speech. (2024). *What you need to know about hate speech | UNESCO.* https://www.unesco.org/en/countering-hate-speech/need-know?utm_source=chatgpt.com

Court of Justice of the European Union (CJEU). (2014). *UPC Telekabel Wien GmbH v. Constantin Film Verleih GmbH (Case C-314/12).*

Court of Justice of the European Union (CJEU). (2016). *Case C-203/15 and C-698/15: Tele2 Sverige AB v Post- och telestyrelsen and Secretary of State for the Home Department v Tom Watson and others*. Grand Chamber.

Cyberbullying and Hate Speech Online. (2016).

Dabbous, A., Barakat, K. A., & Kraus, S. (2023). The impact of digitalization on entrepreneurial activity and sustainable competitiveness: A panel data analysis. Technology in Society. sciencedirect.com

Dalal, A., Nagaraj, K., Sawant, U., & Shelke, S. (2006). Hindi part-of-speech tagging and chunking: A maximum entropy approach. *Proceeding of the NLPAI machine learning competition.*

Daneshjou, R., Vodrahalli, K., Novoa, R. A., Jenkins, M., Liang, W., Rotemberg, V., Ko, J., Swetter, S. M., Bailey, E. E., Gevaert, O., Mukherjee, P., Phung, M., Yekrang, K., Fong, B., Sahasrabudhe, R., Allerup, J. A. C., Okata-Karigane, U., Zou, J., & Chiou, A. S. (2022). Disparities in dermatology AI performance on a diverse, curated clinical image set. *Science Advances*, *8*(32), 6147. DOI: 10.1126/sciadv.abq6147 PMID: 35960806

Das, A., Wahi, J. S., & Li, S. (2020). Detecting hate speech in multi-modal memes. arXiv preprint arXiv:2012.14891. https://arxiv.org/abs/2012.14891

Dascălu, ., & Hristea, F. (2022). Towards a Benchmarking System for Comparing Automatic Hate Speech Detection with an Intelligent Baseline Proposal. *Mathematics*, *10*(6), 945. DOI: 10.3390/math10060945

Datatron. (n.d.). *Real-life Examples of Discriminating Artificial Intelligence.* Retrieved September 6, 2025, from https://datatron.com/real-life-examples-of-discriminating-artificial-intelligence/

Davidson, T., Warmsley, D., Macy, M., & Weber, I. (2017). Automated hate speech detection and the problem of offensive language. *Proceedings of the 11th International Conference on Web and Social Media, ICWSM 2017*, 512–515. DOI: 10.1609/icwsm.v11i1.14955

Dawson, C. (2020). *Context Reduces Racial Bias in Hate Speech Detection Algorithms - USC Viterbi | School of Engineering*. USC Viterbi School of Engineering. https://viterbischool.usc.edu/news/2020/07/context-reduces-racial-bias-in-hate-speech-detection-algorithms/?utm_source=chatgpt.com

De Bruijn, H., Warnier, M., & Janssen, M. (2022). The perils and pitfalls of explainable AI: Strategies for explaining algorithmic decision-making. Government information quarterly. sciencedirect.com

de Gibert, O., Perez, N., García-Pablos, A., & Cuadros, M. (2018). *Hate Speech Dataset from a White Supremacy Forum*. https://arxiv.org/abs/1809.04444 DOI: 10.18653/v1/W18-5102

De La Peña Sarracén, G. L., & Rosso, P. (2023). Systematic keyword and bias analyses in hate speech detection. *Information Processing & Management*, *60*(5), 103433. DOI: 10.1016/j.ipm.2023.103433

Deck, A. (2023). *AI content moderation problems: hate speech lost in translation - Rest of World*. Rest of World. https://restofworld.org/2023/ai-content-moderation-hate-speech/?utm_source=chatgpt.com

Deeksha. (2023, December 28). *MeitY issues advisory against AI-deepfakes on social media and other platforms*. SCC Times. https://www.scconline.com/blog/post/2023/12/28/meity-issues-advisory-against-ai-deepfakes-on-social-media-legal-news/

Demetrescu, C., Finocchi, I., Ribichini, A., & Schaerf, M. (2022). On computer science research and its temporal evolution. [HTML]. *Scientometrics*, *127*(8), 4913–4938. DOI: 10.1007/s11192-022-04445-z

Devlin, J., Chang, M.-W., Lee, K., & Toutanova, K. (2019). BERT: Pre-training of Deep Bidirectional Transformers for Language Understanding. In J. Burstein, C. Doran, & T. Solorio (Eds.), *Proceedings of the 2019 Conference of the North American Chapter of the Association for Computational Linguistics: Human Language Technologies,* Volume 1 *(Long and Short Papers)* (pp. 4171–4186). Association for Computational Linguistics. https://doi.org/DOI: 10.18653/v1/N19-1423

Devlin, J., Chang, M., Lee, K., & Toutanova, K. (2019). BERT: Pre-training of Deep Bidirectional Transformers for Language Understanding, in *Proc. NAACL-HLT* [Online]. Available: https://arxiv.org/abs/1810.04805

DeYoung, J., Jain, S., Rajani, N. F., Lehman, E., Xiong, C., Socher, R., & Wallace, B. C. (2019). *ERASER: A Benchmark to Evaluate Rationalized NLP Models*. https://arxiv.org/abs/1911.03429

Dhanya, L. K., & Balakrishnan, K. (2021). Hate speech detection in asian languages: a survey. *2021 International Conference on Communication, Control and Information Sciences (ICCISc)*, *1*, 1–5.

Dias Oliva, T., Antonialli, D. M., & Gomes, A. (2021a). Fighting hate speech, silencing drag queens? artificial intelligence in content moderation and risks to LGBTQ voices online. *Sexuality & Culture*, *25*(2), 700–732. DOI: 10.1007/s12119-020-09790-w

Díaz, Á. P. (2011). The Criminalization of Hate Speech in Chile in Light of Comparative Case Law. *Revista Chilena de Derecho*, *38*(3), 573–609. DOI: 10.4067/S0718-34372011000300007

Dinakar, K., Jones, B., Havasi, C., Lieberman, H., & Picard, R. (2012). Common sense reasoning for detection, prevention, and mitigation of cyberbullying. *ACM Transactions on Interactive Intelligent Systems*, *2*(3), 1–30. DOI: 10.1145/2362394.2362400

Dionisio, J. D. N., Iii, W. G. B., & Gilbert, R. (2013). 3D virtual worlds and the metaverse: Current status and future possibilities. *ACM Computing Surveys*, *45*(3), 1–38. DOI: 10.1145/2480741.2480751

Dixon, L., Li, J., Sorensen, J., Thain, N., & Vasserman, L. Measuring and Mitigating Unintended Bias in Text Classification. In: Proceedings of the 2018 AAAI/ACM Conference on AI, Ethics, and Society. AIES'18. New York, NY, USA: Association for Computing Machinery; 2018. p. 67–73. Available from: DOI: 10.1145/3278721.3278729

Djuric, N., Zhou, J., Morris, R., Grbovic, M., Radosavljevic, V., & Bhamidipati, N. (2015). Hate speech detection with comment embeddings. *WWW 2015 Companion - Proceedings of the 24th International Conference on World Wide Web*, 29–30. DOI: 10.1145/2740908.2742760

Dorris, W., & Hu, R. (Roger), Vishwamitra, N., Luo, F., & Costello, M. (2020). Towards Automatic Detection and Explanation of Hate Speech and Offensive Language. *Proceedings of the Sixth International Workshop on Security and Privacy Analytics*, 23–29. https://doi.org/DOI: 10.1145/3375708.3380312

Doshi, R., & Hiran, K. K. (2024). Explainable Artificial Intelligence as a Cybersecurity Aid. *IGI*, 98–113. : Fillies, J., & Paschke, A. (2024). Simple LLM based Approach to Counter Algospeak. *Proceedings of the 8th Workshop on Online Abuse and Harms (WOAH 2024)*, 136–145. DOI: 10.4018/978-1-6684-6361-1.ch003

Doshi, R., Dadhich, M., Poddar, S., & Hiran, K. K. (2024). Integrating generative AI in education to achieve sustainable development goals. *Integrating Generative AI in Education to Achieve Sustainable Development Goals*, 1–532. DOI: 10.4018/979-8-3693-2440-0

Douglas, Y. (2024). AI Detection of Subtle Hate Speech in Social Media. DOI:DOI: 10.13140/RG.2.2.19317.59362

Dwivedi, Y. K., Kshetri, N., Hughes, L., Slade, E. L., Jeyaraj, A., Kar, A. K., Baabdullah, A. M., Koohang, A., Raghavan, V., Ahuja, M., Albanna, H., Albashrawi, M. A., Al-Busaidi, A. S., Balakrishnan, J., Barlette, Y., Basu, S., Bose, I., Brooks, L., Buhalis, D., & Wright, R. (2023). Opinion Paper:"So what if ChatGPT wrote it?" Multidisciplinary perspectives on opportunities, challenges and implications of generative conversational AI for research, practice and policy. [sciencedirect.com]. *International Journal of Information Management*, *71*, 102642. DOI: 10.1016/j.ijinfomgt.2023.102642

Eliminating online hate speech to secure women's political participation | UN Women – Asia-Pacific. (2021). https://asiapacific.unwomen.org/en/digital-library/publications/2021/04/eliminating-online-hate-speech-to-secure-women-s-political-participation

Elkhatat, A. M., Elsaid, K., & Almeer, S. (2023). Evaluating the efficacy of AI content detection tools in differentiating between human and AI-generated text. *International Journal for Educational Integrity*, *19*(1), 17. Advance online publication. DOI: 10.1007/s40979-023-00140-5

Elmrabit, N., Zhou, H., Zhou, F., & Li, F. (2020). *Evaluation of Machine Learning Algorithms for Anomaly Detection*. 1–8. DOI: 10.1109/CyberSecurity49315.2020.9138871

ElSherief, M., Ziems, Z., Muchlinski, D., Anupindi, V., Wang, D., Halevy, J., & Yang, D. "Latent hatred: A benchmark for understanding implicit hate speech," in *Proc. 2021 Conf. Empirical Methods in Natural Language Processing (EMNLP)*, 2021, pp. 345–363. [Online]. Available: https://aclanthology.org/2021.emnlp-main.27

Emery-Xu, N., Jordan, R., & Trager, R. (2024). International governance of advancing artificial intelligence. AI & SOCIETY. springer.com

European Court of Human Rights. (n.d.). *Case of Halet v. Luxembourg*. Grand Chamber. https://hudoc.echr.coe.int/fre#%22itemid%22:[%22001-223259%22]

European Parliament and Council. (2024, June 13). *Regulation (EU) 2024/1689 laying down harmonised rules on artificial intelligence and amending Regulations*. [2024] OJ L 2024/1689. https://eur-lex.europa.eu/legal-content/EN/TXT/?uri=CELEX%3A32024R1689

European Union. (2016). *General Data Protection Regulation, Article 5*. https://gdpr-info.eu/art-5-gdpr

Express News Service. (2024, November 4). *Deepfake videos of Narayana Murthy, Mukesh Ambani: Bengaluru residents lose Rs 87 lakh in trading scam*. The Indian Express. https://indianexpress.com/article/cities/bangalore/deepfake-videos-narayana-murthy-mukesh-ambani-bengaluru-trading-scam-9654607/

Fabiano, N., Gupta, A., Bhambra, N., Luu, B., Wong, S., Maaz, M. G., Fiedorowicz, J. L., Smith, A., & Solmi, M. (2024). How to optimize the systematic review process using AI tools. ncbi.nlm.nih.gov

Facts and figures: Ending violence against women. (2022).

Fan, N., Cai, W., & Zhao, Y. (2008, December). Research on the Model of Multiple Levels for Determining Sentiment of Text. In *2008 IEEE Pacific-Asia Workshop on Computational Intelligence and Industrial Application* (Vol. 1, pp. 267-271). IEEE.

Fazil, A. W., Akbari, R., Quchi, M. M., Khaliqyar, K. Q., & Hakimi, M. (2023). Comparative Analysis of Machine Learning Models for Data Classification: An In-Depth Exploration. *Journal of Computer Science and Technology Studies*, *5*(4), 160–168. DOI: 10.32996/jcsts.2023.5.4.16

Feinberg, T., & Robey, N. (2009). Cyberbullying. *Education Digest*, *74*(7), 26.

Fersini, E., Gasparini, F., Rizzi, G., Saibene, A., Chulvi, B., Rosso, P., Lees, A., & Sorensen, J. (2022). *SemEval-2022 Task 5: Multimedia Automatic Misogyny Identification*. https://cloud.google.com/vision/docs/

Fersini, E., Nozza, D., & Rosso, P. (2018). *Overview of the Evalita 2018 Task on Automatic Misogyny Identification (AMI)*. https://figure-eight.com/

Fersini, E., Nozza, D., & Rosso, P. (2020a). *AMI @ EVALITA2020: Automatic Misogyny Identification*.

Fersini, E., Nozza, D., & Rosso, P. (2020b). *AMI @ EVALITA2020: Automatic Misogyny Identification*.

Fersini, E., Rosso, P., & Anzovino, M. (2018). *Overview of the Task on Automatic Misogyny Identification at IberEval 2018*. https://figure-eight.com/

Fleck, A. (2024). *Chart: 2 in 3 People Often Encounter Hate Speech Online | Statista*. Statista Content & Design. https://www.statista.com/chart/33299/online-hate-speech-encounters/

Fortuna, P., & Nunes, S. (2018a). A survey on automatic detection of hate speech in text. In *ACM Computing Surveys* (Vol. 51, Issue 4). Association for Computing Machinery. DOI: 10.1145/3232676

Fortuna, P., Domínguez, M., Wanner, L., & Talat, Z. (2022). *Directions for NLP Practices Applied to Online Hate Speech Detection.*

Fortuna, P., Dominguez, M., Wanner, L., & Talat, Z. (2022). Directions for NLP Practices Applied to Online Hate Speech Detection. *Proceedings of the 2022 Conference on Empirical Methods in Natural Language Processing*, 11794–11805. https://doi.org/DOI: 10.18653/v1/2022.emnlp-main.809

Fortuna, P., Soler-Company, J., & Wanner, L. (2021). How well do hate speech, toxicity, abusive and offensive language classification models generalize across datasets? *Information Processing & Management, 58*(3), 102524. Advance online publication. DOI: 10.1016/j.ipm.2021.102524

Founta, A., Djouvas, C., Chatzakou, D., Leontiadis, I., Blackburn, J., Stringhini, G., Vakali, A., Sirivianos, M., & Kourtellis, N. (2018). Large scale crowdsourcing and characterization of twitter abusive behavior. *Proceedings of the International AAAI Conference on Web and Social Media, 12*(1). DOI: 10.1609/icwsm.v12i1.14991

Francis, N. & Tóth, G. (2022). Trend and network analysis to reveal disciplinary position of soil science and its sub-disciplines. Agrokémia és Talajtan. akjournals.com

Fraser, K. C., Dawkins, H., & Kiritchenko, S. (2025). Detecting ai-generated text: Factors influencing detectability with current methods. *Journal of Artificial Intelligence Research, 82*, 2233–2278. DOI: 10.1613/jair.1.16665

Frenda, S. (2018). *The role of sarcasm in hate speech. A multilingual perspective*. https://alt.qcri.org/semeval2019/index

Frenda, S., Ghanem, B., Montes-Y-Gómez, M., & Rosso, P. (2019). Online hate speech against women: Automatic identification of misogyny and sexism on twitter. *Journal of Intelligent & Fuzzy Systems, 36*(5), 4743–4752. DOI: 10.3233/JIFS-179023

Gandhi, A., Ahir, P., Shah, P., Cambria, E., Hussain, A., Lohiya, R., Adhvaryu, K., & Poria, S. (2024). Hate speech detection: A comprehensive review of recent works. *Expert Systems: International Journal of Knowledge Engineering and Neural Networks, 41*(8), e13562. Advance online publication. DOI: 10.1111/exsy.13562

Gao, J. & Wang, D. (2023). Quantifying the Benefit of Artificial Intelligence for Scientific Research. [PDF]

Gao, L., & Huang, R. (2017). Detecting Online Hate Speech Using Context-Aware Models. *RANLP 2017 - Recent Advances in Natural Language Processing Meet Deep Learning*, 260–266. https://doi.org/DOI: 10.26615/978-954-452-049-6_036

García-Díaz, J. A., Cánovas-García, M., Colomo-Palacios, R., & Valencia-García, R. (2021). Detecting misogyny in Spanish tweets. An approach based on linguistics features and word embeddings. *Future Generation Computer Systems*, *114*, 506–518. DOI: 10.1016/j.future.2020.08.032

García-Díaz, J. A., Jiménez-Zafra, S. M., & Valencia-García, R. (2021). UMUTeam at MeOffendEs 2021: Ensemble learning for offensive language identification using linguistic features, fine-grained negation, and transformers. In *MeOffendEs at IberLEF 2021* (pp. 157–166). CEUR Workshop Proceedings., https://ceur-ws.org/Vol-2943/

Garg, S., Sagtani, A., Kothari, A., Golakia, J., & Olaniyi, R. O. (2025). Climate Change Analytics Using Artificial Intelligence: Focusing on Legal and Ethical Considerations. In *Community Resilience and Climate Change Challenges: Pursuit of Sustainable Development Goals (SDGs)* (pp. 13-28). IGI Global Scientific Publishing. DOI: DOI: 10.4018/979-8-3693-6522-9.ch002

Garg, S., Jadia, U., Sagtani, A., & Hiran, K. K. (2024, July). ECG-Lense: Benchmarking ML & DL Models on PTB-XL Dataset. In *2024 International Conference on Emerging Trends in Networks and Computer Communications (ETNCC)* (pp. 1-8). IEEE. DOI: DOI: 10.1109/ETNCC63262.2024.10767459

Gašević, D., Siemens, G., & Sadiq, S. (2023). Empowering learners for the age of artificial intelligence. [sciencedirect.com]. *Computers and Education: Artificial Intelligence*, *4*, 100130.

Gaurav, A., Gupta, B. B., Chui, K. T., Arya, V., & Chaurasia, P. (2023). Deep learning- based hate speech detection on Twitter. 2023 IEEE 13th International Conference on Consumer Electronics - Berlin (ICCE-Berlin), 1–6. DOI: 10.1109/ICCE- Berlin58801.2023.10375620

Gavi, K. (2025) *Ethical Challenges in AI-Powered Hate Speech Detection: Balancing Automated Moderation and Dataset Creation*. 12 Jan. 2025. www.researchgate.net/publication/387949183

Geetanjali, & Kumar, M. (2025). Exploring hate speech detection: challenges, resources, current research and future directions. *Multimedia Tools and Applications*, 1–37. DOI: 10.1007/S11042-025-20716-2/METRICS

Geng, Y. (2023, January). Comparing "deepfake" regulatory regimes in the United States, the European Union, and China. *Georgetown Law Technology Review, 7*(1), 157. https://georgetownlawtechreview.org/comparing-deepfake-regulatory-regimes-in-the-united-states-the-european-union-and-china/GLTR-01-2023/

Ghiurău, D., & Popescu, D. E. (2025). Distinguishing Reality from AI: Approaches for Detecting Synthetic Content. *Computers, 14*(1), 1. DOI: 10.3390/computers14010001

Ghosh, S., & Caliskan, A. (2023). ChatGPT Perpetuates Gender Bias in Machine Translation and Ignores Non-Gendered Pronouns: Findings across Bengali and Five other Low-Resource Languages. *Proceedings of AAAI/ACM Conference on AI, Ethics, and Society (AIES '23), 1.* XXXXXXX.XXXXXXX

Giorgi, T., Cima, L., Fagni, T., Avvenuti, M., & Cresci, S. (2024). Human and LLM Biases in Hate Speech Annotations: A Socio-Demographic Analysis of Annotators and Targets. *arXiv (Cornell University).* https://doi.org//arxiv.2410.07991DOI: 10.48550

Giyanani, R., & Desai, M. (2014). Spam detection using natural language processing. IOSR Journal of Computer Engineering (IOSR-JCE), 16(5), 116-119.

Goenaga, I., Atutxa, A., Gojenola, K., Casillas, A., Díaz De Ilarraza, A., Ezeiza, N., Oronoz, M., Pérez, A., & Perez De Viñaspre, O. (2018). *Automatic Misogyny Identification Using Neural Networks.* http://ixa.si.ehu.es/

Gómez, R., Gibert, A., Gómez-Adorno, A., & Pardo, L. "Exploring hate speech detection in multimodal publications," in *Proc. IEEE Winter Conf. Applications of Computer Vision Workshops (WACVW)*, 2020, pp. 45–52. [Online]. Available: https://arxiv.org/abs/2005.04790 DOI: 10.1109/WACV45572.2020.9093414

Gov.UK. (n.d.). *AI Safety Summit 2023: The Bletchley Declaration.* https://www.gov.uk/government/publications/ai-safety-summit-2023-the-bletchley-declaration

Government of India. (2000). *The Information Technology Act, 2000.*

Government of India. (2023). *The Bhartiya Nyay Sanhita.* BNS.

Government of India. (2025). *The Digital Personal Data Protection Rules 2025.* https://innovateindia.mygov.in/dpdp-rules-2025/

Gowrishankar, J., Deepak, S., & Srivastava, M. (2024, September). Countering the Rise of AI-Generated Content with Innovative Detection Strategies and Large Language Models. In *2024 International Conference on Advances in Computing Research on Science Engineering and Technology (ACROSET)* (pp. 1-6). IEEE.

Graham, M. (2024, June 26). *Deepfakes: Federal and state regulation aims to curb a growing threat*. Thomson Reuters Practical Law. https://www.thomsonreuters.com/en-us/posts/government/deepfakes-federal-state-regulation/

Guenduez, A. A. & Mettler, T. (2023). Strategically constructed narratives on artificial intelligence: What stories are told in governmental artificial intelligence policies?. Government Information Quarterly. sciencedirect.com

Guest, E., Vidgen, B., Sastry, N., Tyson, G., & Margetts, H. (2021). *An Expert Annotated Dataset for the Detection of Online Misogyny*. https://github.com/ellamguest/

Guiding Principles on Business and Human Rights – Implementing the United Nations. *"Protect, Respect and Remedy" Framework, United Nations Human Rights Office of the High Commissioner, 2011*. (2011).

Gunning, D., Stefik, M., Choi, J., Miller, T., Stumpf, S., & Yang, G. Z. (2019). XAI-Explainable artificial intelligence. *Science Robotics*, *4*(37), eaay7120. Advance online publication. DOI: 10.1126/scirobotics.aay7120 PMID: 33137719

Gupta, M., & Agrawal, P. (2022). Compression of Deep Learning Models for Text: A Survey. *ACM Transactions on Knowledge Discovery from Data*, *16*(4), 1–55. DOI: 10.1145/3487045

Guragain, A., Poudel, N., Piryani, R., & Khanal, B. (2024). *NLPineers@ NLU of Devanagari Script Languages 2025: Hate Speech Detection using Ensembling of BERT-based models*. https://arxiv.org/abs/2412.08163

Gursoy, F., & Kakadiaris, A. I. (2023). Artificial intelligence research strategy of the United States: critical assessment and policy recommendations. ncbi.nlm.nih.gov

Hajari, S. (2025). *Exploring the Limitations of Generative AI in Understanding Social Media Acronyms and Slang*. https://www.academia.edu/127544762/Exploring_the_Limitations_of_Generative_AI_in_Understanding_Social_Media_Acronyms_and_Slang

Hall, H. K. (2018). Deepfake videos: When seeing isn't believing. *Catholic University Journal of Law & Technology*, *27*(1), 51. https://scholarship.law.edu/jlt/vol27/iss1/4

Hana, K. M., Bramantoro, A., Adiwijaya, A., & Faraby, S. A. (2020). *Multi-label Classification of Indonesian Hate Speech on Twitter Using Support Vector Machines. 2018 janua*, 1–7. DOI: 10.1109/ICoDSA50139.2020.9212992

Haq, I., Qiu, W., Guo, J., & Tang, P. (2023). Pashto offensive language detection: A benchmark dataset and monolingual Pashto BERT. *PeerJ. Computer Science*, *9*, e1617. DOI: 10.7717/peerj-cs.1617 PMID: 38077561

Hardt, M., Price, E., & Srebro, N. (2016). Equality of opportunity in supervised learning. *Advances in Neural Information Processing Systems*, •••, 3323–3331.

Hashmi, E., Yayilgan, S. Y., & Abomhara, M. (2025). Metalinguist: Enhancing hate speech detection with cross-lingual meta-learning. *Complex & Intelligent Systems*, *11*(4), 179. Advance online publication. DOI: 10.1007/s40747-025-01808-w

Hate crime: Law Commision United Kingdom Government. (2022).

Helmus, T. C. (2022). *Artificial intelligence, deepfakes, and disinformation: A primer*. RAND Corporation. https://www.jstor.org/stable/resrep42027

Hettiachchi, D., Holcombe-James, I., Livingstone, S., de Silva, A., Lease, M., Salim, F. D., & Sanderson, M. (2023). How Crowd Worker Factors Influence Subjective Annotations: A Study of Tagging Misogynistic Hate Speech in Tweets. *Proceedings of the AAAI Conference on Human Computation and Crowdsourcing*, *11*, 38–50. DOI: 10.1609/hcomp.v11i1.27546

Hill, C. (2023, June 29). *OpenAI and Microsoft face class action lawsuits for allegedly violating copyright and privacy laws*. Legal Insider. https://legaltechnology.com/2023/06/29/openai-and-microsoft-face-class-action-lawsuit-for-allegedly-violating-copyright-and-privacy-laws/

Hiran, K. K., Doshi, R., & Patel, M. (Eds.). (2024). *Modern Technology in Healthcare and Medical Education: Blockchain, IoT, AR, and VR: Blockchain, IoT, AR, and VR*. IGI Global.

Hiran, K. K., Hemachandran, K., Pise, A., & Rabi, B. J. (Eds.). (2023). *Handbook of Research on AI and Knowledge Engineering for Real-Time Business Intelligence*. IGI global. DOI: 10.4018/978-1-6684-6519-6

Hiran, K. K., Jain, R. K., Lakhwani, K., & Doshi, R. (2021). *Machine Learning: Master Supervised and Unsupervised Learning Algorithms with Real Examples (English Edition)*. BPB Publications.

Hiran, K. K., Khazanchi, D., Vyas, A. K., & Padmanaban, S. (Eds.). (2021). *Machine learning for sustainable development* (Vol. 9). Walter de Gruyter GmbH & Co KG. DOI: 10.1515/9783110702514

How Facebook uses super-efficient AI models to detect hate speech. (n.d.). Ai.meta.com. https://ai.meta.com/blog/how-facebook-uses-super-efficient-ai-models-to-detect-hate-speech/

https://irlab.org/metahate.html

Huang, F., An, J., & Kwak, H. (2023). Is ChatGPT better than Human Annotators? *Potential and Limitations of ChatGPT in Explaining Implicit Hate Speech, 294–297*, 294–297. Advance online publication. DOI: 10.1145/3543873.3587368

Hussain, W., Mabrok, M., Gao, H., & Rabhi, A. F., & A. Rashed, E. (2024). Revolutionising healthcare with artificial intelligence: A bibliometric analysis of 40 years of progress in health systems. ncbi.nlm.nih.gov

Ilhan, S. S., Sivakumar, S. N. J., Ramesh, S., Sreeram, N., & Rajalakshmi, R. (2024). Hate speech detection and classification using NLP. *2024 Second International Conference on Advances in Information Technology (ICAIT)*, 1–7. DOI: 10.1109/ICAIT61638.2024.10690655

India, A. I. (n.d.). *AI Task Force: Ministry of Commerce and Industry initiatives.* https://indiaai.gov.in/government/ministry-of-commerce-and-industry

Iqbal, M., Abid, M. M., Ahmad, M., & Khurshid, F. (2016). Study on the effectiveness of spam detection technologies. [IJITCS]. *International Journal of Information Technology and Computer Science*, *8*(1), 11–21.

Iyengar, S., & Kalpana, M. (2017). Integrated SPAM detection for multilingual emails. In *2017 International Conference on Advances in Computing, Communication and Informatics (ICACCI)*, pp. 2352-2357.

Jacobs, J. B., & Potter, K. (2000). *Hate crimes: Criminal law and identity politics.* Oxford University Press.

Jahan, M. S., & Oussalah, M. (2023). A systematic review of hate speech automatic detection using natural language processing. *Neurocomputing*, *546*, 126232. DOI: 10.1016/j.neucom.2023.126232

Jaikishan Kakubhai Saraf v. Peppy Store, 2024 SCC OnLine Del 3664 (India).

Jain, A., Virwani, H., Shrotriya, N., & Somwanshi, D. (2023). Information retrieval using data mining. In Machine Vision and Augmented Intelligence: Select Proceedings of MAI 2022 (pp. 287-293). Singapore: Springer Nature Singapore.

Jaswal, V., & Sood, M. (2013). Spam Detection System Using Hidden Markov Model. *International Journal of Advanced Research in Computer Science and Software Engineering*, *3*(7), 137–141.

Javidan, A. P., Li, A., Lee, M. H., Forbes, T. L., & Naji, F. (2022). A systematic review and bibliometric analysis of applications of artificial intelligence and machine learning in vascular surgery. [HTML]. *Annals of Vascular Surgery*, *85*, 395–405. DOI: 10.1016/j.avsg.2022.03.019 PMID: 35339595

Jedličková, A. (2024). Ethical considerations in Risk management of autonomous and intelligent systems. *Ethics & Bioethics*, *14*(1–2), 80–95. DOI: 10.2478/ebce-2024-0007

Jha, A., & Mamidi, R. (2017). *When does a Compliment become Sexist? Analysis and Classification of Ambivalent Sexism using Twitter Data*. Association for Computational Linguistics. https://twitter.com/chicagotribune/status/762401317050605568

Jha, R., & Kumar, A. (2013). Feature Level Opinion Mining of Movie Reviews. *International Journal of Computer Applications*, *62*(10), 7–12.

Jindal, N., & Liu, B. (2008, February). Opinion spam and analysis. In *Proceedings of the 2008 international conference on web search and data mining* (pp. 219-230).

Joshy, A., & Sundar, S. (2022, December 16). *Analyzing the Performance of Sentiment Analysis using BERT, DistilBERT, and RoBERTa*. DOI: 10.1109/IPRECON55716.2022.10059542

Kamyab, M., Liu, G., & Adjeisah, M. (2021). Attention-Based CNN and Bi-LSTM Model Based on TF-IDF and GloVe Word Embedding for Sentiment Analysis. *Applied Sciences (Basel, Switzerland)*, *11*(23), 11255. DOI: 10.3390/app112311255

Karim, M. R., Dey, S. K., Islam, T., Sarker, S., Menon, M. H., Hossain, K., Hossain, M. A., & Decker, S. (2021a). Deephateexplainer: Explainable hate speech detection in under-resourced bengali language. *2021 IEEE 8th International Conference on Data Science and Advanced Analytics (DSAA)*, 1–10.

Karim, M. R., Dey, S. K., Islam, T., Sarker, S., Menon, M. H., Hossain, K., Hossain, M. A., & Decker, S. (2021b). Deephateexplainer: Explainable hate speech detection in under-resourced bengali language. *2021 IEEE 8th International Conference on Data Science and Advanced Analytics (DSAA)*, 1–10.

Kar, S., Mullick, S., Roy, C., Saha, R., & Das, M. (2023). AI Horizons: Unveiling the Future of Generative Intelligence. *International Journal of Advanced Research in Science. Tongxin Jishu*, *387–391*, 387–391. Advance online publication. DOI: 10.48175/IJARSCT-12969

Kasthuriarachchy, B. H., De Zoysa, K., & Premaratne, H. L. (2014, December). Enhanced bag-of-words model for phrase-level sentiment analysis. In 2014 14th International Conference on Advances in ICT for Emerging Regions (ICTer) (pp. 210-214). IEEE.

Kaur, G., Kaushik, A., & Sharma, S. (2019). Cooking is creating emotion: A study on hinglish sentiments of youtube cookery channels using semi-supervised approach. *Big Data and Cognitive Computing*, *3*(3), 1–19. DOI: 10.3390/bdcc3030037

Kesarwani, T., Mittal, R., Panwar, D., Saini, G. L., & Kumar, S. (2023, December). Facial Recognition Model Using Custom Designed Deep Learning Architecture. In International Conference on Communication and Intelligent Systems (pp. 457-467). Singapore: Springer Nature Singapore.

Ketsbaia, L., Issac, B., Chen, X., & Jacob, S. M. (2023). A Multi-Stage Machine Learning and Fuzzy Approach to Cyber-Hate Detection. *IEEE Access : Practical Innovations, Open Solutions, 11*, 56046–56065. DOI: 10.1109/ACCESS.2023.3282834

Khalifa, M., Albadawy, M., & Iqbal, U. (2024). Advancing clinical decision support: The role of artificial intelligence across six domains. Computer Methods and Programs in .... sciencedirect.com

Khan, A., & Baharudin, B. (2011, September). Sentiment classification using sentence-level semantic orientation of opinion terms from blogs. In *2011 National Postgraduate Conference* (pp. 1-7). IEEE.

Khan, A., Yousaf, J., Muhammad, T., & Ismail, M. (2023). HATE SPEECH DETECTION USING MACHINE LEARNING AND N-GRAM TECHNIQUES. [Jurnal Teknik Informatika Dan Sistem Informasi]. *JATISI, 10*(1). Advance online publication. DOI: 10.35957/jatisi.v10i1.4711

Khandelwal, A., Swami, S., Akhtar, S. S., & Shrivastava, M. (2018). *Humor Detection in English-Hindi Code-Mixed Social Media Content : Corpus and Baseline System*. https://github.com/Ankh2295/

Khan, M. M., Shahzad, K., & Malik, M. K. (2021). Hate Speech Detection in Roman Urdu. *ACM Transactions on Asian and Low-Resource Language Information Processing, 20*(1), 1–19. DOI: 10.1145/3414524

Khan, S., Abbasi, R. A., Sindhu, M. A., Arafat, S., Khattak, A. S., Daud, A., & Mushtaq, M. (2024). Predicting the victims of hate speech on microblogging platforms. *Heliyon, 10*(23), e40611. Advance online publication. DOI: 10.1016/j.heliyon.2024.e40611 PMID: 39698099

Kim, J., Lee, B., & Sohn, K.-A. (2022). *Why Is It Hate Speech? Masked Rationale Prediction for Explainable Hate Speech Detection*. https://arxiv.org/abs/2211.00243

Kiritchenko, S., Nejadgholi, I., & Fraser, K. C. (2021). Confronting Abusive Language Online: A Survey from the Ethical and Human Rights Perspective. *Journal of Artificial Intelligence Research, 71*, 431–478. DOI: 10.1613/jair.1.12590

Kirk, H. R., Yin, W., Vidgen, B., & Röttger, P. (2023). *SemEval-2023 Task 10: Explainable Detection of Online Sexism*. https://arxiv.org/abs/2303.04222 DOI: 10.18653/v1/2023.semeval-1.305

Kolotouchkina, O., Barroso, C. L., & Sánchez, J. L. M. (2022). Smart cities, the digital divide, and people with disabilities. *Cities (London, England)*, *123*, 103613. DOI: 10.1016/j.cities.2022.103613

Koren, Y., Bell, R., & Volinsky, C. (2009). Matrix factorization techniques for recommender systems. *Computer*, *42*(8), 30–37. DOI: 10.1109/MC.2009.263

Kumar Patra, A., Praharaj, A., Sudarshan, D., & Prasad Chhatoi, B. (2023). AI and business management: Tracking future research agenda through bibliometric network analysis. ncbi.nlm.nih.gov

Kumar, A. (2022). A study: Hate speech and offensive language detection in textual data by using RNN, CNN, LSTM and BERT model. 2022 6th International Conference on Intelligent Computing and Control Systems (ICICCS), 1–6. DOI: 10.1109/ICICCS53718.2022.9788347

Kumar, R., Ojha, A. K., Malmasi, S., & Zampieri, M. (2018). *Benchmarking Aggression Identification in Social Media* (Issue 1). https://competitions.codalab.org/

Kumar, R., Ojha, A. K., Malmasi, S., & Zampieri, M. (2020). *Evaluating Aggression Identification in Social Media*. https://competitions.codalab.org/

Kumarage, T., Bhattacharjee, A., & Garland, J. (2024). Harnessing artificial intelligence to combat online hate: Exploring the challenges and opportunities of large language models in hate speech detection. *arXiv preprint arXiv:2403.08035*.

Kumar, P. (2017). SVM with Gaussian kernel-based image spam detection on TREC07 dataset. In *2017 International Conference on Wireless Communications, Signal Processing and Networking (WiSPNET)*, pp. 1234-1238.

Kunchukuttan, A., Mehta, P., & Bhattacharyya, P. (2018, May). The IIT Bombay English-Hindi Parallel Corpus. *Proceedings of the Eleventh International Conference on Language Resources and Evaluation (LREC 2018)*. https://aclanthology.org/L18-1548

Kurban, C. F., & Şahin, M. (2024). Exploring ChatGPT's Impact on Higher Education–A Case Study. In The Impact of ChatGPT on Higher Education: Exploring the AI Revolution (pp. 1-6). Emerald Publishing Limited. [HTML] DOI: 10.1108/978-1-83797-647-820241001

Kwok, I., & Wang, Y. (2013). *Locate the Hate: Detecting Tweets against Blacks*. http://tempest.wellesley.edu/~ywang5/aaai/paper.html

Lala, C., & Dwivedi, P. (2023). Hate speech detection network using LSTM. *2023 International Conference for Advancement in Technology (ICONAT)*, 1–6. DOI: 10.1109/ICONAT57137.2023.10080786

Lal, Y. K., Kumar, V., Dhar, M., Shrivastava, M., & Koehn, P. (2019). De-mixing sentiment from code-mixed text. *Proceedings of the 57th Annual Meeting of the Association for Computational Linguistics: Student Research Workshop*, 371–377. DOI: 10.18653/v1/P19-2052

Landauer, T. K., Foltz, P. W., & Laham, D. (1998). An introduction to latent semantic analysis. *Discourse Processes*, *25*(2–3), 259–284. DOI: 10.1080/01638539809545028

Lau, R. Y., Zhang, W., Bruza, P. D., & Wong, K. F. (2011, October). Learning domain-specific sentiment lexicons for predicting product sales. In 2011 IEEE 8th International Conference on e-Business Engineering (pp. 131-138). IEEE.

Laurer, M., Van Atteveldt, W., Welbers, K., & Casas, A. (2023). Less Annotating, More Classifying: Addressing the Data Scarcity Issue of Supervised Machine Learning with Deep Transfer Learning and BERT-NLI. *Political Analysis*, *32*(1), 84–100. DOI: 10.1017/pan.2023.20

Leading countries based on YouTube audience size as of January 2023. (2023).

Lee, K., & Ram, S. (2024). Deep learning for hate speech detection: A personality-based approach. In Companion Proceedings of the ACM Web Conference 2024 (WWW '24 Companion) (pp. 1667–1671). DOI: 10.1145/3589335.3652502

Li, S., Zhang, H., Xu, W., Chen, G., & Guo, J. (2010, August). Exploiting combined multi-level model for document sentiment analysis. In 2010 20th International Conference on Pattern Recognition (pp. 4141-4144). IEEE.

Liao, X., Yao, C., Jin, F., Zhang, J., & Liu, L. (2024). … intelligence-assisted decision-making software in hospitals in China: a qualitative study using the updated Consolidated Framework for Implementation Research. BMJ open. bmj.com

Limbago, J. (2023). Designing User-Centric Private Conversation Methods in the Metaverse (Master's thesis).

Lim, E. P., Nguyen, V. A., Jindal, N., Liu, B., & Lauw, H. W. (2010, October). Detecting product review spammers using rating behaviors. In *Proceedings of the 19th ACM international conference on Information and knowledge management* (pp. 939-948).

Lin, D. (2023). Appliance of Deep Learning on hate speech detection: A systematic review. *Highlights in Science. Engineering and Technology*, *31*, 76–81. DOI: 10.54097/hset.v31i.4816

Lin, G., Sun, N., Nepal, S., Zhang, J., Xiang, Y., & Hassan, H. (2017). Statistical Twitter Spam Detection Demystified: Performance, Stability and Scalability. *IEEE Access : Practical Innovations, Open Solutions*, *5*, 11142–11154.

Liu, L., Nie, X., & Wang, H. (2012, October). Toward a fuzzy domain sentiment ontology tree for sentiment analysis. In 2012 5th International Congress on Image and Signal Processing (pp. 1620-1624). IEEE.

Liu, B., Cen, S., He, X., Jiang, X., Xiao, B., & Dou, W. (2023). Adversarial Attacks on Large Language Model-Based System and Mitigating Strategies: A Case Study on ChatGPT. *Security and Communication Networks*, *2023*, 1–10. DOI: 10.1155/2023/8691095

Li, X., Sun, A., & Datta, A. (2016). Identifying Informative Reviews Using Dependency Parsing and Sentiment Analysis. In *Proceedings of the 2016 Conference on Empirical Methods in Natural Language Processing (EMNLP)*, pages 1249-1259. Association for Computational Linguistics.

Lundberg, S. M., & Lee, S.-I. (2017). A unified approach to interpreting model predictions. *Advances in Neural Information Processing Systems*, •••, 30.

Lynn, T., Endo, P. T., Rosati, P., Silva, I., Santos, G. L., & Ging, D. (2019a). *A Comparison of Machine Learning Approaches for Detecting Misogynistic Speech in Urban Dictionary*. https://deepmind.com

Lynn, T., Endo, P. T., Rosati, P., Silva, I., Santos, G. L., & Ging, D. (2019b). Data set for automatic detection of online misogynistic speech. *Data in Brief*, *26*, 104223. Advance online publication. DOI: 10.1016/j.dib.2019.104223 PMID: 31508461

MacAvaney, S., Yao, H.-R., Yang, E., Russell, K., Goharian, N., & Frieder, O. (2019). Hate speech detection: Challenges and solutions. *PLoS One*, *14*(8), e0221152. DOI: 10.1371/journal.pone.0221152 PMID: 31430308

Madhavi, M., Agal, S., Odedra, N. D., Chowdhary, H., Ruprah, T. S., Vuyyuru, V. A., & El-Ebiary, Y. A. B. (2024). Elevating Offensive Language Detection: CNN-GRU and BERT for Enhanced Hate Speech Identification. *International Journal of Advanced Computer Science and Applications*, *15*(5). Advance online publication. DOI: 10.14569/IJACSA.2024.01505118

Madiega, T. (2022, November 11). *Digital Services Act (EU legislation in progress)*. European Parliamentary Research Service (EPRS). https://www.europarl.europa.eu/RegData/etudes/BRIE/2021/689357/EPRS_BRI(2021)689357_EN.pdf

Mahrishi, M., Hiran, K. K., Meena, G., & Sharma, P. (2020). *Machine Learning and Deep Learning in Real-Time Applications*. IGI Global. https://www.igi-global.com/book/machine-learning-deep-learning-real/240152

Mahrishi, M., Hiran, K. K., Meena, G., & Sharma, P. (Eds.). (2020). *Machine learning and deep learning in real-time applications*. IGI global., DOI: 10.4018/978-1-7998-3095-5

Malarvizhi, R., & Saraswathi, K. (2013). Content-Based Spam Filtering and Detection Algorithms-An Efficient Analysis & Comparison. [IJETT]. *International Journal of Engineering Trends and Technology*, *4*(9).

Malhotra, C., & Malhotra, U. (2024). Putting interests of digital nagriks first: Digital Personal Data Protection (DPDP) Act 2023 of India. *The Indian Journal of Public Administration*, *70*, 516. DOI: 10.1177/00195561241271575

Mallic, A., & Ganguli, P. (2024, September 27). *Understanding of digital arrest: Definition, methods and implications. SSRN*. http://dx.doi.org/DOI: 10.2139/ssrn.5019885

Manda, D. P., & Misra, A. N. (2024). Report: India will replace the Information Technology Act with the proposed Digital India Act: Out with the old, in with the new? *Global Privacy Law Review*, *5*(1), 50. DOI: 10.54648/gplr2024002

Mandl, T., Modha, S., Shahi, G. K., Jaiswal, A. K., Nandini, D., Patel, D., Majumder, P., & Schäfer, J. (2020). Overview of the HASOC track at FIRE 2020: Hate speech and offensive content identification in Indo-European languages. In CEUR Workshop Proceedings. https://ceur-ws.org/Vol-2757/

Mandl, T., Modha, S., Shahi, G. K., Kumar Jaiswal, A., Nandini, D., Patel, D., & Schäfer, J. (2020). *Overview of the HASOC track at FIRE 2020: Hate Speech and Offensive Content Identification in Indo-European Languages under Creative Commons License Attribution 4.0 International (CC BY 4.0)*. http://ceur-ws.org

Mandl, T., Modha, S., Shahi, G. K., Madhu, H., Satapara, S., Schäfer, J., Ranasinghe, T., Zampieri, M., Nandini, D., Kumar Jaiswal, A., & Zampieri, M. (2021). *Overview of the HASOC Subtrack at FIRE 2021: Hate Speech and Offensive Content Identification in English and Indo-Aryan Languages under Creative Commons License Attribution 4.0 International (CC BY 4.0)*. http://ceur-ws.org

Mandl, T., Modha, S., Majumder, P., Patel, D., Dave, M., Mandlia, C., & Patel, A. (2019). Overview of the hasoc track at fire 2019: Hate speech and offensive content identification in indo-european languages. *Proceedings of the 11th Annual Meeting of the Forum for Information Retrieval Evaluation*, 14–17. DOI: 10.1145/3368567.3368584

Manning, D., Raghavan, P., & Schütze, H. (2008). *Introduction to Information Retrieval*. Cambridge University Press. DOI: 10.1017/CBO9780511809071

Mansur, Z., Omar, N., & Tiun, S. (2023). Twitter Hate Speech Detection: A Systematic Review of Methods, Taxonomy Analysis, Challenges, and Opportunities. *IEEE Access : Practical Innovations, Open Solutions*, *11*, 16226–16249. DOI: 10.1109/ACCESS.2023.3239375

Manuel, M., Dongre, P., Alhamadani, A., & Gračanin, D. (2021, July). Supporting embodied and remote collaboration in shared virtual environments. In *International Conference on Human-Computer Interaction* (pp. 639-652). Cham: Springer International Publishing. DOI: 10.1007/978-3-030-77599-5_44

Maragno, G., Tangi, L., Gastaldi, L., & Benedetti, M. (2023). Exploring the factors, affordances and constraints outlining the implementation of Artificial Intelligence in public sector organizations. [sciencedirect.com]. *International Journal of Information Management*, *73*, 102686. DOI: 10.1016/j.ijinfomgt.2023.102686

Marolla-Gajardo, J., & Riquelme Plaza, I. (2025). Teacher Education, Diversity, and the Prevention of Hate Speech: Ethical and Political Foundations for Inclusive Citizenship. *Societies (Basel, Switzerland)*, *15*(5), 139. DOI: 10.3390/soc15050139

Marra, M. (2024). Co-creating evaluation for policy relevance: The challenges of the post-truth world. Evaluation in the Post-Truth World. [HTML] Letterie, G. (2021). Three ways of knowing: the integration of clinical expertise, evidence-based medicine, and artificial intelligence in assisted reproductive technologies. Journal of Assisted Reproduction and Genetics. nih.gov

Mathew, B., Mukherjee, A., Yimam, S. M., Goyal, P., Biemann, C., & Saha, P. (2021). HateXplain: A Benchmark Dataset for Explainable Hate Speech Detection. *Proceedings of the AAAI Conference on Artificial Intelligence*, *35*(17), 14867–14875. DOI: 10.1609/aaai.v35i17.17745

Mathur, P., Ratn Shah, R., Sawhney, R., & Mahata, D. (2018). *Detecting Offensive Tweets in Hindi-English Code-Switched Language*. http://t... Mathur, P., Sawhney, R., Ayyar, M., & Ratn Shah, R. (2018). *Did you offend me? Classification of Offensive Tweets in Hinglish Language*. www.github.com/pmathur5k10/

Mathur, P., Sawhney, R., Ayyar, M., & Shah, R. (2018). Did you offend me? classification of offensive tweets in hinglish language. *Proceedings of the 2nd Workshop on Abusive Language Online (ALW2)*, 138–148. DOI: 10.18653/v1/W18-5118

Maturana, B., Salama, A. M., & McInneny, A. (2021). Architecture, urbanism and health in a post-pandemic virtual world. *Archnet-IJAR: International Journal of Architectural Research, 15*(1), 1–9. DOI: 10.1108/ARCH-02-2021-0024

Matusitz, J., & Dacas, J. (2024). Other Problems: Privacy Concerns, Surveillance, and Hate Speech. In *Communication in the Metaverse* (pp. 161–179). Springer Nature Switzerland. DOI: 10.1007/978-3-031-63485-7_9

Meena, G., Dhanwal, B., Mahrishi, M., & Hiran, K. K. (2021, August). Performance comparison of network intrusion detection system based on different pre-processing methods and deep neural network. In *Proceedings of the International Conference on Data Science, Machine Learning and Artificial Intelligence* (pp. 110-115). DOI: 10.1145/3484824.3484878

Mehta, H., & Passi, K. (2022). Social Media Hate Speech Detection Using Explainable Artificial Intelligence (XAI). *Algorithms, 15*(8), 291. DOI: 10.3390/a15080291

Mienye, I. D., Obaido, G., & Swart, T. G. (2024). Recurrent Neural Networks: A Comprehensive Review of Architectures, Variants, and Applications. *Information (Basel), 15*(9), 517. DOI: 10.3390/info15090517

Mihalcea, R., Liu, H., & Lieberman, H. (2006). NLP (Natural Language Processing) for NLP (Natural Language Programming). In Gelbukh, A. (Ed.), Lecture Notes in Computer Science: Vol. 3878. *Computational Linguistics and Intelligent Text Processing* (pp. 319–330). Springer., DOI: 10.1007/11671299_34

Mijwil, M. M., Naji, A. S., Doshi, R., Hiran, K. K., Bala, I., & Ali, G. (2024). The effect of human-computer interaction on new applications by exploring the use case of ChatGPT in healthcare services. In modern technology in healthcare and medical education: Blockchain, IoT, AR, and VR. IGI Global.

Mijwil, M. M., Naji, A. S., Doshi, R., Hiran, K. K., Bala, I., & Ali, G. (2024). The effect of human-computer interaction on new applications by exploring the use case of ChatGPT in healthcare services. In modern technology in healthcare and medical education: Blockchain, IoT, AR, and VR. IGI Global. DOI: 10.4018/979-8-3693-5493-3.ch005

Mijwil, M. M., Gök, M., Doshi, R., Hiran, K. K., & Kösesoy, I. (2023). Utilizing Artificial Intelligence Techniques to Improve the Performance of Wireless Nodes. In *Applications of Artificial Intelligence in Wireless Communication Systems* (pp. 150–162). IGI Global., DOI: 10.4018/978-1-6684-7348-1.ch010

Mijwil, M. M., Hiran, K. K., Doshi, R., Dadhich, M., Al-Mistarehi, A. H., & Bala, I. (2023). ChatGPT and the future of academic integrity in the artificial intelligence era: A new frontier. *Al-Salam Journal for Engineering and Technology*, *2*(2), 116–127. DOI: 10.55145/ajest.2023.02.02.015

Miller, G. (2024, March 14). Transcript: US House Subcommittee hearing on the harms of deepfakes. *TechPolicy.Press*. https://www.techpolicy.press/house-hearing-addressing-deepfake-harms

Ministry of Electronics and Information Technology (MeitY). (2023). *Information Technology (Intermediary Guidelines and Digital Media Ethics Code) Amendment Rules, 2022: Rule 3(1)(b)*. https://www.meity.gov.in/writereaddata/files/Information%20Technology%20%28Intermediary%20Guidelines%20and%20Digital%20Media%20Ethics%20Code%29%20Rules%2C%202021%20%28updated%2006.04.2023%29-.pdf

Ministry of Electronics and Information Technology. (2024, March 15). *Advisory on due diligence by intermediaries/platforms outlined under the Information Technology Act and Information Technology (Intermediary Guidelines and Digital Media Ethics Code) Rules, 2021*. https://www.meity.gov.in/writereaddata/files/Advisory%2015March%202024.pdf

Ministry of Electronics and Information Technology. (2025, January 3). *Draft Digital Personal Data Protection Rules 2025*. https://www.meity.gov.in/writereaddata/files/259889.pdf

Miok, K., Škrlj, B., Robnik-Šikonja, M., & Zaharie, D. (2021). To BAN or Not to BAN: Bayesian Attention Networks for Reliable Hate Speech Detection. *Cognitive Computation*, *14*(1), 353–371. DOI: 10.1007/s12559-021-09826-9

Mittal, R., Pathak, V., & Mithal, A. (2020, October). A novel approach to optimize SLAM using GP-GPU. In Proceedings of International Conference on Data Science and Applications: ICDSA 2019 (pp. 273-280). Singapore: Springer Singapore.

Mittal, R., Agarwal, N., Shukla, P. K., & Khatri, N. (2024, November). An Intelligent Self- Balancing Robot with Integrated Object Detection Using MobileNetV2 and PID Control. In *2024 International Conference on Intelligent & Innovative Practices in Engineering & Management (IIPEM)* (pp. 1-5). IEEE.

Mittal, U. (2023). Detecting Hate Speech Utilizing Deep Convolutional Network and Transformer Models. *IEEE International Conference on Electrical, Electronics, Communication and Computers, ELEXCOM 2023*. DOI: 10.1109/ELEXCOM58812.2023.10370502

Mnassri, K., Rajapaksha, P., Farahbakhsh, R., & Crespi, N. (2022). BERT-based Ensemble Approaches for Hate Speech Detection. *GLOBECOM 2022 - 2022 IEEE Global Communications Conference*, 4649–4654. https://doi.org/DOI: 10.1109/GLOBECOM48099.2022.10001325

Mnassri, K., Farahbakhsh, R., & Crespi, N. (2024). Multilingual Hate Speech Detection: A Semi-Supervised Generative Adversarial Approach. *Entropy (Basel, Switzerland)*, *26*(4), 344. DOI: 10.3390/e26040344 PMID: 38667898

Mohanty, A., & Sahu, S. (2024, November 21). India's advance on AI regulation. *Carnegie India*. https://carnegieendowment.org/research/2024/11/indias-advance-on-ai-regulation?lang=en&center=india

Mohapatra, S. K., Bebarta, D. K., Hu, Y.-C., Srinivasan, K., Das, T. K., & Prasad, S. (2021). Automatic Hate Speech Detection in English-Odia Code Mixed Social Media Data Using Machine Learning Techniques. *Applied Sciences (Basel, Switzerland)*, *11*(18), 8575. DOI: 10.3390/app11188575

Mollas, I., Chrysopoulou, Z., Karlos, S., & Tsoumakas, G. "ETHOS: An online hate speech detection dataset," *arXiv preprint arXiv:2006.08328*, 2020. [Online]. Available: https://arxiv.org/abs/2006.08328

Mollas, I., Chrysopoulou, Z., Tsoumakas, G., & Karlos, S. (2022). ETHOS: A multi-label hate speech detection dataset. *Complex & Intelligent Systems*, *8*(6), 4663–4678. DOI: 10.1007/s40747-021-00608-2

Moneta, A. N. D. R. E. A. (2020). Architecture, heritage, and the metaverse. *Traditional Dwellings and Settlements Review*, *32*(1), 37–49.

Moreno, M. A., Gower, A. D., Brittain, H., & Vaillancourt, T. (2019). Applying Natural Language Processing to Evaluate News Media Coverage of Bullying and Cyberbullying. *Prevention Science*, *20*(8), 1274–1283. DOI: 10.1007/s11121-019-01029-x PMID: 31414277

Mouthami, K., Devi, K. N., & Bhaskaran, V. M. (2013, February). Sentiment analysis and classification based on textual reviews. In 2013 international conference on Information communication and embedded systems (ICICES) (pp. 271-276). IEEE.

Mozafari, M., Farahbakhsh, R., & Crespi, N. (2020). Hate speech detection and racial bias mitigation in social media based on BERT model. *PLoS One*, *15*(8), e0237861. DOI: 10.1371/journal.pone.0237861 PMID: 32853205

Mubarak, H., Hassan, S., & Chowdhury, S. A. (2023). Emojis as anchors to detect Arabic offensive language and hate speech. *Natural Language Engineering*, *29*(6), 1436–1457. DOI: 10.1017/S1351324923000402

Mullah, N. S., & Zainon, W. M. N. W. (2021). Advances in Machine Learning Algorithms for Hate Speech Detection in Social Media: A Review. *IEEE Access : Practical Innovations, Open Solutions*, *9*, 88364–88376. DOI: 10.1109/ACCESS.2021.3089515

Murray, S. O. (1979). The art of gay insulting. *Anthropological Linguistics*, *21*(5), 211–223.

Mutanga, R. T., & Naicker, N., & O, O. (2020). Hate Speech Detection in Twitter using Transformer Methods. *International Journal of Advanced Computer Science and Applications*, *11*(9). Advance online publication. DOI: 10.14569/IJACSA.2020.0110972

Narula, R., & Chaudhary, P. (2025). A comprehensive review on detection of hate speech for multi-lingual data. *Social Network Analysis and Mining*, *14*(1), 244. Advance online publication. DOI: 10.1007/s13278-024-01401-y

Nascimento, F. R. S., Cavalcanti, G. D. C., & Da Costa-Abreu, M. (2023). Exploring Automatic Hate Speech Detection on Social Media: A Focus on Content-Based Analysis. *SAGE Open*, *13*(2). Advance online publication. DOI: 10.1177/21582440231181311

Nascimento, F. R. S., Cavalcanti, G. D. C., & Da Costa-Abreu, M. (2025). Gender bias detection on hate speech classification: An analysis at feature-level. *Neural Computing & Applications*, *37*(5), 3887–3905. DOI: 10.1007/s00521-024-10841-8

Naseeb, A., Ahmad, F., Gelbukh, A., Hussain, N., Zain, M., Sidorov, G., & Qasim, A. (2025). Machine Learning- and Deep Learning-Based Multi-Model System for Hate Speech Detection on Facebook. *Algorithms*, *18*(6), 331. DOI: 10.3390/a18060331

Năstasă, A., Dumitra, T. C., & Grigorescu, A. (2024). Artificial intelligence and sustainable development during the pandemic: An overview of the scientific debates. ncbi.nlm.nih.gov

Newman, J., & Mintrom, M. (2023). Mapping the discourse on evidence-based policy, artificial intelligence, and the ethical practice of policy analysis. Journal of European Public Policy. tandfonline.com Kim, E. S. (2024). Can data science achieve the ideal of evidence-based decision-making in environmental regulation? [HTML]. *Technology in Society*.

Nguyen, T. (2024). Merging public health and automated approaches to address online hate speech. *AI and Ethics*, *4*(2), 441–450. DOI: 10.1007/s43681-023-00281-w PMID: 37360146

Nockleby, J. T. (2000). Hate speech. *Encyclopedia of the American Constitution, 3*(2), 1277–1279.

Nozza, D., Volpetti, C., & Fersini, E. (2019). Unintended bias in misogyny detection. *Proceedings - 2019 IEEE/WIC/ACM International Conference on Web Intelligence, WI 2019*, 149–155. DOI: 10.1145/3350546.3352512

Ohana, B., & Tierney, B. (2009). Sentiment classification of reviews using SentiWordNet.

Okoye, K., Nganji, J. T., Hiran, K. K., & Hosseini, S. (2024, May). Impact and implications of AI methods and tools for the future of education. []). Frontiers Media SA.]. *Frontiers in Education*, *9*, 1434052. DOI: 10.3389/feduc.2024.1434052

Olatunji, S. O. (2017). Extreme Learning Machines and Support Vector Machines Models for Email Spam Detection. In 2017 IEEE 30th Canadian Conference on Electrical and Computer Engineering (CCECE), pp. 1-6.

Omran, E., Al Qundus, J., & Al Tararwah, E. (2023). A comparative analysis of machine learning algorithms for hate speech detection in social media. *Online Journal of Communication and Media Technologies*, *13*(4), e202348. DOI: 10.30935/ojcmt/13603

Osipov, D. V.School Shooting Cases. (2024). Ethics of AI technologies in "Sensitive" content creation and Evaluation. School shooting cases. *Galactica Media Journal of Media Studies*, *6*(3), 44–65. DOI: 10.46539/gmd.v6i3.530

Padilla Montani, J., & Schüller, P. (2018). TUWienKBS at GermEval 2018: German Abusive Tweet Detection. *Proceedings of GermEval 2018, 14th Conference on Natural Language Processing (KONVENS 2018)*, 5. http://hdl.handle.net/20.500.12708/57438

Pandey, S., & Jadhav, G. (2023, March 17). Emerging technologies and law: Legal status of tackling crimes relating to deepfakes in India. *SCC Online*. https://www.scconline.com/blog/post/2023/03/17/emerging-technologies-and-law-legal-status-of-tackling-crimes-relating-to-deepfakes-in-india/

Pang, B., Lee, L., & Vaithyanathan, S. (2002). Thumbs up? Sentiment classification using machine learning techniques. arXiv preprint cs/0205070.

Panwar, K. S., & Roy, N. D. (2024). Rising menace of deepfakes with the help of AI: Legal implications in India. *Indian Journal of Integrated Research in Law*, *4*(3), 94. https://ijirl.com/wp-content/uploads/2024/05/RISING-MENACE-OF-DEEPFAKES-WITH-THE-HELP-OF-AI-LEGAL-IMPLICATIONS-IN-INDIA.pdf

Parihar, A. S., Thapa, S., & Mishra, S. (2021). *Hate speech detection using natural language processing: Applications and challenges*. Machine Learning Research Lab.

Park, S. M., & Kim, Y. G. (2022). A metaverse: Taxonomy, components, applications, and open challenges. *IEEE Access : Practical Innovations, Open Solutions*, *10*, 4209–4251. DOI: 10.1109/ACCESS.2021.3140175

Paszke, A., Gross, S., Massa, F., Lerer, A., Bradbury, J., Chanan, G., Killeen, T., Lin, Z., Gimelshein, N., Antiga, L., Desmaison, A., Köpf, A., Yang, E., DeVito, Z., Raison, M., Tejani, A., Chilamkurthy, S., Steiner, B., Fang, L., . . . Chintala, S. (2019). PyTorch: An Imperative Style, High-Performance Deep Learning Library (Version 1). arXiv. DOI: 10.48550/ARXIV.1912.01703

Patil, P., Nagarhalli, T., Raul, S., & Raut, D. (2023). *Hate Speech Detection using Deep Learning and Text Analysis*. 322–330. DOI: 10.1109/ICICCS56967.2023.10142895

Patil, S., Patil, S., & Kulkarni, U. (2017). Visual and CSS-based Phishing Website Detection using SVM with MapReduce. In 2017 International Conference on Intelligent Computing and Control (I2C2), pp. 1-6.

Pereira-Kohatsu, J. C., Quijano-Sánchez, L., Liberatore, F., & Camacho-Collados, M. (2019). Detecting and Monitoring Hate Speech on Twitter. *Sensors (Basel)*, *19*(21), 4654. DOI: 10.3390/s19214654 PMID: 31717760

Pérez, J. M., Debandi, N., Luque, F. M., Cotik, V., Gravano, A., Moro, A., Kondratzky, M., Zayat, D., Serrati, P. S., Miguel, P., & Zajac, J. (2023). Assessing the Impact of Contextual Information in Hate Speech Detection. *IEEE Access : Practical Innovations, Open Solutions*, *11*, 30575–30590. DOI: 10.1109/ACCESS.2023.3258973

Pérez, J. M., Furman, D. A., Alonso Alemany, L., & Luque, F. (2022). RoBERTuito: A pre-trained language model for social media text in Spanish (arXiv:2111.09453v3). https://arxiv.org/abs/2111.09453

Perkins, M., & Roe, J. (2024). Academic publisher guidelines on AI usage: A ChatGPT supported thematic analysis. ncbi.nlm.nih.gov

Perry, B. & Uuk, R. (2019). AI Governance and the Policymaking Process: Key Considerations for Reducing AI Risk. [PDF]

Pfeiffer, C. (2022). Future scenarios on multilateralism: global governance models for efficient (economic) policy coordination. uniroma1.it

Piazza, J. A. (2020). Politician hate speech and domestic terrorism. *International Interactions*, *46*(3), 431–453. DOI: 10.1080/03050629.2020.1739033

Pizzolante, M., Borghesi, F., Sarcinella, E., Bartolotta, S., Salvi, C., Cipresso, P., Gaggioli, A., & Chirico, A. (2023). Awe in the metaverse: Designing and validating a novel online virtual-reality awe-inspiring training. *Computers in Human Behavior*, *148*, 107876. DOI: 10.1016/j.chb.2023.107876

Potla, R. T. (2025). AI-Powered Threat Detection in Online Communities: A Multi-Modal Deep Learning Approach. *Journal of Computer and Communications*, *13*(2), 155–171. DOI: 10.4236/jcc.2025.132010

Prabhu, R., & Seethalakshmi, V. (2025). A comprehensive framework for multi-modal hate speech detection in social media using deep learning. *Scientific Reports*, *15*(1), 13020. Advance online publication. DOI: 10.1038/s41598-025-94069-z PMID: 40234479

Prajapati, M., Baliarsingh, S. K., Dora, C., Bhoi, A., Hota, J., & Mohanty, J. P. "Detection of AI-Generated Text Using Large Language Model," *2024 International Conference on Emerging Systems and Intelligent Computing (ESIC)*, Bhubaneswar, India, 2024, pp. 735-740, DOI: 10.1109/ESIC60604.2024.10481602

Puri, S., Gosain, D., Ahuja, M., Kathuria, I., & Jatana, N. (2013). Comparison and analysis of spam detection algorithms. *International Journal of Application or Innovation in Engineering and Management*, *2*(4), 255–261.

Qi, H., Guo, Q., Juefei-Xu, F., Xie, X., Ma, L., Feng, W., Liu, Y., & Zhao, J. (2020). DeepRhythm. *Proceedings of the 28th ACM International Conference on Multimedia*, 4318–4327. https://doi.org/DOI: 10.1145/3394171.3413707

Qureshi, K. A., & Sabih, M. (2021). Un-Compromised Credibility: Social Media Based Multi-Class Hate Speech Classification for Text. *IEEE Access : Practical Innovations, Open Solutions*, *9*, 109465–109477. DOI: 10.1109/ACCESS.2021.3101977

Radanliev, P. (2024). Artificial intelligence: reflecting on the past and looking towards the next paradigm shift. *Journal of Experimental & Theoretical Artificial Intelligence, ahead-of-print*(ahead-of-print), 1–18. DOI: 10.1080/0952813X.2024.2323042

Radford, A., Kim, J. W., Hallacy, C., Ramesh, A., Goh, G., Agarwal, S., Sastry, G., Askell, A., Mishkin, P., Clark, J., Krueger, G., & Sutskever, I. (2021). *Learning Transferable Visual Models From Natural Language Supervision*. https://arxiv.org/abs/2103.00020

Rafsanjani, H. N., & Nabizadeh, A. H. (2023). Towards digital architecture, engineering, and construction (AEC) industry through virtual design and construction (VDC) and digital twin. *Energy and Built Environment*, *4*(2), 169–178. DOI: 10.1016/j.enbenv.2021.10.004

Rahman, M. M., Balakrishnan, D., Murthy, D., Kutlu, M., & Lease, M. (2021). *An Information Retrieval Approach to Building Datasets for Hate Speech Detection*. https://github.com/mdmustafizurrahman/An-Information-Retrieval-Approach-to-Build

Rajamohana, S. P., Umamaheswari, K., & Abirami, B. (2017). Adaptive binary flower pollination algorithm for feature selection in review spam detection. *Journal of Computer Security*, *25*(4), 357–372.

Rajamohana, S. P., Umamaheswari, K., & Keerthana, S. V. (2017). An effective hybrid Cuckoo Search with Harmony Search for review spam detection. In *Proceedings of the 3rd IEEE International Conference on Advances in Electrical and Electronics, Information, Communication and Bio-Informatics (AEEICB)*, pp. 524-527.

Rajat Sharma & Anr. v. Tamara Doc & Ors., CS(Comm) 1147 of 2024 (India).

Ramos, J. (2003). Using TF-IDF to determine word relevance in document queries, *Proceedings of the First Instructional Conference on Machine Learning*.

Ramponi, A., Testa, B., Tonelli, S., & Jezek, E. (2022). Addressing religious hate online: From taxonomy creation to automated detection. *PeerJ. Computer Science*, *8*, e1128. DOI: 10.7717/peerj-cs.1128 PMID: 37346317

Ramteke, A., Malu, A., Bhattacharyya, P., & Nath, J. S. (2013, August). Detecting turnarounds in sentiment analysis: Thwarting. In *Proceedings of the 51st Annual Meeting of the Association for Computational Linguistics* (Volume 2: Short Papers) (pp. 860-865).

Ranasinghe, T., Zampieri, M., & Hettiarachchi, H. (2019). BRUMS at HASOC 2019: Deep learning models for multilingual hate speech and offensive language identification. In Working Notes of FIRE 2019 - Forum for Information Retrieval Evaluation. https://ceur-ws.org/Vol-2517/

Rane, N., Choudhary, S., & Rane, J. (2023). Metaverse for Enhancing Customer Loyalty: Effective Strategies to Improve Customer Relationship, Service, Engagement, Satisfaction, and Experience. Service, Engagement, Satisfaction, and Experience (November 1, 2023).

Rangan, K., & Yin, Y. (2024). A fine-tuning enhanced RAG system with quantized influence measure as AI judge. *Scientific Reports*, *14*(1), 27446. Advance online publication. DOI: 10.1038/s41598-024-79110-x PMID: 39523408

Rao, K. N., Arora, R. D., Dange, P., & Nagarkar, N. M. (2023). NLP AI Models for Optimizing Medical Research: Demystifying the Concerns. *Indian Journal of Surgical Oncology*, *14*(4), 854–858. DOI: 10.1007/s13193-023-01791-z PMID: 38187847

Raschka, S. (2015). *Python Machine Learning*. Packt Publishing.

Rathi, M., & Pareek, V. (2013). Spam mail detection through data mining-A comparative performance analysis. *International Journal of Modern Education and Computer Science*, *5*(12), 31.

Rathi, S., Kant Hiran, K., & Sakhare, S. (2023). Affective state prediction of E-learner using SS-ROA based deep LSTM. *Array (New York, N.Y.)*, *19*, 100315. DOI: 10.1016/j.array.2023.100315

Rawat, A., Samant, S. S., & Kumar, S. (2024). Hate speech detection in social media: Techniques, recent trends, and future challenges. *Wiley Interdisciplinary Reviews: Computational Statistics*, *16*(2), e1648. Advance online publication. DOI: 10.1002/wics.1648

Raza Ur Rehman, H. M., Saleem, M., Jhandir, M. Z., Alvarado, E. S., Garay, H., & Ashraf, I. (2025). Detecting hate in diversity: a survey of multilingual code-mixed image and video analysis. *Journal of Big Data 2025 12:1*, *12*(1), 1–28. DOI: 10.1186/s40537-025-01167-w

Rekha, S. N. (2014). A review on different spam detection approaches. [IJETT]. *International Journal of Engineering Trends and Technology*, *11*(6), 315–318.

Reza Saeidnia, H., Hosseini, E., Abdoli, S., & Ausloos, M. (2024). *Unleashing the Power of AI. A Systematic Review of Cutting-Edge Techniques in AI-Enhanced Scientometrics*. Webometrics, and Bibliometrics. [PDF]

Ribeiro, M. T., Guerra, P. H. C., Vilela, L., Veloso, A., Guedes, D., & Meira, W., Jr. & Hoepers, C. (2011, September). Spam detection using web page content: a new battleground. In Proceedings of the 8th annual collaboration, electronic messaging, anti-abuse and spam conference (pp. 83-91).

Ribeiro, M. T., Singh, S., & Guestrin, C. (2016). "Why should i trust you?" Explaining the predictions of any classifier. *Proceedings of the ACM SIGKDD International Conference on Knowledge Discovery and Data Mining, 13-17-August-2016*, 1135–1144. DOI: 10.1145/2939672.2939778

Ricci, F., Rokach, L., & Shapira, B. (2015). Recommender Systems: Introduction and Challenges. In Ricci, F., Rokach, L., & Shapira, B. (Eds.), *Recommender Systems Handbook*. Springer., DOI: 10.1007/978-1-4899-7637-6_1

Rizos, G., Hemker, K., & Schuller, B. (2019). Augment to prevent: Short-text data augmentation in deep learning for hate-speech classification. In *Proceedings of the 28th ACM International Conference on Information and Knowledge Management (CIKM '19)* (pp. 991–1000). DOI: 10.1145/3357384.3358040

Roberts, H., Hine, E., Taddeo, M., & Floridi, L. (2024). Global AI governance: barriers and pathways forward. International Affairs. oup.com

Rodriguez, A., & Argueta, C. (2019). Automatic detection of hate speech on Facebook using sentiment and emotion analysis. In *2019 International Conference on Artificial Intelligence in Information and Communication (ICAIIC)* (pp. 215–219). IEEE. DOI: 10.1109/ICAIIC.2019.8669073

Rodriguez, A., Chen, Y.-L., & Argueta, C. (2022). FADOHS: Framework for Detection and Integration of Unstructured Data of Hate Speech on Facebook Using Sentiment and Emotion Analysis. *IEEE Access : Practical Innovations, Open Solutions, 10*, 22400–22419. DOI: 10.1109/ACCESS.2022.3151098

Rojko, K., & Lužar, B. (2022). Scientific performance across research disciplines: Trends and differences in the case of Slovenia. [HTML]. *Journal of Informetrics, 16*(2), 101261. DOI: 10.1016/j.joi.2022.101261

Romero Moreno, F. (2024). Generative AI and deepfakes: A human rights approach to tackling harmful content. *International Review of Law Computers & Technology, 38*(3), 297–326. DOI: 10.1080/13600869.2024.2324540

Romim, N., Ahmed, M., Talukder, H., & Saiful Islam, M. (2021). *Hate Speech Detection in the Bengali Language: A Dataset and Its Baseline Evaluation* (pp. 457–468). springer singapore. DOI: 10.1007/978-981-16-0586-4_37

Ross, B., Rist, M., Carbonell, G., Cabrera, B., Kurowsky, N., & Wojatzki, M. (2017). *Measuring the Reliability of Hate Speech Annotations: The Case of the European Refugee Crisis*. DOI: 10.17185/duepublico/42132

Rudy Salim, C. E., & Suhartono, D. (2020). A Systematic Literature Review of Different Machine Learning Methods on Hate Speech Detection. *JOIV: International Journal on Informatics Visualization, 4*(4), 213–218. DOI: 10.30630/joiv.4.4.476

Saddozai, F. K., Badri, S. K., Alghazzawi, D., Khattak, A., & Asghar, M. Z. (2025). Multimodal hate speech detection: A novel deep learning framework for multilingual text and images. *PeerJ. Computer Science, 11*, e2801. DOI: 10.7717/peerj-cs.2801 PMID: 40567705

Saeed, A., Kamran, M., Khan, H. U., Shankar, A., Imran, T., Khan, D., & Khan, M. A. (2023). *Topic Modeling based Text Classification Regarding Islamophobia using Word Embedding and Transformers Techniques*. ACM Transactions on Asian and Low-Resource Language Information Processing., DOI: 10.1145/3626318

Şahi, H., Klç, Y., & Sa lam, R. B. (2018). Automated detection of hate speech towards woman on Twitter. *2018 3rd International Conference on Computer Science and Engineering (UBMK)*, 533–536.

Saifullah, S., Aribowo, A. S., Cahyana, N. H., Dreżewski, R., Fauziah, Y., & Dwiyanto, F. A. (2024). Automated Text Annotation Using a Semi-Supervised Approach with Meta Vectorizer and Machine Learning Algorithms for Hate Speech Detection. *Applied Sciences (Basel, Switzerland), 14*(3), 1078. DOI: 10.3390/app14031078

Salar Khan, M., Shoaib, A., & Arledge, E. (2023). How to Promote AI in the US Federal Government: Insights from Policy Process Frameworks. osf.io

Saleh, H., Alhothali, A., & Moria, K. (2023). Detection of Hate Speech using BERT and Hate Speech Word Embedding with Deep Model. *Applied Artificial Intelligence, 37*(1), 2166719. Advance online publication. DOI: 10.1080/08839514.2023.2166719

Sallam, M., Snygg, J., & Sallam, M. (2024). Assessment of artificial intelligence credibility in evidence-based healthcare management with "Aerus" innovative tool. J Artif Intell Mach Learn Data Sci. academia.edu

Salton, G., & Buckley, C. (1988). Term-weighting approaches in automatic text retrieval. *Information Processing & Management, 24*(5), 513–523. DOI: 10.1016/0306-4573(88)90021-0

Sánchez, J. M., Rodríguez, J. P., & Espitia, H. E. (2022). Bibliometric analysis of publications discussing the use of the artificial intelligence technique agent-based models in sustainable agriculture. Heliyon. cell.com

Saner, E. (2024, January 31). Inside the Taylor Swift deepfake scandal: "It's men telling a powerful woman to get back in her box." *The Guardian*. https://www.theguardian.com/technology/2024/jan/31/inside-the-taylor-swift-deepfake-scandal-its-men-telling-a-powerful-woman-to-get-back-in-her-box

Sanghvi, H., Bhavsar, R., Sharma, R., Hundlani, V., Vyas, T., Gohil, L., Nair, A., Jadav, N. K., Desai, S., Yamsani, N., & Tanwar, S. (2023). *MetaHate*: AI-based hate speech detection for secured online gaming in metaverse using blockchain. *Security and Privacy*, *7*(2), e343. Advance online publication. DOI: 10.1002/spy2.343

Santra, P. P., & Majhi, D. (2023). Scholarly Communication and Machine-Generated Text: Is it Finally AI vs AI in Plagiarism Detection? *Journal of Information and Knowledge*, 175–183. DOI: 10.17821/srels/2023/v60i3/171028

Sanu, K. (2024, May 31). Deepfakes in poll season: Experts say India needs to evolve AI-specific regulations. *India Today*. https://www.indiatoday.in/law/story/deepfakes-in-poll-season-experts-say-india-needs-to-evolve-ai-specific-regulations-2546018-2024-05-31

Sap, M., Card, D., Gabriel, S., Choi, Y., Smith, N. A., & Allen, P. G. (2019). *The Risk of Racial Bias in Hate Speech Detection*. Association for Computational Linguistics. www.figure-eight.com

Sarwar, S. M., & Murdock, V. (2022). Unsupervised Domain Adaptation for Hate Speech Detection Using a Data Augmentation Approach. *Proceedings of the International AAAI Conference on Web and Social Media, 16*, 852–862. https://doi.org/ DOI: 10.1609/icwsm.v16i1.19340

Satapara, S., Modha, S., Mandl, T., Madhu, H., & Majumder, P. (2021). *Overview of the HASOC Subtrack at FIRE 2021: Conversational Hate Speech Detection in Code-mixed language*. http://ceur-ws.org

Satapara, S., Majumder, P., Mandl, T., Modha, S., Madhu, H., Ranasinghe, T., Zampieri, M., North, K., & Premasiri, D. (2022). Overview of the HASOC Subtrack at FIRE 2022: Hate Speech and Offensive Content Identification in English and Indo-Aryan Languages. *ACM International Conference Proceeding Series*, 4–7. DOI: 10.1145/3574318.3574326

Savaget, P., Chiarini, T., & Evans, S. (2019). Empowering political participation through artificial intelligence.. [PDF]

Schiff, K. J., Schiff, D. S., Adams, I. T., McCrain, J., & Mourtgos, S. M. (2025). Institutional factors driving citizen perceptions of AI in government: Evidence from a survey experiment on policing. [wiley.com]. *Public Administration Review, 85*(2), 451–467. DOI: 10.1111/puar.13754

Schmidt, A., & Wiegand, M. (2017). *A Survey on Hate Speech Detection using Natural Language Processing*. https://en.wikipedia.org/wiki/List_

Schmidt, A., & Wiegand, M. (2017). A Survey on Hate Speech Detection using Natural Language Processing. *Proceedings of the Fifth International Workshop on Natural Language Processing for Social Media*, 1–10. https://doi.org/DOI: 10.18653/v1/W17-1101

Schwartz, M. J. (2020, November 20). The dark side of AI: Previewing criminal uses. *Bank Info Security*. https://www.bankinfosecurity.com/blogs/dark-side-ai-police-preview-likely-attacks-p-2971

Sedhai, S., & Sun, A. (2017). Semi-Supervised Spam Detection in Twitter Stream. *IEEE Transactions on Computational Social Systems*, *5*(2), 169–175.

Segovia, M., & Garcia-Alfaro, J. (2022). Design, modeling and implementation of digital twins. *Sensors (Basel)*, *22*(14), 5396. DOI: 10.3390/s22145396 PMID: 35891076

Sengupta, A., Bhattacharjee, S. K., Akhtar, M. S., & Chakraborty, T. (2022). Does aggression lead to hate? Detecting and reasoning offensive traits in hinglish code-mixed texts. *Neurocomputing*, *488*, 598–617. DOI: 10.1016/j.neucom.2021.11.053

Serrano, S., & Smith, N. A. (2019). Is Attention Interpretable? https://arxiv.org/abs/1906.03731 DOI: 10.18653/v1/P19-1282

Shahbaz, M., Guergachi, A., & ur Rehman, R. T. (2014, May). Sentiment miner: A prototype for sentiment analysis of unstructured data and text. In 2014 IEEE 27th Canadian Conference on Electrical and Computer Engineering (CCECE) (pp. 1-7). IEEE.

Shaikh, M. A. M., Prendinger, H., & Ishizuka, M. (2007, December). An analytical approach to assess sentiment of text. In 2007 10th international conference on computer and information technology (pp. 1-6). IEEE.

Shang, Y. (2019). Consensus and clustering of expressed and private opinions in dynamical networks against attacks. *IEEE Systems Journal*, *14*(2), 2078–2084. DOI: 10.1109/JSYST.2019.2956116

Sharma, D., Gupta, V., Nath, T., & Singh, V. K. (2025). Hate Speech Detection Research in South Asian Languages: A Survey of Tasks, Datasets and Methods. *ACM Transactions on Asian and Low-Resource Language Information Processing, 24*(3), 1–44. DOI: 10.1145/3711710

Sharma, K., & Kaur, M. (2013). Spam Detection Techniques: A Review. *International Journal of Computer Applications, 67*(20), 20–23.

Sheppard, B., Richter, A., Cohen, A., Smith, E. A., Kneese, T., Pelletier, C., Baldini, I., & Dong, Y. (2023). Subtle Misogyny Detection and Mitigation: An Expert-Annotated *Dataset*. https://arxiv.org/abs/2311.09443

Shinde, S., Joshi, S., & Pawar, M. (2016). A Decision Support Engine: Heuristic Review Analysis on Information Extraction System and Mining Comparable Objects from Comparable Concepts. In 2016 International Conference on Advances in Computing, Communication, & Automation (ICACCA), pp. 1-7.

Shishah, W., & Maulana Fajri, R. (2022). Large Comparative Study of Recent Computational Approaches in Automatic Hate Speech Detection. *TEM Journal*, 82–93. https://doi.org/DOI: 10.18421/TEM111-10

Shridhara, M. G., Pristaš, V., Kotvytskiy, A., Antoni, L., & Semanišin, G. (2023). A short review on hate speech detection: Challenges towards datasets and techniques. In *Proceedings of the 2023 World Symposium on Digital Intelligence for Systems and Machines (DISA)* (pp. 204–209). IEEE. DOI: 10.1109/DISA59116.2023.10308906

Silva, L., Mondal, M., Correa, D., Benevenuto, F., & Weber, I. (2016). *Analyzing the Targets of Hate in Online Social Media*. www.aaai.org

Singh, N. (2024, October 1). Digital arrest and Rs 7 crore heist: How Vardhman Group head was tricked. *Business Standard*. https://www.business-standard.com/companies/news/digital-arrest-and-rs-7-crore-heist-how-vardhman-group-head-was-tricked-124100100832_1.html

Singh, R., Choudhary, N., & Shrivastava, M. (2018). Automatic normalization of word variations in code-mixed social media text. *ArXiv Preprint ArXiv:1804.00804*.

Singh, S., Haridasan, A., & Mooney, R. (2023). *"Female Astronaut: Because sandwiches won't make themselves up there!": Towards multi-modal misogyny detection in memes*. https://www.forbes.com/sites/ewelinaochab/2023/03/08/when-

Singh, A., Sharma, D., & Singh, V. K. (2024). *MIMIC: Misogyny Identification in Multimodal Internet Content in Hindi-English Code-Mixed Language*. ACM Transactions on Asian and Low-Resource Language Information Processing., DOI: 10.1145/3656169

Singh, N., & Mundra, S. (2023). *Hinglish HateBERT: Hate Speech Classication in Hinglish language*. DOI: 10.21203/rs.3.rs-3436709/v1

Sipahioğlu, B. Ö. (2023). The Effects Of Hate Speech On Social Media: The Case Of Syrian Refugees In Türkiye. *Journal of Erciyes Communication, 10*(1), 149–164. DOI: 10.17680/erciyesiletisim.1159037

Smith, H., & Mansted, K. (2020). What's a deepfake? In *Weaponised deepfakes: National security and democracy* (pp. 05–10). Australian Strategic Policy Institute. https://www.jstor.org/stable/resrep25129.6

Somers, M. (2020, July 21). *Deepfakes, explained.* MIT Management Sloan School. https://mitsloan.mit.edu/ideas-made-to-matter/deepfakes-explained

Sopher, H., & Lescop, L. (2023). Learning in metaverse: The immersive atelier model of the architecture studio. *Archnet-IJAR: International Journal of Architectural Research, 17*(3), 536–553. DOI: 10.1108/ARCH-10-2022-0213

Statista. (2024). *Leading countries based on YouTube audience size as of July 2024 (in millions)* .

Steen, E., Yurechko, K., & Klug, D. (2023). You Can (Not) Say What You Want: Using Algospeak to Contest and Evade Algorithmic Content Moderation on TikTok. *Social Media + Society, 9*(3), 20563051231194586. Advance online publication. DOI: 10.1177/20563051231194586

Steiger, M., Bharucha, T. J., Venkatagiri, S., Riedl, M. J., & Lease, M. (2021, May 6). The psychologicalwell-being of content moderators the emotional labor of commercial moderation and avenues for improving support. *Conference on Human Factors in Computing Systems - Proceedings*. DOI: 10.1145/3411764.3445092

Stix, C. (2022). Foundations for the future: institution building for the purpose of artificial intelligence governance. ncbi.nlm.nih.gov

Struß, J. M., Siegel, M., Ruppenhofer, J., Wiegand, M., & Klenner, M. (2019). *Overview of GermEval Task 2, 2019 Shared Task on the Identification of Offensive Language*. http://nbn-resolving.de/urn:nbn:de:bsz:mh39-93197

Subcommittee on AI Governance and Guidelines Development. (2025, January 2). *Report on AI governance guidelines development*. Ministry of Electronics and Information Technology. https://indiaai.s3.ap-south-1.amazonaws.com/docs/subcommittee-report-dec26.pdf

Subcommittee on AI Governance and Guidelines Development. 'Report on AI Governance Guidelines Development'. (2025, January 2). Ministry of Electronics and Information Technology. https://indiaai.s3.ap-south-1.amazonaws.com/docs/subcommittee-report-dec26.pdf

Sumsub. (n.d.). *Deepfake cases surge in countries holding 2024 elections*. https://sumsub.com/newsroom/deepfake-cases-surge-in-countries-holding-2024-elections-sumsub-research-shows/

Swami, S., Khandelwal, A., Singh, V., Akhtar, S. S., & Shrivastava, M. (2018). *A Corpus of English-Hindi Code-Mixed Tweets for Sarcasm Detection*. https://arxiv.org/abs/1805.11869

Syed, T. A., Siddiqui, M. S., Abdullah, H. B., Jan, S., Namoun, A., Alzahrani, A., Nadeem, A., & Alkhodre, A. B. (2022). In-depth review of augmented reality: Tracking technologies, development tools, AR displays, collaborative AR, and security concerns. *Sensors (Basel)*, *23*(1), 146. DOI: 10.3390/s23010146 PMID: 36616745

Tchuente Foguem, G., & Teguede Keleko, A. (2023). Artificial intelligence applied in pulmonary hypertension: a bibliometric analysis. ncbi.nlm.nih.gov

Thapliyal, N. (2024, May 8). Journalist Rajat Sharma moves Delhi High Court against non-regulation of deepfake technology, notice issued. *LiveLaw.in*. https://www.livelaw.in/high-court/delhi-high-court/delhi-high-court-deepfake-videos-rajat-sharma-pil-257393

Thapliyal, N. (2024, May 8). *Journalist Rajat Sharma Moves Delhi High Court Against Non-Regulation of Deepfake Technology, Notice Issued*. LiveLaw.in. https://www.livelaw.in/high-court/delhi-high-court/delhi-high-court-deepfake-videos-rajat-sharma-pil-257393

The AB-2355 Political Reform Act. 1974 ('political advertisements & artificial intelligence'). https://calmatters.digitaldemocracy.org/bills/ca_202320240ab2355

The AB-2655 Defending Democracy from Deepfake Deception Act. 2024. https://leginfo.legislature.ca.gov/faces/billNavClient.xhtml?bill_id=202320240AB2655

The Bhartiya Nyay Sanhita (BNS) 2023, Section 319.

The Deepfakes Accountability Act. 2023. https://www.congress.gov/bill/118th-congress/house-bill/5586/text

The Digital Personal Data Protection Rules. 2025. https://innovateindia.mygov.in/dpdp-rules-2025/

The Digital Services Act package | Shaping Europe's digital future. (n.d.). Retrieved September 6, 2025, from https://digital-strategy.ec.europa.eu/en/policies/digital-services-act-package

The EU Artificial Intelligence Act. Up-to-date developments and analyses of the EU AI Act. EU Artificial Intelligence Act. https://artificialintelligenceact.eu/

The H.R.6088 - Deepfakes in Federal Elections Prohibition Act 2020.

The Information Technology Act 2000.

Thombre, M. (2021). Deconstructing deepfake: Tracking legal implications and challenges. *International Journal of Law, Management and Humanities, 4*(4), 2267–2274. https://doij.org/10.10000/IJLMH.111463

Thombre, M. (2021). Deconstructing Deepfake: Tracking Legal Implications and Challenges. *International Journal of Law, Management and Humanities. 4*(4), 2267 – 2274. https://doij.org/10.10000/IJLMH.111463

Tiwari, K., Yuan, S., & Zhang, L. (2022). *Robust Hate Speech Detection via Mitigating Spurious Correlations*. 51–56. DOI: 10.18653/v1/2022.aacl-short.7

Tiwari, S., Sharma, R., Sikarwar, R. S., Dubey, G. P., Bajpai, N., & Singhatiya, S. (2023, January). Detecting AI generated content: A study of methods and applications. In *International Conference on Communication and Computational Technologies* (pp. 161-176). Singapore: Springer Nature Singapore. DOI: 10.1007/978-981-97-7423-4_13

Tiwari, A., & Agrawal, A. (2022). Comparative analysis of different machine learning methods for hate speech recognition in Twitter text data. *2022 Third International Conference on Intelligent Computing Instrumentation and Control Technologies (ICICICT)*, 1016–1020. DOI: 10.1109/ICICICT54557.2022.9917752

Topal, K., & Özsoyoglu, G. (2016). Movie review analysis: Emotion analysis of IMDb movie reviews. In *2016 IEEE/ACM International Conference on Advances in Social Networks Analysis and Mining (ASONAM)*, pp. 1170-1176.

Toraman, C., Şahinuç, F., & Yilmaz, E. H. (2022). Large-scale hate speech detection with cross-domain transfer. *ArXiv Preprint ArXiv:2203.01111*.

Toxic Twitter – The Solution. Chapter 8. (2018).

Trend Micro Research, United Nations Interregional Crime and Justice Research Institute (UNICRI), & Europol's European Cybercrime Centre (EC3). (n.d.). *Malicious uses and abuses of artificial intelligence*. https://unicri.it/sites/default/files/2020-11/Abuse_ai.pdf

Tsou, M. H., & Mejia, C. (2024). Beyond mapping: Extend the role of cartographers to user interface designers in the Metaverse using virtual reality, augmented reality, and mixed reality. *Cartography and Geographic Information Science*, *51*(5), 659–673. DOI: 10.1080/15230406.2023.2264748

Tweets That Chill: Analyzing Online Violence Against Women in Politics | National Democratic Institute. (2019, June 14). https://www.ndi.org/tweets-that-chill

Twitter's policy on hateful conduct | Twitter Help. (2023). https://help.twitter.com/en/rules-and-policies/hateful-conduct-policy

U.S. Congress. (2020). *H.R.6088 - Deepfakes in Federal Elections Prohibition Act of 2020*.

U.S. Congress. (2023). *The Deepfakes Accountability Act, H.R. 5586*. https://www.congress.gov/bill/118th-congress/house-bill/5586/text

U.S. Congress. (2023–2024). *H.R. 6943 – No AI FRAUD Act, 118th Congress*. https://www.congress.gov/bill/118th-congress/house-bill/6943

Ugarte Querejeta, M., Illarramendi Rezabal, M., Unamuno, G., Bellanco, J. L., Ugalde, E., & Valor Valor, A. (2022). Implementation of a holistic digital twin solution for design prototyping and virtual commissioning. *IET Collaborative Intelligent Manufacturing*, *4*(4), 326–335. DOI: 10.1049/cim2.12058

United Nations Interregional Crime and Justice Research Institute (UNICRI). (n.d.). *Artificial intelligence and robotics for law enforcement*. https://unicri.it/sites/default/files/2020-11/Abuse_ai.pdf

United States Congress. H.R. 6943 – No AI FRAUD Act, 118th Congress (2023–2024). https://www.congress.gov/bill/118th-congress/house-bill/6943

Unogwu, O. J., Doshi, R., Hiran, K. K., Mijwil, M. M., Catherine, A. T., & Abotaleb, M. (2024). Exploring the implications of emerging artificial intelligence technologies at edge computing in higher education. In *Integrating generative AI in education to achieve Sustainable Development Goals* (pp. 169–182). IGI Global Scientific Publishing. DOI: 10.4018/979-8-3693-2440-0.ch009

UPC Telekabel Wien GmbH v. Constantin Film Verleih GmbH (Case C-314/12) [2014] (ECJ).

Valakunde, N. D., & Patwardhan, M. S. (2013, November). Multi-aspect and multi-class based document sentiment analysis of educational data catering accreditation process. In *2013 International Conference on Cloud & Ubiquitous Computing & Emerging Technologies* (pp. 188-192). IEEE.

Valiaiev, D. (2024). Detection of machine-generated text: Literature survey. *arXiv preprint arXiv:2402.01642*.

Vaswani, A., Shazeer, N., Parmar, N., Uszkoreit, J., Jones, L., Gomez, A. N., Kaiser, L., & Polosukhin, I. (2017). Attention Is All You Need (Version 7). arXiv. DOI: 10.48550/ARXIV.1706.03762

Velickovic, V., & Elbassuoni, S. (2024). Detecting Hate Speech: Deep Learning Techniques for Text Analysis and Classification. DOI: 10.13140/RG.2.2.27435.04641

Venema, A. (n.d.). Deepfakes as a security issue: Why gender matters. *Women in International Security*. https://wiisglobal.org/deepfakes-as-a-security-issue-why-gender-matters/

Venema, A. *Deepfakes as a Security Issue: Why Gender Matters*. Women in International Security. https://wiisglobal.org/deepfakes-as-a-security-issue-why-gender-matters/

Vetagiri, A., Mogha, P., & Pakray, P. (2024). Multilate Classifier: A Novel Emsemble of Cnn-Bilstm with Resnet-Based Multimodal Classifier for Ai-Generated Hate Speech Detection. DOI: 10.2139/ssrn.4951337

Vetagiri, A., & Pakray, P. Mitigating Adversarial Attacks in Ai-Generated Multimodal Hate. DOI: 10.2139/ssrn.5193751

Vig, S. (2024). Regulating deepfakes: An Indian perspective. *Journal of Strategic Security*, *17*(3), 70–93. DOI: 10.5038/1944-0472.17.3.2245

VOSviewer. Retrieved 2025, https://www.vosviewer.com/

Walter, Y. (2024). … the race to the moon: Global policy and governance in artificial intelligence regulation—A contemporary overview and an analysis of socioeconomic consequences. Discover Artificial Intelligence. springer.com

Wang, H., Lee, R. K.-W., Choo, K. T. W., Awal, M. R., & Hee, M. S. (2023). *Evaluating GPT-3 Generated Explanations for Hateful Content Moderation*. 6255–6263. DOI: 10.24963/ijcai.2023/694

Wang, G., Xie, S., Liu, B., & Yu, P. S. (2012). Identify online store review spammers via social review graph. [TIST]. *ACM Transactions on Intelligent Systems and Technology*, *3*(4), 1–21.

Wang, Q. (2023). Advanced Deep Learning Approaches for Hate Speech Detection. *Highlights in Science. Engineering and Technology*, *41*, 158–164. DOI: 10.54097/hset.v41i.6801

Wang, Y. (2024). Survey for detecting AI-generated content. *Advances in Engineering Technology Research, 11*(1), 643–643. DOI: 10.56028/aetr.11.1.643.2024

Warner, W., & Hirschberg, J. (2012). *Detecting Hate Speech on the World Wide Web*. http://info.yahoo.com/legal/us/yahoo/utos/utos-173.html

Warner, W., & Hirschberg, J. (2012, June 1). *Detecting hate speech on the world wide web*. ACL Anthology. https://aclanthology.org/W12-2103/

Waseem, Z. (2016). *Are You a Racist or Am I Seeing Things? Annotator Influence on Hate Speech Detection on Twitter*. www.spacy.io

Waseem, Z., & Hovy, D. (2016). Hateful symbols or hateful people? predictive features for hate speech detection on twitter. *Proceedings of the NAACL Student Research Workshop*, 88–93. DOI: 10.18653/v1/N16-2013

Watanabe, H., Bouazizi, M., & Ohtsuki, T. (2018). Hate Speech on Twitter: A Pragmatic Approach to Collect Hateful and Offensive Expressions and Perform Hate Speech Detection. *IEEE Access : Practical Innovations, Open Solutions, 6*, 13825–13835. DOI: 10.1109/ACCESS.2018.2806394

Weber-Wulff, D., Anohina-Naumeca, A., Bjelobaba, S., Foltýnek, T., Guerrero-Dib, J., Popoola, O., Šigut, P., & Waddington, L. (2023). Testing of detection tools for AI-generated text. *International Journal for Educational Integrity, 19*(1), 1–39. DOI: 10.1007/s40979-023-00146-z

Wiedemann, G., Ruppert, E., Jindal, R., & Biemann, C. (2018). *Transfer Learning from LDA to BiLSTM-CNN for Offensive Language Detection in Twitter*. https://arxiv.org/abs/1811.02906

Wiegand, M., Ruppenhofer, J., & Kleinbauer, T. (2019a). *Detection of Abusive Language: the Problem of Biased Datasets*. www.kaggle.com/c/jigsaw-toxic-comment-

Wiegand, M., Ruppenhofer, J., & Kleinbauer, T. (2019b). Detection of abusive language: the problem of biased datasets. *Proceedings of the 2019 Conference of the North American Chapter of the Association for Computational Linguistics: Human Language Technologies*, Volume 1 *(Long and Short Papers)*, 602–608.

Wiegand, M., Siegel, M., & Ruppenhofer, J. (2018). *Overview of the GermEval 2018 Shared Task on the Identification of Offensive Language*. https://www.kaggle.com/c/

William, P., Chaudhari, R. E., Gade, R., Pawar, A. B., & Jawale, M. A. (2022). *Machine Learning based Automatic Hate Speech Recognition System*. 315–318. DOI: 10.1109/ICSCDS53736.2022.9760959

Wireko, J. K., Hiran, K. K., & Doshi, R. (2018). Culturally based User Resistance to New Technologies in the Age of IoT in Developing Countries: Perspectives from Ethiopia. International Journal of Emerging Technology and Advanced Engineering, https://vbn.aau.dk/en/publications/culturally-based-user-resistance-to-new-technologies-in-the-age-o

Wu, C., Wang, Y., Zhang, Y., Wang, H., & Pang, Y. (2025). Confront hate with AI: How AI-generated counter speech helps against hate speech on social Media? *Telematics and Informatics*, *101*, 102304. DOI: 10.1016/j.tele.2025.102304

Wullach, T., Adler, A., & Minkov, E. (2021). Towards Hate Speech Detection at Large via Deep Generative Modeling. *IEEE Internet Computing*, *25*(2), 48–57. DOI: 10.1109/MIC.2020.3033161

Xia, M., Field, A., & Tsvetkov, Y. (2020). *Demoting Racial Bias in Hate Speech Detection.* 7–14. DOI: 10.18653/v1/2020.socialnlp-1.2

Xiao, J., Dut, W., Xu, Z., & Qian, Y. (2023). Cross-system data integration based on rule-based NLP and Node2Vec. In 2023 8th International Conference on Data Science in Cyberspace (DSC) (pp. 566–570). IEEE. DOI: 10.1109/DSC59305.2023.00088

Xie, S., Wang, G., Lin, S., & Yu, P. S. (2012, April). Review spam detection via time series pattern discovery. In *Proceedings of the 21st International Conference on World Wide Web* (pp. 635-636).

Yadav, S., Kaushik, A., & Sharma, S. (2023). Comprehensive Analysis of the Artificial Intelligence Approaches for Detecting Misogynistic Mixed-Code Online Content in South Asian Countries: A Review. *Cyberfeminism and Gender Violence in Social Media*, 350–368.

Yadav, Y., Bajaj, P., Gupta, R. K., & Sinha, R. (2021). A comparative study of deep learning methods for hate speech and offensive language detection in textual data. In Proceedings of the 2021 IEEE 18th India Council International Conference (INDICON) (pp. 1–6). IEEE. Available at: https://ieeexplore-ieee.org.muj.remotlog.com/stamp/stamp.jsp?tp=&arnumber=9691704DOI: 10.1109/INDICON52576.2021.9691704

Yadav, S., & Kaushik, A. (2022). Contextualized Embeddings from Transformers for Sentiment Analysis on Code-Mixed Hinglish Data: An Expanded Approach with Explainable Artificial Intelligence. *International Conference on Speech and Language Technologies for Low-Resource Languages*, 99–119.

Yadav, S., Kaushik, A., & McDaid, K. (2023). Hate Speech is not Free Speech: Explainable Machine Learning for Hate Speech Detection in Code-Mixed Languages. *2023 IEEE International Symposium on Technology and Society (ISTAS)*, 1–8. DOI: 10.1109/ISTAS57930.2023.10305996

Yin, W., Agarwal, V., Jiang, A., Sastry, N., & Zubiaga, A. (2023). AnnoBERT: Effectively Representing Multiple Annotators' Label Choices to Improve Hate Speech Detection. *Proceedings of the International AAAI Conference on Web and Social Media*, *17*, 902–913. DOI: 10.1609/icwsm.v17i1.22198

Yin, W., & Zubiaga, A. (2021a). Towards generalisable hate speech detection: A review on obstacles and solutions. *PeerJ. Computer Science*, *7*, 1–38. DOI: 10.7717/peerj-cs.598 PMID: 34239978

Yont, S. (2024, March). *The deepfake menace: Legal challenges in the age of AI*. TRT World Research Centre. https://researchcentre.trtworld.com/wp-content/uploads/2024/03/The-Deepfake-Menace_v2.pdf

Yousif, N. (2022, October 15). *Amanda Todd: Dutchman sentenced for fatal cyberstalking - BBC News*. BBC News, Toronto. https://www.bbc.com/news/world-us-canada-63218797

YouTube Community Guidelines: Hate Speech. (2023).

Zahid, I. A., Joudar, S. S., Albahri, A. S., Albahri, O. S., Alamoodi, A. H., Santamaría, J., & Alzubaidi, L. (2024). Unmasking large language models by means of OpenAI GPT-4 and Google AI: A deep instruction-based analysis. *Intelligent Systems with Applications*, *23*, 200431. DOI: 10.1016/j.iswa.2024.200431

Zhang, B. H., Lemoine, B., & Mitchell, M. (2018). Mitigating Unwanted Biases with Adversarial Learning. *AIES 2018 - Proceedings of the 2018 AAAI/ACM Conference on AI, Ethics, and Society*, 335–340. DOI: 10.1145/3278721.3278779

Zhang, Y., Pan, C. L., & Liao, H. T. (2021). Carbon neutrality policies and technologies: A scientometric analysis of social science disciplines. Frontiers in Environmental Science. frontiersin.org

Zhou, Y., Yang, Y., Liu, H., Liu, X., & Savage, N. (2020). Deep learning based fusion approach for hate speech detection. *IEEE Access : Practical Innovations, Open Solutions*, *8*, 128889–128898. DOI: 10.1109/ACCESS.2020.3009244

Zmigrod, R., Mielke, S. J., Wallach, H., & Cotterell, R. (2019). *Counterfactual Data Augmentation for Mitigating Gender Stereotypes in Languages with Rich Morphology*. https://arxiv.org/abs/1906.04571 DOI: 10.18653/v1/P19-1161

Zuckerberg, M. (2019). *Facebook's Hate Speech Algorithms Leave Out Some Languages | TIME.* https://time.com/5739688/facebook-hate-speech-languages/?utm_source=chatgpt.com

About the Contributors

Mohammad Arsalan received his Ph.D. in Electronics and Electrical Engineering from Dongguk University, Seoul, South Korea, in August 2020. His Ph.D. major includes Computer Vision and Artificial Intelligence. He has more than 07 years of teaching and research experience in utilizing custom Deep Learning Networks for various Computer Vision tasks. He has vast research experience in Biometric Recognition, Human Activity Recognition, Autonomous Driving, and Computer-Aided Disease Diagnosis. Based on his research achievements, in September 2020 he Joined the Division of Electronics and Electrical Engineering at Dongguk University as a full-time Assistant Professor. He has also worked as a Research Professor at The Institute for Future of Education, in the Center for Educational Innovation, Tecnologico de Monterrey. Along with multidisciplinary research experience, he has enormous experience in teaching various Computer Vision and Artificial Intelligence-related graduate courses. He has numerous publications published as Journal Articles and International Conference Proceedings in high-quality Q1/Q2 reputable journals around Artificial Intelligence (AI), Machine Learning (ML), and Deep Learning (DL) for multidisciplinary applications. He has good experience of editorial/gest editorial roles in reputable journals. Currently, he is working as a Research Assistant Professor at the KINDI Center of Computing Research, College of Engineering and Qatar University, Doha, Qatar. His research interests include Artificial Intelligence/Machine Learning/ Deep Learning/ Computer Vision applications for multidisciplinary applications, medical image analysis, and computer-aided disease diagnosis.

Mehul Mahrishi has 18+ years of teaching and research experience; I currently work as a professor and Head in the Department of Computer Science & Engineering, Swami Keshvanand Institute of Technology, Management, and Gramothan, Jaipur – India. Before this assignment, I was a postdoctoral researcher at the Institute for the Future of Education Writing Lab, Tecnologico de Monterrey,

Mexico. I also served as an Assistant Professor at the Central University of Rajasthan, Ajmer, Rajasthan. I am a Senior Member of the IEEE-Delhi Section, a Life Member of the Institution of Engineers, India (L-IEI), and a Life Member of the International Association of Engineers (IAENG). I was a member of an Indian contingent of the BRICS International Forum that traveled to Moscow, Russia, to attend Russian Energy Week 2018 and the BRICS Youth Energy Summit. I have over 35 publications in reputed international journals, conferences, book chapters and authored books on Operating Systems and Cloud Computing. I have participated in and delivered at various national and international forums. My research activities are twofold: the first is to explore the developmental enhancements in education technology and innovation; the second research theme focuses on Natural Language Processing, Machine Learning, and Sentiment Analysis.

Ruchi Doshi has more than 16 years of academic, research and software development experience in Asia, Europe, and Africa. Currently she is working as Research Supervisor and Associate Professor at the Azteca University, Mexico and Adjunct Professor at the Jyoti Vidyapeeth Women's University, Rajasthan, India. She worked at the BlueCrest University College, Liberia, Africa; BlueCrest University College, Ghana, Africa; Amity University, India; Trimax IT Infrastructure & Services, India. She is interested in the field of Machine Learning and Cloud computing framework development. She has published research papers in peer-reviewed international journals and conferences; 3 Indian Patents; 3 books on Cloud Computing, Machine Learning, Mobile Cloud computing, Intelligent IoT Systems for Big Data Analysis and Mobile application development. She is Reviewer, Advisor, Ambassador and Editorial board member of various reputed International Journals and Conferences with IEEE, Springer, and Elsevier. She is an active member in organizing many international seminars, workshops, and conferences. She is nominated from by IEEE Headquarter, USA for the Chair, Women in Engineering (WIE) position in Liberia, West Africa.

Archika Jain currently working as an Assistant Professor in the Department of Computer Science & Engineering, Swami Keshvanand Institute of Technology, Management and Gramothan, Jaipur - India. She received her Ph.D. degree in Computer Science from Suresh Gyan Vihar University, Jaipur, India in July 2024. Her research interests are Image processing, Machine Learning. She has more than 09 years of teaching experience. She has authored/co-authored over 20 research publications in peer-reviewed reputed journals, book chapters, and conference proceedings. Her research interests include Image Processing, Artificial Intelligence, Machine Learning, Deep Learning and Sentiment analysis.

Chandrashekhar Goswami is working as Deputy Dean and Associate Professor in Faculty of Computing and Informatics, Sir Padampat Singhania University, Udaipur, India. He is having more than 15+ years of Teaching, Research, and Institutional Experience. He has completed his Ph.D from Vellore Institute of Technology (VIT), Vellore in 2021. Dr. Goswami holds M.Tech. in Computer Science and Engineering from Chhattisgarh Swami Vivekanand Technical University (CSVTU), Bhilai. He also holds MBA degree in Human Resource Management (HRM). He has completed B.E. in Information Technology from Rashtrasant Tukadoji Maharaj Nagpur University (RTMNU), Nagpur. He had presented several papers in International conferences, published 24 International journal papers in SCOPUS and Web of Science, and 4 patents filed. One Copyright has been granted. He is a Life member of CSI and IAENG. His research interest includes Database System, Mobile Ad Hoc Network, Internet of Things (IoT), Deep Learning, Wireless Sensor Networks and Smart City Application.

***

Indu Bala is a Professor in the School of Electrical and Electronics Engineering (SEEE) at Lovely Professional University, Phagwara, Punjab, India. She has completed her B.Tech and M.Tech from Punjab Technical University, Jalandhar, Punjab, and Ph.D. from Punjabi University, Patiala, India in 2003, 2008, and 2018, respectively. She has published more than 50 papers in various national/ international conferences and international journals including wireless networks (Springer), Wireless personal Communication (Springer), International Journal of Communication Systems (Wiley), etc. She has contributed more than 10 book chapters in various books from renowned publishers like Springer, Wiley, Elsevier, IET, IGI Global, CRC press, etc. She has recently edited a book on IoT from CRC press and served as a guest editor for a special thematic issue on Advancements and Trends in Green Computing and Communication from Bentham Science Publishers. Currently, she is also serving as a lead guest editor for a special issue on Unmanned Aerial vehicles from Bentham Science Publishers. She has served as a reviewer for several international journals including Telecommunication Systems, IEEE Transac

Kashvi Chaturvedi, is studying B.Tech, specialisation in Artificial Intelligence and Data Science at Ajeenkya DY Patil University. She started solidifying her programming skills by completing various certification courses like Data Structures in C, Tableau functions and Operating Systems along with doing few projects using languages like Python, C, C++ and creating Web Page using HTML, CSS and Java Script. She had also attended an Arduino-Based Automation course at Dolphin Labs to enhance her software knowledge. There, she learned how to work with sensors, microcontrollers, and circuit design. She has also written multiple review papers on topics such as Geographic Information Systems, Comparative Analysis of BJT Configurations, Swiss Bank vs. European Central Bank: Data Analysis. She is also researching on and learning many topics such as Small Modular Reactors, Bibliometric Analysis, UNSDGs etc. Because of her interest in latest technologies, she also participated in Global Hyperloop Competition hosted by IIT Madras representing her college as team Vac-Vectoor where she learnt more about various subtopics from the mentors.

Susanta Das is a seasoned educator with a proven record of teaching and mentoring diverse students, working at multiple institutions, and providing service to the various initiatives of organizations. He received his Ph.D. and M.A. degrees from Western Michigan University (WMU), USA, and M.Sc. degree from Banaras Hindu University (BHU), India all in Physics. He continued his research as a Marie-Curie post-doctoral fellow at Stockholm University, Stockholm, Sweden on beam diagnostics for the DESIREE (Double ElectroStatic Ion Ring ExpEriment) in the project DITANET (Diagnostic Techniques for particle Accelerators – a Marie-Curie initial training NETwork), at the Indian Institute of Science Education and Research-Kolkata, India on high-pressure physics as a Project Scientist-B, and at the University of Electro-Communications, Tokyo, Japan on ion-surface interactions as a Post-doctoral fellow. Throughout his career, Dr. Das worked and collaborated with many researchers, Ph.D., master, and visiting students from different countries. He further visited many countries to discuss research and an international conference participant (UK, Italy, Germany, Greece, Belgium, Bulgaria, Romania, Brazil etc.). He worked at several institutions before assuming his current role at Ajeenkya D Y Patil University. He received the Marie-Curie post-doctoral fellowship in Sweden, Science Academies' Summer Research Fellowship in India, Gowen Frostic Doctoral Fellowship, Department Graduate Research and Creative Scholar Award by WMU, and Leo R. Parpart Doctoral Fellowship by Dept. of Physics, WMU, among many others, throughout his academic journey. He co-authored several research articles in WoS/Scopus indexed international journals, conference proceedings, and scholarly book chapters and co-edited several books published by renowned international publishing houses (IGI-Global, Springer Nature, Nova Science Publishers, Wiley, Scrivener-Wiley, Notion Press). At present, Dr. Das continues to delve into cutting-edge fields, with a keen interest in nanotechnology, UN SDGs, and data science. His multifaceted contributions, spanning teaching, research, and administrative leadership, showcase a dedicated professional who is instrumental in advancing the vision and mission of the institutions he serves.

Kamal Kant Hiran moved to Academic City College, Ghana, West Africa to be the Head of School of Technology from the Amity University, Rajasthan where he held the Senior Lecturer in the Department of Computer Engineering and IT.He has more than nine years of experience in academia and research. His earlier appointments were at Amity University, Suresh Gyan Vihar University and Govt. Engineering College, Ajmer as an Assistant Professor. He has published papers in refereed international journals and International conferences. Mr. Hiran has obtained M.Tech Honors (Gold Medalist) in ICT from India and B. Engineering in IT with first class from University of Rajasthan, India. He is Life member of various professional bodies like IEEE (USA), IET (UK), International Association of Engineers (IAENG), Universal Association of Computer and Electronics Engineers (UACEE), IACSIT (Singapore). He is Reviewer & member of Editorial Board team in various reputed International Journals like IJSET, IJTEE, IJSTR and IJERT.

Rituraj Jain is currently working in the Department of Information Technology, Marwadi University, Rajkot, Gujarat, India. He has published many papers in International Journals and Conferences. He has published 4 books. He is an Oracle Database SQL Certified Expert. He is also associated with professional bodies like the Indian Society of Technical Education (ISTE), Computer Science Teachers Association (CSTA), Academy & Industry Research Collaboration Center (AIRCC), International Association of Computer Science and Information Technology (IACSIT), International Association of Engineers (IAENG). His research interests include Cloud Computing, Machine Learning, Deep Learning, Fuzzy Logic, IoT, Genetic Algorithms, Big Data and Software Engineering.

Yadnyesh Khapekar is a student of Ajeenkya D. Y. Patil University, pursuing a Bachelor of Technology degree in Computer Science and Engineering. With a sharp analytical mind and a natural inclination for problem-solving, he thrives in tackling complex challenges with precision and creativity. His proficiency in C++ programming enables him to develop efficient algorithms and software solutions, making him an asset in the world of coding. Beyond programming, He has honed his skills in Computer-Aided Design (CAD) software, allowing him to conceptualize and create innovative designs with technical accuracy. His enthusiasm for 3D printing technology further complements his expertise, as he seamlessly translates digital models into tangible prototypes. His ability to design in three dimensions showcases his blend of technical prowess and artistic vision. An active participant in academic and technical competitions, he has proudly represented his university on multiple occasions, demonstrating his capability to perform under pressure and excel in competitive settings. His dedication to research and knowledge dissemination is evident in the numerous review papers he has authored and published in books and journals relating to concepts like artificial intelligence, lead nanoparticles, climate risks, and many more, contributing valuable insights to the fields. With a strong foundation in engineering principles and a drive to push boundaries, he aspires to innovate and lead in the realm of technology. His blend of coding expertise, design acumen, and research experience positions him as a future visionary in the ever-evolving field of computer science and engineering.

Maad Mijwil is an Iraqi Academician; he was born in Baghdad, Iraq, in 1987. He received his B.Sc. degree in software engineering from Baghdad college of economic sciences university, Iraq, in 2009. He received a M.Sc. degree in 2015 from the computer science department, university of Baghdad in the field of wireless sensor networks, Iraq. Currently, he is a director of the Division of Quality Assurance and Performance at the College of Administration and Economics, Al-Iraqia University. He is working as a Assistant Professor and an academic member of staff in the Computer Techniques Engineering Department at Baghdad College of Economic Sciences University, Iraq. He has over ten years of experience in teaching, guiding projects for undergraduates, and laboratory sessions. He has published 201 works, including research papers, review articles, book chapters, and preprints in national and international journals and conferences. He is also an editor in more than 10 international/national journals and a reviewer in more than 100 international/national journals. He has served on technical program committees for many prestigious conferences. Also, he graduated from Publons Academy as a peer reviewer. His Google citations are over the 4700 mark.

Manish Mittal holds a Doctor of Philosophy (Ph.D.) in Management and a Master of Business Administration (MBA) in Marketing with Honours, awarded with a Merit Scholarship. He also possesses a Bachelor of Legislative Law (LL.B.) and a Bachelor of Commerce (B.Com.). Additionally, he has completed an advanced Postgraduate Certification Programme in Business Analytics (PGBA) from IISc Bangalore. With over 23 years of combined industry and academic experience, Manish currently serves as Assistant Professor and Programme Coordinator (MBA) at Brainware University, Kolkata, India. He has authored six academic research papers published in refereed journals, including one in a Scopus-indexed journal, and holds two patents.

Ujwal Prabhakar Nandekar is an Assistant Professor at Symbiosis Law School, Pune, and a researcher at the Intellectual Property Cell, Symbiosis International (Deemed University). He holds a Ph.D. in Law with a specialization in Intellectual Property Laws and has over nine years of teaching experience spanning undergraduate, postgraduate, and doctoral programs. His areas of academic interest include copyright, patent, trademark, and information technology law. Dr. Nandekar has recently co-authored a notable paper: "Impact of the Biological Diversity (Amendment) Act 2023 on Biodiversity Protection Regime in India: An Empirical Study" (2025, Journal of Intellectual Property Rights). He is actively involved in the 21st Teach Skills Project funded by the European Union, contributing to international study visits and collaborative training initiatives in legal education and technology skills development. In addition to authoring a book and several scholarly publications, Dr. Nandekar serves on the editorial board of the International Journal for Business Law Studies and has reviewed for multiple peer-reviewed journals, including the Journal of Intellectual Property Rights (Scopus), Asian Journal of Agricultural Extension, Economics & Sociology, Journal of Pharmaceutical Research International (WoS), and Asian Journal of Research and Reports in Endocrinology.

Snehal Rathi is an accomplished and student-focused professor with 21 years teaching experience in diverse classroom environments. She inspires students to pursue academic and personal excellence for becoming life-long learners. She has wide experience in the areas of curriculum development and evaluation methodologies. She is awarded Ph.D. in (Computer Engineering) from Vishwakarma University, Pune, India. She is presently working as an associate professor in Computer Engineering department at Vishwakarma Institute of Technology, Pune. She has taught multiple subjects which includes Data Structures, Data Mining and Machine Learning. Her research interest includes machine learning, deep learning, soft computing and human computer interaction.

Sunil Sankathala is pursuing B. Tech Computer Science and Engineering at Ajeenkya DY Patil University, with a diverse range of interests that bridge technology, sustainability, and innovation. His academic focus lies in computer science fundamentals like programming, data structures, algorithms, and software development. He actively supplements this with hands-on experience in web development and robotics. Beyond the core curriculum, He has a strong research inclination in emerging and impactful fields. His current research interests include Artificial Intelligence in Healthcare, bioplastics, nano bioplastics, e-waste management, and solid waste management—areas where he believes technology can make a meaningful difference in solving real-world problems. He has been publishing research articles and book chapters in reputed national and international journals and books. He is also part of an ambitious Hyperloop project, which involves interdisciplinary collaboration and cutting-edge engineering aimed at revolutionizing transportation. Working on this project has enhanced his skills in teamwork, innovation, and systems thinking. In the tech domain, he has developed proficiency in web development using technologies such as HTML, CSS, JavaScript, and React. His interests in robotics further reflect building smart, responsive systems that interact with the physical world. Throughout his course, he has helped strengthen problem-solving and collaborative skills. He is proficient in languages such as Python, C, C++, MySQL, Ubuntu, Machine Learning and familiar with frameworks and tools like React, Git. He actively participates in hackathons, coding competitions, and tech events to challenge himself and learn from peers. He is also a quick learner and highly adaptable, with an eagerness to stay updated with the latest trends in the tech world. He aspires to become a skilled software engineer and contribute to building innovative solutions that have a positive impact on society. The long-term goal is to work in a dynamic environment where knowledge, grow professionally, and make meaningful contributions to the field of technology. Driven by a spirit of exploration and sustainability, he aims to contribute to technological solutions that address both human and environmental needs. The long-term goal is to become a versatile engineer and researcher, working at the intersection of computer science, environmental innovation, and human well-being.

Atharva Saraf is currently pursuing a B. Tech degree in Computer Science Engineering at Ajeenkya D Y Patil University. Throughout his academic journey, he has developed a strong foundation in various programming languages, including C, C++, and Python. His interests and focus areas lie in algorithm-based programs, artificial intelligence (with a special emphasis on neural networks), and cybersecurity. His has successfully undertaken several projects that reflect my proficiency and passion in these domains. For instance, he developed a PC-Tuner application aimed at optimizing system performance by employing various methods such as defragmentation. Additionally, he created an automated backup utility capable of securely backing up selected files, folders, and stores them in compressed backup folder in system itself it can also store backups on external hard disk and cloud storages. Beyond project work, he has contributed to the academic community through research articles and book chapters. Notable among these is my co-authored chapter on federated learning techniques, exploring their applications and advancements in the field of machine learning. Moreover, he is currently working on writing a book chapter focusing on federated learning, delving deeper into its methodologies and practical implementations. His academic experiences have honed his skills in problem-solving, critical thinking, and collaborative teamwork. He is eager to further expand His knowledge and expertise in computer science, particularly in areas that intersect with his interests in algorithms, artificial intelligence, and their practical applications.

Aditya Shrivastav is an aspiring technologist currently pursuing a Bachelor of Technology (B. Tech.) in Computer Science and Engineering at Ajeenkya D. Y. Patil University. He holds solid programming expertise in C, C++, and Python, alongside strong command over data and business tools such as Microsoft Excel and Tally software. Aditya is a member of Team Vac-Vectoor Hyperloop and participated with the team in the Global Hyperloop Competition organized by IIT Madras, contributing to cutting-edge transportation solutions. He actively engages in hackathons and various technical events to expand his skills and contribute to innovative problem-solving. He has authored and co-authored book chapters in the domains of solid waste management, bioplastics, nanotechnology applications, and artificial intelligence, showcasing his multidisciplinary approach and research acumen. Aditya is also working on an innovative project on predictive e-waste management. The project is targeted toward IT departments, schools, and colleges, aiming to support sustainable practices and resource optimization. In parallel with his academic journey, Aditya is serving as a faculty intern at Disha Computer Institute, where he teaches C, C++, basic Python, basic Java, Excel formulas, and Tally software. His dedication and teaching proficiency earned him a Letter of Appreciation and the opportunity to conduct a workshop on Advanced Excel at G. H. Raisoni College of Arts, Commerce and Science. With a strong foundation in technology, a passion for sustainability, and hands-on experience in both teaching and project development, Aditya Shrivastav is committed to driving impact through research, education, and innovation.

Mayank Singh is currently working as Professor and Head CSE (AIML) department at JSS University Noida, UP, India. Prior to this he worked as Dean (Research) at G. L. Bajaj Institute of Technology and Management, Greater Noida, India and Director at Consilio Research Lab, Tallinn, Estonia. He also worked as Postdoctoral Fellow at Univeristy of KwaZulu-Natal Durban, South Africa, and Professor & Head, Department of Computer Science and Engineering at Krishna Engineering College, Ghaziabad from January 2013 to September 2017. He has 21+ years of extensive experience in IT industry, Academics and Research in India and abroad. Dr. Singh has published around 100+ research papers in peer reviewed Transaction, Journals and Conferences of National and International repute and has supervised 14 M. Tech and 9 PhD students. He is currently also serving as a Life Member of Computer Society of India (CSI), Life Member of Indian Science Congress Association (ISCA), Senior Member of IEEE, Senior Member of ACM, Senior Member of IACSIT, and Member of Indian Society for Technical Education (ISTE). He is also serving for IEEE Committees as a TPC Member and designated Reviewer for various IEEE Conferences. He has organized several international conferences with reputed publishers like IEEE, Springer, Taylor and Francis, IOP etc.

Dr. Singh is currently serving as Review Member, Research Grants Council (RGC), Hong Kong (Research Council) since 2016. He is also serving as Reviewer for IET Software, IEEE Communications, IEEE TENCON, IEEE Sensors, The Journal of Engineering, IET Wireless Sensor Networks, and Program Committee Member of innumerable IEEE & Springer International Journals and Conferences Worldwide.

Devendra Kumar Somwanshi did B.E. in 2007 from Govt. Eng. College, Bikaner, and M.E. in Electronics Instrumentation & Control from Thapar University, Patiala in 2009 and awarded his Ph. D. on SDN Based Handover Management in 5G Networks. He started his teaching career as Assistant Professor, in JNIT, Jaipur (RTU) in 2009. He authored 3 technical books. He joined Poornima Group, as M. Tech. Coordinator and worked in Advanced Studies and Research Center for more than 8 years. During this time he coordinated and supported to design and execute the curriculum for M. Tech and Ph. D. course work. He guided more than 40 M. Tech. research scholars till now. He has expertise in Artificial Intelligence, Data Analysis, Image Processing, Instrumentation and Process Control. He has published more than 80 research papers in National and International conferences and journals including IEEE, ACM, Springer, Elsevier etc. He has also expertise to organize International Conferences as publication chair including IEEE, Springer, and Elsevier conferences. He worked as IEEE Student Branch chair for more than 4 years. Currently he is working as Registrar, Poornima College of Engineering since 2019.

Pallavi Tiwari is a doctoral researcher at Maharashtra National Law University, Nagpur, and former Assistant Professor of Law at Symbiosis Law School, Pune. A gold medallist in LL.M. (IPR specialization), she is UGC-NET qualified and currently pursuing her Ph.D. in the field of intellectual property rights. Her scholarly interests lie in the intersection of IPR, technology law, and competition law. She has co-authored several research articles in UGC-CARE and Scopus-indexed journals, including "Impact of the Biological Diversity (Amendment) Act 2023 on Biodiversity Protection Regime in India: An Empirical Study" (JIPR, 2025), and "Deepfake Technology and the Quagmire of Artificial Intelligence: An Analysis of National and International Legal Frameworks", presented at Manipal University Jaipur in 2025. Pallavi is actively involved in international academic collaborations through the 21st Teach Skills project under the Erasmus+ programme, focusing on life and information technology skills in legal education. She currently serves on the editorial team of the Journal of the Institute of Legal Education and is a reviewer for Contemporary Law Review (MNLU Nagpur).

Vipin Tyagi is a distinguished academician, researcher and author, currently serving as Dean (Academic and Research) at Jaypee University of Engineering and Technology in Guna, Madhya Pradesh. With a rich background in Computer Science, his expertise spans across Image Processing, Cyber Forensics, and Speech Recognition. He is also Director – IQAC of JUET Guna. Prof. Tyagi has a prolific publication record, contributing significantly to his fields of interest. His scholarly work includes numerous journal articles, conference papers, and books. Some of his notable publications are in the areas of image forgery detection, image denoising, and content-based image retrieval. He has authored and edited several books and papers in the field of computing and data sciences, such as "Predictive Computing and Information Security" and "Content-Based Image Retrieval: Ideas, Influences, and Current Trends" published by Springer Singapore. His book "Understanding Digital Image Processing" using MATLAB, published by Taylor and Francis is highlighted by Mathworks at: https://in.mathworks.com/academia/books/understanding-digital -image-processing-tyagi.html His scholarly work has earned him a respectable h-index and numerous citations in the academic community.

Neha Yadav Assistant Professor, Department of Computer Science and Engineering (Data Science) G. L. Bajaj Institute of Technology and Management, Greater Noida, India ORCID Id: 0000-0002-7793-2063 Ms. Neha Yadav, Ph.D. (Submitted), is currently serving as an Assistant Professor of Engineering in the Department of Computer Science (Data Science) at G. L. Bajaj Institute of Technology and Management, Greater Noida, India. She is pursuing her PhD and has earned an M.Tech in Computer Science and Engineering from Jaypee Institute of Information Technology (JIIT), Noida, as well as a B.Tech. in Computer Science from Bundelkhand University, India. She is in the final stage of her doctoral studies (PhD submitted) at JIIT. Noida. She has over 10 publications in reputable journals and conferences. She serves as a reviewer in various reputable journals, including Informatica and IEEE Access.

Index

A

B

C

D

E

G

M

N

O

P

R

S

T

U

www.ingramcontent.com/pod-product-compliance
Lightning Source LLC
LaVergne TN
LVHW080911300926
849162LV00003B/640